Needlework & History
Hand in Hand

Piecework Magazine Presents

A FACSIMILE EDITION OF

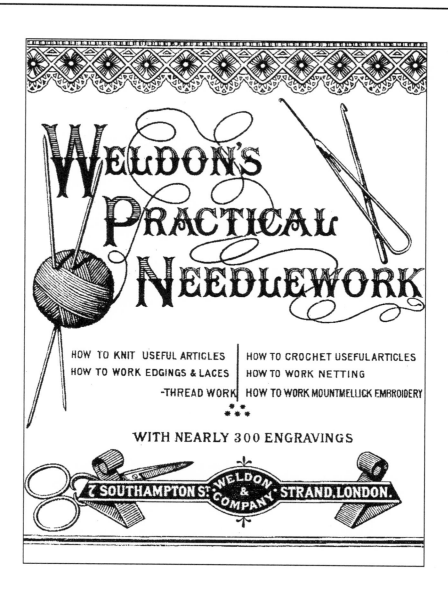

VOLUME 5

Sincere thanks to Lilo Markrich for her help, encouragement, and support.

Weldon's Practical Needlework, Volume 5

Project editor, Jeane Hutchins

Cover design, Dean Howes

Interweave Press

201 East Fourth Street

Loveland, Colorado, 80537-5655

USA

Printed in the United States of America

ISBN 1–883010-95-0

First printing: 2M:IWP:701:WP

*T*his book opens a window on another time and another place. The time is the turn of the twentieth century and the place is London, England. In an effort to bring needlework to a then emerging middle class, several companies in the late 1800s in London began publishing patterns and instructions for various needlework projects. Unlike other magazines available at the time, which ran one or two needlework projects in an issue filled with other editorial (including fiction, recipes, and housekeeping hints), these new publications were devoted solely to needlework.

Many of the companies involved in these publishing ventures were thread companies, and their purpose, of course, was to sell more thread by making patterns and instructions more readily available. One company, however, Weldon's, began as a paper pattern company and became one of the most recognized needlework publishers in Victorian England.

In approximately 1885, Weldon's began publishing monthly newsletters, available by subscription, featuring patterns and instructions for projects. Each fourteen-page newsletter was devoted to one technique and cost 2 pence. Thus, there was *Weldon's Practical Knitter, Weldon's Practical Patchwork, Weldon's Practical Crochet, Weldon's Practical Cross-Stitch,* and so on. By about 1915, Weldon's had published 159 issues of *Practical Crochet* and 100 issues of *Practical Knitting.*

Around 1888, the company began to publish a series of books titled *Weldon's Practical Needlework,* each volume consisting of twelve issues of the various newsletters (one year of publications) bound together with a cloth cover; each book cost 2 shilling/6 pence.

Editions feature instructions for making flowers from crinkled paper or leather, items suitable for selling at bazaars (pincushions, for example), tatting, smocking, netting, beading, torchon lace, and much more. In addition to knitting and crocheting, which were frequently covered, *Weldon's Practical Needlework* books contain extensive coverage of decorative needlework, including crewel work, appliqué, cross-stitch, mountmellick embroidery, drawn thread work, ivory embroidery, hardanger, and canvas work. Each volume is filled with hundreds of projects, illustrations, information on little-known techniques, fashion as it was at the turn of the century, and brief histories of needlework.

PIECEWORK magazine is pleased to present this limited edition, exact reproduction (neither alterations nor corrections were made to the original) of *Weldon's Practical Needlework,* Volume 5. It is a fitting example of needle-work and history, hand in hand.

The Staff of PIECEWORK

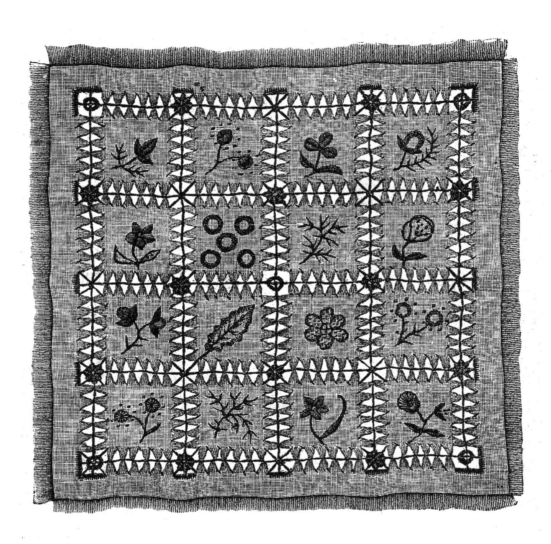

WELDON'S
PRACTICAL NEEDLEWORK

COMPRISING—

KNITTING, CROCHET, DRAWN THREAD WORK, NETTING, KNITTED EDGINGS & SHAWLS, MOUNTMELLICK EMBROIDERY.

WITH FULL WORKING DESCRIPTIONS.

NEARLY 300 ILLUSTRATIONS.

* * *

LONDON:
WELDON & Co., 7, SOUTHAMPTON STREET, STRAND, W.C.,

AND ALL BOOKSELLERS AND FANCY REPOSITORIES IN UNITED KINGDOM AND COLONIES.

INDEX.—Vol. V.

KNITTING.

WELDON'S
PRACTICAL KNITTER.

(TWELFTH SERIES.)

HOW TO KNIT USEFUL GARMENTS FOR LADIES, GENTLEMEN, AND CHILDREN.

TWENTY-FIVE ILLUSTRATIONS.

The Yearly Subscription to this Magazine, post free to any Part of the World, is 2s. 6d.
Subscriptions are payable in advance, and may commence from any date and for any period.

The Back Numbers are always in print. Nos. 1 to 109 now ready, Price 2d. each, postage ½d. Over 5,000 Engravings.

BEADED TRIMMING FOR A DRESS.

KNITTED LENGTHWAYS.

THE substitution of a knitted beaded edging for the neck and sleeves of a dress in place of the usual frilling is a pretty and economical fashion that just now is very much in vogue. Our engraving shows an edging composed of three rows of beads, knitted lengthways, which looks very nice indeed in actual wear, and is besides very durable, and easily washed when necessary. The beads may be either white, pale blue, or pink, according to taste, either clear glass or opaque, and of a size to slip easily along the wool, about one hank will be sufficient, and a skein of white Andalusian wool, and a pair of No. 16 steel knitting needles will be required. The beads must first of all be threaded upon the wool, to accomplish which thread a sewing needle with a six-inch or seven-inch length of fine sewing cotton and tie the ends together in a tiny knot, take the end of the wool and loop it into the noose of cotton, and as you pick up the beads with the needle they will pass easily from the cotton to the wool. When sufficient beads are threaded begin knitting by casting on as many stitches as will make the length required to be knitted, any even number, about 140 or 150 stitches for the neck, and 60 or 70 stitches for each sleeve. **1st row**—Knit 2 stitches, * push up 7 beads close to the needle, knit 2 stitches, and repeat from * to the end; great care must be taken in this row to knit rather tightly and to keep the loops of beads in the right position. **2nd row**—Plain. **3rd row**—Knit 1 stitch, * push up 7 beads close to the needle, knit 2 stitches, and repeat from * to the end, where will be only 1 stitch to knit. **4th row**—Plain. **5th row**—Same as the first row. **6th row**—Plain. Knit 4 rows of all plain knitting, and cast off.

BEADED TRIMMING FOR THE NECK AND SLEEVES OF A DRESS.

KNITTED SHORTWAYS.

A PRETTY and fashionable trimming for the neck and sleeves of a dress can be made from the following instructions, it will keep clean a long time, and may easily be washed when occasion requires. Procure a skein of white Andalusian wool, a hank of clear white glass beads, or coloured beads, not too large, but yet of a size to slip easily along the wool, and a pair of No. 16 steel knitting needles. First of all, thread the beads upon the wool, this can best be managed by threading a sewing needle with a six-inch or seven-inch length of fine sewing cotton, and tying the two ends together in a small knot, pass the end of the wool through the noose loop so formed, and when you pick up the beads with the needle they will pass from the cotton down upon the wool. When the beads are threaded, cast on 7 stitches, and knit one plain row. **2nd row**—Insert the needle in the first stitch as if about to purl, but instead slip it off on to the right-hand needle, pass the wool between the first and second stitch to the back of the work, knit 3 stitches, slip the 2 next stitches on to the right-hand needle without knitting them, push up 7 beads close to the needle at the back of the work and keeping them firmly in place, knit the last stitch plain. **3rd row**—Slip the first stitch as if about to purl, knit 6 stitches. Repeat the last two rows for the length required. The first stitch in every row being slipped as if about to purl gives a neat chain-like edge smoother than the edge of ordinary knitting.

Beaded Trimming for a Dress.

Beaded Trimming for the Neck and Sleeves of a Dress.

BABY'S BOOT AND SOCK COMBINED.

THIS is a pretty fine boot knitted with Shetland wool and Andalusian wool, the Shetland being employed for the sock and the Andalusian for the shoe; the sock is worked in "shell" pattern, the shoe in plain knitting, and there is a little strap which buttons round the instep. Procure ½ oz. of white and ¼ oz. of pale-blue Shetland wool, ½ oz. of blue Andalusian of a shade to match the Shetland, three No. 18 steel knitting needles, the third needle is not used until you come to the foot, and two pearl buttons as small as glove buttons. With white Shetland cast on 71 stitches. **1st row**—Slip 1, * purl 1, knit 11, purl 1, knit 1, and repeat from * to the end of the row. **2nd row**—Slip 1, * knit 1, purl 11, knit 1, purl 1, and repeat from *. **3rd row**—Same as the first row. **4th row**—Same as the second row. This is the edge. Now for the Shell pattern. **1st row**—Still with white Shetland—Slip 1, * purl 1, slip 1, knit 1, pass the slipped stitch over, knit 1, make 1 and knit 1 alternately six times, knit 2 together, purl 1, knit 1, and repeat from * to the end. **2nd row**—Slip 1, * knit 1, purl 15, knit 1, purl 1, and repeat from * to the end. **3rd row**—Slip 1, * purl 1, slip 1, knit 1, pass the slipped stitch over, knit 11, knit 2 together, purl 1, knit 1, and repeat from * to the end. **4th row**—Slip 1, * knit 1, purl 2 together, purl 9, purl 2 together, knit 1, purl 1, and repeat from * to the end. Knit the same 4 rows with blue Shetland. Again 4 rows with white. Then 4 rows with blue. Then 44 rows with white. And now there are 15 shell patterns knitted down the leg. Break off white wool; and slipping the first 27 stitches from off the left-hand needle on to the right-hand needle, begin on the next stitch of the left-hand needle to work the instep, using white Shetland wool. **1st row**—Knit 2 stitches, purl 1, slip 1, knit 1, pass the slipped stitch over, knit 1, make 1 and knit 1 alternately six times, knit 2 together, purl 1, knit 2, and turn, leaving 27 stitches unknitted on the left-hand needle. **2nd row**—Slip 1, purl 1, knit 1, purl 15, knit 1, purl 2. **3rd row**—Slip 1, knit 1, purl 1, slip 1, knit 1, pass the slipped stitch over, knit 11, knit 2 together, purl 1, knit 2. **4th row**—Slip 1, purl 1, knit 1, purl 2 together, purl 9, purl 2 together, knit 1, purl 2. Repeat these 4 rows six times. Break off the white wool, and slip the 17 instep stitches on to the spare needle. Take the blue Andalusian wool, and for the strap cast 12 stitches on to the right-hand needle and knit the 27 stitches off the left-hand needle thus,—knit 2, * knit 2 together, knit 3, and repeat from *. Knit 4 plain rows on the 34 stitches. **Next row**—Knit 24, cast the last stitch but one over the last stitch, and continue casting off to the end of the strap; break off blue wool. Slip the 27 stitches back from the right-hand needle upon the left-hand needle, take the blue Andalusian, and * knit 3 stitches, knit 2 together, repeat from * four times, knit 2, cast on 12 stitches for the strap. Knit 1 plain row. **Next row**—Knit 30, cast off 3, knit 2. **Next row**—Knit 3, cast on 3, knit 28. **Next row**—Plain. **Next row**—Cast off 12 strap stitches, knit 21 stitches. Now for the **Shoe**—Still with blue Andalusian—Knit plain 22 stitches, miss two loops up the side of the flap, pick up and knit a stitch in each of the next two loops, * make 1, pick up and knit a stitch in each of the next 2 loops, and repeat from * four times, which brings you to the end of the side of the flap; work off the instep needle, knit 2 together, * knit 3, knit 2 together, repeat from * twice more; with the spare needle pick up and knit a stitch in each of the first 2 loops along the other side of the flap, * make 1, pick up and knit a stitch in each of the next two loops, and repeat from * four times, which brings you to the end all but two loops that are to be missed to lie under the strap, knit plain 22 stitches off the left-hand pin. **2nd row**—Knit plain 91 stitches, either all upon one needle or on two needles, the latter will be found most convenient. **3rd row**—Plain. **4th row**—Plain. **5th row**—Knit 42, increase 1 by picking up the thread that lies directly below the next stitch and knitting it, knit 7, increase 1, knit 42. Knit 3 plain rows. **9th row**—Knit 42, increase 1, knit 9, increase 1, knit 42. Knit 1 plain row. **11th**

Baby's Boot and Sock combined.

row—Knit 43, increase 1, knit 9, increase 1, knit 43. Knit 3 plain rows. **15th row**—Knit 44, increase 1, knit 9, increase 1, knit 44. Knit 1 plain row. **17th row**—Knit 45, increase 1, knit 9, increase 1, knit 45. Knit 5 plain rows, there are now 101 stitches in the row. **23rd row**—Knit 2, knit 2 together, knit 43, knit 2 together, knit 3 together, knit 2 together, knit 43, knit 2 together, knit 2. Knit 1 plain row. **25th row**—Knit 2, knit 2 together, knit 40, knit 2 together, knit 3 together, knit 2 together, knit 40, knit 2 together, knit 2. Knit 1 plain row. **27th row**—Knit 2, knit 2 together, knit 35, knit 2 together twice, knit 3 together, knit 2 together twice, knit 35, knit 2 together, knit 2. Knit 1 plain row. Cast off. Sew up the sole and the leg of the sock, also sew the tiny holes left at the junction of the strap; sew a tiny button on the left strap. Knit the other boot in the same manner.

BABY'S BONNET.

THIS is a very pretty yet easily made bonnet, and, being lined with knitting is very warm and comfortable. Procure 1½ ozs. of white and 1 oz. of pale salmon pink single Berlin wool, a pair of No. 10 bone knitting needles, a yard of ribbon for strings, and a lace cap front. The piece of knitting which forms the lining of the bonnet is worked first. With white wool cast on 67 stitches. **1st row**—Plain. **2nd row**—Purl. And continue these two rows alternately, always slipping the first stitch of every row, till 34 rows are done for the lining. Now join on the pink wool and begin the pattern. **1st row**—Slip 1, knit 1, * make 1, knit 2 together, and repeat from * to the end of the row, and knit plain the last stitch. **2nd row**—Purl. **3rd row**—Plain. **4th row**—Plain. Now take the white wool and repeat these four rows. Then use pink again, and continue the pattern alternately with white and with pink till four pink patterns, 28 rows, are done. Take the white wool and knit a plain row. Purl a row. Knit a row. Purl a row. Knit 2 rows. Purl a row. Knit a row. Purl 2 rows, all this with white. Now use the pink wool and repeat from the 1st pattern row to the 4th row, and the pink now can be fastened off. Knit the first 3 pattern rows with white wool. Then a purl row and a plain row alternately for 5 rows. And to cast off, fold the knitting the right side out, with the cast on stitches behind and parallel with the stitches on the left-hand pin, and pick up a cast on loop with each stitch that you knit, so joining and casting off at the same time. For the **Curtain**—Cast on 105 stitches with white wool. Knit a row and purl a row alternately till 16 rows are done. Work the 4 pattern

rows with pink wool, then with white wool, and then with pink wool again. Then with white wool knit the first 2 pattern rows. **Next row**—Plain, taking up a loop of the cast on stitches with every stitch that you knit. **Next row**—Purl 6, purl 2 together, and repeat the same to the end of the row, and purl the last stitch. Knit 4 plain rows, all with white wool. **Next row**—Knit 2, make 1, knit 2 together, and repeat the same to the end. **Next row**—Plain. **Next row**—Knit 4, knit 2 together, and repeat the same to the end. Knit 2 plain rows. Cast off. Sew the cast off stitches along the bottom of the bonnet. For the **Tuft**—This may be made with either pink or white wool, according to fancy; cast on 4 stitches. **1st row**—Slip the first stitch, knit the 2 next stitches in looped knitting, knit the last stitch. **2nd row**—Plain. Repeat the two rows until sufficient is worked to make a pretty tuft, which sew in its place on the top of the bonnet. Put in the lace cap, and strings to tie under the chin.

GENTLEMAN'S STOCKING.

KNITTED IN SCOTCH PLAID PATTERN.

POPULAR taste at the present time runs upon bicycling and shooting stockings, knitted with wool of two or three good contrasting or nicely blending colours in patterns of checks and plaids. The stocking shown in our illustration is likely to become a favourite, the plaid being clear and distinct, yet neat, and the shape good. Required, Scotch fingering wool of the best quality, 6 ozs. of dark blue and 4 ozs. of light grey, or blue and brown may be used, or grey and white, according to taste. Four steel knitting needles, No. 14. Cast on with blue wool, 40 stitches on each of three needles, 120 stitches in all. Work in ribbing, 2 stitches plain and 2 stitches purl for 4 rounds. **5th round**—Take the grey wool and work the same. Repeat these five rounds six times, or till you have done 7 grey lines; then do 4 more rounds with blue; and this completes the ribbing. Now commence the PATTERN, beginning of course on the first needle; the stitch is plain throughout. **1st round**—Knit 4 stitches with blue wool, * 1 stitch grey and 1 stitch blue alternately eight times, 1 stitch grey, 7 stitches blue, and repeat from *, till at the end of the third needle there are 3 stitches to be knitted with blue. **2nd round**—Knit 5 stitches with blue, * 1 stitch grey and 1 stitch blue alternately seven times, 1 grey, 9 blue, and repeat from *, till at the end of the third needle there are 4 stitches to be knitted with blue. **3rd round**—Knit 2 stitches blue, * 2 grey,

Baby's Bonnet.

2 blue, 1 grey and 1 blue alternately six times, 1 grey, 2 blue, 2 grey, 3 blue, and repeat from *, and there will be only 1 blue stitch to knit at the end of the third needle. **4th round**—Knit 1 stitch grey, 2 blue, 2 grey, 2 blue, 1 grey and 1 blue alternately five times, 1 grey, 2 blue, 2 grey, 2 blue, and repeat the same to the end of the third needle. **5th round**—Knit 1 stitch blue, 1 grey, 2 blue, 2 grey, 2 blue, 1 grey and 1 blue alternately four times, 1 grey, 2 blue, 2 grey, 2 blue, 1 grey, and repeat. **6th round**—Knit 1 stitch blue, 1 grey, 2 blue, 2 grey, 2 blue, 1 grey and 1 blue alternately three times, 1 grey, 2 blue, 2 grey, 2 blue, 1 grey, 1 blue, and repeat. **7th round**—Knit 1 stitch blue, 1 grey, 1 blue, 1 grey, 2 blue, 2 grey, 2 blue, 1 grey and 1 blue alternately twice, 1 grey, 2 blue, 2 grey, 2 blue, 1 grey, 1 blue, 1 grey, 1 blue, and repeat. **8th round**—Knit 1 stitch grey, 1 blue, 1 grey, 1 blue, 1 grey, 2 blue, 2 grey, 2 blue, 1 grey, 1 blue, 1 grey, 2 blue, 2 grey, 2 blue, 1 grey, 1 blue, 1 grey, 1 blue, and repeat. **9th round**—Knit 1 stitch blue and 1 grey three times, 2 blue, 2 grey, 2 blue, 1 grey, 2 blue, 2 grey, 2 blue, 1 grey and 1 blue twice, 1 grey, and repeat. **10th round**—Knit one stitch grey, 1 blue and 1 grey alternately three times, 2 blue, 2 grey, 3 blue, 2 grey, 2 blue, 1 grey and 1 blue alternately three times, and repeat. **11th round**—Knit 1 stitch blue and

1 grey alternately four times, 9 blue, 1 grey and 1 blue alternately three times, 1 grey, and repeat. **12th round**—Knit 1 stitch grey, 1 blue and 1 grey alternately four times, 7 blue, 1 grey and one blue alternately four times, and repeat. **13th round**—Knit 1 stitch blue and 1 grey alternately four times, 9 blue, 1 grey and 1 blue alternately three times, 1 grey, and repeat. **14th round**—Knit 1 stitch grey, 1 blue and 1 grey alternately three times, 2 blue, 2 grey, 3 blue, 2 grey, 2 blue, 1 grey and 1 blue alternately three times, and repeat. **15th round**—Knit 1 stitch blue and 1 grey alternately three times, 2 blue, 2 grey, 2 blue, 1 grey, 2 blue, 2 grey, 2 blue, 1 grey and 1 blue alternately twice, 1 grey, and repeat. **16th round**—Knit 1 stitch grey, 1 blue and 1 grey alternately twice, 2 blue, 2 grey, 2 blue, 1 grey, 1 blue, 1 grey, 2 blue, 2 grey, 2 blue, 1 grey, 1 blue, 1 grey, 1 blue, and repeat. **17th round**—Knit 1 stitch blue and 1 grey alternately twice, 2 blue, 2 grey, 2 blue, 1 grey and 1 blue alternately twice, 1 grey, 2 blue, 2 grey, 2 blue, 1 grey, 1 blue, 1 grey, and repeat. **18th round**—Knit 1 stitch grey, 1 blue, 1 grey, 2 blue, 2 grey, 2 blue, 1 grey and 1 blue alternately three times, 1 grey, 2 blue, 2 grey, 2 blue, 1 grey, 1 blue, and repeat. **19th round**—Knit 1 stitch blue, 1 grey, 2 blue, 2 grey, 2 blue, 1 grey and 1 blue alternately four times, 1 grey, 2 blue, 2 grey, 2 blue, 1 grey, and repeat. **20th round**—Knit 1 stitch grey, 2 blue, 2 grey, 2 blue, 1 grey and 1 blue alternately five times, 1 grey, 2 blue, 2 grey, 2 blue, and repeat. **21st round**—Knit 2 stitches blue, 2 grey, 2 blue, 1 grey and 1 blue alternately six times, 1 grey, 2 blue, 2 grey, 1 blue, and repeat. **22nd round**—Knit 5 stitches blue, 1 grey and 1 blue alternately seven times, 1 grey, 4 blue, and repeat. Repeat from the first pattern round till four whole patterns are accomplished; and also go on to do 4 rounds of the fifth pattern. In the 5th round of the fifth pattern, and also in the 12th and 19th rounds, decrease by knitting together the third and fourth stitches on the first needle and the third and second stitches from the end of the third needle; and as you decrease of course allow in succeeding rounds by omitting as necessary a few stitches of the pattern each side the seam stitch (the first stitch on the first needle), keep the two slanting stitches always in their right position and no mistake can occur. Decrease similarly in the 5th, 12th, and 19th rounds of each of the three next repetitions of the pattern. And now you will have eight patterns knitted, 176 rounds, and the plaid pattern comes in evenly with 96 stitches in the round; work the length of two more patterns on the 96 stitches for the ankle, which makes 10 diamonds in all for the length of the leg. For the **Heel**, which is knitted entirely with blue wool — After the completion of the last round of the pattern, knit with black wool 24 stitches off the first needle, slip the remaining 4 stitches on to the second needle, and turn the work, slip the first stitch and purl 46 stitches, slip 20 stitches from the second needle on to the third needle which now has only 5 stitches upon it; you now have 49 stitches divided upon two needles for the instep, and 47 stitches all on one needle for the heel. Work a plain row and a purl row forwards and backwards on the 47 heel stitches for 40 rows. To **Turn the Heel**—Slip the first stitch, knit 25, slip 1, knit 1, pass the slipped stitch over, knit 1 ; turn, slip the first stitch, purl 6, purl 2 together, purl 1 ; turn, slip 1, knit 7, slip 1, knit 1, pass the slipped stitch over, knit 1 ; turn, slip 1, purl 8, purl 2 together, purl 1 ; turn, slip 1, knit 9, slip 1, knit 1, pass the slipped stitch over, knit 1 ; turn, slip 1, purl 10, purl 2 together, purl 1, and continue thus widening the centre and taking in the stitches each side, till all the side stitches are knitted in, and you get 27 stitches on the needle for the top of the heel, the last row being a purled row, and break off the wool. For the **Gussets**—Pick up on one needle, and knit 26 stitches (alternately 1 stitch blue and 1 stitch grey) along the right-hand side of the heel flap, and on the same needle knit also 13 stitches off the top of the heel ; on a second needle knit (always 1 stitch blue and 1 stitch grey alternately) the remaining 14 stitches off the top of the heel, and pick up and knit 26 stitches along the opposite side of the flap ; on the third needle knit along the 49 instep stitches in pattern. For the **Foot**—Work alternately 1 stitch with blue and one stitch with grey on the two foot needles, the stitch that is blue in one round to be grey in the next, decrease for the gussets every alternate round till reduced to 47 stitches on the two foot needles, and always knit the 49 instep stitches in pattern ; continue till three whole patterns are done on the instep which makes the length required for the foot ; or if for a tall man, and required longer, knit 4 or 5 rounds all plain witb blue. Then begin the **Toe**—which is all plain knitting with blue wool. Knit 5 plain rounds on the full complement of stitches, 96 stitches. **6th round**—Knit 6, knit 2 together, and repeat the same all round. Knit 6 rounds plain on 84 stitches. **13th round**—Knit 5, knit 2 together, and repeat the same. Knit 6 rounds plain on 72 stitches. **20th round**—Knit 4, knit 2

together, and repeat. Knit 5 rounds plain on 60 stitches. **26th round**—Knit 3, knit 2 together, and repeat. Knit 5 rounds plain on 48 stitches. **32nd round**—Knit 2, knit 2 together and repeat. Knit 4 rounds plain on 36 stitches. **37th round**—Knit 1, knit 2 together, and repeat. Knit 4 rounds plain on 24 stitches. **40th round**—Knit 2 together all round. Now 12 stitches on ; break off the wool and threading the end in a darning needle, run the wool through the stitches and sew them up neatly.

LADY'S MITTEN.

REQUIRED, 1 oz. of black Andalusian wool and 1 skein of black knitting silk, and 4 steel knitting needles, No 16. Commence with silk, and cast 21 stitches on each of three needles, 63 stitches in all, for the wrist. Purl 3 rounds. **4th round**—With wool—Knit plain. **5th round**—Still with wool—Make 1, knit 1, make 1, knit 1, knit 2 together twice, knit 1, and repeat the same to the end of the round. Repeat the last two rounds six times. **18th round**—With silk—Knit plain. Purl three rounds with silk as before. Work 14 rounds with wool in pattern as before. Again purl 3 rounds with silk, and work 14 rounds with wool, and this completes the knitting for the wrist. The rest of the mitten is knitted with all wool. Knit two plain rounds increasing 1 stitch in each round, 65 stitches now on. **1st round of the Hand**—Knit 1, purl 2, knit 1, purl 1, and repeat. **2nd round**—The same. **3rd round**—Plain. **4th round**—Plain. **5th round**—Knit 1, purl 1, knit 1, purl 2, and repeat. **6th round**—The same. **7th round**—Plain. **8th round**—Plain. These 8 rounds constitute the pattern. **9th round**—Begin to increase for the thumb by picking up and knitting a stitch after the first stitch, and picking up and knitting a stitch before the fifth stitch, working all else in pattern as before. Continue the pattern and increase again in the **13th round** after the first stitch and before the seventh stitch. Go on increasing in every fourth round, each time knitting 2 more stitches in pattern between the increasings, till there are 20 stitches increased for the thumb. Now work without any more increasing till there are 11 patterns in all done from the wrist. For the **Thumb**—Knit in pattern the first 20 stitches, cast on 5 stitches, and join round on three needles. Work 3 patterns—i.e., 24 rounds ; do 8 rounds of ribbing, 2 stitches plain and 2 stitches purl ; and cast off. Resume upon the **hand** stitches, picking up 5 over those cast on for the thumb. Knit 5 patterns ; then 12 rounds of ribbing ; and cast off. The mitten for the right hand is worked in the same manner, only the thumb is knitted at the end of the third needle instead of at the beginning of the first needle.

Gentleman's Stocking. Knitted in Scotch Plaid Pattern.

ANKLET.

THESE anklets are warm and comfortable for riding and driving, and also are useful to wear when walking on the moors in stormy weather. They are worked in ribbed knitting and have a lining of plain knitting. One of our engravings depicts the anklet as it is intended to be worn on the leg over the top of the boot, the other represents the anklet with the bottom turned up to show the lining. Procure 2 ozs. of dark brown Berlin fingering, and 1 oz. of white Shetland wool ; knitting needles No. 12 and No. 8. Either four needles or two needles may be used as preferred. The pattern will appear the same, the only difference being that, if knit upon two needles, there will be a seam to sew up at the back of the leg, while with four needles you would knit round and round and have no join. With brown wool and No. 12 needles cast on 64 stitches, and work in ribbing, 1 stitch plain and 1 stitch purl, for 80 rows (or rounds), and cast off. Work a crochet edge at the top and bottom of the anklet—1 double crochet in a stitch of the knitting, miss three stitches, 6 treble in the next, miss three stitches, and repeat to the end of the round. Make the other anklet in the same manner. Then for the **Lining**—Take the Shetland wool and No. 8 needles, and cast on 40 stitches. Knit plain 46 rows, and cast off loosely. Knit another similar piece of lining. Sew the lining inside the anklet to reach from the casting on to the casting off of the ribbed knitting.

D'OYLEY. EIGHT-POINTED STAR.

PROCURE two skeins of Strutt's knitting cotton, No. 16, or Coats' crochet cotton the same size, and four steel knitting needles, No. 18. Cast 3 stitches on the first needle, 3 stitches on the second, and 2 stitches on the third needle. Knit 2 rounds plain, and every alternate round throughout the d'oyley is knitted plain unless otherways stated. **3rd round**—Make 1, knit 1, and repeat seven times. **5th round**—Make 1, knit 2, and repeat. **7th round**—Make 1, knit 3, and repeat. **9th round**—Make 1, knit 4, and repeat. **11th round**—Make 1, knit 5, and repeat. **13th round**—Make 1, knit 6, and repeat. **15th round**—Make 1, knit 7, and repeat. **17th round**—Make 1, knit 8, and repeat. **19th round**—Make 1, knit 1, make 1, slip 1, knit 1, pass the slip stitch over, knit 6, and repeat the same seven times. **21st round**—Make 1, knit 3, make 1, slip 1, knit 1, pass the slipped stitch over, knit 5, and repeat. **23rd round**—Make 1, knit 2, make 1, slip 1, knit 1, pass the slipped stitch over, knit 1, make 1, slip 1, knit 1, pass the slipped stitch over, knit 4, and repeat. **25th round**—Make 1, knit 2, make 1, slip 1, knit 1, pass the slipped stitch over, make 1, slip 1, knit 1, pass the slipped stitch over, knit 1, make 1, slip 1, knit 1, pass the slipped stitch over, knit 3, and repeat. **27th round**—Make 1, knit 2, * make 1, slip 1, knit 1, pass the slipped stitch over, repeat from *, make 1, slip 1, knit 1, pass the slipped stitch over, knit 2, and repeat. **29th round**—Make 1, knit 2, * make 1, slip 1, knit 1, pass the slipped stitch over, repeat from * twice, make 1, slip 1, knit 1, pass the slipped stitch over, knit 1, make 1, slip 1, knit 1, pass the slipped stitch over, knit 1, and repeat. **31st round**—Make 1, knit 2, * make 1, slip 1, knit 1, pass the slipped stitch over, repeat from * three times, make 1, slip 1, knit 1, pass the slipped stitch over, knit 1, make 1, slip 1, knit 1, pass the slipped stitch over, and repeat. **33rd round**—Make 1, slip 1, knit 1, pass the slipped stitch over, repeat this six times, make 1, knit 2, and repeat. **35th round**—Knit 1, * make 1, slip 1,

knit 1, pass the slipped stitch over, repeat from * five times, make 1, knit 4, and repeat. **37th round**—Make 1, slip 1, knit 1, pass the slipped stitch over, repeat this five times, make 1, knit 6, and repeat. **39th round**—Knit 1, * make 1, slip 1, knit 1, pass the slipped stitch over, repeat from * four times, make 1, knit 8, and repeat. **41st round**—Make 1, slip 1, knit 1, pass the slipped stitch over, repeat this four times, make 1, knit 10, and repeat. **43rd round**—Knit 1, * make 1, slip 1, knit 1, pass the slipped stitch over, repeat from * three times, make 1, knit 12, and repeat. **45th round**—Make 1, slip 1, knit 1, pass the slipped stitch over, repeat this three times, make 1, knit 14, and repeat. **47th round**—Knit 1, * make 1, slip 1, knit 1, pass the slipped stitch over, repeat from * twice, make 1, knit 16, and repeat. **49th round**—Make 1, slip 1, knit 1, pass the slipped stitch over, repeat this twice, make 1, knit 18, and repeat. **51st round**—Knit 1, * make 1, slip 1, knit 1, pass the slipped stitch over, repeat from * once, make 1, knit 20, and repeat. **53rd round**—Make 1, slip 1, knit 1, pass the slipped stitch over, make 1, slip 1, knit 1, pass the slipped stitch over, make 1, knit 22, and repeat. **55th round** — Knit 1, make 1, slip 1, knit 1, pass the slipped stitch over, make 1, knit 24, and repeat. **57th round**—Make 1, slip 1, knit 1, pass the slipped stitch over, make 1, knit 26, and repeat. **59th round**—Knit 1, make 1, knit 28, and repeat. **60th round**—Plain; 30 stitches in each division of the star, 240 stitches in the round. Purl 3 rounds. **64th round**—Plain, and increase by knitting 1 in the front and 1 in the back of every fifth stitch; this will bring 300 stitches in the round. **65th round**—Make 1, knit 2 together, and repeat the same all round. Knit 6 more rounds the same. **72nd round**—Knit 1, * make 1, slip 1, knit 1, pass the slipped stitch over, repeat from * to the end of the round; the holes that was made in the last round is to be knit in this round and the holes are now to slant from right to left; there is an odd stitch at the end of each needle, slip it, knit the first stitch off the next needle and pass the slipped stitch over. Knit four more

rounds the same. **77th round**—Make 1, knit 2 together, and repeat the same all round, the holes now slant in the same direction as at first, i.e., from left to right. Knit 4 more rounds the same. **82nd round**—Knit 7, knit 2 in the next stitch, and repeat. Purl 3 rounds. Cast off somewhat loosely. For the **Border**—Cast on 8 stitches. **1st row**—Slip 1, knit 1, make 1, knit 2 together, make 1, knit 2 together, make 2, knit 2. **2nd row**—Knit 3, purl 5, knit 2. **3rd row**—Slip 1, knit 1, make 1, knit 2 together, make 1, knit 2 together, knit 4. **4th row**—Cast off 2, knit 1, purl 4, knit 2. Repeat these four rows till sufficient is knitted to go round the d'oyley, when cast off, and sew it neatly on.

GENTLEMAN'S UNDER-VEST.

REQUIRED, 10 ozs. of the best white unshrinkable vest wool, a pair of long bone knitting needles No. 9 for working the body of the vest, steel knitting needles No. 12 and also No. 9, four needles of each size, for knitting the sleeves, and four white linen buttons. Take the bone knitting needles, and for the front half of the vest, beginning at the bottom, cast on 156 stitches. Work in ribbing, 2 stitches plain and 2 stitches purl, every row the same, for 140 rows, or till the work measures 16 inches in length; it will then be time to begin the opening on the chest, which as is usual in a gentleman's vest is made a little to the right-hand side. **141st row**—Work in ribbing 102 stitches, and leaving 54 stitches unknitted on the left-hand pin, turn the work, slip the first stitch, purl the next, knit ten stitches plain, and rib to the end of the needle. **Next row**—Rib 88 stitches, knit 14 stitches plain; turn the work, slip the first stitch, purl the next, knit 10 stitches plain, and rib to the end of the needle. Continue in this manner forwards and backwards on the 102 stitches till about 20 rows are done, then make a buttonhole in the edge, thus, when within 6 stitches of the end, cast the last stitch but one on the right-hand needle over the last stitch, knit a stitch and cast off another, and so on

Lady's Mitten.

Anklet, as Worn.

Anklet with Bottom turned up,
showing the Knitted Lining.

till 4 stitches are cast off, knit the 3 last stitches; turn, slip the first stitch, purl the next, knit 2, cast on 4, knit 8, and rib to the end. Proceed in the same manner till you have done three buttonholes with 20 rows between each. After the third buttonhole is made knit 13 rows. **1st Neck row**—Beginning on the buttonhole side—Cast off 48 stitches, rib to the end. **2nd row**—Rib 54 stitches. **3rd row**—Cast off 4, rib to the end. **4th row**—Rib 50 stitches. **5th row**—Cast off 4 more, rib to the end. **6th row**—Rib 46 stitches. **7th row**—Again cast off 4, rib to the end. Now there are 42 stitches on the needle. Still work in ribbing, and at the beginning of every row shoulder end, cast off seven stitches, till all are cast off. Resume where you divided the stitches for the opening, and pick up and knit 12 stitches at the back of the plain knitted edge and rib the 54 stitches off the left-hand needle. **Next row**—Rib 56, knit 10. **Next row**—Knit 12, rib 54. Continue these two rows till this half of the front is equal in length to the first half. Then, for the **1st row** of the **Neck**—Beginning on the plain edge side—Cast off 12 stitches, rib to the end. **2nd row**—Rib 54 stitches. **3rd row**—Cast off 4, rib to the end. **4th row**—Rib 50 stitches. **5th row**—Cast off 4 more, rib to the end. **6th row**—Rib 46 stitches. **7th row**—Again cast off 4, rib to the end. Now there are 42 stitches on the needle. Still work in ribbing, and at the beginning of every row shoulder end, cast off 7 stitches, till all are cast off. This finishes the front of the vest. For the **Back**—Cast on 156 stitches, and work in ribbing of 2 stitches plain and 2 stitches purl, till the piece of knitting is as long as the front piece, measuring to the shoulders. Work 42 shoulder stitches on each side in the same way as directed for the front, and cast off the 72 centre stitches for the neck. Sew the shoulder pieces together, and join up the sides of the vest, leaving space for the arm-holes. For the **Neck**—Pick up stitches all round the top of the vest, knitting each stitch as you pick it up; then knit a plain row, in the course of which decrease to 96 or 100 stitches, by taking 2 stitches together at regular intervals.

Work 10 rows of ribbing; do not forget to make a buttonhole in the fifth row of this ribbing on the buttonhole side. When the 10 rows of ribbing are finished cast all the stitches off. Strengthen the buttonholes by sewing round them with white silk. For the **Sleeves**—Take the four steel knitting needles No. 12, and cast 22 stitches on each of three needles, 66 stitches in all; join round for the wrist, and knit in rounds, in ribbing of 1 stitch plain and 1 stitch purl, for 50 rounds. **51st round**—Plain, and increase 5 stitches at equal distances from each other. Now there will be 71 stitches in the round. Now use the four bone knitting needles, and work in ribbing 2 stitches plain and 2 stitches purl, with the 1 odd stitch for a seam stitch, for 14 rounds. Increase in the next round, and in every sixth round afterwards, 1 stitch on each side the seam stitch, till the sleeve is finished; always have 2 stitches between the increased stitch and the seam stitch. When the sleeve is about 11 inches long begin to lengthen one half of it more than the other half to make it sit well on the arm, this is done by working from the seam stitch to a little beyond the half of the round and then turning back to the seam stitch again, do this about every tenth round, still increasing as before every sixth round on each side of the seam stitch. The sleeve will be long enough when it measures about 20 inches from the beginning. Cast off very loosely. Knit the other

beads to three consecutive stitches. Slip the first stitch at the beginning of every beaded row, but knit it at the beginning of all the rows that commence along the scalloped edge. Cast on 20 stitches. Knit 1 plain row. **1st beaded row**—Knit 4 stitches plain, knit 1 bead stitch, 5 plain, 1 bead, 5 plain, 1 bead, 2 plain, increase by knitting 1 in the front of the last stitch. **2nd row—and every alternate row,**—Plain knitting. **3rd row**—Knit 3 stitches plain, knit 3 bead stitches, 3 plain, 3 beads, 3 plain, 3 beads, 2 plain, increase by knitting 1 in the back and 1 in the front of the last stitch. **5th row**—4 plain, 1 bead, 5 plain, 1 bead, 5 plain, 1 bead, 4 plain, increase in the last stitch. **7th row**—7 plain, 1 bead, 5 plain, 1 bead, 5 plain, 1 bead, 2 plain, increase in the last stitch. **9th row**—6 plain, 3 beads, 3 plain, 3 beads, 3 plain, 3 beads, 2 plain, increase in the last stitch. **11th row**—7 plain, 1 bead, 5 plain, 1 bead, 5 plain, 1 bead, 5 plain, 1 bead, 4 plain, increase in the last stitch. **13th row**—4 plain, 1 bead, 5 plain, 1 bead, 5 plain, 1 bead, 5 plain, 1 bead, 2 plain, increase in the last stitch. **15th row**—3 plain, 3 beads, 3 plain, 3 beads, 3 plain, 3 beads, 3 plain, 3 beads, 2 plain, increase in the last stitch. **17th row**—4 plain, 1 bead, 5 plain, 1 bead, 5 plain, 1 bead, 5 plain, 1 bead, 4 plain, increase in the last stitch. **19th row**—7 plain, 1 bead, 5 plain, 1 bead, 5 plain, 1 bead, 5 plain, 1 bead, 2 plain, increase in the last stitch. **21st row**—6 plain,

D'Oyley. Eight-Pointed Star.

sleeve in the same manner, remembering to do the half-rounds on the opposite side, that the sleeves may be right and left. Sew the sleeves into the armholes, the seam stitch by the seam of the vest, and the middle of the sleeve to the middle of the shoulder, with the longest half of the sleeve to the back of the vest.

BEADED COLLARETTE.

REQUIRED, 3 or 4 skeins of medium-sized black purse silk and 3 hanks of the best quality small black cut beads; a pair of steel knitting needles No. 17; and for the neck-band a piece of black ribbon velvet 16 inches long and ¾ inch wide, which has to be lined with a piece of thin black ribbon of the same length and width. The beads must first of all be threaded upon the silk, scattering them thereupon conveniently to be ready for knitting up; if too few beads are threaded upon one skein of silk the ball can be unwound and more threaded at the other end. The collarette is worked every stitch in plain knitting, and the beads are placed so as to form a pattern of tiny stars or crosses. When instructed to put "1 bead," you push one bead close up to the needle at the back of the work and knit one stitch plain, and when it says "3 beads" you do the same thing three consecutive times and thereby place 3

3 beads, 3 plain, 3 beads, 3 plain, 3 beads, 3 plain, 3 beads, 2 plain, increase in the last stitch. **23rd row**—7 plain, 1 bead, 5 plain, 1 bead, 5 plain, 1 bead, 5 plain, 1 bead, 3 plain, knit the last 2 stitches together. **25th row**—4 plain, 1 bead, 5 plain, 1 bead, 5 plain, 1 bead, 5 plain, 1 bead, 5 plain, knit the last two stitches together. **27th row**—3 plain, 3 beads, 3 plain, 3 beads, 3 plain, 3 beads, 3 plain, 3 beads, 3 plain, knit the last two together. **29th row**—4 plain, 1 bead, 5 plain, 1 bead, 5 plain, 1 bead, 5 plain, 1 bead, 3 plain, knit the last 2 together. **31st row**—7 plain, 1 bead, 5 plain, 1 bead, 5 plain, 1 bead, 5 plain, knit the last 2 together. **33rd row**—6 plain, 3 beads, 3 plain, 3 beads, 3 plain, 3 beads, 3 plain, knit the last 2 together. **35th row**—7 plain, 1 bead, 5 plain, 1 bead, 5 plain, 1 bead, 3 plain, knit the last two together. **37th row**—4 plain, 1 bead, 5 plain, 1 bead, 5 plain, 1 bead, 5 plain, knit the last 2 together. **39th row**—3 plain, 3 beads, 3 plain, 3 beads, 3 plain, 3 beads, 3 plain, knit the last 2 together. Repeat from the fifth row till you have five scallops knitted. The sixth scallop is both deeper and wider than the preceding. Work first from the 5th row to the 21st row as above. Then work the following rows. **23rd row**—7 plain, 1 bead, * 5 plain, 1 bead, repeat from * twice, 4 plain, increase in the last stitch. **25th row**—4 plain, 1 bead, * 5 plain, 1 bead, repeat from * three times, 2 plain, increase in the last stitch. **27th row**—3 plain, 3 beads, repeat this four times, 2 plain, increase in the

last stitch. **29th row**—4 plain, 1 bead, * 5 plain, 1 bead, repeat from * three times, 3 plain, knit the last two stitches together. **31st row**—7 plain, 1 bead, * 5 plain, 1 bead, repeat from * twice, 5 plain, knit the last 2 stitches together. **33rd row**—6 plain, 3 beads, * 3 plain, 3 beads, repeat from * twice, 3 plain, knit the last two together. Now make your 35th row the same as the 23rd row of the preceding scallops, and proceed thence to the 39th row. Knit one more scallop the same. Now for the centre scallop, which again is deeper and wider than the foregoing. Work the same as last scallop till you get to the 27th row. Then work the following rows. **29th row**—4 plain, 1 bead, * 5 plain, 1 bead, repeat from * three times, 4 plain, increase in the last stitch. **31st row**—7 plain, 1 bead, * 5 plain, 1 bead, repeat from * three times, 2 plain, increase in the last stitch. **33rd row**—6 plain, 3 beads, * 3 plain, 3 beads, repeat from * three times, 2 plain, increase in the last stitch. **35th row**—7 plain, 1 bead, * 5 plain, 1 bead, repeat from * three times, 3 plain, knit the last 2 stitches together. **37th row**—4 plain, 1 bead, * 5 plain, 1 bead, repeat from * three times, 5 plain, knit the last 2 stitches together. **39th row**—3 plain, 3 beads, repeat this four times, 3 plain, knit the last 2 stitches together. Now make the **39th row** similar to the **29th row** of last scallop and work according to those instructions till the scallop is brought to three beaded stars with 22 stitches on the needle. Work 2 more scallops to match those on the opposite side of the centre scallop, and finish the collarette with 5 scallops the

BEADED CUFFS TO MATCH THE COLLARETTE.

(Not Illustrated.)

To be knitted with the same silk and beads as used for the collarette. Cast on 30 stitches. Knit 1 plain row. Slip the first stitch at the beginning of every beaded row, but knit it at the beginning of the plain rows. **1st Beaded row**—Knit 4 stitches plain, knit 1 bead stitch, 5 plain, 1 bead, 5 plain, 1 bead, 5 plain, 1 bead, 5 plain, knit the last 2 stitches together. **2nd row**—Plain knitting. **3rd row**—Knit 3 stitches plain, knit three bead stitches do this three more times, 3 plain, knit the last 2 stitches together. **5th row**—4 plain, 1 bead, 5 plain, 1 bead, 5 plain, 1 bead, 5 plain, 1 bead, 4 plain, increase by knitting 1 in the back of the last stitch. **7th row**—7 plain, 1 bead, 5 plain, 1 bead, 5 plain, 1 bead, 5 plain, 1 bead, 2 plain, increase by knitting 1 in the back and 1 in the front of the last stitch. **9th row**—6 plain, 3 beads, 3 plain, 3 beads, 3 plain, 3 beads, 3 plain, 3 beads, 2 plain, increase in the last stitch. **11th row**—7 plain, 1 bead, 5 plain, 1 bead, 5 plain, 1 bead, 5 plain, 1 bead, 4 plain, increase in the last stitch. **13th row**—4 plain, 1 bead, * 5 plain, 1 bead, repeat from * three times, 2 plain, increase in the last stitch. **15th row**—3 plain, 3 beads, do this four more times, 2 plain, increase in the last stitch. **17th row**—4 plain,

Gentleman's Under-Vest.

Bea

same as the five with which you began, reducing the number of stitches to 20, and cast off. For the **Neckband**—Take the piece of black ribbon velvet, and after mitring it in the centre to make it fit more shapely round the neck, embroider it with triple feather stitch, putting 3 beads to each stitch, as shown in the engraving. Seam the ribbon lining to the ribbon velvet at the top of the band, and as you seam put in a bead with every alternate stitch of the seaming. Sew the straight edge of the knitting to the lower edge of the neckband, fulling it in nicely to the required size. For **Beaded Fringe**—Work with a needleful of silk, and to begin, bring the needle up at the end corner of the neckband, thread 4 beads, miss the bead last threaded and pass the silk back through 3 beads to the neckband again; now thread 1 bead, and go back to the neckband; next thread 5 beads, and go back through 4 into the neckband again, now thread 1 bead, and again go back to the neckband; continue thus, and as you go down the edge of the neckband and the front edge of the knitting increase the length of the "fringes" to 18 beads; proceed round the scallops putting 20 beads in every fringe, and remember always to put 1 bead close to the knitting between each fringe; work the opposite front edge of the collarette to correspond with the front edge already done. Sew a small black hook to one end of the neckband and make a buttonhole stitch loop at the other end.

1 bead, * 5 plain, 1 bead, repeat from * three times, 3 plain, knit the last 2 stitches together. **19th row**—7 plain, 1 bead, 5 plain, 1 bead, 5 plain, 1 bead, 5 plain, 1 bead, 5 plain, knit the last 2 together. **21st row**—6 plain, 3 beads, 3 plain, 3 beads, 3 plain, 3 beads, 3 plain, 3 beads, 3 plain, knit the last two together. **23rd row**—7 plain, 1 bead, 5 plain, 1 bead, 5 plain, 1 bead, 5 plain, 1 bead, 3 plain, knit the last 2 together. Repeat from the first beaded row till six of the small scallops are knitted, when cast off. Work for the **Top of the Cuff** in ribbing, which causes the cuff to cling and draw closely to the arm. Hold the beaded knitting the right side towards you, and pick up along the straight edge 64 stitches, knitting each stitch as you pick it up. Work in ribbing, 2 stitches plain and 2 stitches purl, every row alike, for 40 rows, and cast off loosely. Sew up the cuff. Thread a needle with a needleful of silk, and seam over the scalloped edge of the knitting, sewing a bead on thereto with each stitch, so finishing off the scallops with a line of beads set rather closely together. Knit the other cuff in the same manner. These cuffs may be knitted with Andalusian wool and coloured beads if desired, and will be durable and look well for every-day wear. Very handsome dressy cuffs for evening are made with black silk and gold beads.

GENTLEMAN'S DRAWERS.

In No. 46 of "Weldon's Practical Needlework Series" will be found a pair of gentleman's drawers knitted with thick warm wool and intended specially for winter wear, and as it may be useful to some of our readers to knit a similar garment with finer wool, we here give a pair of drawers suitable for spring and autumn, or for those gentlemen who do not care for heavy clothing. Required, 10 ozs. of best white Peacock fingering, AA quality, Faudel and Phillips' make; or the same quantity of unshrinkable vest wool; two No. 5 bone knitting needles, four steel knitting needles, No. 9, and four No. 11; $\frac{1}{4}$ yard of white sateen for lining, 3 buttons, 1 yard of tape, and a skein of white sewing silk. Commence for the bottom of the left leg with No. 11 steel needles, by casting on 64 stitches divided upon three needles; work with the fourth needle, going round and round, in ribbing of 1 stitch plain and 1 stitch purl, for 40 rounds. **41st round**—With No. 9 steel needles—Beginning on the first needle—Knit 3, * increase 1 by picking up the thread that lies close under the next stitch and knitting it, knit 3, and repeat from * to the end of the third needle where will be 4 stitches to knit; and now there should be 84 stitches in the round. **42nd round**—Knit 3, purl 1, and repeat the same to the end of the round. Knit 11 more rounds the same. **54th round**—Begin the leg increasings—the last stitch upon the third needle is a purl stitch, and must be considered as a seam

gusset will afterwards be placed. When the $4\frac{1}{2}$ inches are worked, at the end of the forward row (the right side of the work being towards you), cast on 9 stitches for lapping over in front; turn, slip the first stitch, purl the next, knit 8 plain, and rib the remainder as before. Always knit 10 plain stitches at the end of the forward row, and in the back row, slip 1, purl 1, knit 8, and continue in ribbing; it so makes a nice even edge for the opening in front of the garment. After commencing this edge there are no more increasings at either end of the row. When about 10 rows are knitted thus, you begin to decrease at the back of the drawers—*i.e.*, at the beginning of the forward rows, and also begin to make the back half of the leg longer than the front—you do it this way—knit 4, knit 2 together, rib along as far as the centre of the row, turn the work and rib back, then do 8 rows from end to end, and continue the same till the top of the drawers is reached. When the front edge of the plain knitting measures $3\frac{1}{2}$ inches make in it a button hole, thus, when within 5 stitches of the end of the forward row draw the last stitch but one of the right-hand needle over the last stitch, knit 1, draw over again, knit 3; turn, slip the first stitch, purl the next, knit 2, cast on 3, knit 3, and continue in ribbing. Make two more buttonholes as you go along, doing about $3\frac{1}{2}$ inches of knitting between. When the front, from the beginning of the plain knitted edge, measures about $11\frac{1}{2}$ inches, cast off, and in the casting off lessen the number of stitches by taking 2 stitches together off

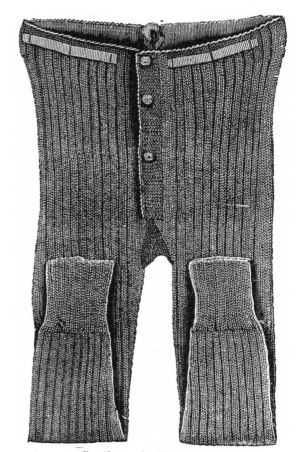

Gentleman's Drawers.

ette.

stitch on each side of which increases are to be made, thus—Knit 2, increase 1, knit 1, purl 1, knit 3, purl 1, rib to within 4 stitches of the end of the third needle, knit 1, increase 1, knit 2, purl 1. **55th round**—Knit 4, purl 1, rib to within 5 stitches of the end of the third needle, knit 4, purl 1. Work 7 more rounds the same as last round. **Next round**—Rib as before, and increase 1 stitch each side the seam stitch. Continue working 8 rounds of ribbing without increasing, and increase every ninth round, always bringing the increased stitches into "ribs" as soon as sufficient stitches are formed. When your work measures 27 inches from the beginning the leg will probably be long enough, and henceforth you work *in rows* backwards and forwards, but for the present you had better keep the stitches divided as they are upon three needles, and take to the bone needles as soon as they can conveniently be used. **1st row**—Having turned the work after knitting to the end of the third needle, knit the first stitch (the seam stitch, which now is not needed as a seam stitch any more), purl the knit stitches and knit the purl stitch to the end of the row. **2nd row**—Ribbing in the ordinary manner. **3rd row**—Knit the first stitch, purl the knit stitches and knit the purl stitch to the end of the row. Still increase every ninth row from the last increase, *i.e.*, at 2 stitches from the beginning and at 2 stitches from the end of the row, till the length of $4\frac{1}{2}$ inches is worked in rows; this space is where a

the left-hand needle at every fourth stitch that you cast off. Now in the space that was left for the gusset, pick up and knit 24 stitches on the front of the leg beginning where the plain knitted edge began, knit them 3 plain, 1 purl, alternately, and back 3 purl, 1 plain, till you have a perfect square, when cast off, and this finishes the left leg, The right leg is worked exactly the same as the left till the space for the gusset is reached, and then the shaping is reversed, and you make the plain knitted edge at the beginning of the forward rows and do the decreasing and the lengthening for the back at the end; no buttonholes are required on this side, and you may cast on 6 stitches instead of nine, as the edge need not be very wide. The drawers are now to be put together; by looking at another pair of drawers you will see how the gusset is to be joined in, one point must be straight up the front and the other point up the back. Sew the two backs of the drawers together to within about 4 inches from the top. Line the top of the drawers and down the front with sateen; cut buttonholes in the sateen to correspond with those in the knitting, and work them with silk over and over the knitting; sew on the buttons. Make two eyelet holes on each side of the back where it is left open, one eyelet hole near the top, the other near the bottom of the opening, and put in a piece of tape to draw in and tie to the required size. Sew a piece of tape about 7 inches long on each leg, about $\frac{1}{2}$ inch from the top and about 2 inches from the fronts, stitching each piece firmly down at each end and also across the centre, as shown in the engraving; this is for suspenders to pass through. Stitch the cast-on stitches of the plain knitted edge to lie perfectly flat one over the other, the buttonhole edge being on the top.

LADY'S STOCKING.

THIS stocking is worked in plain knitting, the leg and the instep are knitted with black wool, and the heel and the under part of the sole with white wool, as is now so fashionable. Procure 4 ozs. of black and ½ oz. of white Andalusian wool, and four No. 17 steel knitting needles. Cast on with black wool 40 stitches on each of three needles, 120 stitches in all. Work in ribbing, 2 stitches plain and 2 stitches purl, round and round, for 30 rounds, for the welt of the stocking. **31st round**—Knit plain, and pick up and knit an additional stitch at the end of the third needle, which stitch is for the seam stitch. Knit 170 rounds of plain knitting, doing the seam stitch purl in one round and plain in the next, for by alternating it in this manner the number of rounds are more easily counted. **Next round**—Begin decreasing the leg—* Knit 2 stitches off the first needle, slip 1, knit 1, pass the slipped stitch over, knit plain to within 5 stitches of the end of the third needle, knit 2 together, knit 2, purl the seam stitch. Knit 7 plain rounds with the seam stitch alternated as before. Repeat from * ten times. You will now have 99 stitches on the three needles for the ankle. Work round and round for about 76 rounds. Then for the **Heel**—Still with black wool—Knit plain 25 stitches from off the first needle, turn the work, slip the first stitch, purl 24 stitches, and purl also 26 stitches off the end of the third needle, making 51 stitches on one needle for the flap of the heel; the remaining 48 stitches should be divided equally on two needles and left for the present. Work the heel stitches thus—**1st row**—Slip the first stitch, knit 24, purl the seam stitch, knit 25. **2nd row**—Slip the first stitch, purl 50. Repeat the two rows till 26 rows are knitted with black wool; then break off black, join on the white wool, and knit 14 rows the same. To **shape the Heel**—Still with white wool, slip the first stitch, knit 19, knit 2 together, knit 3, purl the seam stitch, knit 3, slip 1, knit 1, pass the slipped stitch over, knit 20. Purl back. **Next row**—Slip the first stitch, knit 18, knit 2 together, knit 3, purl the seam stitch, knit 3, slip 1, knit 1, pass the slipped stitch over, knit 19. Purl back. Decrease thus in every forward row till you reduce the heel to 16 purl stitches on each side the seam stitch. Then slip the end 16 stitches on to another needle, hold the two needles parallel together, and cast off by knitting together a stitch from each needle. Now for the **Instep** and **Gussets**—Using black wool—Hold the flap of the heel the right side towards you, pick up and knit 17 stitches along the portion of the flap that is knitted with black wool, on the same needle knit plain the 48 instep stitches, and still on the same needle pick up and knit 17 stitches along the black portion of the other side of the heel flap; this makes 82 stitches all on one needle. Purl a row. **3rd row**—Slip the first stitch, knit 4, knit 2 together, knit plain to within 7 stitches of the end of the needle, slip 1, knit 1, pass the slipped stitch over, knit 5. **4th row**—Purl. **5th row**—Plain. **6th row**—Purl. Repeat these four rows till reduced to 66 stitches. Knit without any more decreasing, a plain row and a purl row alternately, till about 100 rows in all are knitted from the heel. For the **Toe—1st row**—Still with black wool—Slip the first stitch, knit 4, knit 2 together, knit plain to within 7 stitches of the end of the needle, slip 1, knit 1, pass the slipped stitch over, knit 5. **2nd row**—Purl. **3rd row**—Plain. **6th row**—Purl. Repeat these four rows eight times. Then decrease every alternate row till reduced to 26 stitches from the point of the toe. Join on the white wool, and knit forwards plain and backwards purl on the 26 stitches, increasing them in the course of every eighth row to 36 stitches, and when sufficient length is knitted to reach to the heel, the sole will be complete and may be cast off. Sew the sole neatly along each side of the instep, and fit it to the lower portion of the heel. The other stocking is knitted in the same manner.

RIBBED STOCKING FOR BOY OF SIX OR SEVEN YEARS.

THIS will be found a particularly nice shaped stocking, and if knitted with fine fingering wool and needles No. 16 will be of a size to fit a boy of six or seven years, or if a coarser wool such as Alloa be employed the stocking will be suitable for an older boy. Procure from 3 ozs. to 4 ozs. of wool of a pretty grey shade and four steel knitting needles. Cast 28 stitches on the first needle, and 24 stitches on each of two other needles, 76 stitches in all. Work in ribbing of 1 stitch plain and 1 stitch purl for 20 rounds, this forms the top of the

Lady's Stocking.

stocking. Rib 3 stitches plain and 1 stitch purl for 64 rounds. **Next round**—With a thread of cotton mark 1 purl stitch for a seam stitch (the 16th stitch on the first needle), * proceed in ribbing, and when 2 stitches before the seam stitch increase a stitch (by picking up the thread that lies directly below the next stitch and knitting it), and when 2 stitches beyond the seam stitch increase a stitch, and rib on to the end of the round. Work 3 ribbed rounds doing the increased stitches plain. Repeat from * till there are 4 additional stitches each side the seam stitch. Work 12 rounds entirely 3 plain, 1 purl. **110th round**—Begin the leg decreasing—Rib till within 5 stitches of the seam stitch, then slip 1, knit 2 together, pass the slipped stitch over, knit 2, purl the seam stitch, knit 2, knit 3 together, knit 2, purl 1, and rib on to the end of the round. Rib 7 intermediate rounds, doing 5 plain stitches over each decrease. **Next round**—Rib till within 4 stitches of the seam stitch, then slip 1, knit 2 together, pass the slip stitch over, knit 1, purl the seam stitch, knit 1, knit 3 together, knit 1, purl 1, and rib on to the end of the round. Rib 11 intermediate rounds, the ribs come in regularly. Repeat from the 110th round twice, and there will be 60 stitches in the round. Continue in ribbing for the ankle, doing 44 rounds. Then for the **Heel**—Rib as far as 15 stitches beyond the seam stitch; turn, rib 31 stitches; leave 29 stitches for the instep divided upon two pins, and with the other two pins continue ribbing on these 31 heel stitches for 28 rows. To turn the **Heel**—Slip the first stitch, knit plain 18 stitches, slip 1, knit 1, pass the slipped stitch over; turn, slip the first stitch, purl 7, purl 2 together; * turn, slip the first stitch, knit 7, slip 1, knit 1, pass the slipped stitch over; turn, slip the first stitch, purl 7, purl 2 together; and repeat from * till all the side stitches are knitted in, and 9 stitches remain on the needle for the top of the heel. For the **Foot**—Knit plain these 9 heel stitches, and on the same needle pick up and knit 18 stitches along the flap of the heel; rib the 29 instep stitches all on one needle; and on the third needle pick up and knit 18 stitches along the other side of the flap and knit 4 stitches off the top of the heel; now 74 stitches are arranged on three needles. Knit 1 round plain on two foot needles and ribbed on the instep needle. **Next round**—The same, but decrease at the gusset end of each foot needle. Repeat these two rounds till reduced to 29 stitches on the two foot needles. Continue now without any more decreasing, working plain on foot and ribbed on instep, for 42 rounds. For the **Toe—1st round**—On the instep needle, knit 1, slip 1, knit 1, pass the slipped stitch over, knit plain to within 3 stitches of the end of the needle, knit 2 together, knit 1; on the foot needle, knit 1, slip 1, knit 1, pass the slipped stitch over, knit plain to within 3 stitches of the end of the second foot needle, knit 2 together, knit 1. **2nd round**—Plain. Repeat these two rounds till the toe is reduced to 13 stitches on the instep needle and 13 stitches on the two foot needles, slip these last all on to one pin, place it parallel with the instep needle, and cast off by knitting a stitch from each needle at the same time.

LONG SOCK FOR A CHILD.

KNITTED ON TWO NEEDLES, AND WITH A BERLIN PATTERN STRIPE IN FRONT.

THIS is a very pretty sock and equally suitable for a boy or a girl of from three years to five years of age. The front of the sock is knitted in a fancy Berlin pattern stripe with wool of two colours, the back is in simple ribbed knitting. Only two needles are employed, therefore the sock may readily be accomplished by any fairly good knitter, the leg is nicely shaped, and the sole which is knitted separately from the instep can easily be taken out and renewed when necessary, a great advantage as those know who have much to do with children's socks. Our model is worked with Andalusian wool, 2 ozs. of a bright dark blue and ½ oz. of white being required, and a pair of No. 17 steel knitting needles; or Berlin fingering and No. 16 needles may be used if preferred. With blue wool cast on 74 stitches, and work in ribbing. **1st row**—Slip 1, knit 1,* purl 2, knit 2, and repeat from * to the end of the row. **2nd row**—Slip 1, purl 1,* knit 2, purl 2, and repeat from *. Repeat these 2 rows till 6 rows are knitted. Then do 2 rows with white wool. 6 rows with blue wool. 2 rows with white. 6 rows with blue. 2 rows with white. 6 rows with blue. Now 30 rows are done, which completes the ribbed welting for the top of the sock. **31st row**—Still with blue wool—Slip 1, knit 1, purl 2, knit 2 and purl 2 alternately five times, knit 13, increase 1 by picking up the thread that lies close under the next stitch and knitting it, knit 13, purl 2 and knit 2 alternately six times. **32nd row**—Slip 1, purl 1, knit 2, purl 2 and knit 2 alternately five times, purl 27, knit 2 and purl 2 alternately six times. **33rd row**—Here the stripe begins—Slip 1, knit 1, purl 2 and knit 2 alternately five times, knit 13, take the white wool and knit 1 stitch, resume blue and knit 13, and purl 2 and knit 2 alternately six times. **34th row**—Slip 1, purl 1, knit 2, purl 2 and knit 2 alternately five times, purl 12, purl 3 stitches with white, resume blue, purl 12, knit 2 and purl 2 alternately six times. **35th row**—Slip 1, knit 1, purl 2, knit 2 and purl 2 alternately five times, knit 11, knit 2 with white, knit 1 with blue, knit 2 with white, knit 11 with blue, and purl 2 and knit 2 alternately six times. **36th row**—Slip 1, purl 1, knit 2, purl 2, and knit 2 alternately five times, purl 10, purl 2 with white, purl 3 with blue, purl 2 with white, purl 10 with blue, and knit 2 and purl 2 alternately six times. **37th row**—Slip 1, knit 1, purl 2, knit 2 and purl 2 alternately five times, knit 9, knit 2 with blue, 2 with blue, 1 white, 2 blue, 2 white, 9 blue, and purl 2 and knit 2 alternately six times. **38th row**—Slip 1, purl 1, knit 2, purl 2 and knit 2 alternately five times, purl 8, purl 2 with white, 2 with blue, 1 white, 1 blue, 1 white, 2 blue, 2 white, 8 blue, and knit 2 and purl 2 alternately six times. **39th row**—Slip 1, knit 1, purl 2, knit 2 and purl 2 alternately five times, knit 7, knit 2 with white, 2 with blue, 1 white, 1 blue, 1 white, 1 blue, 1 white, 2 blue, 2 white, 7 blue, and purl 2 and knit 2 alternately six times. **40th row**—Slip 1, purl 1, knit 2, purl 2 and knit 2 alternately five times, purl 6, purl 2 with white, 2 with blue, 1 white and 1 blue alternately three times, 1 white, 2 blue, 2 white, 6 blue, and knit 2 and purl 2 alternately six times. **41st row**—Slip 1, knit 1, purl 2, knit 2 and purl 2 alternately five times, knit 5, knit 2 with white, 2 with blue, 1 white and 1 blue alternately four times, 1 white, 2 blue, 2 white, 5 blue, and purl 2 and knit 2 alternately six times. **42nd row**—Slip 1, purl 1, knit 2, purl 2 and knit 2 alternately five times, purl 4, purl 2 with white, 2 with blue, 1 white and 1 blue alternately five times, 1 white, 2 blue, 2 white, 4 blue, and knit 2 and purl 2 alternately six times. **43rd row**—Slip 1, knit 1, purl 2, knit 2 and purl 2 alternately five times, knit 3,

together, knit 16 ; turn, purl back. **25th row**—Slip 1, knit 2 together, knit 15 ; turn, purl back. **27th row**—Slip 1, knit 2 together, knit 14 ; turn, purl back. **29th row**—Slip 1, knit 2 together, knit 3, knit 2 together, knit 8 ; turn, and purl back. Cast off 14 heel stitches. Recommence where you divided for the heel, take blue wool and slip 1, knit 1, purl 2, knit 9, knit 2 stitches with white wool, 2 with blue, 1 white, 2 blue, 2 white, 9 blue, and still with blue, purl 2, knit 1, increase 1, knit 4, increase 1, knit 4, increase 1, knit 5. **2nd row**—Purl 19 stitches ; turn the work, knit 19, and continue thus till 22 little rows are knitted for the other side of the heel. **23rd row**—Slip 1, knit 15, knit 2 together, knit 1 ; turn, purl back. **25th row**—slip 1, knit 14, knit 2 together, knit 1 ; turn, purl back. **27th row**—Slip 1, knit 13, knit 2 together, knit 1 ; turn, purl back. **29th row**—Slip 1, knit 3, knit 2 together, knit 3, knit 2 together, knit 1 ; turn, and purl back. Cast off 14 heel stitches. For the **Instep**—Recommence where you last divided for the heel, take blue wool, and slip 1, purl 1, knit 2, purl 8, purl 2 with white, purl 2 with blue, 1 white, 1 blue, 1 white, 2 blue, 2 white, 8 blue, and knit 2 and purl 2 also with blue. Now continue the diamond pattern on these 35 stitches for the instep, till you have in all six complete diamonds down the sock, when you must finish off the last diamond in a point of 1 white stitch as at the commencement ; this is done by working the 35th, 34th, and 33rd rows in rotation after doing the 36th row in the ordinary course. Work now entirely with blue wool—the forward row—Slip 1, knit 1, purl 2, knit 27, purl, 2, knit 2 ; and the back row—Slip 1, purl 1, knit 2, purl 27, knit 2, purl 2 ; and when 8 rows or 12 rows are accomplished the foot will be long enough. For the **Toe—1st row**—Slip 1, knit 1, slip 1, knit 1, pass the slipped stitch over, knit plain to within 4 stitches of the end, knit 2 together, knit 2. **2nd row**—Purl. Repeat these two rows till the toe is reduced to 13 stitches ; and cast off. For the **Sole**—Now sew together the cast-off stitches at the bottom of the heel, and holding the work the right side towards you, pick up, with blue wool, 43 stitches along the straight side of the heel, knitting each stitch as you pick it up ; turn the work, and purl back all 43 stitches, entirely with blue wool. **3rd row of the Sole**—Slip 1, knit 1, pass the slipped stitch over, knit plain to within 2 stitches of the end, knit those two together. **4th row**—Purl. Repeat these two rows till reduced to 33 stitches. Then knit forwards and backwards 1 row plain and 1 row purl for about 42 rows, or till the foot is long enough, which it will be when it is as long as the corresponding part of the

Ribbed Stocking for a Boy of Six or Seven Years.

knit 2 with white, 2 blue, 1 white and 1 blue alternately six times, 1 white 2 blue, 2 white, 3 blue, and purl 2 and knit 2 alternately six times. **44th row**—Slip 1, purl 1, knit 2, purl 2 and knit 2 alternately five times, purl 2, purl 2 with white, 2 blue, 1 white and 1 blue alternately seven times, 1 white, 2 blue, 2 white, 2 blue, and knit 2 and purl 2 alternately six times. **45th row**—Slip 1, knit 1, purl 2, knit 2 and purl 2 alternately five times, knit 1, knit 2 with white, 2 blue, 1 white and 1 blue alternately eight times, 1 white, 2 blue, 2 white, 1 blue, and purl 2 and knit 2 alternately six times. **46th. row**—The same as the forty-fourth row. **47th row**—Same as the forty-third. **48th row**—Same as the forty-second. **49th row**—Same as the forty-first. **50th row**—Same as the fortieth. **51st row**—Same as the thirty-ninth. **52nd row**—Same as the thirty-eighth. **53rd row**—Same as the thirty-seventh. **54th row**—Decrease the leg by taking 2 stitches together at the beginning and 2 stitches together at the end of the row ; keep the ribbed part straight, and knit the pattern in front of the sock as directed in the thirty-sixth row. **55th row**—The ribbing is to be kept straight at the beginning and at the end of the needle (minus 1 stitch that has been decreased away), the pattern in front is to be worked as in the thirty-seventh row. Continue now, widening the diamond pattern, till you get to the repetition of the forty-fifth row, where make another decrease at the beginning and at the end of the needle. And then, proceeding with the diamond pattern as before, again decrease when you repeat the fifty-fourth row. Continue still, and decrease again when you repeat the forty-fifth row. This makes 81 rows done and there are now 67 stitches on the needle. Now you rib 20 stitches at the beginning and 20 stitches at the end of each row, and work the front 27 stitches in the diamond pattern as already instructed, till you have knitted 108 rows in all down the leg, ending with the thirty-sixth row of the pattern. For the **Heel** Knit plain with blue wool, always slipping the first stitch of every row. **1st row**—Knit 5, increase 1, knit 4, increase 1, knit 4, increase 1, knit 3 ; turn the work, and purl 19 stitches. **3rd row**—Knit 19 ; turn, purl 19, and continue thus till 22 little rows are knitted. **23rd row**—Slip 1, knit 2

Long Sock for a Child.

instep. Decrease the toe as directed above till reduced to 13 stitches, and cast off. Sew the sole of the foot neatly to the upper part, and sew up the back of the leg. The other sock is to be knitted in the same way.

BABY'S SPENCER.

PETTIFER PATTERN.

THIS is a delightful spencer for a baby to wear in summer or at any time when a pretty light garment is desired. It is much in the shape of the Garibaldi jackets now so fashionable, and being fine work and an open stitch it is very elastic and fits any figure to perfection. Required, 2 ozs. of white Shetland wool, a pair of No. 13 bone knitting needles, and about 3½ yards of inch-wide ribbon for strings and bows. For the **Right Front** of the Spencer—Cast on 57 stitches, and knit in ribbing of 3 stitches plain and 3 stitches purl for 30 rows. **31st row**—Slip 1, knit 2, * make 1, knit 2 together knit 1, repeat from * to the end of the row. **32nd row**—Purl. This is the waist, and the small holes are to run a ribbon in. Now begin the **Body Pattern**—**1st row**—Slip 1, knit 1, * make 1, knit 1, slip 1, knit 2 together, pass the slipped stitch over, knit 1, make 1, knit 1, repeat from*, and knit the last stitch plain. **2nd row**—Purl. **3rd row**—Slip 1, knit 2, * make 1, slip 1, knit 2 together, pass the slipped stitch over, make 1, knit 3, and repeat from *. **4th row**—Purl. **5th row**—Slip 1, knit 2 together, knit 1, * make 1, knit 1, make 1, knit 1, slip 1, knit 2 together, pass the slipped stitch over, knit 1, repeat from *, and when within 5 stitches of the end of the row, make 1, knit 1, make 1, knit 1, knit 2 together, knit 1. **6th row**—Purl. **7th row**—Slip 1, knit 2 together, * make 1, knit 3, make 1, slip 1, knit 2 together, pass the slipped stitch over, repeat from *, and when within 6 stitches of the end of the row, make 1, knit 3, make 1, knit 2 together, knit 1. **8th row**—Purl. Repeat from the first row eight times more, which will make 72 pattern rows. **73rd row**—Cast off 20 stitches for the neck, and knit the remaining 37 stitches in pattern for three repeats, 24 rows, and then cast off all. For the **Left Front**—Cast on 57 stitches, and knit a piece to match that already done, the only difference being to cast off the 20 neck stitches in the last row (the purl row) of the pattern to bring the shoulder on the opposite side. For the **Back**—Cast on 90 stitches, and knit the same as directed for the fronts till you have a straight piece of twelve repeats of the pattern, then cast off all. Sew the shoulder pieces of the fronts to the back piece; it will be a perfectly straight seam, but the knitting will stretch to the figure of the child when on. Sew up the side seams leaving space for the sleeves. For the **Sleeves**—Cast on 57 stitches. Knit 22 rows of ribbing; then the 31st row and 32nd row the same as the spencer fronts; and proceed to the pettifer pattern, working nine repeats of the pattern, and cast off loosely. Knit the other sleeve the same. Sew the sleeves in the armholes. Work a **Crochet Edging** down the two fronts and along the neck of the spencer—**1st row**—1 treble in a stitch of the knitting,* 1 chain, miss one stitch of the knitting, 1 treble in the next, and repeat from *. **2nd row**—1 double crochet under one chain of last row,* 1 treble under the next one chain, 3 chain, 1 double crochet in the top of the treble stitch just done, another treble under the same loop of one chain, do a picot loop and a treble stitch twice more in the same place, then 1 double crochet under the next one chain of last row, and repeat from *. Run a piece of ribbon in the holes round the waist, and also round the neck to tie, also at the wrists, and sew on ribbon to make a bow in front of the spencer.

WEDGE PATTERN VEST FOR CHILD OF THREE YEARS.

THIS pretty vest is knitted with white Berlin fingering wool, of which about 3 ozs. will be required, and a pair of No. 10 bone knitting needles. Cast on 64 stitches. **1st row**—Knit 4, * purl 7, knit 7 and repeat from * three times, and knit the last 4 stitches plain. **2nd row**—Knit 4, * purl 6, knit 1, purl 1, knit 6, repeat from * and knit 4 at the end of the row. **3rd row**—Knit 4, * purl 5, knit 2, purl 2, knit 5, repeat from *, and end with knit 4. **4th row**—Knit 4, * purl 4, knit 3, purl 3, knit 4, repeat from, * and end with knit 4. **5th row**—Knit 4, * purl 3, knit 4, purl 4, knit 3, repeat from *, and knit the last 4 stitches plain. **6th row**—Knit 4, * purl 2, knit 5, purl 5, knit 2, repeat from *, and knit the last 4 stitches plain. **7th row**—Knit 4, * purl 1, knit 6, purl 6, knit 1, repeat from *, and end with knit 4. **8th row**—Knit 4, * knit 7, purl 7, repeat from *, and end with knit 4. It will be seen that the four stitches that are knitted plain at the beginning and at the end of each row form a nice even edge, the first stitch should be slipped in every row. Repeat from the first row till 12 patterns, 96 rows, are knitted. The shoulders are worked entirely in plain knitting. Knit 4 rows plain from end to end. **5th row**—Knit 27 stitches, cast the last stitch but one over the last stitch and cast off altogether 14 stitches, and knit to the end of the needle, this gives 25 stitches for each shoulder. Knit each shoulder separately all plain knitting and take 2 stitches together at the neck end in every row till reduced to 12 stitches, knit 12 rows on the 12 stitches, and cast off. Work the other half of the vest in the same manner. Sew the two pieces together leaving space for armholes. With a fine bone crochet needle work an edge round the armholes, the neck, and the bottom of the vest, 1 double crochet in a stitch of the knitting, 3 chain, 3 treble in the same place the double crochet is worked into, miss two stitches of the knitting, and repeat. This will complete the vest.

Baby's Spencer in Pettifer Pattern.

GENTLEMAN'S TARTAN HOSE.

THE stocking shown in our engraving is knitted in Scotch tartan plaid in good sized diamonds of three colours; the colours in most general use as worn by Highland regiments are red, black, and mottled red and black, or else white, black, and mottled white and black, and either combination is equally well suited for bicycle stockings and shooting stockings. The wool must be wound in separate balls, ½ oz. in each ball, and to avoid long loose threads passing along the inside of the stocking one ball is kept for each diamond, and practically 12 balls are in use at the same time; this is rather troublesome, and great care must be taken that they do not get entangled. The most durable wool for wear is the best Scotch fingering yarn, of which 2 ozs. of red, 2 ozs. of black, and 4 ozs. of red and black mixture will be required, and four steel knitting needles, No. 15. A novice in this kind of knitting may use only two needles (long ones) and work for the leg forwards and backwards in rows, and shape the foot in two separate pieces in the manner explained in knitting the gentleman's striped sock, page 10, No. 12 of "Weldon's Practical Work Series;" the tartan pattern will work quite correctly on two needles by the following directions, the seam stitch not being observed but being knitted like an ordinary stitch, the heel also will shape nicely as below, and the instep and the sole will be worked separately, and the stocking when completed will be sewn round the foot and up the leg. For working the stocking on four needles, as our model is worked, the first stitch upon the first needle must be employed as a seam stitch, and after working it at the *end* of *every round*, turn the work, slip the seam stitch and *work back*, as the stocking must, for convenience of neatness in having no loose threads at the back, be knitted forwards and backwards alternately plain and purl. Begin for the turnover of the leg with mottled wool, by casting 40 stitches on each of three needles, 120 stitches in all. **1st round**—Plain. **2nd round**—Purl. **3rd round**—Plain. **4th round**—Purl. **5th round**—Make 1, knit 2 together, and repeat the same to the end of the round. **6th round**—Purl. **7th round**—Plain. **8th round**—Purl. These eight rounds are to form a hem. **1st round** of the Tartan plaid—Slip the first stitch (which is the seam stitch), knit plain 11 stitches with mottled wool, 1 stitch with red, 23 stitches with mottled, 1 stitch with black, 23 stitches with mottled, 1 stitch with red, 23 stitches with mottled, 1 stitch with black, 23 stitches with mottled, 1 stitch with red, 12 stitches with mottled, the last of these being the seam stitch which is to be knitted off the end of the first needle, and turn the work. **2nd round**—Slip the first stitch, purl 10 stitches with mottled, purl 3 with red, 21 with mottled, 3 with black, 21 with mottled, 3 with red, 21 with mottled, 3 with black, 21 with mottled, 3 with red, 11 with mottled, and turn the work. **3rd round**—Slip the first stitch, knit plain 9 with mottled, 5 with red, 19 with mottled, 5 with black, 19 with mottled, 5 with red, 19 with mottled, 5 with black, 19 with mottled, 5 with red, 10 with mottled. **4th round**—Slip the first stitch, purl 8 with mottled, 7 with red, 17 with mottled, 7 with black, 17 with mottled, 7 with black, 17 with mottled, 7 with black, 17 with mottled, 7 with red, 9 with mottled. **5th round**—Slip the first stitch, knit plain 7 with mottled, 9 with red, 15 with mottled, 9 with black, 15 with mottled, 9 with red, 15 with mottled, 9 with black, 15 with mottled, 9 with red, 8 with mottled. **6th round**—Slip the first stitch, purl 6 with mottled, 11 with red, 13 with mottled, 11 with black, 13 with mottled, 11 with red, 13 with mottled, 11 with black, 13 with mottled, 11 with red, 7 with mottled. **7th round**—Slip the first stitch, knit plain 5 with mottled, 13 with red, 11 with mottled, 13 with black, 11 with mottled, 13 with red, 11 with mottled, 13 with black, 11 with mottled, 13 with red, 6 with mottled. **8th round**—Slip the first stitch, purl 4 with mottled, 15 with red, 9 with mottled, 15 with black, 9 with mottled, 15 with red, 9 with mottled, 15 with black, 9 with mottled, 15 with red, 5 with mottled. **9th round**—Slip the first stitch, knit plain 3 with mottled, 17 with red, 7 with mottled, 17 with black, 7 with mottled, 17 with red, 7 with mottled, 17 with black, 7 with mottled, 17 with red, 4 with mottled. **10th round**—Slip the first stitch, purl 2 with mottled, 19 with red, 5 with mottled, 19 with black, 5 with mottled, 19 with red, 5 with mottled, 19 with black, 5 with mottled, 19 with red, 3 with mottled. **11th round**—Slip the first stitch, knit plain 1 with mottled, 21 with red, 3 with mottled, 21 with black, 3 with mottled, 21 with red, 3 with mottled, 21 with black, 3 with mottled, 21 with red, 2 with mottled. **12th round**—Slip the first stitch with mottled, purl 23 with red, 1 with mottled, 23 with black, 1 with mottled, 23 with red, 1 with mottled, 23 with black, 1 with mottled, 23 with red, 1 with mottled. **13th round**—Same as the eleventh round; and proceed thence successively backwards, widening the mottled diamonds and narrowing the coloured ones, till you have in all done 22 rounds, the 22nd round will be the same as the second round. **23rd round**—Slip the first stitch, knit plain 11 stitches with mottled, 1 with black, 23 with mottled, 1 with red, 23 with mottled, 1 with black, 23 with mottled, 1 with red, 23 with mottled, 1 with black, 12 with mottled.

24th round—Slip the first stitch, purl 10 with mottled, 3 with black, 21 with mottled, 3 with red, 21 with mottled, 3 with black, 21 with mottled, 3 with red, 21 with mottled, 3 with black, 11 with mottled. **25th round**—Slip the first stitch, knit plain 9 with mottled, 5 with black, 19 with mottled, 5 with red, 19 with mottled, 5 with black, 19 with mottled, 5 with red, 19 with mottled, 5 with black, 10 with mottled. **26th round**—Slip the first stitch, purl 8 with mottled, 7 with black, 17 with mottled, 7 with red, 17 with mottled, 7 with black, 17 with mottled, 7 with red, 17 with mottled, 7 with black, 9 with mottled. **27th round**—Slip the first stitch, knit plain 7 with mottled, 9 with black, 15 with mottled, 9 with red, 15 with mottled, 9 with black, 15 with mottled, 9 with red, 15 with mottled, 9 with black, 8 with mottled. **28th round**—Slip the first stitch, purl 6 with mottled, 11 with black, 13 with mottled, 11 with red, 13 with mottled, 11 with black, 13 with mottled, 11 with red, 13 with mottled, 11 with black, 7 with mottled. **29th round**—Slip the first stitch, knit plain 5 with mottled, 13 with black, 11 with mottled, 13 with red, 11 with mottled, 13 with black, 11 with mottled, 13 with red, 11 with mottled, 13 with black, 6 with mottled. **30th round**—Slip the first stitch, purl 4 with mottled, 15 with black, 9 with mottled, 15 with red, 9 with mottled, 15 with black, 9 with mottled, 15 with red, 9 with mottled, 15 with black, 5 with mottled. **31st round**—Slip the first stitch, knit plain 3 with mottled, 17 with black, 7 with mottled, 17 with red, 7 with mottled, 17 with black, 7 with mottled, 17 with red, 7 with mottled, 17 with black, 4 with mottled. **32nd round**—Slip the first stitch, purl 2 with mottled, 19 with black, 5 with mottled, 19 with red, 5 with mottled, 19 with black, 5 with mottled, 19 with red, 5 with mottled, 19 with black, 3 with mottled. **33rd round**—Slip the first stitch, knit plain 1 with mottled, 21 with black, 3 with mottled, 21 with red, 3 with mottled, 21 with black, 3 with mottled, 21 with red, 3 with mottled, 21 with black, 2 with mottled. **34th round**—Slip the first stitch with mottled, purl 23 with black, 1 with mottled, 23 with red, 1 with mottled, 23 with black, 1 with mottled, 23 with red, 1 with mottled, 23 with black, 1 with mottled. **35th round**—Same as the thirty-third round; and proceed thence successively backwards to the twenty-third round, which closes this series of coloured diamonds, 45 rounds now being done. Break off the black and the red wool and with a rug needle run the ends in neatly. **46th round**—Purl, entirely with mottled wool. This completes the turnover, and you now reverse the right side of the work and knit for the under part. **1st row**—Purl. **2nd round**—Plain, and take 2 stitches together at the end of the round. Continue now for 10 plain rounds purling the seam stitch as in ordinary stocking knitting. **13th round**—Purl the seam stitch, knit 6, * purl 2, knit 6, and repeat from * to the end of the round. Rib 23 more rounds in the same manner. **37th round**—Purl the seam stitch, and knit plain round. Knit 11 more rounds the same, and in the last of these rounds increase a stitch to compensate for the stitch that was lately decreased. This finishes the under part, and you now recommence the **Tartan plaid pattern** for the **leg**. Begin with the **23rd round** of the turnover, as instructed above and work thence for 22 rounds which will form one series of diamonds, and they will be on the reverse side of the knitting so that the turnover may fold in place above them. The second series of diamonds will then begin, and is worked according to the above instructions from the **1st round** of the tartan plaid to the **22nd round** thereof; only in the *first round* of *this* series *increase* a stitch on each side the seam stitch (allowing 2 plain stitches between the seam and the increase) and decrease the same stitch in the last of these rounds. Then follow the tartan plaid in the same manner, but decrease each side the seam stitch every eighth row eight times, and then every sixth row four times, which will reduce the number of stitches to 96, and the tartan plaid pattern comes in evenly for the ankle. Continue in pattern till eight whole diamonds (four black and four red) are knitted down the leg. The **Heel** is knitted entirely with mottled wool—After purling the seam stitch at the completion of the third needle, knit plain 23 stitches off the first needle; turn, slip the first stitch, purl 22, knit the seam stitch, purl 23; * turn, slip the first stitch, knit 22, purl the seam stitch, knit 23; turn, slip the first stitch, purl 22, knit the seam stitch, purl 23; repeat from * till 48 of these little rows are knitted for the flap of the heel. **To turn the Heel**—Slip the first stitch, knit 25, slip 1, knit 1, pass the slipped stitch over, knit 1; turn, slip the first stitch, purl 6, purl 2 together, purl 1; turn, slip the first stitch, knit 7, slip 1, knit 1, pass the slipped stitch over, knit 1; turn, slip the first stitch, purl 8, purl 2 together, purl 1; turn, slip the first stitch, knit 9, slip 1, knit 1, pass the slipped stitch over, knit 1; turn, slip the first stitch, purl 10, purl 2 together, purl 1; and go on thus widening the centre of the heel and taking in the outside stitches, till in the last row you work slip 1, purl 14, purl 2 together, purl 1; which gives 27 stitches on the needle for the top of the heel. For **Gusset and Foot**—Still with mottled wool—Slip the first stitch, knit 26, and on the same needle pick up and knit 27 stitches along the side of the flap; on another needle knit the 49 instep stitches in the tartan pattern,

and on the third needle pick up and knit with mottled wool 27 stitches along the opposite side of the heel and knit 15 stitches from off the top of the heel. * Turn the work, slip the first stitch (treating it always now like a seam stitch), purl to the end of the needle; purl the instep stitches in pattern; purl along the third needle and purl the seam stitch; turn, slip the seam stitch, knit plain to within 3 stitches of the end of the needle, knit 2 together, knit 1; knit instep in pattern; and on third needle knit 1, slip 1, knit 1, pass the slipped stitch over, knit to the end, and knit the seam stitch; repeat from * till reduced to 49 stitches on the two foot needles, 49 stitches still being on the instep needle. As you work from the instep needle to the foot needles, twist the wools together to connect the work. Continue now, without more decreasing, with mottled wool in the sole and tartan pattern on instep, till you can count twelve whole diamonds (six black and six red) in all from the beginning of the leg. Then work on plain, round and round with mottled wool, for 12 or more rounds, as required for the length of the foot. For the **Toe**—Beginning on the instep needle—Knit 1, knit 2 together, knit plain to within 3 stitches of the end of the needle, slip 1, knit 1, pass the slipped stitch over, knit 1; on foot needle, knit 1, knit 2 together, knit plain to within 3 stitches of the end of the other foot needle, slip 1, knit 1, pass the slipped stitch over, knit 1; knit 1 round plain. Repeat these two rounds till reduced to 9 stitches on the instep and 9 stitches on the two foot needles, and cast off. Work the other stocking to correspond. The cast on stitches are folded over and hemmed on the wrong side of the turnover, the row of holes making a little notched edge to turn by. The stockings, when complete, must be well pressed with a very hot iron on the wrong side, a damp cloth being laid between.

Wedge Pattern Vest for Child of Three Years.

BO-PEEP BOOT FOR AN INFANT.

THESE pretty boots are suitable for an infant's first size. Procure ¼ oz. of white Berlin fingering, and a pair of No. 12 steel knitting needles, also ¼ oz. of white Shetland to knit a lining for additional warmth, and half a yard of narrow ribbon to run round the leg. Begin by casting on 30 stitches with the Berlin fingering wool for the top of the leg. Knit 2 plain rows. **3rd row**—Make 1, slip 1 inserting the needle in the stitch as if about to purl, knit 1, and repeat the same to the end. **4th row**—Make 1, slip 1, inserting the needle as if about to purl, knit 2 stitches together, and repeat. Knit 4 more rows the same as the last row. **9th row**—Slip 1, knit 2 together, * purl 1, knit 2 together, and repeat from * to the end. Knit 3 plain rows. **13th row**—Purl 3, * make 1, purl 2 together, purl 1, and repeat from * to the end. Knit 10 plain rows. **24th row**—Knit 1 and purl 1 alternately six times, increase 1, purl 6, increase 1, purl 1 and knit 1 alternately six times. **25th row**—Knit 13, increase 1, knit 6, increase 1, knit 13. **26th row**—Knit 1 and purl 1 seven times, increase 1, purl 6, increase 1, purl 1, and knit 1 seven times. **27th row**—Knit 15, increase 1, knit 6, increase 1, knit 15. **28th row**—Knit 1 and purl 1 eight times, increase 1, purl 6, increase 1, purl 1 and knit 1 eight times. **29th row**—Knit 17, increase 1, knit 6, increase 1, knit 17. Continue thus increasing twice in the same places in every row till after doing the **36th row** you get 56 stitches on the needle. Knit 10 plain rows. **47th row**—Slip 1, knit 1, knit 2 together, knit 20, knit 2 together, knit 4, knit 2 together, knit 20, knit 2 together, knit 2. **48th row**—Slip 1, knit 1, knit 2 together, knit 20, knit 2 together twice, knit 20, knit 2 together, knit 2. **49th row**—Slip 1, knit 1, knit 2 together, knit 16, knit 2 together four times, knit 16, knit 2 together, knit 2. Cast off all the stitches. Knit the other boot in the same manner. Sew up the bottom of the boot, and sew up the leg. For the **Lining**—Cast on 35 stitches with Shetland wool and work 25 rows of plain knitting, and sew up; and sew in inside the leg of the boot. Run the ribbon through the row of open holes and tie it in a bow in front.

EGG COSY, FLUTED PATTERN.

FOR this pretty cosy single Berlin wool of two colours will be required, about 3 small skeins (one pennyworth) of each colour, blue and white are used in our model, but black and red, green and amber, and other colours may be employed as best will correspond with the breakfast service with which the cosies will be laid. Four steel knitting needles No 16. With blue wool cast 40 stitches on the first needle and 30 stitches on each of two other needles, 100 stitches in all, for the width round the bottom of the cosy. **1st round**—With blue wool, knit plain. **2nd round**—Knit 10 stitches with blue wool, take the white wool and knit 10 stitches, twist the two wools round each other and knit 10 stitches with blue wool, twist the two wools round each other and knit 10 stitches with white wool, and continue blue and white alternately to the end of the round—the wool not used in the knitting passes at the back of the work, and must be rather tightly (but no too tightly) drawn in, just sufficiently so to make the knitting sit in "flutes." **3rd round**—Purl 10 stitches with blue and purl 10 stitches with white twisting the wools each time of changing colours, and keeping the threads on the same side as before. Repeat the last two rounds. When 40 rounds are knitted keep to the blue wool and knit two stitches together all round. Cast off tightly. With a wool needle threaded with the tag end of blue wool sew up closely the stitches that form the top of the cosy; make a tuft of blue and white wool mingled, and sew on the top, as shown in the illustration. For the **Edging** round the bottom of the egg-cosy, work with a fine bone crochet needle. **1st round**— With white wool, 1 double crochet in the first stitch of the flute, 8 treble stitches along the flute, and 1 double crochet in the last stitch of the flute, and repeat the same nine times. **2nd round**—With blue wool, 1 double crochet between the two double crochet stitches of last round, 1 single crochet on each of the treble stitches, and repeat. By casting on a larger number of stitches and knitting more rounds a handsome tea-cosy can be made to match.

which there are five beads in the middle, and working two loops each with four beads on each side of it. By counting carefully the numbers of beads required, and threading them in rotation, it is quite possible to make the fringe at the edge of one and the middle pattern of a second colour.

The cuffs could be utilised for finger napkin rings, mounted upon a card foundation to render them stiff, the card being covered with a piece of satin or sarcenet. I have seen these beaded cuffs made about 1½ inches wide to form wristlets or bracelets, and which suit those who do not want to use themselves to woollen cuffs, and yet feel the cold in the wrist. They are very pretty in this narrow form, lending the effect of a beaded bracelet, and are chiefly worn in black, with gold, steel, or jet beads. In pale grey and steel they look most delicate and pretty, and this colour has the advantage of going with almost any dress, and is really as useful as black, and far prettier.

Bo-Peep Boot for an Infant.

Gentleman's Tartan Hose.

KNITTED AND BEADED CUFFS.

(Not Illustrated.)

THESE narrow bands, which resemble bracelets rather than cuffs, are always much appreciated by old ladies, who like to wear them in summer when longer ones are too warm. They are equally useful for young people who feel the cold to their wrists, and they can be made in all widths. They look very delicate in white wool and milky white beads, but of course quickly soil, therefore black and dark colours have the preference. They may be made in a great variety of colours of beads upon any shade of wool, and can be arranged so as to match any dress. Brown and gold always look well together, so do grey and steel, while metallic beads may now be had in various shades of ruby, peacock blue, bronze, or green, besides the more commonplace gold and silver. The wool may be either single Berlin or Andalusian, the latter by preference, as being softer and more elastic. Knitting silk makes handsome cuffs, but is less pleasant than wool to work with. The beads, of No. 8 size, must be threaded first, and the greater part of them passed along the wool for a long distance before the work is commenced.

Cast on twenty-four stitches, and knit one plain row. Remember that every alternate row must be plain knitting without any beads, or the beads will come on the wrong side of the work. **2nd row**—Slip 3 stitches, as if for purling, from the left-hand to the right-hand needle, pass 4 beads along the wool till they are close to the work, knit 1 stitch. The stitches that are slipped in one row must be very loosely knitted in the next, or the work will be drawn out of place and the cuff rendered too tight. Knit 3 stitches, passing a bead up to each, knit 3, knit 5 stitches with beads, knit 3, knit 3 bead stitches, slip 3, pass along 4 beads. Knit the next row plain. **4th row**—Slip 3, pass along 4 beads, knit 1, knit 3 bead stitches, knit 2, slip 1, pass along 4 beads, slip 2, pass along 5 beads, slip 1, pass along 4 beads, knit 2, knit 3 bead stitches, slip 3, pass along 4 beads. Repeat 2nd and 4th rows until the cuff is long enough to fit closely round the wrist. It will probably require about a hundred rows in all. Cast off and sew the ends together on the wrong side.

By casting on about forty-five or fifty stitches and omitting one fringe, the same pattern may be adapted to longer cuffs, and should the bead-work be considered too narrow in proportion to its length, it is easy to add a couple more of the centre loops of slipped beads, remembering to keep the loop in

Egg Cosy, Fluted Pattern.

WELDON'S
PRACTICAL KNITTER.

(THIRTEENTH SERIES.)

How to Knit Useful Garments for Ladies, Children, and the Home.

TWENTY-SEVEN ILLUSTRATIONS.

Telegraphic Address—] "Consuelo," London.] The Yearly Subscription to this Magazine, post free to any Part of the World, is 2s. 6d. Subscriptions are payable in advance, and may commence from any date and for any period. [Telephone-2745.

The Back Numbers are always in print. Nos. 1 to 96 now ready, Price 2d. each, or post free for 17s. 6d. Over 5,000 Engravings.

BABY'S RING AND RATTLE.

THIS ring and rattle is quite a new design, and a baby may be **kept** amused for hours playing with the pretty drops, rattling them, and admiring the bright colours of the wool. Required, single Berlin Wool of three cheerful colours, about ¼ of an ounce of each colour, mauve, yellow, and cherry colour, a pair of No. 14 knitting needles, a bone ring about 1½ inches in diameter, three small pill boxes, six or nine dry peas (or a little shot), and a small quantity of wadding. Cast on twenty stitches with mauve wool, and work in all plain knitting for 28 ribs, 56 rows, and cast off, leaving a long end of wool. Fold the knitting wrong side out, and sew the cast on stitches to the cast off, which makes a kind of long narrow tube; run the needle with double wool round one end of the tube, and draw it in close, and sew it up like the bottom of a bag. Do the same with two other wools, so making three little tubes for rattles. Partly fill each tube with wadding, put in a pill box with two or three peas inside to rattle, and fill up the tubes tightly with wadding, pressing each into a good shape. Leave the tubes open while you do the plait which is to attach them to the ring. For this plait cut six pieces of wool of each colour 3) inches long, hold them smoothly together in one thick strand, and draw the ring to the middle of the strand, then fold the wool double, and make a thick plait of three colours, 12 threads of wool in each colour; plait for a length of about five inches, then tie a thread of wool round the plait to confine the threads all firmly together; and now divide the colours, and plait each colour separately for a length of four inches, tie the end of each plait in a knot, and put each knot into its own coloured tube, and draw up and sew the knitting closely round enclosing the knot firmly in, which will keep the plait secure. You now will have the three drops hanging from the ring as shown in the engraving.

BEECH LEAF PATTERN.

THIS pattern is almost identical with the old Lyre pattern and is practically a re-arrangement of that once well-known and favourite stitch; it represents a succession of well defined, gracefully curved leaves, and therefore may very appropriately be designated the Beech Leaf pattern. Either cotton or wool may be used for the knitting, selecting the material according to the purpose for which the work is required. For moderately fine work, such as a pin-cushion cover or a tray-cloth, employ Coats' No. 18 crochet cotton, and a pair of No. 17 steel knitting needles. Cast on any number of stitches divisible by 18, and 7 stitches over to keep the pattern even. **1st row**—Purl 3, make 1 by passing the cotton *over* the needle, knit 1, make 1 by passing the cotton twice *round* the needle, purl 3, knit 2 together, knit 9, and repeat the same; and the row will end with make 1, knit 1, make 1, purl 3. **2nd row**—Knit 3, purl 3, knit 3, purl 8, purl 2 together, and repeat. **3rd row**—Purl 3, knit 1, make 1, knit 1, make 1, knit 1, purl 3, knit 2 together, knit 7, and repeat the same; and the row will end with make 1, knit 1, purl 3. **4th row**—Knit 3, purl 5, knit 3, purl 6, purl 2 together, and repeat. **5th row**—Purl 3, knit 2, make 1, knit 1, make 1, knit 2, purl 3, knit 2 together, knit 5, and repeat; and the row will end with make 1, knit 2, purl 3. **6th row**—Knit 3, purl 7, knit 3, purl 4, purl

---

2 together, and repeat; on the completion of this row there will be *six* more stitches on the needle than the number with which you began. **7th row**—Purl 3, knit 3, make 1, knit 1, make 1, knit 3, purl 3, knit 2 together, knit 3, and repeat; and the row will end with make 1, knit 3, purl 3. **8th row**—Knit 3, purl 9, knit 3, purl 2, purl 2 together, and repeat. **9th row**—Purl 3, knit 4, make 1, knit 1, make 1, knit 4, purl 3, knit 2 together, knit 1, and repeat; and the row will end with make 1, knit 4, purl 3. **10th row**—Knit 3, purl 11, knit 3, purl 2 together, and repeat; on the completion of this row there will be *ten* more stitches on the needle than the number with which you began, and the following rows will gradually diminish them to the original number. **11th row**—Purl 3, knit 2 together, knit 9, purl 3, make 1 by passing the cotton *over* the needle, knit 1, make 1 by passing the cotton twice *round* the needle, and repeat the same; and the row will end with knit 9, purl 3. **12th row**—Knit 3, purl 8, purl 2 together, knit 3, purl 3, and repeat. **13th row**—Purl 3, knit 2 together, knit 7, purl 3, knit 1, make 1, knit 1, make 1, knit 1, and repeat the same; and the row will end with knit 7, purl 3. **14th row**—Knit 3, purl 6, purl 2 together, knit 3, purl 5, and repeat. **15th row**—Purl 3, knit 2 together, knit 5, purl 3, knit 2, make 1, knit 1, make 1, knit 2, and repeat; and the row will end with knit 5, purl 3. **16th row**—Knit 3, purl 4, purl 2 together, knit 3, purl 7, and repeat. **17th row**—Purl 3, knit 2 together, knit 3, purl 3, knit 3, make 1, knit 1, make 1, knit 3, and repeat; and the row will end with knit 3, purl 3. **18th row**—Knit 3, purl 2, purl 2 together, knit 3, purl 9, and repeat. **19th row**—Purl 3, knit 2 together, knit 1, purl 3, knit 4, make 1, knit 1, make 1, knit 4, and repeat; and the row will end with knit 1, purl 3. **20th row**—Knit 3, purl 2 together, knit 3, purl 11, and repeat; the same number of stitches will be on the needle as at the beginning. Repeat from the first row, and continue for the length desired.

Baby's Ring and Rattle.

ANOTHER BEECH LEAF PATTERN.

SIMILAR TO THE ILLUSTRATION IN APPEARANCE, BUT SMALLER IN PATTERN.

A SMALLER form of the above pattern can be knitted by casting on any number of stitches divisible by 14, with 5 stitches additional to ensure the symmetry of the pattern. **1st row**—Purl 2, make 1 by passing the cotton *over* the needle, knit 1, make 1, by passing the cotton twice *round* the needle, purl 2, knit 2 together, knit 7, repeat the same; and end the row with make 1, knit 1, make 1, purl 2. **2nd row**—Knit 2, purl 3, knit 2, purl 6, purl 2 together, and repeat. **3rd row**—Purl 2, knit 1, make 1, knit 1, make 1, knit 1, purl 2, knit 2 together, knit 5, repeat the same; and end with make 1, knit 1, purl 2. **4th row**—Knit 2, purl 5, knit 2, purl 4, purl 2 together, and repeat; and on the completion of this row there will be *four* more stitches on the needle than the number with which you began. **5th row**—Purl 2, knit 2, make 1, knit 1, make 1, knit 2, purl 2, knit 2 together, knit 3, and repeat; and end with make 1, knit 2, purl 2. **6th row**—Knit 2, purl 7, knit 2, purl 2, purl 2 together, and repeat. **7th row**—Purl 2, knit 3, make 1, knit 1, make 1, knit 3, purl 2, knit 2 together, knit 1, and repeat; and end with make 1, knit 3, purl 2. **8th row**—Knit 2, purl 9, knit 2, purl 2 together, and repeat; and on the completion of this row there will be *eight* more stitches on the needle than the number with which the work began, and the following rows will gradually diminish them to the original number. **9th row**—Purl 2, knit 2 together, knit 7, purl 2, make 1 by passing the cotton *over* the needle, knit 1, make 1 by passing the cotton twice *round* the needle, and repeat the same; and end the row with knit 7, purl 2. **10th row**—Knit 2, purl 6, purl 2 together, knit 2, purl 3, and repeat. **11th row**—Purl 2, knit 2 together, knit 5, purl 2, knit 1, make 1, knit 1, make 1, knit 1, and repeat; and end the row with knit 5, purl 2. **12th row**—Knit 2, purl 4, purl 2 together, knit 2, purl 5, and repeat. **13th row**—Purl 2, knit 2 together, knit 3, purl 2, knit 2, make 1, knit 1, make 1, knit 2, and repeat; and end the row with knit 3, purl 2. **14th row**—Knit 2, purl 2, purl 2 together, knit 2, purl 7, and repeat. **15th row**—Purl 2, knit 2 together, knit 1, purl 2, knit 3, make 1, knit 1, make 1, knit 3, and repeat; and end the row with knit 1, purl 2. **16th row**—Knit 2, purl 2 together, knit 2, purl 9, and repeat; the same number of stitches will now be on the needle as at the commencement. This completes one pattern, and the work is continued by repeating from the first row to the sixteenth row until the required length is attained.

Beech Leaf Pattern.

INFANT'S BOOT.

HONEYCOMB-STITCH.

REQUIRED, 1 oz. of white and ½ oz. of red single Berlin, and a pair of No. 14 steel knitting needles. With red wool cast on 28 stitches. **1st row**—Plain. **2nd row**—With white wool, knit 4, * slip 2 stitches on to the right-hand needle without knitting them, knit 4, and repeat from * to the end of the row. **3rd row**—Slip 1, increase 1, purl 3, * slip the same 2 stitches as were slipped in last row taking them backwards so as not to twist them, purl 4, and repeat from *, and at the end after slipping 2, purl 3, increase 1, purl 1. **4th row**—Slip 1, knit 4, * slip 2, knit 4, repeat from *, and knit the last stitch plain. **5th row**—Slip 1, increase 1, purl 4, * slip 2, purl 4, repeat from *, and at the end, after purling 4 stitches, increase 1, purl 1. **6th row**—Take red wool, and knit plain 32 stitches. **7th row**—Slip 1, increase 1, knit 30, increase 1, knit 1. **8th row**—Resume with white wool—Knit 4 *, slip 2, knit 4, and repeat from * to the end, the slipped stitches will now come intermediately between the stitches that were slipped in the second row. **9th row**—Slip 1, purl 3, * slip 2, purl 4, and repeat from *, and at the end after slipping 2, purl 3, increase 1, purl 1. **10th row**—Slip 1, knit 4, * slip 2, knit 4, repeat from * to the end. **11th row**—Slip 1, purl 3, * slip 2, purl 4, repeat from *, and at the end after purling 4, increase 1, purl 1. **12th row**—With red wool—Knit plain 36 stitches. **13th row**—Knit 35, increase 1, knit 1. **14th row**—Resume with white—Knit 4, * slip 2, knit 4, repeat from *, and when within 3 stitches of the end, slip 2, knit 1. **15th row**—Purl 1, * slip 2, purl 4, and repeat from *, and at the end after slipping 2, purl 3, increase 1, purl 1. **16th row**—Slip 1, knit 4, * slip 2, knit 4, repeat from *, and at the end after slipping 2, knit the last stitch plain. **17th row**—Purl 1, * slip 2, purl 4, and repeat from *, and at the end after slipping 2, purl 4, increase 1, purl 1. **18th row**—With red—Knit plain 39 stitches. **19th row**—Knit 38, increase 1, knit 1. **20th row**—With white wool—For the toe—Knit 4, slip 2, knit 4, slip 2, knit 4; and turn the work leaving 24 red stitches unknitted on the left-hand needle. **21st row**—Slip 1, purl 3, slip 2, purl 4, slip 2, purl 3, increase 1, purl 1. **22nd row**—Slip 1, knit 4, slip 2, knit 4, slip 2, knit 4. **23rd row**—Slip 1, purl 3, slip 2, purl 4, slip 2, purl 4, increase 1. purl 1. **24th row**—With red—Knit plain 18 stitches. **25th row**—Knit 17, increase 1, knit 1.

26th row—With white—Knit 4, slip 2, knit 4, slip 2, knit 4, slip 2, knit 1. **27th row**—Purl 1, slip 2, purl 4, slip 2, purl 4, slip 2, purl 4, cast on 34 stitches for the sole, which is knitted in all plain knitting with white wool, at the end of the toe, and afterwards folded under. **28th row**—Knit 38, slip 2, knit 4, slip 2, knit 4, slip 2, knit 1. **29th row**—Purl 1, slip 2, purl 4, slip 2, purl 4, slip 2, purl 4, knit 33, increase 1, knit 1. **30th row**—Knit 35 stitches with white wool, take red and knit 19 stitches. **31st row**—Knit 19 with red, take white and knit 34, increase 1, knit 1. **32nd row**—With white—Knit 37, slip 2, knit 4, slip 2, knit 4, slip 2, knit 4. **33rd row**—Purl 4, slip 2, purl 4, slip 2, purl 4, slip 2, purl 1, knit 35, increase 1, knit 1. **34th row**—Knit 38, slip 2, knit 4, slip 2, knit 4, slip 2, knit 4. **35th row**—Purl 4, slip 2, purl 4, slip 2, purl 4, slip 2, purl 1, knit 37. **36th row**—Knit 37 stitches with white wool, take red and knit 19 stitches. **37th row**—Knit 19 with red, take white and knit 34, knit 2 together, knit 1. **38th row**—With white—Knit 40, slip 2, knit 4, slip 2, knit 4, slip 2, knit 1. **39th row**—Purl 1, slip 2, purl 4, slip 2, purl 4, slip 2, purl 4, knit 33, knit 2 together, knit 1. **40th row**—Knit 39, slip 2, knit 4, slip 2, knit 4, slip 2, knit 1. **41st row**—Purl 1, slip 2, purl 4, slip 2, purl 4, slip 2, purl 4, knit 32, knit 2 together, knit 1. **42nd row**—Cast off 33 sole stitches with white wool, knit 1 stitch with red and cast the white stitch over it, knit 18 stitches with red. **43rd row**—With red—Knit 16, knit 2 together, knit 1. **44th row**—With white—Knit 6, slip 2, knit 4, slip 2, knit 4. **45th row**—Slip 1, purl 3, slip 2, purl 4, slip 2, purl 3, purl 2 together, purl 1. **46th row**—Slip 1, knit 4, slip 2, knit 4, slip 2, knit 4. **47th row**—Slip 1, purl 3, slip 2, purl 4, slip 2, purl 2, purl 2 together, purl 1. **48th row**—With red—Knit 16 plain stitches, and cast on 24 stitches for the other side of the boot. **49th row**—Knit 37, knit 2 together, knit 1. **50th row**—With white—Knit 6, * slip 2, knit 4, and repeat from *, and end with slip 2, knit 1. **51st row**—Purl 1, * slip 2, purl 4, repeat from *, and at the end after slipping 2, purl 3, purl 2 together, purl 1. **52nd row**—Slip 1, knit 4, * slip 2, knit 4, repeat from *, and end with slip 2, knit 1. **53rd row**—Purl 1, * slip 2, purl 4, repeat from *, and at the end after slipping 2, purl 2, purl 2 together, purl 1. **54th row**—With red—Knit plain 37 stitches. **55th row**—Knit 34, knit 2 together, knit 1. **56th row**—With white—Knit 6, * slip 2, purl 4, repeat from * to the end. **57th row**—Slip 1, purl 3, * slip 2, purl 4, repeat from *, and at the end after slipping 2, purl 3, purl 2 together, purl 1. **58th row**—Slip 1, knit 4, * slip 2, knit 4, and repeat from * to the end. **59th row**—Slip 1, purl 3, * slip 2, purl 4, repeat from *, and at the end after slipping 2, purl 2, purl 2 together, purl 1. **60th row**—With red—Knit plain 34 stitches. **61st row**—Slip 1, knit 2 together, knit 28, knit 2 together, knit 1. **62nd row**—Slip 1, knit 5, * slip 2, knit 4, repeat from *, and knit the last 2 stitches. **63rd row**—Slip 1, purl 2 together, purl 3, * slip 2, purl 4, repeat from *, and at the end after slipping 2, purl 3, purl 2 together, purl 1. **64th row**—Slip 1, knit 4, * slip 2, knit 4, repeat from *, and knit the last stitch. **65th row**—Slip 1, purl 2 together, purl 2, * slip 2, purl 4, repeat from *, and at the end after slipping 2, purl 2, purl 2 together, purl 1. **66th row**—With red—Knit plain 28 stitches. Cast off. Hold the work the right side

Infant's Boot. Honeycomb-Stitch.

towards you, and with the red wool pick up and knit 24 stitches along the upper rim of the cast-on stitches of the second side of the boot, pick up and knit 13 stitches across the instep, and knit the 24 stitches that have been standing all this time on the left-hand pin; now there are 61 stitches on the needle; knit 2 plain rows; cast off all. For the **Sock**—Take the white wool, and holding the boot the right side towards you, pick up and knit a row of stitches at the back of the work under the stitches just cast off, 24 stitches on each side and 13 stitches across the instep, 61 stitches in all. Purl 37 stitches, leave 24 stitches on the left-hand needle; turn the work, slip 1, knit 2, make 1, knit 1, knit 2 together, knit 1, slip 1, knit 1, pass the slipped stitch over, knit 1, make 1, knit 2, slip 1, knit 1, pass the slipped stitch over, leave 23 stitches on the left-hand needle; turn the work, slip 1, purl 11, purl 2 together; * turn, slip 1, knit 2, make 1, knit 1, knit 2 together, knit 1, slip 1, knit 1, pass the slipped stitch over, knit 1, make 1, knit 2, slip 1, knit the next stitch, pass the slipped stitch over it; turn, slip 1, purl 11, purl 2 together; and repeat from * till you can count eight holes in a straight line, when you will find several of the side stitches have been absorbed into the instep, and you will have 13 stitches on the instep and 16 stitches on each side thereof; purl the stitches to the end of the left-hand needle, and there will be 45 stitches on the needle for knitting the sock. **1st row** of the **Sock**—Still with white wool—Slip 1, knit 2, make 1 and knit 2 together alternately nine times, make 1, slip 1, knit 2 together, pass the slipped stitch over, make 1 and knit 2 together alternately ten times, knit 1. **2nd row**—Purl; 44 stitches on. **3rd row**—Plain. **4th row**—Purl. **5th row**—Slip 1, knit 1, make 1 and knit 2 together alternately twenty-one times. Repeat from the second row twice. **14th row**—Purl. **15th row**—Knit 2, purl 2, and repeat all along. Do the same

Cape in Looped Fringed Knitting.

ribbing for six more rows. **22nd row**—With red wool—Purl. **23rd row**—Still with red—Slip 1, knit 1, make 1 and knit 2 together alternately twenty-one times. **24th row**—Purl. **25th row**—Plain. **26th row**—Purl. **27th row**—Same as the twenty-third row. **28th row**—Purl. Do 4 rows of ribbing, 2 stitches plain and 2 stitches purl. Cast off loosely. Knit the other boot in the same manner. Sew up the back of the leg and join the sole evenly to the lower part of the boot.

CAPE IN LOOPED FRINGED KNITTING.

THIS elegant shoulder cape is worked in looped knitting, but has a very different appearance to the ordinary capes knitted in imitation of thick fur; here the loops are so arranged as to resemble a series of fringes, and the effect in very pretty; the cape is lighter than the old style of cape, and is useful to wear at any time, either in summer or winter. The work is executed in six sections, which are afterwards joined together. Procure 12 ozs. of grey single Berlin wool, and a pair of No. 7 bone knitting needles. Begin for the bottom of one of the back sections by casting on 38 stitches. Knit 3 plain rows. **4th row**—This is a fringe row—Slip the first stitch, insert the needle in the next stitch as if going to knit it, pass the wool over the point of the needle and round the first and second fingers of the left hand twice, and then again over the point of the needle, and knit all three threads of wool in as you knit the stitch, knit all the other stitches in the same manner except the last stitch, which knit plain. Knit 5 plain rows. Repeat from the fourth row till you have done nine of the fringed rows. Then in the third of the plain-knit rows make the first decrease by taking together the second and third stitches from the beginning, the two centre stitches together, and the third and second stitches from the end together. Proceed doing a fringe row and five plain rows, and always in the third of the plain-knit rows decrease as above till there are eighteen fringed rows, and the section is reduced to 11 stitches on the needle, and then cast off. Knit three more sections in the same manner; these four sections are intended for the back of the cape, but five sections can be made if the cape is required for a very stout figure. For the **Left Front**—Cast on 40 stitches. Knit as before until nine fringed rows are accomplished without any decreasing at all, and then in the third of the plain-knit rows only decrease at the beginning and in the centre, leaving the other edge perfectly straight until after the seventeenth fringed row is done, when in each row that begins on the straight side cast off 2 stitches to give a slight slope towards the neck. Cast off all when the section is knitted to the same length as the back sections. For the **Right Front**—Cast on

40 stitches. Knit nine fringed rows without decreasing, then in the third of the plain-knit rows decrease in the centre and at the end of the row, keeping the first edge perfectly straight until after the seventeenth fringed row, and then cast off 2 stitches at the beginning of each row on the straight side till the section is long enough to cast off all. When this section is finished, the six sections can be sewn neatly together. For the **Neck Band**—Cast on 8 stitches. Knit 3 plain rows. **4th row**—Work in fringed knitting. Knit 3 plain rows. Repeat from the fourth row until a length of about 14 inches is knitted, and cast off. Attach the neck band to the cape. Line the neck band with a piece of grey ribbon, and leave ends of ribbon to tie in front; or put on a hook and eye to fasten the neck band.

PLAIN KNIT BALL.

THIS ball is worked throughout in a simple plain knitting; it is quickly and easily made, and is much appreciated by children, who always take delight in possessing a pretty ball. Procure single Berlin wool of two bright contrasting colours, say red and grey, ¼ of an ounce of each colour, and a pair of No. 15 steel knitting needles. Cast on 32 stitches with the red wool. Knit 1 plain row. Then, * knit 18 stitches; turn the work, knit 4 stitches; turn the work, knit 5 stitches; turn, knit 6 stitches; turn, knit 7; turn, knit 8; turn, knit 9; and so on, doing 1 more stitch each time of turning till you knit quite to the end of the pin, when 32 stitches should be on the needle, the same as at the beginning. Join on the grey wool, and repeat from * with grey. When that is done, work another section with red, and then another section with grey, and proceed in the same manner till eight sections in all are knitted, when cast-off the stitches. **Always slip** the first stitch after turning the work, but **count** it just the same as if it were knitted. Make up the foundation of the ball with wadding, flock, or scraps of wool knotted together, and wound up, pressing it into a nicely-rounded shape, or use an india-rubber ball of the right size. Draw the knitting over the ball, and sew the cast-off stitches to the cast-on stitches; join the ends neatly round, and decorate each end with a small tuft of wool.

FIFE COLLARETTE AND CUFFS.
FOR A LADY.

THIS collarette is knitted to stand high up the neck, in the style of the Fife collars that are now so fashionable; it is very warm for winter wear, and, with the cuffs, makes a very pretty finish to a walking costume. The work is executed in looped knitting in imitation of grey Astrachan fur. Procure 5 ozs. of grey partridge-speckled single Berlin wool, a pair of No. 9 bone

Plain Knit Ball.

knitting needles, 6 large black hooks and eyes, and 2½ yards of two-inch wide grey ribbon. Wind two balls of wool, and knit with a strand from each ball. Cast on 12 stitches with the wool thus double. **1st row**—Work the 12 stitches in looped knitting, thus—insert the needle in the first stitch, put the wool over the point of the needle and round the first finger of the left hand twice, then the wool over the point of the needle again and knit the stitch in the usual manner, drawing all the threads of wool through; and knit all the other stitches in the same way. **2nd row**—Knit plain 12 stitches. **3rd row**—Looped knitting, and increase by dividing the strands of the second stitch and knitting a looped stitch in each strand. **4th row**—Plain, 13 stitches. **5th row**—Same as the third row. **6th row**—Plain, 14 stitches. **7th row**—Same as the third row. **8th row**—Knit plain 2 stitches, and turn the work. **9th row**—Work the 2 stitches in looped knitting. **10th row**—Knit plain.

4 stitches, and turn the work. **11th row**—Work the 4 stitches in looped knitting. **12th row**—Knit plain 6 stitches, and turn the work. **13th row**—Work the 6 stitches in looped knitting. **14th row**—Knit plain 4 stitches, and turn the work. **15th row**—Work the 4 stitches in looped knitting. **16th row**—Knit plain 2 stitches, and turn the work. **17th row**—Work the 2 stitches in looped knitting; the last ten rows make a kind of gore on the lower edge of the collarette. **18th row**—Knit plain 13 stitches, knit the 2 last stitches together. **19th row**—Looped knitting, 14 stitches. **20th row**—Knit plain 12 stitches, knit the 2 last stitches together. **21st row**—Looped knitting, 13 stitches. **22nd row**—Knit plain 11 stitches, knit the 2 last stitches together; and now 12 stitches are on the needle as at the commencement. Repeat from the third row until seven scollops are completed for the length of the collarette, and cast off. Recommence, and work three scollops for each cuff. The scolloped side of the knitting is the top of the collarette and it comes up high nearly to the ears, and the gores widen

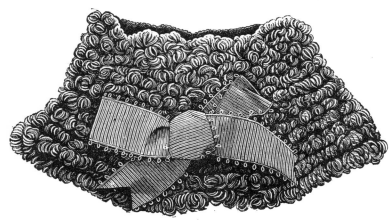

Fife Collarette.

the lower edge and cause it to set nicely. Put two hooks and two eyes to fasten the collarette, and the same on each cuff. Make pretty bows of ribbon to place on the collarette and cuffs, as shown in the engraving.

SAILOR DOLL.

PROCURE ½ oz. of white and ½ oz. of navy blue single Berlin wool, and three steel knitting needles, No. 14; the work is done upon two needles throughout, but one needle is required for a spare needle. For the **Trousers**—Cast on 36 stitches with white wool. Work 1 row plain and 1 row purl alternately, until 50 rows are knitted for the length of one leg; break off the wool and leave this piece of work on the needle as it is; and re-commence, and knit another piece exactly similar. Now divide, and take the last 18 stitches of the last piece of knitting on one pin together with the first 18 stitches of the first piece of knitting, and take the last 18 stitches of the first piece of knitting on another pin together with the first 18 stitches of the second piece of knitting, this joins the two pieces together for the front and the back of the trousers, and now the rows are carried on from hip to hip. Work front and back separately, doing as before a plain row and a purl row alternately, and if the shape of the doll requires it decrease a few stitches where the two pieces join in front, and increase a few stitches in the same place at the back. Knit in all about 30 rows for the top of the trousers, front and back, and cast off; join up the legs. For the **Jersey**—With navy wool—Cast on 50 stitches, and work all plain knitting for 36 rows. Continue still in plain knitting and decrease by taking 2 stitches together at the beginning and at the end of every third row three times, when 45 rows will be knitted. **Next row**—Knit 2 together, knit 9; turn the work, cast off 2 stitches for the armhole, and knit plain back. Proceed forwards and backwards on these stitches for one side of the front of the jersey, decreasing occasionally to shape the **V** in front till 24 rows are done and the work is reduced to 6 stitches for the shoulder, and cast off. Work on the next 20 stitches without any decrease whatever for 22 rows for the back of the jersey, and cast off. Work the remaining 11 stitches to correspond with the first front. Join the shoulders to the back; and sew up the front from the bottom edge to where the decreasings begin. For the **Sleeve**—With navy wool—Cast on 24 stitches; knit 18 plain rows. **Next row**—Take 2 stitches together all along. Knit 4 plain rows for the wrist, and cast off. Knit the other sleeve in the same manner, and sew the sleeves in the armholes. For the **Collar** and **Revers**—With white wool—Cast on 18 stitches and knit 24 plain rows, and cast off; this is the back piece, and a small anchor should be embroidered with navy wool in the two lower corners. Cast on for the revers 4 stitches with white wool, knit plain a sufficient length to reach from the bottom of the **V**-shaped opening to the shoulder, increasing gradually on one side of the revers to 9 stitches, and cast off. Knit another piece the same, and sew the straight edges along the opening to the shoulder, and the collar at the back. For the **Vest**—Cast on with navy wool 14 stitches, and work alternately a plain row and a purl row, 2 rows with navy and 2 rows with white, till 15 stripes are done; cast off the middle 4 stitches; and work

5 stitches on each side thereof for 6 stripes to go round the neck, and cast off; put a tag of wool at each corner of this vest to tie it on the doll. Finish the costume with a lanyard made of a piece of white whipcord. The costume will fit an ordinary sized sixpenny doll.

CHILD'S TOY WHIP.

PROCURE a straight stick about 14 inches long and not very thick, a piece of cane will do, but it should be rather tapering at one end; besides this you will require ¼ an ounce of scarlet Scotch fingering, a little black fingering, a little scarlet double Berlin, about a yard of gold tinsel thread, and a pair of No. 15 steel knitting needles. The knitting has to be just wide enough to bind closely over the stick. Cast on with scarlet fingering 10 or 12 stitches according to the size of the top of your stick, and knit 16 plain rows; join on black, and knit 12 rows; join on scarlet, and knit 16 rows; join on black, and knit 12 rows; join on scarlet, and knit till the strip is about ten inches long; decrease in the middle and knit another two inches; decrease again and knit sufficient to bring you to the bottom of the stick. Decrease again and knit seven inches; decrease, and knit another seven inches; decrease, and knit three inches; decrease, and knit another three inches; and then bring the work gradually to a point of 3 stitches, when knit a few rows to form a twist, thus, slip the 3 knit stitches to the other end of the needle (without turning the needle round), and bringing the wool to the right-hand side knit them from thence. Fasten off, leaving a three-inch tag of wool. Sew the widest end of the piece of knitting over the stick; ornament the top of the stick with a plait composed of wool and gold tinsel, and put on three tufted tassels made with scarlet double Berlin, arranged as represented in the illustration. Tie a knot in the knitting near the thong of the whip, and also another knot further up; and tie a small tuft of scarlet Berlin on the point of the thong.

BASSINETTE COVER, OR QUILT FOR CHILD'S COT.

MOUSE PATTERN.

A VERY pretty cot cover can be knitted in the Mouse pattern, as shown in our engraving, using Andalusian wool of two colours, ruby and grey. The quantity of wool will depend upon the size the quilt is to be, and it will take double as much ruby wool as grey, because the whole of the border is knitted with ruby. Work with a pair of No. 14 steel knitting needles. Commence with ruby wool, with a long end, casting on 1 stitch; the end will be used afterwards for sewing up. **1st row**—Make 1, knit 1. **2nd row**—Make 1, knit 2. **3rd row**—Make 1, knit 1, make 1, knit 1, make 1, knit 1. **4th row**—Make 1, knit 1,

Fife Cuffs.

purl 3, knit 2. **5th row**—Make 1, knit 2, make 1, knit 3, make 1, knit 2. **6th row**—Make 1, knit 2, purl 5, knit 3. **7th row**—Make 1, knit 3, make 1, knit 5, make 1, knit 3. **8th row**—Make 1, knit 3, purl 7, knit 4. **9th row**—Make 1, knit 4, make 1, knit 7, make 1, knit 4. **10th row**—Make 1, knit 4, purl 9, knit 5. **11th row**—Make 1, knit 5, make 1, knit 9, make 1, knit 5. **12th row**—Make 1, knit 5, purl 11, knit 6. **13th row**—Make 1, knit 6, make 1, knit 11, make 1, knit 6. **14th row**—Make 1, knit 6, purl 13, knit 7. **15th row**—Make 1, knit 7, make 1, knit 13, make 1, knit 7. **16th row**—Make 1, knit 7, purl 15, knit 8. **17th row**—Make 1, knit plain to the end. **18th row**—Make 1, knit 8, purl 15, knit 9. **19th row**—Make 1, knit 9, slip 1, knit 1, pass the slipped stitch over, knit 11, knit 2 together, knit 9. **20th row**—Make 1, knit 9, purl 13, knit 10. **21st row**—Make 1, knit 10, slip 1, knit 1, pass the slipped stitch over, knit 9, knit 2 together, knit 10. **22nd row**—Make 1, knit 10, purl 11, knit 11. **23rd row**—Make 1, knit 11, slip 1, knit 1, pass the slipped stitch over, knit 7, knit 2 together, knit 11. **24th row**—

Make 1, knit 11, purl 9, knit 12. **25th row**—Make 1, knit 12, slip 1, knit 1, pass the slipped stitch over, knit 5, knit 2 together, knit 12. **26th row**—Make 1, knit 12, purl 7, knit 13. **27th row**—Make 1, knit 13, slip 1, knit 1, pass the slipped stitch over, knit 3, knit 2 together, knit 13. **28th row**—Make 1, knit 13, purl 5, knit 14. **29th row**—Make 1, knit 14, slip 1, knit 1, pass the slipped stitch over, knit 1, knit 2 together, knit 14. **30th row**—Make 1, knit 14, purl 3, knit 15. **31st row**—Make 1, knit 15, slip 1, knit 2 together, pass the slipped stitch over, knit 15. **32nd row**—Make 1, knit plain to the end. **33rd row**—Make 1, knit plain to the end. **34th row**—Plain, no increase, this is the middle of the section, break off the wool at the end of the row. **35th row**—Take the grey wool, and knit plain. **36th row**—Purl the 2 first stitches together, purl each stitch to the end of the row. **37th row**—Knit 2 together, knit plain to the end. **38th row**—Knit 2 together, knit plain to the end. **39th row**—Purl 2 together, purl to the end. **40th row**—Knit 2 together, knit plain to the end. **41st row**—Knit 2 together, knit plain to the end.

Sailor Doll.

the end. **42nd row**—Purl 2 together, purl to the end. Continue thus knitting 2 plain rows and 1 purl row, always taking 2 stitches together at the beginning of each row, till the work is reduced to only 2 stitches, when slip one stitch over the other, break off the wool with rather a long end, and draw it through the last stitch. Knit three more sections in the same manner. Then sew the four sections together, making the raised knitting meet in the centre, and joining by the made stitches along the edge of the ruby rows so as to give an appearance of two rows of holes. Knit a number of similar squares, and join them together, till you have completed the centre of the quilt.

FLUTED BORDER.

FOR TRIMMING A CHILD'S COT QUILT.

(Not Illustrated.)

THIS is knitted with ruby Andalusian wool, and a pair of No. 14 steel knitting needles. Cast on 40 stitches. **1st row**—Slip 1, knit 3, make 1, knit 2 together, knit 2, make 1, knit 2 together, knit 2, make 1, knit 2 together, knit 25, knit 1 taking the stitch from the back. **2nd row**—Slip 1, purl 22, and turn, leaving 17 stitches unknitted on the pin. **3rd row**—Slip 1, knit 21, knit 1 taking the stitch from the back. **4th row**—Slip 1, purl 22, knit 4, wool twice round the needle, purl 2 together, purl 2, pass the wool over the needle, knit 2 together, knit 2, wool twice round the needle, purl 2 together, purl 3. Repeat these four rows twice. **13th row**—Slip 1, knit 3, make 1, knit 2 together, knit 2, make 1, knit 2 together, knit 2, make 1, knit 2 together, knit 3, purl 23. **14th row**—Slip 1, knit 22, and turn, leaving 17 stitches unknitted on the pin. **15th row**—Slip 1, purl 22. **16th row**—Slip 1, knit 26, wool twice round the needle, purl 2 together, purl 2, pass the wool over the needle, knit 2 together, knit 2, wool twice round the needle, purl 2 together, purl 3. Repeat these four rows twice. Then recommence at the first row, and continue for the length required. The border must be amply full round the corners of the quilt. Our engraving shows a portion of the border attached to a square knitted in mouse pattern.

LADY'S VEST.

KNITTED IN SMALL BASKET PATTERN.

THIS vest is comfortably shaped, fitting to the figure, with gussets, and nicely rounded at the neck. Required, 9 oz. of pink unshrinkable vest wool, and a pair of No. 9 bone knitting needles, or No. 8 needles if a tight knitter. Cast on 111 stitches for the **Border** at the bottom of the front of the vest. Knit 2 plain rows. **3rd row**—Slip 1, * knit 2 together, knit 5, make 1 and knit 1 alternately eight times, knit 4, knit 2 together, purl 1, and repeat from * to the end of the row. **4th row**—Slip 1, * purl 2 together, purl 23, purl 2 together, knit 1, and repeat from * to the end. **5th row**—Slip 1, * knit 2 together, knit 21, knit 2 together, purl 1, and repeat from *. **6th row**—Slip 1, * purl 2 together, purl 19, purl 2 together, knit 1, and repeat from *. Now there are 111 stitches again on the needle. Repeat from the third row twice. **15th row**—Slip 1, purl 2 together, purl to the end; now 110 stitches on the needle. Knit 2 plain rows. Purl 3 rows. This finishes the border. Begin the **Basket Pattern** holding the right side of the border next you. **1st row**—Knit 2, purl 2, and repeat, and end the row with knit 2 as it began. **2nd row**—Purl 2, knit 2, and repeat, and end the row with purl 2. **3rd row**—Plain. **4th row**—Purl. **5th row**—Purl 2, knit 2, and repeat, and end the row with purl 2 as it began. **6th row**—Knit 2, purl 2, and repeat, and end with knit 2. **7th row**—Plain. **8th row**—Purl. **9th row**—Knit 2, purl 2, and repeat, and end the row with knit 2 as it began. **10th row**—Purl 2, knit 2, and repeat, and end the row with purl 2. **11th row**—Slip 1, knit 2 together, knit plain to within 3 stitches of the end, knit 2 together, knit 1. **12th row**—Purl. **13th row**—Slip 1, * knit 2, purl 2, repeat from *, and end with knit 3. **14th row**—Slip 1, * purl 2, knit 2, and repeat from *, and end with purl 3. **15th row**—Slip 1, knit 2 together, knit plain to within 3 stitches of the end, knit 2 together, knit 1. **16th row**—Purl. **17th row**—Purl 2, knit 2, and repeat, and end the row with purl 2. **18th row**—Knit 2, purl 2, and repeat, and end with knit 2. **19th row**—Slip 1, * knit 2 together, knit plain to within 3 stitches of the end, knit 2 together, knit 1. **20th row**—Purl. **21st row**—Slip 1, * purl 2, knit 2, and repeat from * and end with purl 2, knit 1. **22nd row**—Slip 1, * knit 2,

Child's Toy Whip.

purl 2, repeat from *, and end with knit 2, purl 1. **23rd row**—Slip 1, knit 2 together, knit plain to within 3 stitches of the end, knit 2 together, knit 1. **24th row**—Purl. Repeat from the ninth row, until on completion of the **56th row** you find the work reduced to 86 stitches on the needle. Then repeat from the first row to the eighth row till you have done about 26 patterns, 208 rows, when it will be time in the next row to commence the gussets. **1st Gusset row**—Knit 2 and purl 2 alternately till 26 stitches are knitted, increase 1 (by picking up the thread that lies directly under the next stitch and knitting it), purl 2, increase 1, knit 2 and purl 2 alternately till 30 more stitches are knitted, increase 1, purl 2, increase 1, knit 2 and purl 2 alternately to the end; there are 26 stitches always at the beginning and at the end, and 30 stitches in the centre between the gussets. **2nd row**—Purl 2, knit 2, and repeat, and knit 4 instead of 2 where the increased stitches come. **3rd row**—Knit plain 26 stitches, increase 1, knit 4, increase 1, knit 30, increase 1, knit 4, increase 1, knit 26. **4th row**—Purl. **5th** row—Purl 2 and knit 2 alternately till 26 stitches are knitted, increase 1, purl 2, knit 2, purl 2, increase 1, purl 2 and knit 2 alternately till 30 more stitches are knitted, increase 1, purl 2, knit 2, purl 2, increase 1, purl 2 and knit 2 alternately to the end. **6th row** —Knit 2, purl 2, and repeat, and purl the 1 increased stitch of last row. **7th row**—Knit plain 26 stitches, increase 1, knit 8, increase 1, knit 30, increase 1, knit 8, increase 1, knit 26. **8th row**—Purl. **9th row**—Knit 2 and purl 2 alternately till 26 stitches are knitted, increase 1, purl 2, knit 2, purl 2, knit 2, purl 2, increase 1, knit 2 and purl 2 alternately till 30 more stitches are knitted, increase 1, purl 2, knit 2, purl 2, knit 2, purl 2, increase 1, knit 2 and purl 2 alternately to the end. **10th row**—Purl 2, knit 2, and repeat, and knit the 1 increased stitch of last row. **11th row**—Knit plain 26 stitches, increase 1, knit 12, increase 1, knit 30, increase 1, knit 12, increase 1, knit 26. **12th row**—Purl. **13th row**—Purl 2 and knit 2 alternately till 26 stitches are knitted, increase 1, purl 2 and knit 2 alternately for 14 stitches across the gusset, increase 1, purl 2 and knit 2 alternately till 30 more stitches are knitted, increase 1, purl 2 and knit 2 alternately for 14 stitches across the other gusset, increase 1, purl 2 and knit 2 alternately to the end. **14th row**—Knit 2, purl 2, and repeat, and purl the 1 increased stitch of last row. **15th row**—Knit plain 26 stitches, increase 1, knit 16, increase 1, knit 30, increase 1, knit 16, increase 1, knit 26. **16th row**—Purl. **17th row**—Knit 2, and purl 2 alternately till 26 stitches are knitted, increase 1, purl 2 and knit 2 for 18 stitches across the gusset, increase 1, knit 2, and purl 2 alternately till 30 more stitches are knitted, increase 1, purl 2, and knit 2, for 18 stitches across the gusset, increase 1, knit 2, and purl 2 alternately to

stitches from the beginning and before getting to 20 stitches from the end in each forward row, till you have worked the gusset completely out, and have 48 stitches on the needle. Proceed in pattern till three patterns, 24 rows, are knitted above the closing of the gusset, and it will then be time to begin shaping the neck, which is done by casting off 14 stitches at the beginning of a back row by the six edge stitches, and continuing working in pattern, taking 2 stitches together at the beginning of every row at the neck end till reduced to 26 stitches on the needle, and cast off. Recommence where you divided for the opening in front of the vest, and after casting on 6 stitches for a fold-over, work the 68 stitches in pattern ; and proceed in pattern, knitting the 6 edge stitches always plain, reducing the gusset, and shaping the neck to correspond with the half front already knitted, but as you now have two more stitches on the needle than in the first half you must cast off 16 stitches instead of fourteen at the beginning of the neck to bring the rows in evenly to 26 stitches for the shoulder ; and cast off. For the **Back of the Vest**—Cast on 111 stitches, and work as directed for the front till you have decreased to 86 stitches on the needle ; then continue the basket pattern, keeping the same number of stitches in every row, till you have done the same number of patterns that are knitted on the front of the vest, counting from the bottom to the cast off stitches at the neck ; cast off the 14 centre stitches of the back, and then work each shoulder separately, taking 2 stitches together at the beginning of every row that commences at the neck end, till 26 stitches remain, and cast these off. Sew the shoulder pieces neatly together, and join up the sides of the vest leaving room for the armholes. Sew the front folds nicely in position. For the **Sleeves**—Cast on 46 stitches Knit 2 plain rows. **3rd row**—

Bassinette Cover, or Quilt for Child's Cot. Mouse Pattern.

Lady's Vest. Knitte

the end. **18th row**—Purl 2, knit 2, and repeat, and knit the 1 increased stitch of last row. **19th row**—Knit plain 26, increase 1, knit 20, increase 1, knit 30, increase 1, knit 20, increase 1, knit 26. **20th row**—Purl. **21st row**—Purl 2 and knit 2 alternately till 26 stitches are knitted, increase 1, purl 2 and knit 2 for 22 stitches across the gusset, increase 1, purl 2 and knit 2 alternately till 30 more stitches are knitted, increase 1, purl 2 and knit 2 for 22 stitches across the gusset, increase 1, purl 2 and knit 2 alternately to the end. **22nd row**—Knit 2, purl 2, and repeat, and purl the 1 increased stitch of last row. **23rd row**—Knit plain 26, increase 1, knit 24, increase 1, knit 30, increase 1, knit 24, increase 1, knit 26. **24th row**—Purl, 134 stitches are now on the needle. **25th row**—Knit 2 and purl 2 alternately (no more increase at the gusset) till 66 stitches are knitted, then cast on 6 stitches for the fold under ; turn the work, leaving 68 stitches on the left-hand pin, and knit back doing the 6 cast on stitches plain and the 66 vest stitches in pattern; this begins the opening in front, and the 6 additional stitches are edge stitches to be knitted plain in every row. **Next row**—Plain knitting ; and turn, and after knitting 6 edge stitches, purl back. **Next row**—Purl 2 and knit 2 alternately till 26 stitches are knitted, knit 2 together, purl 2 and knit 2 alternately for 22 stitches across the gusset, knit 2 together, purl 2 and knit 2 alternately for 14 stitches, knit 6 ; and turn, and after knitting 6 edge stitches plain, work in pattern back. **Next row**—Knit plain 26 stitches, knit 2 together, knit 20 stitches across the gusset, knit 2 together, knit 20 ; and turn, and after knitting 6 edge stitches, purl back. Continue thus in small basket pattern, and decrease the gusset after doing 26

Slip 1, * knit 2 together, knit 2 together, make 1 and knit 1 alternately three times, make 1, knit 2 together, knit 2 together, and repeat from *, and at the end there will be 1 plain stitch to knit. **4th row**—Purl. Repeat the last two rows five times. **15th row**—Slip 1, purl 2 together, purl 40, purl 2 together, purl 1 : now there are 44 stitches on the needle. Knit 2 plain rows. Purl 3 rows. Work 16 rows of the basket pattern, increasing 1 stitch at the beginning and 1 stitch at the end of *every* row to form the gusset ; there will be 76 stitches on the needle on completion of the 16 pattern rows ; cast off rather loosely. Knit the other sleeve in the same manner. Join up the gussets, and sew the sleeves into the vest. Work a crochet edge round the neck, 1 double crochet in a stitch of the knitting, 2 chain, 2 treble in the same place, miss two stitches, and repeat. Run a ribbon through the open crochet, and tie a pretty bow in front.

SAXON STAR PATTERN.

KNITTED STRIPE FOR A QUILT.

OUR engraving shows a handsome pattern for a quilt knitted in stripes, in a design of stars surrounded by bay leaves. Use Strutt's knitting cotton, No 6, and a pair of No 15 steel knitting needles. Cast on 52 stitches for the width of one stripe. **1st row**—Plain. **2nd row**—Purl. **3rd row**—Plain, of course always slip the first stitch of every row whether plain or purl. **4th row**—Purl 4, * make 1 (by passing the cotton *over* the needle), knit 1, make (by passing the cotton *twice round* the needle), purl 6, repeat from * four times, make 1, knit 1, make 1, purl 7, make 1, knit 1, make 1, purl 4. **5th row**—Knit 4, purl 3, knit 7, purl 3, * knit 6, purl 3, repeat from *, and end with knit 4. **6th row**—Purl 4, * make 1, knit 3, make 1, purl 6, repeat from * four times, make 1, knit 3, make 1, purl 7, make 1, knit 3, make 1, purl 4. **7th row**—Knit 4, purl 5, knit 7, purl 5, * knit 6, purl 5, repeat from *, and end with knit 4. **8th row**—Purl 4, * make 1, knit 5, make 1, purl 6, repeat from * four times, make 1, knit 5, make 1, purl 7, make 1, knit 5, make 1, purl 4. **9th row**—Knit 4, purl 7, knit 7, purl 7, * knit 6, purl 7, repeat from *, and end with knit 4. **10th row**—Purl 4, * make 1, knit 7, make 1, purl 6, repeat from * four times, make 1, knit 7, make 1, purl 7, make 1, knit 7, make 1, purl 4. **11th row**—Knit 4, purl 9, knit 7, purl 9, * knit 6, purl 9, repeat from *, and end with knit 4. **12th row**—Purl 4, * knit 3, slip 1, knit 2 together, pass the slipped stitch over, knit 3, purl 6, repeat from * four times, knit 3, slip 1, knit 2 together, pass the slipped stitch over, knit 3, purl 7, knit 3, slip 1, knit 2 together, pass the slipped stitch over, knit 3, purl 4. **13th row**—Knit 4, purl 7, knit 7, purl 7, * knit 6, purl 7, repeat from *, and end with knit 4. **14th row**—Purl 4, * knit 2, slip 1, knit 2 together, pass the slipped stitch over, knit 2, purl 6, repeat from * four times, knit 2, slip 1, knit 2 together, pass the slipped stitch over, knit 2, purl 7, knit 2, slip 1, knit 2 together, pass the slipped stitch over, knit 2, purl 4. **15th row**—Knit 4, purl 5, knit 7, purl 5, * knit 6, purl 5, repeat from *, and end with knit 4. **16th row**—Purl 4, * knit 1, slip 1, knit 2 together, pass the slipped stitch over, knit 1, purl 6, repeat from * four times, knit 1, slip 1, knit 2 together, pass the slipped stitch over, knit 1, purl 7, knit 1, slip 1, knit 2 together, pass the slipped stitch over, knit 1, purl 4. **17th**

37th row—Knit 4, purl 5, knit 4, purl 9, knit 7, purl 2, knit 7, purl 9, knit 4, purl 5, knit 4. **38th row**—Purl 4, knit 1, slip 1, knit 2 together, pass the slipped stitch over, knit 1, purl 4, knit 34, purl 4, knit 1, slip 1, knit 2 together, pass the slipped stitch over, knit 1, purl 4. **39th row**—Knit 4, purl 3, knit 4, purl 9, knit 16, purl 9, knit 4, purl 3, knit 4. **40th row**—Purl 4, slip 1, knit 2 together, pass the slipped stitch over, purl 4, knit 34, purl 4, slip 1, knit 2 together, pass the slipped stitch over, purl 4. **41st row**—Knit 4, purl 1, knit 4, purl 1, knit 15, purl 1, knit 4, purl 1, knit 4. **42nd row**—Purl 9, knit 34, purl 9. **43rd row**—Knit 9, purl 2, knit 13, purl 2, knit 9. **44th row**—Purl 9, knit 34, purl 9. **45th row**—Knit 9, purl 3, knit 11, purl 6, knit 11, purl 3, knit 9. **46th row**—Purl 9, knit 15, purl 4, knit 15, purl 9. **47th row**—Knit 9, purl 4, knit 9, purl 2, knit 4, purl 2, knit 9, purl 4, knit 9. **48th row**—Purl 4, make 1, knit 1, make 1, purl 4, knit 15, purl 4, knit 15, purl 4, make 1, knit 1, make 1, purl 4. **49th row**—Knit 4, purl 3, knit 4, purl 5, knit 7, purl 3, knit 4, purl 3, knit 7, purl 5, knit 4, purl 3, knit 4. **50th row**—Purl 4, make 1, knit 3, make 1, purl 4, knit 15, purl 4, knit 15, purl 4, make 1, knit 3, make 1, purl 4. **51st row**—Knit 4, purl 5, knit 4, purl 6, knit 5, purl 4, knit 4, purl 4, knit 5, purl 6, knit 4, purl 5, knit 4. **52nd row**—Purl 4, make 1, knit 5, make 1, purl 4, knit 15, purl 4, knit 15, purl 4, make 1, knit 5, make 1, purl 4. **53rd row**—Knit 4, purl 7, knit 4, purl 7, knit 3, purl 4, knit 4, purl 4, knit 1, purl 3, knit 7, purl 4, purl 7, knit 4. **54th row**—Purl 4, make 1, knit 7, make 1, purl 4, knit 11, purl 4, make 1, knit 7, make 1, purl 4. **55th row**—Knit 4, purl 9, knit 4, purl 8, knit 1, purl 2, knit 4, purl 4, knit 4, purl 2, knit 1, purl 8,

Basket Pattern.

Saxon Star Pattern.

row—Knit 4, purl 3, knit 7, purl 3, * knit 6, purl 3, repeat from *, and end with knit 4. **18th row**—Purl 4, * slip 1, knit 2 together, pass the slipped stitch over, purl 6, repeat from * four times, slip 1, knit 2 together, pass the slipped stitch over, purl 7, slip 1, knit 2 together, pass the slipped stitch over, purl 4. **19th row**—Knit 4, purl 1, knit 7, purl 1, * knit 6, purl 1, and repeat from * and end with knit 4. **20th row**—Purl all. 52 stitches. **21st row**—Plain. **22nd row**—Purl. **23rd row**—Plain. **24th row**—Purl 9, knit 34, purl 9. **25th row**—Knit 9, purl 9, knit 1, purl 14, knit 1, purl 9, knit 9. **26th row**—Purl 4, make 1, knit 1, make 1, purl 4, knit 34, purl 4, make 1, knit 1, make 1, purl 4. **27th row**—Knit 4, purl 3, knit 4, purl 9, knit 3, purl 10, knit 3, purl 9, knit 4, purl 3, knit 4. **28th row**—Purl 4, make 1, knit 3, make 1, purl 4, knit 34, purl 4, make 1, knit 3, make 1, purl 4. **29th row**—Knit 4, purl 5, knit 4, purl 9, knit 3, purl 10, knit 3, purl 9, knit 4, purl 5, knit 4. **30th row**—Purl 4, make 1, knit 5, make 1, purl 4, knit 34, purl 4, make 1, knit 5, make 1, purl 4. **31st row**—Knit 4, purl 7, knit 4, purl 9, knit 4, purl 8, knit 4, purl 9, knit 4, purl 7, knit 4. **32nd row**—Purl 4, make 1, knit 7, make 1, purl 4, knit 34, purl 4, make 1, knit 7, make 1, purl 4. **33rd row**—Knit 4, purl 9, knit 4, purl 9, knit 5, purl 6, knit 5, purl 9, knit 4, purl 9, knit 4. **34th row**—Purl 4, knit 3, slip 1, knit 2 together, pass the slipped stitch over, knit 3, purl 4, knit 34, purl 4, knit 3, slip 1, knit 2 together, pass the slipped stitch over, knit 3, purl 4. **35th row**—Knit 4, purl 7, knit 4, purl 9, knit 6, purl 4, knit 6, purl 9, knit 4, purl 7, knit 4. **36th row**—Purl 4, knit 2, slip 1, knit 2 together, pass the slipped stitch over, knit 2, purl 4, knit 34, purl 4, knit 2, slip 1, knit 2 together, pass the slipped stitch over, knit 2, purl 4.

knit 4, purl 9, knit 4; this brings you to the half of the star. **56th row**—Purl 4, knit 3, slip 1, knit 2 together, pass the slipped stitch over, purl 4, knit 11, purl 4, knit 4, purl 4, knit 11, purl 4, knit 3, slip 1, knit 2 together, pass the slipped stitch over, knit 3, purl 4. **57th row**—Knit 4, purl 7, knit 4, purl 8, knit 1, purl 2, knit 4, purl 4, knit 4, purl 2, knit 1, purl 8, knit 4, purl 7, knit 4. **58th row**—Purl 4, knit 2, slip 1, knit 2 together, pass the slipped stitch over, knit 2, purl 4, knit 11, purl 4, knit 4, purl 4, knit 11, purl 4, knit 2, slip 1, knit 2 together, pass the slipped stitch over, knit 2, purl 4. **59th row**—Knit 4, purl 5, knit 4, purl 7, knit 3, purl 1, knit 4, purl 4, knit 4, purl 1, knit 3, purl 7, knit 4, purl 5, knit 4. **60th row**—Purl 4, knit 1, slip 1, knit 2 together, pass the slipped stitch over, knit 1, purl 4, knit 10, purl 1, knit 4, purl 4, knit 4, purl 1, knit 10, purl 4, knit 1, slip 1, knit 2 together, pass the slipped stitch over, knit 1, purl 4. **61st row**—Knit 4, purl 3, knit 4, purl 6, knit 5, purl 4, knit 4, purl 4, knit 5, purl 6, knit 4, purl 3, knit 4. **62nd row**—Purl 4, slip 1, knit 2 together, pass the slipped stitch over, purl 4, knit 15, purl 4, knit 15, purl 4, slip 1, knit 2 together, pass the slipped stitch over, purl 4. **63rd row**—Knit 4, purl 1, knit 4, purl 5, knit 7, purl 3, knit 4, purl 3, knit 7, purl 5, knit 4, purl 1, knit 4. **64th row**—Purl 9, knit 15, purl 4, knit 15, purl 9. **65th row**—Knit 9, purl 4, knit 9, purl 2, knit 4, purl 2, knit 9, purl 4, knit 9. **66th row**—Purl 9, knit 15, purl 4, knit 15, purl 9. **67th row**—Knit 9, purl 3, knit 11, purl 6, knit 11, purl 3, knit 9. **68th row**—Purl 9, knit 34, purl 9. **69th row**—Knit 9, purl 2, knit 13, purl 4, knit 13, purl 2, knit 9. **70th row**—Purl 4, make 1, knit 1, make 1, purl 4, knit 34, purl 4, make 1, knit 1, make 1, purl 4. **71st row**—Knit 4, purl 3, knit 4, purl 1, knit 15, purl 2, knit 15, purl 1, knit 4, purl 3, knit 4. **72nd row**—Purl 4, make 1, knit 3, make 1, purl 4, knit 34, purl 4, make 1, knit 3, make 1, purl 4. **73rd row**—Knit 4, purl 5, knit 4, purl 9, knit 16, purl 9, knit 4, purl 5, knit 4. **74th row**—Purl 4, make 1, knit 5, make 1, purl 4, knit 34, purl 4, make 1, knit 5, make 1, purl 4. **75th row**—Knit 4, purl 7, knit 4, purl 9, knit 7, purl 2, knit 7, purl 9, knit 4, purl 7, knit 4. **76th row**—Purl 4, make 1, knit 7, make 1, purl 4, knit 34, purl 4, make 1, knit 7, make 1, purl 4. **77th row**—Knit 4, purl 9, knit 4, purl 9, knit 6, purl 4, knit 6, purl 9, knit 4, purl 9, knit 4. **78th row**—Purl 4, knit 3, slip 1, knit 2 together, pass the slipped stitch over, knit 3, purl 4, knit 34, purl 4, knit 3, slip 1, knit 2 together, pass the slipped stitch over, knit 3, purl 4. **79th row**—Knit 4, purl 7, knit 4, purl 9, knit 5, purl 6, knit 5, purl 9, knit 4, purl 7, knit 4. **80th row**—Purl 4, knit 2, slip 1, knit 2 together, pass the slipped stitch over, knit 2, purl 4, knit 34, purl 4, knit 2, slip 1, knit 2 together, pass the slipped stitch over, knit 2, purl 4. **81st row**—Knit 4, purl 5, knit 4, purl 9, knit 4, purl 8, knit 4, purl 9, knit 4, purl 5, knit 4. **82nd row**—Purl 4, knit 1, slip 1, knit 2 together, pass the slipped stitch over, knit 1, purl 4, knit 34, purl 4, knit 1, slip 1, knit 2 together, pass

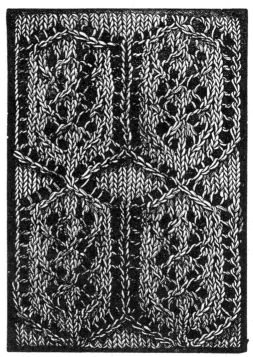

Grecian Pattern.

the slipped stitch over, knit 1, purl 4. **83rd row**—Knit 4, purl 3, knit 4, purl 9, knit 3, purl 10, knit 3, purl 9, knit 4, purl 3, knit 4. **84th row**—Purl 4, slip 1, knit 2 together, pass the slipped stitch over, purl 4, knit 34, purl 4, slip 1, knit 2 together, pass the slipped stitch over, purl 4. **85th row**—Knit 4, purl 1, knit 4, purl 9, knit 2, purl 12, knit 2, purl 9, knit 4, purl 1, knit 4. **86th row**—Purl 9, knit 34, purl 9. **87th row**—Knit 9, purl 9, knit 1, purl 14, knit 1, purl 9, knit 9. **88th row**—Purl 9, knit 34, purl 9. Now work from the first row, repeating the line of bay-leaves, and proceed till the stripe is the length required, which for a full-sized bed will be about two and a half yards; cast off after doing the twenty-second row. Knit more stripes in the same pattern, and the same length, and sew them together to make the width of the quilt.

GRECIAN PATTERN.

THIS lovely pattern may be knit either with cotton or wool, and is suitable for toilet covers, long window curtains, ottoman cloths, couvrepieds, antimacassars, and other purposes. Cast on as many stitches as are required for the width of the article, allowing 12 stitches for each repetition of the pattern, and 1 additional stitch over at the end of the row, say 145 stitches, which number will allow for 11 patterns and for 6 plain stitches as edge stitches on each side. Begin by knitting 12 plain rows. **1st pattern row**—Slip 1, knit 9, knit 2 together, * make 1, knit 1, make 1, slip 1, knit 1, pass the slipped stitch over, knit 7, knit 2 together, repeat from *; and at the end of the row, after knitting 7, knit plain the last three stitches. **2nd row**—Slip 1, knit 5, purl 3, purl 2 together, * make 1, purl 3, make 1, purl 2 together, purl 5, purl 2 together backwards, repeat from *; end the row with purl 3 instead of purl 5, and knit the last 6 stitches plain. To purl 2 together *backwards* you purl 1 stitch first, slip the stitch back on to the left-hand needle and draw the next stitch over it, and then replace the stitch in its position on the right-hand needle; this proceeding makes the 2 together slant

from right to left on the surface of the work in the contrary direction to that taken if purled together in the ordinary way. **3rd row**—Slip 1, knit 7, knit 2 together, * make 1, knit 5, make 1, slip 1, knit 1, pass the slipped stitch over, knit 3, knit 2 together, repeat from *; and at the end after knitting 3 stitches, knit 5 more plain stitches. **4th row**—Slip 1, knit 5, purl 1, purl 2 together, * make 1, purl 7, make 1, purl 2 together, purl 1, purl 2 together backwards, repeat from *; and at the end after purling 1 stitch, knit the last 6 stitches plain. **5th row**—Slip 1, knit 5, knit 2 together, * make 1, knit 9, make 1, slip 1, knit 2 together, pass the slipped stitch over, repeat from *; and at the end after knitting 9, make 1, knit 2 together, knit 6. **6th row**—Slip 1, knit 5, purl 4, purl 2 together, * make 1, purl 1, make 1, purl 2 together, purl 7, purl 2 together backwards, repeat from *; and end with purl 4 instead of purling 7, and knit the last 6 stitches plain. **7th row**—Slip 1, knit 6, * make 1, knit 2 together, knit 2 together, make 1, knit 3, make 1, slip 1, knit 1, pass the slipped stitch over, slip 1, knit 1, pass the slipped stitch over, make 1, knit 1, repeat from *; and end with 6 plain stitches. **8th row**—Slip 1, knit 5, purl all but the last 6 stitches which knit. **9th row**—Slip 1, knit 6, * make 1, knit 2 together, knit 1, make 1, knit 2 together, knit 1, knit 2 together, make 1, knit 1, slip 1, knit 1, pass the slipped stitch over, make 1, knit 1, repeat from *; and end with 6 plain stitches. **10th row**—Slip 1, knit 5, purl 5, * make 1, purl 3 together, make 1, purl 9, repeat from *; and at the end after purling 5 stitches, knit the last 6 stitches plain. **11th row**—Slip 1, knit 6, * make 1, knit 2 together, knit 7, slip 1, knit 1, pass the slipped stitch over, make 1, knit 1, repeat from *; and end with 6 plain stitches. **12th row**—Slip 1, knit 5, purl 4, purl 2 together, * make 1, purl 1, make 1, purl 2 together, purl 7, purl 2 together, repeat from *; and at the end after purling 4 stitches, knit the last six stitches plain. Repeat from the seventh row to the twelfth row inclusive. Repeat from the seventh row to the eleventh row inclusive. This makes twenty-three rows now done. **24th row**—Slip 1, knit 5, purl 2, * make 1, purl 2 together, purl 5, purl 2 together backwards, make 1, purl 3, repeat from *; and end with purl 2 instead of purling 3, and knit the last 6 stitches plain. **25th row**—Slip 1, knit 8, * make 1, slip 1, knit 1, pass the slipped stitch over, knit 3, knit 2 together, make 1, knit 5, repeat from *; and at the end there will be 4 stitches to knit plain. **26th row**—Slip 1, knit 5, purl 4, * make 1, purl 2 together, purl 1, purl 2 together backwards, make 1, purl 7, repeat from *; and end with purl 4 instead of purling 7, and knit the last 6 stitches plain. **27th row**—Slip 1, knit 10, * make 1, slip 1, knit 2 together, pass the slipped stitch over, make 1, knit 9, repeat from *; and at the end there will be 2 stitches to knit plain. **28th row**—Slip 1, knit 5, purl to within 6 stitches of the end, and knit those 6 stitches plain. Repeat from the first row of the pattern.

CARTOON LACE.

CAST on 15 stitches. Knit 1 plain row. **1st row**—Slip 1, knit 2 together, make 2, slip 1, knit 2 together, pass the slipped stitch over, make 2, knit 2 together, knit 2, make 3, knit 2, make 2, knit 1, make 2, knit 1. **2nd row**—Knit 2, purl 1, knit 2, purl 1, knit 2, purl 1, knit 3, purl 1, knit 5, purl 1, knit 2, purl 1, knit 2. **3rd row**—Slip 1, knit 2 together, make 2, slip 1, knit 2 together, pass the slipped stitch over, make 2, knit 2 together, knit 1, knit 2 together, knit 1, * insert the needle in the next stitch, pass the cotton over the needle and draw it through the stitch as if about to knit, move this

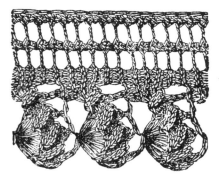

Cartoon Lace.

extra stitch from the right-hand needle on to the left, and cast on in all **7** stitches in this way, then cast off the seven stitches, and let the little strip so formed hang for the present at the back of the work, knit 2 stitches, and repeat from * to the end of the row, and you will have made four little strips. **4th row**—Knit 17, purl 1, knit 2, purl 1, knit 2. **5th row**—Slip 1, knit 2 together, make 2, slip 1, knit 2 together, pass the slipped stitch over, make 2, knit 2 together, knit 15. **6th row**—Knit 17, purl 1, knit 2, purl 1, knit 2. **7th row**—Slip 1, knit 2 together, make 2, slip 1, knit 2 together, pass the slipped stitch over, make 2, knit 2 together, knit 5, take the top thread of the first little strip on the left-hand needle and knit it together with the next stitch, * knit 2 stitches, take up the top thread of the next little strip on the left-hand needle and knit it together with the next stitch, and repeat from * twice more, and you will have the four little strips looped up prettily from the previous row to the present row. **8th row**—Knit 10 stitches, and as you knit draw each stitch up nearly half an inch high, make 3, knit 2 together, knit 5, purl 1, knit 2, purl 1, knit 2. **9th row**—Slip 1, knit 2 together, make 2, slip 1, knit 2 together, pass the slipped stitch over, make 2, knit 2 together, knit 5, purl 1, knit 1, knit the 10 long stitches together, and pass the last stitch but one over this last stitch. **10th row**—Slip 1, knit 8, purl 1, knit 2, purl 1, knit 2. Repeat from the first row.

KNITTED PATTERN FOR A QUILT. OCTAGONS AND SQUARES.

A VERY handsome quilt may be knitted in octagons as shown in our engraving, the spaces between the octagons being filled in with small squares. Use Strutt's knitting cotton No. 6, and four No. 14 steel knitting needles. Cast 3 stitches on each of two needles, two stitches on the third needle, and knit with the fourth needle. **1st round**—Knit plain the 8 stitches each on

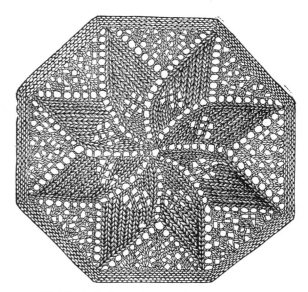

Knitted Pattern for an Octagon Quilt.

their own respective pins. **2nd round**—Make 1, knit 1, and repeat the same all round. **3rd round**—Plain. **4th round**—make 1, knit 2, and repeat. **5th round**—Plain. **6th round**—Make 1, knit 3, and repeat. **7th round**—Plain, and each alternate round is the same. **8th round**—Make 1, knit 4, and repeat. **10th round**—Make 1, knit 5, and repeat. **12th round**—Make 1, knit 2, make 1, knit 2 together, knit 2, and repeat. **14th round**—Make 1, knit 2, make 1, knit 2 together, make 1, knit 2 together, knit 1, and repeat. **16th round**—Make 1, knit 2, make 1, knit 2 together, make 1, knit 2 together, knit 2, and repeat. **18th round**—Make 1, knit 4, make 1, knit 2 together, make 1, knit 2 together, make 1, knit 2 together, knit 1, and repeat. **20th round**—Make 1, knit 1, make 1, knit 7, knit 2 together, and repeat. **22nd round**—Make 1, knit 3, make 1, knit 6, knit 2 together, and repeat. **24th round**—Make 1, knit 1, make 1, slip 1, knit 2 together, pass the slipped stitch over, make 1, knit 1, make 1, knit 5, knit 2 together, and repeat. **26th round**—Make 1, knit 2 together, make 1, knit 3, make 1, knit 2 together, make 1, knit 4, knit 2 together, and repeat. **28th round**—Make 1, knit 3, make 1, slip 1, knit 2 together, pass the slipped stitch over, make 1, knit 3, make 1, knit 3, knit 2 together, and repeat. **30th round**—Make 1, knit 1, make 1, slip 1, knit 2 together, pass the slipped stitch over, make 1, knit 3, make 1, slip 1, knit 2 together, pass the slipped stitch over, make 1, knit 1, make 1, knit 2, knit 2 together, and repeat. **32nd round**—Make 1, knit 2 together, make 1, knit 3, make 1, slip 1, knit 2 together, pass the slipped stitch over, make 1, knit 3, make 1, knit 2 together, make 1, knit 1, knit 2 together, and repeat. **34th round**—Make 1, knit 3, make 1, slip 1, knit 2 together, pass the slipped stitch over, make 1, knit 3, make 1, slip 1, knit 2 together, pass the slipped stitch over, make 1, knit 3, make 1, knit 2 together, and repeat. **35th round**—Plain. Purl 2 rounds. Cast off in the next round in purling it. Now one octagon is finished. Knit several more, and join them together in a straight line. For the **Square**—Cast 2 stitches on each of two needles, and 4 stitches on the third needle. **1st round**—Knit plain. **2nd round**—Make 1, knit 1, and repeat the same all round. **3rd round**—Plain, and each alternate round is the same. **4th round**—Make 1, knit 3, make 1, knit 1, and repeat the same all round. **6th round**—Make 1, knit 5, make 1, knit 1, and repeat. **8th round**—Make 1, knit 7, make 1, knit 1, and repeat. **10th round**—Make 1, knit 4, make 1, knit 2 together, knit 3, make 1, knit 1, and repeat. **12th round**—Make 1, knit 3, knit 2 together, make 1, knit 1, make 1,

knit 2 together, knit 3, make 1, knit 1, and repeat. **14th round**—Make 1, knit 3, knit 2 together, make 1, knit 3, make 1, knit 2 together, knit 3, make 1, knit 1, and repeat. **16th round**—Make 1, knit 3, knit 2 together, make 1, knit 5, make 1, knit 2 together, knit 3, make 1, knit 1, and repeat. **17th round**—Plain. Purl 2 rounds, increasing 1 stitch at each corner. Cast off in the next round in purling it. The squares are used to fill in the interstices between the octagons.

BABY'S BALMORAL BOOTIKINS.

OUR model pair of bootikins are knitted throughout with white wool, they come nice and high up the leg, and are very warm and comfortable. Procure 2 ozs. of the best white Peacock Fingering, a pair of No. 15 or No. 16 steel knitting needles, and a yard of narrow ribbon. Commence by casting on 42 stitches for the top of the leg. **1st row**—Knit plain. **2nd row**—Slip the first stitch, knit 1, * make 1, knit 2 together, and repeat from * to the end of the row, this makes a series of holes in which to run a ribbon. **3rd row**—Plain. **4th row**—Here begins the striped pattern for the leg—Slip 1, * purl 1, knit 1, purl 1, knit 3, repeat from *, and at the end of the row there will be 2 stitches to knit. **5th row**—Slip 1, * knit 1, purl 1, knit 1, purl 3, repeat from *, and end with 2 purl stitches. Repeat the last two rows three times, and there will be eight pattern rows done, and you will be able to see how the pattern sits in stripes. In the next row decrease by taking 2 stitches together at the beginning and at the end of the row. Keep the pattern even, and decrease every fourth row till reduced to 32 stitches for the ankle. Knit thus —**1st row**—Slip 1, knit 1, * purl 1, knit 1, purl 1, knit 3, and repeat from * to the end of the row. **2nd row**—Slip 1, purl 1, * knit 1, purl 1, knit 1, purl 3, and repeat from * to the end. Continue till 16 rows are done on the 32 stitches. **Next row**—Knit plain 14 stitches, then purl 1, knit 1, purl 1, knit 4, and leaving 11 stitches unknitted on the left-hand pin, turn the work, and slip 1, purl 2, knit 1, purl 1, knit 1, purl 4; * turn the work, slip 1, knit 2, purl 1, knit 1, purl 1, knit 4; turn, slip 1, purl 2, knit 1, purl 1, knit 1, purl 4; repeat from * till 16 little rows are knitted for the instep, and break off the instep wool. Resume in continuation of the stitches knitted plain upon the right-hand needle, and pick up and knit 12 stitches along the side of the instep, knit plain the 10 instep stitches, pick up and knit 12 stitches along the other side of the instep and knit plain the 11 stitches off the left-hand needle; now you will have 56 stitches all on one needle for knitting the foot. **2nd row of Foot**—Knit 25, increase 1 (by picking up the thread that lies directly under the next stitch and knitting it), knit 6, increase 1, knit 25. **3rd row**—Purl. **4th row**—Knit 26, increase 1, knit 6, increase 1, knit 26. **5th row**—Knit 29, increase 1, knit 2, increase 1, knit 29. **6th row**—Plain. **7th row**—Knit 29, increase 1, knit 4, increase 1, knit 29. Knit 7 plain rows, 64 stitches on the needle. **15th row**—Knit 2, knit 2 together, knit 24, knit 2 together four times, knit 24, knit 2 together, knit 2. **16th row**—Plain. **17th row**—Knit 2, knit 2 together, knit 21, knit 2 together four times, knit 21, knit 2 together, knit 2. **18th row**—Plain. **19th row**—Knit 2, knit 2 together, knit 18, knit 2 together four times, knit 18, knit 2 together, knit 2. Cast off. For the **Border** on the **Top** of the **Leg**—Hold the knitting the right side towards you and pick up

Knitted Pattern of the Square for Octagon Quilt.

and knit 48 stitches along the top of the leg. **2nd row**—Purl. **3rd row**—Make 1, slip 1, knit 2, draw the slipped stitch over the two knitted stitches, and repeat to the end of the row. **4th row**—Purl. **5th row**—Slip 1, knit 1, * make 1, slip 1, knit 2, draw the slipped stitch over the two knitted ones, and repeat from *, and knit the one stitch at the end of the row. **6th row**—Purl. Repeat the last four rows twice. Cast off. Sew up the back of the leg and the sole of the foot. With a rug needle and wool make a double line of bosses like buttons up the middle stripe of the fancy pattern, and carry the wool across from boss to boss in imitation of a lacing, as represented in the engraving. Take a bone crochet needle, and work a row of scolloped edge, 1 double crochet, 4 treble alternately round the top of the boot. Run a piece of ribbon through the row of holes and tie it in a pretty bow in front. A lining of plain knitting done with Shetland wool may be put in the boot if greater warmth is desired.

INFANT'S BOOTS. DOTTY PATTERN.

THESE are very comfortable boots and not at all difficult to make. Required, 1 oz. of white Andalusian wool, and 3 steel knitting needles No. 16; the third needle is not used until you come to the foot. Cast on one needle 50 stitches for the top of the leg. **1st row**—Knit 2, purl 2, and repeat. **2nd row**—Purl 2, knit 2, and repeat. Continue thus in ribbing till 12 rows are done. **13th row**—Wool over the needle to make a stitch, knit 2 stitches together, and knit each 2 stitches together to the end of the row, which brings 26 stitches on the needle. **14th row**—Knit 1, pick up the thread that lies intermediate between the stitches and knit a stitch in it, knit 1, pick up and knit a stitch, and continue the same except between the last two stitches, and now 50 stitches are again on the needle. **15th row**—Plain. **16th row**—Purl. Repeat the last four rows seven times. **45th row**—Same as the thirteenth row. **46th row**—Same as the fourteenth row. **47th row**—Knit plain 32 stitches, and turn the work leaving 18 stitches on the left-hand needle. **48th row**—Purl 14 stitches, you now again leave 18 stitches unworked, and turn, and work upon the 14 centre stitches for the instep. **1st row**—In pattern the same as the thirteenth row. **2nd row**—Same as the fourteenth row. **3rd row**—Knit 14 stitches. **4th row**—Purl 14 stitches. Repeat the four instep rows

Baby's Balmoral Bootikin.

five times, but the last time of all knit plain the last row instead of purling it. **25th row**—Knit 2, knit 2 together, knit 6, knit 2 together, knit 2. Knit 5 plain rows. **31st row**—Knit 2, knit 2 together, knit 4, knit 2 together, knit 2. Knit 5 plain rows. Break off the wool. For the **Foot**—Begin along the right side of the instep to pick up and knit on the right-hand needle 10 stitches along the edge of the fancy pattern of the knitting and 7 stitches along the plain portion and on the same needle knit 10 stitches off the instep needle; take the spare needle and on it pick up and knit 17 stitches along the opposite edge of the instep and knit 18 stitches off the left-hand needle. Knit 3 plain rows, 80 stitches in each row. **5th row**—Knit 35, increase 1, knit 2, increase 1, knit 6, increase 1, knit 2, increase 1, knit 35. Knit 5 plain rows, 84 stitches in each row. **11th row**—Knit 38, knit 2 together, knit 4, knit 2 together, knit 38. Knit 1 plain row. **13th row**—Knit 38, knit 2, together, knit 2, knit 2 together, knit 38. **15th row**—Knit 38, knit 2 together, knit 2 together, knit 38. Knit 1 plain row. **17th row**—Knit 37, knit 2 together, knit 2 together, knit 37. Knit 1 plain row. **19th row**—Knit 2, knit 2 together, knit 30, knit 2 together four times consecutively, knit 30, knit 2 together, knit 2. Knit 1 plain row. **21st row**—Knit 2, knit 2 together, knit 27, knit 2 together four times, knit 27, knit 2 together, knit 2. Knit 1 plain row. **23rd row**—Knit 2, knit 2 together, knit 24, knit 2 together four times, knit 24, knit 2 together, knit 2. Knit 1 plain row. Fold the two needles together with the same number of stitches (29) upon each, and the wrong side of the work outside, and cast off, knitting together a stitch from each needle. Sew up the leg of the boot. A ribbon can be run round the ankle and tied in a bow in front, if liked. The other boot is knitted in the same manner.

BOY'S SAILOR JERSEY.

KNITTED IN SMALL BASKET PATTERN.

THE jersey jacket shown in our engraving is suitable for a boy from six to eight years of age, it is knitted in the fashionable sailor shape with a collar and vest, and is very comfortable wear. Required, 5 ozs. of navy blue and 1 oz. of best white fingering wool, and a pair of No. 11 long bone knitting needles. Begin for the **Front** of the **Vest** by casting on 90 stitches with navy wool. Knit 8 plain rows. **9th row**—Slip 1, knit 1, * purl 2, knit 2, and repeat from * to the end of the row. **10th row**—Slip 1, purl 1, * knit 2, purl 2, and repeat from * to the end. Knit 10 more rows of this ribbing. Knit 6 plain rows. Now for the **Small Basket Pattern—1st row**—Still with navy wool, and always slipping the first stitch in every row—Knit 2 and purl 2 alternately all along, and end with knit 2. **2nd row**—Purl 2 and knit 2 alternately all along, and end with purl 2. **3rd row**—Plain. **4th row**—Purl. **5th row**—Purl 2 and knit 2 alternately all along, and end with purl 2. **6th row**—Knit 2 and purl 2 alternately all along, and end with knit 2. **7th row**—Plain. **8th row**—Purl. Repeat these eight rows till you have 80 rows of basket pattern knitted. **81st row**—Which is a repetition of the first row—Knit in pattern 45 stitches and here begin the opening—Turn the work, knit the 2 first stitches together and proceed back in pattern; continue in pattern always taking 2 stitches together at the beginning of each "back" row to make the V shape for the front of the jersey till reduced to 21 stitches on the needle, and cast off. Resume where you divided the stitches, knit the 2 first stitches together and thence work in pattern to the end; continue, and always take 2 stitches together at the beginning of every "forward" row till reduced to 21 stitches, and cast off For the **Back** of the **Vest**—Re-commence with 90 stitches, and work the same as directed for the front till you have knitted 80 rows of the basket pattern, and then continue still in basket pattern on the same number of stitches (90) till 127 rows in all of basket pattern are done. In the **128th row**—which is a purl row—Cast off the first 21 stitches, * knit 5, knit 2 together, repeat from * five times, knit 7, draw the last stitch but one over the last stitch, and continue casting off to the end, 21 stitches in all. The 21 stitches cast off on each side are for the shoulders, and the 42 stitches that now remain upon the needle are for the back of the neck; slip these stitches on to a spare needle for the present. Sew up the shoulders and the sides of the vest leaving space for the armholes. For the **Revers** and **Collar**—Use white wool and work entirely in plain knitting. Cast on 4 stitches. Knit 4 plain rows; always now slip the first stitch of each row as if about to purl and pass the wool to the back before knitting the second stitch, this gives a

Infant's Boot. Dotty Pattern.

nice chain-like edge. **5th row**—Slip 1, increase by knitting 1 in the back and 1 in the front of the next stitch, knit plain to the end of the row. Knit 7 plain rows. Repeat from the fifth row, always increasing on the same side of the knitting, and when you have done 84 rows you will find 14 stitches on the needle, and the strip should be long enough to go up one side of the V-shaped opening in the front of the jersey. Slip the 14 stitches on to another spare needle while you knit a similar strip for the opposite side of the opening. Sew the *straight* edge of the strips up the front opening of the vest, the needles with the stitches being of course by the shoulders, and the narrow parts fitting nicely in the angle where the V commences. Fold the strips into their proper position as revers. And now, holding the front of the vest towards you, knit, still with white wool, 14 revers stitches, 42 stitches belonging to the back of the neck, and the other 14 revers stitches, all on one needle. Knit 3 rows plain. Take 2 stitches together at the beginning and at the end of the next row; and decrease likewise every fourth row afterwards, till reduced to 40 stitches for the bottom of the collar, and cast off. For the **Sleeves**—Cast on 66 stitches with navy wool for the top of the sleeve. Knit the eight basket pattern rows, taking 2 stitches together at the beginning and at the end of every fourth row till reduced to 50 stitches, by which means a gusset is formed. Continue still in basket pattern upon the 50 stitches without any more reduction till 80 rows in all are knitted, when the sleeve will be long enough to reach nearly to the wrist. Knit 6 plain rows. Then do 12 rows of ribbing. **Next row**—Plain, but decrease by knitting together every seventh and eighth stitch. Knit 7 plain rows. Cast off loosely. Knit the other sleeve in the same manner. Join the sleeves up, and sew them into the jersey. For the **Vest**—Cast on 12 stitches with navy wool, and knit 1 row plain and 1 row purl. Join on the white wool and knit 1 row plain and 1 row purl. Proceed with the two colours thus, doing two rows with each colour. Increase at the beginning and at the end of every fourth row till there are 21 stripes of colour knitted. Then work only the 12 first stitches for 18 stripes, and cast off. Cast off the centre stitches, and knit the last 12 stitches for 18 stripes, and cast off. Strengthen all round this vest with crochet worked with navy wool, doing first a row of double crochet, and then a row of treble stitches. Sew two buttons and corresponding loops to encircle the ends of the vest round the back of the neck.

BABY'S OVERALLS.

REQUIRED, 4 ozs. of white Berlin fingering, a pair of No 7 bone knitting needles, and 1¼ yards of narrow white ribbon. Each leg is worked separately

Boy's Sailor Jersey.

and sewn together. Cast on 68 stitches, and work in ribbing, 2 stitches plain and 2 stitches purl, forwards and backwards, for 20 rows, for the waistband. Then work in plain knitting, and lengthen for the back of the garment. **1st row**—Knit 6 stitches plain ; turn the work, slip the first stitch, and knit 5 stitches back. **3rd row**—Knit 14 stitches plain ; turn the work, slip the first stitch, and knit 13 stitches back. **5th row**—Knit 22 stitches plain, turn the work, slip the first stitch, and knit 21 stitches back. **7th row**—Knit 30 stitches plain ; turn the work, slip the first stitch, and knit 29 stitches back. **9th row**—Knit 38 stitches plain ; turn the work, slip the first stitch, and knit 37 stitches back. **11th row**—Knit 46 stitches plain ; turn the work, slip the first stitch, and knit 45 stitches back. **13th row**—Knit 54 stitches plain ; turn the work, slip the first stitch, and knit 53 stitches back. **15th row**—Knit plain the whole 68 stitches ; turn the work, slip the first stitch, and knit 67 stitches back. Continue now in plain knitting on the 68 stitches, until 32 complete rows are done from end to end ; always slip the first stitch in every row. **Next row**—Slip 1, increase 1, knit plain to the end. Repeat this row nine times, when there should be 78 stitches on the needle. **Next row**—Slip 1, knit 2 together, knit plain to the end. Repeat this row thirty-nine times, and there will be 38 stitches on the needle. And now the Cable stripe begins on the leg. **1st row**—Slip 1, knit plain to the end. **2nd row**—Slip 1, knit 7, purl 6, knit 10, purl 6, knit 8. Repeat these two rows twice. **7th row**—Slip 1, knit 7, take a spare needle, hold it in front of the work, and slip 3 stitches off the left-hand needle on to it, knit the 3 next stitches, put the 3 slipped stitches back upon the left-hand needle and knit them, knit 10 stitches, take the spare needle and again slip 3 stitches on to it, knit the 3 next stitches, put the 3 slipped stitches back and knit them, knit 8. **8th row**—Slip 1, knit 7, purl 6, knit 10, purl 6, knit 8. Repeat these eight rows four times, and you will have five twists of cable pattern on each side the leg ; break off the wool. Slip 14 stitches on to a spare needle, and for the **Instep**, work plain knitting upon the 10 centre stitches for 32 rows, and break off the wool. For the **Foot**—Knit plain the 14 stitches off the spare needle, pick up and knit 19 stitches along the edge of the instep, knit the 10 stitches across the top of the instep ; pick up and knit 16 stitches along the opposite edge, and knit the remaining 14 stitches ; there now should be 70 stitches all on one needle. Knit 8 plain rows. Knit 8 more plain rows taking 2 stitches together at the beginning of each row. Cast off the 62 stitches now remaining, fold them, and sew them up for the bottom of the boot. Sew up the leg as far

as to where the decreasings begin. Re-commence the **other Leg** with 68 stitches, but work only 19 rows of ribbing so as to begin the lengthening at the opposite side of the work ; do 33 rows instead of 32 rows of plain knitting afterwards to compensate for this ; and the increasings and the decreasings and the cable pattern will follow according to the instructions for the leg already knitted. Join the body part, back and front, and run a ribbon through the ribbing to tie round the waist.

LADY'S UNDER-SLEEVE.

THESE sleeves are very comfortable to wear in winter for extra warmth under the sleeves of a dress. Procure 3 ozs. of the best brown Fingering wool, four steel knitting needles, No. 12, and also four of No. 9. Commence with needles No. 12, and for the wrist cast 12 stitches on each of three needles, and knit with the fourth needle round and round like a stocking, doing a rib of 2 stitches plain and 2 stitches purl until 36 rounds are knitted. **37th round**—Take No. 9 needles, and beginning upon the first needle, knit 10 stitches plain, increase 1 stitch, knit 2 stitches plain, and repeat the same on each of the other two needles, and there should now be 13 stitches on each needle. Knit 9 rounds of all plain knitting. **47th round**—Knit 7 stitches plain, increase 1 stitch, knit 6 stitches plain, and repeat to the end of the round. Knit 9 plain rounds. **57th round**—Knit 1 stitch plain, increase 1 stitch, knit 14 stitches plain, and repeat to the end of one round. Knit 9 plain rounds. **67th round**—Knit 13 stitches plain, increase 1 stitch, knit 2 stitches plain, and repeat to the end of the round ; there should now be 16 stitches on each of the three needles. Knit 9 plain rounds. **77th round**—Begins the gusset for the elbow—Knit the 2 first stitches off the first needle and put them upon the end of the third (or right-hand) needle, knit 12 plain stitches upon the fourth needle, and slip the remaining 2 stitches upon the beginning of the second needle ; count to see that you have the stitches right, there should be 12 stitches on the first (or gusset) needle, and 18 stitches on each of the two other needles ; turn the work, and now proceed backwards and forwards *in rows* for the gusset—Slip the first stitch, purl 11, purl 1 stitch off the next adjoining needle ; turn, slip the first stitch, knit 12, knit 1 stitch off the next adjoining needle ; turn, slip 1, purl 13, purl 1 stitch off the next needle ; turn, slip 1,

Baby's Overalls.

knit 14, knit 1 stitch off the next needle ; turn, slip 1, purl 15, purl 1 stitch off the next needle ; turn, slip 1, knit 16, knit 1 stitch off the next needle ; turn, slip 1, purl 17, purl 1 stitch off the next needle ; turn, slip 1, knit 18, knit 1 stitch off the next needle ; turn, slip 1, purl 19, purl 1 stitch off the next needle ; turn, slip 1, knit 20, knit 1 stitch off the next needle ; turn, slip 1, purl 21, purl 1 stitch off the next needle ; turn, slip 1, knit 22, knit 1 stitch off the next needle ; turn, slip 1, purl 23, purl 1 stitch off the next needle ; turn, slip 1, knit 24, knit 1 stitch off the next needle ; turn, slip 1, purl 25, purl 1 stitch off the next needle ; turn, slip 1, knit 26, knit 1 stitch off the next needle ; turn, slip 1, purl 27, purl 1 stitch off the next needle ; turn, slip 1, knit 28, knit 1 stitch off the next needle ; turn, slip 1, purl 29, purl 1 stitch off the next needle ; turn, slip 1, knit 30, knit 1 stitch off the next needle. There are now 32 stitches on the gusset needle, and there should be 8 stitches on each of the two other needles ; put these 8 stitches altogether to make 16 stitches on one needle, and divide the 32 stitches equally upon two needles, so now you have 16 stitches upon each of three needles for knitting the upper part of the arm. Work round and round—**1st round**—Knit 8 stitches plain, increase 1 stitch, knit 8 stitches plain, and repeat the same on each of the other two needles. Knit 9 plain rounds. **11th round**—Knit 15 stitches plain, increase 1 stitch, knit 2 stitches plain, and repeat to the end of the round. Knit 9 plain rounds. **21st round**—Knit 2 stitches plain, increase 1 stitch, knit 16 stitches plain, and repeat to the end of the round. Knit 9 plain rounds. **31st round**—Knit 9 stitches plain, increase 1 stitch, knit 10 stitches plain, and repeat to the end of the round; there should now be 20 stitches on each of the three needles. Knit 9 plain rounds. Rib 36 rounds of ribbing to correspond with the ribbing at the wrist, and cast off loosely. Work the other sleeve in the same manner.

BARRISTER'S WIG IN PUFFED KNITTING.

OUR engraving shows the fashionable head covering known by the name of the "barrister's wig." Procure 1 oz. of light silver grey single Berlin wool and 2 ozs. of pale blue double Berlin, a pair of No. 9 bone knitting needles, and 2 yards of inch wide pale blue ribbon. Cast on 84 stitches with grey

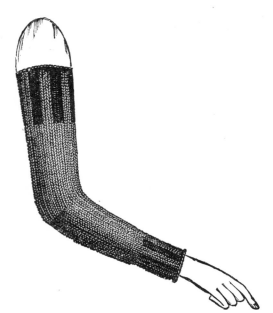

Lady's Under-Sleeve.

wool for the bottom of the curtain. **1st row**—Knit plain. **2nd row**—Purl. **3rd row**—Plain. **4th row**—Purl. **5th row**—Take the blue wool—Knit 3, * pass the wool twice round the needle and knit 1 stitch, do this six times, knit plain the 3 next stitches, and repeat from * to the end of the row. **6th row**—Work in the same way as last row, and as you knit drop the twisted stitches from off the needle so as always to keep 84 *knitted* stitches on the needle. **7th row**—Purl 3, * pass the wool twice round the needle and purl 1 stitch, do this six times, at the same time dropping the twisted stitches of last row, purl the next 3 stitches, and repeat from * to the end. **8th row**—Same as the sixth row. Resume the grey wool and repeat from the first row, carry the wool on from stripe to stripe without breaking it, and when you have completed the fifth ridge of puffed knitting with blue wool there will be 40 rows done and the curtain is complete. **41st row**—With grey wool—Knit plain. **42nd row**—Purl 3 and purl 2 together alternately seven times, purl 2 together four times, purl 3 and purl 2 together alternately seven times, purl 6; now there will be 66 stitches on the needle. **43rd row**—Slip 1, knit 2, * make 1, knit 2 together, repeat from * to the end, and knit the last stitch plain; this makes a row of holes to run ribbon round the neck. **44th row**—Purl. Now take the blue wool, and work as directed for the fifth row and three following rows. Then resume grey wool and work according to the first row and three following rows. And continue till you have completed three ridges of puffed knitting on the 66 stitches. Now the remaining grey stripes are to be knitted with decreasings as follows—**1st grey row**—Knit 5, knit 2 together, continue in plain knitting till you get to the middle of the row, then knit 2 together, and again when 7 stitches from the end knit 2 together, knit 5. **2nd row**—Purl 5, purl 2 together, purl along to within 7 stitches of the end, purl 2 together, purl 5. **3rd row**—Knit 5, knit 2 together, knit to within 7 stitches of the end, then knit 2 together, knit 5. **4th row**—Same as the second row. Take blue wool and work the 4 puffed rows. And repeat the 4 decreasing rows with grey wool and the 4 puffed rows with blue wool, till you have done nine ridges of the puffed knitting for the head of the barrister's wig, when there will be only 12 stitches left on the needle. Knit these with grey wool to a point, thus, **1st row**—Knit 3, knit 2 together three times, knit 3. **2nd row**—Purl. **3rd row**—Knit 2, knit 2 together, knit 1, knit 2 together, knit 2. **4th**

row—Purl. Cast off 4. Draw the casting off up and sew it together. Work a crochet edge all round the wig with grey wool, 1 double crochet in a stitch of kitting, 4 chain, 1 single crochet in the fourth chain from the needle, miss a stitch of the knitting, 1 double crochet in the next, and repeat the same. Run a piece of ribbon through the holes round the neck leaving long ends to tie under the chin. Make a pretty bow to place on the top of the wig, and a smaller bow to go at the back of the neck above the curtain.

BRIOCHE MATS.
(Not Illustrated.)

THESE are usually made of two colours, the circumference being divided into twelve divisions of colour. The first four stitches make the fringed border, which is done by passing the wool three times round the two first fingers of the left hand and knitting it in. Next to the border you always knit 1 stitch plain, the remainder is in brioche. Pink and white double Berlin wool or arrasene, 1 oz. of each colour. Knitting pins, No. 9. With pink wool cast on 17 stitches. **1st row**—Knit 4 border stitches with the wool wound three times round the fingers, knit 1; make 1, slip 1, inserting the needle as if about to purl, knit 2 together four times. **2nd row**—Make 1, slip 1, knit 2 together four times, knit 5. **3rd row**—Knit 4 border stitches, knit 1, make 1, slip 1, knit 2 together three times, leaving 3 on the left-hand pin unknitted. **4th row**—Make 1, slip 1, knit 2 together three times, knit 5. **5th row**—Knit 4 border stitches, knit 1, make 1, slip 1, knit 2 together twice, leaving 6 on the left-hand pin unknitted. **6th row**—Make 1, slip 1, knit 2 together twice, knit 5. **7th row**—Knit 4 border stitches, knit 1, make 1, slip 1, knit 2 together, leaving 9 on the left-hand pin unknitted. **8th row**—Make 1, slip 1, knit 2 together, knit 5. Break off the blue wool and join on the white, and repeat these 8 rows. Then continue the work until you have six sections of blue and six of white. Cast off and sew the casting off to the commencement, drawing the centre in closely.

TUFTED FRINGE FOR MATS.
(Not Illustrated.)

GET skeins of single Berlin wool of different shades of any colour, dark and light, green is preferable; lay it in strands of ten; thread a rug needle with some of the wool, tie it to the end of the strands, and with the wool in the needle tie the stranded wool tightly round twice about an inch down, sewing it in a firm knot. Proceed in this way until you have tied it at

Barrister's Wig in Puffed Knitting.

regular intervals all along. Then break off the wool and cut the strands in the centre of the spaces between the ties. This leaves a series of little tufts on the wool you have been sewing with, and the fringe is complete. Sew it round a foundation, in loops of any length preferred, mixing the shades so as to produce a good effect.

KNITTED MOSS FOR MATS.
(Not Illustrated.)

SINGLE Berlin wool in shades of green. Knitting pins No. 10. Cast on 40 stitches, and do a piece of plain knitting, 10 or 12 rows of each shade from dark to light and to dark again. Having knitted the required length, cast it off. Wet it in warm water in which a little sugar has been melted, bake it, and iron it; then cut through the middle, and unravel all but the 3 edge stitches. Four or six pieces of this moss knitting round a wool-worked centre will make a very pretty drawing-room mat, particularly if a few wool flowers are introduced in it.

WELDON'S
PRACTICAL KNITTER. EDGINGS.

(FOURTEENTH SERIES.)

How to Knit Useful Edgings, Borders, Veils, Shawls, &c., with Fife Lace Yarn.

TWENTY-SEVEN ILLUSTRATIONS.

The Yearly Subscription to this Magazine, post free to any Part of the World, is 2s. 6d. Subscriptions are payable in advance, and may commence from any date and for any period.

The Back Numbers are always in print. Nos. 1 to 109 now ready, Price 2d. each, postage ½d. Over 5,000 Engravings.

DESIGNS FOR FIFE LACE YARN AND OTHER WOOLS.

OUR PRESENT ISSUE contains a variety of useful patterns for knitting shawls, veils, clouds, borders, laces, and edgings; these are prepared especially for working with Faudel, Phillips, and Sons' FIFE LACE YARN, peacock quality, a speciality which has quite recently been manufactured, and supplies a want that has long been felt for a really good wool for shawls, and veils, and lace borders. Fife Lace Yarn is made in all colours, and is sold in the skein and also in balls ready wound. The *finest* Fife Lace Yarn (peacock quality) is almost as small as Pyreneen wool, but much stronger, and this is particularly recommended for making nice fine best shawls; the thicker Fife Lace Yarn is about the size of ordinary Peacock fingering. Ladies who try Fife Lace Yarn (peacock quality) for knitting will certainly be pleased with the result; it has a certain "spring" about it quite distinct from all other wools, that gives play to the knitting and brings the pattern out clearly and prettily.

SPANISH POINT LACE.

THIS design can be worked with Shetland wool and steel needles No. 15; or use the finest Fife Lace Yarn and steel needles No. 16, or the thicker Fife Lace Yarn and needles No. 14. For cotton work for trimming underlinen, &c., use Coats' No. 20 crochet cotton and steel knitting needles No 17. Cast on 19 stitches. Knit 1 plain row. **1st row**—Slip 1, knit 2, make 1, knit 2 together, knit 2; make 1, slip 1, knit 1, pass the slipped stitch over, knit 3, knit 2 together, make 1, knit 3, make 1, knit 2. **2nd row**—Make 1, knit 2 together, knit 15, make 1, knit 2 together, knit 1. **3rd row**—Slip 1, knit 2, make 1, knit 2 together, knit 3, make 1, slip 1, knit 1, pass the slipped stitch over, knit 1, knit 2 together, make 1, knit 5, make 1, knit 2. **4th row**—Make 1, knit 2 together, knit 16, make 1, knit 2 together, knit 1. **5th row**—Slip 1, knit 2, make 1, knit 2 together, knit 4; make 1, slip 1, knit 2 together, pass the slipped stitch over, make 1, slip 1, knit 1, pass the slipped stitch over, knit 2 together, make 3, knit 2 together, knit 1, make 1, knit 2. **6th row**—Make 1, knit 2 together, knit 4, purl 1, knit 12, make 1, knit 2 together, knit 1. **7th row**—Slip 1, knit 2, make 1, knit 2 together, knit 2, knit 2 together; make 1, knit 3, make 1, slip 1, knit 1, pass the slipped stitch over, knit 3, knit 2 together, make 1, knit 2 together, knit 1. **8th row**—Make 1, knit 2 together, knit 16, make 1, knit 2 together, knit 1. **9th row**—Slip 1, knit 2, make 1, knit 2 together, knit 1, knit 2 together; make 1, knit 5, make 1, slip 1, knit 1, pass the slipped stitch over, knit 1, knit 2 together, make 1, knit 2 together, make 1, knit 2 together, knit 1. **10th row**—Make 1, knit 2 together, knit 15, make 1, knit 2 together, knit 1. **11th row**—Slip 1, knit 2, make 1, knit 2 together, knit 2 together; make 1, slip 1, knit 1, pass the slipped stitch over, knit 2 together, make 3, knit 2 together, knit 1, make 1, slip 1, knit 2 together, pass the slipped stitch over, make 1, knit 2 together, knit 1. **12th row**—Make 1, knit 2 together, knit 6, purl 1, knit 7, make 1, knit 2 together, knit 1. Repeat from the first row for the length

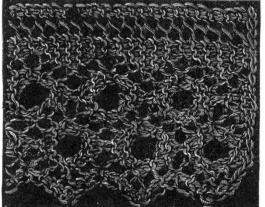

Spanish Point Lace.

required. In the above instructions, where directed to "make 3," it is intended that the wool be turned three times round the needle, and when you get to the same place in the next row you "knit 1, purl 1, and knit 1" in the three "made" stitches.

BARBERRY LEAF BORDER.

OUR example is knitted with Fife Lace Yarn of medium thickness and a pair of No. 14 steel knitting needles. Cast on 25 stitches. Knit 1 plain row. **1st row**—Slip 1, knit 2, make 1, knit 2 together, knit 1, make 1, knit 2 together, knit 2, make 1, knit 2 together, knit 5; make 1, knit 2 together, knit 1, make 2, knit 2 together, make 2, knit 2 together, knit 1. **2nd row**—Knit 3, purl 1, knit 2, purl 1, knit 3; make 1, knit 2 together, knit 12, make 1, knit 2 together, knit 1. **3rd row**—Slip 1, knit 2, make 1, knit 2 together, knit 2, make 1, knit 2 together, knit 2, make 1, knit 2 together, knit 4; make 1, knit 2 together, knit 3, make 2, knit 2 together, make 2, knit 2 together, knit 1. **4th row**—Knit 3, purl 1, knit 2, purl 1, knit 5; make 1, knit 2 together, knit 12, make 1, knit 2 together, knit 1. **5th row**—Slip 1, knit 2, make 1, knit 2 together, knit 3, make 1, knit 2 together, knit 2, make 1, knit 2 together, knit 3; make 1, knit 2 together, knit 5, make 2, knit 2 together, make 2, knit 2 together, knit 1. **6th row**—Knit 3, purl 1, knit 2, purl 1, knit 7; make 1, knit 2 together, knit 12, make 1, knit 2 together, knit 1. **7th row**—Slip 1, knit 2, make 1, knit 2 together, knit 4, make 1, knit 2 together, knit 2, make 1, knit 2 together, knit 2; make 1, knit 2 together, knit 12. **8th row**—Cast off 6, knit 7; make 1, knit 2 together, knit 12, make 1, knit 2 together, knit 1. Repeat from the first row.

STRIPED BORDER.

THIS simple striped border may be knitted with the finest Fife Lace Yarn and No. 16 needles, or, as represented in our engraving, with a thicker Fife Lace Yarn and No. 14 needles. Cast on 25 stitches. **1st row**—Knit plain. **2nd row**—Plain. **3rd row**—Slip 1, knit 3, make 1 and knit 2 together alternately nine times, make 2, knit 2 together, knit 1. **4th row**—Knit 3, purl 1, knit 22. **5th row**—Slip 1, knit 4, make 1 and knit 2 together nine times, make 2, knit 2 together, knit 1. **6th row**—Knit 3, purl 1, knit 23. **7th row**—Slip 1, knit 5, make 1 and knit 2 together nine times, make 2, knit 2 together, knit 1. **8th row**—Knit 3, purl 1, knit 24. **9th row**—Slip 1, knit 27. **10th row**—Plain. **11th row**—Slip 1, knit 27. **12th row**—Cast off 3, knit 24. Repeat from the first row for the length required.

LATTICE PATTERN FOR A SHAWL.

OUR example is worked with white Shetland wool and a pair of No. 8 bone knitting needles, and is extremely light and pretty; when the knitting is stretched width-ways certain stitches appear to run in a vertical direction right and left in clear resemblance of "a lattice," from which the pattern takes its name, but this peculiarity is not so apparent in the illustration as in the actual work. A very fine and gossamer-looking shawl can be made by using the finest Fife Lace Yarn and No. 10 knitting needles; while for a warmer article Andalusian wool may be employed with No. 7 knitting needles. Cast on stitches sufficient for the width of the shawl, any number divisible by 6, and 5 additional stitches for edge stitches; 155 stitches with Shetland wool, 191 stitches with fine Fife Lace Yarn, or 137 stitches with Andalusian wool, will make a good-sized shoulder shawl. **1st row**—Knit plain. **2nd row**—Knit 3, purl all along till within 3 stitches of the end, and knit those plain. **3rd row**—Plain. **4th row**—Knit 3, purl all along till within 3 stitches of the end, and knit those plain. **5th row**—Slip 1, knit 2, * make 1, slip 1, knit 3, pass the slipped stitch over the 3 knitted stitches, put the 3 stitches back upon the left-hand pin and draw the next stitch to the left over them, and then replace the 3 stitches on the right-hand pin, make 1, knit 1, and repeat from * to the end of the row where there will be 2 stitches to knit plain. **6th row**—Knit 3, purl all along till within 3 stitches of the end and knit those plain. **7th row**—Plain knitting. **8th row**—Same as the sixth row. **9th row**—Slip 1, knit 2, knit 2 together, * make 1, knit 1, make 1, slip 1,

Barberry Leaf Border.

knit 3, pass the slipped stitch over the 3 knitted stitches, put the 3 stitches back upon the left-hand pin and draw the next stitch to the left over them, and then replace the 3 stitches on the right-hand pin, and repeat from * till within 6 stitches of the end of the row, where make 1, knit 1, make 1, slip 1, knit 1, pass the slipped stitch over, knit 3. **10th row**—Same as the sixth row. **11th row**—Plain knitting. **12th row**—Same as the sixth row. Repeat from the fifth row till the shawl is a perfect square, when cast off all. The shawl is then to be finished off with one of the knitted edgings illustrated in the present issue, sewing it on to be nicely fulled round the corners.

FAIRFAX BORDER.

THE pretty border shown in our engraving is specially useful for edging shawls; it is knitted with Fife Lace Yarn of medium thickness and a pair of No. 14 steel knitting needles. Cast on 19 stitches, and knit across plain. **1st row**—Slip 1, knit 2, make 1, knit 2 together, knit 5; make 1, knit 2 together, make 1, knit 2 together, knit 1, purl 1, knit 1. **2nd row**—Make 1, knit 2 together, knit 13; make 1, knit 2 together, knit 1. **3rd row**—Slip 1, knit 2, make 1, knit 2 together, knit 3; knit 2 together, make 1, knit 2 together, make 1, knit 2 together, knit 1, make 1, knit 1, make 1, knit 2. **4th row**—Make 1, knit 2 together, knit 14; make 1, knit 2 together, knit 1. **5th row**—Slip 1, knit 2, make 1, knit 2 together, knit 2, knit 2 together; make 1, knit 2 together, make 1, knit 2 together, knit 1, make 1, knit 3, make 1, knit 2. **6th row**—Make 1, knit 2 together, knit 15; make 1, knit 2 together, knit 1. **7th row**—Slip 1, knit 2, make 1, knit 2 together, knit 1, knit 2 together; make 1, knit 2 together, make 1, knit 2 together, knit 1, make 1, knit 5, make 1, knit 2. **8th row**—Make 1, knit 2 together, knit 16; make 1, knit 2 together, knit 1. **9th row**—Slip 1, knit 2, make 1, knit 2 together, knit 2 together; make 1, knit 2 together, make 1, knit 2 together, knit 1, make 1, knit 7, make 1, knit 2. **10th row**—Make 1, knit 2 together, knit 17, make 1, knit 2 together, knit 1. **11th row**—Slip 1, knit 2, make 1, knit 2 together, knit 2; make 1, knit 2 together, make 1, knit 2 together, knit 1, make 1, knit 2 together, knit 3, knit 2 together, make 1, knit 2 together, knit 1. **12th row**—Make 1, knit 2 together, knit 16; make 1, knit 2 together, knit 1. **13th row**—Slip 1, knit 2, make 1, knit 2 together, knit 3; make 1, knit 2 together, make 1, knit 2 together, knit 1, make 1, knit 2 together, knit 1, knit 2 together, make 1, knit 2 together, knit 1. **14th row**—Make 1, knit 2

together, knit 15; make 1, knit 2 together, knit 1. **15th row**—Slip 1, knit 2, make 1, knit 2 together, knit 4; make 1, knit 2 together, make 1, knit 2 together, knit 1, make 1, slip 1, knit 2 together, pass the slipped stitch over, make 1, knit 2 together, knit 1. **16th row**—Make 1, knit 2 together, knit 14; make 1, knit 2 together, knit 1. Repeat from the first row of the pattern.

SWEET-BRIAR LACE.

THIS elegant lace is knitted with the finest Fife Lace Yarn and a pair of No. 16 steel knitting needles. It is suitable for dress trimming, for the borders of shawls, and many various purposes. Cast on 22 stitches. Purl 1 row. **1st row**—Slip 1, knit 2 together, make 1, knit 3, make 1, knit 2 together, knit 5; make 1, knit 3 together, knit 1, make 1, knit 1; make 1, knit 2 together, make 1, knit 2. **2nd row**—Make 1, knit 2 together, purl 21. **3rd row**—Slip 1, knit 2, make 1, slip 1, knit 2 together, pass the slipped stitch over, make 1, knit 6; make 1, knit 3 together, knit 1, make 1, knit 3; make 1, knit 2 together, make 1, knit 2. **4th row**—Make 1, knit 2 together, purl 22. **5th row**—Slip 1, knit 2 together, make 1, knit 3, make 1, knit 2 together, knit 3; make 1, knit 3 together, knit 1, make 1, knit 5; make 1, knit 2 together, make 1, knit 2. **6th row**—Make 1, knit 2 together, purl 23. **7th row**—Slip 1, knit 2, make 1, slip 1, knit 2 together, pass the slipped stitch over, make 1, knit 4; make 1, knit 3 together, knit 1, make 1, knit 7; make 1, knit 2 together, make 1, knit 2. **8th row**—Make 1, knit 2 together, purl 24. **9th row**—Slip 1, knit 2 together, make 1, knit 3, make 1, knit 2 together, knit 1; make 1, knit 3 together, knit 1, make 1, knit 9; make 1, knit 2 together, make 1, knit 2. **10th row**—Make 1, knit 2 together, purl 25. **11th row**—Slip 1, knit 2, make 1, slip 1, knit 2 together, pass the slipped stitch over, make 1, knit 12; make 1, knit 3 together, knit 1; make 1, knit 2 together, make 1, knit 2 together, knit 1. **12th row**—Make 1, knit 2 together, purl 24. **13th row**—Slip 1, knit 2 together, make 1, knit 3, make 1, knit 2 together, knit 9; make 1, knit 3 together, knit 1; make 1, knit 2 together, make 1, knit 2 together, knit 1. **14th row**—Make 1, knit 2 together, purl 23. **15th row**—Slip 1, knit 2, make 1, slip 1, knit 2 together, pass the slipped stitch over, make 1, knit 10; make 1, knit 3 together, knit 1; make 1, knit 2 together, make 1, knit 2 together, knit 1. **16th row**—Make 1, knit 2 together, purl 22. **17th row**—Slip 1, knit 2 together, make 1, knit 3, make 1, knit 2 together, knit 7; make 1, knit 3 together, knit 1; make 1, knit 2 together, make 1, knit 2 together, knit 1. **18th row**—Make 1, knit 2 together, purl 21. **19th row**—Slip 1, knit 2, make

Striped Border.

1, slip 1, knit 2 together, pass the slipped stitch over, make 1, knit 8; make 1, knit 3 together, knit 1; make 1, knit 2 together, make 1, knit 2 together, knit 1. **20th row**—Make 1, knit 2 together, purl 20. Repeat from the first row for the length required.

MYRTLE LEAF PATTERN FOR A SHAWL.

OUR engraving shows the corner of a shawl worked in myrtle leaf pattern, with the finest Fife Lace Yarn and No. 15 steel knitting needles; in this form it is very light and pretty, and though so fine, is yet strong enough to wear for a considerable time. If a warmer shawl is required, a thicker make of Fife Lace Yarn can be procured, and the work be executed with No. 9 or No. 10 bone needles. The number of stitches to be cast on will depend upon the size the shawl is desired to be, 11 stitches are employed in each repetition of the pattern, and 1 extra stitch must be added to keep the pattern even; also 2 or more stitches should be allowed on each side for "edge" stitches to be knitted plain at the beginning and at the end of every row. Two edge stitches are allowed in the example illustrated, but no mention is made of them in the instructions, as they do not interfere with the pattern, and some workers may prefer to put a margin of six or eight plain stitches. Having decided upon the number of stitches to cast on for the width of the shawl, knit 4 rows (or more) of all plain knitting. **1st pattern row**—Knit 1, * make 1, knit 3, slip 1, knit 1, pass the slipped stitch over, knit 2 together, knit 3, make 1, knit 1, and repeat from * to the end of the row. **2nd row**—Purl 1, * make 1, purl 3, purl 2 together, purl 2 together, purl 3, make 1, purl 1, and repeat from *. **3rd row**—Knit 1, * make 1, knit 3, slip 1, knit 1, pass the slipped stitch over, knit 2 together, knit 3, make 1, knit 1, and repeat from *. **4th row**—Purl 2, * make 1, purl 2, purl 2 together, purl 2 together, purl 2, make 1, purl 3, repeat from * to the end of the row, where there will be 2 stitches to purl as at the beginning. **5th row**—Knit 3, * make 1, knit 1, slip 1, knit 1, pass the slipped stitch over, knit 2 together, knit 1, make 1, knit 3, and repeat from *, and at the end there will be 3 stitches to knit as at the beginning. **6th row**—Purl 4, * make 1, purl 2 together, purl 2 together, make 1, purl 7, repeat from *, and at the end there will be 4 stitches to purl to correspond with the beginning. **7th row**—Knit 2 together, knit 3, make 1, knit 2 together, make 1, knit 4, and repeat the same to the end, where instead of knitting 4 stitches, knit 3 stitches and then knit 2 stitches together, which does away with the extra stitch which is not required during the next five rows. **8th row**—Purl 2 together, purl 3,

Lattice Pattern for a Shawl.

make 1, purl 1, make 1, purl 3, purl 2 together, and repeat the same to the end. **9th row**—Knit 2 together, knit 3, make 1, knit 1, make 1, knit 3, slip 1, knit 1, pass the slipped stitch over, and repeat. **10th row**—Purl 2 together, purl 2, make 1, purl 3, make 1, purl 2, purl 2 together, and repeat. **11th row**—Knit 2 together, knit 1, make 1, knit 5, make 1, knit 1, slip 1, knit 1, pass the slipped stitch over, and repeat. **12th row**—Purl 2 together, make 1, purl 7, make 1, purl 2 together and repeat. **13th row**—Knit 1, * make 1, knit 4, knit 2 together, knit 3, make 1, knit 2 together, and repeat from * to the end of the row, and there knit 1 stitch instead of knitting 2 together, and you will find the same number of stitches on the needle with which you began. And now repeat from the second row of the pattern for the length required, and when the work is long enough cast off after finishing with 4 plain rows. You will see the shawl sits in small scallops up each side as well as along the top and bottom; it can be simply finished with a knotted fringe, or bordered with one of the lace edgings illustrated in the present issue.

FRENCH TRELLIS BORDER.

OUR illustration shows a handsome wide trellis border of particularly pleasing appearance, being light and lacy, and yet not difficult of accomplishment. The example is worked with Shetland wool and No. 14 steel knitting needles, but the instructions can equally well be carried out with any other make of wool, with silk, or with cotton, selecting needles of suitable size. If fine Fife Lace Yarn and No. 15 steel needles be employed the border will look very elegant for an apron or dress trimming. Begin by casting on 51 stitches, and to work across, knit 16, purl 19, knit 16. **1st row**—Slip 1, knit 4, knit 2 together, make 1, knit 2 together, make 1, knit 1; make 1, knit 1, slip 1, knit 1, pass the slipped stitch over, knit 5, knit 2 together, make 1, knit 2 together; make 1, knit 3, knit 2 together, make 1, knit 3; make 1, knit 2 together, knit 3, knit 2 together, make 1, knit 3; make 1, knit 2 together, knit 3, knit 2 together, make 1, knit 3. **2nd row**—Make 1, knit 4, make 1, knit 2 together, knit 1, knit 2 together, make 1, knit 5; make 1, knit 2 together, knit 1, knit 2 together, make 1, knit 5; make 1, knit 2 together, knit 1; purl 19, knit 5. **3rd row**—Slip 1, knit 3, knit 2 together, make 1, knit 2 together, make 1, knit 3; make 1, knit 1, slip 1, knit 1, pass the slipped stitch over, knit 3, knit 2 together, knit 1, make 1, knit 2 together; make 1, knit 2 together, make 1, knit 7; make 1, slip 1, knit 2 together, pass the slipped stitch over, make 1, knit 7; make 1, slip 1, knit 2 together, pass the slipped stitch over, make 1, knit 6. **4th row**—Make 1, knit 5, knit 2 together, make

1, knit 1; make 1, knit 2 together, knit 5, knit 2 together, make 1, knit 1; make 1, knit 2 together, knit 5, knit 2 together, make 1, knit 1; purl 19, knit 5. **5th row**—Slip 1, knit 2, knit 2 together, make 1, knit 2 together, make 1, knit 5; make 1, knit 1, slip 1, knit 1, pass the slipped stitch over, knit 1, knit 2 together, knit 1, make 1, knit 2 together; make 1, knit 5, make 1, knit 2 together, knit 3, knit 2 together; make 1, knit 3, make 1, knit 2 together, knit 3, knit 2 together; make 1, knit 3, make 1, knit 2 together, knit 5. **6th row**—Make 1, knit 4, knit 2 together, make 1, knit 5; make 1, knit 2 together, knit 1, knit 2 together; make 1, knit 5, make 1, knit 2 together, knit 1, knit 2 together, make 1, knit 5; purl 19, knit 3. **7th row**—Slip 1, knit 1, knit 2 together, make 1, knit 2 together, make 1, knit 7; make 1, knit 1, slip 1, knit 2 together, pass the slipped stitch over, knit 1, make 1, knit 2 together; make 1, knit 8, make 1, slip 1, knit 2 together, pass the slipped stitch over; make 1, knit 7, make 1, slip 1, knit 2 together, pass the slipped stitch over; make 1, knit 7, make 1, slip 1, knit 1, pass the slipped stitch over, knit 4. **8th row**—Cast off 3, knit 1, make 1, knit 2 together, make 1, knit 1, make 1, knit 2 together, knit 5, knit 2 together; make 1, knit 1, make 1, knit 2 together, knit 6; purl 19, knit 2. **9th row**—Slip 1, knit 3, make 1, knit 2 together, make 1, knit 1; slip 1, knit 1, pass the slipped stitch over, knit 5, knit 2 together; make 1, knit 1, make 1, knit 2 together; make 1, slip 1, knit 1, pass the slipped stitch over, knit 4, knit 2 together, make 1, knit 3; make 1, knit 2 together, knit 3, knit 2 together, make 1, knit 3; make 1, knit 2 together, knit 3, knit 2 together, make 1, knit 3. **10th row**—Make 1, knit 4, make 1, knit 2 together, knit 1, knit 2 together; make 1, knit 5, make 1, knit 2 together, knit 1, knit 2 together; make 1, knit 5, make 1, knit 2 together, knit 3; purl 19, knit 3. **11th row**—Slip 1, knit 4, make 1, knit 2 together, make 1, knit 1, slip 1, knit 1, pass the slipped stitch over, knit 3, knit 2 together, knit 1; make 1, knit 3, make 1, knit 2 together; make 1, slip 1, knit 1, pass the slipped stitch over, knit 1, knit 2 together, make 1, knit 7; make 1, slip 1, knit 2 together, pass the slipped stitch over, make 1, knit 7; make 1, slip 1, knit 2 together, pass the slipped stitch over, make 1, knit 6. **12th row**—Make 1, knit 5, knit 2 together, make 1, knit 1; make 1, knit 2 together, knit 5, knit 2 together, make 1, knit 1; make 1, knit 2 together, knit 5, knit 2 together, make 1, knit 3; purl 19, knit 4. **13th row**—Slip 1, knit 5, make 1, knit 2 together, make 1, knit 1, slip 1, knit 1, pass the slipped stitch over, knit 1, knit 2 together, knit 1; make 1, knit 5, make 1, knit 2 together; make 1, slip 1, knit 1, pass the slipped stitch over, knit 2, make 1, knit 2 together, knit 3, knit 2 together; make 1, knit 3, make 1, knit 2 together, knit 3, knit 2 together; make 1, knit 3, make 1, knit 2 together, knit 5. **14th row**—Make 1, knit 4, knit 2 together, make 1, knit 5; make 1, knit 2 together, knit 1, knit 2 together, make 1, knit 5; make 1, knit 2 together, knit 1, knit 2 together, make 1, knit 3; purl 19, knit 5. **15th row**—Slip 1, knit 6, make 1, knit 2 together, make 1, knit 1, slip 1, knit 2

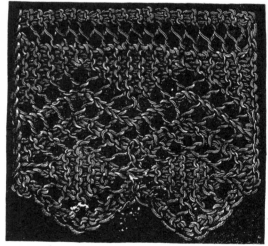

Fairfax Border.

together, pass the slipped stitch over, knit 1; make 1, knit 7, make 1, knit 2 together; make 1, slip 1, knit 1, pass the slipped stitch over, knit 3, make 1, slip 1, knit 2 together, pass the slipped stitch over; make 1, knit 7, make 1, slip 1, knit 2 together, pass the slipped stitch over; make 1, knit 7, make 1, slip 1, knit 1, pass the slipped stitch over, knit 4. **16th row**—Cast off 3, knit 1, make 1, knit 2 together, knit 5, knit 2 together; make 1, knit 1, make 1, knit 2 together, knit 5, knit 2 together; make 1, knit 1, make 1, knit 2 together, knit 2; purl 19, knit 6. Repeat from the first row for the length required.

CORNER OF A SHAWL KNITTED IN BOULE DE NEIGE,

WITH INSERTION OF DUTCH KNITTING, AND A WIDE CROCHET BORDER.

THIS handsome shawl, of which a corner is shown in our illustration, is knitted with medium-sized Fife Lace Yarn and a pair of long bone knitting needles, No. 10. The border is worked in crochet, and the insertion is partly crochet and partly knitting. The centre of the shawl is knitted in Boule de Neige,

For this cast on *loosely* a sufficient number of stitches for the width of the shawl, any uneven number, say 59 stitches, or 71 stitches. **1st row**—Knit plain, loosely. **2nd row**—Slip 1, knit 1, * bring the wool to the front under the needle, purl the next stitch, and before taking it off the left-hand needle pass the wool round the right-hand needle, to make a stitch and purl it again, pass the wool again round the right-hand needle to make a stitch, and purl it again, and now slip the stitch off the left-hand needle and you will find a little group of 5 stitches on the right-hand needle knitted in the one stitch, put the wool to the back, and knit 1 stitch plain; repeat from * to the end of the row, which brings a group of five stitches in every alternate stitch of last row, and there is 1 stitch at the end to be knitted plain. **3rd row**—Plain. **4th row**—Purl. **5th row**—Plain. **6th row**—Purl. **7th row**—Plain. **8th row**—Slip 1, knit 1, * knit 5 stitches together, bring the wool under the needle to the front and purl a group of 5 stitches (as directed in the second row) in the next stitch, put the wool to the back, and repeat from * to the end of the row, where knit plain the 2 last stitches. **9th row**—Plain. **10th row**—Purl. **11th row**—Plain. **12th row**—Purl. **13th row**—Plain. **14th row**—Slip 1, knit 1, * bring the wool to the front and purl a group of 5 stitches in the next, put the wool to the back and knit 5 stitches together; repeat from *, and knit plain the last stitch at the end of the row. **15th row**—Plain. **16th row**—Purl. **17th row**—Plain. **18th row**—Purl. **19th row**—Plain. Repeat

Sweet-Briar Lace.

from the eighth row till the shawl is perfectly square. In the *last* pattern row you should omit working a new group of 5 purl stitches, and so bring upon the needle the original number of stitches with which the shawl commenced; then knit 1 plain row loosely, and cast off loosely. The **Insertion** begins with two rounds of crochet worked all round the square of knitting. Use a No. 10 crochet needle. **1st round**—Hold the right side of the knitting towards you, and work 1 double crochet stitch, 2 chain, and repeat, missing just so much of the knitting below the chain as will permit the crochet to set evenly and smoothly; join at the end of the round, and fasten off. **2nd round**—Make a stitch upon the crochet needle, * wool over the needle, insert the hook under a loop of two chain and draw the wool through, repeat from * twice more in the same place, and 7 stitches will be on the needle; wool over the needle and draw through 6, wool over the needle and draw through 2, do 2 chain; and proceed, making a similar clump of stitches under every loop of two chain of last round, drawing the wool up long and loosely; and do three clumps to turn the corner, as shown in the engraving; join evenly at the end of the round, and fasten off. Now work the **Dutch Knitting**—Employ the same knitting needles as used for the centre of the shawl—Pick up on one needle a row of stitches from corner to corner, knitting each stitch as you pick it up; as you pick up, the *right side* of the work should be towards you. **1st row**—Plain knitting, and increase 1 stitch at the beginning and 1 stitch at the end of the row; and this is to be done at the beginning and at the end of *every row* of this insertion to mitre the corners. **2nd row**—Purl. **3rd row**—Plain. **4th row**—Make, 1, slip 1, knit 3, draw the slipped stitch over the three knitted stitches, and repeat the same to the end. **5th row**—Purl. **6th row**—Work the same as the fourth row, making the holes slant properly; the centre stitch of the three knitted stitches of the previous row is to be the slipped stitch in this row. Repeat the fifth and sixth rows till five slanting holes are knitted. **13th row**—Plain. **14th row**—Purl. **15th row**—Plain. These three rows made a ridge on the right side to correspond with the ridge with which you began. Cast off. Work the insertion along the other three sides of the shawl in the same manner. Join up the corners. For the **Crochet Border**—**1st round**—1 double crochet into a stitch of the knitted insertion, 3 chain, miss two stitches of the knitting, and repeat. **2nd round**—Work clump stitch the same as instructed in a previous round. **3rd round**—Plain double crochet. **4th round**—1 double crochet on a stitch of last round, 5 chain, miss three stitches, and repeat; and turn the corners as shown in the engraving. **5th round**—1 double crochet in the centre stitch of five chain of last round, 5 chain, and repeat; and make an extra loop of chain at each corner. **3th round**—1 double crochet in the centre stitch of a loop of chain of last round, 5 chain, 1 double crochet in the centre stitch of the next loop, 5 chain, 1 double crochet in the centre stitch of the next loop,

3 chain, work a clump in the centre stitch of the next loop, 2 chain, a clump in the same place, 2 chain, another clump in the same place, 3 chain, and repeat; you should commence this round so as to place three clumps in the loop at the corner (as shown in the engraving), and calculate the number of loops along each side of the shawl, that all the corners may be similarly fashioned; join evenly, and fasten off at the end of the round. **7th round**—Work 1 double crochet on the last clump of a group, * 5 chain, 1 double crochet in the centre stitch of the first loop of five chain, 5 chain, 1 double crochet in the centre stitch of the next loop of five chain, 5 chain, 1 double crochet on the first clump of the next group, 5 chain, 1 double crochet on the last clump of the same group, and repeat from *, and turn the corner with extra loops as shown in the engraving. **8th round**—1 double crochet in the centre stitch of five chain of last round, 5 chain, and repeat the same; make an extra loop at the corners; fasten off on the completion of the round. **9th round**—Looking at the work you will see there are two loops of five chain, as it were, *above* each group of clumps of the sixth round—begin on a loop of five chain to the right above a group of clumps—* do 1 treble in the centre stitch of the loop, 3 chain, another treble in the same place, 1 treble in the centre stitch of the next loop, 3 chain, another treble in the same place, draw up a long chain stitch on the needle and make a clump on the top (edgeways) of the treble stitch last worked, make a clump in the centre stitch of each of the two next loops of five chain, insert the hook in the top of the first clump and draw the wool through to hold the three clumps closely together, draw up a long chain-stitch on the needle and make a clump on the top of the last clump, then go to the next loop of five chain and repeat from *; the four clumps stand together in the form of a semi-circle, as seen represented in the engraving; and the corner is eased by doing a clump in the second stitch and a clump in the fourth stitch of the corner loop of five chain. **10th round**—Work 1 double crochet under the first chain loop between the treble stitches of last round, 5 chain, 1 double crochet under the next chain loop between the treble stitches, 3 chain, 1 clump in the exact centre of the group of clumps of last round, 3 chain, another clump in the same place, 3 chain, another clump in the same place, 3 chain, and repeat, and as you go on you will see the rosettes forming as in the illustration, seven clumps being in each rosette along the sides of the shawl, and nine clumps in the rosette at each corner. **11th round**—Do 1 double crochet under the loop of five chain of last round, 2 chain, 1 treble under the first loop of three chain, 2 chain, another treble in the same place, * 2 chain, 1 treble under the next loop of three chain, 2

Myrtle Leaf Pattern for a Shawl.

chain, another treble in the same place, repeat from * till 8 treble stitches in all are worked, then 2 chain, 1 double crochet under the loop of five chain, 2 chain, 1 treble under the first loop of three chain, 2 chain, another treble in the same place, and repeat from *; at the corner there will be 10 treble stitches to work instead of eight as in the other scallops. **12th round**—1 double crochet on the double crochet stitch of last round, 4 chain, work 1 treble edgeways on the top of the double crochet stitch, * 1 treble in the space between two treble stitches, 4 chain, 1 treble edgeways on the top of the treble just done, and repeat from * till 7 treble stitches are worked round the scallop; then 1 double crochet on double crochet, 4 chain, 1 treble edgeways on the top of the double crochet stitch, and repeat from *, and ease round the corner with additional stitches as represented in the engraving.

A VEIL, KNITTED IN AN OPEN STITCH, WITH WAVE PATTERN BORDER.

OUR example is worked with the finest Fife Lace Yarn and a pair of No. 15 steel knitting needles. The pattern is very light and open, and the border is pretty. Commence for the **Border** by casting on the requisite number of stitches to make the width required for the bottom of the veil, allowing 12 stitches for each scallop, and 2 stitches over for edge stitches. **1st row**— Knit 2, purl 10, and repeat to the end of the row, where there will be 2 stitches to knit as at the beginning. **2nd row**—Purl 2, * make 1 (by passing the yarn over the needle), knit 3, slip 1, knit 1, pass the slipped stitch over, knit 2 together, knit 3, make 1 (by passing the yarn twice round the needle), purl 2, and repeat from * to the end of the row. **3rd row**—Same as the first row. **4th row**—Purl 2, * knit 1, make 1, knit 2, slip 1, knit 1, pass the slipped stitch over, knit 2 together, knit 2, make 1, knit 1, purl 2, and repeat from *. **5th row**—Same as the first row. **6th row**—Purl 2, * make 1, knit 1, slip 1, knit 1, pass the slipped stitch over, knit 2 together, knit 1, make, 1, knit 2, purl 2, and repeat from *. **7th row**—Same as the first row. **8th row** Purl 2, * knit 3, make 1, slip 1, knit 1, pass the slipped stitch over, knit 2 together, make 1, knit 3, purl 2, and repeat from *. **9th row**—Same as the first row. Repeat from the second row till four patterns, thirty-three rows are done. **34th row**—Purl 2 together, knit 4, knit 2 together, knit 4, and repeat the same to the end of the row, where purl 2 together; now 10 stitches are in each scallop. **35th row**— Purl all along. **36th row**—Plain. **37th row**—Purl. This completes the border. **1st row of the Veil**—Slip 1, knit 1, * make 1, knit 2 together, and repeat from * to the end of the row, where knit the last stitch. **2nd row**—Purl. **3rd row**—Slip 1, knit 2, * make 1, knit 2 together, and repeat from * to the end of the row, and knit the 2 last stitches plain. **4th row**—Purl. **5th row**—Plain. **6th row**—Purl. Repeat these six rows till the veil is the length desired. Knit 4 or 5 plain rows; and cast off.

MELON PATTERN FOR A SHAWL OR SCARF.

THE accompanying illustration shows a very pretty striped pattern for a shawl or scarf, arranged with a border to correspond. Worked with the finest Fife Lace Yarn and a pair of No. 14 steel knitting needles, this makes a most charming light wrap, but if greater warmth be required, a thicker Fife Lace Yarn can be used with No. 11 bone needles. Commence by casting on the requisite number of stitches to make the width of the shawl, allowing 10 stitches for each repetition of the pattern. Knit 1 or 2 plain rows. **1st pattern row**—Slip 1, knit 9, * make 1, knit 2 together, knit 8, and repeat from * to the end of the row. **2nd row**— Slip 1, knit 1, purl 6, * knit 2, make 1, knit 2 together, purl 6; repeat from * and end the row with 2 plain knit stitches. **3rd row**—The same as the first row. **4th row** —Same as the second row. **5th row**— Slip 1, knit 1, * draw the fourth stitch on the left-hand needle over the three stitches nearest to the point of the needle, also draw over the fifth and sixth stitches in the same way, which makes 3 stitches drawn over 3, keeping the first 3 stitches still on the left-hand needle, make 1, knit 1 of these stitches, make 1, knit 2 stitches, make 1, knit 2, make 1, knit 2 together, and repeat from * to the end of the row, which finish with make 1, knit 2. **6th row**—Same as the second row. Repeat from the first pattern row until the shawl is as long as desired. Then after working the fourth row, knit 1 or 2 plain rows, and cast off all. For the **Border**—Cast on 13 stitches. **1st row**—Slip 1, knit 2, make 1, knit 2 together, knit 1, make 2, knit 2 together, knit 5. **2nd row**—Knit 7, purl 1, knit 3, make 1, knit 2 together, knit 1. **3rd row**—Slip 1, knit 2, make 1, knit 2 together, knit 9. **4th row**— Knit 11, make 1, knit 2 together, knit 1. **5th row**—Slip 1, knit 2, make 1, knit 2 together, knit 1, make 2, knit 2 together, make 2, knit 2 together, knit 4. **6th row**—Knit 6, purl 1, knit 2, purl 1, knit 3, make 1, knit 2 together, knit 1. **7th row**—Slip 1, knit 2, make 1, knit 2 together, knit 11. **8th row**—Cast off 3, knit 9, make 1, knit 2 together, knit 1. Repeat from the first row till a sufficient length is knitted to go round the shawl, with plenty of fulness at the corners; and sew it on firmly and neatly.

French Trellis Border.

POMPADOUR LACE.

THIS handsome lace may be used for many purposes; if knitted with fine Fife Lace Yarn or with knitting silk it makes a nice dress trimming or apron border, or it may be worked with Shetland or Berlin wool as a border for a shawl, or with fine crochet thread as an edging for serviettes and d'oyleys. This design can be worked with Shetland wool and steel needles No. 15; or use the finest Fife Lace Yarn and steel needles No. 16; or the thicker Fife Lace Yarn and needles No. 14. For cotton work for trimming underlinen, &c., use Coats' No. 20 crochet cotton and steel knitting needles No. 17. Cast on 24 stitches. Knit 1 plain row. **1st row**—Slip 1, knit 2, make 1, knit 2 together, make 1, knit 2 together, knit 12, knit 2 together; make 2, knit 2 together, knit 1. **2nd row**—Knit 3, purl 1, knit 20. **3rd row**—Slip 1, knit 3, make 1, knit 2 together, knit 11, knit 2 together; make 2, knit 2 together, knit 3. **4th row**—Knit 5, purl 1, knit 18. **5th row** —Slip 1, knit 2, make 1, knit 2 together, make 1, knit 2 together, knit 8, knit 2 together; make 2, knit 2 together, knit 3, make 2, knit 2. **6th row**—Knit 3, purl 1, knit 5, purl 1, knit 16. **7th row**—Slip 1, knit 3, make 1, knit 2 together, knit 7, knit 2 together; make 2, knit 2 together, knit 3, make 1, knit 1, make 1, knit 5. **8th row**—Knit 13, purl 1, knit 14. **9th row**—Slip 1, knit 2, make 1, knit 2 together, make 1, knit 2 together, knit 4, knit 2 together; make 2, knit 2 together, knit 3, knit 2 together, make 1, knit 3, make 1, knit 2 together, make 2, knit 2 together, knit 1, **10th row**—Knit 3, purl 1, knit 12, purl 1, knit 12. **11th row**—Slip 1, knit 3, make 1, knit 2 together, knit 3, knit 2 together; make 2, knit 2 together, knit 4, knit 2 together, make 1, knit 5, make 1, knit 5. **12th row**—Knit 19, purl 1, knit 10. **13th row**—Slip 1, knit 2, make 1, knit 2 together, make 1, knit 2 together, knit 2 together; make 2, knit 2 together, knit 5, knit 2 together, make 1, knit 1, slip 1, knit 2 together, pass the slipped stitch over, make 3, knit 2 together, knit 1, make 1, knit 2 together, make 2, knit 2. **14th row** —Knit 3, purl 1, knit 6, purl 1, knit 12, purl 1, knit 8. **15th row**—Slip 1, knit 3, make 1, knit 2 together, knit 3, knit 2 together; make 2, knit 2 together, knit 5, make 1, knit 2 together, knit 3, knit 2 together, make 1, knit 1, knit 1, knit 2 together, knit 4. **16th row**—Knit 20, purl 1, knit 10. **17th row**—Slip 1, knit 2, make 1, knit 2 together, make 1, knit 2 together, knit 4, knit 2 together; make 2, knit 2 together, knit 4, make 1, knit 2 together, knit 1, knit 2 together, make 1, knit 1, knit 2 together, make 2, knit 2 together, knit 2 together. **18th row**—Knit 3, purl 1, knit 13, purl 1, knit 12. **19th row**—Slip 1, knit 3, make 1, knit 2 together, knit 7, knit 2 together; make 2, knit 2 together, knit 3, make 1, slip 1, knit 2 together, pass the slipped stitch over, make 1, knit 1, knit 2 together, knit 4. **20th row**—Knit 14, purl 1, knit 14. **21st row**—Slip 1, knit 2, make 1, knit 2 together, make 1, knit 2 together, knit 8, knit 2 together; make 2, knit 2 together, knit 2 together, knit 2 together, knit 2 together, make 2, knit 2 together, knit 2 together. **22nd row**—Knit 3, purl 1, knit 5, purl 1, knit 16. **23rd row**—Slip 1, knit 3, make 1, knit 2 together, knit 11, knit 2 together; make 1, slip 1, knit 2 together, pass the slipped stitch over, make 1, knit 2, knit 2 together, knit 1, make 1, knit 2 together, knit 12, knit 2 together; **24th row**— Knit 5, purl 1, knit 18. **25th row**—Slip 1, knit 2, make 1, knit 2 together, make 1, knit 2 together, knit 12, knit 2 together; make 2, knit 2 together, knit 1. **26th row**—Knit 3, purl 1, knit 20. **27th row**—Slip 1, knit 3, make 1, knit 2 together, knit 18. **28th row**—Knit 24 stitches plain. Repeat from the first row of the pattern.

CITRON LEAF BORDER.

THIS is a pretty pointed leaf border with an insertion, suitable for a variety of purposes, according to the material, either wool or cotton, with which it is knitted. This design can be worked with Shetland wool and steel needles No. 15; or use the finest Fife Lace Yarn and steel needles No. 16; or the thicker Fife Lace Yarn and needles No. 14. For cotton work for trimming underlinen, &c., use Coats' No. 20 crochet cotton and steel knitting needles No. 17. Cast on 24 stitches. Purl 1 row. **1st row**—Slip 1, knit 2, make 1, knit 2 together, knit 11; make 1, knit 2 together, knit 1, make 1, knit 2 together, make 2, knit 2 together, knit 1. **2nd row**—Knit 3, purl 1, knit 5; make 1 (by passing the wool twice round the needle), purl 2 together, purl 10, knit 1, make 1, knit 2 together, knit 1. **3rd row**—Slip 1, knit 2, make 1, knit 2 together, make 1 and knit 2 together four times, knit 2; make 1, knit 2 together, knit 2, make 1, knit 2 together, make 2, knit 2 together, knit 1.

4th row—Knit 3, purl 1, knit 6 ; make 1 (always here by passing the wool twice round the needle), purl 2 together, purl 10, knit 1, make 1, knit 2 together, knit 1. **5th row**—Slip 1, knit 2, make 1, knit 2 together, knit 11 ; make 1, knit 2 together, knit 3, make 1, knit 2 together, make 2, knit 2 together, knit 1. **6th row**—Knit 3, purl 1, knit 7 ; make 1, purl 2 together, purl 10, knit 1, make 1, knit 2 together, knit 1. **7th row**—Slip 1, knit 2, make 1, knit 2 together, knit 1, make 1 and knit 2 together four times, knit 2 ; make 1, knit 2 together, knit 4, make 1, knit 2 together, make 2, knit 2 together, knit 1. **8th row**—Knit 3, purl 1, knit 8 ; make 1, purl 2 together, purl 10, knit 1, make 1, knit 2 together, knit 1. **9th row**—Slip 1, knit 2, make 1, knit 2 together, knit 11 ; make 1, knit 2 together, knit 5, make 1, knit 2 together, make 2, knit 2 together, knit 1. **10th row**—Knit 3, purl 1, knit 9 ; make 1, purl 2 together, purl 10, knit 1, make 1, knit 2 together, knit 1. **11th row**—Slip 1, knit 2, make 1, knit 2 together, knit 11 ; make 1, knit 2 together, knit 6, make 1, knit 2 together, make 2, knit 2 together, knit 1. **12th row**—Knit 3, purl 1, knit 10 ; make 1, purl 2 together, purl 10, knit 1, make 1, knit 2 together, knit 1. **13th row**—Slip 1, knit 2, make 1, knit 2 together, knit 11 ; make 1, knit 2 together, knit 12. **14th row**—Cast off 6, knit 7 ; make 1, purl 2 together, purl 10, knit 1, make 1, knit 2 together, knit 1. Repeat from the first row for the length required.

IRISH LACE.

This lace is a nice width for edging shawls, and may be used for other

HEM-STITCH PATTERN FOR A VEIL.

Our illustration shows a portion of a veil knitted in Hem-stitch with a deep Ladder pattern border ; the work is executed with the finest white Fife Lace Yarn and a pair of No. 16 steel knitting needles. Black Fife Lace Yarn will perhaps be the most generally useful, and a tight knitter had better use No. 15 needles. About 2 ozs. will be ample to knit a veil, as, being very fine, the quantity goes a long way. Of course the number of stitches to be cast on will entirely depend upon the width the veil is required to be, there are thirteen stitches in each repetition of the pattern, and 5 stitches over for edge stitches,— therefore 200 stitches will be needed to make a veil of fifteen scallops in width, and 278 stitches for a width of twenty-one scallops. Knit 1 row plain. 1 row purl. **1st Pattern row** of the **Border**—Slip 1, knit 2, * make 1, knit 4, knit 2 together, slip 1, knit 1, pass the slipped stitch over, knit 4, make 1, knit 1, and repeat from * to the end of the row, and knit the last 2 stitches plain. **2nd row**—Slip 1, knit 1, purl all along to within 2 stitches of the end of the row, and knit those plain. Repeat these two rows till 36 pattern rows are knitted, when you will be able to count eighteen holes running up in a straight line. **37th row**—Slip 1, knit 6, * knit 2 together, slip 1, knit 1, pass the slipped stitch over, knit 9, repeat from *, and at the end knit only 7 plain stitches, now there are 11 stitches in each pattern. **38th row**— Slip 1, knit 1, purl all along to within 2 stitches of the end of the row, and knit those plain. **39th row**—Slip 1, knit 6, * knit 2 together, knit 9, repeat from *, and end with 7 plain knit stitches, now the stitches are reduced to ⁀ stitches in each pattern. **40th row**—Slip 1, knit 1, purl along to within 2

Corner of a Shawl Knitted in Boule de Neige Pattern, with Insertion of Dutch Knitting and a Wide Crochet Border.

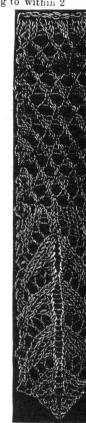

A Veil. Knitted in an

purposes according to the material with which it is knitted. This design can be worked with Shetland wool and steel needles No. 15 ; or use the finest Fife Lace Yarn and steel needles No. 16 ; or the thicker Fife Lace Yarn and needles No. 14. For cotton work for trimming underlinen, &c., use Coats' No. 20 crochet cotton and steel knitting needles No. 17. Cast on 20 stitches. Purl 1 row. **1st row**—Slip 1, knit 1, make 1 and knit 2 together four times, purl 3, knit 2 together, make 1, knit 3, make 1, knit 2. **2nd row**—Make 1, knit 2 together, knit 19. **3rd row**—Slip 1, knit 2, make 1 and knit 2 together three times, purl 3, knit 2 together, make 1, knit 2. **4th row**—Make 1, knit 2 together, knit 20. **5th row**—Slip 1, knit 1, make 1 and knit 2 together three times, purl 3, knit 2 together, make 1, knit 2 together, knit 2 together, make 3, knit 2 together, knit 1, make 1, knit 2. **6th row**— Make 1, knit 2 together, knit 4, purl 1, knit 16. **7th row**—Slip 1, knit 2, make 1 and knit 2 together three times, purl 3, knit 1, make 1, knit 2 together, knit 3, knit 2 together, make 1, knit 2 together, knit 1. **8th row**—Make 1, knit 2 together, knit 20. **9th row**—Slip 1, knit 1, make 1 and knit 2 together four times, purl 3, knit 1, make 1, knit 2 together, knit 1, knit 2 together, make 1, knit 2 together, knit 1. **10th row**—Make 1, knit 2 together, knit 19. **11th row**—Slip 1, knit 2, make 1 and knit 2 together four times, purl 3, knit 1, make 1, slip 1, knit 2 together, pass the slipped stitch over, make 1, knit 2 together, knit 1. **12th row**—Make 1, knit 2 together, knit 18. Repeat from the first row of the pattern.

stitches of the end, and knit those plain. **41st row**—Plain. **42nd row**— Slip 1, knit 1, purl to within 2 stitches of the end, and knit those. This completes the border. **1st Pattern row** of the **Veil**—Slip 1, knit 2, * make 1, knit 2 together, repeat from * to the end of the row and knit the last 2 stitches plain. **2nd row**—Slip 1, knit 1, purl 1, * make 1, purl 2 together, repeat from * to the end of the row, and knit the last two stitches plain. Repeat the last two rows till you have knitted sufficient for the length of the veil. Then do a plain row ; a purl row ; and 4 plain rows ; and cast off all.

SEA-SHELL BORDER.

This elegant border is useful for a variety of purposes according to the material with which it is knitted, it looks equally well worked with wool, silk, or cotton, and may be employed for dress trimming if knitted with the finest Fife Lace Yarn and No. 16 steel knitting needles. Cast on 23 stitches, and knit across doing 12 stitches plain, 6 stitches purl, and the remaining 5 stitches plain. **1st row**—Slip 1, knit 2, make 1, knit 2 together, knit 8, make 1, knit 2 together, knit 1 ; make 2, knit 2 together, make 2, knit 2 together, make 2, knit 2 together, knit 1. **2nd row**—Knit 3, purl 1, knit 2, purl 1, knit 2 ; purl 1, knit 3 ; make 1, knit 2 together, purl 6, knit 2, make 1, knit 2 together, knit 1. **3rd row**—Slip 1, knit 2, make 1, knit 2 together, knit 8, make 1, knit

2 together, knit 11. **4th row**—Knit 13; make 1, knit 2 together, purl 6, knit 2, make 1, knit 2 together, knit 1. **5th row**—Slip 1, knit 2, make 1, knit 2 together, draw the fourth stitch on the left-hand needle over the 3 stitches that are nearest to the point of the needle, also draw over the fifth and sixth stitches in the same way, which makes three stitches drawn over three, all still on the left-hand needle, now make 1, knit 1 stitch off the left-hand needle, make 1, knit 2 stitches off, which works over the "tie," make 1, knit 2; make 1, knit 2 together, knit 1, make 2, knit 2 together, knit 8. **6th row**—Knit 10, purl 1, knit 3; make 1, knit 2 together, purl 6, knit 2, make 1, knit 2 together, knit 1. **7th row**—Slip 1, knit 2, make 1, knit 2 together, knit 8, make 1, knit 2 together, knit 12. **8th row**—Knit 14; make 1, knit 2 together, purl 6, knit 2, make 1, knit 2 together, knit 1. **9th row**—Slip 1, knit 2, make 1, knit 2 together, knit 8, make 1, knit 2 together, knit 1; make 2, knit 2 together, make 2, knit 2 together, knit 7. **10th row**—Knit 9, purl 1, knit 2, purl 1, knit 3; make 1, knit 2 together, purl 6, knit 2, make 1, knit 2 together, knit 1. **11th row**—Slip 1, knit 2, make 1, knit 2 together, draw the fourth, the fifth, and the sixth stitches on the left-hand needle over the 3 stitches that are nearest to the point of the needle as instructed in the fifth row, make 1, knit 1, make 1, knit 2, make 1, knit 2, make 1, knit 2 together, knit 14. **12th row**—Knit 7, slip 6 of these stitches over the stitch you *last knitted* and you will have that 1 stitch only remaining on the right-hand needle (while the six slipped stitches will be puckered up into a kind of shell instead of being cast off in the usual manner), knit 9; make 1, knit 2 together, purl 6, knit 2, make 1, knit 2 together, knit 1. Repeat from the first row for the length required.

times, make 1, knit 2. **10th row**—Knit 32, make 1, knit 2 together, knit 1, make 1, knit 2 together, knit 1. **11th row**—Slip 1, knit 2, make 1, knit 2 together, knit 1, make 1, knit 2 together, knit 2; knit 2 together and knit 2 alternately seven times. **12th row**—Cast off 8, knit 2 together and knit 1 alternately four times, knit 2 together, knit 2; make 1, knit 2 together, knit 1, make 1, knit 2 together, knit 1. Repeat from the first row for the length required.

BELGRAVE EDGING.

SELECT material and needles suitable for the purpose for which the edging is required. This design can be worked with Shetland wool and steel needles No. 15; or use the finest Fife Lace Yarn and steel needles No. 16; or the thicker Fife Lace Yarn and needles No. 14. For cotton work for trimming underlinen, &c., use Coats' No. 20 crochet cotton and steel knitting needles No. 17. Cast on 23 stitches, and knit across plain. **1st row**—Slip 1, knit 2, make 2, purl 2 together, knit 2, make 1, knit 2 together, knit 2, make 1, knit 2 together, knit 4, make 2, purl 2 together, knit 2, make 2, knit 2. **2nd row**—Knit 3, purl 1, knit 2, make 2, purl 2 together, knit 12, make 2, purl 2 together, knit 3. **3rd row**—Slip 1, knit 2, make 2, purl 2 together, knit 3, make 1, knit 2 together, knit 2, make 1, knit 2 together, knit 3, make 2, purl 2 together, knit 6. **4th row**—Knit 6, make 2, purl 2 together, knit 12, make 2, purl 2 together, knit 3. **5th row**—Slip 1, knit 2, make 2, purl 2 together, knit 4, make 1, knit 2 together, knit 2, make 1, knit 2 together, knit 2, make 2,

Melon Pattern for a Shawl or Scarf.

...tch, with Wave Pattern Border.

WIDE POINT LACE BORDER.

SELECT materials suitable for the purpose for which the lace is required. This design can be worked with Shetland wool and steel needles No. 15; or use the finest Fife Lace Yarn and steel needles No. 16; or the thicker Fife Lace Yarn and needles No. 14. For cotton work for trimming underlinen, &c., use Coats' No. 20 crochet cotton and steel knitting needles No. 17. Cast on 18 stitches, and knit 1 plain row. **1st row**—Slip 1, knit 2, make 1, knit 2 together, knit 1, make 1, knit 2 together, knit 1, make 2, knit 2 together, make 2, knit 2 together, make 2, knit 2 together, knit 1. **2nd row**—Knit 3, purl 1, knit 2, purl 1, knit 2, purl 1, knit 2, purl 1, knit 3; make 1, knit 2 together, knit 1, make 1, knit 2 together, knit 1. **3rd row**—Slip 1, knit 2, make 1, knit 2 together, knit 1; make 2 and knit 2 together six times, knit 1. **4th row**—Knit 3, purl 1, knit 2 and purl 1 alternately five times, knit 3; make 1, knit 2 together, knit 1, make 1, knit 2 together, knit 1. **5th row**—Slip 1, knit 2, make 1, knit 2 together, knit 1, make 1, knit 2 together, make 2 and knit 2 together nine times, knit 1. **6th row**—Knit 3, purl 1, knit 2 and purl 1 alternately eight times, knit 3; make 1, knit 2 together, knit 1, make 1, knit 2 together, knit 1. **7th row**—Slip 1, knit 2, make 1, knit 2 together, knit 1, make 1, knit 2 together, knit 29. **8th row**—Knit 31, make 1, knit 2 together, knit 1, make 1, knit 2 together, knit 1. **9th row**—Slip 1, knit 2, make 1, knit 2 together, knit 1, make 1, knit 2 together, knit 1; make 1 and knit 2 together thirteen

purl 2 together, knit 2, make 2, knit 2 together, make 2, knit 2. **6th row**—Knit 3, purl 1, knit 2, purl 1, knit 2, purl 1, knit 2, make 2, purl 2 together, knit 3. **7th row**—Slip 1, knit 2, make 2, purl 2 together, knit 5, make 1, knit 2 together, knit 2, make 1, knit 2 together, knit 1, make 2, purl 2 together, knit 9. **8th row**—Cast off 5, knit 3, make 2, purl 2 together, knit 12, make 2, purl 2 together, knit 3. Repeat the pattern from the first row.

CYPRUS EDGING.

THIS is a pretty edging to use for a shawl or scarf when only a narrow bordering is required, in which case it should be worked with the same wool and needles as the shawl itself; it also is appropriate for trimming underlinen. This design can be worked with Shetland wool and steel needles No. 15; or use the finest Fife Lace Yarn and steel needles No. 16; or the thicker Fife Lace Yarn and needles No. 14. For cotton work for trimming underlinen, &c., use Coats' No. 20 crochet cotton and steel knitting needles No. 17. Cast on 12 stitches. Knit 1 plain row. **1st row**—Slip 1, knit 5, knit 2 together, make 1, knit 1, knit 2 together, knit 1. **2nd row**—Knit 4, make 1, knit 2 together, knit 2, make 1, knit 2 together, knit 1. **3rd row**—Slip 1, knit 3, knit 2 together, make 1, knit 1, knit 2 together, knit 2. **4th row**—Knit 7, make 1, knit 2 together, knit 1. **5th row**—Slip 1, knit 4, make 1, knit 2 together, knit 1, make 2, knit 2. **6th row**—Knit 3, purl 1, knit 2, make 1, knit 3, make 1, knit 2 together, knit 1. **7th row**—Slip 1, knit 6, make 1, knit 2 together, knit 4. **8th row**—Cast off 2, knit 2, make 1, knit 5, make 1, knit 2 together, knit 1. Repeat from the first row for the length required.

WILLOW LEAF EDGING.

THIS pretty leaf edging may be employed for various purposes according to the material with which it is worked. If knitted with Fife Lace Yarn, or Shetland, or Berlin wool, it makes a neat and sufficient border for a small square shawl or fichu; and if worked with fine cotton it is useful for trimming underlinen and children's things. This design can be worked with Shetland wool and steel needles No. 15; or use the finest Fife Lace Yarn and steel needles No. 16; or the thicker Fife Lace Yarn and needles No. 14. For cotton work for trimming underlinen, &c., use Coats' No. 20 crochet cotton and steel knitting needles No. 17. Cast on 12 stitches. Purl 1 row. **1st row** —Make 1 by passing the wool round the needle, knit 1, make 1, knit 2, knit 2

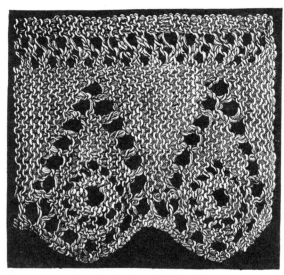

Pompadour Lace.

together, knit 2 together, knit 2, make 1, knit 2 together, knit 1. **2nd row**— Slip 1, knit 1, purl 10. **3rd row**—Make 1, knit 3, make 1, knit 1, knit 2 together, knit 2 together, knit 1, make 1, knit 2 together, knit 1. **4th row**— Slip 1, knit 1, purl 10. **5th row**—Make 1, knit 5, make 1, knit 2 together, knit 2 together, make 1, knit 2 together, knit 1. **6th row**—Slip 1, knit 1, purl 10. **7th row**—Make 1, knit 3, knit 2 together, knit 2, make 1, knit 2 together, make 1, knit 2 together, knit 1. **8th row**—Slip 1, knit 1, purl 10. Repeat from the first row for the length required. You will observe there are 12 stitches retained upon the needle at the completion of every row, and the scalloped edge is formed by the stitch that is made by passing the wool round the needle at the beginning of each alternate row, the looser this stitch is made the better the edging will look.

NARROW POINT LACE BORDER.

THIS is a useful lace for bordering shawls, as the edge sits rather full and nicely pointed. Our example is worked with Shetland wool and No. 15 steel knitting needles. Cast on 11 stitches. Knit 1 plain row. **1st row**—Slip 1, knit 2, make 1, knit 2 together, knit 1; make 2, knit 2 together, make 2, knit 2 together, knit 1. **2nd row**—Knit 3, purl 1, knit 2, purl 1, knit 3; make 1, knit 2 together, knit 1. **3rd row**—Slip 1, knit 2, make 1, knit 2 together, knit 1; make 2 and knit 2 together three times, knit 1. **4th row**—Knit 3, purl 1, knit 2, purl 1, knit 2, purl 1, knit 3; make 1, knit 2 together, knit 1. **5th row**—Slip 1, knit 2, make 1, knit 2 together, knit 1; make 2 and knit 2 together four times, make 2, knit 2. **6th row**—Knit 3, purl 1, knit 2 and purl 1 alternately four times, knit 3; make 1, knit 2 together, knit 1. **7th row**—Slip 1, knit 2, make 1, knit 2 together, knit 17. **8th row**—Knit 19; make 1, knit 2 together, knit 1. **9th row**—Slip 1, knit 2, make 1, knit 2 together, knit 1; make 1 and knit 2 together seven times, make 1, knit 2. **10th row**—Knit 20; make 1, knit 2 together, knit 1. **11th row**—Slip 1, knit 2, make 1, knit 2 together, knit 2, knit 2 together and knit 2 alternately four times. **12th row**—Cast off 5, knit 2 together, knit 1, knit 2 together, knit 1, knit 2 together, knit 2; make 1, knit 2 together, knit 1. Repeat from the first row of the pattern.

HAREBELL LACE.

THIS pretty lace is knitted with Fife Lace Yarn of medium thickness, and a pair of No. 14 steel knitting needles. It is suitable for the borders of shawls and many other purposes; if worked with the finest Fife Lace Yarn and needles No. 16 it makes an elegant trimming for dresses. Cast on 21 stitches. Purl 1 row. **1st row**—Slip 1, knit 2, make 1, knit 2 together, knit 1, make 1, knit 2 together, knit 1; make 1, knit 1, make 1, knit 1, make 1, knit 1, make 1, knit 2; make 1, knit 2 together, make 1, knit 1, make 1, knit 1, make 1, knit 2. **2nd row**—Purl 29. **3rd row**—Slip 1, knit 2, make 1, knit 2 together, knit 1, make 1, knit 2 together, knit 1; make 1, knit 3, make 1, knit 1, make 1, knit 3, make 1, knit 2; make 1, knit 2 together, make 1, knit 3, make 1, knit 1, make 1, knit 3, make 1, knit 2. **4th row**—Purl 37. **5th row**—Slip 1, knit 2, make 1, knit 2 together, knit 1, make 1, knit 2 together, knit 1; make 1, knit 5, make 1, knit 1, make 1, knit 5, make 1, knit 2; make 1, knit 2 together, make 1, slip 1, knit 4 together, pass the slipped stitch over, make 1, knit 1, make 1, slip 1, knit 4 together, pass the slipped stitch over, make 1, knit 2. **6th row**—Cast off 4, purl 32. **7th row**—Slip 1, knit 2, make 1, knit 2 together, knit 1, make 1, knit 2 together, knit 1; make 1, slip 1, knit 1, pass the slipped stitch over, knit 2, knit 2 together, make 1, knit 3, make 1, slip 1, knit 1, pass the slipped stitch over, knit 2, knit 2 together, make 1, knit 2; make 1, knit 2 together, make 1, knit 1, make 1, knit 1, make 1, knit 1, make 1, knit 2. **8th row**—Purl 37. **9th row**—Slip 1, knit 2, make 1, knit 2 together, knit 1, make 1, knit 2 together, knit 1; make 1, slip 1, knit 2 together, pass the slipped stitch over, knit 2 together, make 1, knit 5, make 1, slip 1, knit 1, pass the slipped stitch over, knit 3 together, make 1, knit 2; make 1, knit 2 together, make 1, knit 3, make 1, knit 1, make 1, knit 3, make 1, knit 2. **10th row**—Purl 39. **11th row**—Slip 1, knit 2, make 1, knit 2 together, knit 1, make 1, knit 2 together, knit 1; make 1, slip 1, knit 3 together, pass the slipped stitch over, make 1, knit 5, make 1, slip 1, knit 3 together, pass the slipped stitch over, make 1, knit 2; make 1, knit 2 together, make 1, slip 1, knit 4 together, pass the slipped stitch over, make 1, knit 1, make 1, slip 1, knit 4 together, pass the slipped stitch over, make 1, knit 2. **12th row**—Cast off 4, purl 28. **13th row**—Slip 1, knit 2, make 1, knit 2 together, knit 1, make 1, knit 2 together, slip 1, knit 1, pass the slipped stitch over; make 1, knit 1, slip 1, knit 2 together, pass the slipped stitch over, knit 1, knit 3 together, make 1, knit 2 together, knit 1; make 1, knit 2 together, make 1, knit 1, make 1, knit 1, make 1, knit 1, make 1, knit 2. **14th row**—Purl 29. **15th row**—Slip 1, knit 2, make 1, knit 2 together, knit 1, make 1, knit 2 together, slip 1, knit 1, pass the slipped stitch over; make 1, slip 1, knit 2 together, pass the slipped stitch over, knit 2 together, make 1, knit 2 together, knit 1; make 1, knit 2 together, make 1, knit 3, make 1, knit 1, make 1, knit 3,

Citron Leaf Border.

make 1, knit 2. **16th row**—Purl 30. **17th row**—Slip 1, knit 2, make 1, knit 2 together, knit 1, make 1, knit 2 together, slip 1, knit 1, pass the slipped stitch over; make 1, knit 2 together, make 1, knit 2 together, knit 1; make 1, knit 2 together, make 1, slip 1, knit 4 together, pass the slipped stitch over, make 1, knit 1, make 1, slip 1, knit 4 together, pass the slipped stitch over, make 1, knit 2. **18th row**—Cast off 4, purl 20. Repeat the pattern from the first row.

COBURG LACE.

A USEFUL lace for general purposes; may be knitted with either cotton or wool. This design can be worked with Shetland wool and steel needles No. 15; or use the finest Fife Lace Yarn and steel needles No. 16; or the thicker Fife Lace Yarn and needles No. 14. For cotton work for trimming underlinen, &c., use Coats' No. 20 crochet cotton and steel knitting needles No. 17. Cast on 20 stitches. Knit 1 plain row. **1st row**—Slip 1, knit 2, make 1, knit 2 together, knit 1, make 1, knit 2 together, make 1, knit 2 together, knit 1; make 1 and knit 2 together three times, make 2, knit 2 together, knit 1. **2nd row**—Knit 3, purl 1, knit 11; make 1, knit 2 together, knit 4. **3rd row**—Slip 1, knit 2, make 1, knit 2 together, knit 1, make 1, knit 2 together, make 1, knit 2 together, knit 2; make 1 and knit 2 together three times, make 2, knit 2 together, knit 1. **4th row**—Knit 3, purl 1, knit 12; make 1, knit 2 together, knit 4. **5th row**—Slip 1, knit 2, make 1, knit 2 together, knit 1, make 1, knit 2 together, make 1, knit 2 together, knit 3; make 1 and knit 2 together three times, make 2, knit 2 together, knit 1. **6th row**—Knit 3, purl 1, knit 13; make 1, knit 2 together, knit 4. **7th row**—Slip 1, knit 2, make 1, knit 2 together, knit 1, make 1, knit 2 together, make 1, knit 2 together, knit 4; make 1 and knit 2 together three times, make 2, knit 2 together, knit 1. **8th row**—Knit 3, purl 1, knit 14; make 1, knit 2 together, knit 4. **9th row**—Slip 1, knit 2, make 1, knit 2 together, knit 1, make 1, knit 2 together, make 1, knit 2 together, knit 5; make 1 and knit 2 together three times, make 2, knit 2 together, knit 1. **10th row**—Knit 3, purl 1, knit 15; make 1, knit 2 together, knit 1. **11th row**—Slip 1, knit 2, make 1, knit 2 together, knit 1, make 1, knit 2 together, make 1, knit 2 together, knit 6; make 1 and knit 2 together three times, make 2, knit 2 together, knit 1. **12th row**—Knit 3, purl 1, knit 16; make 1, knit 2 together, knit 4. **13th row**—Slip 1, knit 2, make 1, knit 2 together, knit 1, make 1, knit 2 together, make 1, knit 2 together, knit 16. **14th row**—Cast off 6, knit 13; make 1, knit 2 together, knit 4. Repeat from the first row for the length required.

PHEASANT'S EYE PATTERN.

FOR A SHAWL.

THIS pattern is copied from a fine old woven Shetland shawl, and though it may not be quite so easy to work as some other patterns, owing to *every* row being a fancy row, the effect when finished will amply repay any little

Irish Lace.

Hem-Stitch Pattern for a Veil.

extra trouble, from the extreme lightness and beauty of the design. The finest Fife Lace Yarn should be used, and a pair of No. 14 steel knitting needles; or Shetland wool and No. 10 needles. Cast on for the width of the shawl any number of stitches divisible by 10, and 5 over for edge stitches. Knit 4 plain rows. **1st pattern row**—Knit 3, * make 1, knit 2, slip 1, knit 1, pass the slipped stitch over, knit 1, knit 2 together, knit 2, make 1, knit 1; repeat from *, and end with knit 2. **2nd row**—Knit 2, purl 1, * make 1, purl 2, purl 2 together, purl 1, purl 2 together, purl 2, make 1, purl 1, and repeat from *, and end with knit 2. **3rd row**—The same as the first row. **4th row**—The same as the second row. **5th row**—Knit 3, * make 1, knit 2, slip 1, knit 1, pass the slipped stitch over, knit 6; repeat from *, and end with knit 2. **6th row**—Knit 2, purl all along to within 2 stitches of the end and knit those. **7th row**—Knit 3, * knit 2 together, knit 2, make 1, knit 1, make 1, knit 2, slip 1, knit 1, pass the slipped stitch over, knit 1; repeat from *, and end with knit 2. **8th row**—Knit 2, purl 1, * purl 2 together, purl 2, make 1, purl 1, make 1, purl 2, purl 2 together, purl 1; repeat from *, and end with knit 2. **9th row**—The same as the seventh row. **10th row**—The same as the eighth row. **11th row**—Knit 8, * make 1, knit 2, slip 1, knit 1, pass the slipped stitch over, knit 6; repeat from *, and end with knit 3 only. **12th row**—Knit 2, purl all along to within 2 stitches of the end, and knit those. Repeat from the first row of the pattern until the shawl attains the length desired. Finish by knitting 4 plain rows; and cast off. The shawl must be edged with a pretty knitted lace. The Irish lace given in the present issue is a very suitable pattern, and should be nicely fulled in round the corners.

A PLAIN-KNIT SCARF OR CLOUD,

THAT MAY ALSO BE USED AS A FASCINATOR.

(Not Illustrated.)

THIS is simply a long strip of plain knitting, measuring about two yards in length, one end of which is gathered up and finished off with a handsome wool tassel, while the other end is ornamented with a bow of ribbon, and may either be worn on the head, after the manner of a fascinator, or be thrown over the left shoulder to hang down behind. The peculiarity of the work is that the knitting is executed with thick wooden pins and with wool of two different colours and qualities, the one fine and the other thick. Pale pink, blue, or crimson Andalusian wool will knit prettily with white or grey double Berlin, using needles about an inch and a quarter in circumference—or silk may be substituted for the Andalusian wool if the scarf is required to be very elegant. About 2 ozs. of Andalusian wool (or silk) and 4 ozs. of double Berlin should be procured, and 1½ yards of inch-wide ribbon. Cast on 60 stitches with the double Berlin wool, and knit 2 plain rows; take the Andalusian wool and knit 2 plain rows; and continue in the same way, doing 2 rows with each wool alternately, not breaking off the wool, but carrying it on along the edge of the knitting, till the scarf is the necessary length, when cast off after doing 2 rows with the double Berlin. Gather up one end of the knitting and put on a good full tassel made with Andalusian wool. Fold the other end in half and seam it together in such a way that the knitting is doubled; a bow of ribbon is then placed on the seam; this end of the scarf may hang down behind, or be worn as a covering for the head, in which case the bow comes on the top of the head. A similar scarf can be more lightly knitted by combining the finest Fife Lace Yarn with single Berlin wool, using needles No. 1, measured by Walker's Bell Gauge, and casting on 76 stitches for the width of the scarf.

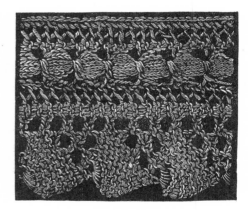

Sea Shell Border.

THE OLD-FASHIONED SHELL PATTERN.

FOR A SHAWL OR SCARF.

(Not Illustrated.)

THIS favourite shell pattern can be most satisfactorily employed for knitting a shawl or scarf, and is quite easy of accomplishment. Procure a sufficient quantity of Fife Lace Yarn and a pair of No. 14 steel knitting needles; or Shetland Wool and No. 10 bone needles. Cast on a multiple of 26 stitches for each repetition of the pattern, and 5 additional stitches for edge stitches. **1st row**—Slip 1, knit 1, purl 1, * knit 25, purl 1, and repeat from * to the end of the row, and knit the last 2 stitches plain. **2nd row**—Slip 1, knit 2, * purl 25, knit 1, and repeat from * to the end, and knit the last 2 stitches plain. **3rd row**—Slip 1, knit 1, purl 1, * knit 2 together four consecutive times, knit 1, make 1 and knit 1 alternately eight times, knit 2 together four consecutive times, purl 1, and repeat from * to the end of the row, and knit the last 2 stitches plain. **4th row**—Slip 1, knit 2, * purl 25, knit 1, and repeat from * to the end, and knit the last 2 stitches plain. **5th row**—Slip 1, knit 1, purl 1, * knit 25, purl 1, and repeat from * to the end of the row, and knit the last 2 stitches plain. **6th row**—Slip 1, knit 2, * purl 25, knit 1, and repeat from * to the end, and knit the last 2 stitches plain. Repeat the pattern from the third row till the shawl or scarf is the required length, when cast off all the stitches. Finish the shawl or scarf with a pretty border, or tie in a knotted fringe.

CRESCENT PATTERN FOR A SHAWL OR SCARF.
(Not Illustrated.)

THIS elegant pattern looks well knitted with Fife Lace Yarn and a pair of No. 14 steel knitting needles; with Shetland wool and No. 11 needles; or with Andalusian wool and No. 8 bone needles. The crescents are arranged in stripes, and each stripe requires 20 stitches cast on loosely, also 5 additional stitches must be allowed for edge stitches. About 245 stitches cast on will make a good sized shawl; or 165 stitches for a scarf. **1st row**—Slip 1, knit

1, purl 1, * knit 9, purl 1, and repeat from *, and end with knit 2. **2nd row**—Slip 1, knit 2, * purl 9, knit 1, and repeat from *, and knit the last 2 stitches plain. **3rd row**—Slip 1, knit 1, purl 1, * knit 2, make 1, slip 1, knit 1, pass the slipped stitch over, make 1, knit 3, slip 1, knit 1, pass the slipped stitch over, purl 1, knit 2 together, knit 3, make 1, knit 2 together, make 1, knit 2, purl 1, and repeat from * to the end of the row, and knit the last 2 stitches plain. **4th row**—The same as the second row, and every alternate row is worked in the same manner. **5th row**—Slip 1, knit 1, purl 1, * knit 2 together, knit 1, make 1, knit 2, make 1, knit 2, slip 1, knit 1, pass the slipped stitch over, purl 1, knit 2 together, knit 2, make 1, knit 2, make 1, knit 1, slip 1, knit 1, pass the slipped stitch over, purl 1, and repeat from * to the end of the row, and knit the last 2 stitches plain. **7th row**—Slip 1, knit 1, purl 1, * knit 2 together, knit 1, make 1, knit 3, make 1, knit 1, slip 1, knit 1, pass the slipped stitch over, purl 1, knit 2 together, knit 3, make 1, knit 1, slip 1, knit 1, pass the slipped stitch over, purl 1, and repeat from * to the end of the row, and knit the last 2 stitches plain. **9th row**—Slip 1, knit 1, purl 1, * knit 2 together, make 1, knit 1, make 1, slip 1, knit 1, pass the slipped stitch over, knit 2, make 1, knit 1, slip 1, knit 1, pass the slipped stitch over, purl 1, knit 2 together, make 1, knit 2, knit 2 together, make 1, knit 1, make 1, slip 1, knit 1, pass the slipped stitch over, purl 1, and repeat from * to the end of the row, and knit the last 2 stitches plain. **10th row**—Slip 1, knit 2, * purl 9, knit 1, and repeat from *; and knit the last 2 stitches plain. Repeat from the third

row, and knit the last 2 stitches plain. **2nd row**—Slip 1, knit 1, purl all along to within 2 stitches of the end of the row, and knit those. **3rd row**—Slip 1, knit 1, * bring the wool to the front under the needle and purl the next three stitches together, pass the wool to the back under the needle and knit 1 and purl 1 and knit 1 in the next stitch, and repeat from * to the end of the row, and knit plain the last 2 stitches. **4th row**—Slip 1, knit 1, purl all along to within 2 stitches of the end of the row, and knit those. Repeat from the first pattern row till the shawl is a perfect square. Then finish with 4 plain rows, and cast off. The raised side of the knitting is the right side of the shawl. It may be bordered with a fringe, or with one of the pretty edgings illustrated on the foregoing pages.

PINE PATTERN FOR A SHAWL.
(Not Illustrated.)

THIS is a pretty striped pattern for a shawl, and each stripe is knitted to represent a series of "pines." Procure the finest Fife Lace Yarn and a pair of No. 14 steel knitting needles, or Shetland wool and No. 11 needles. The number of stitches to cast on will depend upon the size the shawl is required to be, 18 stitches are employed for working each stripe, and 2 stitches

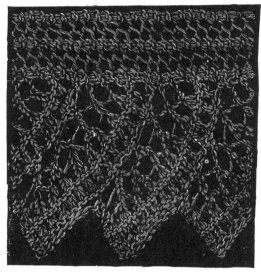

Wide Point Lace Border.

Belgrave Edging.

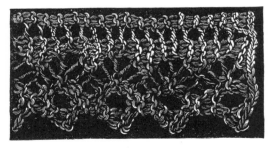

Cyprus Edging.

Willow Leaf Edging.

row till the shawl or scarf is the length required, when cast off loosely. Border the piece of work with one of the pretty edgings illustrated in the present issue of this Practical Work Series.

TRINITY STITCH FOR A SHAWL.
(Not Illustrated.)

THIS is a very pretty spotted stitch for a shawl. It will be effective knitted with the thickest make of Fife Lace Yarn and a pair of No. 4 bone knitting needles, or with Peacock fingering or Andalusian wool and the same sized needles. Cast on an even number of stitches, 200 will make a good-sized shawl that will require about 12 ozs. of wool. Begin by knitting 4 plain rows. **1st pattern row**—Slip 2, knit 1, * make 3 stitches out of the next stitch by first knitting 1, then purling 1, and then knitting 1 in it, bring the wool to the front under the needle and purl the next 3 stitches together, pass the wool to the back under the needle and knit 1 and purl 1 and knit 1 in the next stitch, bring the wool to the front under the needle and purl the next 3 stitches together, pass the wool to the back under the needle, and repeat from * to the end of the

additional should be cast on at each end of the needle for edge stitches to be knitted plain at the beginning and at the end of every row over and above the stitches detailed in the following directions. 234 stitches will suffice for knitting thirteen stripes, and will be a nice size for a shoulder shawl. Begin by knitting a plain row and a purl row. **1st pattern row**—Knit 1, make 1, knit 2 together, knit 12, slip 1, knit 1, pass the slipped stitch over, make 1, knit 1, and repeat to the end of the row. **2nd row**—Purl. **3rd row**—Knit 1, make 1, knit 2 together, knit 4, make 1, knit 2 together, knit 6, slip 1, knit 1, pass the slipped stitch over, make 1, knit 1, and repeat the same. **4th row**—Purl. **5th row**—Knit 1, make 1, knit 2 together, knit 2, knit 2 together, make 1, knit 1, make 1, knit 2 together, knit 5, slip 1, knit 1, pass the slipped stitch over, make 1, knit 1. **6th row**—Purl. **7th row**—Knit 1, make 1, knit 2 together, knit 1, knit 2 together, make 1, knit 3, make 1, knit 2 together, knit 4, slip 1, knit 1, pass the slipped stitch over, make 1, knit 1. **8th row**—Purl. **9th row**—Knit 1, make 1, knit 2 together, knit 2, make 1, knit 2 together, knit 1, knit 2 together, make 1, knit 5, slip 1, knit 1, pass the slipped stitch over, make 1, knit 1. **10th row**—Purl. **11th row**—Knit 1, make 1, knit 2 together, knit 2, make 1, knit 2 together, knit 1, knit 2 together, make 1, knit 2, make 1, knit 2 together, knit 1, slip 1, knit 1, pass the slipped stitch over, make 1, knit 1. **12th row**—Purl. **13th row**—Knit 1, make 1, knit 2 together, knit 1, slip 1, knit 1, pass the slipped stitch over, make 1, knit 2, knit 2 together, make 1, knit 2, make 1, knit 2 together, knit 1, slip 1, pass the slipped stitch over, make 1, knit 1. **14th row**—Purl. **15th row**—Knit 1, make 1, knit 2 together, knit 1, slip 1, knit 1, pass the slipped stitch over, make 1, knit 6, make 1, knit 2 together, knit 1, slip 1, knit 1, pass the slipped stitch over, make 1, knit 1. **16th row**—Purl. **17th row**—Knit 1, make 1, knit 2 together, knit 3, make 1, slip 1, knit 1, pass the slipped stitch over, make 1, knit 2 together, make 1, knit 3, slip 1, knit 1, pass the slipped stitch over, make 1, knit 1. **18th row**—Purl. **19th row**—Knit 1, make 1, knit 2 together, knit 4, make 1, slip 1, knit 1, pass the slipped stitch over, knit 2, make 1, knit 2 together, knit 2, slip 1, knit 1, pass the slipped stitch over, make 1, knit 1. **20th row**—Purl. **21st row**—Knit 1, make 1, knit 2 together, knit 5, make 1, slip 1, knit 2 together, pass the slipped stitch over, make 1, knit 4, slip 1, knit 1, pass the slipped stitch over, make 1, knit 1. **22nd row**—Purl. **23rd row**—Knit 1, make 1, knit 2 together, knit 12, slip 1, knit 1, pass the slipped stitch over, make 1, knit 1. **24th row**—Purl. Repeat from the first pattern row till the shawl is the length required. Cast off. This shawl may be bordered with one of the lace edgings illustrated in the present issue, or finished off with fringe according to taste.

A PRETTY SMALL DIAMOND PATTERN

FOR A SHAWL OR CLOUD.

(Not Illustrated.)

PROCURE the finest Fife Lace Yarn and a pair of No 14 steel knitting needles; or Shetland wool and No. 12 needles; or Andalusian wool and No. 10 needles; and cast on as many stitches as are required for the width of the shawl, allowing 6 stitches for each repetition on the pattern, and 5 stitches over for edge stitches. Begin by

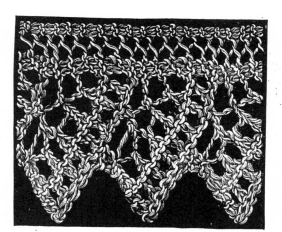

Narrow Point Lace Border.

Harebell Lace.

working a plain row, a purl row, and a plain row. **1st Pattern row**—Slip 1, knit 2, * knit 2 together, make 1, knit 1, make 1, knit 2 together, knit 1 and repeat from * to the end of the row, where knit the 2 last stitches plain. **2nd row**—Purl. **3rd row**—Slip 1, knit 1, knit 2 together, * make 1, knit 3, make 1, slip 1, knit 2 together, pass the slipped stitch over, and repeat from *; and when within 4 stitches of the end of the row, make 1, knit 2 together, knit 2. **4th row**—Purl. **5th row**—Slip 1, knit 2, * make 1, knit 2 together, knit 1, knit 2 together, make 1, knit 1, and repeat from *; and end by knitting the last 2 stitches plain. **6th row**—Purl. **7th row**—Slip 1, knit 3, * make 1, slip 1, knit 2 together, pass the slipped stitch over, make 1, knit 3, and repeat from *; and end by knitting the last stitch plain. **8th row**—Purl. Repeat from the first pattern row till the shawl or cloud is the length desired. Then knit a plain row, and a purl row, and cast off. Worked as above the shawl has a right side and a wrong side; it can be made both sides alike by substituting plain knitting in those rows which are directed to be purled. This makes a sweetly pretty shawl when worked in pale blue, coral pink, grey, or crimson wool, or it is very delicate and nice in white or cream wool. There are many pretty mixed wools now to be had, such as wool and silk, mossy looking wools, &c., all of which work up very effectively. It can be worked in two colours, doing so many rows of the one shade, and so many rows of another colour, or to render the shawl still more choice, add a lacy border of any depth desired, as there are a number of pretty designs in the present issue.

COBWEB STITCH FOR A SHAWL OR CLOUD.

(Not Illustrated.)

THIS is a pretty open stitch for a shawl, and may be knitted with the finest Fife Lace Yarn and a pair of No. 14 steel knitting needles, or with Shetland wool and No. 13 needles. Cast on any number of stitches divisible by 5 stitches over for edge stitches. Work 4 plain rows. **1st pattern row**—Slip 1, knit 1, knit 2 together, * make 1, knit 5, make 1, knit 3 together, and repeat from *; and at the end of the row, make 1, knit 5, make 1, knit 2 together, knit 2. **2nd row**—Slip 1, knit 3, * make 1, knit 2 together, knit 1, knit 2 together, make 1, knit 3, and repeat from * to the end of the row, where knit plain the last stitch. **3rd row**—Slip 1, knit 4, * make 1, knit 3 together, knit 2, knit 2 together, * make 1, knit 3, make 1, knit 2 together, * make 1, knit 3, make 1, knit 2 together, knit 1, knit 2 together, and repeat from *; and at the end of the row, make 1, knit 3, make 1, knit 2 together, knit 3. Repeat from the first pattern row for the length required. Then knit 4 plain rows, and cast off. The shawl may be bordered with any of the pretty edgings illustrated in the present number.

PRETTY OPEN STITCH FOR A SHAWL.

(Not Illustrated.)

REQUIRED, the finest Fife Lace Yarn and a pair of No. 14 steel knitting needles; or Shetland Wool and No. 12 needles. Cast on any number of stitches divisible by 3. **1st row**—Plain. **2nd row**—Purl. **3rd row**—Plain. **4th row**—Purl. **5th row**—Slip 1, knit 1, * make 2, knit 3 together, and repeat from * to the end, knitting the last stitch plain. **6th row**—Slip 1, purl 2, knit 1, * purl 2, knit 1, and repeat from * to the end, where purl the last 2 stitches. **7th row**—Plain. **8th row**—Purl. **9th row**—Plain. **10th**

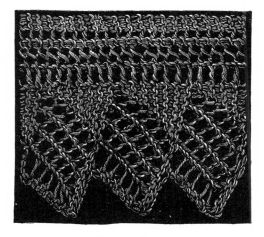

Coburg Lace.

row—Purl. **11th row**—Slip 1, knit 3, * make 2, knit 3 together, and repeat from * to the end, and knit the last 2 stitches plain. **12th row**—Slip 1, purl 3, knit 1, * purl 2, knit 1, and repeat from * to the end, where purl the last 4 stitches. **13th row**—Plain. **14th row**—Purl. **15th row**—Plain. **16th row**—Purl. **17th row**—Slip 1, knit 2, * make 2, knit 3 together, and repeat from * to the end, and knit the last 3 stitches plain. **18th row**—Slip 1, purl 4, knit 1, * purl 2, knit 1, and repeat from * to the end, where purl the last 3 stitches. **19th row**—Plain. **20th row**—Purl. **21st row**—Plain. **22nd row**—Purl. Repeat from the fifth row. Cast off when a sufficient length is knitted. Edge the shawl with the Irish Lace shown on page 11 and described on page 8.

CANADIAN CLOUD.

(Not Illustrated.)

SHETLAND Wool and knitting pins No. 6. Cast on 124 stitches, and knit 2 plain rows. **3rd row**—Slip 1, knit 3, knit 2 together, * make 1, knit 1, make 1, knit 2 together, knit 3, knit 2 together; repeat from *, and end the row with 3 plain. **4th row**—Plain. Repeat the third and fourth row 3 times. Knit 2 plain rows. **13th row**—Slip 1, knit 7, knit 2 together, * make 1, knit 1, make 1, knit 2 together, knit 3, knit 2 together; repeat from *, and end the row with 7 plain. **14th row**—Plain. Repeat the thirteenth and fourteenth rows 3 times. Knit 2 plain rows. Repeat from the third row for the length required, and cast off after having completed the twelfth row of the pattern. A cloud should be about two yards long, to go twice round the neck and once over the head. One end is to be drawn together and finished off with a large tassel, the other end may be fringed. Or if you like to have a lace along the sides of the cloud continue it round the end also. A pretty lace border for a cloud, shawl, &c., is made by casting on 19 stitches. **1st row**—Slip 1, knit 2, make 1, knit 2 together, knit 1, make 1 and knit 2 together six times, knit 1. **2nd row**—Slip 1, knit 2, purl 1 and knit 2 five times, purl 1, knit 3, make 1, knit 2 together, knit 1. **3rd row**—Slip 1, knit 2, make 1, knit 2 together, knit 20. **4th row**—Cast off 6, knit 15, make 1, knit 2 together, knit 1. Repeat from the first row.

GENTLEMAN'S COMFORTER.

(Not Illustrated.)

DECIDEDLY the best stitch for comforters is the Brioche stitch, as it is thick and elastic, and yet is alike on both sides. With single Berlin wool of any colour, and No. 9 needles, cast on any even number of stitches according to the width required; then work as follows—make 1, slip 1, putting the needle in front as if about to purl it, knit 1 all along. Every succeeding row is the same, excepting that when knitting 1 you will knit the stitch that was slipped in the preceding row and the thread that lies over it together. A comforter should be about two yards long, to go twice round the neck, and with ends to wrap over and cover the chest. Add a fringe at each end.

LADY'S CAP IN PUFFED KNITTING.

(Not Illustrated.)

MATERIALS required are ½ oz. of white single Berlin wool, 1 oz. of blue double Berlin wool. Knitting pins No. 11. With the white wool cast on 66 stitches, and knit 4 rows as follows: **1st row**—Plain. **2nd row**—Purl. **3rd row**—Plain. **4th row**—Purl. Then commence knitting with the blue wool. **1st row**—Knit 3, * wool over the needle, knit 1, wool over the needle, knit 1, wool twice over the needle, knit 1, wool twice over the needle, knit 1, wool once over the needle, knit 1, wool over the needle, knit 4; repeat from *. **2nd row**—The same as the preceding row, letting the wool that was passed round the needle slip off without being knitted, and this will form a series of graduated puffs. **3rd row**—The same, but purled instead of knitted. **4th row**—Same as the second row. The work is continued in alternate colours, 4 rows of white and 4 of blue; do not break off the wool, but carry it on from stripe to stripe. The blue is to be knitted in puffs (as above) throughout the cap, but when you have completed 3 stripes of each colour, the remaining white stripes are to be knitted with decreasings as follows, to bring the cap to shape; it slopes off from the ears, and forms a point at the back of the head. **1st row**—Knit 5, knit 2 together, continue knitting until you get to the middle of the row; then knit 2 together, and when 7 stitches from the end knit 2 together, knit 5. **2nd row**—Purl 5, purl 2 together, purl along to within 7 stitches from the end, then purl 2 together, purl 5. **3rd row**—Knit 5, knit 2 together, knit to within 7 stitches of the end, then knit 2 together, knit 5. **4th row**—The same as the second row. When you have knitted 9 stripes of each colour there will be only 12 stitches left, finish these off with white wool so as to form a point. **1st row**—Knit 3, knit 2 together three times, knit 3. **2nd row**—Purl. **3rd row**—Knit 2, knit 2 together, knit 1, knit 2 together, knit 2. **4th row**—Purl. **5th row**—knit 1, knit 2 together, knit 1, knit 2 together, knit 1. **6th row**—Purl. **7th row**—Knit 2 together, knit 1, pass the first stitch over the second, knit 2 together, pass the first stitch over the last, and fasten off. Add blue ribbon strings to tie under the chin, and a small bow on the point.

CROSS-STITCH KNITTING FOR A SHAWL OR CLOUD.

(Not Illustrated.)

USE single Berlin Wool and knitting pins No. 7. Cast on any number of stitches divisible by six, and 4 extra for edge stitches. **1st row**—Plain. **2nd row**—Plain. **3rd row**—Knit 3, twist the wool three times round the pin before knitting each succeeding stitch, and end the row by knitting the last stitch plain without making a twist. **4th row**—Knit 2, * let the twist slip off the left-hand needle, insert the right-hand needle in the knitted stitch as if about to purl it, and slip it on to the right-hand needle in one long loop, slip the next 5 stitches in the same way, and then with the left-hand needle lift the 3 first loops over the 3 last loops, and having all 6 in regular order on the left-hand pin, knit them plain one after the other; this forms a cross; repeat from *, and knit 2 at the end of the row. **5th row**—Plain. **6th row**—Plain. **7th row**—Knit 6, twist the wool three times round the pin before knitting each succeeding stitch, and end the row by knitting the last 4 stitches plain without making a twist. **8th row**—Knit 5, proceed as in the fourth row, and knit the last 5 stitches plain. Repeat from the first row for the length

required. When the shawl is large enough cast off after doing the sixth row A pretty border for a shawl or cloud is arranged by casting on 16 stitches. **1st row**—Slip 1, knit 3, make 1, knit 2 together, knit 1, make 2, knit 2 together, make 2, knit 2 together, knit 5. **2nd row**—Knit 7, purl 1, knit 2, purl 1, knit 3, make 1, knit 2 together, knit 2. **3rd row**—Slip 1, knit 3, make 1, knit 2 together, knit 12. **4th row**—Knit 14, make 1, knit 2 together, knit 2. **5th row**—Slip 1, knit 3, make 1, knit 2 together, knit 1, make 2, knit 2 together, make 2, knit 2 together, knit 5. **6th row**—Knit 7, purl 1, knit 2, purl 1, knit 2, purl 1, knit 3, make 1, knit 2 together, knit 2. **7th row**—Slip 1, knit 3, make 1, knit 2 together, knit 15. **8th row**—Cast off 5, knit 11, make 1, knit 2 together, knit 2. Repeat from the first row; and when a sufficient length is done sew it to the shawl, fulling it in round the corners.

SHAWL KNITTED WITH ARRASENE.

(Not Illustrated.)

ARRASENE wool, which may be had in white or any colour desired, is employed for this effective shawl; and for which the best size knitting needles are No. 6. Cast on as many stitches as are required for the width of the shawl, allowing 6 stitches for each pattern, and 6 over for edge stitches. Knit 4 plain rows. **5th row**—Knit 4, * knit 1, knit 2 together, make 1, knit 1, make 1, knit 2 together; repeat from *, and end the row with knit 4. **6th row**—Plain. **7th row**—Knit 5, * make 1, knit 3, make 1, slip 1, knit 2 together, pass the slip stitch over; repeat from *, and end the row with make 1, knit 2 together, knit 3. **8th row**—Plain. **9th row**—Knit 4, * make 1, knit 2 together, knit 1, knit 2 together, make 1, knit 1; repeat from *, end with knit 3. **10th row**—Plain. **11th row**—Knit 5, * make 1, slip 1, knit 2 together, pass the slip stitch over, make 1, knit 3; repeat from *, end with make 1, knit 5. **12th row**—Plain. Repeat from the fifth row until the shawl forms a perfect square. It is a small diamond pattern alike on both sides. Cut some arrasene into lengths of seven inches for fringe, and knot one piece into every row of the knitting.

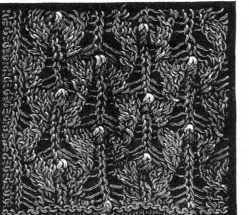

Pheasant's Eye Pattern for a Shawl.

CUFFS. BRIOCHE KNITTING.

THESE simple yet useful little articles are not illustrated. They merely require 1½ ozs. of red, ½ oz. of grey double Berlin wool, and knitting needles No. 10 size. Cast on 28 stitches with the red wool. **1st row**—Make 1, slip 1, putting the needle in as if about to purl, knit 1; repeat. **2nd row**—Make 1, slip 1, knit the next stitch and the thread that lies over it together; repeat. The whole of the cuff is worked as the second row. Knit 4 rows with the red wool, 4 with grey, 2 with red, 4 with grey, 12 with red, 4 with grey, 2 with red, 6 with grey, 2 with red, 4 with grey, 12 with red, 4 with grey, 2 with red, 4 with grey, 4 with red, and cast off. Sew the cuff up neatly, bringing the stripes together colour to colour.

FANCHON.

THIS pretty article is not illustrated, but owing to the explicit directions, no difficulty will be experienced in copying it. Use pink and white, blue and white, grey and pink, or red and grey Shetland wool, and knitting needles No. 16 and No. 10. This fanchon is knitted throughout in plain knitting; it covers the head, and has long ends to wind round the neck, thus making it both dressy and protective. Use No. 16 pins for the pink wool, and No. 10 pins for the white wool. Cast on 20 stitches with the pink wool, and knit 6 plain rows. Join on the white wool and knit 18 plain rows, increasing 1 stitch at the end of every alternate row by picking up the wool that lies under the second stitch from the end and knitting it. All the increasings are to come at the same side of the fanchon, and the two colours are to be repeated in this manner alternately until there are 9 pink stripes done. Then decreasings are to be made by knitting 2 stitches together at the end of every alternate white row, until there are 20 stitches again as at the commencement. Knit 6 rows with the pink wool, and cast off. Make four tassels, and sew two on each end of the fanchon.

CHILD'S KNITTED BALL.

THERE is no need to illustrate so simple an article as this little ball, and which can be made in any two bright well-contrasting colours preferred, such for instance, as black and amber, blue and white, red and black, &c., and of which 1 oz. of each colour will be necessary, using No. 14 knitting needles. The ball is composed of twelve sections of Brioche knitting arranged first by casting on 16 stitches with the black wool. **1st row**—Make 1, slip 1, putting the needle in as if about to purl, knit 1, and repeat to the end. **2nd row**—Make 1, slip 1, knit the next stitch and the thread that lies over it together; repeat six times, and leave 3 stitches unknitted. **3rd row**—The same, leaving 3 stitches unworked at the other end of the knitting. Turn, and work as before until you have only 2 ribs left to knit upon in the centre, knit these 2 ribs, turn, and knit all the stitches off, and then knit 2 whole rows of all the stitches. Join on the amber wool, knit 2 whole rows with it, and then repeat from the second row. When you have worked the twelve sections, cast off the stitches, and sew together along the ribs, drawing in at one end, and for the present leaving the other end open. Find a ball that will fit into the knitting, or stuff it with wadding, then draw up the end, and work a few fancy stitches on each end to imitate the little brown tufts of an orange.

WELDON'S
PRACTICAL KNITTER.

(FIFTEENTH SERIES.)

How to Knit Useful Articles for Ladies, Gentlemen, and Children.

TWENTY-SEVEN ILLUSTRATIONS.

Telegraphic Address—]
"Consuelo," London.]

The Yearly Subscription to this Magazine, post free to any Part of the World, is 2s. 6d.
Subscriptions are payable in advance, and may commence from any date and for any period.

[Telephone
2745.

The Back Numbers are always in print. Nos. 1 to 106 now ready, Price 2d. each, postage ½d. Over 5,000 Engravings.

HANDSOME WIDE MECHLIN LACE.

Our illustration shows a handsome wide Mechlin lace knitted with the finest make of Faudel, Phillips and Sons' Fife Lace Yarn, peacock quality, and a pair of No. 16 steel knitting needles, forming a very elegant pattern for a dress trimming, for the border of an apron, or any purpose for which a wide lace is desired. Cast on 60 stitches. Knit 1 plain row. **1st row**—Slip 1, knit 6, draw the 3 stitches knitted previous to the last stitch one by one over the last stitch, make 1, knit 7; make 1, knit 1 and purl 1 in the next stitch, knit 1, make 1, slip 1, knit 1, pass the slipped stitch over, purl 1, knit 2 together, slip 1, knit 2 together, pass the slipped stitch over, slip 1, knit 1, pass the slipped stitch over, purl 1, knit 2 together, make 1, knit 1, make 1, purl 1 and knit 1 in the next stitch; make 1, knit 7, draw the three stitches knitted previous to the last stitch over the last stitch, make 1, knit 9, knit 2 together; make 1, knit 2 together, make 1, knit 1, make 1, knit 2 together, make 1, knit 2 together, make 2, knit 2 together, knit 2. **2nd row**—Knit 4, purl 1, knit 1, purl 3, knit 14, knit 1 purl 1 and knit 1 in the loop that is formed by the made stitch of last row, knit 4, purl 6, knit 1, purl 1, knit 1, purl 1, knit 1, purl 6, knit 7, knit 1 purl 1 and knit 1 in the loop, knit 4. **3rd row**—Slip 1, knit 13, make 1, knit 5, make 1, slip 1, knit 2 together, pass the slipped stitch over, purl 1, knit 3 together, make 1, knit 5, make 1, knit 15, knit 2 together; make 1, knit 3, make 1, knit 2 together, make 1, knit 2 together, make 2, knit 1, make 1, knit 3. **4th row**—Knit 6, purl 1, knit 3, purl 5, knit 11, draw the 3 stitches knitted previous to the last stitch over the last stitch, make 1, knit 7, purl 8, knit 1, purl 8, knit 7, draw 3 stitches over, make 1, knit 7. **5th row**—Slip 1, knit 6, knit 1 purl 1 and knit 1 in the loop, knit 4, make 2, knit 1, slip 1, knit 1, pass the slipped stitch over, purl 1, knit 2 together, knit 1, make 1, slip 1, knit 2 together, pass the slipped stitch over, make 1, knit 1, slip 1, knit 1, pass the slipped stitch over, purl 1, knit 2 together, make 1, knit 2, knit 7, knit 1 purl 1 and knit 1 in the loop, knit 4, knit 2 together; make 1, knit 2 together, make 1, knit 5, make 1, knit 2 together, make 1, knit 2 together, make 2, knit 2 together, make 2, knit 2 together, knit 2. **6th row**—Knit 4, purl 1, knit 2, purl 1, knit 3, purl 7, knit 18, purl 3, knit 1, purl 7, knit 1, purl 3, knit 15. **7th row**—Slip 1, knit 6, draw 3 stitches over, make 1, knit 7; make 1, knit 1 and purl 1 in the next, knit 1, make 1, slip 1, knit 1, pass the slipped stitch over, purl 1, knit 2 together, slip 1, knit 2 together, pass the slipped stitch over, slip 1, knit 1, pass the slipped stitch over, purl 1, knit 2 together, make 1, knit 1, purl 1 and knit 1 in the next; make 1, knit 7, draw 3 stitches over, make 1, knit 8, make 1, knit 2 together; make 1, slip 1, knit 1, pass the slipped stitch over, knit 3, knit 2 together; make 1, knit 2 together, make 1, knit 2 together, make 2 and knit 2 together

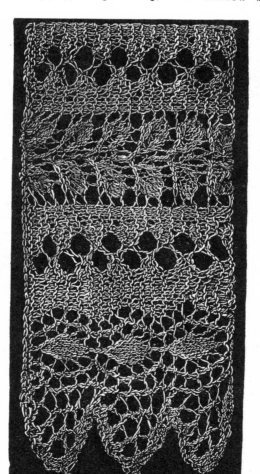

Handsome Wide Mechlin Lace.

three times, knit 1. **8th row**—Knit 3, purl 1, knit 2, purl 1, knit 2, purl 1, knit 4, purl 5, knit 11; knit 1 purl 1 and knit 1 in the loop, knit 4; purl 6, knit 1, purl 1, knit 1, purl 1, knit 1, purl 6; knit 7, knit 1 purl 1 and knit 1 in the loop, knit 4. **9th row**—Slip 1, knit 13, make 1, knit 5, make 1, slip 1, knit 2 together, pass the slipped stitch over, purl 1, knit 3 together, make 1, knit 5; make 1, knit 16, make 1, slip 1, knit 1, pass the slipped stitch over, make 1, slip 1, knit 1, pass the slipped stitch over, knit 1, knit 2 together; make 1, knit 2 together, make 1, knit 2 together, make 2 and knit 2 together four times, knit 2. **10th row**—Knit 4, purl 1, knit 2, purl 1, knit 2, purl 1, knit 2, purl 1, knit 4, purl 3; knit 12, draw 3 stitches over, make 1, knit 7; purl 8, knit 1, purl 8, knit 7, draw 3 stitches over, make 1, knit 7. **11th row**—Slip 1, knit 6, knit 1 purl 1 and knit 1 in the loop, knit 4; make 2, knit 1, slip 1, knit 1, pass the slipped stitch over, purl 1, knit 2 together, knit 1, make 1, slip 1, knit 2 together, pass the slipped stitch over, make 1, knit 1, slip 1, knit 1, pass the slipped stitch over, purl 1, knit 2 together, knit 1; make 2, knit 7, knit 1 purl 1 and knit 1 in the loop, knit 7, make 1, slip 1, knit 1, pass the slipped stitch over, make 1, slip 1, knit 2 together, pass the slipped stitch over, make 1, knit 2 together, make 1, knit 2 together, knit 14. **12th row**—Cast off 10 stitches, knit 7, purl 1, knit 21, purl 3, knit 1, purl 7, knit 1, purl 3, knit 15. Repeat from the first row for the length required.

AMERICAN OVER-SHOES,
OR BAG SLIPPERS.

These shoes, which are made exactly in the shape of a bag, are intended to draw over a kid boot for extra warmth when travelling. The Americans wear them over their boots for walking in frosty weather, as the roughness of the wool upon the icy ground is a sure preventive against slipping. They also are useful as bedroom slippers, and will fit quite closely on any sized foot by reason of the elasticity of the knitting. Our engravings show one slipper in actual wear drawn over a boot, and the other slipper as it appears in bag shape when off the foot. Procure 1½ ozs. of claret colour and ½ oz. of black good quality Scotch fingering, or single Berlin wool, and a pair of No. 12 steel knitting needles. Cast on 60 stitches with claret wool, and work in ribbing of 2 stitches plain and 2 stitches purl, for 30 rows. Take black wool, and work in the same ribbing for 12 rows. Resume claret, and continue ribbing for 50 rows, and cast off. Fold the knitting double, selvedge to selvedge. Sew the selvedges together to form the front of the shoe; and sew the cast-off stitches together, these will be in the centre of the sole. Fold the cast-on stitches inside to reach the top of the black knitting, and hem down. Make a bow and ends, or a rosette of ribbon to smarten the instep. Knit the other shoe in the same manner.

CABLE-KNIT BABY'S BOOT.

THESE are pretty nicely-fitting boots for a baby three or four months old. Our model boots are worked throughout with pale pink Andalusian wool, of which about 1 oz. will be required, and three No. 15 steel knitting needles, the third needle is used only for slipping the cable stitches and in knitting the shoe; if liked in two colours the sock can be knitted with white Andalusian and the shoe with pink or cardinal. Cast on 62 stitches for the scolloped edge at the top of the leg. **1st row**—Plain knitting. **2nd row**—Slip 1, knit 1, * make 1, slip 1, knit 2 together, pass the slipped stitch over, make 1, knit 2, and repeat from * to the end of the row. **3rd row**—Purl. Repeat the last two rows twice. This completes the edge, and now the **Cable** pattern begins. **1st row**—Slip 1, knit 1, * purl 2, knit 4, purl 2, knit 2, and repeat from * to the end of the row. **2nd row**—Slip 1, purl 1, * knit 2, purl 4, knit 2, purl 2, and repeat from * to the end. **3rd row**—Same as the first row. **4th row**—Same as the second row. **5th row**—Slip 1, knit 1, * purl 2, twist the cable, which is done thus: slip 2 stitches on to the spare pin, knit the 2 next stitches

American Over-Shoe as Worn.

replace the 2 slipped stitches on the left-hand needle and knit them, purl 2, knit 2, and repeat from * to the end. **6th row**—Slip 1, purl 1, * knit 2, purl 4, knit 2, purl 2, and repeat from * to the end. Repeat from the first row of the cable pattern five times, when thirty-six rows will be knitted. **37th row**—Same as the first row. **38th row**—Same as the second row. **39th row**—Knit plain 22 stitches (these 22 stitches should be knitted with coloured wool if the sock has been worked with white), then in cable pattern for the **Instep**, purl 2, knit 4, purl 2, knit 2, purl 2, knit 4, purl 2; turn the work, and slip 1, knit 1, purl 4, knit 2, purl 2, knit 2, purl 4, knit 2; turn the work, slip 1, purl 1, twist the cable, purl 2, knit 2, purl 2, twist the cable, purl 2; turn the work, and slip 1, knit 1, purl 4, knit 2, purl 2, knit 2, purl 4, knit 2; and turn, and continue the cable pattern on the 18 stitches for the instep for 14 more little rows. **Next row**—Holding the right side of the work towards you, slip 1, knit 2, knit 2 together, knit 1, knit 2 together, knit 2, knit 2 together, knit 1, knit 2 together, knit 3; now 14 instep stitches are on the needle. Knit 16 plain rows on the 14 instep stitches; then 8 plain rows, taking 2 stitches together at the end of each, and when the instep is reduced to 6 stitches break off the wool and let the 6 stitches remain on the left-hand needle by the side of the 22 stitches that have not yet been knitted. Now, holding the right side of the work towards you, resume with the right-hand needle where you have knitted 22 plain stitches, on the same needle, with coloured wool, pick up and knit 22 stitches along the side of the instep (11 stitches on the cable part and 11 on the plain part), knit 3 of the six toe stitches, take the spare needle, and knit the other 3 toe stitches, pick up and knit 22 stitches along the other side of the instep, and knit plain the 22 stitches that all this time have been remaining on the left-hand needle. Now there are 47 stitches on each of two needles for knitting the **Shoe**, 94 stitches in all. Keep them equally divided, and knit 9 plain rows from end to end of the 94 stitches. **10th row**—With the right side of the sock towards you, knit plain to within 4 stitches of the end of the first needle, knit 2 together, knit 2, on the second needle knit 2, knit 2 together, knit plain to the end. **11th row**—Plain. Repeat the last two rows five times. **22nd row**—Slip 1, knit 1, knit 2 together, knit 33, knit 2 together, knit 2, on next pin, knit 2, knit 2 together, knit 33, knit 2 together, knit 2. **23rd row**—Plain. **24th row**—Slip 1, knit 1, knit 2 together, knit 31, knit 2 together twice, on next pin knit 2 together twice, knit 31, knit 2 together, knit 2. **25th row**—Plain. Cast off all the stitches, and break off the wool with a long end. Join up the sole of the shoe, and sew up the leg. Knit the other boot to correspond.

GENTLEMAN'S CUFFS.

IN HONEYCOMB KNITTING.

REQUIRED, 1 oz. of white and ½ oz. of ruby single Berlin wool, and a pair of No. 14 steel knitting needles, or, if a large wrist, No. 13 needles. Cast on with ruby wool 40 stitches for the length of the cuff. **1st row**—Knit plain. **2nd row**—Take the white wool, knit 4 stitches, * slip 2 stitches on to the right-hand needle without knitting them, knit 4, and repeat from * to the end of the row. **3rd row**—Still with white wool—slip 1, purl 3, * slip the same two stitches that were slipped in the last row, taking them backwards so as not to twist them, purl 4, and repeat from * to the end. **4th row**—Slip 1, knit 3, * slip 2, knit 4, and repeat from * to the end. **5th row**—Same as the third row. **6th row**—With red wool—Knit plain 40 stitches. **7th row**—also with red wool—plain knitting. **8th row**—Resume white wool—knit 1 stitch, * slip 2, knit 4, and repeat from * ; and end the row with slip 2, knit 1; in this row the slipped stitches should always come intermediately between the stitches slipped in the previous rows. **9th row**—Slip the white stitch, * slip 2 red stitches, purl 4, and repeat from * ; and end the row with slip 2, purl 1. **10th row**—Slip 1 white stitch, * slip 2 red stitches, knit 4, and repeat from * ; and end the row with slip 2, knit 1. **11th row**—Same as the 9th row. **12th row**—With red wool—knit plain 40 stitches. **13th row**—Also with red wool—plain knitting. Repeat from the second row seven times. Then work from the second row to the twelfth row. Cast off. Sew the casting off to the cast on stitches, joining the honeycomb pattern evenly. For the **Edge**—With a No. 12 crochet needle and ruby wool, work round the top and bottom of the cuff. **1st round**—Plain double crochet, 1 double crochet on the seam, 1 double crochet on each perpendicular red line, 1 double crochet on the small white space of honeycomb, 2 double crochet on the largest white space of honeycomb, and join evenly at the end of the round. **2nd round**—1 double crochet on the first double crochet stitch of the previous round, 3 chain, * insert the hook in the next stitch of last round and draw the wool through, insert the hook in the next successive stitch of last round and draw the wool through, now 3 stitches on the needle, wool over the needle and draw through the three stitches, do 3 chain, and repeat from * to the end of the round, where join neatly and fasten off. Knit the other cuff in the same manner.

BABY'S SHETLAND VEST.

PROCURE 1½ ozs. of white Shetland wool, and a pair of No. 14 or No. 15 steel knitting needles. Cast on 78 stitches for the bottom of the vest. Work in ribbing—**1st row**—Knit 2, * purl 2, knit 2, and repeat from * to the end of the row. **2nd row**—Purl 2, * knit 2, purl 2, and repeat from * to the end. Continue these two rows till 20 rows are done. Always throughout the vest slip the first stitch in every row. **21st row**—Knit plain. **22nd row**—Purl. Repeat these two rows four times. **31st row**—Slip 1, knit 1, knit 2 together, knit plain to within 4 stitches of the end, knit 2 together, knit 2. **32nd row**

American Over-Shoe in Bag Shape.

—Purl. Knit a row plain and a row purl alternately for 6 rows. Repeat from the thirty-first row till reduced to 66 stitches on the needle. Work a row purl and a row plain for 25 rows, ending with a purl row. Cast on 8 stitches at the end of the purl row. **Next row**—Purl 18, knit 2, purl 2 and knit 2 alternately 11 times, purl 10, cast on 8. **2nd row**—Knit 18, purl 2, knit 2 and purl 2 alternately 11 times, knit 18. **3rd row**—Purl 18, knit 2, purl 2 and knit 2 alternately 11 times, purl 18. **4th row**—Same as the second row. **5th row**—Knit 20, purl 2, knit 2 and purl 2 alternately 10 times, knit 20. **6th row**—Purl 20, knit 2, purl 2 and knit 2 alternately 10 times, purl 20. **7th row**—Same as the fifth row. Repeat from the second row twice, when 19 rows will be done of the ridged knitting upon the sleeves and of the ribbing across the chest. **20th row**—Knit 18 stitches, knit 2 more, draw the last stitch but one over the last stitch, knit another stitch, and again draw a stitch over, and go on casting off till you have cast off the 46 ribbed stitches rather tightly, then knit plain to the end of the needle, 17 stitches, 1 stitch being already on the pin. **21st row**—Purl 18 sleeve stitches. **22nd row**—Knit 18 stitches. Then knit a row; purl a row; knit a row. And continue thus working in ridges for the shoulder, till you can count 8 raised ridges; knit 1 plain row, and cast off. Go to the other shoulder, and beginning at the neck end continue in ridges to correspond with the shoulder already worked; and cast off. Recommence with 78 stitches, and knit a similar piece for the back of the vest. Sew the shoulder pieces together. Sew up the under part of the sleeves and the sides of the vest. Crochet a little edging round the neck and sleeves,—1 double crochet in a depressed rib of the knitting, 2 chain, 3 treble in the same rib as the double crochet, and repeat. This completes the vest.

GENTLEMAN'S COTTON NIGHTCAP.

PROCURE 2 ozs. of Strutt's best white knitting cotton, No. 8, and a pair of No. 14 steel knitting needles, or No. 15 needles if a loose knitter or if the cap is required a small size. The cap is knitted in rows and is sewn up on completion. Cast on 156 stitches for the size round the head. Work in ribbing, 2 stitches plain and 2 stitches purl, for 26 rows for the band. Then do 1, purl row; 1 plain row; and 1 purl row. **1st Pattern row**—Slip 1, knit 1,

Cable-Knit Baby's Boot.

* make 1, knit 2 together, knit 11, and repeat from * to the end of the row, where there will be only 9 stitches to knit. **2nd row**—Purl. **3rd row**—Plain. **4th row**—Plain. Repeat these four rows four times. **21st row**—Slip 1, knit 1, * make 1, knit 2 together, knit 2 together, knit 9, and repeat from * to the end, where there will be only 7 stitches to knit; the holes in this row and the succeeding rows should come straight above the holes made previously. **22nd row**—Purl, 144 stitches on the needle. **23rd row**—Plain. **24th row**—Plain. **25th row**—Slip 1, knit 1, * make 1, knit 2 together, knit 10, and repeat from * to the end, where there will be 8 stitches to knit. **26th row**—Purl. **27th row**—Plain. **28th row**—Plain. **29th row**—Slip 1, knit 1, * make 1, knit 2 together, knit 8, and repeat from * to the end, where there will be 6 stitches to knit. **30th row**—Purl, 132 stitches on. **31st row**—Plain. **32nd row**—Plain. **33rd row**—Slip 1, knit 1, * make 1, knit 2 together, knit 9, and repeat from * to the end, where there will be 7 stitches to knit. **34th row**—Purl. **35th row**—Plain. **36th row**—Plain. **37th row**—Slip 1, knit 1, * make 1, knit 2 together, knit 2 together, knit 7, and repeat from * to the end, where there will be 5 stitches to knit. **38th row**—Purl, 120 stitches on. **39th row**—Plain. **40th row**—Plain. **41st row**—Slip 1, knit 1, * make 1, knit 2 together, knit 8, and repeat from * to the end, where there will be 6 stitches to knit. **42nd row**—Purl. **43rd row**—Plain. **44th row**—Plain. **45th row**—Slip 1, knit 1, * make 1, knit 2 together, knit 6, and repeat from * to the end, where there will be 4 stitches to knit. **46th row**—Purl, 108 stitches on. **47th row**—Plain. **48th row**—Plain. **49th row**—Slip 1, knit 1, *make 1, knit 2 together, knit 7, and repeat from * to the end, where there will be 5 stitches to knit. **50th row**—Purl. **51st row**—Plain. **52nd row**—Plain. **53rd row**—Slip 1, knit 1, * make 1, knit 2 together, knit 2 together, knit 5, and repeat from * to the end, where there will be 3 stitches to knit. **54th row**—Purl, 96 stitches on. **55th row**—Plain. **56th row**—Plain. **57th row**—Slip 1, knit 1, * make 1, knit 2 together, knit 6, and repeat from * to the end, where there will be 4 stitches to knit. **58th row**—Purl. **59th row**—Plain. **60th row**—Plain. **61st row**—slip 1, knit 1, * make 1, knit 2 together, knit 2 together, knit 4, and repeat from * to the end, where there will be 2 stitches to knit. **62nd row**—Purl, 84 stitches on. **63rd row**—plain. **64th row**—Plain. **65th row**—Slip 1, knit 1, * make 1, knit 2 together, knit 2 together, knit 3, and repeat from * to the end, where there will be 1 stitch to knit. **66th row**—Purl, 72 stitches on. **67th row**—Plain. **68th row**—Plain. **69th row**—Slip 1, knit 1, * make 1, knit 2 together, knit 2 together, knit 2, and repeat from * to the end. **70th row**—Purl, 60 stitches on. **71st row**—Plain. **72nd row**—Plain. **73rd row**—

Knit 2 together, knit 1, knit 2 together, and repeat the same to the end of the row. **74th row**—Purl, 36 stitches on. **75th row.**—Knit 2 stitches together all along; this will bring 18 stitches on the needle for the top of the cap; break off the cotton with a long end. Run the end of the cotton through the 18 stitches and tie it round in a circle. Join the side of the cap, making the ridged rows meet one another. Make a nice full cotton tassel, and place it on the point at the top of the cap. If it is preferred to knit the cap round like a stocking, without making a join, it can be done by using four needles and working in *rounds* instead of rows following the above instructions, but substituting plain knitting where directed to purl, and always purling the fourth round of the pattern to form the ridge on the right side of the work.

BABY'S SHORT-WAISTED JACKET.

THIS jacket comes down to the child's waist and affords sufficient protection to the chest and back, and as it opens all the way down the front it can readily be drawn on and off. It is knitted in a pretty fancy pattern. The back of the jacket is shown in the engraving. Required, 2 ozs. of white Peacock wool, or Andalusian, a pair of No. 11 bone knitting needles, 2 yards of inch-wide sarcenet ribbon, and four small pearl buttons. Commence for the bottom of the **Back** of the **Jacket** by casting on 58 stitches. Knit 4 plain rows. **5th row**—Slip 1, knit 1, * make 1, knit 2 together, and repeat from * to the end. **6th row**—Slip 1, purl 1, rib knit 2 and purl 2 alternately to the end. **7th row**—Slip 1, knit 1, rib purl 2 and knit 2 alternately to the end. **8th row**—Same as the sixth row. Repeat the two last rows till 13 rows of the ribbing are done. Then 1 plain row and 1 purl row. **21st row**—Beginning the pattern of the jacket—Slip 1, knit 1, * make 1, knit 2 together, and repeat from * to the end. **22nd row**—Plain. **23rd row**—Plain. **24th row**—Purl. Repeat the four pattern rows 10 times, making eleven lines of open holes. **65th row**—Slip 1, knit 1, rib purl 2 and knit 2 alternately to the end. **66th row**—Slip 1, purl 1, rib knit 2 and purl 2 alternately to the end. Repeat the two rows of ribbing 5 times, that is, till 12 rows are done. Then do 1 plain row and 1 purl row. This completes the back. Now work for the right **Shoulder**. **1st row**—Slip 1, knit 1, make 1 and knit 2 together 7 times, knit 1, turn the work. **2nd row**—Plain, 17 stitches. **3rd row**—Plain. **4th row**—Purl. Repeat these four rows till 30 little rows are done. Now the other stitches can be slipped for the present upon a spare pin unless you have another No. 11 needle at hand to work with. **Next row**—Beginning the Front—Knit the 17 shoulder stitches, and cast on 17 stitches for the right side front of the jacket. **Next row**—Knit plain the 17 cast on stitches, purl the 17 shoulder stitches, 34 stitches on the needle. **1st row of ribbing**—Slip 1, knit 1, rib purl 2 and knit 2 alternately 6 times, purl 2, knit 6. **2nd row**—Slip 1, knit 7, purl 2, knit 2 and purl 2 alternately to the end. Repeat these two rows till 12 rows of ribbing are done, but when you get to the edge stitches at the end of the seventh of these rows form a buttonhole by knitting 3 edge stitches, draw the last stitch but one over the last stitch, knit 1, draw another stitch over, knit the 2 last stitches; and in the next row cast on 2 stitches to replace those cast off. **13th row**—Plain. **14th row**—Knit 6, purl 28. **15th row**—Slip 1, knit 1, * make 1, knit 2 together, and repeat from * twelve times, knit 6. **16th row**—Plain. **17th row**—Plain. **18th row**—Knit 6, purl 28. Repeat the last four rows 10 times, *i.e.,*

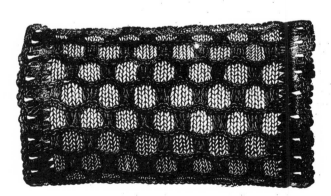

Gentleman's Cuff in Honeycomb Knitting.

till eleven lines of open holes are done, and form a buttonhole at intervals of every twelve rows. **59th row**—Slip 1, knit 1, rib purl 2 and knit 2 alternately 6 times, purl 2, knit 6. **60th row**—Slip 1, knit 7, purl 2, knit 2 and purl 2 alternately to the end. Repeat these two rows till 12 rows of ribbing are done. **Next row**—Slip 1, knit 1, * make 1, knit 2 together, and repeat from * twelve times, knit 6. Knit 4 plain rows. Cast off. *Resume* where you divided for the shoulder, and cast off 24 stitches across the back of the jacket, knit 2 stitches, now you have 3 stitches on the right-hand needle and 15 stitches on the left-hand needle, make 1 and knit 2 together 7 times. **2nd row** of the shoulder—Plain, 17 stitches. **3rd row**—Plain. **4th row**—Purl. Continue the open pattern to correspond with the first shoulder till 30 little rows are done, and at the end of the thirtieth row cast on 17 stitches; now 34 stitches on the needle. **Next row**—Plain. **Next row**—Purl. **Next row**—Beginning on the front edge—Knit 6, and rib purl 2 and knit 2 alternately to the end. **2nd row**—Purl 2 and knit 2 alternately 6 times, purl 2, knit 8. Repeat these two rows till 12 rows of ribbing are done. **13th row**—Plain. **14th row**—Purl 28, knit 6. **15th row**—Knit 6, make 1 and knit 2 together to the end.

16th row—Plain. **17th row**—Plain. **18th row**—Purl 28, knit 6. Repeat the last four rows 10 times, *i.e.*, till eleven lines of open holes are knitted. **59th row**—Knit 6, rib purl 2 and knit 2 alternately to the end. **60th row**—Purl 2 and knit 2 alternately 6 times, purl 2, knit 8. Repeat these two rows till 12 rows of ribbing are done. **Next row**—Knit 6, make 1 and knit 2 together to the end. Knit 4 plain rows. Cast off. For the **Sleeves**—Pick up along the edge of the armhole, that is, across the two upper lines of ribbing and along the intermediate shoulder rows of open work, 40 stitches, knitting each stitch as you pick it up. **2nd row**—Purl. **3rd row**—Slip 1, knit 1, * make 1, knit 2 together, and repeat from * to the end. **4th row**—Plain. **5th row**—Knit 2 together at the beginning, knit plain along, and knit 2 together at the end. **6th row**—Purl 2 together at the beginning, purl along, and purl 2 together at the end ; now 36 stitches on the needle. **7th row**—Slip 1, knit 1, * make 1, knit 2 together, and repeat from * to the end. **8th row**—Plain. **9th row**—Plain. **10th row**—Purl. Repeat the last four rows 9 times, when eleven lines of open rows will be knitted. Work 16 rows of ribbing for the wrist, and cast off rather loosely. Knit the other sleeve in the same manner. Sew the sleeves up, and sew up the sides of the jacket. For the **Crochet Edge** round the **Neck**—**1st row**—Work plain double crochet, missing a stitch occasionally to draw the neck in a little. **2nd row**—Turn with 5 chain, miss one double crochet, 1 treble on the next, * 1 chain, miss one stitch, 1 treble on the next, and repeat from *. **3rd row**—Turn the work, do 1 double crochet in the first space, 3 treble in the same place, * 1 double crochet in the next space, 4 treble in the next space, and repeat from * to the end of the row, and fasten off. Put four pearl buttons down the left front of the jacket. Divide the ribbon into two pieces, and run one piece through the treble stitches at the neck, and the other piece through the holes at the waist, and tie the ends in pretty bows in front.

LADY'S VEST.

Worked in a New Wedge Pattern.

Our engraving shows a lady's vest knitted in a handsome wedge pattern, and nicely shaped to the figure. Required, 7 ozs. of unshrinkable vest wool, Peacock quality, and a pair of No. 9 bone knitting needles. Begin for the **Back of the Vest**, for which cast on 98 stitches. Always slip the first stitch in every row. **1st row**—Knit 1, purl 6, and repeat the same to the end. **2nd row**—Knit 5, purl 2, and repeat. **3rd row**—Knit 3, purl 4, and repeat. **4th row**—Knit 3, purl 4, and repeat. **5th row**—Knit 5, purl 2, and repeat. **6th row**—Knit 1, purl 6, and repeat. **7th row**—Plain knitting. **8th row**—Knit 6, purl 1, and repeat. **9th row**—Knit 2, purl 5, and repeat. **10th row**—Knit 4, purl 3, and repeat. **11th row**—Knit 4, purl 3, and repeat. **12th row**—Knit 2, purl 5, and repeat. **13th row**—Knit 6, purl 1, and repeat. **14th row**—Purl all along. These fourteen rows are repeated throughout the vest. The first decrease takes place in the fourteenth row, a plain row, when you should take 2 stitches together at the beginning and 2 stitches together at the end of the row ; the first and the last wedge in the six following rows will, therefore, be minus 1 stitch, but the other wedges will not be affected, and must be carried on in a straight perpendicular line, as you will see by the work already done. The second decrease is made in the twenty-eighth row, a purl row, when you will purl 2 stitches together at the beginning and at the end of the row ; this will bring the first and the last wedge each minus 2 stitches in knitting the following rows, but the other wedges will consist each of 7 stitches as before, and must be kept in perpendicular line. Decrease in the same way in further repeats of the pattern, always in the plain row and in the purl row, until seven decreases have been made, when you will have 84 stitches on the needle, and the pattern will again work evenly, as in the fourteen commencing rows, one entire stripe of wedges being knitted out on each side. Continue therefore straight on in pattern until you can count 27 wedges, 189 rows from the beginning. **190th row**—Which is a repetition of the eighth row of the pattern,—Work 28 stitches in pattern ; knit 2 stitches, draw the stitch before the last over the last stitch, knit 1, draw over another stitch, and proceed till 28 stitches are cast off ; then knit in pattern to the end of the row. Continue working in pattern on the 28 shoulder stitches, taking 2 stitches together at the neck end in every row, till reduced to 21 stitches, when cast off. Shape the other 28 stitches for the other shoulder, and cast them off. This finishes the back of the vest. For the **Front of the Vest**—Recommence with 98 stitches, and work exactly the same as the back until you can count 17 wedges, 119 rows from the beginning ; there should be 84 stitches on the needle. The **Gussets** must now be commenced. **120th row**—Which is a repetition of the eighth row of the pattern,—Work 21 stitches in pattern, increase 1, work 42 stitches in pattern, increase 1, work 21 stitches in pattern. **121st row**—Work 21 stitches in pattern, increase 1, knit 1, increase 1, work 42 stitches in pattern, increase 1, knit 1, increase 1, work 21 stitches in pattern. **122nd row**—You will now discern the position of the gussets, the wedge pattern stripes continuously follow the preceding instructions, and need not be alluded to any further ; in this row there are 3 gusset stitches, and you knit 2 stitches and

Baby's Shetland Vest.

purl 1 stitch in each gusset. **123rd row**—In the gussets, increase 1, knit 2, purl 1, increase 1. **124th row**—Gussets, knit 1, purl 4. **125th row**—Gussets, increase 1, knit 4, purl 1, increase 1. **126th row**—Purl all. **127th row**—Gussets, increase 1, knit 1, purl 6, increase 1. **128th row**—Gussets, purl 1, knit 5, purl 2, knit 1. **129th row**—Gussets, increase 1, purl 1, knit 3, purl 4, knit 1, increase 1. **130th row**—Gussets, purl 2, knit 3, purl 4, knit 2. **131st row**—Gussets, increase 1, purl 2, knit 5, purl 2, knit 2, increase 1. **132nd row**—Gussets, purl 3, knit 1, purl 6, knit 1, purl 2. **133rd row**—Gussets, increase 1, knit 13, increase 1. **134th row**—Gussets, knit 3, purl 1, knit 6, purl 1, knit 4. **135th row**—Gussets, increase 1, purl 4, knit 2, purl 5, knit 2, purl 2, increase 1. **136th row**—Gussets, knit 2, purl 3, knit 4, purl 3, knit 4, purl 1. **137th row**—Gussets, increase 1, knit 2, purl 3, knit 4, purl 3, knit 4, purl 1, increase 1. **138th row**—Gussets, knit 1, purl 5, knit 2, purl 5, knit 2, purl 4. **139th row**—Gussets, increase 1, knit 5, purl 1, knit 6, purl 1, knit 5, purl 1, increase 1. **140th row**—Purl all the row, there are now 21 stitches across each gusset. **141st row**—Here the gussets begin to decrease, and here also commences the opening in the front of the vest.—Work 21 stitches in wedge pattern, on gusset knit 2 together, purl 5, knit 1, purl 6, knit 1, purl 4, slip 1, knit 1, pass the slipped stitch over, work 21 stitches in wedge pattern on the front of the vest, cast on 7 stitches for edge stitches ; turn the work, you may slip the stitches belonging to the other side of the first on to a spare needle till wanted. **2nd row** of **Front**—Knit 6 edge stitches, purl 1, work 21 stitches in wedge pattern, on gusset knit 4, purl 2, knit 5, purl 2, knit 5, purl 1, work 21 stitches in wedge pattern. **3rd row**—Work 21 stitches in wedge pattern, on gusset knit 2 together, purl 4, knit 3, purl 4, knit 3, purl 1, slip 1, knit 1, pass the slipped stitch over, work 21 stitches in wedge pattern, knit plain 7 edge stitches. **4th row**—Knit 6 edge stitches, purl 1, work 21 stitches in wedge pattern, on gusset knit 1, purl 4, knit 3, purl 4, knit 3, purl 2, work 21 stitches in wedge pattern. Proceed in this manner, always decreasing on each side of the gusset in each forward row, till the gusset is quite knitted out, and you find 49 stitches on the needle, inclusive of the 7 edge stitches. Work four more wedge patterns. Then to form the **Neck**—Cast off 14 stitches at the beginning of a row on the plain edge side, and continuing in pattern take 2 stitches together at the neck end in every row, till reduced to 21 stitches, when cast off. Work the other half of the front to correspond, and make a buttonhole in every fourteenth row of the plain edge. Sew up the shoulder pieces, and join the sides of the vest leaving space for armholes. Sew the cast on edge stitches to lie smoothly over the front of the knitting. For the **Sleeves**—Cast on 56 stitches, and work in ribbing 2 stitches plain and 2 stitches purl, for 16 rows. At the end of the sixteenth row cast on 21 stitches, now 77 stitches on the needle. Work 21 rows of the wedge pattern, and cast off loosely. Commence the other sleeve with 56 stitches, and work in ribbing for 15 rows, when cast on 21 stitches, and knit 21 rows of the wedge pattern, and cast off. The difference of one row in the ribbing brings the gusset of the second sleeve on the opposite side to the first, so that when the gusset is folded and the sleeves sewn up, they will fit right and left into the vest. The gusset seams should be put against the back of the vest. For the **Crochet Edging** round the **Neck**—Do 1 double crochet in a stitch of the knitting, miss two stitches, 5 treble in the next, miss two stitches, and repeat the same. Make a crochet chain to run through the openings in the crochet, to tie the vest round the neck, and put tassels on each end. Sew small pearl buttons up the front edge to fasten into the buttonholes.

LADY'S PETTICOAT.

Knitted in Cable Plait and Ridged Stitch.

A very elegant petticoat for a lady can be worked in two breadths in cable plait knitting and ridged stitch, as shown in the engraving. Required, 14 ozs. of white Peacock fingering wool, and a pair of long bone knitting needles, No. 9. Cast on 277 stitches for the front breadth. **1st row**—Knit plain. **2nd row**—Purl. **3rd row**—Plain. **4th row**—Slip 1, * make 1, knit 4, slip 1, knit 2 together, pass the slipped stitch over, knit 4, make 1, knit 1, and repeat from * to the end. **5th row**—Purl. Repeat the two last rows four times ; this forms the border. **14th row**—Slip 1, * purl 3, knit 2, knit 2 together, knit 1, purl 3, knit 1, and repeat from * to the end : the stitches are now reduced to 254 on the needle. **15th row**—Slip 1, * knit 3, purl 4, knit 3, purl 1, and repeat from * to the end. **16th row**—Begins the cable pattern—Slip 1, * purl 3, knit 4, purl 3, knit 1, and repeat from * to the end of the row. **17th row**—Slip 1, * knit 3, purl 4, knit 3, purl 1, and repeat from * to the end. **18th row**—Same as the sixteenth row. **19th row**—Same as the seventeenth row. **20th row**—Slip 1, * purl 3, slip the 2 next stitches on to a spare needle, knit the 2 following stitches, put the 2 stitches from off the spare needle back again upon the left-hand needle and knit them, which twists the cable, purl 3, knit 1, and repeat from * to the end. **21st row**—Slip 1, * knit 3, purl 4, knit 3, purl 1, and repeat from * to the end. Repeat from the sixteenth row, till eight twists of the cable plait are knitted. **64th row**—Slip 1, * purl 1, purl 2 together, knit 1, knit 2 together, knit 1, purl 2 together, purl 1, knit 1, and repeat from * to the end of the row, and the stitches are now reduced to 198 for knitting the upper portion of the skirt. **65th row**—Slip 1, * knit 2, purl 3, knit 2, purl 1, and repeat from * to the end. **66th row**—Begins the ridged pattern—Slip 1, * purl 3, knit 1, and repeat from * to the end. **67th row**—Slip 1, purl 1, knit 1, * purl 3, knit 1, and repeat from * to the end of the row, which finishes with 2 stitches purl. Repeat the last two rows till a length of from 16 inches to 18 inches is knitted of this ridged pattern. For the **Waist**—Beginning with the right side of the skirt towards you—**1st row**—Slip 1, knit 1, * purl 2 together, knit 2, and repeat from * to the end, where there will be 1 stitch only to knit. **2nd row**—Slip 1, * knit 1, purl 2, and repeat from * to the end; and there are now 145 stitches on. **3rd row**—Knit 2, purl 1, and repeat the same to the end of the row, where there will be 1 stitch to knit. **4th row**—Slip 1, * knit 1, purl 2, and repeat from * to the end. Repeat the two last rows till you have done about 28 rows of ribbing for the waist, and then cast off rather tightly. Recommence for the back breadth by casting on 277 stitches, and work the same as instructed for the front till you get about half-way up the ridged knitting; then, in the forward row, knit in the ridged pattern till you get 97 stitches on the right-hand needle, turn the work, and knit back in pattern, and continue on these stitches till you have accomplished the required length of ridged knitting, when proceed to the ribbing, doing the same number of rows as are on the front of the petticoat, and cast off. The

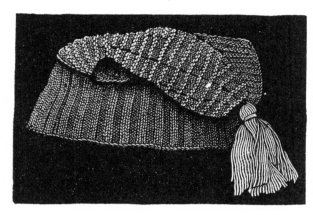

Gentleman's Cotton Nightcap.

opening is for a placket. Cast 8 stitches on the right-hand needle, and work remaining stitches off the left-hand needle, thus, * purl 3, knit 1, and repeat from * to the end. **Next row**—Slip 1, purl 1, knit 1, * purl 3, knit 1, and repeat from * till within 9 stitches of the end, when purl 2, knit 7. **Next row**—Slip 1, knit 7, * purl 3, knit 1, and repeat from * to the end. **Next row**—Slip 1, purl 1, knit 1, * purl 3, knit 1, and repeat from * till within 9 stitches of the end, when purl 2, knit 7. Continue working the last two rows till sufficient is done of the ridged pattern; and then go on to the ribbing, always working the 7 edge stitches plain in every row; and when this side of the placket is the same length as the other side, cast off all the stitches. A straight band of calico may be sewn either on the top, or at the back of the ribbing, for a waistband, or the petticoat can be secured by a ribbon run through the ribbing to tie round the waist.

PETTICOAT FOR GIRL OF FIVE TO SEVEN YEARS.

THIS stylish garment consists of a petticoat and bodice combined; the petticoat is knitted in a pretty ridged pattern, edged round the bottom with an insertion and a scolloped border; a repetition of the insertion forms a waistband; and the bodice is simply worked in ribs, with a line running across at intervals to mark the number of rows; the neck is nicely rounded to shape, and the sleeves correspond with the insertion and border. Our model is knitted with 7 ozs. of the best white Scotch Fingering and a pair of No. 10 bone knitting needles, and is of a size to fit a girl of from five to seven years. If the same instructions be followed with Petticoat yarn and No. 9 needles the garment will be large enough for an older child. Or a nice skirt can be made for a girl of twelve by using 3 thread Fleecy wool and No. 9 needles, and casting off the stitches on the completion of the waistband. Begin by casting on 171 stitches for the **Front Breadth** of the petticoat, and knit plain along. **1st row** of the **Border**—Slip 1, * make 1, knit 3, knit 3 together, knit 3, make 1, knit 1, and repeat from * to the end of the row. **2nd row**—Purl. **3rd row**—Same as the first row. **4th row**—Plain. Repeat these four rows four times. **21st row**—Slip 1, * make 1, knit 3, knit 3 together, knit 3, make 1, knit 1, and repeat from * to the end. **22nd row**—Purl. **23rd row**—Slip 1, knit 2, * slip 1, knit 1, pass the slipped stitch over, knit 1, knit 2 together, knit 5, and repeat from * to the end of the row, where there will be only 3 stitches to knit. **24th row**—Plain knitting; the border is finished, and the insertion is begun, and there should now be 137 stitches on the needle. **25th row**—Purl. **26th row**—Plain; these last three rows make a raised ridge on the right side of the petticoat. **27th row**—Plain; still 137 stitches on the needle. **28th row**—Slip 1, knit 1, purl 3, * knit 3, purl 3, and repeat from * to the end. **29th row**—Slip 1, * knit 3, purl 3; repeat from *; and end with knit 3, purl 1. **30th row**—Slip 1, purl 2, * knit 3, purl 3; repeat from *; and end with 2 stitches knit plain. **31st row**—The same as last row. **32nd row**—Slip 1, * knit 3, purl 3; repeat from *; and end with knit 3, purl 1.

33rd row—Slip 1, knit 1, purl 3, * knit 3, purl 3, and repeat from * to the end. **34th row**—The same as last row. **35th row**—Plain. **36th row**—Plain. **37th row**—Purl. **38th row**—Plain; the last three rows make a raised ridge on the right side of the petticoat, and this is the completion of the insertion. **39th row**—Plain; still 137 stitches on the needle. **40th row**—Purl. **41st row**—Beginning of the ridged pattern for the **Skirt**—Slip 1, knit 1, * purl 1, knit 3; repeat from *, and end with purl 1, knit 2. **42nd row**—Slip 1, * knit 3, purl 1, and repeat from * to the end of the row. Repeat the last two rows till 60 rows of the ridged pattern are knitted, keeping always 137 stitches on the needle. Now 100 rows are done from the commencement of the border, and if the skirt is required longer a few additional rows can be added. **101st row**—To decrease to shape the waist, rib as follows—Slip 1, knit 1, purl 2 together, * knit 2, purl 2 together; repeat from *, and there will be 1 plain stitch to knit at the end of the row; now 103 stitches on the needle. **102nd row**—Slip 1, * knit 2, purl 1, and repeat from * to the end. **103rd row**—Slip 1, * purl 2, knit 1, and repeat from *. **104th row**—Slip 1, * knit 2, purl 1, and repeat from * to the end. Repeat the last two rows till 14 rows of ribbing are accomplished, when there still should be 103 stitches on the needle. **Next row**—is a decrease row—Slip 1, knit 3, then knit 2 together and knit 1 alternately till you get to the last 3 stitches which knit plain; there should now be 71 stitches on the needle. For the **Waistband**—Work the insertion, beginning at the twenty-fourth row and continuing to the thirty-eighth row. For the **Front** of the **Bodice**—**1st row**—Plain knitting, 71 stitches on the needle. **2nd row**—Purl. **3rd row**—Ribbing, always slip the first stitch of every row—Purl 2, knit 1, and repeat the same, and end the row with 2 purl stitches. **4th row**—Knit 2, purl 1, and repeat the same, and end the row with 2 plain stitches. Repeat the last two rows twice. **9th row**—Purl 2, knit 1, and repeat the same, and end the row with 2 purl stitches. **10th row**—Plain. Repeat from the third row to the tenth row seven times, i.e., 64 rows in all of the ribbing, and eight plain lines will be seen running across the surface of the work. For the **First Shoulder**—**1st row**—Purl 2 and knit 1 alternately 7 times, purl 2 together; turn the work, knit 2 together, knit 2, * purl 1, knit 2, and repeat from * to the end. **3rd row**—Purl 2 and knit 1 alternately 6 times, purl 1, purl 2 together; turn the work, knit 2 together, * purl 1, knit 2, and repeat from * to the end. **5th row**—Purl 2 and knit 1 alternately 5 times, purl 2, purl 2 together; turn the work, knit 2 together, knit 1, * purl 1, knit 2, and repeat from * to the end. **7th row**—Purl 2 and knit 1 alternately 5 times, purl 2 together; turn the work, knit 2 together, knit 14. **9th row**—Purl 2 and knit 1 alternately 4 times, purl 1, purl 2 together; turn the work, knit 2, * purl 1, knit 2, and repeat from * to the end. **11th row**—Purl 2 and knit 1 alternately 4 times, purl 2; turn the work, knit 2, * purl 1, knit 2 and repeat from * to the end. **13th row**—Purl

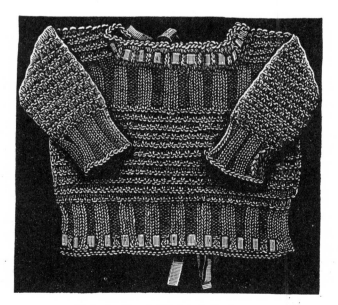

Baby's Short-Waisted Jacket.

2 and knit 1 alternately 4 times, purl 2; turn the work, knit 2, * purl 1, knit 2, and repeat from * to the end. **15th row**—Purl 2 and knit 1 alternately 4 times, purl 2; turn the work, knit 14. Cast off 14 stitches, and break off the wool. Resume where you divided for the shoulder, and cast off 27 stitches rather tightly along the front of the body, then for the **Other Shoulder**—Purl 1, knit 1, and purl 2 alternately 7 times. **2nd row**—Knit 2 and purl 1 alternately 7 times, knit 2 together; turn the work, purl 2 together, purl 2, * knit 1, purl 2, and repeat from * to the end. **4th row**—Knit 2 and purl 1 alternately 6 times, knit 1, knit 2 together; turn the work, purl 2 together, * knit 1, purl 2, and repeat from * to the end. **6th row**—Knit 2 and purl 1 alternately 5 times, knit 2, knit 2 together; turn the work, purl 2 together, purl 1, * knit 1, purl 2, and repeat from * to the end. **8th row**—Knit 15, knit 2 together; turn the work, purl 2 together, purl 2, * knit 1, purl 2, and repeat from * to the end. **10th row**—Knit 2 and purl 1 alternately 4 times, knit 1, knit 2 together; turn the work, purl 2, * knit 1, purl 2, and repeat from * to the end. **12th row**—Knit 2 and purl 1 alternately 4 times, knit 2; turn the work, purl 2, * knit 1,

purl 2 and repeat from * to the end. **14th row**—Knit 2 and purl 1 alternately 4 times, knit 2; turn the work, purl 2, * knit 1, purl 2, and repeat from * to the end. **16th row**—Knit 14 stitches; turn the work, cast off the 14 stitches, and break off the wool. For the **Back Breadth** of the petticoat—Cast on 171 stitches, and work the same as the front breadth till you have done 46 rows of the ridged pattern. Then **next row**—Work up to 69 stitches only, so as to divide the knitting into two pieces to form a placket, cast on 2 stitches, and turn, and knit 2, purl 1, * knit 3, purl 1, and repeat from * to the end. Continue the ridged pattern on the 69 stitches and always knit the 2 extra stitches plain, till the full complement of 60 ridged rows are worked, making 100 rows in all from the commencement of the border. **101st row**—To decrease to shape the waist—Slip 1, knit 1, purl 2 together, * knit 2, purl 2 together, and repeat from *, and end by knitting 2 plain stitches; now there are 54 stitches on the needle. **102nd row**—Slip 1, knit 1, purl 1, * knit 2, purl 1, and repeat from * to the end. Continue the ribbing, keeping the 2 extra stitches for a plain edge, till 14 rows of ribbing are accomplished the same as on the front breadth. **Next row**—is a decrease row—Slip 1, then knit 2 together and knit 1 alternately till you get to the 2 last stitches which knit plain; now 37 stitches on the needle. For the **Waistband**—Work the insertion as directed from the twenty-fourth row to the thirty-eighth row, still always doing the 2 extra stitches plain. Now work for the **Back** of the **Body—1st row**—Plain, 37 stitches. **2nd row**—Knit 7, purl the remainder. **3rd row**—Purl 2, knit 1, and repeat the

together, * knit 2, purl 2 together, and repeat from *, and there will be 1 plain stitch to knit at the end of the row; now 57 stitches on the needle. **102nd row**—Slip 1, * knit 2, purl 1, and repeat from * to within 2 stitches of the end which knit plain. Continue ribbing till 14 rows are accomplished. **Next row**—is a decrease row—Slip 1, knit 2, then knit 2 together and knit 1 alternately to the end; now 39 stitches on the needle. Work for the **Waistband** as instructed from the twenty-fourth row to the thirty-eighth row, but decrease 2 stitches in the course of the plain row that there may be 37 stitches in the row to bring the pattern in evenly, allowing for 2 edge stitches to be always knitted plain by the placket. Next, work for the **Back** of the **Body—1st row**—Plain, 37 stitches. **2nd row**—Purl to within 7 stitches of the end, and knit those. **3rd row**—Knit 5, purl 2, knit 1 and purl 2 alternately to the end. **4th row**—Knit 2 and purl 1 alternately till within 7 stitches of the end, and knit those plain. Repeat the last two rows twice. **9th row**—Knit 5, purl 2, knit 1 and purl 2 alternately to the end. **10th row**—Plain. Repeat from the third row to the tenth row seven times. There are no buttonholes on this side the body. When 64 rows are done, cast off the first 14 stitches of the next row, then purl 1, and knit 1 and purl 2 alternately 7 times, and proceed to shape the shoulder by the instructions given for the second front shoulder, and cast off. For the **Sleeves**. Cast on 61 stitches, and knit plain along. Work the first 12 rows of the border. **13th row**—Slip 1, * make 1, knit 3, knit 3 together, knit 3, make 1, knit 1, and repeat

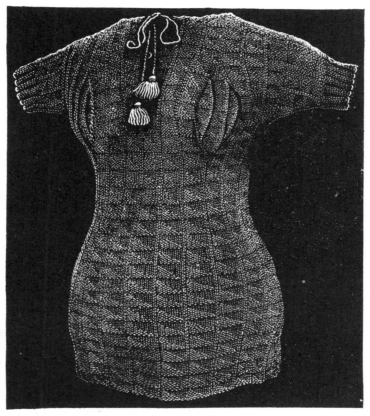

Lady's Vest, Worked in the New Wedge Pattern.

Lady's Petticoat, Knitted in

same, and end with purl 2, knit 5. **4th row**—Knit 7, purl 1, and knit 2 alternately to the end. Repeat the last two rows twice. **9th row**—Purl 2, knit 1, and repeat the same, and when within 7 stitches of the end, purl 2, knit 2, draw the last stitch but one over the last stitch, knit 1, draw another stitch over, knit 2 stitches. **10th row**—Knit 3, cast on 2, knit plain to the end. Repeat from the third row to the tenth row seven times, that is 64 rows in all of the ribbing, eight plain lines as on the front. You need not make a buttonhole in the first repeat, but when repeating the second time and the fourth and sixth times. For the **Shoulder—1st row**—Purl 2 and knit 1 alternately 7 times, purl 2 together, knit 2, draw the last stitch but one over the last stitch, knit 1, cast off 1 again, and continue casting off to the end of the needle, and break off the wool; resume, and turning the work, knit 2 together, knit 2, * purl 1, knit 2, and repeat from * to the end; and proceed upon this shoulder, shaping it as the first shoulder is shaped, and cast it off. Recommence where you divided for the placket,—pick up and knit 7 stitches behind the 7 last stitches of the row on the first side (these are for a fold under, and the two extra stitches on the first side will fold over), then knit 1, * purl 1, knit 3, and repeat from *, and end with purl 1, knit 2. **Next row**—Slip 1, * knit 3, purl 1, and repeat from *, and knit plain the 2 last stitches; 75 stitches on the needle. **Next row**—Slip 1, knit 3, * purl 1, knit 3, and repeat from *, and end with purl 1, knit 2. **Next row**—Slip 1, * knit 3, purl 1, and repeat from *, and knit plain the 2 last stitches. Continue working as the last two rows, till in all 60 rows of the ridged pattern are knitted, making 100 rows from the commencement of the border. **101st row**—To decrease to shape the waist—Slip 1, knit 3, purl 2

from * to the end. **14th row**—Purl. **15th row**—Slip 1, knit 2, * slip 1, knit 1, pass the slipped stitch over, knit 1, knit 2 together, knit 5, and repeat from * to the end of the row, where there will be only 3 stitches to knit; and there should now be 49 stitches on the needle. Now work the insertion from the twenty-fourth row to the thirty-eight row, allowing 1 extra stitch at the beginning and at the end of *every* row, to bring the pattern in evenly; cast off loosely. Knit the other sleeve in the same manner. Make gussets by casting on 10 stitches and knitting 14 plain rows and cast off. Join up the border of the sleeve and put a gusset in corner ways by the insertion; be careful to put the gusset right and left in each sleeve. Sew up the side seams of the petticoat, leaving space for armholes; join the shoulder pieces, and sew the sleeves in. Crochet a little edge round the neck, 1 double crochet in a stitch of the knitting, 3 chain, 2 treble in the same place the double crochet is worked into, miss two stitches of the knitting, and repeat. Sew four pearl buttons to fasten into the buttonholes. Stitch the opening of the placket smoothly in place.

MUFFLER AND CHEST PROTECTOR COMBINED.

THE article represented in our engraving is a great comfort, and in fact almost a necessity, to omnibus drivers, cabmen, and others, who are much exposed to wind and weather; it consists of a piece of ribbed knitting folded double which encircles the neck closely round, and from which a flap depends.

In front to lay over the chest, thereby forming a safeguard against bronchitis and other chest complaints. Required, 3 ozs. of 4 or 5 ply fingering wool, or Alloa yarn, and four No. 10 steel knitting needles, or bone needles with points at both ends. Cast 28 stitches on each of two needles and 32 stitches on the third needle, 88 stitches in all, and work in rounds, in ribbing, doing 2 stitches plain and 2 stitches purl, continuously, every round alike, for about 60 rounds, or to about 8 inches deep of the ribbing; this is the piece that goes round the neck. When sufficient rounds are accomplished, cast off 44 stitches, and then purl 1 stitch, * knit 1, purl 1, and repeat from * to the end of the stitches, and you will have 44 stitches on the needle for knitting the flap in moss stitch, proceeding now in rows backwards and forwards. **2nd row**—Slip 1, knit 1, * purl 1, knit 1, and repeat from * to the end of the row. **3rd row**—Slip 1, purl 1, * knit 1, purl 1, and repeat from * to the end. Repeat the last two rows till you have a length of from 10 inches to 12 inches is knitted, when cast off. The muffler is folded double, and slipped over the head into its position on the neck. For those who do not like knitting with four pins we append instructions for making the muffler and chest-protector upon two needles only; the work looks exactly the same, the only difference being that the muffler must be joined up one side. Cast 88 stitches all on one needle, and work in rows of 2 stitches plain and 2 stitches purl, every row the same, for 60 rows, or to the depth of 8 inches. **61st row**—Cast off 44 stitches, purl 1, and knit 1 and purl 1 alternately to the end of the row, when 44 stitches should remain on the

first stitch of every row to make a smooth edge. **25th row**—Slip 1, knit 4, cast the last stitch but one over the last stitch, knit 1, cast off another, knit 1, cast off another (thus 3 stitches are cast off to make a buttonhole), knit 3, purl 2, knit 2 and purl 2 alternately, and when 4 stitches from the end, knit 2 and purl 2 together, so decreasing a stitch. **26th row**—Purl along to within 2 stitches of the buttonhole, knit 2, cast on 3, knit 3. **27th row**—Knit 10, purl 2, knit 2 and purl 2 alternately, and end the row with knit 1, knit 2 together. **28th row**—Purl to within 8 stitches of the end, and knit those. **29th row**—Knit 10, purl 2, knit 2 and purl 2 alternately, and end the row with knit 2. **30th row**—Purl to within 8 stitches of the end, and knit those. **31st row**—Same as the twenty-ninth row. **32nd row**—Same as the thirtieth row. **33rd row**—Knit 10, purl 2, knit 2 and purl 2 alternately, and end by knitting the last 2 stitches together. **34th row**—Purl to within 8 stitches of the end, and knit those. **35th row**—Knit 10, purl 2, knit 2 and purl 2 alternately, and end with knit 2, purl 1, purl 2 together. **36th row**—Purl to within 8 stitches of the end, and knit those. **37th row**—Knit 10, purl 2, knit 2 and purl 2 alternately to the end. **38th row**—Purl to within 8 stitches of the end, and knit those. **39th row**—Same as the thirty-seventh row. **40th row**—Same as the thirty-eighth row. Repeat from the twenty-fifth row three times, and you will have the stitches reduced to 72 on the needle. Continue in pattern upon the 72 stitches until 144 rows are accomplished, making buttonholes as usual at intervals of every

lait and Ridged Stitch.

Petticoat for Girl of Five to Seven years.

needle for knitting the flap. **62nd row**—Slip 1, knit 1, * purl 1, knit 1, and repeat from * to the end of the row. **63rd row**—Slip 1, purl 1, * knit 1, purl 1, and repeat from * to the end. Continue working as the last two rows till you have a length of from 10 inches to 12 inches worked in moss stitch, and cast off. A muffler for a gentleman should be made with the best white peacock wool, or 3-thread or 4-thread Lady Betty, using No. 11 needles, and casting on 96 or 100 stitches for the part that goes round the neck, from which 48 stitches may be retained for the flap; also the finer quality of the wool and the small size of the needles will necessitate a few more rows being knitted in each part to ensure the muffler and chest-protector being the right dimensions.

LADY'S BED JACKET.

THE jacket, of which we here give an illustration, is a simply-made comfortable garment for an invalid to wear over a nightdress when sleeping, or when sitting up in bed. Procure 12 ozs. of white Peacock fingering wool, a pair of No. 9 bone knitting needles, a pair of No. 14 steel needles, and about a dozen white pearl buttons. With the bone needles cast on 88 stitches for the bottom of the **Right Side Front** of the **Jacket. 1st row**—Knit 10, purl 2, * knit 2, purl 2, and repeat from * to the end of the row. **2nd row**—Purl along to within 8 stitches of the end, and knit the 8 stitches plain for the front edge. These two rows constitute the pattern. Repeat the same till 24 rows are knitted. By this time you will see the effect of the pattern, which though simple is very pretty, forming little narrow stripes. Always slip the

sixteen rows. **145th row**—Work in pattern, and begin to shape the shoulder by taking 2 stitches together at the end of the row. Decrease in the same way every front row till reduced to 64 stitches. **161st row**—Knit 10, purl 2 together, * knit 2, purl 2 together, and repeat to the end; now 50 stitches on. **162nd row**—Purl to within 8 stitches of the end, and knit those. **163rd row**—Knit 10, purl 1, * knit 2, purl 1, and repeat from * to the end. **164th row**—Purl to within 8 stitches of the end, and knit those. Repeat the last two rows twice. **169th row**—Make a buttonhole in the edge stitches, knit the ninth and tenth stitches together, purl 1, * knit 2 together, purl 1, and repeat from * to the end; now 36 stitches on. **170th row**—Purl to within 8 stitches of the end, and knit those. **171st row**—Knit 9, purl 1, * knit 1, purl 1, and repeat from * to the end of the row. **172nd row**—Knit 1 and purl 1 alternately to within 8 stitches of the end, and knit those. Repeat the last two rows twice. **177th row**—Knit 9, * make 1, knit 2 together, and repeat from *, and knit the last stitch plain. **178th row**—Use No. 11 needles, and work for the neck band, knit 1 and purl 1 alternately to within 8 stitches of the end, and knit those; the made stitch of last row is the plain knit stitch in this row. **179th row**—Knit 9, purl 1, * knit 1, purl 1, and repeat from * to the end. Cast off after doing 12 rows of this ribbing. For the **Left Front**—Cast on 88 stitches. **1st row**—Purl 2 and knit 2 alternately to within 12 stitches of the end, purl 2, knit 10. **2nd row**—Knit 8 edge stitches, purl to the end. Repeat these two rows till 24 rows are knitted. You will see that the stitches are now reversed, and the edge stitches come at the *end* of the fancy rows instead of at the beginning. All decreasings are therefore to be made at the *beginning* of the fancy rows. The shaping is exactly similar to the first front, and you can work row by row from the preceding instructions, but *reversely*, that is, beginning each row of work at the end of the row of instructions and following the instructions backwards. The front edge is perfectly straight as no buttonholes are now required. For the **Back of the Jacket** —Cast on 158 stitches. **1st row**—Purl 2, * knit 2, purl 2, and repeat from * to the end. **2nd row**—Purl all along. Repeat these two rows till 24 rows are knitted. Decrease at both ends of the needle in the same rows where the fronts are decreased; knit exactly the same number of rows in length, shaping the neck in ribbing, and fasten off. For the **Sleeves**—Begin at the wrist with the steel needles, by casting on 52 stitches. **1st row**—Knit 2, purl 2, and repeat to the end. **2nd row**—Purl all along. Do 20 rows thus with the steel needles. Then 20 rows with the bone needles on the same number of stitches. Continue on the bone needles, and increase at each end of the needle in the 41st row, and in every sixth row afterwards, always keeping the pattern straight, till 16 or 18 increases have been made according to the length the sleeve is desired. To shape the top of the sleeve, work thus—Cast off 10 stitches and knit in pattern to the end of the needle; cast off 10 stitches, and purl to the end of the needle. Cast off 4 stitches, and knit in pattern to the end of the needle; cast off 4 stitches and purl to the end of the needle.

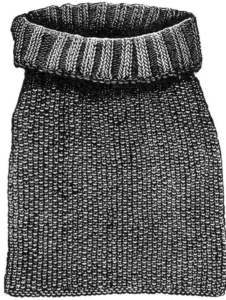

Muffler and Chest Protector Combined.

Repeat the last two rows till reduced to 14 stitches in the middle of the top of the sleeve, and cast off these. Knit the other sleeve in the same way. Sew up the shoulders and the side seams of the jacket. Sew up the sleeves and put them in. Place buttons down the front to fasten into the buttonholes; run a ribbon through the holes round the neck. The neck may be prettily finished off with a crochet edging.

SLEEPING SOCKS. QUEEN'S PATTERN.

THESE sleeping socks are quickly and easily knitted and are very warm and comfortable. If they are wished to come higher up the leg a few additional rows of ribbing can be worked. Procure 3 ozs. of white double Berlin wool, and a pair of No. 9 bone knitting needles, or for a large size sock No. 8 needles. Cast on 40 stitches for the top of the leg. Work in ribbing, 2 stitches plain and two stitches purl, for 20 rows. At the end of the twentieth row cast on 14 stitches. **21st row**—Knit plain 54 stitches, cast on 14 stitches at the end, now 68 stitches on the needle. Work in all plain knitting, increasing 1 stitch at the end of each row for 10 rows. Work 2 rows without any increase. Then work 10 plain rows taking 2 stitches together at the end of each row, and cast off. Sew up the ribbing for the front of the leg, join the fourteen cast on stitches together for the instep, sew round the toe, and fold the cast off stitches side by side and sew them together to form the bottom of the sole. Knit the other sock in the same manner. If the socks are intended for a present or for sale a little bow of ribbon placed on the instep will make them look pretty.

WANZER BORDER.

USE Fife Lace Yarn of medium thickness and a pair of No. 14 steel knitting needles. Cast on 26 stitches, and knit 1 plain row. **1st row**—Slip 1, knit 1, knit 2 together, make 1, knit 8, purl 2 together, make 1, knit 1, purl 2 together, make 1, knit 1, purl 2 together, make 1, knit 1; make 1, knit 2, make 1, knit 2 together, knit 1. **2nd row**—Knit 4, make 1, knit 2 together, knit 21. **3rd row**—Slip 1, knit 1, knit 2 together, make 1, knit 7, purl 2 together, make 1, knit 1, purl 2 together, make 1, knit 1, purl 2 together, make 1, knit 1; make 1, knit 1, make 1, knit 2 together, knit 1, make 1, knit 2 together, knit 1. **4th row**—Knit 4, make 1, knit 2 together, make 1, knit 2 together, knit 20. **5th row**—Slip 1, knit 1, knit 2 together, make 1, knit 6,

purl 2 together, make 1, knit 1, purl 2 together, make 1, knit 1, purl 2 together, make 1, knit 1; make 1, knit 1, make 1, knit 2 together, make 1, knit 2 together, knit 1, make 1, knit 2 together, knit 1. **6th row**—Knit 4, make 1, and knit 2 together three times, knit 19. **7th row**—Slip 1, knit 1, knit 2 together, make 1, knit 5, purl 2 together, make 1, knit 1, purl 2 together, make 1, knit 1, purl 2 together, make 1, knit 1; make 1, knit 1, make 1 and knit 2 together three times, knit 1, make 1, knit 2 together, knit 1. **8th row**—Knit 4, make 1 and knit 2 together four times, knit 18. **9th row**—Slip 1, knit 1, knit 2 together, make 1, knit 4, purl 2 together, make 1, knit 1, purl 2 together, make 1, knit 1, purl 2 together, make 1, knit 1; make 1, knit 1, make 1 and knit 2 together four times, knit 1, make 1, knit 2 together, knit 1. **10th row**—Knit 4, make 1 and knit 2 together five times, knit 17. **11th row**—Slip 1, knit 1, knit 2 together, make 1, knit 3, purl 2 together, make 1, knit 1, purl 2 together, make 1, knit 1, purl 2 together, make 1, knit 1; make 1, knit 1, make 1 and knit 2 together five times, knit 1, make 1, knit 2 together, knit 1. **12th row**—Knit 4, make 1 and knit 2 together six times, knit 16. **13th row**—Slip 1, knit 1, knit 2 together, make 1, knit 2, purl 2 together, make 1, knit 1, purl 2 together, make 1, knit 1, purl 2 together, make 1, knit 1; make 1, knit 1, make 1 and knit 2 together six times, knit 1, make 1, knit 2 together, knit 1. **14th row**—Knit 4, make 1 and knit 2 together seven times, knit 15. **15th row**—Slip 1, knit 1, knit 2 together, make 1, knit 1, purl 2 together, make 1, knit 1, purl 2 together, make 1, knit 1, purl 2 together, make 1, knit 1; make 1, knit 1, make 1 and knit 2 together seven times, knit 1, make 1, knit 2 together, knit 1. **16th row**—Knit 4, make 1 and knit 2 together eight times, knit 14. **17th row**—Slip 1, knit 1, knit 2 together, make 1, knit 3, make 1, knit 2 together, knit 1, make 1, knit 1, make 1, knit 3 together, knit 2 together; make 1 and knit 2 together six times, knit 1, make 1, knit 2 together, knit 1. **18th row**—Knit 4, make 1, and knit 2 together seven times, knit 14. **19th row**—Slip 1, knit 1, knit 2 together, make 1, knit 4, make 1, knit 2 together, knit 1, make 1, knit 2 together, knit 1, make 1, knit 2 together, knit 1; make 1 and knit 2 together five times, knit 1, make 1, knit 2 together, knit 1. **20th row**—Knit 4, make 1 and knit 2 together six times, knit 15. **21st row**—Slip 1, knit 1, knit 2 together, make 1, knit 5, make 1, knit 2 together, knit 1, make 1, knit 2 together, knit 1, make 1, knit 2 together, knit 2 together,

Lady's Bed Jacket.

make 1 and knit 2 together four times, knit 1, make 1, knit 2 together, knit 1. **22nd row**—Knit 4, make 1 and knit 2 together five times, knit 16. **23rd row**—Slip 1, knit 1, knit 2 together, make 1, knit 6, make 1, knit 1, make 1, knit 2 together, knit 1, make 1, knit 2 together, knit 2 together; make 1 and knit 2 together three times, knit 1, make 1, knit 2 together, knit 1. **24th row**—Knit 4, make 1 and knit 2 together four times, knit 17. **25th row**—Slip 1, knit 1, knit 2 together, make 1, knit 7, make 1, knit 2 together, knit 1, make 1, knit 2 together, knit 1, make 1, knit 2 together, knit 2 together; make 1 and knit 2 together twice, knit 1, make 1, knit 2 together, knit 1. **26th row**—Knit 4, make 1 and knit 2 together three times, knit 18. **27th row**—Slip 1, knit 1, knit 2 together, make 1, knit 8, make 1, knit 2 together, knit 1, make 1, knit 2 together, knit 1, make 1, knit 2 together, knit 2 together; make 1, knit 2 together, knit 1, make 1, knit 2 together, knit 1. **28th row**—Knit 4, make 1 and knit 2 together twice, knit 19. **29th row**—Slip 1, knit 1, knit 2 together, make 1, knit 9, make 1, knit 2 together, knit 1, make 1, knit 2 together, knit 1, make 1, knit 2 together, knit 2 together; knit 1, make 1, knit 2 together, knit 1. **30th row**—Knit 4, make 1, knit 2 together, knit 20. Repeat the pattern from the first row.

A SHAWL WORKED IN CROSS-STITCH KNITTING.

OUR engraving represents a corner of a shawl, with a border, worked with medium-sized Fife Lace Yarn and a pair of No. 10 bone knitting needles. The pattern is cross-stitch knitting. The quantity of wool will greatly depend upon the size the shawl is required to be ; a dozen one-ounce balls should be procured to begin with. Cast on any number of stitches divisible by 6, with 4 stitches additional for edge stitches. **1st row**—Knit plain. **2nd row**—Plain. **3rd row**—Knit 3 stitches, * pass the wool three times round the needle, and knit the next stitch, and repeat from * till you get to the last stitch in the row, which knit plain without previously passing the wool round the needle. **4th row**—Knit 2 stitches, * let the twisted wool slip off the left-hand needle, insert the point of the right-hand needle in the knitted stitch as if about to purl it, but instead of doing so, slip it on to the right-hand needle, drawing it

Sleeping Sock. Queen's Pattern.

up in a long loose loop, take the next 5 stitches in the same way, and then with the point of the left-hand needle lift the 3 first long loops over the 3 last loops, and placing all 6 long stitches in regular order on the left-hand pin, knit them consecutively in plain knitting; this produces a "cross;" repeat from * to the end of the row, where knit plain the last 2 stitches. **5th row**—Plain knitting. **6th row**—Plain. **7th row**—Knit 6 stitches, * pass the wool three times round the needle and knit the next stitch, and repeat from * till you get within 4 stitches of the end of the row, and knit those 4 stitches plain, without passing the wool round the needle. **8th row**—Knit 5 stitches, proceed with the "crossing" as in the fourth row, and knit the last 5 stitches plain. **9th row**—Plain knitting. **10th row**—Plain. Repeat from the third row until the shawl is as long as required, and then cast off after knitting the sixth row. The crossed knitting will appear as in the illustration covering the surface of the work. A pretty variation of the pattern can be made by working the first four rows, and repeating the same over and over again till the shawl has attained the necessary length, and in this way the "crossed" stitches take the form of a stripe. The **Border** is knitted in a cross-stitch and open pattern to correspond with the shawl. Cast on 16 stitches. Knit 1 plain row. **1st row**—Slip 1, knit 3, pass the wool three times round the needle and knit the next stitch, and knit 5 stitches in the same way, knit 1 stitch plain, make 2, knit 2 together, make 2, knit 2 together, knit 1. **2nd row**—Knit 3, purl 1, knit 2, purl 1, knit 2, let the twisted wool slip off the left-hand needle and take the knitted stitch on the right-hand needle as if about to purl it, drawing it up in a long loose loop, take the next five stitches in the same way, and then with the left-hand needle lift the 3 first long stitches over the 3 last long stitches, and having all 6 in inverted order on the left-hand pin, knit them consecutively in plain knitting, and knit the 3 last stitches plain. **3rd row**—Slip 1, knit 17. **4th row**—Cast off 2, knit 15. Repeat from the first row. When a sufficient length is knitted, sew it neatly and firmly upon the margin of the shawl, fulling it in nicely round the corners.

VEST, KNITTED IN BASKET PATTERN.

OUR engraving shows a vest knitted in the favourite basket pattern and of a size suitable for a girl of from twelve to fifteen years, and the same is equally well fitted for a grown-up young lady if additional rows be worked to add a little to the length of the vest. Procure 4½ ozs. of pink unshrinkable vest wool, or of white Andalusian wool, and a pair of No. 10 bone knitting needles. Begin by casting on 111 stitches for the bottom of the front of the vest, and work for the **Border** ; always slip the first stitch of every row. **1st row**—Plain. **2nd row**—Purl. **3rd row**—Plain. **4th row**—Slip 1, * make 1, knit 3, slip 1, knit 1, pass the slipped stitch over knit 2 together, knit 3,

make 1, knit 1; repeat from * to the end. **5th row**—Purl. **6th row**—Same as the fourth row. **7th row**—Plain. **8th row**—Purl. **9th row**—Plain. Repeat from the fourth row to the ninth row. **16th row**—Knit 1, knit 2 together, * knit 2 together, knit 9, and repeat from * till within 7 stitches of the end of the row, when knit 2 together, knit 2, knit 2 together, knit 1. Now the border is finished, and there are 98 stitches on the needle. Work for the **Basket Pattern** as follows. **1st row**—Knit 5, purl 3, * knit 7, purl 3, and repeat from * to the end. **2nd row**—Knit 3, purl 7, and repeat, and end with purl 5 only. **3rd row**—Same as the first row. **4th row**—Plain. **5th row**—Purl 3, knit 7, and repeat, and end with purl 5 only. **6th row**—Purl 5, knit 3, * purl 7, knit 3, and repeat from * to the end. **7th row**—Same as the fifth row. **8th row**—Plain. Repeat these eight rows till you can count 18 blocks of the basket pattern, 144 rows; or 21 blocks of the basket pattern, 168 rows; according to the length required. Then for the **Shoulders**—**1st row**—Knit 5, purl 3, knit 7, purl 3, knit 7, purl 3, knit 1, cast the last stitch but one over the last stitch, and continue casting off till 26 stitches remain on the left-hand needle, then knit 3, purl 3, knit 7, purl 3, knit 7, purl 3. **2nd row**—Knit 3, purl 7, knit 3, purl 7, knit 3, purl 2, purl 2 together. **3rd row**—Knit 3, purl 3, knit 7, purl 3, knit 7, purl 3. **4th row**—Knit 24, knit 2 together. **5th row**—Knit 7, purl 3, knit 7, purl 3, knit 5. **6th row**—Purl 5, knit 3, knit 3, purl 5, purl 2 together. **7th row**—Knit 6, purl 3, knit 7, purl 3, knit 5. **8th row**—Knit 22, knit 2 together. **9th row**—Purl 3, knit 7, purl 3, knit 7, purl 3. **10th row**—Knit 3, purl 7, knit 3, purl 7, knit 1, knit 2 together. **11th row**—Purl 2, knit 7, purl 3, knit 7, purl 3. **12th row**—Knit 20, knit 2 together. **13th row**—Knit 3, purl 3, knit 7, purl 3, knit 5. **14th row**—Purl 5, knit 3, purl 7, knit 3, purl 1, purl 2 together. **15th row**—Knit 2, purl 3, knit 7, purl 3, knit 5. **16th row**—Knit 20. **17th row**—Knit 7, purl 3, knit 7, purl 3. **18th row**—Knit 3, purl 7, knit 3, purl 7. **19th row**—Knit 7, purl 3, knit 7, purl 3. **20th row**—Plain. Cast off. Now work upon the other shoulder, beginning inside the neck (the first row being already knitted). **2nd row**—Knit 2 together, purl 7, knit 3, purl 7, knit 3, purl 5. **3rd row**—Knit 5, purl 3, knit 7, purl 3, knit 7, purl 1. **4th row**—Knit 2 together, knit 24. **5th row**—Purl 3, knit 7, purl 3, knit 7, purl 3, knit 2. **6th row**—Purl 2 together, knit 3, purl 7, knit 3, purl 7, knit 3. **7th row**—Purl 3, knit 7, purl 3, knit 7, purl 4. **8th row**—Knit 2 together, knit 22. **9th row**—Knit 5, purl 3, knit 7, purl 3, knit 5. **10th row**—Knit 2 together, purl 3, knit 3, purl 7,

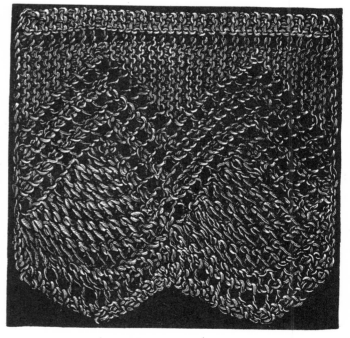

Wanzer Border.

knit 3, purl 5. **11th row**—Knit 5, purl 3, knit 7, purl 3, knit 4. **12th row**—Knit 2 together, knit 20. **13th row**—Purl 3, knit 7, purl 3, knit 8. **14th row**—Purl 2 together, purl 6, knit 3, purl 7, knit 3. **15th row**—Purl 3, knit 7, purl 3, knit 7. **16th row**—Knit 20. **17th row**—Knit 5, purl 3, knit 7, purl 3, knit 2. **18th row**—Purl 2, knit 3, purl 7, knit 3, purl 5. **19th row**—Knit 5, purl 3, knit 7, purl 3, knit 2. **20th row**—Plain. Cast off. Knit another similar piece for the back of the vest. Sew the shoulder pieces together; and sew up the sides of the vest, from the bottom, leaving space for the armholes. For the **Sleeves**—Cast on 69 stitches, and work 15 rows of the border the same as at the bottom of the vest, but doing 1 additional plain stitch at the beginning and at the end of each row. **16th row**—Plain knitting, and take 2 stitches together once in the course of the row to bring 68 stitches on the needle. Now knit 8 rows of the basket pattern, and cast off loosely. Make a little gusset by casting on 16 stitches, and knitting 26 plain rows, and cast off. Knit another sleeve and another gusset in the same manner. Sew up the sleeves, taking care that the gussets are placed properly. Crochet a little edge round the neck of the vest—1 double crochet in a stitch of the knitting, 2 chain, 3 treble in the same place as the double crochet stitch is worked, miss three stitches of the knitting, and repeat the same. A narrow ribbon can be run through the open holes of the crochet to tie in a bow in front.

GAITER FOR A CHILD OF TWO.

PROCURE 2 ozs. of white and ¼ oz. of pale blue single Berlin wool, and a pair of No. 11 bone knitting needles. Cast on 47 stitches with white wool. **1st row**—Knit 2, purl 1, and repeat, and the row will end with knit 2 as it began. **2nd row**—Purl 2, knit 1, and repeat, and end with purl 2. Repeat these two rows of ribbing until 16 rows are accomplished. **17th row**—For the striped pattern,—Still with white wool,—Purl 2, knit 1, and repeat, and the row will end with purl 2. Take the blue wool, and purl a row, and **knit** a row. **20th row**—With white wool,—Purl. **21st row**—Purl 2, knit 1, and repeat, and end with purl 2. Still with white wool,—purl a row, knit a row, and purl a row. Repeat from the seventeenth row till you have worked

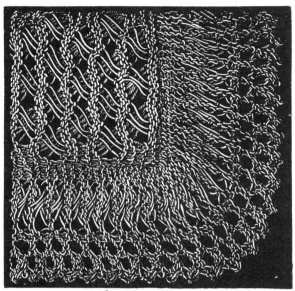

Shawl Worked in Cross-Stitch Knitting.

four blue stripes and four white stripes, when 48 rows will be knitted, counting from the top of the gaiter; the blue wool may be broken off as it is not required any more. **49th row**—With white wool which now is used to the completion of the gaiter,—Purl 2, knit 1, and repeat, and end with purl 2. **50th row**—Purl, taking 2 stitches together at the beginning of the needle, and 2 stitches together at the end. **51st row**—Plain. **52nd row**—Purl. **53rd row**—Purl 1, knit 1, * purl 2, knit 1, repeat from *, and the row will end with purl 1. **54th row**—Purl, taking 2 stitches together at the beginning and 2 stitches together at the end. **55th row**—Plain.—**56th row**—Purl. **57th row**—Knit 1, * purl 2, knit 1, and repeat from * to the end. **58th row**—Purl, taking 2 stitches together at the beginning and 2 stitches together at the end. **59th row**—Plain. **60th row**—Purl. **61st row**—Purl, and take 2 stitches together at the end; this is a raised row, and there should be 40 stitches on the needle. The pattern now changes to a small basket pattern. **1st row**—Purl. **2nd row**—Slip 1, * knit 2, purl 2, and repeat from *, and the row will end with knit 3. **3rd row**—Slip 1, * purl 2, knit 2, and repeat from *, and there will be only 1 stitch to knit at the end. **4th row**—Plain. **5th row**—Purl. **6th row**—Slip 1, * purl 2, knit 2, and repeat from *, and there will be only 1 stitch to knit at the end. **7th row**—Slip 1, * knit 2, purl 2, and repeat from * and the row will end with knit 3. **8th row**—Plain. **9th row**—Purl. **10th row**—Slip 1, * knit 2, purl 2, and repeat from *, and the row will end with knit 3. **11th row**—Slip 1, * purl 2, knit 2, and repeat from *, and there will be only 1 stitch to knit at the end. **12th row**—Plain. **13th row**—Purl, 40 stitches still on the needle. **14th row**—Slip 1, purl 2, knit 2, purl 2, knit 2, purl 2, increase 1 (by picking up the thread that lies directly under the next stitch and knitting it), knit 2 and purl 2 alternately four times, knit 2, increase 1, purl 2, knit 2, purl 2, knit 2, purl 2, knit 1. **15th row**—Slip 1, knit 2, purl 2, knit 2, purl 2, knit 2, purl 3, knit 2 and purl 2 alternately four times, purl 1 more stitch, knit 2, purl 2, knit 2, purl 2, knit 3. **16th row**—Knit 11, increase 1, knit 20, increase 1, knit 11. **17th row**—Purl, 44 stitches. **18th row**—Slip 1, knit 2, purl 2, knit 2, purl 2, knit 2, increase 1, knit 2 and purl 2 five times, knit 2, increase 1, purl 2, knit 2, purl 2, knit 3. **19th row**—Slip 1, purl 2, knit 2, purl 2, knit 2, purl 2, knit 1, purl 2, knit 2 and purl 2 five times, knit 2, purl 2, knit 2, purl 2, knit 1. **20th row**—Knit 11, increase 1, knit 24, increase 1, knit 11. **21st row**—Purl, 48 stitches. **22nd row**—Slip 1, purl 2, knit 2, purl 2, knit 2, purl 2, increase 1, knit 2 and purl 2 six times, knit 2, increase 1, purl 2, knit 2, purl 2, knit 1. **23rd row**—Slip 1, knit 2, purl 2, knit 2, purl 3, knit 2 and purl 2 six times, purl 1 more stitch, knit 2, purl 2, knit 2, purl 2, knit 3. **24th row**—Knit 11 ,increase 1, knit 28, increase 1, knit 11. **25th row**—Purl, 52 stitches. **26th row**—Slip 1, knit 2, purl 2, knit 2, purl 2,

knit 2, increase 1, knit 2 and purl 2 seven times, knit 2, increase 1, knit 2, purl 2, knit 2, purl 2, knit 3. **27th row**—Slip 1, purl 2, knit 2, purl 2, knit 2, purl 2, knit 1, purl 2, knit 2 and purl 2 seven times, knit 1, purl 2, knit 2, purl 2, knit 2, purl 2, knit 1. **28th row**—Cast off 13, knit the remaining 40 stitches. **29th row**—Cast off 13, purl the remaining 27 stitches. Now work for the **Instep**. **1st row**—Knit 2 together, knit 1, purl 2, knit 2 and purl 2 alternately five times, knit 1, knit 2 together. **2nd row**—Purl 2, knit 2 and purl 2 alternately six times. **3rd row**—Knit 2 together, knit 22, knit 2 together. **4th row**—Purl, 24 stitches. **5th row**—Knit 2 together, knit 1, purl 2, knit 2 and purl 2 four times, knit 1, knit 2 together. **6th row**—Purl 2, knit 2 and purl 2 five times. **7th row**—Knit 2 together, knit 18, knit 2 together. **8th row**—Purl, 20 stitches. **9th row**—Knit 2 together, knit 1, purl 2, knit 2 and purl 2 three times, knit 1, knit 2 together. **10th row**—Purl 2, knit 2 and purl 2 four times. **11th row**—Knit 2 together, knit 14, knit 2 together. **12th row**—Purl, 16 stitches. **13th row**—Knit 2 together, knit 1, purl 2, knit 2, purl 2, knit 2, purl 2, knit 1, knit 2 together. **14th row**—Purl 2, knit 2 and purl 2 three times. **15th row**—Knit 14 stitches. **16th row**—Purl 14. **17th row**—Knit 2 together, knit 2, purl 2, knit 2, purl 2, knit 2, knit 2 together. **18th row**—Slip 1, purl 2, knit 2, purl 2, knit 2, purl 3. **19th row**—Knit 12 stitches. **20th row**—Purl 12. Cast off. Now along the bottom of the gaiter pick up stitches, knitting each stitch as you pick it up, 13 stitches where cast off at the bottom of the heel, 17 stitches along the side, 12 stitches across the front, 17 stitches along the other side, and 13 stitches again at the bottom of the heel—72 stitches in all; and knit 1 and purl 1 alternately for two rows, and cast off. Or a row of double crochet may be worked, if preferred. Sew up the leg of the gaiter. The other gaiter is to be knitted in the same manner.

A VEIL: KNITTED IN AN OPEN DIAMOND PATTERN, WITH VINE LEAF PATTERN BORDER.

THIS veil should be knitted with the finest Fife Lace Yarn and a pair of No. 15 steel knitting needles; the pattern is particularly elegant, and yet not at all difficult to execute. Begin for the **Border** by casting on stitches sufficient to make the width for the bottom of the veil, allowing an ample number, as four stitches are decreased away in the formation of each scollop. Calculate therefore to give 16 stitches for each scollop, and 6 stitches over for edge stitches; it will take twenty-one scollops for a good-sized veil, i.e., 336 stitches, which will afterwards be reduced to 216 stitches. **1st row**—Knit plain. **2nd row**—Purl. **3rd row**—Slip 1, knit 2, knit 2 together, * knit

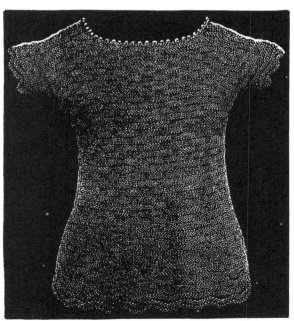

Vest Knitted in Basket Pattern.

2 together, knit 2, make 1, knit 2 together, make 1, knit 2 together, make 1, knit 2, knit 2 together, slip 1, knit 3 together, pass the slipped stitch over, and repeat from * till you get to within 5 stitches of the end of the row, and then finish with knit 2 together, knit 3. **4th row**—Purl; and every alternate row is to be purled. **5th row**—Slip 1, knit 2, knit 2 together, * knit 2, make 1, knit 2 together, make 1, knit 1, make 1, knit 2 together, make 1, knit 2, slip 1, knit 2 together, pass the slipped stitch over, and repeat from * till you get within 5 stitches of the end of the row, and then finish with knit 2 together, knit 3. **7th row**—Slip 1, knit 2, knit 2 together, * knit 1, make 1, knit 2 together, make 1, knit 3, make 1, knit 2 together, make 1, knit 1, slip 1, knit 2 together, pass the slipped stitch over, and repeat from * till you get within 5 stitches of the end of the row, and then finish with knit 2 together, knit 3. **9th row**—Slip 1, knit 2, knit 2 together, * make 1, knit 2 together, make 1, knit 5, make 1, knit 2 together, make 1, slip 1, knit 2 together, pass the slipped

stitch over, and repeat from * till you get within 5 stitches of the end of the row, and then finish with knit 2 together, knit 3. **11th row**—Slip 1, knit 3, * make 1, knit 1, make 1, knit 2 together, knit 1, slip 1, knit 2 together, pass the slipped stitch over, knit 1, knit 2 together, make 1, knit 1, make 1, knit 1, and repeat from * to the end of the row, and knit plain the last 3 stitches. **13th row**—Slip 1, knit 3, * make 1, knit 3, make 1, knit 1, slip 1, knit 2 together, pass the slipped stitch over, knit 1, make 1, knit 3, make 1, knit 1, and repeat from * to the end of the row, and knit plain the last 3 stitches. **15th row**—Slip 1, knit 3, * make 1, knit 5, make 1, slip 1, knit 2 together, pass the slipped stitch over, make 1, knit 5, make 1, knit 1, and repeat from * to the end of the row, and knit plain the last 3 stitches. **17th row**—Slip 1, knit 3, * make 1, knit 2, slip 1, knit 2 together, pass the slipped stitch over, knit 5, knit 3 together, knit 2, make 1, knit 1, and repeat from * to the end of the row, and knit plain the last 3 stitches. **19th row**—Slip 1, knit 3, * make 1, knit 1, make 1, knit 1, slip 1, knit 2 together, pass the slipped stitch over, slip 1, knit 2 together, pass the slipped stitch over, knit 3 together, knit 1, make 1, knit 1, make 1, knit 1, and repeat from * to the end of the row, and knit plain the last 3 stitches. **21st row**—The same as the thirteenth row. **23rd row**—Same as the fifteenth row. **25th row**—Same as the seventeenth row. **27th row**—Slip 1, knit 1, knit 2 together, knit 1, * make 1, knit 1, slip 1, knit 2 together, pass the slipped stitch over, slip 1, knit 2 together, pass the slipped stitch over, knit 3 together, make 1, knit 3, and repeat from * till you get within 5 stitches of the end of the row, and then finish with make 1, knit 1, knit 2 together,

make 1, slip 1, knit 2 together, pass the slipped stitch over, make 1, knit 2 together, make 1, knit 3, and repeat from * to the end of the row, and knit the last stitch plain. **41st row**—Slip 1, knit 2, make 1, slip 1, knit 1, pass the slipped stitch over, * make 1, slip 1, knit 1, pass the slipped stitch over, knit 1, knit 2 together, make 1, knit 2 together, make 1, knit 1, make 1, slip 1, knit 1, pass the slipped stitch over, and repeat from * till you get within 2 stitches of the end of the row, and knit those plain. **43rd row**—Slip 1, knit 3, make 1, slip 1, knit 1, pass the slipped stitch over, * make 1, slip 1, knit 2 together, pass the slipped stitch over, make 1, knit 2 together, make 1, knit 3, make 1, slip 1, knit 1, pass the slipped stitch over, and repeat from * to the end of the row, and knit plain the last stitch. Now repeat the open diamond pattern from the thirty-third row till a sufficient length is knitted for the veil. Then work 6 plain rows, and cast off.

SOCK FOR CHILD OF TWO.

WORKED IN HONEYCOMB KNITTING.

THE model socks are knitted with white and black wool, and are very pretty for a child to wear with black patent leather shoes. Required, 2 ozs. of white and ¾ oz. of black Andalusian wool and four steel knitting needles No. 15. Commence with white wool, and cast 21 stitches on each of three needles

Gaiter for a Child of Two.

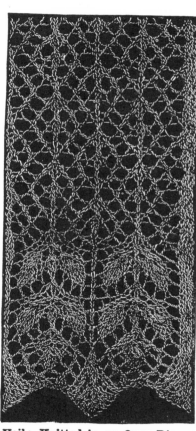

A Veil: Knitted in an Open Diamond Pattern, with Vine Leaf Pattern Border.

Sock for a Child of Two Years, Worked in Honeycomb Knitting.

knit 2 : now there should be 10 stitches in each pattern, and 5 edge stitches over ; and the border is finished, and you proceed with the open diamond pattern for the veil. **29th row**—Slip 1, knit 2, * make 1, knit 2 together, make 1, knit 1, slip 1, knit 2 together, pass the slipped stitch over, knit 1, make 1, knit 2 together, make 1, knit 1, and repeat from * to the end of the row, and knit plain the 2 last stitches. **31st row**—Slip 1, knit 3, * make 1, knit 2 together, make 1, slip 1, knit 2 together, pass the slipped stitch over, make 1, knit 2 together, make 1, knit 3, and repeat from * to the end of the row, and knit plain the last stitch. **33rd row**—Slip 1, knit 1, knit 2 together, * make 1, knit 2 together, make 1, knit 3, make 1, slip 1, knit 1, pass the slipped stitch over, make 1, slip 1, knit 2 together, pass the slipped stitch over, and repeat from * till you get to within 4 stitches of the end of the row, and then finish with make 1, slip 1, knit 1, pass the slipped stitch over, knit 2. **35th row**—Slip 1, knit 2, knit 2 together, * make 1, knit 2 together, make 1, knit 1, make 1, slip 1, knit 1, pass the slipped stitch over, make 1, slip 1, knit 1, pass the slipped stitch over, knit 1, knit 2 together, and repeat from * till you get to within 5 stitches of the end of the row, and then finish with make 1, knit 2 together, knit 3. **37th row**—Slip 1, knit 1, knit 2 together, * make 1, knit 2 together, make 1, knit 3, make 1, knit 1, knit 1, pass the slipped stitch over, make 1, slip 1, knit 2 together, pass the slipped stitch over, and repeat from * till you get within 4 stitches of the end of the row, and then finish with make 1, slip 1, knit 1, pass the slipped stitch over, and knit 2. **39th row**—Slip 1, knit 3, * make 1, slip 1, knit 1, pass the slipped stitch over,

63 stitches in all for the top of the leg, and work in ribbing of 2 stitches plain and 2 stitches purl, for 20 rounds. Then take the black wool and begin the honeycomb pattern. **1st round**—Knit plain, and increase 1 stitch somewhere upon the third needle, so as to get 64 stitches in the round. Purl 2 round with the black wool. **4th round**—With white wool—Knit 6 stitches, slip the next 2 stitches on to the right-hand needle without knitting them, and repeat the same to the end of the round. Knit 5 more rounds the same. **10th round**—With black wool—Plain knitting. Purl 2 rounds with black wool. **13th round**—With white wool—Knit 2 *, slip 2, knit 6, and repeat from *, and there will be 4 stitches to knit at the end of the third needle to complete the round. Knit 5 more rounds the same. **19th round**—With black wool—Plain knitting. Purl 2 rounds with black wool. Repeat from the fourth round till 66 rounds are knitted, when you have seven blocks of the honeycomb pattern, ending with three rounds worked with black wool ; break off the black wool. Knit the **Heel** entirely with white. Slip the last 18 stitches from off the end of the third needle upon the spare needle and slip the remaining stitches upon the second needle, so now you have the third needle free. **1st row** of the **Heel**—Knit plain with white wool 17 of the stitches you slipped on the spare needle, pick up 1 stitch for a seam stitch, this stitch should be picked up between the two bar stitches of the honeycomb, knit plain the remaining stitch and also 16 stitches off the first needle, which brings 35 stitches on one needle for the heel ; keep the 30 instep stitches divided upon two needles for the present, to be worked upon after the heel is

finished. **2nd row** of the **Heel**—Slip 1, purl 16, knit the seam stitch, purl 17. **3rd row**—Slip 1, knit 16, purl the seam stitch, knit 17. **4th row**—slip 1, purl 16, knit the seam stitch, purl 17. Repeat the last two rows till 24 rows are knitted for the flap of the heel. Then to **Turn the Heel**—Slip the first stitch, knit 16, purl the seam stitch, slip 1, knit 1, pass the slipped stitch over, knit 1; turn the work, slip the first stitch, purl 1, knit the seam stitch, purl 2 together, purl 1; turn, slip 1, knit 1, purl the seam stitch, knit 1, slip 1, knit 1, pass the slipped stitch over, knit 1; turn, slip 1, purl 2, knit the seam stitch, purl 1, purl 2 together, purl 1; turn, slip 1, knit 2, purl the seam stitch, knit 2, slip 1, knit 1, pass the slipped stitch over, knit 1; turn, slip 1, purl 3, knit the seam stitch, purl 2, purl 2 together, purl 1; turn, slip 1, knit 3, purl the seam stitch, knit 3, slip 1, knit 1, pass the slipped stitch over, knit 1; turn, slip 1, purl 4, knit the seam stitch, purl 3, purl 2 together, purl 1, and proceed thus widening the heel till all the side stitches are knitted in, and ending with a purled row, 19 stitches remain on the needle for the top of the heel: break off the wool. Keep the heel stitches as they are on one pin while you work upon the **Instep**, which is done in rows forwards and backwards using two needles. **1st row** of the instep—With white wool—Knit 2, * slip 2, knit 6, and repeat from * twice, and then slip 2, knit 2. **2nd row**—Slip 1, purl 1, * slip 2, purl 6, and repeat from * twice, and break off the wool. **7th row**—With black wool—Knit plain. Knit a row and purl a row with black wool. **10th row**—With white wool—Purl 6, * slip 2, purl 6, and repeat from * to the end. **11th row**—Slip 1, knit 5, * slip 2, knit 6, and repeat from * to the end. Repeat the

Infant's Boot and Sock.

last two rows twice, and break off the wool. **16th row**—With black wool—Purl. Purl a row and knit a row with black wool. Repeat these eighteen rows twice, and 54 rows will be done for the length of the instep. If required longer work a few rows with all white wool. For the **Toe**—With white wool—**1st row**—Slip 1, knit 1, slip 1, knit 1, pass the slipped stitch over, knit plain to within four stitches of the end, knit 2 together, knit 2. **2nd row**—Slip 1, purl to the end. Repeat these two rows till reduced to 10 stitches, and cast off. For the **Sole**—With white wool—**1st row**—Pick up and knit 12 stitches along the side of the flap, knit 19 heel stitches, pick up and knit 12 stitches along the other side of the flap, 43 stitches on the needle. **2nd row**—Purl 21, purl 2 together, purl 20. **3rd row**—Slip 1, knit 1, slip 1, knit 1, pass the slipped stitch over, knit plain to within four stitches of the end, knit 2 together, knit 2. **4th row**—Purl. Repeat the last two rows till you have reduced to 28 stitches on the needle. Then knit a plain row and a purl row alternately on the 28 stitches till the sole is the same length as the instep. Work the toe as instructed above, and cast off. Sew the sole and the instep together rounding the toe nicely. Make the other sock in the same manner.

INFANT'S BOOT AND SOCK.

REQUIRED, 1 oz. of white and ¼ oz. of pink wool, either Beehive yarn, Saxony yarn, or Cocoon, a pair of knitting needles No. 14 or No. 15, and a yard of very narrow ribbon. Cast on with pink wool, for the sole of the boot, 25 stitches. **1st row**—Purl, and increase by purling a stitch in the back as well as in the front of the last stitch but one from the end, and break off the pink wool. **2nd row**—Take the white wool, knit plain, and increase by knitting a stitch in the back as well as in the front of the last stitch but one from the end. Continue working as the last row till in the ninth row you get 34 stitches on the needle. **10th row**—Plain, no increase. Knit 2 more rows the same **13th row**—Plain, and decrease by knitting together the third and second stitches from the end. Continue as the last row till in the nineteenth row you have reduced to 27 stitches. **20th row**—Beginning on the side where the pink wool was broken off, resume with pink, and knit plain, decreasing again at the end. **21st row**—Purl, and again decrease at the end, and now there are 25 stitches on the needle, and a long narrow piece with a

point at each end is knitted to form the sole of the boot. The remainder of the boot is knitted as alternately 6 rows with white wool and 2 rows with pink, carrying on the colours without breaking off the wool. **22nd row**—With white wool, knit plain, and cast on 6 stitches at the end of the row. **23rd row**—Plain, and increase a stitch at the end; the side where the cast-on stitches are the heel, the increase stitches are to shape the toe. **24th row**—Plain, no increase. **25th row**—Same as the twenty-third row. **26th row**—Plain. **27th row**—Same as the twenty-third. **28th row**—Take pink wool, and knit plain. **29th row**—Purl, and increase a stitch at the end. **30th row**—Resume white wool, and knit plain. **31st row**—Plain, and increase a stitch at the end. **32nd row**—Plain. **33rd row**—Same as the thirty-first row. **34th row**—Plain. **35th row**—Plain, and increase a stitch at the end, and now there are 38 stitches on the needle. **36th row**—This is the **Beginning** of the **Toe**—Take pink wool, and knit plain 22 stitches, and turn the work leaving 16 stitches unknitted on the left-hand pin. **37th row**—Purl 22 stitches. Resume with white wool, and knit 6 plain rows. Take the pink wool, and knit a row plain and a row purl. And continue thus doing 6 rows with white and 2 rows with pink upon 22 stitches till three white stripes and four pink stripes are knitted in short rows for the toe and instep. Then for the **1st row** of the **other Side** of the **Boot**—Resume the white wool, knit 1, knit 2 together, knit 19 to the end of the instep stitches, cast on 16 stitches for the other side of the boot. **2nd row**—Plain, 37 stitches. **3rd row**—Slip 1, knit 2 together, knit plain to the end. **4th row**—Plain. **5th row**—Slip 1, knit 2 together, knit plain to the end. **6th row**—Plain. **7th row**—Take pink wool, knit 1, knit 2 together, knit plain to the end. **8th row**—Purl, 34 stitches on the needle, and break off the pink wool. **9th row**—Resume white wool, knit 1, knit 2 together, knit plain to the end. **10th row**—Plain. **11th row**—Slip 1, knit 2 together, knit plain to the end. **12th row**—Plain. **13th row**—Slip 1, knit 2 together, knit plain to the end. **14th row**—Cast off. Now for the **Sock**—**1st row**—With pink wool, and holding the right side of the work towards you, pick up and knit 16 stitches in the cast-on stitches of the second side of the boot, pick up and knit 13 stitches along the top of the instep, knit the 16 stitches of the first side of the boot that are still standing upon the left-hand needle; now there are 45 stitches in all on one needle. **2nd row**—Plain. **3rd row**—Slip 1, knit 1, make 1 and knit 2 together twenty-one times, knit 1. **4th row**—Plain, still 45 stitches on the needle. **5th row**—Break off pink wool and tie on white, work in brioche knitting, thus * make 1, slip 1 inserting the needle in the stitch as if about to purl, knit 2 together, and repeat from * to the end of the row. **6th row**—Work in the same manner, taking together the two stitches that lie one over the other. Continue the brioche knitting with white wool till about two inches length is knitted. Then holding the right side of the work next you, take the pink wool, and knit 2 plain rows; take white wool and knit 4 plain rows; pink wool again, and knit 2 plain rows, and cast off. Sew up the back of the leg and the bottom of the sole and mitre the little gusset at the heel. Sew the toe in a nicely-rounded shape. Run a piece of ribbon through the holes round the ankle and tie the ends in a pretty bow in front, as shown in the illustration.

Pretty Knitted Cuff.

PRETTY KNITTED CUFFS.

THESE cuffs are knitted in a variation of the fluted banister pattern, which is very elastic, therefore the cuffs fit closely round the wrist and are warm and comfortable. Procure from ½ oz. to ¾ oz. of Andalusian wool of any colour that is preferred, and a pair of No. 15 steel knitting needles. Cast on 50 stitches for a lady's small size cuff, or 60 stitches for a gentleman's size. **1st row**—Knit 3, purl 2, and repeat to the end. **2nd row**—Knit 2, purl 3, and repeat to the end. Continue these two rows of ribbing till 13 rows are done; always throughout the cuff slip the first stitch in every row. **14th row**—Knit 4, purl 1, and repeat the same to the end. **15th row**—Beginning on the side where the tag of wool hangs—Knit 4, purl 1, and repeat the same to the end. **16th row**—Knit 2, purl 3, and repeat to the end. **17th row**—Knit 2, purl 3, and repeat. **18th row**—Knit 4, purl 1, and repeat. The last four rows constitute the banister pattern; repeat the same eight more times. Then do 13 rows of the same ribbing as at the beginning of the cuff; and cast off loosely, and sew up. The pattern is alike on both sides. If knitted with stronger wool these cuffs are very useful for charitable purposes.

WELDON'S PRACTICAL
MOUNTMELLICK EMBROIDERY

(THIRD SERIES.)

New and Original Designs for Toilet Covers, Pincushions, Quilts, Brush and Comb Bags; also Grouped Sprays for Decorative Purposes.

SEVENTEEN ILLUSTRATIONS.

Telegraphic Address—
"Consuelo," London.

The Yearly Subscription to this Magazine, post free to any Part of the World, Is 2s 6d.
Subscriptions are payable in advance, and may commence from any date and for any period.

[Telephone 2745.

The Back Numbers are always in print. Nos. 1 to 105 now ready, Price 2d. each, postage ½d. Over 5,000 Engravings.

MOUNTMELLICK EMBROIDERY.

WE now place before our readers our third issue on Mountmellick Embroidery, feeling sure that the ladies who have taken so much interest in working from the two previous numbers will be pleased with a further selection of new designs for this charming variety of useful fancy work. Unlike most other kinds of fancy work, it is strong and durable, washes perfectly, and really looks well to the last; it also is a work one never gets tired of seeing, therefore it is particularly suitable for sideboard cloths, five-o'clock tea-slips, and bedroom accessories. The present issue contains valuable designs for working a nightdress sachet, brush and comb bag, duchesse table cloth, and a corner for a quilt, also designs for several lovely borders and sprays, &c. Other handsome subjects are illustrated and fully explained in No. 47 of "Weldon's Practical Needlework Series," while No. 45 is devoted to preliminary instructions regarding the different stitches made use of in this fascinating work, all of which are fully illustrated and described, together with a few simple examples of the uses to which they can be turned, and also a lovely nightdress case in a design of passion flowers and asters. The three numbers together form the most complete arrangement of Mountmellick Embroidery that has hitherto been published.

Coat of Arms.

COAT OF ARMS.

A COAT of Arms forms an appropriate subject to place in the centre of a quilt, at the corner of a pillow sham, upon a nightdress sachet, or on any piece of work where such a design will look well. It is, of course, not intended that the accompanying illustration should be copied in detail, it is given rather as an example of the purposes to which Mountmellick Embroidery can be applied, and to afford an idea to be adapted to a family coat of arms, or may be varied to represent a shield. It may either be worked straight upon the article it is purposed to adorn, or it may be executed upon a separate piece of satin jean, and placed in position when complete. The outline in either case should be worked in button-hole stitching over one or two strands of coarse cotton to raise the stitching well above the level of the foundation; the quarterings may be defined with crewel stitch, chain stitch, or cable stitch, or any other stitches the worker can successfully master.

NIGHTDRESS SACHET.
DESIGN OF OAK LEAVES AND ACORNS, GRASSES, THISTLES, MARGUERITES, AND BUTTERFLIES.

THE accompanying design represents a nightdress sachet executed in Mountmellick Embroidery in a combination of subjects, conventionally treated, and producing altogether a particularly effective and pleasing piece of work. The foundation is of white satin jean material of the best quality, of which rather more than three-quarters of a yard will be required, and must be cut into three pieces, allowing a piece 13 inches long by 18 inches wide for the back of the sachet, a piece 10 inches long by 18 inches wide for the front, and a piece 4½ inches long by 18 inches wide for the flap. Trace the design upon the front of the sachet, and on the flap, as shown in the illustration; the procedure of enlarging and tracing a design is explicitly detailed on page 4, No. 47, of "Weldon's Practical Needlework Series," which is entirely devoted to handsome designs for Mountmellick Embroidery, as also is No. 45, and the two numbers are obtainable through any bookseller or fancy repository, price 2d. each, or from this office for 2½d. each, post free. The back of the sachet is quite plain. Use

Bring up the needle and cotton close by the cable plait, insert the needle to take up a few threads of the material about half-an-inch distant and in a nearly straight direction, and draw through, then pass the needle and cotton twice or three times round the long stitch just formed, and finally return the needle to the back of the work a mere thread or two from where the stitch started; work seven or eight more stitches in the same manner, making some longer and some shorter, as shown in the engraving. The leaf has a serrated edge and is worked in flake stitch. Proceed next with the spray of marguerites in the right-hand corner of the flap. The stem is formed of couching stitch worked over one strand of cotton, and consequently is more slender than the stem in the spray of

Nightdress Sachet. Design of Oak Leaves and Acorns, Grasses, Thistles, Marguerites, and Butterflies.

Strutt's knitting cotton No. 6 and No. 8, for working the flowers and leaves, and No. 12 for the butterflies.

Commence with the flap, on which work first the spray of thistles in the left-hand corner. This consists of a stem, three flowers, and one leaf; the stem is executed in couching stitch, with three strands of coarse cotton laid down to work upon, and when this is done, a line of small spike stitches is added at regular intervals along each side of the couching; the thistles are prettily outlined with cable plait stitch, from which, at the top, springs a tuft of long twisted stitches, and the remaining portion of the outline is embellished with spike stitch similar to the spike stitches on the stem, while the interior is occupied with French knots dotted not too closely together. The long twisted stitches are worked thus—

thistles; the leaves are long and thin, and are worked simply in flake stitch from the base to the tip; the flowers are prettily devised with a centre or eye composed of a cluster of small French knots, surrounded by a circle of numerous petals, which are simulated by working long bullion stitches in pairs, and afterwards connecting the pairs together by inserting a tiny French knot close to their tips. The butterfly is first of all traced entire on a piece of fine cambric muslin, then the outline of four wings is worked in small button-hole stitch overcasting, using No. 12 cotton. Nothing as yet is done upon a very narrow rib of material that must be left vacant between the wings for the future working of the body, but you proceed to fill up the wings, decorating each with a tiny circlet of button-hole stitches to simulate the coloured blotches usually seen on butterflies' wings, and the remainder of the space is filled with ornamental stitches, as flat satin stitch, feather stitch, outline stitch, and French knots, all of which are clearly visible in the illustration; when complete lay the butterfly in position upon the centre of the flap of the nightdress sachet, and work the body in highly raised satin stitch in such a way that the wings are attached to the satin jean by the process of working the raised satin stitch over the narrow line of cambric that has hitherto been left void between the wings. The wings now are in two sections, and are moveable from the satin jean; work a small cluster of French knots to represent the head of the butterfly and add two long spike stitches to simulate the antennæ; this completes the Mountmellick Embroidery for the flap. A bold spray of oak leaves and acorns occupies the left-hand side of the front of the nightdress sachet; here the principal stem is worked in thick couching, while the smaller stems are represented variously in thin couching, small close overcasting, and snail-trail stitch; there are six leaves, of which only four are visible in the engraving, the other two being concealed under the fringe; the large leaf in the corner is outlined with button-hole stitch worked over a foundation thread, and the veining is composed of French knots; the leaf to the right is defined with a double margin of French knots, and copiously filled with crewel-stitch veining. The serrated leaf, still further to the right, is a pretty leaf, outlined with cable plait stitch, with small veinings worked in crewel stitch, snail-trail stitch, and feather stitch, tastefully blended; the small leaf to the left is represented with an outline of cable stitch and veining of crewel stitch, while of the two other small leaves hidden beneath the fringe, one is worked with a couched outline and the other defined with an outline of cable-plait stitch, and both are ornamented with a veining of feather stitch. The acorns are beautifully executed, all in highly raised work, and each one

snail-trail stitch, and bullion stitch, as represented in the engraving. The butterfly in the right-hand corner is worked in the same manner as the butterfly on the flap, the wings only being just a little differently filled in with honeycomb stitch, feather stitch, crewel stitch, and French knots. The scallops of the nightdress case are worked round with indented button-hole stitching, and a straight line of the same is used to finish off the top of the front (under the flap), and the top of the sachet; this can be done at pleasure, either before or after the Mountmellick Embroidery is worked. Cut away the surplus material from the outside

Corner for a Quilt. Design of Vine Leaves and Grapes.

varying in detail; for instance, some of the nuts are composed of highly raised satin stitch and some of raised bullion stitches worked across from side to side. The cups are prettily fashioned in good contrasting style; an acorn with a nut worked in satin stitch has a cup of raised bullion stitches worked longitudinally; other cups are composed of large French knots massed thickly and closely together, and two or three acorns with nuts of raised satin stitches worked down to meet the stem, have their cups embroidered in a kind of honeycombed network, apart from, yet lying closely around the nut. The grasses are tastefully worked in couching stitch, crewel stitch,

of the scallops, and make up the sachet in the usual manner, joining the pieces neatly together. A border of knitted fringe is used for trimming, which is worked as follows: Wind a supply of No. 12 knitting cotton upon four separate balls, and use from all four balls together, working with a pair of No. 11 steel knitting needles. Cast on 12 stitches. **1st row**—Make 1 (by passing all four strands of cotton round the needle), knit 2 together, knit 1, and repeat this three times. Every row is the same. When you have knitted a sufficient length to go nicely round the article you intend trimming, cast off 7 stitches, break off the cotton, and draw the end through the last stitch on the right-hand needle. Slip the 5 remaining stitches off the left-hand needle, and unravel them all the way along, and a pretty crinkled fringe will be produced. Sew the fringe by the loop stitches that are at the top of the heading to the edge of the indented button-hole stitching that borders the nightdress case.

This fringe is fully illustrated and detailed in No. 45 of "Weldon's Practical Needlework Series," which contains all the preliminary instructions for this most attractive and durable of Needleworks.

An elegantly designed Nightdress Case of Passion Flowers and Asters appears in No. 45 of "Weldon's Practical Needlework Series."

CORNER FOR A QUILT.
DESIGN IN VINE LEAVES AND GRAPES.

THIS elegant design of vine leaves and grapes is intended for working on the four corners of a quilt, and should extend from 36 inches to 40 inches along each side from the corner. As satin jean is not manufactured wider than 32 inches or 36 inches from selvedge to selvedge, three widths must be joined together to make a quilt.

The method of enlarging and tracing a design is fully explained on page 4, No. 47, of "Weldon's Practical Needlework Series," and need not again be repeated. The stem throughout the design now under consideration is worked in cable stitch (for description of which see illustration 6, page 5, No. 45, of "Weldon's Practical Needlework Series"); two lines of cable stitch are arranged closely parallel to simulate the thickest portion of the stem, or rather to form that part of the stem that represents the branch of the vine, and a single line denotes the stems leading to the leaves and the grapes. The tendrils are all executed in crewel stitch, or may be variously worked in cording stitch and in snail-trail stitch. The leaves throughout are alike embroidered with an outline of French knots and a copious filling of feather stitch, and the grapes are prettily outlined with a margin of cable-plait stitch (see illustration 8, page 5, No. 45, "Weldon's Practical Needlework Series") and a centre filling composed of two bullion stitches placed thus ( ).

The centre of the quilt may be ornamented with the owner's crest, or coat-of-arms, or with a flight of swallows, or with cog-wheel rings (see page 12, No. 45, of "Weldon's Practical Needlework Series") dotted about at intervals about six inches apart from each other. The sides and the top and bottom of the quilt are worked in deep button-hole stitching in large scallops, the head of the button-hole stitching is decorated with a scalloped line of bullion stitches, as is clearly apparent by reference to the engraving; and the quilt is finished with a border of the knitted fringe, fully described at end of description of Nightdress Sachet, on page 5 of this issue, and which forms such an appropriate trimming for all articles of Mountmellick Embroidery.

SPRAY OF IVY, COBWEB AND SPIDERS.

THIS is a lovely design, and may be utilised for various purposes. If worked exactly as represented in the illustration, it is suitable for a d'oyley, cheese cloth, or small tray cloth or the spray of ivy may be enlarged and continued, adding here and there more leaves, and another spider, or a small cobweb, till the design is brought to a size sufficiently large for a nightdress sachet or a pillow sham; it also may be still more enlarged, and a spray or two of passion flowers

and grasses introduced, to form a splendid design for a duchesse table-cloth or a five o'clock tea-table slip.

The stem, as shown in our engraving, is worked in close overcast stitches well raised over a couching of three or four strands of cotton. All the tendrils are simulated by snail-trail stitch, which so easily lends itself to graceful curves. The centre leaf is first of all highly raised with padding darned forwards and backwards within the allotted space, and then worked smoothly and thickly in long satin stitches, the stitches reaching from the margin on each side to the centre of the leaf, where they meet and form an indented line or mid-rib. There are two leaves at the top of the spray, one of which is worked in darning stitch, and the other is outlined with cable-plait stitch, and filled with an ample veining of crewel stitch. The large leaf at the bottom of the spray is formed of heavy raised darning stitch, and the other leaf is prettily outlined with French knots and filled in with feather stitch. Next proceed with the spider at the top of the spray, and work the body smoothly and evenly in raised satin stitch; the head is simulated by three French knots grouped closely together, the horns by tiny spike stitches, and the legs are simply loose threads of cotton in which, previously to inserting the needle, two knots have been tied to represent the joints in the legs. The other spider is worked in the same way, but is not quite so large. The spider's web is commenced by working eight long stitches in the form of a star, at equal distances one from the other, as shown in the engraving. The centre is then darned round and round, over one thread and under one thread, and in each successive round going over the thread you before went under, till a circle about the size of a sixpence is closely worked, when fasten off neatly; the same stitch is employed to work four rounds with a space left between each round, which completes the web.

Spray of Ivy. Cobweb and Spiders.

GROUP OF BUL-RUSHES AND A MOTH.

A GRACEFUL and pretty design of bulrushes is a favourite subject for Mountmellick Embroidery, and invariably looks natural and pleasing. The subject of the annexed engraving may be employed for traycloths and d'oyleys, and ladies who are skilful in designing will be able to carry the same on to a larger and more spreading pattern, and by the addition of sprays of double marsh marigolds (see page 11, No. 47, of "Weldon's Practical Needlework Series"), or water-lilies and rushes, as worked upon the brush and comb-bag, page 11 of the present issue, a lovely design can be arranged, suitable for a toilet cover or sideboard slip. The stems of the bulrushes are worked in snail-trail stitch, but may equally well be produced in crewel stitch or cording stitch, according to fancy. The leaves are thin and long, and are worked in overcast stitching, either flat or raised, as preferred. The rushes are beautifully executed in fluffy rug stitch, which is worked in a parallel direction from left to right, over a netting mesh about three-quarters of an inch wide, or a slip of stout cardboard cut to the same width will serve the purpose; bring up the needle and cotton on the outline of the bulrush on the right side of the material, hold the mesh upon the material, keeping it in place by pressure of the left-hand thumb, pass the cotton over the mesh, then under, and take two small stitches into the material to secure the loop. Every stitch is worked in the same way, and when the length of the bulrush is completed the mesh is drawn out, the cotton is fastened off, and another row is worked in the same manner quite close to the row that has just been done; when sufficient rug stitch is accomplished to cover the surface of the bulrush, the cotton is cut, and combed out and clipped to the shape, desired. Bulrushes are also very properly worked in French knots, and sometimes in bullion stitch. The moth is embroidered in finer cotton than is used for the other portion of the design; the outline is worked in chain stitch, then the wings and the head are formed with a few very tiny French knots and feather stitches, and two spike stitches project from the head to simulate horns.

CHRYSANTHEMUMS.

ARRANGED FOR A BORDER.

THIS is a very handsome design, and though executed for the most part in a novel and pretty arrangement of stitches is not beyond the capability of a fairly experienced worker. Chrysanthemums may otherways be arranged to form a solid all-over pattern for working on nightdress sachets, and for other purposes; or a few ears of wheat, barley, and grasses may be introduced, and the whole arranged in a tasteful design to suit the size and shape of the article it is intended to adorn.

The chrysanthemum stem, as shown in our engraving, is worked entirely in fine close overcast stitching. The first leaf at the bottom of the stem at the right-hand side is prettily executed in two sections; the upper section is of close evenly-worked satin stitch raised on a slightly padded foundation the needle being so placed as to slant the stitches from the mid-rib to the margin of the leaf; the under-section is composed of a series of bullion stitches worked in the form of spikes extending from the mid-rib to the other margin of the leaf. The upper division of the next leaf is embroidered in elongated trellis stitch (for instruction in working see page 11, No. 45, "Weldon's Practical Needlework Series"), it has a mid-rib of overcast stitch, and the lower division is outlined with small button-hole stitches, between which and the mid-rib runs a row of French knots of graduated sizes, the smaller knots being towards the tip of the leaf. Work the petals of the full-blown flower in slightly raised satin stitch, and fill the centre with a cluster of French knots. The leaf next above is tastefully executed with a row of spiked stitches

Group of Bulrushes and a Moth.

carried along its upper section, each spike stitch being dotted on the tip with a French knot, while the lower portion of the leaf is entirely composed of French knots, small, and arranged quite closely together. The three chrysanthemum buds are all worked similarly with petals of flat satin or overcast stitches and base of French knots. The leaf at the top of the stem is outlined with overcast stitch, a mid-rib of the same passes up the centre of the leaf, which then is completed with a filling of diamond stitch worked quite evenly and held in place by one small bind stitch confining the cross threads of each diamond. The small leaf on the left-hand side is neatly delineated with overcast stitching, and in the centre, taking the place of a mid-rib, is a line of four wafer-like spots worked in slightly raised satin stitch. The next leaf is most tastefully elaborated in two sections, the one section being worked in thick raised satin stitch graduated in length to the formation of the leaf, and the other section occupied with rows of small loops of button-hole stitches worked upon a thread of cotton as if making the loops used upon dresses. The large wide leaf next demands attention, and is simply worked with an outline of cable-plait stitch, and an ample veining of crewel stitch. The very small leaf worked close

DUCHESSE TABLE CLOTH.

DESIGN OF POPPIES AND HONEYSUCKLE SPRAYS.

THE toilet cloth shown in our engraving is specially adapted for a duchesse table, and the original measures 54 inches long and 16 inches deep, and is shaped a little at the back to accord with the table it is destined to cover. Most cloths for duchesse tables would be shaped in the same way, unless a long straight slip fringed all round is preferred. The material selected for the cloth is white satin jean, of the best quality, and the work is executed with No. 8 knitting cotton, in a simple yet pretty design of poppies and honey-suckle. The poppies are grouped together in the centre of the cloth, and again at each corner, and the intermediate space, and also a small space on each side, is occupied with honeysuckle. The centre spray consists of two full blown poppies, three buds, and three seed pods, and leaves of different sizes. Work the stems according to taste in cable-plait stitch, cable stitch, and snail-trail stitch. The large flower to the right has five petals all outlined with snail-trail stitch and filled with good-sized French knots, the centre of the flower is composed of a circle of French knots grouped closely together, and round this is an almost circular ray of bullion stitches with just a few flat satin stitches breaking the circle at the base of the flower. The petals of the other large flower are outlined with crewel stitch and filled with French knots, while the centre is formed by a round spot of thickly raised satin stitch, from which extends an " arc " of spike stitches that would be circular were it not broken into by a few flat satin stitches worked near the junction of the stem. The seed pods are effectively executed in French knots worked thickly and closely together, and a tuft of long indented satin stitches protrudes as it were from the mouth of the pod in the manner shown in the engraving. Some of the buds are larger than others, but all are worked in the same way in raised satin stitches in two unequal-sized divisions or sections, the larger section being the most raised, the buds are supposed to be just bursting forth, and a few stitches of flat satin stitch are inserted in such a manner as to represent the opening. The leaves are variously worked—the large leaf to the right is outlined with small French knots and filled with a copious veining of crewel stitch and bullion stitches; the other leaf is also defined by a margin of French knots, and is completed with a veining of crewel stitch and double bullion stitches; while the leaf to the left-hand side is worked in the same manner as the leaf to the right. The other leaves are embroidered in simple flat satin stitch, taking the stitches in two divisions, and of different lengths, to simulate a serrated edge; the working of the stitches forms of itself a kind of mid-rib down the centre of the leaf. All the tendrils are worked in snail-trail stitch. The poppy sprays at each corner are worked in style to correspond with the centre spray. The

upon the stem of the bud is defined with small overcast stitches, the same stitches being used for a mid-rib up the centre of the leaf. The leaf at the bottom of the stem, opposite the first leaf, is embroidered in two divisions, the lower division is outlined and partially filled with indented satin stitch, and the upper division after being outlined with crewel stitch, is entirely filled with rows of tiny close back stitching.

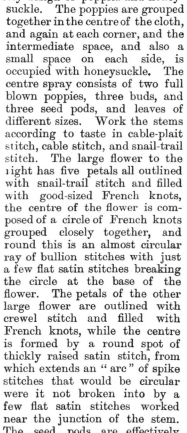

honeysuckle sprays are very easy to work, and consist of leaves only, as this portion of the design is secondary to the flowers and leaves of the poppy sprays, and therefore must not be made too conspicuous; the stem is of cording stitch, and the leaves raised satin stitch, for the mode of working which see page 11, No. 45, of "Weldon's Practical Needlework Series," where a spray of honeysuckle is depicted in nearly full working size

The table-cloth is edged round three sides with an edging of saw-tooth, button-holing, and on the fourth side (which is the back of the cloth) with plain button-holing. Then the cloth is completed by the addition of a handsome knitted fringe, described at foot of design of Nightdress Sachet, on page 5. A handsomely designed Toilet Cover of White Lilies and Passion Flowers appears in No. 47 of "Weldon's Practical Needlework Series."

Chrysanthemums Arranged for a Border.

ORANGES.
CONVENTIONAL DESIGN FOR A BORDER.

THE oranges represented in our engraving are a very effective subject for a border, which may be from eight inches to fourteen or sixteen inches wide. The stem winds alternately from right to left, and is worked throughout in close firm overcast stitch, and great care should be taken that the stitches lie smoothly side by side, closely together, yet not in the least overlapping each other. The leaves afford a good example of the variety obtainable in Mount-mellick Embroidery, almost every known stitch being called into requisition. We will describe each leaf separately in rotation, begin-ning at the bottom of the stem. A very pretty leaf is that on the

right-hand side, with the outline worked in fine overcast stitch, round which runs an edge of very tiny French knots, and up the centre of the leaf occupying the place of a mid-rib, is a line of six wafer-like spots, worked in raised satin stitch. The next leaf is quite different in style, being embroidered in two sections or divisions, the lower section is composed entirely of raised satin stitches, slanting from the outside to the centre of the leaf, while the upper section is simply outlined with crewel stitch along the margin, and filled with small French knots worked at intervals in a line from the base to the tip of the leaf. The third leaf on the right-hand side is defined with an outline of cable-plait stitch, and filled in with a mid-rib and veining of crewel stitch. The next leaf is formed simply of two rows of flake stitch extending from the outside to the centre of the leaf where a mid-rib of crewel stitch is afterwards put in. The next is an elaborate leaf, one half being of raised satin stitch and the other half being outlined with small fine overcasting and worked with diamond filling. The top leaf is defined with button-hole stitching, it has a mid-rib of cable-plait stitch, and on each side between this and the button-hole stitching is an ornamental line of French knots running from the base to the top of the leaf. The small leaf on the left-hand side is composed entirely of bullion stitches, worked very evenly in a slanting direction from the margin to the centre of the

Duchesse Dressing-Table Cover.

leaf, where the stitches meet and form a natural vein. The next is a pretty leaf. One side of it is formed of satin stitches of various lengths, the indentations being arranged to come on the inside instead of as usual on the margin of the leaf; the mid-rib is of closely worked overcast stitch, and the other side of the leaf is worked in trellis stitch expanded to the required shape. The next leaf is handsomely worked, and, from its novel effect, will repay careful attention. It is divided into two sections; one section is composed of small French knots, all exactly the same size, worked closely together, while the other section is embroidered in rows of small loops of button-hole stitch, thus ‿, in the same way that the loops are made that are sometimes placed for the fastenings of dresses. The leaf next below is worked on one side with the indented satin stitch described in a previous leaf, and it has a mid-rib of close firm overcasting, from which a line of bullion stitches extend as far as the opposite outline of the leaf. The oranges are not difficult of ex-ecution, but care must be taken in tracing to get them a correct shape. The illustration shows four different styles of working oranges, and other combinations of stitches may be invented as the work proceeds, or the same may be repeated over and over again for the length of the border. The rim of the first orange is defined by a circle of cable-plait stitch, inside which is worked four circles of crewel stitch, each at a little distance one from the other; the orange is then com-pleted by the addition of a few ornamental stitches depending from the stem. The second orange has its outer rib delineated with button-hole stitch, then a circle of French knots about the size of a threepenny piece is worked in the middle of the orange, and from this the space as far as the outer rim is filled with a series of long stitches radiating from the circle of French knots towards the button-hole stitching, and these long threads are ornamented with lace stitches, grouping them together in clusters of four threads, as will be seen by reference to the engraving. The third orange is prettily surrounded with cable-plait stitch, and filled in with a double circle of round wafer-like spots, worked in slightly raised satin stitch. The fourth orange is outlined with crewel stitch, beyond which is an edging of small French knots, and the centre is tastefully occupied by a circle of crewel stitch, with long spike stitches radiating therefrom, each spike stitch being finished off with a French knot at the tip.

SUNFLOWERS.

OUR engraving shows a design of sunflowers adapted for a border, and worked in a very effective style, in a combination of the many pretty stitches applicable to this description of art needlework; both flowers and leaves are large and bold, and therefore the subject is

f Poppies and Honeysuckle Sprays.

well suited to Mountmellick Embroidery, and ladies who are clever in sketching will be able to re-arrange the same in various forms for working upon toilet covers, nightdress cases, and brush and comb bags, or for pillow shams and quilts.

The stalk of the sunflower, which for the most part is thick and solid, is worked throughout in cable-plait stitch, and the stems belonging to each leaf and flower, being thinner, are successfully represented by snail-trail stitch and cable stitch—these three stitches will be found illustrated in full working size on page 5, No. 45, of "Weldon's Practical Needlework Series." The leaf at the bottom of the stalk on the right-hand side is outlined with button-hole stitch, the stitches being taken a little apart from each other, and the veining which occupies nearly all the centre of the leaf is worked in feather stitch. The leaf at the top is depicted with a line of small French knots worked closely together round the margin, and is filled entirely with the pretty stitch known as honeycomb stitch; for details see pages 9 and 10, No. 45, of "Weldon's Practical Needlework Series," which is the first issue on Mountmellick Embroidery, and contains all the elementary stitches. The large leaf to the left is simply worked with an outline of French knots, and a mid-rib of crewel stitch, and veining of long bullion stitches. The full-blown flower on the right-hand side of the stalk has petals of bullion stitches worked evenly across from side to side, the stitches vary in length, and of course get quite short as they approach the tip of

each petal; the centre of the flower, that is, the part that is usually full of seeds, is composed of good-sized French knots worked with thicker cotton than that employed for the petals, or a double cotton is sometimes used, but in this event great care must be taken to get the two threads to draw together with just the same degree of tightness. The top flower is composed of petals worked in satin stitch, highly raised, the satin stitches being embroidered from side

Oranges. Conventional Design for a Border.

to side over a padded foundation, and graduated in size to the contour of the tracing, a circlet of bullion stitches is then worked closely and firmly for filling in the middle of the flower.

Briggs' Transfer design, No. 329, of sunflowers for a border, will work out very effectively in Mountmellick Embroidery in the stitches that are here described, or in any other combination of stitches that may be preferred.

THREE-SIDED COMB AND BRUSH BAG.

DESIGN OF WATER LILY AND BULRUSHES.

OUR illustration represents a comb and brush bag of novel shape, which being made with three sides is more roomy and capacious than bags made with two sides only, besides being much prettier. It is composed of three pieces of the best white satin jean, each piece measuring 14 inches long and 7 inches wide. Cut a piece of paper to the shape shown in the engraving, and outline the same upon each piece of material, and work down each side and the bottom of the bag with indented button-holing, after which the outer margin of material is cut away. The work is executed with Strutt's No. 10 knitting cotton. Trace on each piece of material the design of water lily and bulrushes as in the engraving, making some little alteration in the arrangement, so that all three sides may present a pleasing variation of the idea. The leaf of the water lily is outlined partly in button-hole stitch and partly in French knots, and veined with cording stitch and feather stitch. The flower stands as it were *upon* the leaf, and, by clever manipulation of the stitches, appears as if raised therefrom. The petals are first of all thickly padded with darning and then worked in satin stitch over and over from side to side, and the centre is filled with a circlet of bullion stitches placed quite thickly and closely together. A few lines of crewel stitches give the appearance of water. There are two bulrushes and two blades of grass upon the side of the bag selected for representation. The bulrush to the right is worked across from side to side in close even rows of bullion stitches, and tapered off to a point at the top with a few overcast stitches and one spike stitch, and the stem is depicted by a line of crewel stitch. The other bulrush is embroidered entirely in French knots, the head tapered with overcast stitches and a spike stitch, and the stem worked in snail-trail stitch. Both blades of grass are defined by overcast stitching.

On the other sides of the bag the work may be carried out in a slightly different style; for instance, the bulrushes may both be worked in French knots or both in bullion stitch, and the outlining of the water-lily leaf may be cable-plait stitch, or cable plait and overcasting combined, which pretty stitch is shown on page 6, No. 45, of "Weldon's Practical Needlework Series,"

Sunflowers.

where also will be found instructions for working all the different stitches to which allusion is made in this present issue.

The three sides of the bag are sewn together by the edge of the button-hole stitches at the same time as the fringe (which should be previously knitted) is put on. The top of the bag is finished off with a narrow hem. A tape is laid in position below the hem, on the inside of the bag, to contain drawing strings, and is held in place by two rows of French knots, as will be seen by the engraving.

A nightdress sachet, with a design of water lilies and bulrushes, should be made to use with the bag.

A differently shaped Brush and Comb Bag in a design of Marsh Marigolds appears in No. 47 of "Weldon's Practical Needlework Series."

A SWALLOW.

THIS bird lends itself most favourably for reproduction in Mountmellick Embroidery, and is a very useful subject for working upon a table cover, pillow sham, or cot quilt, in combination with a simple spray of flowers and leaves, or a group of bulrushes and grasses. A flight of five or six swallows makes a splendid centre for a bed spread; they should vary in size, the largest bird being placed as leader of the flight, and the others following in gradation. Our illustration is taken from a swallow beautifully executed in highly raised work, and measuring from five to six inches from head to tail.

The outline of the swallow should be traced in the usual manner. Then the body is darned over and over with thick cotton till it stands as highly raised as is desired, most particularly so in the top wing, the upper part of the body, and the top of the head over the eye, for which a space or hollow should be left to receive one French knot, which can be put in when the body of the bird is completed. The head is worked in satin stitch; the beak is composed of a few small flat satin stitches. The upper portions of the wings are elaborated of long twisted stitches, or flake stitches, alternated with bullion stitches of medium length, and prettily mingled together; and one or two very long bullion stitches (unpadded) stretch down quite to the extreme end of the wings. It is rather difficult at first to get into the way of working these very long stitches as round and as roll-like as they should be, but practice will lead to perfection. The tail is worked in loose large chain stitches. The swallow looks most effective if not too fine cotton be employed in the working, No. 6 is not any too coarse for large birds such as would be used on a bed spread or pillow sham, while No. 8 will do nicely for all other purposes.

Several good designs of swallows and other birds can be obtained in Briggs' series of patent transfer papers in full size for working. These are most convenient for ladies not wishing to design for themselves, as they are readily transferred by means of a warm iron.

SPRAY OF POMEGRANATE.

A DESIGN of pomegranates forms a good subject for Mountmellick Embroidery, and is very suitable for the borders and corners of quilts, for curtains, five-o'clock teacloths, and any purpose for which a bold important looking design is required. The spray shown in our illustration may be employed as a powdering, dotted here and there over the entire surface of the material, and also will serve as a guide for designing and working a running border, while three sprays prettily grouped together will form a corner.

The stem of the pomegranate, which is rather thick, is effectively represented by a series of close even overcast stitches, from which, at intervals, spike stitches are worked jutting out to simulate the hairy fibres of the natural stem. The leaf to the left at the bottom of the stem is outlined with small button-hole stitches, and the veining is worked in crewel stitch. Above this leaf will be seen two small protuberances proceeding from the stem, and intended to represent leaves just bursting forth, these are worked in flat satin stitch and spike stitches. The next leaf on the left-hand side is very tastefully devised entirely in bullion stitches, extending in a slanting direction from each margin to the centre of the leaf, where the stitches meet and form a natural mid-rib. The leaf next above this is outlined with very small close overcast stitches, and filled in with diamond pattern filling, with a cross-stitch worked at intervals to secure the threads at the angle of each diamond. On the right-hand side of the spray are two exceedingly pretty leaves worked each in two sections or divisions with stitches of contrasting character ;— the larger leaf has its lower division embroidered in raised

one section is filled with back-stitching in the same manner as the leaf just described, while the other section is tastefully elaborated in rows of small loops of button-hole stitches worked on a thread or "loop" of cotton, in just the same way that the loops are made that are used upon dresses to receive hooks. The pomegranate is outlined with cable-plait stitch (see instructions, page 5, No. 45, of "Weldon's Practical Needlework Series") in two semicircular sections, and surmounted with a tuft worked in button-hole stitches

Three-Sided Brush and Comb Bag. Design of Water Lily and Bulrushes.

satin stitch, slanting from the margin to the centre of the leaf, the stitches being in length graduated to the contour of the leaf, while the upper division is outlined with crewel-stitch, which also is carried as a mid-rib by the side of the satin stitches to form the centre of the leaf, and the entire space between the crewel stitch outline and the mid-rib is occupied with close even lines of small fine back-stitching ; the other leaf is partly outlined with crewel stitch, and

indented from half-an-inch to three-eighths of an inch in height, according to the requirement of the design, and embellished on the top with a row of very tiny French knots. The centre is defined by lines of small fine overcast stitches, and is filled with diamond filling held in place by a bind stitch at the angles, and further ornamented with a small French knot in the middle of each diamond ; then between this centre and the cable plait are two small bars of cable plait on each side. If working a large design, other stitches can be employed for some of the pomegranates, so as to afford a pleasing variety; these can be selected from the preliminary examples issued in No. 45, or will suggest themselves as one gets accustomed to the work. As a rule the more stitches that can conveniently be introduced, and the greater attention that is paid to minute details, the better and handsomer will be the appearance of the work when finished.

PINCUSHION.

Conch Shell and Seaweed.

The top of this pincushion is composed of a circular piece of white satin jean, measuring 9 inches in diameter, of which about 6 inches form the covering of the pincushion itself, and is delineated by the level round of crewel stitch that is apparent in the engraving, and the margin thence beyond constitutes a border or frill. A straight strip of jean, 19 inches long and 2 inches wide, is required for the band or side of the cushion, and a circle of calico, 6 inches in diameter, for the bottom; turnings in are not included in this

ornamentation as in the engraving on each side of this line. The little loops that appear something in the shape of an "O," are composed of two bullion stitches placed rather closely together, and a small space is left between every pair of stitches. The little tiny dots on the outer side of the crewel stitch line are in representation of a double row of small French knots. The scallops are worked in button-hole stitch, and the head of the button-holing is ornamented with eight or nine bullion stitches, each a little distance apart, and in an upward position as shown in the illustration. Knit a sufficient quantity of fringe to go easily round the scallops, or if preferred, an edging of torchon lace may be substituted; but knitted fringe, such as is described at end of description of Nightdress Sachet on page 5, will last as long as the pincushion itself, and is the best kind of trimming for work of this description.

PRACTICAL SUGGESTIONS
For the Further Development of Mountmellick Embroidery.

Though Mountmellick Embroidery in its modern form is almost

A Swallow.

Spray of Pomegranate.

measurement. A round collar box, measuring 6 inches across the bottom and 2 inches high, will be a capital foundation for making up the shape of the pincushion, which may be stuffed with either bran or wadding.

Trace the design upon the piece of jean with which you intend covering the top of the cushion; the shell must be exactly in the middle, the line for the crewel stitch must be marked to correspond with the exact size of the foundation, and the margin must be outlined with an even number of scallops, and work with Strutt's best knitting cotton, No. 12. Commence with the shell. The outline of this and also the markings of all the "crinkles" on the outside of the shell are worked in cable-plait stitch, and the intervening spaces are filled with bullion stitches on the lower half of the shell, and with bullion stitches and French knots alternately on the upper half. A glance at the illustration will show clearly how this is accomplished. The mouth of the shell is occupied with a series of rows of small button-hole stitches. The sprays of seaweed that surround the shell, as well as the small sprigs of seaweed in the scallops, are worked with the stem of crewel stitch and fronds of bullion knots. Work the circular line of crewel stitch, then do the

exclusively worked according to the instructions contained in the pages of this Work Series, with white knitting cotton upon white satin jean, in which materials it is most particularly suitable for making toilet covers, nightdress sachets, comb and brush bags, pillow shams, quilts, and other domestic appurtenances, which, as a rule, being in constant use, require to be strong and serviceable, it must not be supposed that the work is unsuited to other materials and other purposes; it is, in fact, capable of much development, and there is a growing disposition to employ the Mountmellick stitches upon fine material for table linen, as well as for ornamenting children's little pelisses, frocks, and pinafores, for ladies' fancy aprons, and for the panels and borders of ladies' dresses; and for these purposes either flax thread or embroidery silk would be employed.

It is considered good taste to use nothing but white for table linen; and many leaders of fashion oppose the introduction of colour either in the linen itself or in the embroidery with which the linen is decorated. Certainly white always looks well, and presents a delicacy and elegance peculiar to itself. The introduction of heavy colouring is not to be commended, but lovely tints are now manufactured in Messrs. Harris's flax threads—notably pale blue, pink, old gold, and art greens in every delicate gradation—and remarkable for their fine gloss and brilliancy of finish. These threads are quite well suited for Mountmellick Embroidery upon linen, and may be depended upon for washing perfectly and retaining their glossy appearance. Of course one would not carry out a piece of Mountmellick work in a variety of shades and colours in the style of crewel embroidery, but one shade of flax thread inter-mingled with white can be made to produce a very pleasing effect.

A dining table-cloth of fine white linen will look very handsome embroidered with a running border of flowers and leaves, or bunches of flowers, or clusters of fruit may be introduced on the corners of the cloth, or small scattered sprays may be powdered lightly over the entire surface. It is customary to have dinner napkins embroidered to correspond.

D'oyleys are usually about 7 inches square, and may have a fruit, or a single flower, or a small spray of flowers in the centre, with a little border of feather stitch, and a fringe of drawn threads; or the centre may be left void and a narrow border be worked round, and the edge finished with a button-hole stitching and a narrow torchon lace.

Large d'oyleys and serviettes are worked with a pretty border, which may be of forget-me-nots, ivy, honeysuckle, or other designs, according to taste.

An elegant sideboard slip is made of white linen or sateen, about 2½ yards long and 14 or 15 inches wide, embroidered with a running border of pomegranates, or oranges, or bulrushes and water-lilies and grasses, with a button-hole stitched edge worked in scallops, and a border of deep torchon lace.

A bread-cloth should be a square or oblong piece of linen, worked with a border of wheat and barley, or other appropriate designs, with a button-hole stitched edge and a border of knitted fringe

Afternoon tea has become quite a recognised feature in modern society, and the cus-tom has brought tea-cloths and tea-slips into great demand, these therefore present an im-portant and almost unlimited scope for ornamentation. A tea-cloth may be as large as the table requires; a good size for a small occasional table is from 1 yard to 48 inches square; a tea-slip is about 1½ yards long, and 14 or 15 inches wide, and is intended to lay across the head of the table to receive the cups and saucers instead of using a tea-tray. Most of the designs we have illustrated can be turned to account for a bordering, and an arrangement of the "blackberry flowers, berries, and leaves," on page 13, No. 45, will be found very effective and pleasing; the cloth can be finished off with button-hole stitching in scallops, and a lace border, or simply with a fringing of drawn threads. Or the "swallow" page of the present number, might be embroidered in each corner of the cloth, with a trailing design of passion flowers extending half-way along each side. Or a cobweb and spiders with trails of ivy.

Those ladies who like making quilts in patchwork sections will enjoy the idea of preparing a number of squares measuring about eight inches each way, each square being embroidered with a different subject, and the whole sewn together and then prettily feather stitched over the seams; this might be quickly executed after the manner of a "friendship quilt," by a number of friends joining in the enterprise and contributing two or three squares each.

Pillow slips, or pillow shams, may be decorated with little sprigs of flowers dotted about at intervals; or discs, or half-moons, drawn from any good-sized circle, and filled with small flowers in solid work, makes a handsome slip; or a "spread" design after the style of the design of "double marsh marigolds" on the front of the brush and comb bag, page 5, No. 47, might be arranged, and will look very effective made up with a border of knitted fringe.

Children's pelisses and frocks, if of cashmere or soft woollen material, may be effectively embroidered in Mountmellick stitches with Pearsall's embroidery silks or Duncan's washing silks, of shade exactly to match the material; embroidery is rarely now executed with silk of contrasting colour, and it must be owned a self-colour is far the neatest and prettiest. Endless designs for this purpose will be found among Briggs' Transfer patterns, originally prepared for crewel embroidery, but which can well be reproduced in Mount-mellick work if only care be taken in selecting such as have a bold, well-defined outline, and plenty of space between the different parts of the design.

Ladies' morning aprons, or work aprons, can be ornamented with a border of Mountmellick work, executed either with flax thread or embroidery silk, according to the material of which the apron is composed.

Pincushion. Conch Shell and Seaweed.

A flannel dressing-gown, embroidered in a trailing design of "honeysuckle" (see page 13, No. 45) up each side of the front and round the collar and cuffs, will be a great success; and the work is easily accomplished in satin stitch and French knots.

We have seen a lady's bodice made with a yoke em-broidered with a honeysuckle design, both bodice and em-broidery being one shade of myrtle green, and it looked very pretty and becoming. Many other designs will work out equally well

A deep border for the bottom of the front breadth of a dress might very tastefully be ar-ranged and worked in Mount-mellick Embroidery.

Also the ends of sashes are capable of being embroidered in a dainty manner.

Bands of material or bands of silk may be embroidered separately and put on dresses as an appliqué trimming, either by a neat feather stitching or a couching and spike stitch. A couching consists simply of long strands of cotton, silk, or wool, laid down level with the edge of the band, and fastened at regular intervals by stitches taken across the couching line, then spike stitches are taken at equal distances from each other, from the couched thread over the edge of the band, which thus is held in place.

Many other purposes to which Mountmellick Embroidery can pleasantly and profitably be employed will, doubtless, present them-selves to an accomplished worker.

Design of Lilies and Leaves for Mountmellick Embroidery.

Convolvulus and Leaves for Embroidery Purposes.

WELDON'S
PRACTICAL CROCHET.
(TENTH SERIES.)

HOW TO CROCHET MITTENS, CAPES, PETTICOATS, QUILTS, CHEMISE TRIMMINGS, Etc.

TWENTY-FOUR ILLUSTRATIONS.

Telegraphic Address—] "Consuelo," London.]

The Yearly Subscription to this Magazine, post free to any Part of the World, is 2s. 6d. Subscriptions are payable in advance, and may commence from any date and for any period.

[Telephone— 2745.

The Back Numbers are always in print. Nos. 1 to 106 now ready, Price 2d. each, postage ½d. Over 5,000 Engravings.

DOLL'S WALKING COSTUME.

THIS costume consists of pelisse, cape, hat, muff, shoes, and handkerchief bag, worked in wool crochet, with a pair of knitted drawers, and a knitted petticoat with bodice, and fits a doll measuring 11 inches high. Procure 8 ozs. of Eider wool of a light fawn colour for the out-door apparel, 1 oz. of white Beehive wool, 1 oz. of white Andalusian, and ½ oz. of white Shetland for the underclothing, a fine bone crochet needle, a pair of steel knitting needles No. 13, four knitting needles No. 14, nine or ten small hooks and eyes, and a few small ornamental buttons.

Commence with the fawn wool and fine crochet needle for the **Pelisse**, which excepting the looped crochet rows at the bottom is worked throughout in plain double crochet, in rows forwards and backwards, closely and firmly, taking up the two top threads of the stitches of the preceding row, and always doing 1 chain to turn at the end of every row. Make 115 chain for the width round the bottom. **1st row**—Loop crochet—Twist the wool four times over the first finger of the left hand, insert the hook in a stitch of the work and draw all four threads of wool through, wool over the needle and draw through all on the needle; every stitch is worked in the same way, and forms a loop of three strands of wool on the side of the work farthest from you. **2nd row**—Plain double crochet. **3rd row**—Looped crochet **4th row**—Double crochet. **5th row**—Looped crochet. Work 4 rows of double crochet of 114 stitches. **10th row**—Work 32 double crochet, miss one stitch, 48 double crochet, miss one stitch, 32 double crochet. Work 3 rows of double crochet of 112 stitches. **14th row**—Work 31 double crochet, miss one stitch, 48 double crochet, miss one stitch, 31 double crochet. Work 3 rows of double crochet of 110 stitches. **18th row**—30 double crochet, miss one stitch, 48 double crochet, miss one stitch, 30 double crochet. Work 3 rows of 108 stitches. **22nd row**—29 double crochet, miss one stitch, 48 double crochet, miss one stitch, 29 double crochet. Work 3 rows of double crochet, 106 stitches. **26th row**—28 double crochet, miss one stitch, 48 double crochet, miss one stitch, 28 double crochet. Work three rows of double crochet, 104 stitches. **30th row**—13 double crochet, miss one, 13 double crochet, miss one, 48 double crochet, miss one, 13 double crochet, miss one, 13 double crochet. Work 4 rows of double crochet, 100 stitches. **35th row**—12 double crochet, miss one, 12 double crochet, miss one, 48 double crochet, miss one, 12 double crochet, miss one, 12 double crochet. Work 3 rows of double crochet, 96 stitches. **39th row**—11 double crochet, miss one, 11 double crochet, miss one, 48 double crochet, miss one, 11 double crochet, miss one, 11 double crochet. Work 3 rows of double crochet, 92 stitches. **43rd row**—10 double crochet, miss one, 10 double crochet, miss one, 48 double crochet, miss one, 10 double crochet, miss one, 10 double crochet. Work 3 rows of double crochet, 88 stitches. **47th row**—9 double crochet, miss one, 9 double crochet, miss one, 48 double crochet, miss one, 9 double crochet, miss one, 9 double crochet. Work 1 row of double crochet, 84 stitches. **49th row**—25 double crochet, * wool over the needle and insert the hook in the next stitch and draw the wool through, wool over the needle and draw through 2 stitches on the needle, repeat from * till you have done 13 stitches in this way, then wool over the needle and draw through all on the needle, 6 double crochet, 13 stitches as before, 25 double crochet; the groups of 13 stitches drawn together form two pleats at the back of the pelisse **50th row**—Plain double crochet, 60 stitches. **51st row**—8 double crochet, miss one, 8 double crochet, miss one, 8 double crochet, miss one, 6 double crochet, miss one, 8 double crochet, miss one, 8 double crochet, miss one, 8 double crochet, miss one, 8 double crochet, miss one, 8 double crochet. **52nd row**—Double crochet. **53rd row**—24 double crochet, miss one, 4 double crochet, miss one, 24 double crochet. **54th row**—Double crochet **55th row**—7 double crochet, miss one, 7 double crochet, miss one, 20 double crochet, miss one, 7 double crochet, miss one, 7 double crochet. Work 3 rows of double crochet, 48 stitches. **59th row**—6 double crochet, 2 double crochet on the next, 6 double crochet, 2 double crochet on the next, 20 double crochet, 2 double crochet on the next, 6 double crochet, 2 double crochet on the next, 6 double crochet. **60th row**—Double crochet, 52 stitches. **61st row**—6 double crochet, 2 double crochet on the next, 38 double crochet, 2 double crochet on the next, 6 double crochet. **62nd row**—Double crochet. **63rd row**—7 double crochet, 2 double crochet on the next, 8 double crochet, 2 double crochet on the next, 20 double crochet, 2 double crochet on the next, 8 double crochet, 2 double crochet on the next, 7 double crochet. **64th row**—Double crochet. **65th row**—7 double crochet, 2 double crochet on the next, 42 double crochet, 2 double crochet on the next, 7 double crochet. **66th row**—Double crochet. **67th row**—7 double crochet, 2 double crochet on the next, 7 double crochet, 1 chain to turn the work, and now proceed for the first half of the front **68th row**—Miss the first stitch, do 15 double crochet Work 2 more rows of 15 double crochet. Work 4 rows of 14 double crochet. **75th row**—14 double crochet, 2 chain. **76th row**—2 double crochet into second chain stitch, 8 double crochet, 1 chain, and turn. **77th row**—9 double crochet. **78th row**—Miss two stitches, 7 double crochet **79th row**—7 double crochet. **80th row**—Miss two stitches, 5 double crochet. **81st row**—5 double crochet **82nd row**—Miss two stitches, 3 double crochet. **83rd row**—3 double crochet. **84th row**—Miss two stitches, do 1 double crochet, and fasten off. Recommence upon the sixteenth stitch from the end of the sixty-sixth row, that is, missing twenty-nine stitches from the half front already done, and work for the other half of the front, for the **67th row**—7 double crochet, 2 double crochet on the next, 8 double crochet. **68th row**—15 double crochet, omit the last stitch. **69th row**—15 double crochet. **70th row**—14 double crochet, omit the last stitch. Work 5 rows of 14 double crochet. **76th row**—14 double crochet, 2 chain. **77th row**—1 double crochet in the second chain stitch, 8 double crochet. **78th row**—9 double crochet. **79th row**—Miss two stitches, 7 double crochet. **80th row**—7

Doll's Walking Costume.

double crochet. **81st row**—Miss two stitches, 5 double crochet. **82nd row**—5 double crochet. **83rd row**—Miss two stitches, 3 double crochet. **84th row**—3 double crochet. **85th row**—Miss two stitches, 1 double crochet, and fasten off. Now work for the **Back** of the **Pelisse**: Miss two stitches on the sixty-sixth row from the first half of the front, and for the **67th row**—Work 9 double crochet, 2 double crochet on the next, 5 double crochet, 2 double crochet on the next, 9 double crochet, 1 chain to turn. **68th row**—26 double crochet. **69th row**—Miss one stitch, 24 double crochet. **70th row**—Miss one stitch, 22 double crochet. Work 4 rows of 22 double crochet. **75th row**—Miss two stitches, 20 double crochet. **76th row**—Miss 2 stitches, 18 double crochet. **77th row**—Miss two stitches, 16 double

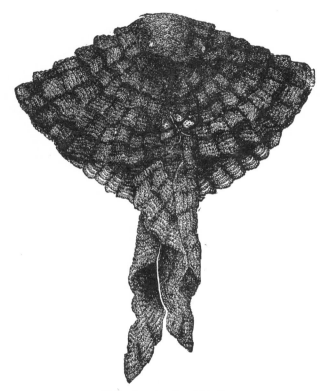

Pelerine in Ice Wool.

crochet. **78th row**—Miss two stitches, 14 double crochet. **79th row**—Miss two stitches, 12 double crochet. **80th row**—Miss two stitches, 10 double crochet. **81st row**—Miss two stitches, 8 double crochet. **82nd row**—Miss two stitches, 6 double crochet, and fasten off. Sew up the shoulder pieces. For the **Right Sleeve**—Work 24 double crochet stitches round the armhole, beginning under the arm at the lowest part of the hole, do not join in a round, but crochet backwards and forwards to match the stitch used for the pelisse. Do 4 rows with 24 double crochet in each row. **5th row**—5 double crochet, miss one stitch, 2 double crochet, miss one, 2 double crochet, miss one, 2 double crochet, miss one, 2 double crochet, miss one, 6 double crochet. Work 3 rows of 19 double crochet. **9th row**—7 double crochet, miss one, 3 double crochet, miss one, 7 double crochet. Work 10 rows of 17 double crochet. **20th row**—Work 2 stitches of looped crochet, miss one stitch, 11 looped crochet, miss one, 2 looped crochet. **21st row**—15 double crochet. **22nd row**—14 looped crochet. **23rd row**—14 double crochet; fasten off, and sew up the sleeve. The **Left Sleeve** is the same, except in the **5th row**, which should be thus—6 double crochet, miss one stitch, 2 double crochet and miss one stitch 4 times, end with 5 double crochet. Stitch back the corners of the breast of the pelisse to imitate a coat front. Fasten the pelisse with hooks and eyes, and sew a row of ornamental buttons down the front.

For the **Cape**—which is worked in **Looped Crochet**—Begin with a chain of 72 stitches. **1st row**—Looped crochet as already instructed in the first row of the pelisse. **2nd row**—Plain double crochet. **3rd row**—Looped crochet. **4th row**—Double crochet. **5th row**—Looped crochet. **6th row**—Double crochet. **7th row**—Work 16 stitches of looped crochet, miss one stitch, 2 looped crochet, miss one, 31 looped crochet, miss one, 2 looped crochet, miss one, 16 looped crochet. **8th row**—Double crochet. **9th row**—15 looped crochet, miss one, 2 looped crochet, miss one, 29 looped crochet, miss one, 2 looped crochet, miss one, 15 looped crochet. **10th row**—Double crochet. **11th row**—14 looped crochet, miss one, 2 looped crochet, miss one, 27 looped crochet, miss one, 2 looped crochet, miss one, 14 looped crochet. **12th row**—Double crochet. **13th row**—13 looped crochet, miss one, 2 looped crochet, miss one, 25 looped crochet, miss one, 2 looped crochet, miss one, 13 looped crochet. **14th row**—12 double crochet, miss one, 2 double crochet, miss one, 23 double crochet, miss one, 2 double crochet, miss one, 12 double crochet. **15th row**—11 looped crochet, miss one, 2 looped crochet, miss one, 21 looped crochet, miss one, 2 looped crochet, miss one, 11 looped crochet. **16th row**—10 double crochet, miss one, 2 double crochet, miss one, 19 double crochet, miss one, 2 double crochet, miss one, 10 double crochet. **17th row**

—Single crochet along 5 stitches, and beginning at the sixth stitch, do 4 looped crochet, miss one, 2 looped crochet, miss one, 6 looped crochet, miss one, 3 looped crochet, miss one, 6 looped crochet, miss one, 2 looped crochet, miss one, 4 looped crochet. **18th row**—3 double crochet, miss one, 2 double crochet, miss one, 13 double crochet, miss one, 2 double crochet, miss one, 3 double crochet. **19th row**—2 looped crochet, miss one, 2 looped crochet, miss one, 5 looped crochet, miss one, 1 looped crochet, miss one, 5 looped crochet, miss one, 2 looped crochet, miss one, 2 looped crochet. **20th row**—2 double crochet, miss one, 1 double crochet, miss one, 18 double crochet, miss one, 1 double crochet, miss one, 2 double crochet, and fasten off. **21st row**—To finish the **Neck**—Begin at the left-hand side of the front, that is holding the work the wrong side towards you, and work a row of loop stitch, missing one stitch at each corner, so as to render the shape more even; fasten off the wool.

For the **Muff**—which also is worked in **Looped Crochet**—Make a chain of 10 stitches, and work alternately a row of looped crochet and a row of double crochet till you have sufficient rows done to make the muff a proper size. Fold the crochet over on the wrong side and join it. Turn it, and run a thread of wool on each side to draw in the edge a little, and fasten off. The muff is hung round the doll's neck with a strand of fawn wool.

For the **Hat**—Make 2 chain, work 4 double crochet in the second chain from the needle, proceed in rounds. **1st round**—2 double crochet on each stitch of the double crochet with which you commenced. **2nd round**—Increase by working 2 double crochet on each alternate stitch. Work 2 more rounds in the same manner. **5th round**—Increase on every third stitch. **6th round**—The same. Work 5 rounds of plain double crochet, no increase. **12th round**—Double crochet, and miss every fifth stitch. **13th round**—Double crochet, and miss every fourth stitch. Work 2 rounds of double crochet, and fasten off.

For the **Shoes**—Begin with 3 chain. **1st row**—1 chain to turn, do 1 double crochet in the next, 1 double crochet in the end stitch. **2nd row**—1 chain to turn, 2 double crochet on consecutive stitches, 3 double crochet on the centre stitch, 2 more double crochet. **3rd row**—1 chain to turn, 3 consecutive double crochet, 3 double crochet in the centre stitch, 3 consecutive double crochet. **4th row**—1 chain to turn, 4 consecutive double crochet, 3 double crochet in the centre stitch, 4 consecutive double crochet. **5th row**—1 chain to turn, 5 consecutive double crochet, 3 double crochet in the centre stitch, 5 consecutive double crochet. This is sufficient for the front of the shoe. For the **6th row**—Do 1 chain to turn, 4 consecutive double crochet; and repeat the same till you have enough to go round the doll's heel and meet at the other side, where join it to the front. Proceed thus for the **Sole**—8 chain, work double crochet down one side of the chain, 3 double crochet in the end stitch, and double crochet down the other side increasing at the end, and continue round till the sole is the right size to fit nicely in the upper part; then sew them together. A few loops of red wool on the front of each slipper, on the muff, and on the hat, is a set-off to the doll's costume.

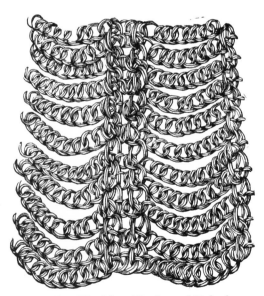

Full Size Working Design of Pelerine.

For the **Petticoat.**—This is knitted partly with white Beehive wool and partly with Andalusian, with No. 13 knitting needles; it has a fluted flounce round the bottom, and a beautifully shaped body and sleeves. Begin for the flounce with Beehive wool by casting on 24 stitches. **1st row**—Plain. **2nd row**—Plain. **3rd row**—Purl, and leave the last 2 stitches unknitted on the left-hand needle. **4th row**—Plain 22 stitches. **5th row**—Purl 22, knit 2. **6th row**—Knit 2, purl 22. **7th row**—Plain, and leave the last 2 stitches unknitted. **8th row**—Purl 22 stitches. **9th row**—Plain 24 stitches. Repeat from the second row twenty-three times more, and end by casting off instead of knitting the last plain row. Join the flounce round. For the back of the petticoat, take the Andalusian wool, and along 13 ribs of the flounce pick up 29 stitches. Knit alternately purl and plain for 9 rows. **10th row**—Knit 2, slip 1, knit 1, pass the slipped stitch over the knitted one, knit plain till you come within 4 stitches of the end, then knit 2 together, knit 2. **11th row**—Purl. **12th row**—Plain **13th row**—Purl. **14th row**—Same as the tenth row. Knit purl and plain rows alternately until you have done about 48 rows.

Next row, cast off all but 5 stitches, and continue purl and plain rows alternately on the 5 stitches for 5 rows, and cast off. Next work the front of the petticoat, pick up 25 stitches along the 11 ribs of the flounce, and work alternately purl and plain rows until you have done about 48 rows, when cast off all but 5 stitches, and knit those for 5 rows, and cast off. Sew the shoulder pieces to the corresponding place on the opposite side. Now fashion the **Sleeves,**— thus, commence at the thirty-sixth row to pick up stitches along the side of the body, in this way, * pick up 3 stitches knitting each as you pick it up, make a stitch by passing the wool round the needle, repeat from * till you have 19 stitches. **1st row**—Purl. **2nd row**—Plain. **3rd row**—Purl. **4th row**— Plain, decreasing a stitch at the beginning and at the end of the row **5th row** —Purl. **6th row**—Same as the fourth row. **7th row**—Purl. **8th row**—

Child's Tricot Petticoat.

Cast off. Knit the other sleeve in the same manner. When both sleeves are knitted sew up the sides of the petticoat. Finish the petticoat with a crochet edge round the neck and sleeves. **1st round**—1 double crochet, * 2 chain, miss one stitch, 1 double crochet in the next, and repeat from *. **2nd round** —1 double crochet under the loop of two chain, 3 chain, and repeat; fasten off at the end of the round. Make a cord of chain stitch, and run it through the holes round the neck, and tie in front.

For the **Drawers.**—Use white Shetland wool and four No. 14 knitting needles. Cast 9 stitches on each of two needles, and twelve stitches on a third needle, and work round and round like a stocking, doing first of all a ribbing of 2 stitches plain, 1 stitch purl, for ten rounds. **11th round**—Plain knitting. **12th round**—Knit 2, increase 1, knit plain to within 2 stitches of the end of the round, increase 1, knit 2. **13th round**—Plain. **14th round** —The same as the twelfth round. Repeat the last two rounds till you get 40 stitches on the needles. Then you commence to work in rows, alternately purl and plain, till you have completed 48 rows from the beginning. **49th row**—Purl. **50th row**—Knit 2, knit 2 together, knit plain to within 4 stitches of the end, knit 2 together, knit 2. **51st row**—Purl. **52nd row** —Plain. **53rd row**—Purl. **54th row**—Plain. **55th row**—Purl. **56th row**—Same as the fiftieth row. Repeat the last six rows. **63rd row**—Purl. **64th row**—Slip 1, * make 1, knit 2 together, repeat from * seven times, knit plain to the end. **65th row**—Purl. **66th row**—Cast off 17 stitches, make 1, knit 2 together, knit plain to the end. **67th row**—Purl. **68th row**— Cast off 2 stitches, make 1, knit 2 together, knit plain to the end. Repeat the last two rows till all the stitches are cast off; this is the right leg. Work for the left leg the same as for the right until you have completed the sixty-third row. **64th row**—Knit 17, make 1, knit 2 together; turn, and purl back. **66th row**—Knit 15, make 1, knit 2 together; turn, and purl back. Continue thus knitting 2 stitches less at the beginning of every forward row, till you come to knit 1, make 1, knit 2 together, and turn, and purl back. **Next row**—Plain the whole way across. **Next row**—Cast off in purling. Now make a gusset; cast on 5 stitches, and knit a row and purl a row alternately till you have a perfect square, when cast off. Sew the gusset into its place, and join up the seams of the drawers. Run a crochet cord through the holes at the top of the drawers.

Dolls' Handkerchief Bag.—Begin with 6 chain, and work double crochet down each side thereof, and go on crocheting round and round, without increasing, until you have finished four rounds. **5th round**—12 chain, 6 double crochet, 12 chain, 6 double crochet, and fasten off; the loops of chain stitches form the handles. This completes the costume of this pretty doll.

PELERINE IN ICE WOOL.

THE foundation of this pretty pelerine is worked in plain tricot, in two pieces, which subsequently are joined together down the back; the frills are fashioned separately, and afterwards sewn upon the tricot, there are six frills upon the pelerine, and a narrower frill is made to form a kind of ruching round the neck. You will require ½ lb. of double Berlin wool for the founda-

tion, and 5 or 6 balls of ice wool for the frills, and the colour may be a pretty pale blue, or light grey, or any colour in which you can get the two wools of a shade to match; procure also a No. 5 bone tricot needle, and a No 9 bone crochet needle Commence with the foundation, using double Berlin wool and the tricot needle, and work 21 chain for the half of the neck of the pelerine. **1st row**—Plain tricot; work rather loosely. For the following 14 rows increase a stitch at the beginning of each row for the front of the pelerine, increase a stitch in the middle of every row for the shoulder, and increase a stitch at the end of every alternate row for the back, therefore on the completion of the fifteenth row you will have 56 tricot stitches in the row. **16th row**—Pick up 32 stitches for the front of the pelerine (leaving 24 stitches to be worked upon presently for the back) and draw through in the usual manner. For the following 5 rows increase a stitch at the beginning of each row and decrease a stitch at the end of every alternate row. **22nd row**—Pick up 18 stitches and draw back. For the following 5 rows increase a stitch at the beginning and decrease a stitch at the end of each row Then keep the beginning straight and still decrease a stitch at the end for 16 rows, which will reduce to 2 stitches for the corner of the left-hand side front of the pelerine. Next resume the working of the 16th row—Pick up the 24 stitches you left, and draw back; then for 8 rows increase a stitch every fourth row at the beginning, and increase a stitch every alternate row at the end; and then for 5 rows keep straight at the beginning and leave 3 stitches unworked every row at the end; the last row consists of 15 tricot stitches, and completes this portion of the back of the pelerine. Next leave 5 stitches from the 18 stitches you picked up in the twenty-second row, and pick up thence to the end of the front portion, 10 stitches, and draw back. **Next row**—Slip along the first two stitches, pick up to the end, and draw back. Work three more rows the same, and fasten off. Join this portion of the front to the corresponding portion of the back of the pelerine. Recommence with 21 chain for the other half of the pelerine. **1st row**—Plain tricot For the following 14 rows increase a stitch at the beginning of every alternate row for the back of the pelerine, increase a stitch in the middle of every row for the shoulder, and increase a stitch at the end of every row for the front, and on the completion of the fifteenth row you will have 56 stitches in the row. **16th row**—Pick up 24 stitches for the back of the pelerine (leaving 32 stitches to be worked afterwards for the front) and draw through in the usual manner; then for 8 rows increase a stitch every alternate row at the beginning and increase a stitch every fourth row at the end; and then for 5 rows slip along 3 stitches at the commencement of every row, and keep straight at the end; the last row consists of 15 tricot stitches, and completes this portion of the back of the

Vest for a Child of Five.

pelerine. Next resume the working of the **16th row**—Pick up the 32 stitches you left, and draw back. For the following 5 rows decrease a stitch at the beginning of each alternate row and increase a stitch at the end of each row. **22nd row**—Pick up 10 stitches, and draw back. **Next row**— Pick up 8 stitches and draw back And for the three following rows pick up 2 stitches less each time, and fasten off. Resume where you left off in the 22nd row—Omit 5 stitches from the ten already worked, and pick up thence to the end, 18 stitches and draw back. For the following five rows decrease a stitch at the beginning and increase a stitch at the end of each row Then still decrease a stitch at the beginning for 16 rows but keep the end straight, which will reduce to two stitches for the corner of the right-hand side front of the pelerine. Join together the two portions of the tricot where divided below the shoulders; and crochet the two pieces of work together down the back of the pelerine. For the **Frills.**—Work with ice wool and No. 9 crochet needle. Commence for the bottom frill with 530 chain **1st row**— Work 1 double crochet in the second chain from the needle, 1 chain, 1 double crochet in the next stitch of the foundation, * 7 chain, miss six of the foundation, 1 double crochet in the next, 1 chain, 1 double crochet in the next, and repeat from *, making 66 scallops in the row; break off at the end of this and every row, and recommence on the right hand side. **2nd row**—Work 1 double crochet on double crochet stitch of last row, 1 chain, 1 double crochet on double crochet, 7 chain, and continue the same to the end. **3rd row**—1 double crochet on double crochet stitch of last row, 1 chain, 1 double crochet on double crochet, 8 chain, and proceed thus to the end. Work 2 more rows the same as last row. Work 3 rows in the same manner, but doing nine chain instead of eight chain. Work 2 rows doing 10 chain in each long loop. **11th row**—Work in the same manner, but doing 11 chain in each loop. This finishes the first frill. Do another frill on a foundation of 387 chain stitches, making 48 scallops. Do two frills on foundations of 323 chain, making 40 scallops. Do two frills on foundations of 227 chain, making 28 scallops. Do another frill on 168 chain as a foundation, and work only 6 rows. You will observe that the first frill is the longest; thread a rug needle with a strand of the ice wool, and tack this frill all along the bottom of the pelerine and round the narrow ends of the front to where the tricot on eighteen stitches begins, the edge of the frill falls just upon the edge of the tricot and does not extend any lower whatever. The second frill is tacked a little higher upon the pelerine, and is so arranged as to entirely fill in the centres of the two front end pieces, which so far are finished. The third frill is placed a little higher still upon the pelerine. And the other three frills rise successively and cover the tricot to the neck; the last and smallest frill being tacked

with ruby and 25 stitches with grey (leaving 6 unworked), and draw back. Repeat from the second row till you have done 112 rows, that is, 14 whole points round the bottom of the skirt. Sew up the back of the skirt, leaving about twelve stitches open at the top for a placket hole; strengthen the placket with a row of single crochet. For the **Edge** round the bottom of the skirt—Work with a crochet needle, 1 double crochet in a stitch of the tricot, miss 1 stitch, 4 treble in the next, miss 1, and repeat all round. This edge should be done with ruby wool. For the **Waistband**—Use two No 14 steel knitting needles, and pick up stitches along the top of the skirt, about 100 stitches or 104 stitches, missing a stitch here and there; work in ribbing, 2 stitches plain and 2 stitches purl for 16 rows, and cast off. Put on a button, and sew a hole for a buttonhole, or if liked have ribbon to tie round the waist.

VEST FOR CHILD OF FIVE.

THIS is worked simply in treble stitch, and is a comfortable and nice fitting vest. Required, 2½ ozs of the best pink unshrinkable vest wool, and a No 11 bone crochet needle. Commence across the chest with 65 chain. **1st row**—Work 1 treble in the fourth chain from the needle, and continue in treble stitches to the end of the row, doing 62 stitches. **2nd row**—3 chain to turn 1 treble on the second treble stitch of preceding row, inserting the hook to take up the two top threads, and work altogether 62 treble stitches to the end

Handsome Wide Border.

along the edge of the neck by one of its middle rows so that the foundation chain stands up loosely round the neck, while the last row falls level with the commencing chain of the previous frill. The neck should have previously been strengthened with a row of double crochet worked along it.

CHILD'S TRICOT PETTICOAT.

WORKED IN TWO COLOURS.

FOR this little petticoat procure 4 ozs. of grey and 1½ ozs. of ruby single Berlin wool, or the best Scotch fingering, or Petticoat fingering, and a No 7 long bone tricot needle. Or a larger petticoat can be made by using fleecy wool and a No. 5 needle. Commence with grey wool with 30 chain, take the ruby wool and joining into the grey do 13 chain. **1st row**—Pick up 12 tricot stitches with ruby wool, and pick up 31 stitches with grey wool, and draw back as in ordinary tricot, through each stitch with its own colour. **2nd row**—Pick up 10 tricot stitches with ruby, and 33 stitches with grey, and draw back as in the previous row. **3rd row**—Pick up 8 tricot stitches with ruby, and 35 stitches with grey, and draw back. **4th row**—Pick up 6 tricot stitches with ruby, and 37 stitches with grey, and draw back. **5th row**—Pick up 4 tricot stitches with ruby, and 33 stitches with grey (leaving 6 unworked), and draw back. **6th row**—Pick up 6 tricot stitches with ruby, and 37 stitches with grey, and draw back. **7th row**—Pick up 8 tricot stitches with ruby, and 35 stitches with grey, and draw back. **8th row**—Pick up 10 stitches with ruby and 33 stitches with grey, and draw back. **9th row**—Pick up 12 stitches

of the row, the last stitch being upon the chain that turned. Do 4 more rows the same as the last row, and break off the wool. Begin again with 65 chain, and work another piece of 6 rows in the same manner. **7th row**—3 chain to turn, 1 treble on the second treble stitch of previous row, and work 62 treble stitches in the row, take the first piece of crochet and do 1 treble on the first treble stitch by the tag of wool, and continue in treble to the end, in all 63 stitches, the last stitch being upon the chain that turned, work 1 single crochet in the top stitch of chain on the second piece of crochet to join the work round. **1st round**—3 chain to stand for a treble stitch, turn the work, and do 125 treble stitches in the round, and when you get to the end join with a single crochet stitch to the top stitch of chain with which the round commenced. Work each successive round in the same manner. In the **6th round** increase a stitch on each side (that is, under each armhole), and increase in the same place every third round five times. Then proceed without increasing till you can count 29 lines of treble stitches from the commencement. Work for the **last round**—1 double crochet on a treble stitch, * 5 chain, 1 double crochet in the fourth chain from the needle, 1 double crochet on the next treble stitch, 1 double crochet on the next, and repeat from * to the end of the round and fasten off. Now work for the **Shoulders**—Hold the work with the wrong side of the first row towards you, and do a row of treble stitches along the commencing chain. **1st Shoulder row**—3 chain to turn, miss the first stitch, do 10 consecutive treble. **2nd row**—3 chain to turn, miss the 2 first stitches, do 9 treble. **3rd row**—3 chain to turn, miss the first stitch, 8 treble. **4th row**—3 chain to turn, miss the two first stitches, 7 treble **5th row**—3 chain to turn, miss the first stitch, 6 treble. **6th row**—3 chain to turn, miss the first stitch, 6 treble, and fasten off. Miss 41 stitches from the shoulder you have just worked, and for the **1st row** of the other shoulder do 11 treble stitches. **2nd row**—3 chain to turn, miss the first stitch, do 9 treble, omit the last. **3rd row**—3 chain to turn, miss the two first stitches, 8 treble **4th row**—3 chain to turn, miss the first stitch, 7 treble. **5th row** —3 chain to turn, miss the two first stitches, 6 treble. **6th row**—3 chain to turn, miss the first stitch, 6 treble, and fasten off. Work shoulders upon the other half of the vest in the same way. Sew the shoulder pieces together. For the **Neck**—Work 1 round of treble stitches. **Next round**—1 single crochet on a stitch of last round, 3 chain, 1 double crochet in the same place as the single crochet is worked into, miss 1 stitch, and repeat; fasten off at the end of the round For the **Sleeves**—Work 3 rounds of treble stitches; then 1 round of edging the same as you have just worked round the neck Make a crochet chain to run through the treble stitches at the neck to tie in a bow in front; put a little tassel on each end of the chain.

Baby's Pilch.

HANDSOME WIDE BORDER.

THIS border is useful to go round quilts, or may be employed for a mantle drape, or for any purpose for which a handsome wide border is required. Select a crochet needle of suitable size, and cotton, silk, or wool, as is considered most desirable for the article it is intended to make. The border is worked in separate scallops which are joined together previous to working the last row, and before the heading is put on. Commence with 7 chain; work 1 treble in the seventh chain from the needle, 3 chain, another treble in the same place, 3 chain, another treble in the same place. **2nd row**—Turn the work, and do 1 double crochet, 5 treble, and 1 double crochet under the first loop of three chain, and the same under each of the other two loops. **3rd row**— Turn the work, 5 chain, 1 double crochet on the treble stitch of the first row, 5 chain, 1 double crochet on the next treble stitch, 5 chain, 1 double crochet on the treble stitch at the end. **4th row**—Turn the work, do 1 double crochet, 7 treble, 1 double crochet under the first loop of five chain, and the same under each of the other two loops. **5th row**—Turn, do 6 chain, 1 double crochet on the first double crochet of the third row, 6 chain, 1 double crochet on the next double crochet of the third row, 6 chain, 1 double crochet on the double crochet at the end. **6th row**—Turn, do 8 chain, 1 single crochet in the sixth chain from the needle, do 9 treble and 1 long treble under the first loop of six chain, do 1 long treble, 8 treble, and 1 long treble under the second loop of six chain, and do 1 long treble and 9 treble under the third loop. **7th row**—Turn, do 6 chain, 1 single crochet on the first treble stitch of last row, 3 chain, 1 treble on each of 9 consecutive stitches taking up the one top thread only, 2 treble on the next stitch, 4 consecutive treble, 2 treble on the next, 4 consecutive treble, 2 treble on the next, 9 consecutive treble to the end. **8th row**—Turn, do 6 chain, 1 single crochet on the first treble stitch of last row, 1 treble on each of 6 consecutive stitches taking up the back thread only; turn the work, 6 chain, 1 single crochet on the first treble stitch of last row, 3 chain, 6 treble worked consecutively and taking up the one top thread; turn the work, make a picot as before (i.e., 6 chain, 1 single crochet on the first treble stitch of last row), 3 chain, 7 treble worked consecutively and taking up the back thread; turn, make a picot, 3 chain, 8 consecutive treble taking up the one top thread; turn, a picot, 8 chain, 1 single crochet in the sixth chain from the needle, and taking up the top thread work 1 treble on each of the first 2 treble stitches, a picot, 5 consecutive treble, a picot, 2 treble, a picot, another picot, and fasten off evenly ; this forms one of the four divisions You will notice the little rows are crocheted on the back thread and on the top thread alternately of previous rows, and the "ridge" so formed always shows on the right side of the scallop. Turn the work, and first making a picot by doing 6 chain, 1 single crochet in the sixth chain from the needle, resume working upon the stitches of the seventh row, miss two stitches from the first division and do 1 treble on the

third treble stitch, and 6 more treble consecutively, taking up the back thread; turn the work, make a picot, 3 chain, 8 consecutive treble taking up the one top thread ; turn, 8 chain, 1 single crochet in the sixth chain from the needle, 9 consecutive treble taking up the back thread ; turn, make a picot, 8 chain, 1 single crochet in the sixth chain from the needle, and taking up the top thread work 1 treble on each of the second and third treble stitches, make a picot, 5 consecutive treble, a picot, 2 treble, a picot, and fasten off evenly. The third division is worked the same as the second division. For the fourth division, after turning the work, first make a picot by doing 6 chain, 1 single crochet in the sixth chain from the needle, miss two stitches from the third division and do 7 consecutive treble to the end of the row taking up the back thread ; turn, make a picot, 3 chain, 7 consecutive treble taking up the one top thread, turn, 8 chain, 1 single crochet in the sixth chain from the needle, 8 consecutive treble taking up the back thread ; turn, make a picot, 8 chain, 1 single crochet in the sixth chain from the needle, 6 chain, 1 single crochet in the same place to make another picot, and taking up the top thread work 1 treble on each of the first and second treble stitches, make a picot, 5 consecutive treble, a picot, 2 treble, a picot, and fasten off evenly ; this completes the four divisions. Now for the **Tufted Part**—This is worked in rows, and each row commences on the right-hand side and is fastened off at the end, the tags of cotton should be folded down and worked over in the next following row to ensure perfect neatness. **1st row**—Begin with 1 double crochet in the fifth picot (counting along the right-hand side from the centre of the semi-circle) 5 chain, 1 double crochet in the next picot, * 3 chain, 1 treble on the centre stitch of the five treble stitches between the picots, 3 chain, 1 double crochet in the next picot, 6 chain, miss a picot, and do 1 long treble in the next picot of the same division, 1 long treble in the corresponding picot of the next division, 6 chain, miss one picot, 1 double crochet in the next picot, and repeat from * twice, then 3 chain, 1 treble on the centre stitch of the five treble stitches between the picots, 3 chain, 1 double crochet in the next picot, 5 chain, 1 double crochet in the next picot, and fasten off. **2nd row**—Work 1 treble on the first double crochet stitch of preceding row and proceed with 1 treble on each successive stitch till 45 treble are done, do 2 treble on the next stitch, then 44 successive treble to the end, and fasten off. **3rd row**—Work 15 consecutive double crochet, taking up the top thread of the stitches of previous row, cotton over the needle. insert the hook from right to left *under* the next treble stitch of last row and draw the cotton through, cotton over the needle and draw through 2 stitches on the needle, cotton over the needle and draw through the other 2 stitches on the needle ; this is simply a treble stitch, and 4 more treble are to be worked in the same place in the same way, when the 5 treble are done take the hook out of the stitch and insert the hook in the first treble and draw the stitch through, so forming a "tuft," do 1 chain to tighten the tuft, miss one stitch behind the tuft, * do 11 double crochet, a

Raised Diamond Lattice Pattern.

tuft, and repeat from * till 6 tufts are done, then work 15 consecutive double crochet, and fasten off. **4th row**—Work 13 consecutive double crochet, * work a tuft into the lower part of the next double crochet stitch of last row, 1 double crochet, a tuft on the tuft of previous row, 1 double crochet, a tuft, 7 double crochet, and repeat from *, and end the row with 13 double crochet, and fasten off **5th row**—Work 14 double crochet, * a tuft, 1 double crochet, a tuft, 9 double crochet, and repeat from *, and end with 14 double crochet, and fasten off **6th row**—Work 15 double crochet, * a tuft, 11 double crochet, and repeat from *, and end with 15 double crochet, and fasten off **7th row**—Treble, working 91 stitches in the row When a sufficient number of scallops are worked in this manner join them by sewing together to the depth of seven stitches on each side For the **Edge**—Begin crocheting on the eighth stitch of the first scallop, work 5 consecutive double crochet, * 5 chain, 1 single crochet in the fourth chain from the needle, miss three stitches of last row, 1 treble on the next (this should be the centre stitch over the group of tufts). § 5 chain, 1 single crochet in the fourth chain from the needle, another treble in the same place, repeat from § twice more, 5 chain, 1 single crochet in the fourth chain from the needle, miss three stitches of last row, 1 double crochet on the next, and work 4 more double crochet consecutively; repeat from * five times; and then proceed in the same way round the next scallop For the **Heading—1st row**—Work single crochet along the thick part of the scallops, doing 2 chain or 3 chain as required across the space between the picots, and do 2 chain and 1 treble five times in the centre of each scallop where there are no picots; fasten off at the end of the row, and recommence on the right-hand side **2nd row**—Plain double crochet. **3rd row**—Begin with a stitch secured on the needle, * pass the cotton twice round the needle, insert the hook in the first stitch of last row and draw the cotton through, cotton over the needle and draw through 2 stitches on the needle, cotton over the needle, miss two stitches of last row, insert the hook in the next stitch and draw the cotton through, then 4 times cotton over the needle and draw through 2 stitches on the needle, do 2 chain, cotton over the needle, insert the hook to take up the two centre threads of the twisted stitch just made, draw the cotton through, then twice cotton over the needle and draw through 2 stitches on the needle ; the entire row is worked in the same manner, repeating from *, and presents the appearance of a number of small crosses. **4th row**—1 treble on the first stitch of preceding row, * 1 chain, miss one stitch, 1 treble on the next, and repeat from * to the end of the row.

BABY'S PILCH.

A WARM woollen pilch will prevent many a chill, and is almost a necessity in winter for a baby to wear in its perambulator. The p n shown in our

the row, with of course 1 chain stitch between each double crochet stitch. **Next row**—Work as far as the twenty-first double crochet stitch ; turn the work, miss the first double crochet stitch, and work back. **Next row**—Work as far as the nineteenth double crochet stitch; turn the work, miss the first double crochet stitch, and work back. **Next row**—Work as far as the seventeenth double crochet stitch ; turn the work, miss the first double crochet stitch, and work back, and break off the wool. Recommence 21 stitches from the other side of the pilch, and work another side piece to correspond with the side piece you have just done. Now for the **Middle Piece** or **Flap**—Miss four double crochet stitches from the first side piece, and beginning with 1 double crochet upon the fifth stitch, work 1 chain and 1 double crochet alternately till 37 double crochet stitches are done, which will leave four double crochet stitches from the other side piece ; turn the work, miss the first double crochet stitch, do 1 double crochet on the second double crochet stitch, and work 1 chain and 1 double crochet alternately till you come to the end, where leave 1 double crochet stitch unworked, and proceed in this manner, decreasing a stitch at the beginning and a stitch at the end of every row till you work 19 double crochet stitches in the row Keep to 19 double crochet stitches for 20 rows. **Next row**—1 double crochet on the first double crochet stitch of preceding row, increase by doing 1 chain and 1 double crochet twice on the next double crochet stitch, then 1 chain and 1 double crochet alternately to the end. Repeat this row till you get 33 double crochets in the row. **Next row**—Work in the usual manner, no increase For the **next 6 rows** decrease a stitch at the beginning of each row ; and for the **next 15 rows** decrease a stitch at the beginning and at the end of each row, to form the point; and

D'Oyley with Fan Pattern Lace Border.

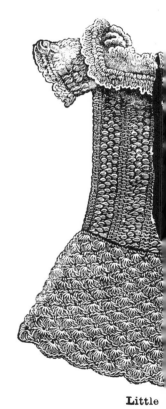

Little

illustration is very simply made, the stitch being nothing more than 1 chain and 1 double crochet worked alternately, always putting a double crochet stitch upon a double crochet stitch of the preceding row, yet though so easy, it is a pretty and tasteful little garment. Procure 3 ozs. of white Peacock fingering, a No. 10 bone crochet needle, 4 white linen buttons, and 1½ yards of inch-wide ribbon. Commence with 14 chain for the top of the pilch. **1st row**—Work 1 double crochet in the second chain from the needle, and continue plain double crochet to the end, doing in all 145 stitches. **2nd row**—Turn the work, do 1 double crochet on the first double crochet stitch of preceding row, * 1 chain, miss one stitch, 1 double crochet on the next, and repeat from * to the end, and there will be 73 double crochet in the row with a chain stitch between each double crochet stitch. **3rd row**—The same as the second row. **4th row**—Turn the work, do 1 double crochet on the first stitch of preceding row, 1 chain and 1 double crochet alternately 19 times, increase by doing 1 chain and 1 double crochet twice on the next double crochet stitch, which is the twenty-first double crochet stitch of the preceding row, then work 1 chain and 1 double crochet alternately till you come to the twenty-first double crochet stitch from the other end, increase again upon that stitch by doing 1 chain and 1 double crochet twice, then 1 chain and 1 double crochet alternately 20 times to the end of the row. **5th row**—Turn the work, do 1 double crochet on the first stitch of the preceding row, and 1 chain and 1 double crochet alternately to the end. Work 2 more rows the same as last row. Repeat from the fourth row until you work 87 double crochet stitches in

fasten off. For the **Edging round the Legs**—Work 1 row of plain double crochet along the opening for the leg, doing about 65 stitches ; turn with 1 chain, * do 1 treble in the third stitch of double crochet of last row, § 3 chain, 1 single crochet in the third chain from the needle, another treble in the same stitch of double crochet, repeat from § twice, then miss two stitches, 1 double crochet on the next, miss two stitches, and repeat from * nine times, and fasten off. Work the same along the other leg. For the **Waistband**—**1st row**—Work double crochet into the commencing chain. **2nd row**—Long treble stitches, made by turning the wool twice round the needle, decrease twice on each side of the pilch by taking up two double crochet stitches together as one. **3rd row**—Double crochet. Run ribbon through the row of long treble stitches to tie in a bow in front. Make a buttonhole at each of the three points by sewing a chain stitch round with a needleful of wool, also make one buttonhole at the bottom of the front piece. Sew buttons on the corresponding part underneath.

RAISED DIAMOND LATTICE PATTERN.
FOR A SOFA BLANKET.

THIS handsome pattern looks well worked with four shades of Berlin, either crimson, art green, peacock blue, brown, or whatever colour will best harmonise or contrast with the furniture of the room. A blanket worked with double Berlin will be warm and useful, and the pattern looks just as nice in single

Berlin if a less weighty article is desired, work the former with a No. 8 bone crochet needle, the latter with a No. 12 needle. Commence with the darkest shade of wool with chain sufficient for the length of the sofa blanket, any number of stitches divisible by 6, and 4 stitches over. **1st row**—Work 1 double crochet in the second chain from the needle, and double crochet all along to the end. **2nd row**—Turn the work, and always inserting the hook to take up the two top threads of the stitches of preceding row, work 1 double crochet on the first stitch, and proceed in double crochet to the end, making any number of stitches divisible by 6, and 3 stitches over, **3rd row**—The same as the second row. **4th row**—Still with the darkest shade of wool, turn the work, do 4 consecutive double crochet, pass the wool thrice round the needle loosely, insert the hook from right to left to take up the chain stitch below the second double crochet on the first row and draw the wool through, wool over the needle and draw through two stitches on the needle, wool over the needle and draw through two more stitches on the needle, wool twice round the needle loosely, insert the hook from right to left to take up the chain stitch below the sixth double crochet from the previous lattice stitch and draw the wool through, wool over the needle and draw through two stitches on the needle, wool over the needle and draw through two more stitches on the needle, wool over the needle and draw through three stitches on the needle, miss one double crochet of last row, work 5 consecutive double crochet, * then wool twice round the needle loosely, insert the hook from right to left to take up the chain stitch next to the previous lattice stitch and draw the wool through, wool over the needle and draw through two stitches on the needle, wool over the needle and again draw through two stitches on the needle, wool twice round the needle

the row work the last lattice stitch off by drawing the wool through two stitches three times, miss one double crochet, and do 1 double crochet on the last stitch of previous row. Join on the next lightest shade of crimson, and work 3 rows the same as the second row; then work the lattice as directed in the fourth row, but looping the long lattice stitches into the lattices that are already made. Join the lightest shade of crimson and work 8 rows. Then do 4 rows with each shade back again to the darkest, with which work 8 rows, and continue shading in the same manner till the blanket is sufficiently wide, ending with 4 dark rows as it began. The blanket may be finished off with a knotted fringe, or with a border of tufted balls like those represented on the Cot Quilt, page 13 of this present issue.

D'OYLEY WITH FAN PATTERN LACE BORDER.

VERY pretty d'oyleys are made with a centre of diaper or fine damask linen, bordered with wide crochet lace. The diaper is cut to a convenient size, round or oval, as desired; the edge is then turned down and neatly hemmed, and ornamented with a feather stitching as shown in the engraving. For the feather stitching a reel of Evans' crochet cotton, No. 2, will be required; and for the border procure a ball of Finlayson's Scotch crochet thread, No. 40, or a reel of Evans' crochet cotton, No. 25, and a medium-sized steel crochet needle When the centre is prepared take a crewel needle, and having threaded it with a rather long length of the same coarse cotton you have been using for the feather stitching, proceed to work the **1st round** by making a series of loops round the material as a foundation for crocheting into; thus—tie a knot at the

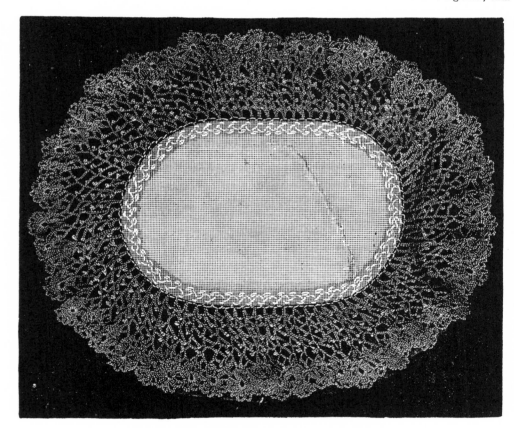

D'Oyley with Greek Lace Border.

loosely, insert the hook to take up the chain stitch below the sixth double crochet from the last lattice stitch and draw the wool through, wool over the needle and draw through two stitches on the needle, wool over the needle and draw through two more stitches on the needle, wool over the needle and draw through three stitches on the needle, repeat from * to the end, where work only 4 double crochet instead of five. Join on the next lightest shade of crimson, work 3 rows the same as the second row. **8th row**—Turn the work, and still with crimson the next shade to the darkest, do 1 double crochet on the first stitch, pass the wool twice round the needle loosely, insert the hook from right to left under the two lattice stitches of the fourth row and draw the wool through, wool over the needle and draw through two stitches on the needle, wool over the needle and draw through two more stitches on the needle, wool over the needle and again draw through two stitches on the needle. * miss one double crochet of last row, work 5 consecutive double crochet, wool twice round the needle loosely, insert the hook under the lattice stitch of the present row and under the same two lattice stitches that already have been worked under and draw the wool through, wool over the needle and draw through two stitches on the needle, wool over the needle and draw through two more stitches on the needle, wool twice round the needle loosely, insert the hook from right to left under the next two lattice stitches of the fourth row and draw the wool through, wool over the needle and draw through two stitches on the needle, wool over the needle and draw through two more stitches on the needle, wool over the needle and draw through three stitches on the needle; repeat from * and at the end of

end of the needleful o cotton, bring the needle and cotton up from the wrong to the right side of the damask just on the margin of the hem, * let the cotton hang over the fingers of the left hand, insert the needle from the wrong side to the right side of the material about an eighth of an inch to the right of where it previously was brought up, and draw the cotton through in a rather loose loop; keep the cotton to the right, and insert the needle upwards through the loop and draw the cotton through; twist a similar stitch again in the loop, and then repeat from *, going all round the damask centre, and making the loops all the same size; join evenly at the end of the round, and fasten off. **2nd round**—With flax thread and crochet needle, work 3 treble stitches under the first loop, do 1 long treble under the next loop, then 1 chain and 1 long treble alternately four times in the same place, and continue the same all round, working loosely; and join evenly at the end of the round. **3rd round**—Still working loosely, do 1 double crochet on the centre stitch of the three treble of last round, 4 chain, 1 double crochet under the first loop of one chain, 2 chain, 1 double crochet under the next, 2 chain, 1 double crochet under the next, 2 chain, 1 double crochet under the next, 4 chain, and repeat; join at the end of the round, and fasten off. **4th round**—Begin with 1 treble under the first loop of four chain, 2 chain, 1 treble under the next loop of four chain, 2 chain, 1 treble under the centre loop of two chain, 2 chain, another treble in the same place, 2 chain, and repeat to the end of the round, and join evenly. **5th round**—Work 3 treble under the first loop of two chain of last round 1 chain, 1 long treble under the loop between the two treble stitches that are worked together, 1 chain and 1 long treble alternately four times in the same place, 1 chain, and repeat. **6th round**—Work just the same as the third round; you miss the one chain stitch on each side the three treble stitches, and fasten off at the end of the round. **7th round**—Same as the 4th round. **8th round**—Work 3 treble under the first loop of two chain of last round, 1 chain 1 long treble under the loop between the two treble stitches that are worked together, 1 chain and 1 long treble alternately six times in the same place, 1 chain and repeat. **9th round**—Same as the sixth round, but do two more loops of 2 chain 1 double crochet. **10th round**—Begin with 1 treble under the first loop of four chain, 2 chain, 1 treble under the next loop of four chain, 3 chain 1 treble under the centre loop of two chain, 3 chain, another treble in the same place, 3 chain, and repeat to the end of the round, and join evenly. **11th round**—Same as the eighth round. **12th round**—Same as the ninth round. This completes the border, which is worked loosely throughout. It looks very light and lacy if crocheted with Coats' No. 20 sewing cotton if the flax thread is not easily procurable.

LITTLE GIRL'S FROCK.

THIS pretty frock will fit a child of about three years of age; the body is worked in striped tricot and the skirt in crochet, and a handsome wide silk sash should be tied loosely round the waist, but is not represented in our engraving that the method of working the frock may be more clearly seen. Procure 6 ozs. of Peacock Fingering wool, any colour that may be preferred, white always looks nice for a best frock, but of course a dark colour such as cardinal or peacock blue is more serviceable, use a No 9 bone tricot needle, and a No. 10 crochet needle. Commence lengthways for the back of the body with 50 chain stitches. **1st row**—Pick up 1 tricot stitch in the second chain from the needle, and thence pick up 1 stitch in every chain to the end, making 49 tricot stitches on the needle, draw back in the ordinary manner. Work 2 more rows of plain tricot. 49 stitches in each row. **4th row**—

Full Size Working Design of Trimming for Chemise.

to shape the neck nicely. Next, **two Frills** are to be worked, the one to stand up round the neck, the other to fall over the body, the top frill is crocheted into the upper edge of the row of double crochet stitches, and the lower frill is fashioned by holding the body upside down and working into the lower edge of the same row of stitches; each row must be commenced on the right-hand side, holding the right side of the work towards you and fastened off at the end. **1st row**—Treble crochet, 1 treble in every stitch of the double crochet. **2nd row**—2 double crochet in the first stitch, * miss one stitch, 2 double crochet in the next, and repeat from * to the end. **3rd row**—1 double crochet on each of two double crochet stitches, 3 chain, 1 single crochet in the third chain from the needle, and repeat the same to the end. For the **Sleeves**—Work from where the armhole begins underneath to the same place again, forwards and backwards, in the same tricot stitch as used for the body, doing 3 plain rows and 3 fancy rows; next row, slip stitch; then 1 row of treble crochet; and then the last 2 rows of the frill. Sew up the under part of the sleeves. For the **Skirt**—Use the No. 10 crochet needle, and work a row of double crochet all along the bottom of the body getting 96 double crochet in the row, join the last stitch to the first, thereby uniting the two back pieces. Henceforth work in rounds, joining the work on the completion of every round. **1st round**—Work 1 double crochet on a double crochet stitch, miss one stitch, 4 treble on the next, miss one stitch, and repeat, and there will be 24 patterns in the round. **2nd round**—Work 1 double crochet, in the centre of the group of treble stitches in the last round, and 4 treble on the double crochet stitch. Work 2 more rounds the same. Then work 8 rounds with 5 treble in a group instead of four treble. Then 4 rounds with 6 treble stitches in a group. Then 3 rounds with 7 treble in a group. Now the skirt will probably be long enough, but if required longer more rounds can be done. Work a row of double crochet up each side the back of the body, and as you do this on the right-hand side work at intervals 2 chain stitches and miss two stitches of the body, so forming a little loop to use as a buttonhole. Sew on buttons to correspond. Run a length of narrow ribbon through the row of treble

Trimming for a Chemise.

You have 1 stitch already on the needle to begin with, wool over the needle and insert the hook to take up the second tricot stitch of the last row but one and draw the wool through, wool over the needle and draw through one stitch on the needle, wool over the needle and draw through two stitches on the needle, do 1 plain tricot stitch in the last row, do 1 raised tricot stitch in the last row but one, 1 plain tricot stitch in the last row, and so on, a raised stitch and a plain stitch alternately to the end. **5th row**—Pick up a plain tricot stitch in the second tricot stitch of last row, and work a raised stitch in the tricot stitch of the last row but one, in this way the raised stitches will come intermediately between the raised stitches of the last row. **6th row**—Work the same as the fourth row. There should be 24 raised stitches in the fourth row and in the sixth row, and 23 raised stitches in the fifth row, and all the remaining stitches plain. Repeat these six rows till you have worked 18 rows in all from the commencement. You then begin to shape for the shoulder by making 10 chain at the end of the eighteenth fancy row and picking up these as additional tricot stitches at the beginning of the next plain tricot row, now doing 59 stitches in each row for 3 plain and 2 fancy rows, then slip stitch along 20 tricot stitches and work only 39 stitches of the next fancy row to allow of space for an armhole, and when drawing back do 20 chain at the end to restore the shoulder piece to its original height. Work 3 plain tricot rows and 2 fancy rows on 59 stitches; then at the beginning of the third fancy row slip stitch along 10 stitches and complete the row on 49 stitches as previously worked for the back of the body. Continue on 49 stitches for the front, doing altogether 6 stripes of plain and 5 stripes of fancy tricot, 33 rows in all. Next row do fancy tricot and work 10 chain at the end to shape for the other shoulder; do 2 rows of fancy tricot and 3 rows of plain tricot on 59 stitches, then slip stitch along 20 stitches and work only 39 stitches in the next fancy row and when drawing back do 20 chain at the end on which to complete the shoulder. Work 2 fancy rows and 3 plain rows on 59 stitches; then at the beginning of the next fancy row slip stitch along 10 stitches and work along 49 stitches for the back of the body, continuing the striped pattern till 3 fancy stripes and 3 plain stripes are worked, slip stitch along the last row and fasten off. Sew the shoulder pieces together. Work a row of plain double crochet round the neck, using a No. 10 needle, and contracting a little

stitches at the bottom of the sleeves, and the same through the treble stitches in the upper frill.

D'OYLEY WITH GREEK LACE BORDER.

THIS useful d'oyley is composed of a centre of diaper or fine damask linen, bordered with a pretty crochet lace. Cut the damask the size the d'oyley is required to be, and after hemming it round, embroider the margin with feather stitching. The feather stitching should be done with coarse crochet cotton, the size of Evans' No. 2, while for the crochet border you will require a reel of No. 20 or No. 24, and a fine steel crochet needle. The **1st round** of the d'oyley consists of a series of buttonhole stitch loops, worked with a crewel needle and a rather long length of the same coarse cotton you have been using for the feather stitching, and is simply for the purpose of making a foundation for working the crochet into; proceed thus—tie a knot to secure the end of the needleful of cotton, bring the needle and cotton up from the wrong side to the right side of the damask, just on the margin of the hem, * let the cotton hang over the fingers of the left hand, insert the needle from the wrong side to the right side of the material, about an eighth of an inch to the right of where it previously was brought up, and draw the cotton through to form a rather loose loop, keep the cotton to the right while you insert the needle upwards through the loop and draw the cotton through twist another similar stitch in the loop, and then repeat from *, making the loops all of even size, and when you have gone entirely round the material, join neatly, and fasten off. **2nd round**—With No. 20 cotton and fine crochet needle—Work 1 double crochet under the first buttonhole stitch loop of last round, * 9 chain, 1 single crochet in the fifth chain from the needle, 5 chain, 1 double crochet under the next buttonhole loop, and repeat from *; fasten off at the end of this and every round, and recommence in a fresh place. **3rd round**—1 double crochet in the next chain stitch but one *after* the picot of last round, 9 chain, 1 single crochet in the fifth chain from the needle, 5 chain, and repeat to the end of the round. Work three more rounds the same as last round. **7th round**—1 treble in the next chain stitch but one *after* the picot of last round, 8 chain, 1 single crochet in the fifth chain from the needle, 3 chain, another treble in the same place as last treble is worked into, 8 chain, 1 single crochet in the fifth chain from the needle, 5 chain, 1 single crochet in the same place, 5 chain, another single crochet in the same place (making three picots), 3 chain, and repeat. **8th round**—1 double crochet in the little picot of last round that stands by itself, 3 chain, 1 double crochet in the first picot of the group of three picots, 5 chain, 1 double crochet in the centre picot, 5 chain, 1 double crochet in the third picot, 3 chain, and continue the same to the end of the round **9th round**—1 double crochet on the double crochet stitch that in last round is worked into the solitary picot, 5 chain, 1 double crochet in the fourth chain stitch of the first loop of five chain of last round, 5 chain, 1 double crochet in the second stitch of the next loop of five chain of last round, 5 chain, and repeat. **10th round**—1 double crochet on the double crochet stitch above the solitary picot, 5 chain, 1 double crochet in the centre loop of five chain of last round, 5 chain, another double crochet in the same place, 5 chain, another double crochet in the same place, 5 chain, another double crochet in the same place, 5 chain, 1 double crochet on the double crochet stitch above the next solitary picot, 5 chain, 1 double crochet in the centre loop of five chain of last round, * 3 chain, 2 treble in the same loop, 3 chain, 1 double crochet in the same loop, repeat from * twice, then do 5 chain, and repeat all. **11th round**—1 double crochet in the first of the chain picot loops of last round, 5 chain, 1 double crochet in the next loop, 5 chain, 1 double crochet in the next loop, 1 chain, * 1 double crochet in the loop of chain before the two treble stitches of last round, 5 chain, 1 double crochet in the loop of chain before the double crochet of last round, 5 chain, repeat from * twice, which makes five loops round the treble stitches of the scallop, 1 chain, and proceed in the same manner to the end of the round. This finishes the d'oyley.

Full Size Working Design for Set for Chemise Trimming.

of last row, 2 chain, 1 double crochet in the space to the left of the double crochet stitch of last row, 4 chain, and repeat from * to the end, where join neatly; this finishes the scalloped edge. For the **Heading**—Work along the opposite side of the insertion,—**1st round**—2 treble under the loop of chain at the top of a point, * 5 chain 2 treble under the loop of the next point, and repeat from * to the end of the round, and join neatly. **2nd round**—Slip stitch between the two treble stitches of last round, 5 chain, 1 treble in the centre stitch of the five chain of last round, 2 chain, 1 treble between the two next treble stitches, 2 chain, * 1 treble in the centre stitch of five chain of last round, 2 chain, 1 treble between the two next treble stitches, 2 chain, and repeat from *; and at the end of the round join to the third stitch of the chain with which the round commenced. Sew the trimming upon the chemise, and run the narrow blue ribbon in and out through the open part of the heading, finishing with a little bow in front and on the top of each shoulder, as represented in the engraving. This border is also very suitable as a trimming for drawers.

SET FOR CHEMISE TRIMMING.

THIS trimming is worked with Evans' crochet cotton, No. 24, of which two reels will be required, and a very fine steel crochet needle. Commence with 30 chain, and work closely and firmly. **1st row**—1 treble in the sixth chain from the needle, 2 chain, another treble in the same place, 1 chain, miss one, 1 double crochet in the next, 8 consecutive treble, 5 chain, miss one, 8 more consecutive treble, 1 chain, miss one, 1 double crochet in the next, 1 chain, miss one, 1 treble in the last, 2 chain, another treble in the same place. **2nd row**—5 chain to turn, 1 treble under the loop of two chain, 2 chain, another treble in the same place, 2 chain, 4 treble on the first four

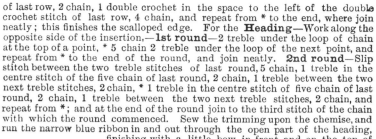

Set for Chemise Trimming.

TRIMMING FOR A CHEMISE.

PROCURE two reels of Evans' crochet cotton No. 18 or No 20, a fine steel crochet needle, and 2 yards of blue ribbon measuring three-eighths of an inch in width. The trimming is first of all worked the short way, and when a sufficient length is thus executed the scallops and the heading are added on either side. Commence with 9 chain; miss the eight chain stitches nearest the needle, and work 5 treble in the next stitch **2nd row**—5 chain to turn, miss the first treble stitch, do 1 treble on the next, 2 chain, 1 treble on the next, 2 chain, miss one stitch, 1 treble on the next, 2 chain, 5 treble under the loop at the end **3rd row**—Do 5 chain to turn, miss the first treble stitch, and do 1 treble on the next, 2 chain, 1 treble on the next, 2 chain, miss one stitch, 1 treble on the next, 2 chain, 5 treble under the first loop of two chain of last row. Repeat the last row till you can count 102 points along each side of the insertion. Then work in the same manner 34 points for each sleeve. Join the pieces in three separate rounds. Now work for the **Scallop—1st round**—1 double crochet under a point of the insertion, 4 chain, 5 treble 2 chain and 5 treble all under the next point, * 1 double crochet, under the next point, 4 chain, 5 treble 2 chain and 5 treble all under the next point, and repeat from * to the end, where join neatly round. **2nd round**—Turn the work, recommence with 1 double crochet under the loop of four chain, * 2 chain, 1 treble on the second treble stitch, 2 chain, 1 treble on the third treble stitch, 2 chain, miss one, 1 treble on the fifth treble stitch, 2 chain, 1 treble under the loop of two chain at the point of the scallop, 3 chain, another treble in the same place, 2 chain, 1 treble on the first treble stitch, 2 chain, miss one, 1 treble on the third treble stitch, 2 chain, 1 treble on the next treble stitch, 2 chain, 1 double crochet under the loop of four chain, and repeat from * to the end of the round, and join neatly **3rd round**—Turn the work, * do 1 double crochet under the space to the left of the first treble stitch, 4 chain, 1 double crochet under the next, 4 chain, 1 double crochet under the next, 4 chain, 1 double crochet under the loop at the point of the scallop, 4 chain, another double crochet in the same place, 4 chain, 1 double crochet under the next space, 4 chain, 1 double crochet under the next space, 4 chain, 1 double crochet under the next space, 4 chain, 1 double crochet in the space to the right of the double crochet stitch

treble of last row, 5 chain, 1 double crochet under the five chain of last row, 5 chain, 4 treble on the last four treble stitches, 2 chain, 1 treble under the loop of two chain, 2 chain, another treble in the same place. **3rd row**—5 chain to turn, 1 treble under the loop of two chain, 2 chain, another treble in the same place, 1 chain, 1 double crochet under two chain, 1 chain, 2 treble on the first two treble stitches, 4 chain, 1 double crochet under the first loop of five chain, 5 chain, 1 double crochet under the next loop of five chain, 4 chain, 2 treble on the last two treble stitches, 1 chain, 1 double crochet under two chain, 1 chain, 1 treble under the loop of two chain, 2 chain, another treble in the same place. **4th row**—5 chain to turn, 1 treble under the loop of two chain, 2 chain, another treble in the same place, 2 chain, 4 consecutive treble beginning over the two treble stitches of last row, 5 chain, 1 double crochet under the loop of five chain, 5 chain, 4 consecutive treble ending over the two treble stitches of last row, 2 chain, 1 treble under the loop of two chain, 2 chain, another treble in the same place. **5th row**—5 chain to turn, 1 treble under the loop of two chain, 2 chain, another treble in the same place, 1 chain, 1 double crochet under two chain, 1 chain, 8 consecutive treble beginning over the four treble stitches of last row, 5 chain, 8 more consecutive treble ending over the four treble stitches of last row, 1 chain, 1 double crochet under two chain, 1 chain, 1 treble under the loop of two chain, 2 chain, another treble in the same place. Repeat from the second row until 68 patterns are done, (or the length desired to go round the neck), then fasten off, and join the work in a round. Recommence with 30 stitches, and proceed with the same pattern for a sleeve; when 12 patterns are done join the scalloped edge of the next 8 patterns to the edge of the 8 corresponding patterns of the neck piece; work 12 more patterns, and fasten off. Work for the other sleeve in the same manner, and join the 8 centre patterns to the opposite side of the neck piece. Join both the sleeve pieces in a round Now work for the **Scalloped Edge** on the top of the neck piece and on the outside of each sleeve piece—**1st round**—Do 2 long treble, 3 chain, and 2 long treble, all under every point of five chain stitches; join evenly at the end of the round. **2nd round**—1 double crochet under a loop of three chain of last round, 1 chain, 1 treble under the next loop of three chain, 1 chain and 1 treble six times in the same place, 1 chain, and repeat to the end of the round. **3rd round**—1 double crochet under the chain stitch next after the double crochet stitch of last round, 5 chain, 1 double crochet under the next chain stitch, 5 chain and 1 double crochet six more times under successive chain stitches, and continue the same to the end of the round, where join neatly; this finishes the scalloped edge. For the **Heading**—Work along the under side of the neck piece and on the inside of the sleeves—3 treble under every point of five chain stitches, doing 2 chain between each group of treble stitches. This completes the trimming, which now is ready for sewing upon the chemise. The same border is also pretty as a trimming for drawers.

THE BURLINGTON CAPE.

THIS is one of the shoulder capes that are now so fashionably worn and gradually are usurping the place of shawls as they are warm and comfortable, and are not liable to fall off being secured round the neck with a ribbon. Our model is worked throughout in a pretty fancy stitch, with a soft shade of grey double Berlin wool, of which 10 ozs. are required, with 1¾ yards of two inch wide ribbon to match, and three bone crochet needles, No 9, No. 7, and No. 5. The pattern is worked in rows forwards and backwards. Wind two balls of

The Burlington Cape.

wool to begin with. Use No. 9 crochet needle, and commence with the first ball of wool with 63 chain stitches for the top of the cape. Leave this, and take the other ball, and leaving 17 chain unworked from the end where the first ball of wool is, begin with 1 double crochet in the eighteenth stitch of the chain, * miss one chain stitch, do 5 treble in the next, miss one, do 1 double crochet in the next, and repeat from * till 7 little patterns are worked, ending with a double crochet stitch as you began, and leaving 17 stitches unworked at the other end of the foundation chain. **2nd row**—1 chain to turn, and work back along the seven little patterns you have just done—thus—insert the hook from right to left behind the double crochet stitch and draw the wool through loosely, insert the hook from right to left behind the first treble stitch and draw the wool through loosely, insert the hook in the same manner behind the next treble stitch and draw the wool through loosely, now 4 loops are on the needle, wool over the needle and draw through all, do 1 chain to bind the cluster together, * insert the hook to take up the two top threads of the next treble stitch and draw the wool through, wool over the needle and draw through the two loops on the needle (this is practically a double crochet stitch and is always to be worked thus upon the centre treble stitch of a group), raise a loop upon the stem of each of the 2 next treble stitches (*always* inserting the hook from right to left at the back of the stitch), a loop upon the double crochet stitch, and a loop upon each of the 2 next treble stitches, all the loops to be as loose and as long as possible, now 6 loops are on the needle, wool over the needle and draw through all, do 1 chain to bind the loops together, and repeat from *, and when you come to the end of the seven patterns you will have only 3 stitches to raise loops upon for the last cluster, wool over the needle and draw through the loops, 1 chain, and break off the wool; tie the two ends of wool together **3rd row**—Resume the last stitch of the foundation chain, and proceed now with the first ball of wool; do 1 double crochet in the first chain stitch by the needle, * miss one, do 5 treble in the next, miss one, do 1 double crochet in the next, and repeat from * along the seventeen stitches of the foundation chain; when you get to the small portion that is already worked do a double crochet on the double crochet stitch of the first little row, and do 5 treble stitches in the loop of one chain that binds the little half pattern together, then * 1 double crochet on the double crochet of last row, and 5 treble in the one chain that binds the cluster of loops together, repeat from * five times, do 1 double crochet on the double crochet stitch, 5 treble in the loop of one chain that binds the half patterns together, 1 double crochet on the double crochet stitch at the end of the first little row, * miss one of the foundation chain, 5 treble in the next, miss one, 1 double crochet in the next, and repeat from * to the end of the row; there are 16 groups of five treble in this row, i.e., 4 groups at each end of the foundation chain, and 8 groups on the little rows that are worked in the middle of the back; the object of working the little rows is to make the back of the cape longer than the front. **4th row**—1 chain to turn, and work as instructed for the second row, doing 15 clusters of five loops in a cluster, and half a cluster at the beginning and end of the row. **5th row**—1 chain to turn, work 6 treble in the chain stitch that binds the half cluster together, * 1 double crochet on the double crochet stitch of last row, 5 treble in the chain stitch that binds the entire cluster

together, repeat from *, and end the row with 6 treble stitches as it began; there are 17 groups in this row. **6th row**—1 chain to turn, and work as directed for the fourth row, but doing 16 clusters and two half clusters. **7th row**—The same as the fifth row, but doing 18 groups. **8th row**—Take the No 7 needle, and work as instructed for the sixth row, doing 17 clusters and two half clusters. **9th row**—Keep to No. 7 needle, and work in the same manner as the seventh row, but do 8 treble at the beginning of the row, 7 treble always in each pattern instead of five treble, and end with 8 treble; there will be 19 groups in the row. **10th row**—Work as the eighth row, but raise 7 loops in a cluster instead of five loops, and make 18 clusters and two half clusters. **11th row**—Work the same as the ninth row, but make 20 groups in the row. **12th row**—The same as the tenth row, but to consist of 19 clusters and two half clusters. **13th row**—The same as the eleventh row, but make 21 groups in the row. **14th row**—The same as the twelfth row, but to consist of 20 clusters and two half clusters. **15th row** The same as the thirteenth row, but make 22 groups in the row. **16th row**—The same as the fourteenth row, but to consist of 21 clusters and two half clusters. **17th row**—The same as the fifteenth row, but make 23 groups in the row. **18th row**—Take the No. 5 needle, and work the same as in the sixteenth row, but doing 22 clusters and two half clusters. **19th row**—Keep to No. 5 needle, and work in the same manner as the seventeenth row, but do 24 groups in the row. **20th row**—Work as the eighteenth row, but to consist of 23 clusters and two half clusters **21st row**—2 chain to turn, 3 treble in the chain stitch that binds the half cluster together, 1 double crochet on double crochet stitch of last row, proceed as in the nineteenth row, and end with 4 treble stitches, this row therefore has no increase and will consist of 23 groups of treble stitches and two half groups. **22nd row**—Work a double crochet stitch on the first treble stitch of last row, then a cluster of 7 loops, a double crochet on double crochet, and continue to the end, where the double crochet must be worked upon the chain that turned, and there are 24 whole clusters in the row. **23rd row**—The same as the twenty-first row, and the same number of groups. **24th row**—The same as the twenty-second row. **25th row**—The same as the twenty-third row; leave the wool at the end of this row while you work a few rows for a neck-band. For the **Neck-band**—**1st row**—Use the second ball of the wool and No. 9 crochet needle, and holding the right side of the cape towards you, work along the commencing chain, 1 double crochet into about each alternate stitch of the chain, doing about 30 or 32 double crochet in the row **2nd row**—Turn the work, and do another row of double crochet stitches. **3rd**

Gentleman's Mitten.

row—4 chain to turn, and work long treble stitches (the wool twice round the needle) through which to run the ribbon. **4th row**—Plain double crochet. Now continue the border from the bottom corner of the cape, rounding the corner nicely with additional treble stitches, do scallops up the front, along the neck, and down the other front, and join neatly at the corner. Run the ribbon at the neck through the row of long treble stitches, there will be long ends to tie in a nice bow in front.

GENTLEMAN'S MITTEN.

PROCURE 1½ ozs. of brown Berlin fingering, or a 2 oz. packet of Baldwin's Beehive yarn, and a No. 12 bone crochet needle. Commence with 61 chain for the length of the mitten from the wrist to the top of the hand. **1st row**—Miss the first chain stitch, and work 36 double crochet and 24 single crochet, that is, 60 stitches in the row. **2nd row**—1 chain to turn, and inserting the hook to take up the one thread at the back of the stitches of the preceding row, do 24 single crochet over the twenty-four single crochet and 36 double crochet over the thirty-six double crochet of last row **3rd row**—1 chain to turn, work 36 double crochet and 24 single crochet in the row, always taking up the one back thread **4th row**—Same as the second row. Repeat these two rows till 51 rows are done, or till the mitten is the right size to fit round the hand, the single crochet stitches form the wrist. **52nd row**—Beginning at the wrist end—Do 1 chain to turn, 24 single crochet, 26 double crochet and 6 chain, and leave the other ten double crochet unworked **53rd row**—1 chain to turn, and work back 8 double crochet. **54th row**—Do 8 double crochet. **55th row**—1 chain to turn, and work 10 double crochet. **56th row**—Do 10 double crochet. **57th row**—1 chain to turn, and work twelve double crochet. Continue thus up and down, going 2 stitches further towards the wrist in every downward row till you work 16 stitches down and up again, and fasten off. Sew up the mitten, and work a row of double crochet along the top of the hand and thumb. Work a row of crazy stitch round the wrist. thus—1 double crochet on a rib of the mitten, 3 chain, 3 treble in the same place as the double crochet is worked into, and repeat the same, and join evenly at the end of the round. Crochet the other mitten in the same manner; and when sewing up be careful to fold this mitten to correspond with the mitten already made, one for the right hand and the other for the left, and the seam of each mitten must come inside the hand.

———

BABY'S PETTICOAT WITH BODICE.

WORKED IN RUSSIAN CROCHET.

THE petticoat from which our engraving is taken is very useful for summer wear, as it is worked with unbleached knitting cotton, Strutt's No 10 being the size selected, and of which about 4 ozs. will be required, the work is done with a No. 14 steel crochet needle. A similar petticoat can of course be made

Baby's Petticoat with Bodice.

with Andalusian wool and a bone crochet needle if preferred. Begin for the bottom of the front of the petticoat with a chain of 170 stitches. **1st row**—Commence in the first chain stitch by the needle, and work 5 consecutive double crochet, 3 double crochet in the next chain stitch, 5 more consecutive double crochet, * miss two chain, work 5 consecutive double crochet, 3 double crochet in the next, 5 more consecutive double crochet, and repeat from * to the end of the row. **2nd row**—Turn the work, and now miss the first stitch, and inserting the needle to take up the back thread of the stitches of the previous row, do * 5 consecutive double crochet, 3 double crochet on the next stitch which is the centre stitch of the three double crochet of last row, 5 more consecutive double crochet, miss two stitches, and repeat from * to the end of the row, where you will leave the one last stitch unworked. Continue working every row the same as the second row till 40 rows are done. **41st row**—Turn the work, miss the first stitch, do 11 consecutive double crochet, * miss 2 stitches, 11 consecutive double crochet, and repeat from * ; this forms the first decrease in the skirt. **42nd row**—Turn the work, miss the first stitch, * do 4 consecutive double crochet, 3 double crochet on the next stitch, which is the one stitch that in last row is worked upon the centre stitch of the three double crochet of previous rows, 4 more consecutive double crochet, miss two stitches, and repeat from * to the end, where as before, you will leave the one last stitch unworked. **43rd row**—Turn the work, miss the first stitch, do 9 consecutive double crochet, * miss two stitches, 9 consecutive double crochet, and repeat from * ; this forms a second decrease in the skirt. **44th row**—Turn the work, miss the first stitch, * do 3 consecutive double crochet, 3 double crochet on the next stitch, which is the one stitch that in last row is worked upon the centre stitch of the three double crochet of previous rows, 3 more consecutive double crochet, miss two stitches, and repeat from * to the

end, where as usual you will leave the one last stitch unworked **45th row**—Turn the work, miss the first stitch, do 7 consecutive double crochet, * miss two stitches, 7 consecutive double crochet, and repeat from * ; this forms another decrease, and now the skirt is narrowed sufficiently for the waist **46th row**—Turn the work, miss the first stitch, * do 2 consecutive double crochet, 3 double crochet on the next stitch, which is the one stitch that in last row is worked upon the centre stitch of the three double crochet of previous rows, 2 more consecutive double crochet, miss two stitches, and repeat from * to the end, where as before you will leave the last stitch unworked. Work for the **Body** 20 more rows the same as the last row. Then for the shoulder pieces, work the first 12 stitches forwards and backwards in plain double crochet for 8 rows, and fasten off ; work the last 12 stitches in the same manner for the other shoulder piece. The back of the petticoat commences with 170 chain, and is crocheted in the same manner as the front. Join the shoulder pieces together, and sew up the sides, leaving space at the top for armholes, round which is worked a little narrow edging, thus—* 1 double crochet, miss a little space, work 6 treble all in one loop of the foundation, miss a little space, and repeat from *, and join evenly at the ending of the round. The petticoat has no opening at the back, but slips easily over the child's head.

———

COT QUILT.

THIS cot quilt is worked in squares of tricot, each square being surrounded with three rounds of crochet. It is easily and quickly made, and looks very bright and pretty. The same pattern will serve for a sofa blanket, for a cushion cover, and many other articles. Procure 10 ozs of pink and 10 ozs of white double Berlin wool, a tricot needle No 6, a crochet needle No. 8, and odd lengths of filoselles of various colours. Commence with pink wool, with 15 chain, in which pick up 14 double crochet stitches, and draw back ; continue in rows of plain tricot till you have made a perfect square Then still with pink wool, and holding the tricot the wrong side towards you, take the crochet needle and work double crochet all round the square, doing three double crochet at the turning of the corners, join evenly at the end of the round, and fasten off. **2nd round**—With white wool, hold the tricot the right side towards you, and inserting the hook to take up the back thread of the stitches of last round, work round in treble, doing three or five treble to ease the corners, join at the end, and fasten off. **3rd round**—With pink wool, work a double crochet stitch on each of two successive stitches of last round, insert the hook into a double crochet stitch of the first round (the same stitch as the next treble stitch of last row is worked into) and draw the wool through, wool over the needle and draw through two stitches on the needle loosely, and repeat, and fasten off at the end of the round ; this finishes one square. Work the tricot part of the next square with white wool, and border it with a round of pink, white, and pink again, like the square already done On the white tricot square embroider a rose-bud spray, or other pretty device, with shaded filoselles On the pink tricot square work five double perpendicular lines of coral stitch, all with pink filoselle. When a sufficient number of squares are worked join them together by a pink row of double crochet. For the **Border** round the **Quilt**. **1st round**—Hold the work the wrong side

Cot Quilt.

towards you, and taking up the one top thread, work with pink wool a round of double crochet. **2nd round**—With white wool, hold the work the right side towards you and insert the hook to take up the back thread of the stitches of last round, work 1 double crochet, 6 chain, miss two stitches, and repeat. **3rd round**—Still with white wool, do 1 double crochet under a loop of chain stitches, 6 chain, and repeat Make a number of daisy balls of pink and white wool mixed, and sew one upon every alternate loop of chain stitches, as shown in the engraving, also place one daisy ball at every corner of the square sections.

ST. ANDREW'S CROSS.

SQUARE FOR A QUILT.

PROCURE sufficient quantity of Strutt's knitting cotton No. 6, and a medium sized steel crochet needle. Begin with 52 chain. **1st row**—Miss the two chain stitches nearest the needle and work 50 double crochet in the row, closely and firmly. **2nd row**—Turn the work, and proceed with double crochet, 51 stitches in the row, taking up the back thread of the stitches of the preceding row that the work may sit in ridges, the last double crochet stitch will come upon the chain that turned. Work 3 more rows of ridged crochet doing 51 stitches in each row. **6th row**—Turn, work 3 double crochet, 1 treble in the back thread of double crochet stitch of the second previous row, 3 double crochet, 1 treble in the lower rib, 3 double crochet, 1 treble in the lower rib, 9 double crochet, a tuft (4 treble stitches worked as a group in one stitch of the lower rib), 3 double crochet, a tuft, 3 double crochet, a tuft, 9 double crochet, 1 treble in the lower rib, 3 double crochet, 1 treble in the lower rib, 3 double crochet, 1 treble in the lower rib, 3 double crochet. The treble stitches which form the "cross" are always to be worked into the corresponding stitch of the second previous row, and so also are the groups of four treble stitches that form the "tufts." **7th row**—21 double crochet, 1 treble worked into the lower rib behind the tuft, 3 double crochet, 1 treble, 3 double crochet, 1 treble, 21 double crochet. **8th row**—5 double crochet, 1 treble, 3 double crochet, 1 treble, 3 double crochet, 1 treble, 9 double crochet, a tuft, 3 double crochet, a tuft, 9 double crochet, 1 treble, 3 double crochet, 1 treble, 3 double crochet, 1 treble, 5 double crochet. **9th row**—23 double crochet,

15 double crochet, 1 treble, 3 double crochet, 1 treble, 3 double crochet, 1 treble, 15 double crochet, a tuft, 5 double crochet. **25th row**—5 double crochet, 1 treble, 39 double crochet, 1 treble, 5 double crochet. **26th row**—3 double crochet, a tuft, 3 double crochet, a tuft, 11 double crochet, 1 treble, 3 double crochet, 1 treble, 3 double crochet, 1 treble, 3 double crochet, 1 treble, 11 double crochet, a tuft, 3 double crochet, a tuft, 3 double crochet. **27th row**—3 double crochet, 1 treble, 3 double crochet, 1 treble, 35 double crochet, 1 treble, 3 double crochet, 1 treble, 3 double crochet. **28th row**—The same as the twenty-fourth row. **29th row**—Same as the twenty-third row. **30th row**—Same as the twenty-second row. And so on work backwards, each successive row, till you finish the square with 3 rows of plain double crochet. Do not break off the cotton but proceed for **the Edge**—After working the last double crochet stitch of last row, do 6 chain, 1 treble on that same double crochet stitch (which is a corner stitch), 2 chain, 1 treble on the tip of the second ridge along the side of the square, 2 chain, 1 treble in the depressed space midway between the third and fourth ridges, and continue 2 chain and 1 treble alternately, and get 18 treble stitches along the side of the square from corner to corner, do 3 chain to round the corner, another treble on the corner stitch, and work the same along each side of the square; and on completion of the round join with a single crochet to the third stitch of chain with which the round commenced. **2nd round**—Work 1 double crochet in every stitch of preceding round, and 3 double crochet in the corner stitch; join round neatly, and fasten off. A Border suitable for this quilt appears in No. 39 of "Weldon's Practical Needlework Series."

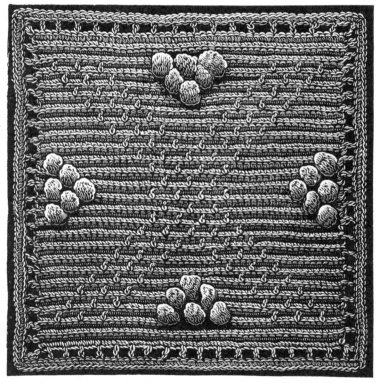

St. Andrew's Cross. Square for a Quilt.

1 treble, 3 double crochet, 1 treble, 23 double crochet. **10th row**—7 double crochet, 1 treble, 3 double crochet, 1 treble, 3 double crochet, 1 treble, 11 double crochet, a tuft, 11 double crochet, 1 treble, 3 double crochet, 1 treble, 3 double crochet, 1 treble, 7 double crochet. **11th row**—25 double crochet, 1 treble, 25 double crochet. **12th row**—9 double crochet, 1 treble, 3 double crochet, 1 treble, 3 double crochet, 1 treble, 15 double crochet, 1 treble, 3 double crochet, 1 treble, 3 double crochet, 1 treble, 9 double crochet. **13th row**—Plain double crochet, 51 stitches. **14th row**—11 double crochet, 1 treble, 3 double crochet, 1 treble, 3 double crochet, 1 treble, 11 double crochet, 1 treble, 3 double crochet, 1 treble, 3 double crochet, 1 treble, 11 double crochet. **15th row**—Plain double crochet. **16th row**—13 double crochet, 1 treble, 3 double crochet, 1 treble, 3 double crochet, 1 treble, 7 double crochet, 1 treble, 3 double crochet, 1 treble, 3 double crochet, 1 treble, 13 double crochet. **17th row**—Plain double crochet. **18th row**—15 double crochet, 1 treble, 3 double crochet, 1 treble, 3 double crochet, 1 treble, 3 double crochet, 1 treble, 3 double crochet, 1 treble, 3 double crochet, 1 treble, 15 double crochet. **19th row**—Plain double crochet. **20th row**—17 double crochet, 1 treble, 3 double crochet, 1 treble, 3 double crochet, 1 treble, 3 double crochet, 1 treble, 17 double crochet. **21st row**—Plain double crochet. **22nd row**—3 double crochet, a tuft, 15 double crochet, 1 treble, 3 double crochet, 1 treble, 3 double crochet, 1 treble, 15 double crochet, a tuft, 3 double crochet. **23rd row**—3 double crochet, 1 treble behind the tuft, 43 double crochet, 1 treble behind the tuft, 3 double crochet. **24th row**—5 double crochet, a tuft,

WELDON'S
PRACTICAL CROCHET.

(ELEVENTH SERIES.)

HOW TO CROCHET HATS, PETTICOATS, QUILTS, BORDERS, PINCUSHIONS, HOODS, &c.

TWENTY-SIX ILLUSTRATIONS.

Telegraphic Address—
"Consuelo," London.]

The Yearly Subscription to this Magazine, post free to any Part of the World, is 2s. 6d.
Subscriptions are payable in advance, and may commence from any date and for any period.

[Telephone—
2745.

The Back Numbers are always in print. Nos. 1 to 101 now ready, Price 2d. each, or post free for 18s. 2d. Over 5,000 Engravings.

CHILD'S PETTICOAT.
SHELL PATTERN

THIS is a pretty and useful petticoat for a girl of about five years of age, and is worked with the best Peacock wool or Petticoat fingering, and a No. 8 or No. 9 bone crochet needle. Of Peacock wool 1 oz. of red and 3 ozs. of white will be sufficient, but of Petticoat fingering rather more will be required, as it is thicker and therefore weighs heavier, and will make a larger sized skirt. Commence with red wool for the 1st round, which forms a line of little scollops along the bottom of the skirt ; * do 7 chain, pick up loosely 1 tricot stitch in each of 6 chain stitches, and there will be 7 stitches on the needle, wool over the needle and draw through all, do 1 chain to tighten the group of stitches ; repeat from * till you have 37 of these shell-like scollops, (or more or less according as you desire for the width of the skirt) ; join round evenly, and fasten off the wool. 2nd round— With white—Join the white wool in the heading of the row of scollops, draw the wool through a round loop where the stitches of last row are gathered together, and do three chain, draw up a tricot stitch in each of the 2 chain stitches below the needle, a stitch in the round loop where the stitches of last row are gathered together, a stitch in the next thread of wool, and a stitch in the next thread of wool, now 6 stitches are on the needle, wool over the needle and draw through all, and do 1 chain to tighten the group ; draw up a tricot stitch in the little round hole under the needle, a stitch in the lower back part of the shell just formed, a stitch in the thread of wool of last row where a stitch is already worked, a stitch in the next thread of wool, and a stitch in the next thread of wool, which is a little round loop where the stitches of last row are gathered together, now 6 stitches are on the needle, wool over the needle and draw through all, and do 1 chain to tighten the group ; proceed in this shell pattern, working two shells above each scollop to the end of the round ; which will make 74 shells in the round if you began with 37 scollops. 3rd round—Also with white wool— Work shell above shell ; break off the wool at the end of this round. 4th round—Shell-stitch worked with red wool. 5th round—Shell stitch worked with white wool. Repeat the last two rounds twice more. Then continue entirely with white wool, retaining the same number of shells in every round, till 10 consecutive rounds are worked with white wool, when break off ; and henceforth work in rows, doing 7 rows, and the beginning and at the end of the rows will form the opening of the placket hole at the back of the skirt. Decrease one shell in every six in the first row, and again one shell in every six in the fifth row. The waistband on our model is knitted with red wool

Child's Petticoat in Shell Pattern.

and a pair of No. 14 knitting needles, picking up a line of stitches along the top of the skirt and working in a rib of 1 stitch plain and 1 stitch purl for 10 rows, and cast off. Or you can make a calico waistband if you like, or work one in plain double crochet.

D'OYLEY WORKED IN MEDALLIONS.

A PRETTY dessert d'oyley can be worked according to the accompanying illustration by using Evans' crochet cotton, No. 18, of which two reels will be required, and a fine steel crochet needle, or for a toilet d'oyley employ red or blue crochet Maltese thread, No. 14. Commence with 8 chain, and join round. 1st round—Do 3 chain to stand for a treble, and work 23 treble stitches in the circle, and join evenly to the third chain with which the round began. 2nd round—3 chain, miss one treble stitch, 1 double crochet on the next, and repeat, doing 12 loops in the round, and join evenly. 3rd round—Slip-stitch to the middle of the loop of three chain, * 5 chain, 1 double crochet in the middle of the next loop, and repeat from * till 12 loops of five chain are done, and join round. 4th round—Slip-stitch to the middle of the loop of five chain, * 4 chain, 1 double crochet under the same loop, 3 chain, 1 double crochet under the next loop, and repeat from *, making 12 loops of four chain, and 12 loops of three chain, and join round. 5th round—Slip-stitch once into the four chain loop, do 3 chain to stand for a treble, 3 treble in the four chain loop, * 3 chain, 4 more treble in the same place, 3 chain, 4 treble in the next four chain loop, and repeat from *, making 12 groups of eight treble stitches, and join round. 6th round —Slip-stitch to the three chain loop in the centre of the group of treble stitches, * do 1 double crochet in the three chain loop, 5 chain, another double crochet in the same place, 5 chain, another double crochet, 5 chain, and another double crochet in the same place, 3 chain, miss one three-chain loop, and in the next loop repeat from *, and fasten off at the end of the round, which completes one medallion. Work 6 more medallions in the same manner, and unite them together in process of working the last round, as shown in the engraving. For the **Border—1st round**— 1 double crochet in the centre loop of the first group of picots round the margin of a medallion, * 8 chain, 1 double crochet in the centre loop of the next group of picots, and repeat from *, doing 6 double crochet stitches into each medallion with 8 chain between ; and join evenly at the end of the round. 2nd round—5 chain, miss one stitch of last round, 1 treble in the next, * 2 chain, miss one stitch, 1 treble in the next, and repeat from * ; and join at the end of the round to the third chain with which the round commenced. **3rd round**—Slip-stitch under a space of last round, 6 chain, 1 treble in the same space, 2 chain, miss one space, * 1 treble in the next, 3 chain, 1 treble in the same space, 2 chain, miss one space, and repeat from *, and at the end join to the third chain with which the round commenced. **4th round**—Slip-stitch to the centre of a loop of three chain where do 1 double crochet, * 3 chain, 1 treble under the next loop of three chain, 2 chain, 1 treble in the same place, 2 chain, another treble, 2 chain, another treble in the same place, 3 chain, 1 double crochet under the next loop of three chain, and repeat from *; and join, and fasten off at the end of this round. **5th round**—1 double crochet under the centre loop of two chain of last round, 5 chain and 1 double crochet three times in the same place, 7 chain, and repeat; and join evenly at the end of the round, and fasten off.

TEA COSY.

REQUIRED, about 1 oz. of each of eight shades of crimson, and 1½ oz. of black single Berlin wool, and a No. 12 bone crochet needle. Begin for the fan-like semicircle with the fourth shade of crimson wool, counting from the lightest, make 37 chain stitches; and for the **1st row**—Work 8 double crochet in the second chain from the needle, 7 double crochet in the next, and continue the same number of double crochet alternately to the end of the foundation chain.

row—Sixth shade. **16th row**—Seventh shade. **17th row**—Darkest shade. **18th row**—Black. **19th row**—Lightest shade. **20th row**—Third shade, **21st row**—Fourth shade. **22nd row**—Sixth shade. **23rd row**—Black. This completes the fan. For the **Sunflower in the Centre**—Commence with the third shade of crimson wool, with 2 chain, and work 4 double crochet in the second chain from the needle, and join the last of the four stitches to the first, in a circle. **1st round**—With same shade of wool—Turn the work, and inserting the hook to take up the back thread of the previous stitches, work 8 double crochet in the round, that is, 2 double crochet on each stitch, and join round. **2nd round**—Still with the same wool—Turn the work, and again do 2 double crochet on each stitch of last round, making 16 double crochet, and join round. **3rd round**—Keep the work on the same side, do 3 chain to stand for a treble, insert the hook to take up both the front threads of last round and work 4 treble on the first stitch, withdraw the hook, insert it in the third stitch of chain and draw the wool through, which binds the treble stitches closely together in a knob, do 1 loose double crochet on the next stitch of last row, 5 treble on the same stitch, withdraw the hook and insert it in the first of the five treble stitches and draw the wool through, which produces another knob; make 7 of these knobs on seven stitches and 1 double crochet between each, then miss one stitch, and do 7 more knobs and 7 more double crochet stitches, making in all 14 knobs and 14 double crochet in the round. **4th round**—With the next darkest shade of crimson—Work 1 knob and 1

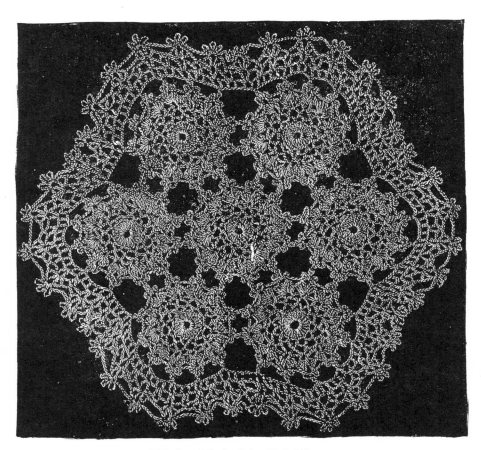

D'Oyley Worked in Medallions.

to the number of 269 stitches; fasten off at the end of this row and every row, and commence the following row on the right-hand side, always inserting the hook to take up the one top thread of the stitches of the previous row, and working closely and evenly. **2nd row**—With the third shade of crimson wool—Work 6 consecutive double crochet stitches (i.e., 1 stitch on each of 6 stitches), 3 double crochet on the next, * 6 consecutive double crochet, miss two stitches, 6 consecutive double crochet, 3 double crochet on the next, and repeat from *, making 18 points of three double crochet stitches, and end as you began with 6 consecutive double crochet. **3rd row**—With the lightest shade of crimson wool—Insert the hook to take up the first and second stitches of last row as one stitch in which to work 1 double crochet, do 5 consecutive double crochet, then 3 double crochet on the centre stitch of three double crochet of last row, * 6 consecutive double crochet, miss two stitches, 6 consecutive double crochet, 3 double crochet on the next, which again is on the centre stitch of three double crochet of last row, and repeat from *, and end the row as you began with 5 consecutive double crochet and the two last stitches taken together in 1 double crochet. Every succeeding row is worked in the same manner as this last row. The only difference being in the shade of the wool. For the **4th row**—Use black wool. **5th row**—The second shade of crimson. **6th row**—Darkest crimson. **7th row**—Sixth shade. **8th row**—Third shade. **9th row**—Black. **10th row**—Sixth shade. **11th row**—Fifth shade. **12th row**—Second shade. **13th row**—Black. **14th row**—Second shade. **15th**

double crochet on every stitch of the preceding round, making 28 knobs, and 28 double crochet in the round, join quite evenly, and fasten off. You now arrange the fan-like portion of the crochet upon the sunflower as shown in the engraving, it stretches over twenty-two of the knobs, and must be neatly joined thereto by stitching or by crocheting at the back; the remaining six knobs lie as they are to the bottom of the cosy. You now, with the darkest shade of crimson, work 2 rows of plain double crochet straight along the bottom of the cosy from end to end. Work the reverse side of the cosy in exactly the same manner. Join the two fan-like pieces together stitch by stitch along the scolloped edge, only when at the bottom of the hollows you take two stitches together twice, the better to preserve the shape of the scollops. The cosy is lined with nicely quilted satin, and finished off with a bow of ribbon on the top.

BULGARIAN HEAD-DRESS.

FOR EVENING WEAR.

THIS head-dress is a novel and exceedingly pretty style for the opera or theatre, and consists of a stiff coronet covered with satin on which a band of tricot is arranged, while the crochet falls like a veil down the back, and may be wrapped closely round the neck as a protection from draught, or be tastefully caught up on one side with a pretty pin or a small glistening brooch. Materials required—9 ozs. of white peacock fingering wool of **A A** quality, a No. 8 bone crochet needle and a No. 9 tricot needle, a piece of stiff buckram this shape, ⌒ measuring 14½ inches along the straight side and 4½ inches in width in the centre but rounded at the corners, ¼ yard of pale blue satin, and ⅛ yard of narrow white elastic. Commence for the top of the veil, with Peacock wool and No. 8 crochet needle, with 31 chain. **1st row**—Miss the three chain stitches nearest the needle, and work 5 long treble stitches (wool twice round the needle) in the fourth chain from the needle, miss two stitches, 1 double crochet in the next, * miss two, 5 long treble in the next, miss two, 1 double crochet in the next, and repeat from *, making five groups of long treble stitches in the row; always work loosely, and draw up the long treble stitches to stand as high as possible. **2nd row**—Make three chain to turn, work 5 long treble on the first long treble stitch of previous row, 1 double crochet on the third long treble which is the middle stitch of the group, * 5 long treble on the double crochet stitch of previous row, 1 double crochet on the middle stitch of the next group, and repeat from *, and at the end of the row work 5 long treble on the last long treble stitch of last row; this makes six groups of long treble stitches in the row. Every successive row is worked in the same way as the last row, and by the time you get 37 rows done for the length of the veil you will have 41 groups of long treble stitches in the row. Now work the **Border** which is crocheted all round the veil excepting along the foundation chain—**1st row**—Beginning on the side of the veil by the foundation chain, work 7 long treble stitches in a group, miss a row, work one double crochet, miss a row, and continue the same until the corner is reached; turn easily; then along the bottom of the veil you work the group of 7 long treble stitches on a double

stitch at the beginning and a stitch at the end of every row till 10 rows in all are worked for the width of the band. Stitch the tricoted band firmly and neatly upon the satin coronet, leaving a margin of satin showing in front, that is along the straight side of the coronet, place the commencing chain of the veil under the band on the opposite side, stitching both band and commencing chain of the veil neatly together : let the veil hang over the band while you stitch down on the slant about two scollops on each end of the coronet, then throw the veil back in its right position. Sew an elastic on each side of the coronet with a button to fasten.

PINCUSHION.

THIS pincushion is made in the shape of a brioche. The cover is worked with red and pink D M C coton à tricoter, No. 20, a ball of each being required and a medium fine steel crochet needle. The cushion measures about 6 inches across, the top is covered with red satin on which the crochet is laid, and the bottom is of pink flannelette. Commence with pink cotton for the centre of the cover; work 8 chain, join round, do 14 double crochet in the circle, and again join evenly. **2nd round**—Do 3 chain to stand for 1 treble stitch, and work 5 treble on the first double crochet of last round, take the hook out and insert it in the top stitch of the three chain and draw the loop through, which binds the group of stitches in the form of a raised tuft, do 4 chain, * miss one double crochet, work 6 treble in the next, withdraw the hook and insert it in the top of the first treble stitch and draw the loop through, which again binds a group of stitches in the similitude of a raised

Tea Cosy.

crochet of last row, and a double crochet on the centre stitch of the previous group; turn the other corner when you come to it, and then proceed up the other side to correspond with the side already done; fasten off after doing the last group of 7 long treble stitches. **2nd row**—Recommencing on the right-hand side—Do 1 double crochet on the first long treble stitch, 1 double crochet on the second long treble stitch, 3 chain, 1 single crochet in the third chain from the needle, 1 double crochet on the third long treble stitch, 3 chain, 1 single crochet in the third chain from the needle, 1 double crochet on the fourth long treble stitch, 3 chain, 1 single crochet in the third chain from the needle, 1 double crochet on the fifth long treble stitch, 1 double crochet on the sixth long treble stitch, miss three stitches, and repeat the same upon every scollop round the veil; which now is completed. For the **Coronet**—Having the buckram cut to the required shape and size, cover it neatly on both sides with pale blue satin, and proceed to work a strip of tricot for the band. Take the tricot needle, and beginning with 62 chain, work a **1st row** of 60 stitches of plain tricot. **2nd row**—1 stitch remains on the needle, wool over the needle, insert the hook to take up the chain stitch below the second tricot stitch of last row, and draw the wool through very loosely, wool over the needle and draw through one loop, wool over the needle and draw through two loops, pick up a tricot loop in the next stitch of previous row, work another raised loop in the chain stitch below the next stitch of previous row, and continue the two stitches alternately to the end; and draw back as in ordinary tricot. **3rd row**—Work alternately a plain tricot and a raised tricot, the raised tricot to be over the plain stitch of preceding row and the plain tricot over the raised stitch. Continue working in the same manner but decrease a

tuft, do 4 chain, and repeat from * five times, making in all 7 tufts in the round with 4 chain between each tuft; join round. **3rd round**—Slip stitch into a four chain loop, do 3 chain to stand for 1 treble stitch, and work 5 treble in the four chain loop, take out the hook and insert it in the top stitch of three chain and draw the loop through so as to bind the group of stitches into a tuft, then 4 chain. 6 treble stitches in the same loop and draw in a tuft, 4 chain, * 6 treble stitches in the next loop and make a tuft, 4 chain, 6 treble stitches in the same loop, and make a tuft, 4 chain, and repeat from * ; and make 14 tufts in the round with 4 chain between each tuft; and join evenly. **4th round**—Work 1 tuft in each loop of last round, making 14 tufts in the round with 4 chain between each tuft. **5th round**—Work the same as the third round, two tufts in each loop, making 28 tufts in the round with 4 chain between each tuft, and join round. **6th round**—Work 1 tuft in the first loop, 1 tuft in the next loop, and 1 tuft in the next loop, then 6 chain, 1 double crochet in the next loop, 6 chain, and repeat the same to the end of the round, and you will have 21 tufts in the round of seven groups of three tufts in a group. **7th round**—Do 1 tuft in the loop between the first and second tufts of preceding round, 4 chain, 1 tuft in the next loop between the second and third tufts of preceding round, 6 chain, 1 double crochet in the next loop, 6 chain, 1 double crochet in the next loop, 6 chain,* 1 tuft in the next loop, 4 chain, 1 tuft in the next, 6 chain, 1 double crochet in the next, 6 chain, 1 double crochet in the next, 6 chain, and repeat from * to the end of the round, and join evenly **8th round**—Do 1 tuft in the loop between the two tufts of last round, 6 chain and 1 double crochet in the next loop three times, 6 chain, and repeat the same to the end of the round, which brings each of the seven groups of tufts to a point of one tuft only. **9th round**—Slip-stitch to the centre of a loop of last round, do 1 double crochet in the loop, * 5 chain, 1 double crochet in the next loop, and repeat from *, and there will be 28 loops of chain in the round. **10th round**—The same. **11th round**—Slip-stitch to the centre of a loop of last round, do 1 double crochet in the loop, 7 chain, 1 double crochet in the fifth chain from the needle, 4 chain, 1 single crochet on the double crochet stitch, 4 chain, another single crochet in the same place where now there are three little pique loops of chain, 2 chain, and work the same to the completion of the round, where join evenly, and fasten off. **12th round**—With red

Bulgarian Head-Dress.

cotton—Work 1 double crochet in the centre pique loop of last round, * 6 chain, 1 double crochet in the next centre pique loop, and repeat from * to the end of the round. **13th round**—Also with red cotton—Plain double crochet. For the **Border**—With pink cotton, **1st round**—Work 1 double crochet on a double crochet stitch of last round, 5 chain, and repeat; you will generally miss two stitches, but occasionally miss three stitches of last round when doing the five chain, as there must be 68 loops of chain stitches in the round. **2nd round**—Work the same as the sixth round, and you will have 51 tufts in the round in seventeen groups of three tufts in a group **3rd round**—Same as the seventh round. **4th round**—Same as the eighth round. **5th round**—With red cotton—Work 1 treble under a loop of last round, 3 chain, another treble in the same place, * 1 treble under the next loop, 3 chain, another treble in the same place, and repeat from * to the end of the round. **6th round**—Also with red cotton—Do 1 double crochet, 4 treble, 1 double crochet, all under each loop of three chain of last round, and join evenly, and fasten off. This finishes the crochet cover. The padded cushion should be just the size of the round of double crochet that is worked with red cotton; the first and second rounds of the cover are scarcely perceptible in the engraving as they sink into the hollow in the centre of the cushion. The cushion is very tightly stuffed with bran except in the exact centre where the red satin and the pink flannelette meet and are secured together by a few stitches.

BORDER FOR A QUILT.

THIS border is worked in rows lengthways, and though specially designed for trimming a quilt executed in the Raised Square Pattern, illustrated on page 13 of the present issue, it can be used with several patterns that have appeared in Nos. 6, 39, 42, and 51 of "Weldon's Practical Needlework Series," price 2d. each of all booksellers, or 2½d. each from this office. The first row may be commenced straight upon the margin or edge of the quilt itself, in

which case the additional fulness required for turning the corners can be ensured row by row, by working three or five extra stitches, in the same way as extra stitches are employed in turning the corners of the quilt squares; or it can be crocheted upon a foundation chain of the required length, with an ample allowance for fulling in round the corners. The same pattern is useful worked with macramé twine for a mantel-drape, or worked with coloured flax thread for furniture trimming. **1st row**—Plain double crochet. **2nd row**—Turn the work; do 1 treble in the back thread of a double crochet stitch of the preceding row, * 3 chain, another treble in the same place, miss two stitches, 1 treble in the back thread of the next double crochet, and repeat from * to the end of the row. **3rd row**—Keep the work on the same side, and do 1 double crochet in the centre stitch of three chain of last row, 2 chain, and continue the same. **4th row**—Plain double crochet. **5th row**—All treble, inserting the hook to take the one *top* thread of the stitches of the previous row, and increase one stitch in every ten. **6th row**—Work 1 double crochet in the *front* thread of a double crochet stitch of the fourth row, miss one stitch, 6 double crochet in the front thread of the next stitch, miss one, and repeat. **7th row**—Turn the work; and do plain double crochet, inserting the hook to take the back thread of the treble stitches of the fifth row. **8th row**—Turn the work; insert the hook into two top threads of the stitches of last row, and do 1 treble, 1 chain, miss one, and repeat. **9th row**—Turn the work; and do plain double crochet, inserting the hook to take the back thread of the stitches of last row. **10th row**—Same as the eighth row. **11th row**—Same as the ninth row. **12th row**—With the right side of the work to the front; work all treble, taking up the *back* thread of the stitches of last row, and increase one treble in every ten. **13th row**—Work 1 double crochet in the *top* thread of a double crochet stitch of the eleventh row, miss one stitch, 6 double crochet in the top thread of the next stitch, miss one, and repeat. **14th row**—With the right side of the work to the front, work double crochet on the treble stitches of the twelfth row. **15th row**—Same as the eighth row. **16th row**—Same as the ninth row. **17th row**—Turn the work; and again do plain double crochet, inserting the hook to take the back thread of the stitches of last row. **18th row**—The same. Now for the **Scollops**—Beginning with the wrong side of the work to the front—Do 1 double crochet on the first stitch, inserting the hook to take the top and back threads, * 5 chain, miss three, 1 double crochet on the next, and repeat from * three times, making four loops of chain stitches, and turn the work. **2nd row**—Do 6 double crochet under each of the three first loops, and 3 double crochet under the fourth loop. **3rd row**—Turn with 5 chain, 1 double crochet between the third and fourth double crochet stitches

Working Design of one Corner of the Bulgarian Head-Dress.

of the first loop, 5 chain, 1 double crochet between the third and fourth stitches of the next loop, 5 chain, 1 double crochet between the third and fourth stitches of the next loop, making three loops of chain stitches, and turn the work. **4th row**—Do 6 double crochet under each of the two first loops, and 3 double crochet under the third loop. **5th row**—Turn with 5 chain, 1 double crochet between the third and fourth double crochet stitches of the first loop, 5 chain, 1 double crochet between the third and fourth stitches of the next loop, making two loops of chain stitches, and turn the work. **6th row**—Do 6 double crochet under the first loop, and 3 double crochet under the second loop. **7th row**—Turn with 5 chain, 1 double crochet between the third and fourth double crochet stitches of the loop, forming one loop only for the top of the scollop, and turn the work. **8th row**—Do 2 double crochet under the loop, 4 chain, 2 more double crochet under the loop, 4 chain, again 2 double crochet, 4 chain, and again 2 double crochet under the loop, then 3 double crochet to fill in the vacant half space of the next loop to the left, 3 double crochet in the next loop, and 3 double crochet in the next loop, which finishes one scollop. The other scollops are formed in the same manner.

D'OYLEY, EDGED WITH VENETIAN LACE.

THE centre of this d'oyley is composed of an oval piece of fine linen damask measuring about six inches from end to end, which after being hemmed round, is bordered with a pretty crochet lace, worked shortways. For this lace procure a skein of Coats' crochet cotton, No. 20, and a fine steel crochet needle. Begin with 24 chain, do 1 treble in the eleventh chain from the needle, 5 chain, 1 treble in the next, 10 chain, miss ten stitches, 1 treble in the next, 5 chain, 1 treble in the next, which is the last of the foundation stitches : * 10 chain, turn the work, do 1 treble under the loop of five chain, 5 chain, another treble in the same place, 5 chain, 1 double crochet under the loop of ten chain, 5 chain, 1 treble under the loop of five chain, 5 chain, another treble in the same place ;

Pincushion.

10 chain, turn the work, do 1 treble under the loop of five chain, 5 chain, another treble in the same place, 10 chain, miss two loops of five chain, 1 treble under the next loop, 5 chain, another treble in the same place ; you are now on the side where the tag of cotton hangs, and must repeat from * twice more, when there will be three loops of ten chain protruding from the edge of the crochet on each side the work. Do 10 chain, turn the work, 1 treble under the loop of five chain, and now for a **Scollop**—1 chain, turn the work, do 11 treble under the last loop of ten chain, 10 chain, 1 treble in the second loop of ten chain (i.e., the second loop), that protrudes on that side the work, 5 chain, another treble in the same place ; 10 chain, turn, do 1 treble under the five chain just done, 5 chain, another treble in the same place, 10 chain, 1 double crochet between the first and second of the eleven treble stitches ; * 10 chain, turn, 1 treble under the last worked loop of five chain, 5 chain, another treble in the same place, 10 chain, turn, 1 treble under the five chain just done, 5 chain, another treble in the same place, 10 chain, 1 double crochet between the two next of the eleven treble stitches, and repeat from * till you have ten loops projecting in the form of a scollop, and ten double crochet stitches worked intermediately between the eleven treble stitches, work 1 single crochet on the one chain stitch with which the scollop began ; then, 5 chain, 1 treble in the same loop in which you see a treble is already worked, 5 chain, 1 double crochet under the loop of ten chain, 5 chain, 1 treble under the loop of five chain, 5 chain, another treble in the same place, and now you are at the top of the edging, and proceed with working the insertion or heading. Do 10 chain, turn the work, 1 treble under the loop of five chain, 5 chain, another treble in the same place, 10 chain, miss two loops of five chain, 1 treble under the next loop, 5 chain, another treble in the same place, 10 chain, turn the work, 1 treble under the loop of five chain, 5 chain, another treble in the same place, 5 chain, 1 double crochet under the loop of ten chain, 5 chain, 1 treble under the loop of five chain, 5 chain, another treble in the same place, which is the top of the edging ; 10 chain, turn the work, 1 treble under the loop of five chain, 5 chain, another treble in the same place, 10 chain, miss two loops of five chain, 1 treble under the next loop, 5 chain, another treble in the same place, then 5 chain, and do 1 double crochet in the five-chain loop in the last row of the scollop, 5 chain, turn the work, 1 treble under the ordinary five-chain loop, 5 chain, another treble in the same place, 5 chain, 1 double crochet under the loop of ten chain, 5 chain, 1 treble under the loop of five chain, 5 chain, another treble in the same place, and this brings you again to the top of the edging, and completes one scollop. Now proceed with working the insertion or heading forwards and backwards for 7 short rows in the manner already instructed, and when these are done crochet another scollop like the preceding,

only when you get to the first, also the second, projecting loops of ten chain, do 5 chain only, do 1 single crochet into the last projecting loop of last scollop, and another 5 chain, and this makes the ordinary projecting loops of the present scollop, and at the same time joins the present scollop to the preceding scollop. Continue the edging until twelve scollops are accomplished, which will be a sufficient length to go round a d'oyley of the size shown in our engraving, though a longer piece can be made if a larger d'oyley is required. Join the last row of the edging very neatly to the foundation row ; then sew the edging to the damask centre by two or three seam stitches set into the tip of each protruding loop. Work a row of coral stitching with coarse crochet cotton round the margin of the damask linen.

PRETTY DRESS FOR A CHILD.

THE dress shown in the accompanying illustration measures about 20 inches from the shoulder to the bottom of the skirt, and is intended for a child of about three years of age ; it is simply and easily made, and yet has a pretty and stylish appearance. The materials required are 5 ozs. of the best white Peacock fingering wool, a No. 10 bone crochet needle, five or six white pearl buttons, and a yard of ribbon to tie round the waist. A good warm petticoat for a poor child can be worked from the same instructions by using ordinary Scotch Yarn of strong quality. Begin with 80 chain for the length of the dress from the neck to the bottom of the skirt at the back. **1st row**—Do 1 treble in the fourth chain from the needle, 1 treble in the next chain, and so on, 1 treble in every stitch of chain, making 77 treble in all in the row. **2nd row**—3 chain to turn, 1 treble on the first treble stitch of preceding row, and 1 treble on each treble successively to the end, 77 treble in all, inserting the hook to take up the two top threads of the stitches. **3rd row**—3 chain to turn, 1 treble on the first treble stitch of last row, and 33 more treble worked consecutively ; then turn with 2 chain, miss the first treble stitch, and work again 33 consecutive treble ; and you are at the bottom edge of the skirt ; the short double row just worked, which is practically *two* rows, is repeated at regular intervals on purpose to increase the fulness of the skirt. **5th row**—3 chain to turn, 1 treble on the first treble stitch of last row, and continue in treble to the end, doing 1 treble on the chain where last row was turned, and making in all 77 treble in the row. **6th row**— 3 chain to turn, and work 77 treble. Repeat from the third row twice. **15th row**—The same as the third row. **17th row**—Same as the fifth row, and do 14 chain at the end to heighten for the shoulder. **18th row** —Work 1 treble in the third chain from the needle, and treble all along 89 stitches to the bottom of the skirt. **19th row**—Same as the third row. **21st row**—3 chain to turn, and 89 treble in the row to the top of the shoulder. **22nd row**—3 chain to turn, and 89 treble to reach to the bottom of the skirt. **23rd row**—Same as the third row. **25th row**—3 chain to turn, and work 66

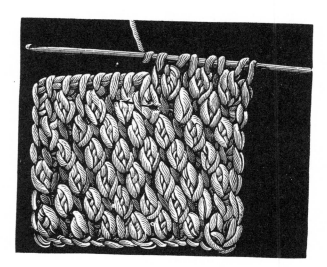

Tricot Design as used for the Coronet of Bulgarian Head-Dress.

treble, and leave the other stitches unworked to afford space for the armhole. **26th row**—3 chain to turn, and work 66 treble stitches. Repeat the last four rows. **31st row**—Same as the third row. **33rd row**—3 chain to turn, work 66 treble, and do 25 chain at the end to heighten for the shoulder. **34th row** —Work 1 treble in the third chain from the needle, and treble consecutively all along, 89 stitches to the bottom of the skirt. **35th row**—Same as the third row. **37th row**—3 chain to turn, and work 89 treble in the row to the top of the shoulder. **38th row**—3 chain to turn, and work 89 treble to reach to the bottom of the skirt. **39th row**—Here you begin the front of the dress by working a short double row the same as the third row. **41st row**—3 chain to turn, and work in all 77 treble in the row. **42nd row**—3 chain to turn, and work 77 treble to the bottom of the skirt. Repeat these four rows seven times, which will count 16 rows along the neck of the dress and 28 rows upon the skirt. **71st row**—Same as the third row. **73rd row**—Same as the seventeenth row. **74th row**—Same as the eighteenth row. And continue hence straight on, row by row, forming the other shoulder, till you come to a repetition of the forty-second row. Thence repeat the last four rows for the other half of the back of the dress till 10 rows are done along the neck, work the last row to the waist only, and fasten off. Sew up the back of the skirt, and sew the first two rows of the body to lap as it were over the last two rows. Join the shoulder pieces together. Work a **Crochet Edge** along the bottom of the skirt. **1st round**—1 double crochet under a loop of three chain, 4 chain, another double crochet in the same place, * 1 double crochet under the next loop of three chain, 4 chain, another double crochet in the same place, and repeat from * to the end of the round. **2nd round**—1 double crochet under a loop of four chain, 4 chain, another double crochet in the same place, and repeat. Work 2 more rounds the same. **5th round**—Work 6 double crochet under each loop of four chain of last round, and fasten off at the end of the round. Work the same crochet edge round the armholes, also round the neck, and down the right-hand side of the back as far as the waist, where put a stitch or two to cause the edge to fold over. Sew pearl buttons on the left-hand side of the back, and they will button into the first row of holes in the edging. Run a ribbon along the top of the skirt to tie round the waist. A broad handsome ribbon sash can be becomingly worn upon this little dress.

OPERA HOOD AND COLLARETTE.

WORKED WITH GIANT WOOL.

GIANT WOOL, or, as it is sometimes called, Leviathan Wool, is a soft wool of many plies, about the thickness of box-cord. Of course being so thick only a short length goes to an ounce, but it works up well in bulk, and the opera hood and collarette combined, as shown in our illustration, is a charming novelty, and is sure to be much liked by ladies who are partial to a pretty

Border for a Quilt.

head covering. Required, 6 ozs. of white and 2 ozs of a pale shade of greeny-blue giant wool, and a large wooden crochet needle of size to measure about 1½ inches round. Commence with white wool for the top of the head, make 2 chain, and work 6 double crochet stitches in the second chain from the needle. **2nd round**—Proceed in a circle, and do 2 double crochet on each of the six double crochet stitches taking up the one top thread. **3rd round**—Again do 2 double crochet on each stitch. **4th round**—Do 2 double crochet on the first stitch, 1 double crochet on the next, and repeat, and there will be 36 double crochet in this round. **5th round**—Do 2 double crochet on the first stitch, * 1 double crochet on each of the two next stitches, 2 double crochet on the next, repeat from * four times, and now turn, and work in rows. **1st row**—2 chain to turn, 1 treble on the first double crochet stitch taking up the two top threads, * miss one stitch, 3 treble on the next, miss one stitch, 1 treble on the next, and repeat from * four times ; the part now about to be done is for the back of the head. **2nd row**—2 chain to turn, 1 treble on the first treble stitch, 3 treble on the centre stitch of three treble of last row, 1 treble on one treble stitch, 3 treble on the centre stitch of three treble, 1 treble on one treble stitch, 7 treble on the centre stitch of three treble, 1 treble on one treble stitch, 3 treble on the centre stitch of three treble, 1 treble on one treble stitch, 3 treble on the centre stitch of three treble, 1 treble on treble stitch at the end. **3rd row**—2 chain to turn, 1 treble on the first treble stitch, 3 treble on the centre stitch of three treble, 1 treble on

treble, 3 treble on the centre stitch of three treble, 1 treble on treble, miss one stitch, 3 treble on the next, 1 treble on the next, 3 treble on the centre stitch of seven treble, 1 treble on the next, 3 treble on the next, miss one stitch, 1 treble on treble, 3 treble on the centre stitch of three treble, 1 treble on treble, 3 treble on the centre stitch of three treble, 1 treble on treble stitch at the end. **4th row**—2 chain to turn, 1 treble on the first treble stitch, * 3 treble on the centre stitch of three treble, 1 treble on treble stitch, and repeat from * six times. **5th row**—3 chain to turn, 3 treble on the centre stitch of three treble of last row, 1 treble on treble, 1 treble on the centre stitch of three treble, 1 treble on treble, 3 treble on centre stitch of three treble, 1 treble on treble, 1 treble on the centre stitch of three treble, 1 treble on treble, 3 treble on the centre stitch of three treble, 1 treble on treble, 3 treble on centre stitch of three treble, one treble on treble stitch at the end. **6th row**—3 chain to turn, 3 treble on the centre stitch of three treble of last row, 1 treble on treble, 3 treble on the centre stitch of three treble, 1 treble on treble, miss one stitch, 1 treble on the next, miss one stitch, 1 treble on the centre stitch of three treble, miss one stitch, 1 treble on the next, miss

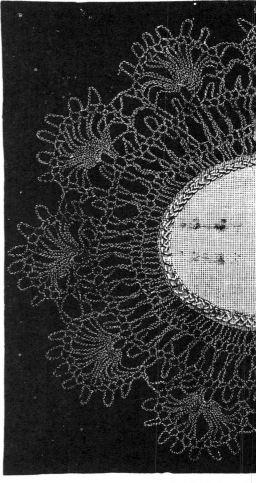

D'Oyley, E

one stitch, 1 treble on the next, 3 treble on the centre stitch of three treble, 1 treble on treble, 3 treble on the centre stitch of three treble, 1 treble on the chain that turned, and break off the wool. **7th row**—The beginning of the collarette,—Begin with 11 chain, do 1 treble on the treble stitch where you broke off, 3 treble on the centre stitch of three treble, 1 treble on treble, 3 treble on the centre stitch of three treble, 1 treble on treble, 3 treble on the next stitch, 1 treble on the next, 1 treble on the next, 3 treble on the centre stitch of three treble, 1 treble on treble, 3 treble on the centre stitch of three treble, 1 treble on the chain at the end, 11 chain, and break off the wool. **8th row**—Begin with 16 chain, and turning the work so as to crochet in the chain where you broke off last row, do 1 single crochet in the first stitch of chain, 1 double crochet in each of the 2 next, 1 treble in the next, miss one, 3 treble in the next, miss one, 1 treble in the next, miss one, 3 treble in the next, miss one, then 1 treble on treble stitch of last row, 3 treble on the centre stitch of three treble, 1 treble on treble, 3 treble on the centre stitch of three treble, and now without missing any do 1 treble on the next stitch and 3 treble on the next stitch alternately six times, then miss one, 1 treble on treble, 3 treble on the centre stitch of three treble, 1 treble on the last treble stitch, miss one chain, 3 treble in the next, miss one, 1 treble in the next, miss one, 3 treble in the next, miss one, 1 treble in the next, 1 double crochet in each of the 2 next, 1 single crochet in the last stitch of chain, do

16 chain, and break off. **9th row**—Recommencing now on the right-hand side, the same side where you began last row, work into the chain, 1 single crochet in the first stitch, 1 double crochet in each of the 2 next, 1 treble in the next, miss one, 3 treble in the next, miss one, 1 treble in the next, * miss one, 3 treble in the next, miss one, 1 treble in the next, and repeat from * till within 3 stitches of the end of the row, when do 1 double crochet in each of the 2 next, and 1 single crochet in the last stitch of chain, and break off; in the centre of this row the 3 treble stitches come always on the centre stitch of three treble of last row. **10th row**—Work into the stitches of last row in the manner there instructed. **11th row**—Work the same again. **12th row**—With blue wool. Holding the work the right side towards you, and working entirely round the hood and collarette, beginning at the corner of the sixth row to go first round the head, do 1 single crochet in a stitch of the hood, * 7 chain, 1 single crochet in the next stitch of the hood, and repeat from * to the opposite corner of the sixth row; then round the collarette do 7 chain, 1 single crochet in each of the two next stitches, till you meet the blue where you commenced, and join neatly. Then work with blue wool the trimming on the top of the head, holding the front of the hood with the blue edge

Venetian Lace.

towards you—Begin on the sixth round, and go just behind the first row of blue edging with 1 single crochet, 9 chain, alternately, always missing about half an inch of crochet between the single stitches, till you get to the fourth double crochet stitch from the middle of the top of the head, when break off, and work similar loops along the opposite side to correspond. The centre of the top of the head is worked with blue wool in the style of a rosette composed of loops of 4 chain, 1 single crochet in a double crochet of the top of the hood, till the front half of the circle of double crochet is covered with loops of blue. Make with blue wool a length of 25 chain, tie it in the back of the hood to embrace the five treble stitches in the middle of the sixth row; make a tassel at each end and tie the chain in a bow.

CHILD'S PELISSE.

THIS pelisse will fit a child of four or five years; it is Princesse shape, and measures 23 inches from the neck to the bottom of the flounce at the back. Materials required are, ¾ lb of pink Heather wool, a bone crochet needle No. 12, and 5 yards of ⅝ of an inch wide ribbon of colour to match the wool. The stitch used for the frock throughout is one row of plain double crochet, and turn, and work back the next row in point-neige or shell-stitch, this stitch is clearly described and illustrated on page 3 of this present issue. For the **Left Front**—Make 51 chain, along which work 50 stitches of double crochet, turn

with 3 chain, and work back 25 point-neige stitches. Begin each point-neige row with 3 chain, and work the double crochet rows with 1 chain, to make a smooth edge. Decrease a point-neige stitch at the beginning of the sixth row, and at the beginning of every fourth row afterwards, till 30 rows are done, counting both double crochet and point-neige rows from the commencement; all these decreasings come at the same end (the right) In the 32nd row, and 2 following rows, decrease 3 stitches at the same end in each row, which shapes for the armhole. Do 6 rows without decreasing Then for the shoulder, increase for 4 consecutive rows, and in the last of these leave 5 stitches unworked at the other end for the neck. Do 5 rows, decreasing 3 stitches at each end, and fasten off **The Right Front** is to be worked in the same manner, but begin with 47 stitches, and make the decreasings come at the other end of the work. For the **Back** of the **Frock**—Make 63 chain, and work in the same stitch as the fronts All decreasings and increasings are now to be done on *both* sides of the work, that is, at the end of the rows as well as at the beginning. Decrease every fourth row till the 16th row; then increase every fourth row till the 24th row; this brings you to the armhole, as the back of the frock is not required to be so long as the fronts in consequence of the flounce which is put on afterwards. Now decrease at the beginning and at the end of each row for 4 rows. Do 3 rows without decreasing. Decrease 2 stitches at each end for 7 rows, and fasten off. For the **Flounce**—Begin with 21 chain, and work forwards and backwards for 70 rows. This makes a long strip which is to be sewn in pleats to the foundation chain of the back piece, and then the whole back is to be joined to the two fronts as far as the armholes, and the shoulders also joined. For the **Sleeves**—Commence with 41 chain, and increase at the beginning and end of every fourth row till there are 56 double crochet worked in the 17th row of the sleeve; now slip along 4 stitches at the beginning, and leave 4 stitches unworked at the end of each row for 5 rows to make the slope for the shoulder, fasten off, and sew up as far as the 17th row. Make the other sleeve similarly. For the **Border** round the **Skirt**—Begin with a single

Pretty Dress for a Child.

crochet stitch into the commencing chain at the corner of the right front, do 10 chain, and now holding the *wrong* side of the frock towards you, do 1 treble in the third chain from the needle, 1 chain, miss one stitch, 1 treble in the next, and continue the same all along the bottom of the frock till you get to the corner of the left front; this open row of treble and chain is to run a ribbon in, and the 10 chain with which you began makes a foundation to jut out to work the front trimming upon. You now do 6 rows of coiled crochet, thus—forwards and backwards, beginning with the right side of the frock towards you, and turning the work at the completion of every row—1 double crochet in the first stitch, insert the hook in the next stitch and draw the wool through and do 5 chain, at the last chain pulling the wool through both loops on the needle, repeat. In succeeding rows do double crochet on the double crochet and the 5 chain into the previous loops of five chain. When the 6 rows are worked round the bottom of the skirt do the same coiled crochet in little rows on the 10 extra chain added to the right front till sufficient length is worked to reach the neck, and sew it up the front. Work the same border, commencing with the 1 chain 1 treble row, round the neck and sleeves Sew the sleeves in Run ribbon in through the open treble row round the neck and sleeves, and round the bottom of the skirt, with ends sufficient to tie in bows Place a ribbon over the pleating of the flounce at the back, with a bow in the centre. Add ribbon strings in front to tie in bows on the chest over the coiled trimming.

TAM O'SHANTER.

THE cap shown in our engraving is worked in a pretty combination of double crochet and point neige, or shell stitch, and can be suitably worn by a child of from five to ten years of age. Procure 2½ ozs. of pale blue single Berlin wool, and work with a No. 8 bone crochet needle. Commence for the centre of the cap with 3 chain stitches, and join round. **1st round**—2 chain to stand up to begin upon, and work 6 shell stitches in the round, and join evenly; shell stitch is fully explained in the instructions for working a Child's Skirt, see page 3 of the present issue. **2nd round**—Begin with 2 chain, and work 10 shell stitches over the six shell stitches of last round, and join evenly

Opera Hood and Collarette.   **Worked with Giant Wool.**

to the commencement. **3rd round**—1 chain to begin, and work 27 double crochet stitches in the round, and again join evenly. **4th round**—1 chain to begin, turn the work, and do 30 double crochet stitches in the round, inserting the hook to take up the back thread of the stitches of the previous round. **5th round**—2 chain, turn the work, and do 25 shell stitches in the round. **6th round**—2 chain, and work 33 shell stitches in the round. **7th round**—1 chain to begin, and do 66 double crochet. **8th round**—1 chain, turn the work, and do plain double crochet, 66 stitches, into the back thread of the stitches of last round. **9th round**—2 chain, turn the work, and do 58 shell stitches in the round. **10th round**—2 chain, and work 64 shell stitches in the round. **11th round**—1 chain to begin, and do 128 double crochet. **12th round**—1 chain, turn the work, and do again 128 double crochet, working into the back thread of the stitches of last round. **13th round**—2 chain, turn the work, and do 80 shell stitches in the round. **14th round**—2 chain, and work 86 shell stitches in the round. **15th round**—1 chain, and do 145 double crochet. **16th round**—1 chain, turn the work, and do again 145 double crochet. **17th round**—Begin to draw in for the under part of the brim, and do 80 shell stitches in the round. **18th round**—74 shell stitches. **19th round**—110 double crochet. **20th round**—Turn, and decrease again, getting 94 double crochet into the back threads of the stitches of last round. **21st round**—Turn, and work 56 shell stitches. **22nd round**—50 shell stitches. **23rd round**—70 double crochet. **24th round**—again 70 double crochet. Work for the **Band** 6 or 8 rounds of single crochet, inserting the hook to take up the one top thread of the stitches of the preceding round. The tuft in the centre of the crown is made of a number of strands of wool

about 3 inches in length, tied tightly together in the centre; the thread of wool that ties them will do to secure the tuft to the cap, and the ends are then pulled into the shape of a pompon and cut smooth and even.

WIDE BORDER IN OPEN RAISED CROCHET.

THIS border is useful for a quilt or for any purpose for which a wide open raised border is desired. It is worked the short way. Begin with 43 chain. **1st row**—Work 1 treble in the third chain from the needle, 2 chain, miss two stitches, 1 treble in the next, 2 chain, miss two, 1 treble in the next, 2 chain, miss two, 1 treble in the next, 2 chain, miss two, 1 treble in the next, 2 chain, miss two, work 4 treble consecutive, 3 chain, miss three, 4 treble consecutive, 3 chain, miss three, 4 treble consecutive, 3 chain, miss three, 4 treble consecutive. **2nd row**—7 chain to turn, work 1 treble in the fourth chain from the needle and 8 more treble consecutive, on the next stitch which is the middle stitch of three chain of last row work a group of 5 treble stitches, withdraw the hook from the stitch on the needle, insert it in the top of the first of the five treble and draw the stitch through, do 1 chain to tighten the group, this is termed a "tuft," and is always to be worked thus, work 6 consecutive treble, then a tuft, 6 more treble, another tuft, 3 treble consecutive, 1 chain, 1 treble on last stitch of four of last row, 2 chain and 1 treble on treble five times, 1 treble on the chain that turned. **3rd row**—3 chain to turn, 1 treble on the treble stitch of last row, 2 chain and 1 treble on treble five times, 1 chain, 1 treble on first stitch of four of last row, 1 chain, miss one, 4 treble consecutive, 3 chain, miss three, 4 treble consecutive, 3 chain, miss three, 4 treble consecutive, 3 chain, miss three, 4 treble consecutive. **4th row**—7 chain to turn, work 1 treble in the fourth chain from the needle and 8 more treble consecutive, a tuft on the centre chain stitch, 6 consecutive treble, a tuft, 6 consecutive treble, a tuft, 3 consecutive treble, 1 chain, 1 treble on the last stitch of four of last row, 1 chain and 1 treble on treble three times, 2 chain and 1 treble on treble five times, 1 treble on the chain that turned. **5th row**—3 chain to turn, 1 treble on treble stitch of last row, 2 chain and 1 treble on treble five times, 1 chain and 1 treble on treble three times, 1 chain, miss one, 4 treble consecutive, 3 chain, miss three, 4 treble consecutive, 3 chain, miss three, 4 treble consecutive, 3 chain, miss three, 4 treble consecutive. **6th row**—7 chain to turn, work 1 treble in the fourth chain from the needle and 8 more consecutive treble, a tuft on the centre chain stitch, 6 consecutive treble, a tuft, 6 consecutive treble, a tuft, 3 consecutive treble, 1 chain, 1 treble on the last stitch of four of last row, 1 chain and 1 treble on treble four times, 2 chain and 1 treble on treble five times, 1 treble on the chain that turned. **7th row**—

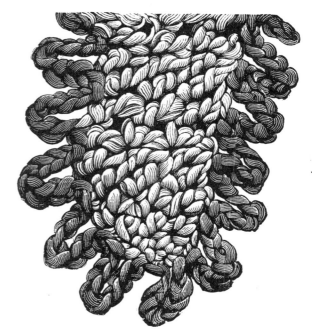

Working Design for Opera Hood and Collarette in Giant Wool.

3 chain to turn, 1 treble on treble stitch of last row, 2 chain and 1 treble on treble five times, 1 chain and 1 treble on treble five times, 1 chain, 1 treble on 4 treble consecutive, 3 chain, miss three, 4 treble consecutive, 3 chain, miss three, 4 treble consecutive, 3 chain, miss three, 4 treble consecutive. **8th row**—3 chain to turn, 1 treble on the first treble stitch of last row and 8 more treble consecutive, a tuft on the next treble stitch, 6 consecutive treble, a tuft on the next treble stitch, 6 consecutive treble, a tuft on the next treble stitch, 3 consecutive treble, 1 chain and 1 treble on treble five times, 2 chain and 1 treble on treble five times, 1 treble on the chain that turned. **9th row**—3 chain to turn, 1 treble on treble stitch of last row, 2 chain and 1 treble on treble five times, 1 chain and 1 treble on treble three times, 1 chain, miss one, 4 treble consecutive, 3 chain, miss three, 4 treble consecutive, 3 chain,

miss three, 4 treble consecutive, 3 chain, miss three, 4 treble consecutive. **10th row**—3 chain to turn, 1 treble on the first treble stitch of last row and 8 more treble consecutive, a tuft on the next treble stitch, 6 consecutive treble, a tuft on the next treble stitch, 6 consecutive treble, a tuft on the next treble stitch, 3 consecutive treble, 1 chain and 1 treble on treble 3 times, 2 chain and 1 treble on treble five times, 1 treble on the chain that turned. **11th row**—3 chain to turn, 1 treble on treble stitch of last row, 2 chain and 1 treble on treble five times, 1 treble on treble, 1 chain, miss one, 4 treble consecutive, 3 chain, miss three, 4 treble consecutive, 3 chain, miss three, 4 treble consecutive, 3 chain, miss three, 4 treble consecutive. **12th row**—3 chain to turn, 1 treble on the first treble stitch of last row and 8 more treble consecutive, a tuft on the next treble stitch, 6 consecutive treble, a tuft on the next treble stitch, 6 consecutive treble, a tuft on the next treble stitch, 3 consecutive treble, 1 chain, 1 treble on treble, 2 chain and 1 treble on treble five times,

Child's Pelisse.

1 treble on the chain that turned. Begin the next row with 3 chain to turn and work according to the first row of the pattern, and continue for the length required.

STRIPE FOR AN ANTIMACASSAR OR COUVRE-PIED PINE PATTERN.

THIS pattern may be worked in stripes with double Berlin wool of two good contrasting colours doing the whole of one stripe with one colour, or if preferred the colours may be arranged in rows, working three rows with each colour successively. Use a No. 6 tricot needle. Begin with a chain of 20 stitches. **1st row**—Wool over the needle and insert the hook in the third chain from the needle and draw the wool through, wool over the needle and draw through two threads on the needle, wool over the needle and insert the hook again in the same chain stitch and draw the wool through, wool over the needle and draw through two threads on the needle, wool over the needle and again insert the hook in the same chain stitch and draw the wool through, wool over the needle and draw through two threads on the needle, wool over the needle and draw through three threads on the needle, this group of stitches is termed "a pine," and every pine is worked in the same manner, raise a plain tricot stitch in the next stitch of the foundation, a pine in the next, a tricot stitch in the next, and so on to the end of the row, keeping all the stitches (19) on the needle; the plain tricot stitches should be raised very loosely; to work back, draw the wool through one stitch first, then wool over the needle and draw through two at a time till all the stitches are off. **2nd row**—Raise a plain tricot stitch over the pine of last row inserting the hook through the perpendicular thread only, * then a pine over the tricot stitch of last row taking up the stitch with a top thread of the chain that lies under it, and a tricot stitch over a pine, and repeat from *, and at the end there will be another plain tricot stitch to

pick up; work back as the first row. **3rd row**—Work a pine over the tricot stitch of last row, and a plain tricot stitch over a pine, and repeat, ending with a stitch of plain tricot. There will be 9 pines in the first row, 8 pines in the second, 9 pines again in the third, and so on alternately to keep the pattern straight. Repeat the second and third rows for the length required. When a sufficient number of stripes are worked for the width of the article join them together with a row of plain double crochet, and finish off the top and the bottom with a fringe of four strands of wool knotted into each pine.

RAISED SQUARE PATTERN FOR A QUILT.

THIS very handsome square should be worked with Strutt's best knitting cotton, No. 6, and a steel crochet needle, No. 15. Begin in the centre by winding the cotton twice round the first finger of the left hand, work 8 double crochet in the loop, draw the loop in closely, then join the last stitch of the double crochet to the first stitch, and this forms the first round of the quilt square. Every successive round is to be joined in same manner quite evenly to its own commencement, and unless otherways directed, always *turn* the work with 1 chain to re-commence a fresh round, and insert the hook to take up the one back thread of the stitches of the previous round, that the work may sit in ridges. **2nd round**—1 double crochet on the first stitch, 3 double crochet on the next stitch, and repeat the same three times, making 16 double crochet in the round. **3rd round**—1 double crochet on each of three double crochet along the side of the square, 3 double crochet on the centre stitch of three double crochet for the corner, making 24 double crochet in the round, and fasten off. **4th round**—Holding the wrong side of last round towards you, do 1 double crochet on the third stitch of the three double crochet at the corner, 1 double crochet on the next stitch, now a "tuft," that is 5 treble stitches worked into a thread of the second previous round, miss the next stitch of last round, 1 double crochet on the next stitch, 1 double crochet on the next, 3 double crochet on the centre stitch of three double crochet at the corner, and repeat the same three times. **5th round**—Plain double crochet, except behind the tufts, where a treble stitch is to be worked into the thread of the stitch that was missed in last round, and 3 double crochet are as usual to be worked on the centre stitch at each corner. **6th round**—Work 1 double crochet on the third stitch of the three double crochet at the corner, 1 double crochet on the next, a tuft, miss one stitch of last round, 3 double crochet consecutive, a tuft, miss one stitch, 1 double crochet on the next, 1 double crochet on the next, 3 double crochet on the centre stitch at the corner. **7th round**—Same as the fifth round. **8th round**—Work 1 double crochet on the third stitch of the three double crochet at the corner, 1 double crochet on the next, a tuft, miss one stitch of last round, 7 double crochet consecutive, a tuft, miss one stitch, 1 double crochet on the next, 1 double crochet on the next, 3 double crochet on the centre stitch at the corner. **9th round**—Same as the fifth. **10th round**—Work 1 double crochet on the third stitch of the three double crochet at the corner, 1 double crochet on the next, a tuft, miss one stitch of last round, 11 double crochet consecutive, a tuft, miss 1 stitch, 1 double crochet on

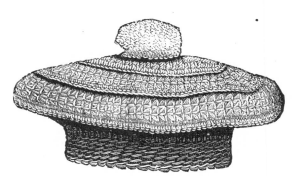

Tam O'Shanter.

the next, 1 double crochet on the next, 3 double crochet on the centre stitch at the corner. **11th round**—Same as the fifth. **12th round**—Work 1 double crochet on the third stitch of the three double crochet at the corner, 1 double crochet on the next, a tuft, miss one stitch of last round, 15 double crochet consecutive, a tuft, miss one stitch, 1 double crochet on the next, 1 double crochet on the next, 3 double crochet on the centre stitch at the corner. **13th round**—Same as the fifth. **14th round**—Work plain double crochet, with 3 double crochet on the centre stitch at each corner. **15th round**—The same; in this round there should be 27 double crochet along each side of the square and 3 double crochet at each corner; fasten off at the end of the round. **16th round**—Hold the right side of the work towards you, do 1 treble on the first of the three double crochet stitches at the corner, inserting the hook to take up the two front threads of the stitches of last round, 1 chain, 1 treble on the corner stitch, 1 chain, another treble on the corner stitch, 1 chain, another treble in the same place, 1 chain, 1 treble on the third of the three double crochet stitches, 1 chain, miss one, 1 treble on the next, and continue thus in 1 chain, miss one, 1 treble on the next, till you get in all, 5 treble worked at the corner, and 13 treble along the side of the square, with 1 chain between each; do 1 chain, and repeat the same to the end of the round, and join evenly. **17th round**—Turn, and work plain double crochet, with 3 double crochet on the centre stitch at each corner.

18th round—The same. **19th round**—Hold the right side of the work towards you, and insert the hook to take up the one *front* thread of the stitches of last round, 5 double crochet on one double crochet stitch of last round, miss one, 1 double crochet on the next, miss one, and repeat the same to the end of the round, and fasten off; this round sits in little scollops, and there must be a scollop at each corner and nine scollops along each side, making 40 scollops in the round. **20th round**—Hold the work the right side towards you and do a round of plain treble stitches, with 5 treble on the centre stitch at each corner, inserting the hook to take up the one *top* thread of the stitches of the eighteenth round, and keeping the little scollops down under the left-hand thumb. **21st round**—With the right side of the work still in front, do 1 double crochet into the top thread of a stitch of last row, do 1 double crochet into the

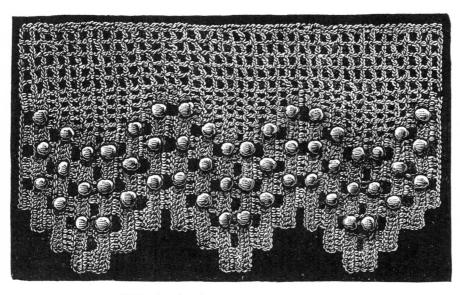

Wide Border in Open Raised Crochet.

front thread of a stitch of last row, and repeat this alternately all round, with 3 double crochet stitches at each corner. **22nd round**—Work in the same manner, taking the top thread now where in last round the front thread was taken. **23rd round**—Turn, and work plain double crochet into the back threads of the stitches of last round, and as before do 3 double crochet on the centre stitch at each corner. **24th round**—The same as last round. **25th round**—Work in little scollops, the same as the nineteenth round, a scollop at each corner and 12 scollops along each side, making 52 scollops in the round. **26th round**—The same as the twentieth round. **27th round**—Turn, and work plain double crochet into the back threads of the stitches of last round, and 3 double crochet on the centre stitch at each corner, and fasten off at the end of the round. **28th round**—Hold the right side of the work towards you and inserting the hook to take up the back thread of the stitches of last round, do 1 treble, 1 chain, miss one, and repeat the same all round, making a little increase to ease the corners. **29th round**—With the right side of the work still in front, do plain double crochet into the top thread of the stitches of last round, and 3 double crochet on the centre stitch at each corner. This finishes the square. When a number of squares are worked they may be joined together by a row of double crochet, or simply sewn together.

THE SYLVESTER CAPE.

FOR this very pretty and stylish cape procure 9 ozs of grey single Berlin wool, a No. 8 and No. 10 bone crochet needle, and 1½ yards of inch-wide grey ribbon for the neck. The cape is worked in four pieces, *i.e*, three frills as shown in the engraving, and an open-work foundation on which the frills are placed. Work first of all the foundation, using No 8 needle, and commencing for the neck with 71 chain. The **1st row** consists of double long treble stitches, worked thus—pass the wool three times round the needle, insert the hook in the sixth chain from the needle and draw the wool through, then four successive times pass the wool over the needle and draw through 2 stitches on the needle; wool three times round the needle, insert the hook in the next stitch of the commencing chain and draw the wool through, and four successive times pass the wool over the needle and draw through 2 stitches on the needle; every stitch is worked in the same manner, rather loosely, and there should be 66 stitches in the row, these form a wide insertion for the neckband in which afterwards to run a piece of ribbon. **2nd row**—3 chain to turn, 1 treble on the first stitch of previous row * 2 chain, miss one, 1 treble on the next, and repeat from * to the end, making in all 33 holes of two-chain stitches. **3rd row**—3 chain to turn, 1 treble on the first treble stitch of preceding row, 2 chain and 1 treble in the first space, * 2 chain and 1 treble in each of the four following spaces, 2 chain and 1 treble in the same place to increase, and

repeat from * to the end, making 42 holes of two-chain stitches. **4th row**—3 chain to turn, 1 treble on the first treble stitch of previous row, 2 chain and 1 treble in the first space, 2 chain and 1 treble in three successive spaces, 2 chain and 1 treble in the same place as last treble, * 2 chain and 1 treble in five successive spaces, 2 chain and 1 treble in the same space as the last treble, repeat from * six times, 2 chain and 1 double crochet in three successive spaces, 2 chain and 1 treble in the same space as the last treble, 2 chain and 1 treble on the chain that turned; making 52 spaces in the row. **5th row**—3 chain to turn, 1 treble on the treble stitch, 2 chain and 1 treble in the first space, 2 chain and 1 treble in each successive space to the end, 2 chain, and 1 treble on the chain that turned. **6th row**—3 chain to turn, * 2 chain and 1 treble in three successive holes, 2 chain and 1 treble in the same hole as the last treble, and repeat from *, and at the end do 2 chain and 1 treble twice, 2 chain and 1 treble in the chain that turned; making 71 spaces in the row. **7th row**—3 chain to turn, 1 treble in the first space, 2 chain and 1 treble all along to the end of the row. **8th row**—3 chain to turn, 1 treble in the first space, do 2 chain and 1 treble sixteen times, 2 chain and 1 treble in the same space as the last treble, increase in the same way in the two next spaces, do 2 chain and 1 treble thirty-four times, 2 chain and 1 treble in the same space as the last treble, increase in each of the two next spaces, 2 chain and 1 treble sixteen times to the end. Work 11 more rows of open spaces without any increase, and fasten off, as now the foundation is long enough. For the **Frills** —Take the No. 10 crochet needle, and work firmer than you worked for the foundation. Begin for the **Top Frill** with 106 chain. **1st row**—1 treble in the third chain from the needle, * 1 chain, miss one stitch, 2 treble in the next, 2 chain, 2 treble in the next, 1 chain, miss one, 1 treble in the next, and repeat from * to the end, finish with 1 extra treble, and fasten off. **2nd row**—Commence this and every row on the right-hand side; 2 treble stitches, 1 chain, 2 treble under the loop of two chain of last row, 2 chain, 2 more treble in the same place, 1 chain, 1 treble on the one treble stitch, and repeat from *, do 1 more treble at the end, and fasten off. Work 5 more rows the same as the last row. Also do 1 more row the same, but work also along the little side at the beginning of the rows and along the little side at the end. **9th row**—

Stripe for an Antimacassar or Couvrepied Pine Pattern.

Begin along the little side, * work 1 treble on the one treble stitch, 1 chain, 8 treble under the loop of two chain, 1 chain, and repeat from * to the end of the other little side. **10th row**—Single crochet along just below the chain edge of the stitches of last row. This finishes the first frill. For the second **Frill**—Begin with 172 chain—**1st row**—1 treble in the third chain from the needle, * 1 chain, miss two stitches, 2 treble in the next, 2 chain, 2 treble in the next, 1 chain, miss two, 1 treble in the next, and repeat from * to the end, finish with 1 extra treble, and fasten off. The remaining rows of the frill are worked in the same way as the corresponding rows in the first frill; there are 20 scollops along the first frill, 24 scollops along the second frill, and 28 scollops along the third frill. For the **Third Frill**—Commence with 256 chain. **1st row**—1 treble in the third chain from the needle, * 1 chain, miss three stitches, 2 treble in the next, 2 chain, 2 treble in the next, 1 chain, miss three, 1 treble in the next, and repeat from * to the end, finish with 1 extra treble, and fasten off. Work the remaining 9 rows in the same way as the corresponding rows of the first frill are worked, being careful to round the corners nicely in the 3 last rows. Sew the last frill upon the stitches of the fifteenth row of the foundation; sew the second frill upon the stitches of the eighth row; and sew the first frill just immediately below the neckband and above the first row of the open crochet; sew the front edge of the frills down in place as shown in the illustration. For the **Ruching** round the **Neck—1st row**—Work 4 treble stitches into every stitch of the foundation chain. **2nd row**—3 chain to turn, and work 1 treble on every stitch of last row. Fasten off all ends of wool securely. Run the ribbon through the open insertion of double long treble stitches weaving it over three and under three to the end.

MANTEL VALANCE, OR BRACKET DRAPE.

PROCURE a number of brass curtain rings about the size of a halfpenny, which can be procured at an ironmonger's for twopence the dozen, 1 oz. or 2 ozs. of shaded crimson Berlin wool, and a No. 10 bone crochet needle. Take the first ring, and to cover the brass outline, work one double crochet over the ring, * 3 chain, 2 double crochet, and repeat from * till you have 10 loops of three chain, when end with one double crochet as you began, join to the first stitch and fasten off; and draw in the ends of wool through two or three stitches on the wrong side of the work. Take the second ring, and work the same as

crochet just worked, 4 chain, 1 single crochet in the same place, 3 chain, another single crochet in the same place, 4 chain, 1 treble also on the double crochet stitch, 1 double crochet in the next loop of the same ring; 4 chain, 1 double crochet in the second loop of the ring at the point of the scollop, * 4 chain, 1 treble on the double crochet just done, 1 double crochet in the next loop of the same ring, repeat from * twice, then do 3 chain, 1 single crochet on the double crochet just worked, 4 chain, 1 single crochet in the same place, 3 chain, another single crochet in the same place, 4 chain, 1 treble on the same double crochet, 1 double crochet in the next loop of the ring, * 4 chain, 1 treble on the double crochet just done, 1 double crochet in the next loop of the same ring, repeat from * once; 4 chain, 1 double crochet in the first loop of the next ring, and proceed up this side of the scollop to correspond with the side already done; and edge along the remaining scollops in the same way. Cut a number of strands of wool in seven-inch lengths, and draw 18 or 20 strands through the centre loop at the bottom of each ring, fold the strands double, and bind the top in resemblance of a handsome tassel.

TOBOGGAN CAP.

PROCURE 3½ ozs. of brown Berlin fingering, and a No. 9 or No. 10 bone crochet needle. Commence with 80 chain for the bottom of the cap; join

Raised Square Pattern for a Quilt.

the first till you have done 8 loops and 2 double crochet stitches, then 1 chain, join to a loop of the first ring, 1 chain, do 2 double crochet in the second ring, 1 chain, join to the next loop of the first ring, 1 chain, 1 double crochet in the second ring, and join and fasten off. Work in the same manner as many rings as you require for the length of the border, joining five rings in a straight line for one scollop, nine rings for two scollops, thirteen rings for three scollops, and so on. Then proceed with a second row of rings in the same manner, but joining them to the first row, as shown in the engraving, where also you will see how to place the additional seven rings to shape the scollops. For the **Edging** of the **Scollops**—Begin with a double crochet stitch in the fourth loop of the first ring of the second row, 4 chain, 1 treble in the double crochet just worked, 1 double crochet in the next loop, 3 chain, 1 single crochet on the double crochet just worked, 4 chain, 1 single crochet in the same place, 3 chain, another single crochet in the same place, 4 chain, 1 treble also on the double crochet stitch, 1 double crochet in the next loop of the same ring; 3 chain, 1 double crochet in the first loop of the next ring (the first ring on the first row of three), 4 chain, 1 treble on the double crochet just done. 1 double crochet in the next loop of the same ring, 4 chain, 1 treble on the double crochet just done, 1 double crochet in the next loop of the same ring, 4 chain, 1 treble on the double crochet last done, 1 double crochet in the next loop of the same ring; 3 chain, 1 double crochet in the first loop of the next ring (the first ring on the second row of three), * 4 chain, 1 treble on the double crochet just done, 1 double crochet in the next loop of the same ring, repeat from * three times, then do three chain, 1 single crochet on the double

round; and work in simple double crochet round and round continuously, inserting the hook to take up the one top thread of the stitches of the previous round, till 20 rounds are done. Continue working in the same manner, but now decrease 2 stitches in every round, at alternate intervals, till the cap is brought to a point at the top. For the **Brim**—Turn the cap upside down, and work a round of double crochet stitches into the commencing chain. **2nd round**—1 double crochet in the first stitch from the needle, insert the hook in the next stitch, draw the wool through and do 3 chain, wool over the needle and draw through the last stitch of the chain and through the stitch on the needle, and repeat the double crochet stitch and the raised chain stitch alternately to the end of the round; this fancy stitch must not take up any more room than the rounds of double crochet in which 80 stitches are worked, therefore if you find it becoming wider miss one stitch in every six or ten stitches to keep it to the required size. **3rd round**—Work a plain double crochet over a raised chain stitch of last round, and a raised chain stitch over a double crochet; and proceed working in the same manner till the turn-up brim is sufficiently deep, when join round evenly, work a round of single crochet stitches, and fasten off. Make a crochet chain with a wool pompon at each end, and loop the chain on the point of the cap as shown in the engraving. How to make a pompon or tuft is given at the end of description of Tam o'Shanter on page 10 of this issue.

LAMP MAT.

THIS lamp mat is crocheted with brown Macramé thread of a rather fine size, and a No. 10 bone crochet needle. Wind the thread once round the first finger of the left hand, and work 6 double crochet in the loop, draw in the loop closely to form a circle. Now proceed round and round in plain double crochet, inserting the hook to take up the top and back threads of the stitches. **1st round**—Work 2 double crochet on each stitch, 12 double crochet in all. **2nd round**—2 double crochet on the first stitch, 1 double crochet on the next, and repeat five times, making 18 stitches in the round. **3rd round**—2 double crochet on the first stitch, 1 double crochet on each of the two next stitches, and repeat five times, making 24 stitches in the round. **4th round**—2 double crochet on the first stitch, 1 double crochet in each of the three next stitches, * 3 double crochet on the next, 1 double crochet on each of the three next, and repeat from * four times. **5th round**—3 double crochet on the first stitch, 1 double crochet on each of the five next stitches, * 3 double crochet on the next, 1 double crochet on each of the five next, and repeat from * four times. **6th round**—3 double crochet on the centre stitch of three double crochet of last round, 7 double crochet worked consecutively and repeat the same five times. **7th round**—3 double crochet on the centre stitch of three double crochet of last round, 9 double crochet worked consecutively, and repeat five times. **8th round**—3 double crochet on the centre stitch of three

2 chain, and 1 treble, to be worked under every loop of chain of last round. **4th round**—1 treble in the small open space in the centre of 2 treble stitches at the point. 2 chain, another treble in the same place, 1 treble, 2 chain, 1 treble, as before, under every loop of chain along the sides of the mat. **5th round**—The same as the second round. **6th round**—Work 1 double crochet, 1 chain, 4 treble, 1 chain, 1 double crochet, *all* under a loop of 2 chain of last round, 1 double crochet in the small open space between 2 treble stitches, and repeat the same to the end of the round. This finishes the mat. A similar mat can be made by working the centre with single Berlin over a thin window blind cord, or picture cord, and doing the border with wool only.

SHORTWAY EDGING.

(Not illustrated.)

THIS simple edging, which is so useful for trimming underlinen, children's clothing, &c., may be worked with Coats' crochet cotton, No. 25, and a fine steel crochet needle; or may be rendered still more lacy-looking by employing a finer cotton, thus rendering it suitable for infants' tiny garments. Begin with 20 chain. **1st row**—1 double crochet in the eleventh chain from the

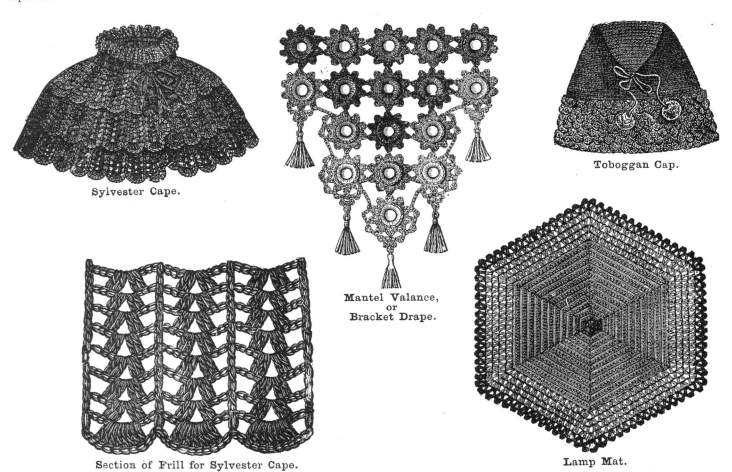

Sylvester Cape.

Mantel Valance,
or
Bracket Drape.

Toboggan Cap.

Section of Frill for Sylvester Cape.

Lamp Mat.

double crochet of last round, 11 double crochet worked consecutively, and repeat five times. **9th round**—3 double crochet on the centre stitch of three double crochet of last round, 13 double crochet worked consecutively, and repeat five times. Continue in this manner, always doing 3 double crochet on the centre stitch of the three double crochet of last round, and 1 double crochet on each of the intervening stitches, increasing 2 stitches on each of the six sides of the mat in every round, till in the 16th round you work 3 double crochet in every point, and 27 double crochet along each side of the mat; when join quite evenly, and fasten off. For the **Border—1st round**—Do 1 treble stitch on the centre stitch of three double crochet at the point, 2 chain, 1 more treble in the same place, miss two stitches, * 1 treble on the next, 2 chain, another treble in the same place, miss two stitches, and repeat from * till you get to the next point, which work the same as the first, and continue to the end of the round, where join to the first treble stitch with which the round began; and fasten off at the end of this and every following round, and commence the next round on one of the other points. **2nd round**—Do 1 treble under the loop of chain at the point, 2 chain, 1 more treble in the same place, 2 chain, another treble in the same place, * 1 treble under the next loop of chain of last round, 2 chain, another treble in the same place, and repeat from * till you get to the next point, which work the same as the first, and continue to the end of the round. **3rd round**—1 treble.

needle, miss two, 5 treble in the next, miss two, 1 double crochet in the next, 5 chain, miss two, 1 double crochet in the next. **2nd row**—3 chain to turn, 5 treble on the first double crochet stitch of last row, 1 double crochet in the centre stitch of five chain, 5 chain, 1 double crochet on the centre stitch of five treble, 5 chain, 1 double crochet in the third stitch of the chain that turned. **3rd row**—7 chain to turn, 1 double crochet in the centre stitch of five chain, 5 chain, 1 double crochet in the centre stitch of next five chain, 5 treble on the double crochet stitch, 1 double crochet on the centre stitch of five treble, 5 chain, 1 double crochet on the stitch at the corner. **4th row**—Slip-stitch over two first treble stitches of last row, 1 treble on the centre stitch of the five treble, 5 treble on the double crochet stitch, 1 double crochet on the centre stitch of the next five treble, 5 chain, 1 double crochet in the centre stitch of five chain, 5 chain, 1 double crochet in the third stitch of the chain that turned. **5th row**—7 chain to turn, 1 double crochet in the centre stitch of five chain, 5 treble on the double crochet stitch, 1 double crochet in the centre stitch of five chain, 5 chain, 1 double crochet on the centre stitch of five treble. Repeat from the second row for the length required. Now work the open edge round the bottom of the scollops: 1 treble on the end treble stitch of the fourth row, 3 chain, 1 treble at the point of the scollop, 5 chain, another treble in the same place, 3 chain, 1 treble on the end treble stitch of the second row; repeat the same on each scollop.

WELDON'S
PRACTICAL CROCHET.

(TWELFTH SERIES.)

How to Crochet Useful Garments for Ladies, Children, and the Home.

TWENTY-SEVEN ILLUSTRATIONS.

The Yearly Subscription to this Magazine, post free to any Part of the World, is 2s. 6d.
Subscriptions are payable in advance, and may commence from any date and for any period.

The Back Numbers are always in print. Nos. 1 to 110 *now ready,* Price 2d. each, postage ½d. *Over 5,000 Engravings.*

LADY'S SHETLAND HOOD.

THIS hood is worked with pale blue Shetland wool in a very open lacy stitch; a piece of thin silk of the same colour is required for lining, and four yards of inch-wide ribbon for trimming; use a bone crochet needle, No. 7, as the work is done loosely; the hood will take about 3 ozs. of wool.

Begin with 53 chain. **1st row**—1 double crochet in the first chain stitch by the needle, 3 chain, 1 double crochet in the third chain from the needle, 4 chain, 1 double crochet in the third chain from the needle, this makes two picots with one chain stitch between the picots, and is called a "bar," miss three of the foundation chain, 1 double crochet in the next, * work a "bar," miss three of the foundation chain, 1 double crochet in the next, and repeat from * to the end, when you will have thirteen picoteed bars in the row. **2nd row**—Make a bar, and turn the work, and do 1 double crochet under the one chain between two piques of last row, then a bar, and 1 double crochet under the chain stitch between the piques of the next bar, and so on, doing 13 bars in the row. Work 4 more rows like the second row; then break off the wool. Gather up the foundation chain, and bring the crochet into a kind of semicircle or fan, this will be on the top of the head, and the gathering will be covered with a bow of ribbon; the middle of row comes directly over the forehead, the opposite side, *i.e.*, the two *ends* of the rows (where turned) are now to be worked upon for the back of the hood. The two ends when brought together should measure about 14 inches across. Now work the pattern along the ends, proceeding forwards and backwards always in "bars": in the second row increase three bars in the middle of the row, increasing is done by working two bars where one bar should be. Increase one bar somewhere about the middle of every row till 12 or 14 rows are done, when the back of the neck will probably be reached. Continue now, increasing 2 bars in every row, for 6 or 8 rows. Then work a little row of 2 bars only, and turn back on the same. **Next row**—Work 3 bars, and then turn back thereon. **Next row**—Work 4 bars, and turn back on the same. And so on, increasing the number of bars in every forward row, till you get to the middle of the back of the hood, when fasten off. Recommence on the other side, and work it in the same manner. Then do 2 rows all along the bottom of the hood from end to end, and fasten off. For the **Border**, which is worked all round the hood—**1st round**—1 double crochet under the one chain stitch in the middle of a bar, * 6 chain, 1 double crochet under the stitch in the middle of the next bar, and repeat from * to the end of the round. **2nd round**—Work 1 double crochet on the double crochet of last round, and 10 treble under every loop of six chain; and fasten off at the end of the round. Line the hood with silk throughout. Cut a fifteen-inch length of ribbon and

run it through the fourteen loops of six chain at the top of the forehead securing it to the crochet at each end, this draws the frill prettily over the face. A thread of double wool is run a row or two behind the ribbon to still further confine the frill. A bow of ribbon is placed on the top of the head over the gathering of the foundation chain, and from this on each side two ribbons are run, as shown in the engraving. Tie a bow of ribbons in the crochet at the back of the neck. Make a bow to sew by the side of the chin, where also put strings to tie.

Lady's Shetland Hood.

LADY'S PETTICOAT.
WORKED IN A VARIETY OF SHELL STITCH.

THE petticoat shown in our engraving can be made with petticoat fingering and a No. 8 crochet needle, or with fleecy wool and a No. 7 needle. Commence with sufficient chain for the length of the petticoat from the waist to the top of the border. **1st row**—Miss the chain stitch next to the needle, work 14 double crochet, then for shell stitch raise 1 stitch in the last double crochet, 1 stitch in the same chain the double crochet is worked into, 1 stitch in each of the next 2 chain, 5 now on the needle, wool over the needle and draw through all and do 1 chain to tighten the group, and now proceed in ordinary shell stitch to the end of the row. **2nd row**—Do 3 chain, and turn, raise 1 stitch in each of 2 chain stitches, 1 stitch in the chain that tightened the group of last row, and 1 stitch on the shell stitch taking up the one back thread, 5 now on the needle, wool over the needle and draw through all and do 1 chain to tighten the group, work ordinary shell stitch over the shell stitches of last row, always inserting the hook to take up the one back thread, work 14 double crochet on the double crochet of last row still taking the one back thread. **3rd row**—Do 1 chain, and turn, and always taking up the one back thread, work 14 double crochet, and then shell stitch as in the first row. Repeat the last two rows until the petticoat is the desired width. You will soon see how the work sits in small perpendicular stripes, and is alike on both sides, and how the double crochet contracts the top of the petticoat to the size of the waist. Sew up the petticoat from the bottom to within eight or nine inches of the top, which leave open for a placket; strengthen the placket with a row of double crochet: work a row of 2 chain 1 treble along the top of the petticoat. For the **Border — 1st round**—Work plain double crochet all round the bottom of the petticoat, and join evenly, and fasten off at the end of this and every succeeding round. **2nd round**—2 treble on a stitch of last round, 1 chain, 2 more treble in the same place, 1 chain, miss one stitch, insert the hook in the next stitch and draw the wool through, miss one stitch, insert the hook in the next stitch and draw the wool through, wool over the needle and draw through 3 stitches on the needle, 1 chain, miss one stitch, and repeat.

3rd round—2 treble under the chain stitch between the treble of last round, 1 chain, 2 more treble in the same place, 1 chain, insert the hook under the next chain stitch and draw the wool through, insert the hook under the next chain stitch and draw the wool through, wool over the needle and draw through 3 stitches on the needle, 1 chain, and repeat. **4th round**—Same as the third round. **5th round**—Double crochet in every stitch of last round. This completes the border. Run a ribbon through the open holes round the top of the petticoat to tie round the waist.

CHEMISE TRIMMING.

REQUIRED, Evan's crochet cotton No. 16 or No. 20, and a fine steel crochet needle. The buds are first to be worked. Begin with 20 chain; miss the first chain by the needle and work 18 double crochet stitches consecutively and 3 double crochet in the end stitch of the foundation chain, and work 16 double

Lady's Petticoat worked in a variety of Shell Stitch.

crochet along the other side of the foundation chain; * turn the work with 1 chain, do 17 consecutive double crochet, taking up always now the one back thread of the stitches of last row, do 3 double crochet on the centre stitch of the previous three double crochet, and 16 double crochet along the opposite side of the work, and repeat from * four times; then turn the work with 1 chain and do 17 double crochet stitches, which brings you to the bottom of the bud, and fasten off. This forms one bud. The other buds are all worked in the same manner, but each one is joined to the preceding with a single crochet worked (instead of the last chain stitch) into the corresponding point of the previous bud. Work sufficient buds to make a length to go round the neck, round the sleeves, and also for a V-shape in front, all in one piece, according to the shape shown in the engraving; and when this is arranged work a heading by which to sew the trimming on to the chemise, and finish off with a simple scolloped border. For the **Heading—1st round**—Do 1 long treble stitch in the fifth double crochet counting from the centre stitch at the bottom of one of the buds, * 4 chain (or 5 chain as may be necessary to make the buds lie flat and even), 1 single crochet in the point at the bottom of the bud, 4 chain (or 5), cotton twice round the needle, insert the hook in the fifth double crochet stitch on the left side of the same bud and draw the cotton through cotton over the needle and draw through 2 loops on the needle, cotton over the needle and draw through 2 more loops on the needle, cotton twice round the needle, and proceed with a long treble stitch on the side of the next bud, finishing off the 2 long trebles as 1 stitch, and repeat from *. **2nd round**—1 treble, 1 chain, miss one, and repeat. For the **Scolloped Border**—Work the first two rounds the same as the two rounds of the heading. **3rd round**—2 treble stitches, 7 chain, miss six stitches, and repeat. **4th round**—3 treble in the second chain stitch, 3 chain, miss three stitches, 3 treble in the next, 3 chain, and repeat. **5th round**—1 double crochet under a loop of three chain, * 4 chain, 1 double crochet in the same loop, 4 chain, 1 double crochet under the next loop, and repeat from *. **6th round**—Work 1 double crochet in the upright loop of four chain of last round, * 3 chain, 1 long treble under the loop over the previous group of treble stitches, 4 chain, 1 single crochet on the long treble stitch, another long treble in the same loop, do another picot and another long treble till you have 3 picots and 4 long treble stitches, then 3 chain, 1 double crochet in the next loop, and repeat from * to the end of the round, which completes the trimming.

INFANT'S CAPE WITH WIDE COLLAR.

THE cape shown in our engraving is particularly handsome for an infant, and may easily be enlarged to suit a lady. Procure ¾ lb. of white double Berlin wool, Peacock quality, and a No. 4 bone crochet needle, 1½ yards of good sarcenet ribbon for strings, and about ½ yard of narrow ribbon to run through the crochet at the neck. Commence for the **front of the cape**, lengthways, with 36 chain. **1st row**—Miss the chain stitch nearest the needle, and work

35 double crochet along the foundation chain. **2nd row**—1 chain to turn, and work 35 double crochet upon the stitches of the preceding row, always throughout the cape inserting the needle to take up the one top thread of the stitches, that the work may appear as shown in the sectional illustration. **3rd row**—1 chain to turn, work 25 double crochet, and 5 single crochet, and leave 5 stitches at the end unworked, this end is the neck end, and the crochet is now to be shaped in a kind of gore. **4th row**—Do 5 single crochet on the single crochet, and 25 double crochet on the double crochet of the previous row. **5th row**—1 chain to turn, work 20 double crochet, and 5 single crochet, and leave 10 stitches unworked. **6th row**—Do 5 single crochet on the single crochet, and 20 double crochet on the double crochet of the previous row. **7th row**—1 chain to turn, work 15 double crochet, and 5 single crochet, and leave 15 end stitches unworked. **8th row**—Do 5 single crochet on the single crochet, and 15 double crochet on the double crochet of the previous row. **9th row**—1 chain to turn, and work all the way up to the neck end, doing 35 double crochet. **10th row**—1 chain to turn, and work 35 double crochet upon the stitches of the preceding row. Repeat from the third row twelve times, which will make 106 rows along the bottom of the cape but only 28 rows along the neck; thus, by means of the gores, the cape is brought to a nice circular shape. For the **Collar—1st row**—Work 42 double crochet along the edge of the stitches at the top of the neck; by doing 2 double crochet on one stitch, and 1 double crochet on the stitch following the required number is exactly managed. **2nd row**—Working as usual into the one top thread of the stitches, increase a stitch at the beginning and at the end, in the middle of the row, and on each shoulder, and so make 47 double crochet in the row. **3rd row**—Increase a stitch on each shoulder, but rather more to the back than the previous increase, and so make 49 double crochet in the row. **4th row**—Increase a stitch at the beginning, in the middle, and at the end, and so make 52 double crochet in the row. **5th row**—Increase twice upon each shoulder, and to make 56 double crochet in the row. **6th row**—Increase

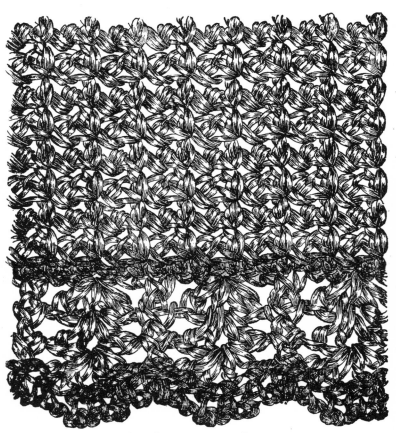

Details of a Lady's Petticoat.

four times at intervals in the row, and you will have 60 double crochet. **7th row**—Increase at the beginning, in the middle, and at the end, and so make 63 double crochet in the row. **8th row**—Increase six times at intervals in the row, and you will have 69 double crochet. **9th row**—Increase at the beginning and end and four times in the middle of the row, and so make 75 double crochet. **10th row**—Increase four times at intervals in the row, and there will be 79 double crochet. **11th row**—Plain double crochet without any increase. Fasten off. For the **Daisy Fringe**—Take about 14 long strands of wool and lay them all evenly together on the table before you, thread a rug needle or a tatting shuttle with another length of wool, and tie the end of this wool firmly round the strands of wool, beginning on the left-hand side about half an inch from the end; make another tie with the wool in the needle upon the stranded wool about an inch from the first tie, sewing it in a perfectly firm knot; and proceed in this manner till you have tied the stranded wool at regular intervals all along, when do more strands in the same way. When the needleful is used up thread another and tie it to the first with a knot. The strands of wool are then cut in the centre of every space between the ties; and a series of little tufts, or "daisies," is thus produced on the wool with which you have been sewing. This daisy fringe is now to be arranged in loops round the cape and round the collar; eight or nine daisies hang downwards in every loop, and two intermediate daisies are sewn straight upon the edge of the crochet, rather closely together, to simulate a kind of heading to the fringe. This daisy fringe uses up a quantity of wool but looks exceedingly stylish. Cut the narrow ribbon to the length required to go round the child's neck, and run it through the crochet, securing it at each end by a few stitches, thus the neck is drawn into shape and kept from stretching. Put on ribbon strings to tie in a bow in front of the neck.

A cape for a lady will take about 1 lb. of double Berlin wool, either grey, or ruby, or any colour that is desired. Begin with 44 chain, and work exactly as instructed above, only doing an additional 8 double crochet stitches always at the bottom of the cape to add to the length. The 106 rows along the bottom of the cape will probably make it quite sufficiently wide, but if for a stout figure another gore can be worked to increase the width. The collar forms a very pretty finish round the neck.

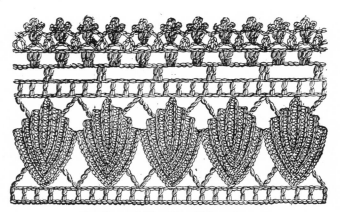

Section of Chemise Trimming.

ALBEMARLE PATTERN QUILT SQUARE.

WITH A PORTION OF BORDER.

THE handsome pattern represented in our engraving may be worked with either knitting cotton or crochet cotton, coarse or fine, according to taste. Strutt's No. 8 and No. 10 knitting cotton are nice sizes, or Coats' crochet cotton No. 12, and with either employ as fine a crochet-needle as you can conveniently use, that the work may be close and firm. Commence with 6 chain, and join round in a circle. 1st round—Work 4 chain to stand for a long treble stitch, do 3 long treble (cotton twice round the needle) in the circle, * 5 chain, 4 long treble in the circle, repeat from * twice, and do 5 chain and join to the top stitch of the chain with which the round commenced. 2nd round—Turn the work, and inserting the needle to take up the one back thread of the stitches of preceding round, do 1 double crochet on each stitch, and 3 double crochet on the centre stitch of the chain at each corner. 3rd round—Turn the work, slip invisibly to the centre chain stitch at the corner, do 4 chain to stand for a long treble stitch, * 2 long treble in the next chain stitch of the first round and 1 long treble in the next chain stitch, then inserting the needle to take always the one top thread of the stitches of the first round, work one long treble upon each long treble stitch, then 1 long treble on the first chain stitch, 2 long treble on the next chain stitch, 1 long treble on the centre chain stitch at the corner, 5 chain, 1 long treble again in the centre chain at the corner, and repeat from * three times; there should be 12 long treble stitches along each side of the square, and a loop of 5 chain at each corner; and finish by joining evenly to the top stitch of chain with which the round commenced: observe to work all the long treble stitches into the stitches of the first round and not into the double crochet stitches at all, these stand upwards in a kind of raised ridge upon the surface of the work as shown in the engraving. 4th round—Work as instructed for the second round. 5th round—Work as instructed for the third round, taking the long treble stitches into the one top thread of the stitches of the third round, and getting 20 long treble stitches along each side of the square, and a loop of 5 chain at each corner. It is a good plan to fasten off on the completion of some of the rounds and recommence in a fresh place, as thus any semblance of a seam on the surface of the work is avoided. Continue working a round of double crochet and a round of long treble stitches alternately, always turning the work on the completion of each round, and always working the double-crochet stitches in the one back thread of the stitches of last round, and the long treble stitches in the one top thread of the same round, and of course increasing the number of stitches in each round as the square gets larger, doing always eight more long treble stitches on each side of the square in each round, till you get to the 15th round, where you will do 60 long treble stitches along each side of the square, and a loop of 5 chain at each corner; join evenly on completion, and fasten off. 16th round—Beginning of the open crochet. Hold the right side of the work towards you, and now always inserting the needle to take up the tiny thread at the back of the stitches of last round, so as to leave the two front threads free, begin with 1 long treble in the centre stitch of chain at the corner, 5 chain, another long treble in the

same place, * cotton twice round the needle, insert the hook in the next chain stitch and draw the cotton through, cotton over the needle and draw through 2 loops on the needle, cotton over the needle, miss one chain stitch, insert the hook in the back thread of the treble stitch of last round and draw the cotton through, cotton over the needle, and draw through 2 loops on the needle four times in succession, 3 chain, cotton once over the needle, insert the hook to take up the two centre threads of the twisted stitch just done, and draw the cotton through, cotton over the needle and draw through 2 loops on the needle, cotton over the needle and draw through the last 2 loops on the needle, 1 long treble on the next stitch of last round, * 3 chain, miss three stitches, 1 long treble in the back thread of the next stitch and complete the "crossed stitch" as from * to * above, but miss two stitches where you before missed only one stitch; 3 chain, miss three stitches, 1 long treble, then a crossed stitch, and continue; and get 8 crossed stitches and 7 open spaces along the side of the square from corner to corner, missing two stitches instead of three under the last open space to get it in evenly, 5 chain at the corner, another long treble in the corner stitch, and repeat from * along the other three sides of the square; and join at the end of the round to the long treble stitch with which the round commenced. 17th round—Keep the square the right side to the front, and now working always into the one top thread of the stitches of the preceding round, begin with 4 chain to stand for a long treble stitch, 2 long treble in the first chain stitch of the corner loop, 1 long treble in the next, 1 long treble in the next (which is the corner stitch), 7 chain, 1 long treble in the same place, 1 long treble in the next, 2 long treble in the next, 1 long treble on long treble stitch of last round, * 4 chain, miss the crossed stitch, 1 long treble on next long treble of last round, and 4 more long treble worked consecutively, and repeat from *; and get 9 groups of long treble stitches and 8 open spaces along each side of the square from corner to corner, with a loop of 7 chain at each corner; and join evenly at the end of the round. 18th round—Work in cross stitches and spaces, getting 10 crossed stitches and 9 open spaces along each side of the square, with a loop of 7 chain at each corner. 19th round—Work in long treble stitches and spaces, and get 11 groups of long treble and 10 open spaces along each side of the square and a loop of 7 chain at each corner. 20th round—Same as the eighteenth round, but get 12 crossed stitches and 11 open spaces along each side, and a loop of 7 chain at each corner. 21st round—Work long treble stitches consecutively along each side of the square, with 5 chain at each corner, and join evenly on completion, and fasten off. This completes one square. The number of squares to be worked will depend greatly upon the coarseness or fineness of the

Chemise Trimming.

cotton and the size the quilt is desired to be. When you have a sufficient number join them together with a row of double crochet, making the stitches stand up in a ridge, to correspond with the ridged rows in the centre of the square. For the Border—The border is, of course, worked round the outside of the quilt after all the squares are joined together. 1st round—Double crochet, holding the wrong side of the quilt towards you, and inserting the hook to take up the back thread of the stitches. 2nd round—Hold the right side of the quilt towards you, and work long treble into the top thread of the stitches the same as in the fifteenth round of the square, and do 3 chain at each corner. 3rd round—1 double crochet on the centre stitch of three chain at the corner, 5 chain, 4 long treble on consecutive stitches taking up the one top thread, 5 chain, miss four stitches, 1 double crochet on the next, * 5 chain, miss four stitches, 4 long treble worked consecutively, 5 chain, miss four stitches, 1 double crochet on the next, and repeat from * till you get to the corner, where after working 4 long treble stitches close by the corner chain as shown in the engraving, do 5 chain, 1 double crochet on the centre stitch of three chain at the corner; and continue to the end of the round, and fasten off. 4th round—1 double crochet between the second and third long treble stitches of last round, 12 chain, and repeat the same; do 13 chain on turning the corner. 5th round—1 double crochet on double crochet of last round,

5 chain, miss four chain of last round, do 4 long treble worked consecutively, miss four stitches, 5 chain, and repeat; at the corner do two groups of 4 long treble stitches with the usual chain, and 1 double crochet on the centre stitch of chain, as shown in the engraving. **6th round**—Same as the fourth round. **7th round**—Same as the fifth round. **8th round**—Same as the fourth round, but 13 chain in each loop. **9th round**—1 double crochet on double crochet of last round, 6 chain, miss four stitches, do 5 long treble consecutively, 6 chain, miss four stitches, and repeat the same to the end of the round. **10th round**—Same as the eighth round. **11th round**—1 double crochet on double crochet of last round, 7 chain, 1 single crochet in the fifth chain from the needle, 2 chain, miss four stitches of last round, 1 long treble in the next, 4

Infant's Cape with Wide Collar.

chain, 1 single crochet in the top of the long treble stitch, 1 long treble on each of the three next stitches, 4 chain, 1 single crochet in the top of the last long treble stitch, 1 long treble on the next stitch, 7 chain, 1 single crochet in the fifth chain from the needle, 2 chain, and repeat the same to the end of the round; a double group of stitches is worked into each corner loop, as will be seen by referring to the engraving. This finishes the border.

LADY'S WARM FLEECY PETTICOAT.

PROCURE 1¾ lbs. of grey four-thread superfine fleecy wool and a No. 8 bone crochet needle. The striped pattern, which constitutes the upper portion of the skirt, is first to be worked, and the skirt is afterwards brought to the length required by the addition of the insertion and the border. Commence therefore for the top of the skirt, lengthways, with 69 chain. **1st row**—Miss the first chain stitch by the needle, and work 7 single crochet, 7 double crochet, and then 1 treble and 1 double crochet alternately twenty-seven times. **2nd row**—3 chain to turn, 1 treble on double crochet stitch and 1 double crochet on treble stitch alternately twenty-seven times, always taking up the one back thread of the stitches of the preceding row that the work may sit in ridges, then 7 double crochet on double crochet, and 7 single crochet on single crochet, still working in the back thread of the stitches. **3rd row**—1 chain to turn, work 7 single crochet, 7 double crochet, and then 1 treble and 1 double crochet alternately twenty-seven times, always taking up the one back thread of the stitches of last row. Continue working up and down in a repetition of the last two rows, till 108 rows, or 120 rows, are worked for the width of the skirt. Do not make it too narrow, as the tendency of the skirt is to drop lengthways by reason of its own weight, and therefore in dropping it narrows itself slightly. You will see how the waist is shaped by the single crochet and double crochet stitches, which serve the purpose as a band; the single crochet should be worked rather tightly, so as to contract as nearly as possible to the size of the figure. In working the last row but one form a button-hole in the single crochet by doing 2 chain and missing two corresponding stitches of the preceding row when 3 stitches from the top, and in the following row work 2 single crochet on the two chain to restore the original number of single crochet stitches. Sew up the skirt from the bottom to within nine inches of the top, which space should be left open for a placket. Strengthen round the placket with a row of plain double crochet, and carry a line of open stitches—viz., 1 chain and 1 treble alternately—along the top edge of the single crochet, in which afterwards to run a tape or a ribbon to tie round the waist. **For the Insertion** round the **Bottom** of the **Skirt**—**1st round**—Work

in plain double crochet; notice how the pattern sits in ridges, each ridge comprising two rows of crochet; do 3 double crochet upon one ridge, and four double crochet upon the next following ridge, alternately, all round the bottom of the skirt; the number of double crochet in the whole round must be some number divisible by eight. **2nd round**—Work 7 double crochet consecutively on double crochet of last round, inserting the hook to take up the two front threads of the stitches, insert the hook to take up two threads of the next stitch, draw the wool through and do 3 double crochet, then draw the wool through the last stitch of chain and through the double crochet stitch on the needle, which makes a "knob" or "tuft;" repeat the same to the end of the round. **3rd round**—Work 1 knob to the left of the knob of last round, 5 double crochet, 1 knob to the right of a knob of last round, and 1 double crochet on the knob of last round. **4th round**—Extend the vandyke in the manner shown in the engraving, working 1 knob and 3 double crochet alternately to the end of the round. **5th round**—Still extending the vandyke, work 1 knob, 1 double crochet, 1 knob, 5 double crochet, and repeat the same to the end of the round. **6th round**—Close the vandyke by working 1 knob on the one double crochet stitch of last round, 7 double crochet consecutively, and repeat. **7th round**—Plain double crochet, taking up the two front threads of the stitches of previous round, and increase 1 double crochet on the centre stitch between each knob; this finishes the insertion. For the **Border**—Work now always into the one top thread of the stitches. **1st round**—Do 3 double crochet on one stitch, 1 double crochet on the next stitch, * miss one stitch, 1 double crochet on the next, 3 double crochet on the next, 1 double crochet on the next, and repeat from * to the end of the round. **2nd round**—Work 1 double crochet on the first of the 3 double crochet stitches of last round, 3 double crochet on the centre stitch, and 1 double crochet on the last stitch of the 3 double crochet stitches of

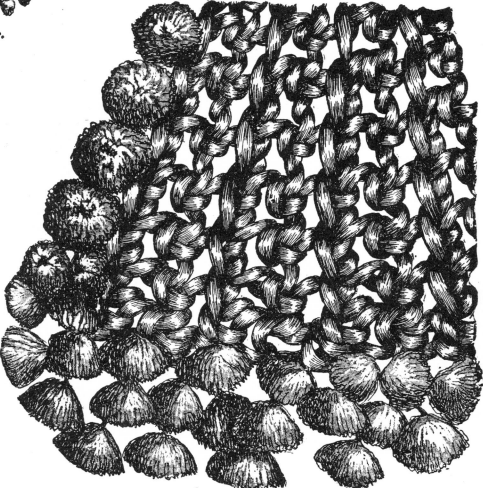

Section of Infant's Cape.

last round, miss two stitches, and repeat the same to the end. Repeat the 2nd round eight times, or till the border is as deep as is desired. **Last round**—To form Scollops—Work 3 treble on the centre stitch of the group of three double crochet, and do 1 double crochet on each of the other double crochet stitches, not missing any in the course of the round. Complete the skirt by sewing a button on the band to correspond with the button-hole; and run a tape or ribbon into the holes round the top of the skirt to tie round the waist.

D'OYLEY, EDGED WITH OLD ENGLISH LACE.

FOR the centre of this d'oyley procure a piece of fine diaper or damask linen measuring about six inches long by four inches and a half wide, or larger or smaller according to the size the d'oyley is required to be, cut this into a nice oval shape, and hem it neatly, either by machine or hand. The edging is crocheted upon this linen centre, working in rounds, with Ardern's crochet cotton, No. 24, and a fine steel crochet needle. **1st round**—Work 1 long treble, 1 chain, and repeat; the long treble stitches are formed by passing the cotton *twice* round the needle, and they are set rather closely together into the margin of the hem; join neatly on the completion of this and every round. **2nd round**—Work 1 double crochet under one chain space of last round, * 5 chain, miss three spaces, 1 long treble in the next, 1 chain, another long treble in the same place, do this twice more making in all 4 long treble divided by 1 chain under a one chain space of last round, 5 chain, miss three spaces, 1 double crochet in the next, and repeat from *. **3rd round**—Slip stitch to nearly the top of the five chain stitches of last round, do 6 chain to stand for a long treble stitch, * 1 long treble under the first one chain space of last round,

loop, 2 chain, and repeat from *; and join at the end of the round to the fourth chain with which the round commenced. **8th round**—Slip stitch under the first two chain space of last round, * 2 chain and 1 treble under the next space four consecutive times, 6 chain, 1 treble under the first two chain space of the next group of stitches, and repeat from *. **9th round**—Slip stitch under the first two chain space of last round, * 2 chain and 1 treble under the next space three consecutive times, 7 chain, 1 treble under the first two chain space of the next group of stitches, and repeat from *; and fasten off at the end of the round. **10th round**—Begin with 1 double crochet under a loop of seven chain of last round, * 9 chain, 1 long treble under the centre space of two chain, 1 chain and 1 long treble three times in the same place, 9 chain, 1 double crochet under the loop of seven chain, and repeat from *. **11th round**—Slip stitch along three chain stitches, 8 chain, 1 long treble under the first small space, * 2 chain, 1 long treble under the next which is the centre space, 2 chain, 1 long treble in the same place, 2 chain, 1 long treble in the same again, 2 chain, 1 long treble under the next space, 5 chain, 1 treble under the loop of nine chain, 1 treble under the next loop of 9 chain, 5 chain, 1 long treble under the first small space of the next group, and repeat from *; and join at the end of the round to the third chain stitch with

Albemarle Pattern Quilt Square, with a Portion of the Border.

2 chain, 1 long treble under the next space, 2 chain, 1 long treble under the next, 2 chain, 1 long treble under the next, 2 chain, 1 long treble under the five chain loop, 5 chain, 1 long treble under the next five chain loop, 2 chain. and repeat from *; and join at the end of the round to the fourth chain stitch with which the round commenced. **4th round**—Slip stitch under the first two chain space of last round, 5 chain to stand for a treble stitch, * 1 treble under the first space, 2 chain, 1 treble under the next space, 2 chain, 1 treble under the next space, 6 chain, and repeat from * to the end of the round, and join, and fasten off: the treble stitches in this round are ordinary treble worked with the cotton *once* round the needle. **5th round**—Begin with 1 double crochet under a loop of six chain of last round, * 5 chain, 1 long treble under the centre space of two chain, 1 chain and 1 long treble three times in the same place, 5 chain, 1 double crochet under the loop of six chain, and repeat from *. **6th round**—The same as the third round. **7th round**—Slip stitch under the five chain to the left, 6 chain to stand for a long treble stitch, * 1 long treble under the first two chain space, 2 chain, 1 long treble under the next two chain space three times, 2 chain, 1 long treble under the loop of five chain, 4 chain, 1 long treble under the same

which the round commenced. **12th round**—Work 5 double crochet under the loop of 5 chain, * 1 double crochet under the two chain space, 4 chain. 2 more double crochet under the same space, repeat the same under each of the next three spaces, 5 double crochet under the first loop of five chain, 5 double crochet under the next loop of five chain, and repeat from * to the end of the round, and fasten off. This finishes the d'oyley.

CROCHET SHAWL. HALF-CRAZY STITCH.

THIS shawl is extremely pretty worked with Shetland wool and a No. 10 bone crochet needle after the manner of the shawl from which our engraving is taken; or Pompadour wool can be employed if a handsome wrap is desired regardless of expense; while Andalusian wool is very suitable and will afford greater warmth. The shawl is worked lengthways, therefore commence with chain sufficient for the length required. **1st row**—1 double crochet in the second chain from the needle, 3 chain, 2 treble in the same stitch of the foundation as the double crochet is worked into, * miss three chain, 1 double crochet in the next, 3 chain, 2 treble in the same place, and repeat from * to the end of the row, where after missing three chain you do 1 double crochet on the last stitch of the foundation; it is wise to make an *even* number of groups in the row. **2nd row**—1 chain to turn, 1 double crochet on the first double crochet stitch of previous row, inserting the needle to take up the two top threads, 3 chain, 2 treble in the same place, * 1 double crochet on the next double crochet of preceding row, 3 chain, 2 treble in the same place, and repeat from *; and end with 1 double crochet on the last double crochet stitch of last row. The remainder of the shawl is a repetition of the second row, working forwards and backwards till the required size is attained, when fasten off. For the **Border**—Beginning at the corner on the double crochet stitch with which you ended the last row of the shawl, and holding the wrong side of last row towards you in the usual way after having turned the work, do 2 treble on the corner stitch, 3 chain, 2 treble in the same place, 3 chain, 2 more treble in the same place, 2 chain, wool over the needle and insert the hook in the next stitch of double crochet of the last row of the shawl and draw the wool through in a loose long loop, * wool over the needle and insert the hook again in the same place and again draw the wool through in a loose long hoop, repeat from * twice more, and there will be 4 loose loops on the needle with the wool between each, pass the wool over the needle and draw through all the loops, wool over the needle and draw through 2 stitches on the

corner. **4th round**—Again beginning at the corner—Work 3 treble 3 chain and 3 treble under the loop of three chain between the treble stitches of last round, 2 chain, a tuft in the loop in front of the tuft of last round, 2 chain, a tuft in the next following loop, 2 chain, 3 treble 3 chain and 3 treble in the loop between the treble stitches of last round, * 2 chain, a tuft in the loop in front of the tuft of last round, 2 chain, a tuft in the next following loop, 2 chain, 3 treble 3 chain and 3 treble in the loop between the treble stitches of last round, and repeat from *; and work the other corners similarly to the first corner. **5th round**—Beginning with a double crochet in any loop between two tufts of last round, * do 3 treble under the three chain loop between the treble stitches of last round, 4 chain, 1 single crochet on the top of the treble stitch last done, 2 more treble in the same loop, 4 chain, 1 single crochet on the top of the treble stitch last done, 2 more treble in the same loop, 4 chain, 1 single crochet on the top of the treble stitch last done, 3 more treble in the same loop, this makes 10 treble in the loop of last round with three little piques jutting out, then do 1 double crochet in the loop between the two tufts of last round, and repeat from *; and work the other corners to correspond; and join evenly at the end of the round, and fasten off securely. This a very handsome border and well worth the trouble of working.

Lady's Warm Fleecy Petticoat.

D'Oyley, Edg

needle, this forms a "tuft;" do 2 chain, then on the next double crochet stitch of last row work 2 treble 3 chain and 2 treble, do 2 chain, and on the next double crochet stitch make a tuft, and so on all along till you reach the corner, which work similarly to the first corner, and proceed along the other three sides of the shawl, and join evenly at the end of each round, and fasten off at the end of this and every round. **2nd round**—Work 2 treble under the first loop of three chain at the corner, 3 chain, 2 more treble in the same place; 2 chain, 2 treble 3 chain and 2 treble between the next two treble stitches of last round; 2 chain, 2 treble 3 chain and 2 treble under the other loop of three chain at the corner; * 2 chain, a tuft in the loop in front of the tuft of last round, 2 chain, a tuft in the loop following the tuft of last round, 2 chain, 2 treble 3 chain and 2 treble in the loop between the treble stitches of last round, and repeat from *; and work the other corners the same as the first corner. **3rd round**—Beginning by the corner in the same place as last round, do 3 treble 3 chain and 3 treble under the loop of three chain between the treble stitches of last round, 2 chain, a tuft under the next loop, 2 chain, 3 treble 3 chain and 3 treble in the corner loop, 2 chain, a tuft under the next loop, 2 chain, 3 treble 3 chain and 3 treble in the loop between the treble stitches of last round, 2 chain, a tuft in the loop between the tufts of last round, 2 chain, 3 treble 3 chain and 3 treble in the loop between the treble stitches of last round, and repeat from *; and work the other corners the same as the first

COUVREPIED.

THIS couvrepied is composed of sectional squares worked in Russian crochet, each square being bordered with a round of open crossed stitches, through which a satin ribbon is run from side to side of the couvrepied. The process of working is clearly shown in the engraving. Select single Berlin wool of any colour that harmonises or contrasts well with the upholstery of the room. Crimson always looks bright and cheerful, and art green gives a pleasant, subdued colouring; a pretty way is to shade the wool from dark in the centre to light outside, doing four or six rounds with each shade. Use a No. 10 bone crochet needle, and work the Russian crochet closely and firmly. If you like to employ double Berlin wool use a No. 8 needle. Begin in the centre of the square with 2 chain; work 8 double crochet in the first stitch of chain, and join round quite evenly. **2nd round**—Turn the work, insert the hook always to take up the one *back* thread of the stitches of the previous round, do 1 double crochet on the first stitch of previous round, 3 double crochet on the next, repeat the same three times, and join evenly at the end of the round, this joining should be made quite invisibly, and that it may be so it is a good plan to break off the wool on the completion of every two or four rounds and recommence in a fresh place. **3rd round**—Turn the work, do 3 double crochet on the centre stitch at each corner, and 3 consecutive double crochet along each side of the square. **4th round**—Turn the work, do 3 double crochet on the centre stitch at each corner, and 5 consecutive double crochet along each side of the square. **5th round**—Turn the work, do 3 double crochet on the centre stitch at each corner, and 7 consecutive double crochet along each side of the square. Continue in this manner, always working 3 double crochet for corner stitches and consecutive double crochet along the sides of the square, till in the **18th round** you work 3 double crochet at the corner and 33 double crochet along each side, and join quite evenly, and fasten off. **19th round**—This round consists of open crossed stitches. Turn the work so as to have, as usual, the wrong side of last round uppermost, make a stitch on the needle, wool twice round the needle, insert the hook to take up the back thread of the centre stitch at the corner, and draw the wool through, wool over the needle and draw through 2 loops on the needle, wool over the needle, miss one stitch of last round, insert the hook in the back thread of the next stitch and draw the wool through, wool over the needle and draw through 2 loops on the needle *four* times, 2 chain, wool over the needle, insert the hook to take up the two centre threads of the twisted stitch just made and draw the wool through, wool over the needle and draw through 2 loops on the needle, wool over the needle and again draw through 2 loops on the needle, this forms 1 crossed stitch, * 1 chain, wool twice round the needle, miss one

off. **2nd round**—Hold the right side of the work uppermost, and take up the one top thread of the stitches, * 3 double crochet in the centre stitch of the loop of eleven chain, 7 double crochet worked consecutively, miss two stitches, work 7 double crochet consecutively, and repeat from * to the end of the round. **3rd round**—Do 3 double crochet on the centre stitch of three double crochet of last round, 7 double crochet on the seven following stitches, miss two stitches, 7 double crochet on the following seven stitches, and repeat the same to the end of the round. Work 4 more rounds the same as last round. **8th round**—Work 1 double crochet on the second stitch of seven double crochet on the rising side of a scollop, then loops of 3 chain, miss one stitch, 1 double crochet on the next, seven times round the scollop, miss two stitches, and continue the same to the end of the round. The fringe is made by cutting strands of wool eight or nine inches in length and knotting 6 or 7 strands into each loop of chain. Procure good satin ribbon of a suitable width to run in through the open crossed stitches, as shown in the illustration; the ribbon is held in place by a few stitches at the beginning and at the end of each line.

CROCHET EDGING.
FOR A SHAWL, OR OTHER PURPOSE.

COMMENCE with a chain the length required, or otherwise work immediately

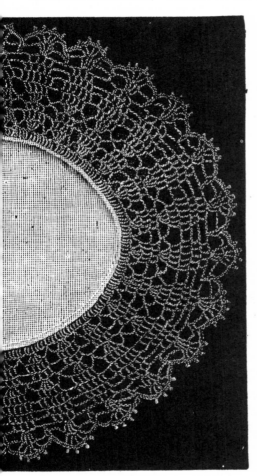

d English Lace.

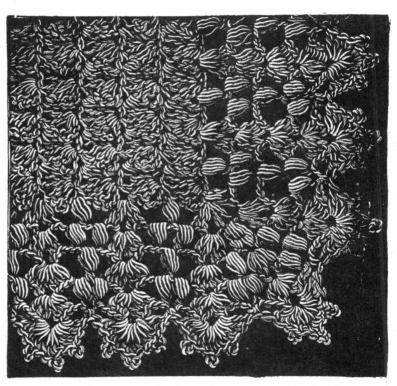

Crochet Shawl. Half-Crazy Stitch.

stitch of last round, insert the hook in the back thread of the next stitch and draw the wool through, wool over the needle and draw through 2 loops on the needle, wool over the needle, miss two stitches of last round, insert the hook in the back thread of the next stitch and draw the wool through, wool over the needle and draw through 2 loops on the needle *four* times, 2 chain, wool over the needle, insert the hook to take up the two centre threads of the twisted stitch just made and draw the wool through, wool over the needle and draw through 2 loops on the needle, wool over the needle and again draw through 2 loops on the needle, and repeat from * till you get to the centre stitch at the next corner, making 8 crossed stitches along the side of the square (one stitch only to be missed under the cross at the end the same as at the beginning), do 7 chain to turn round the corner, and continue the three other sides of the square in the same way, and join evenly at the end of the round, and fasten off. Work a sufficient number of squares for the size of the couvrepied and sew them together. When they are all joined, a row of crossed stitches is worked the whole way round the couvrepied, followed by six rounds of Russian crochet. For the **Border** and **Fringe—1st round**—Beginning on the double crochet stitch next after the three double crochet at the corner, * work 6 double crochet consecutively, 11 chain, miss seven stitches, and repeat from *; make the stitches come in evenly at the corners where only three double crochet should be missed, and join evenly at the end of the round, and fasten

upon the article for which the border is intended; it is very pretty worked with Shetland wool and a fine crochet needle. **1st row**—1 double crochet in a stitch of the foundation, * 5 chain, a picot (that is 1 single crochet in the third chain from the needle), 6 chain, a picot, 2 chain, miss five stitches of the foundation, 1 double crochet in the next, and repeat from * to the end of the row; break off the wool at the end of this and every row. The work may be turned or not, as preferred; if it be turned, both sides of the edging will be alike, and if not turned, there will a right side and a wrong side. **2nd row**—1 single crochet in the centre stitch of the three chain stitches between the picots of last row, * 5 chain, a picot, 6 chain, a picot, 2 chain, 1 single crochet in the centre stitch of the next loop of last row, and repeat from *. **3rd row**—Same as the second row. **4th row**—1 single crochet in the centre stitch of a loop of last row, 9 chain, 1 single crochet in the centre stitch of the next loop, 2 chain, turn the work, and do 7 treble and 1 double crochet under the loop of nine chain, 2 chain, turn the work and do 8 treble in the spaces of the little treble row just done, 6 chain, 1 single crochet in the centre stitch of the next loop of last row, * 2 chain, turn the work, and do 7 treble and 1 double crochet under the loop of six chain, 2 chain, turn the work, and do 8 treble in the spaces of the little treble row, 6 chain, 1 single crochet in the centre stitch of the next loop of last row, and repeat from *. **5th row**—1 single crochet in the two chain at the top of the little scollop of treble stitches, * 5 chain, a picot, 6 chain, a picot, 2 chain, 1 single crochet in the two chain at the top of the next scollop of treble stitches, and repeat from *. **6th row**—Same as the second row. **7th row**—Also like the second row. **8th row**—Same as the fourth row. **9th row**—Same as the fifth row. **10th row**—Same as the second row. **11th row**—Also like the second row. This completes the edging.

INFANT'S BONNET IN TRICOT.

THIS warm comfortable bonnet for an infant is worked entirely in plain tricot, excepting the border, which is done in looped knitting; it comes nicely upon the head, and protects the ears from cold winds. The materials required are 4 ozs. of white single Berlin wool, a No. 6 bone tricot needle, or a No. 7 if a loose worker, a pair of No. 14 steel knitting needles, 3 yards of ribbon for bows and strings, and 1 yard of narrow ribbon for drawing up the front, also a lace cap may be put in and is a decided improvement. Make 60 chain for the *front* of the *bonnet*, and work 14 rows of all plain tricot, 60 stitches in each

Section of Couvrepied.

row. **15th row**—Pick up 12 tricot stitches (1 stitch being already on the needle from last row makes 13 stitches on the needle), pick up 2 stitches together, 14 plain tricot, 2 stitches together, 14 plain tricot, 2 stitches together, 13 plain tricot, and draw back as usual. **16th row**—13 plain tricot, 2 together, 12 plain, 2 together, 13 plain, 2 together, 13 plain tricot. **17th row**—13 plain tricot, 2 together, 11 plain, 2 together, 11 plain, 2 together, 13 plain. **18th row**—13 plain tricot, 2 together, 9 plain, 2 together, 10 plain, 2 together, 13 plain. **19th row**—13 plain tricot, 2 together, 18 plain, 2 together, 13 plain. **20th row**—13 plain tricot, 2 together, 7 plain, 2 together, 7 plain, 2 together, 13 plain. **21st row**—12 plain tricot, 2 together, 6 plain, 2 together, 7 plain, 2 together, 12 plain. **22nd row**—11 plain tricot, 2 together, 6 plain, 2 together, 6 plain, 2 together, 11 plain. **23rd row**—10 plain tricot, 2 together, 5 plain, 2 together, 6 plain, 2 together, 10 plain. **24th row**—9 plain tricot, 2 together, 5 plain, 2 together, 5 plain, 2 together, 9 plain. **25th row**—8 plain tricot, 2 together, 4 plain, 2 together, 5 plain, 2 together, 8 plain. **26th row**—7 plain tricot, 2 together, 4 plain, 2 together, 4 plain, 2 together, 7 plain. **27th row**—11 plain tricot, 2 together, 12 plain tricot, which brings now only 24 stitches on the needle, draw back, and break off the wool with a long end; fold the 24 stitches to form the back of the crown, and sew up. Work a row of treble stitches along the bottom of the bonnet in which afterwards to run a ribbon to confine the bonnet in shape round the back of the neck, do 28 treble on each side and 1 treble on the join that runs up the back of the bonnet, 57 treble in all, and break off the wool. For the **Curtain**—**1st row**—Pick up 57 tricot stitches upon the edge of the treble, and draw back as usual. **2nd row**—Pick up 1 tricot stitch, increase 1, 22 plain, increase 1, 4 plain, increase 1, 5 plain, increase 1, 22 plain, increase 1, 2 plain. **3rd row**—Plain tricot, 62 stitches. **4th row**—Pick up 1 tricot stitch, increase 1, 20 plain, increase 1, 7 plain, increase 1, 4 plain, increase 1, 7 plain, increase 1, 20 plain, increase 1, 2 plain. **5th row**—Plain tricot, 68 stitches. **6th row**—Pick up 1 tricot stitch, increase 1, 24 plain, increase 1, 8 plain, increase 1, 8 plain, increase 1, 24 plain, increase 1, 2 plain. **7th row**—Plain tricot, 73 stitches. **8th row**—Pick up 20 tricot stitches, increase 1, 16 plain, increase 1, 16 plain, increase 1, 20 plain. **9th row**—Plain tricot, 76 stitches. Fasten off. For the **Looped Trimming**—Use the knitting needles and cast on 5 stitches. **1st row**—Plain knitting. **2nd row**—Insert the right-hand needle in the first stitch, pass the wool over the point of the needle and round the first and second fingers of the left hand twice, and then again over the point of the needle and knit the stitch

taking in all three threads of the wool, and knit the 4 other stitches in the same manner. **3rd row**—Plain, taking every group of threads as one stitch, so again you have 5 stitches on the needle. Repeat the last two rows till a sufficient length is knitted to go along the edge of the bottom of the curtain, when fasten off, and sew it on. Make another length of looped trimming to go along the edge of the front of the bonnet, from the bottom of the looped trimming on one side the curtain to the bottom of the looped trimming on the other side, and sew it on. Make a nice bow of ribbon to place on the top of the bonnet. Divide the remainder of the ribbon into four pieces; run two pieces through the row of treble stitches, securing an end firmly on each side under the looped trimming, and tying a bow at the back; use the other two pieces for strings. Run the narrow ribbon in the front of the bonnet alongside the first row of the tricot, and draw it in slightly to suit the child's face, and the bonnet will appear as shown in the engraving. The bonnet may be lined with thin silk if desired, but it is not actually necessary.

SEXAGON FOR A QUILT.

OUR engraving shows a large handsome sexagon for a quilt, also a section of the same to more clearly illustrate the method of working. The model is executed with Coats' crochet cotton, No. 8, and a fine steel crochet needle; each sexagon measures nearly ten inches from side to side, therefore, though there is a great deal of work in the making of one sexagon, not a very great number will be required to complete a quilt, in fact eight or nine sexagons in width and the same number in length are sufficient for a good-sized quilt. Knitting cotton, No. 12, may be employed instead of crochet cotton, if preferred. The work is done closely and rather tightly. **Commence** in the centre of the sexagon, with 2 chain; work 4 double crochet in the second chain from the needle. **1st round**—Work 2 double crochet on each of the four double crochet stitches, inserting the needle to take up the one top thread. **2nd round**—Work again 2 double crochet on each stitch, making 16 double crochet, always inserting the hook in the one top thread of the stitches of previous round, and join evenly at the end of this and every following round. **3rd round**—In this round the raised tufts begin; if you look at the work you will see the front threads of the 4 first double crochet stitches visible in the middle of the circle, raise each a little so as to be more readily noticed, a "tuft" is to be worked into each of these four stitches, * cotton over the needle and insert the hook into the first of these stitches and draw the cotton through, cotton over the needle and draw through 2

Couvrepied.

stitches on the needle, § cotton over the needle and insert the hook again in the same place and draw the cotton through, cotton over the needle and draw through 2 stitches on the needle, repeat from § three times more, and there will be 6 stitches on the needle, cotton over the needle and draw through 5 of these stitches, cotton over the needle and draw through 2 stitches on the needle, miss the stitch of last round at the back of the tuft, do 1 double crochet on the next, 2 double crochet on the next, 1 double crochet on the next, and repeat from * three times, and there will be in all 20 stitches in the round. **4th round**—Double crochet all round, increasing eight times, and making 28 stitches in the round. **5th round**—Double crochet, increasing six times, and making 32 stitches in the round. **6th round**—You now should be in position for working directly beyond one of the tufts of the third round, work a tuft therefore into a stitch of the third round, miss one stitch of last round, 1 double crochet on the next, 2 double crochet on the next, 1 double crochet on the next, and repeat the same to the end of the round, making two tufts between each tuft of the third round, and there will be 8 tufts, and 40 stitches in all in the round. **7th round**—Plain double crochet, 40 stitches, and join *quite* evenly. **8th round**—This is an open round, do 5 chain to stand for a treble, 1 treble on the first stitch of the preceding round, 2 chain, 1 treble on the next, 2 chain, 1 treble on the next, 2 chain, 1 treble on the next, 2 chain, 1 treble on the next, 2 chain, 1 treble on the next, 2 chain, miss 1 stitch, * 1 treble on the next, 2 chain, 1 treble on the next, 2 chain, miss one stitch, and repeat from *, and at the end of the round after doing 2 chain join to the third stitch of the chain with which the round began; the hook should be inserted into both the top and the back threads of the stitches of last round, and there will be 30 treble stitches and 30 open spaces in the round. **9th round**—The beginning of the raised pleated wheel—Do 3 double crochet on the treble stitch of last round, 1 double crochet on each of the two chain stitches, and repeat, working always now into the one top thread, **10th round**—3 double crochet on the centre stitch of the three double crochet of last round, 4 double crochet worked consecutively, and repeat; there should be 30 points of three double crochet stitches in each round. **11th round**—3 double crochet on the centre stitch of the three double crochet of last

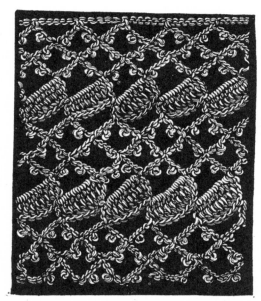

Edging for a Shawl or other purpose.

round, 6 double crochet worked consecutively, and repeat. **12th round**—3 double crochet on the centre stitch of the three double crochet of last round, 8 double crochet worked consecutively, and repeat. **13th round**—3 double crochet on the centre stitch of the three double crochet of last round, 10 double crochet worked consecutively, and repeat. **14th round**—3 double crochet on the centre stitch of the three double crochet of last round, 12 double crochet worked consecutively, and repeat. **15th round**—3 double crochet on the centre stitch of the three double crochet of last round, 14 double crochet worked consecutively, and repeat. Proceed working in the same manner as the last few rounds, always doing 3 double crochet on the centre stitch of the previous three double crochet, and always increasing two plain stitches in every round between the points, till in the **20th round** you do 3 double crochet on the centre stitch of the three double crochet of last round, and 24 double crochet worked consecutively, which completes the wheel, join round quite evenly, and fasten off. **21st round**—Beginning the plain double crochet behind the wheel—work 1 double crochet on the thirteenth stitch of the twenty-four consecutive stitches of the last round of the wheel, inserting the hook to take up the front and top threads of the stitch, * 4 chain, 1 double crochet on the thirteenth stitch of the next division of twenty-four stitches, 5 chain, 1 double crochet on the thirteenth stitch of the next division, 4 chain, 1 double crochet on the thirteenth stitch of the next division, 5 chain, 1 double crochet on the thirteenth stitch of the next division, 5 chain, 1 double crochet on the thirteenth stitch of the next division, and repeat from *, being very careful to make the right number of chain stitches; there should be 30 double crochet stitches and 30 loops of chain in the round, 168 stitches; keep the points of the wheel to the front of the loops of chain stitches, and join evenly on the completion of the round. **22nd round**—Plain double crochet, 168 stitches in the round. **23rd round**—Work 3 double crochet on the first stitch of last round (on the stitch above the double crochet of the preceding round), 27 consecutive double crochet, and repeat, working now into the one top thread of the stitches, and you will have 6 points of three double crochet to denote the six points of the sexagon. **24th round**—3 double crochet on the centre stitch of the three double crochet of last round, 29 double crochet worked consecutively, and repeat. **25th round**.—3 double crochet on the centre stitch of the three double crochet of last round, 31 double crochet worked consecutively, and repeat. **26th round**—3 double crochet on the centre stitch of the three double crochet of last round, 33 double crochet worked consecutively, and repeat. **27th round**—3 double crochet on the centre stitch of the three double crochet of last round, 35 double crochet worked consecutively, and repeat. **28th round**—3 double crochet on the centre stitch of the

three double crochet of last round, 37 double crochet worked consecutively, and repeat; and be careful to join quite evenly on the completion of the round, and fasten off. **29th round**—This is an open round; do 1 treble on the first of the three double crochet stitches on a point, 1 chain, 1 treble on the centre stitch of the point, 1 chain, 1 treble on the third of the three double crochet stitches, * 1 chain, miss one stitch, 1 treble on the next, and repeat from * till you get to the next point, which work like the first, and continue the same to the end of the round, when there should be 126 treble and 126 open spaces, that is 21 treble stitches and 21 open spaces on each of the six sides of the sexagon, and join round. **30th round**—Work 1 treble on the centre stitch of a point, 1 chain, 1 treble in the same place, 1 chain, another treble in the same place, * 1 chain, 1 treble on treble stitch of last round, and repeat from * till you get to the next point, which work like the first, and continue the same open stitch to the end of the round, when there should be 138 treble and 138 open spaces, that is 23 treble stitches, and 23 open spaces on each of the six sides of the sexagon, join round. **31st round**—Work 3 double crochet on the centre stitch of a point, 45 double crochet worked consecutively, and repeat. **32nd round**—Work 3 double crochet on the centre stitch of the three double crochet of last round, 47 double crochet worked consecutively, and repeat. **33rd round**—Beginning the triangles of tufts, * work 3 double crochet on the centre stitch of three double crochet at the point, 12 double crochet worked consecutively, a tuft into a stitch of the second previous round, 3 double crochet and a tuft alternately till 7 tufts are worked, 12 double crochet, and repeat from * to the end of the round. **34th round**—3 double crochet on the centre stitch at the point, 51 double crochet worked consecutively, and repeat. **35th round**—3 double crochet on the centre stitch at the point, 16 consecutive double crochet, a tuft into the middle double crochet between the tufts of the second previous round, 3 double crochet and a tuft alternately till 6 tufts are worked, 16 double crochet, and repeat the same. **36th round**—3 double crochet on the centre stitch at the point, 55 double crochet worked consecutively, and repeat. **37th round**—3 double crochet on the centre stitch at the point, 20 consecutive double crochet, a tuft into the middle stitch between the tufts of the second previous row, 3 double crochet and a tuft alternately till 5 tufts are worked, 20 double crochet, and repeat the same. **38th round**—3 double crochet on the centre stitch at the point, 59 double crochet worked consecutively, and repeat. **39th round**—3 double crochet on the centre stitch at

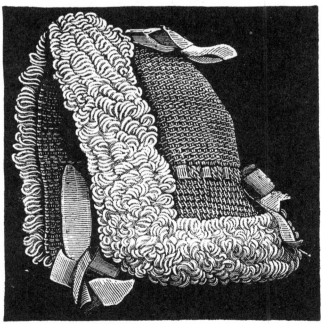

Infant's Bonnet in Tricot.

the point, 24 consecutive double crochet, a tuft into the middle stitch between the tufts of the second previous row, 3 double crochet and a tuft alternately till 4 tufts are worked, 24 double crochet, and repeat the same. **40th round**—3 double crochet on the centre stitch at the point, 63 double crochet worked consecutively, and repeat. **41st round**—3 double crochet on the centre stitch at the point, 28 consecutive double crochet, a tuft into the middle stitch between the tufts of the second previous row, 3 double crochet and a tuft alternately till 3 tufts are worked, 28 double crochet, and repeat the same. **42nd round**—3 double crochet on the centre stitch at the point, 67 double crochet worked consecutively, and repeat. **43rd round**—3 double crochet on the centre stitch at the point, 32 consecutive double crochet, a tuft into the middle stitch between the tufts of the second previous row, 3 double crochet, a tuft, 32 double crochet, and repeat the same. **44th round**—3 double crochet on the centre stitch at the point, 71 double crochet worked consecutively, and repeat. **45th round**—3 double crochet on the centre stitch at the point, 36 consecutive double crochet, a tuft, 36 double crochet, and repeat the same; this completes the triangles of tufts, join evenly, and fasten off. **46th round**—This is an open round, do 1 treble on the first of the three double crochet stitches on a point, 1 chain, 1 treble on the centre stitch of the point, 1 chain, 1 treble on the third of the three double crochet stitches, * 1 chain, miss one stitch, 1 treble on the next, and repeat from *, till you get to the next point, which work like the first, and continue the same to the end of the round. **47th round**—5 treble on the centre stitch at the point, and 77 treble worked consecutively, and repeat, and fasten off at the end of the round. This completes one sexagon. A number of sexagons are very easily joined together by sewing the straight side of one to the straight side of another. The spaces all round the edge of the quilt may be filled with *half* sexagons if the quilt is to be finished with a lace border; but if fringed a longer fringe can be put in the spaces than is put on the extreme outside margin.

INFANT'S BOOTS. TRICOT.

FOR an infant's first-size boots procure ¾ oz. of white and a little pale blue

tricot on the needle; and draw back. **3rd row**—Drop the tricot stitch off the needle, draw the wool through the twentieth, twenty-first, and twenty-second double crochet stitches, resume the dropped stitch, pick up 9 tricot on the tricot stitches, and 3 tricot on double crochet; 16 tricot on the needle; and draw back. **4th row**—Drop the tricot stitch off the needle, draw the wool through the seventeenth, eighteenth, and nineteenth double crochet stitches, resume the dropped stitch, pick up 15 tricot on the tricot stitches, and 3 tricot on double crochet; 22 tricot on the needle; and draw back. **5th row**—Drop the tricot stitch, pick up a tricot stitch in the fourteenth, fifteenth, and sixteenth double crochet stitches, resume the dropped stitch, pick up 5 tricot, pick up 2 stitches together, pick up 6 tricot, pick up 2 stitches together, pick up 6 tricot on tricot stitches, and 3 tricot on double crochet; 26 tricot on the needle; and draw back. **6th row**—Drop the tricot stitch, pick up a tricot stitch in the eleventh, twelfth, and thirteenth double crochet stitches, resume the dropped stitch, pick up 7 tricot, 2 together, 6 tricot for the instep, 2 together, pick up 8 tricot on tricot stitches, and 3 tricot on double crochet; 30 tricot on the needle; and draw back. **7th row**—Drop the tricot stitch, pick up a tricot stitch in the

Sexagon for a Quilt.

Andalusian wool and a No. 9 bone tricot needle; for larger boots 1 oz of white and ¼ oz. of blue single Berlin and a No. 8 needle. The blue wool is only used as a trimming to edge the frill round the top of the boots. Commence for the bottom of the boot with white wool, with 55 chain, and work a row of 54 double crochet stitches, and break off the wool. Now proceed **in tricot**— Miss the first 24 double crochet stitches, draw the wool through the next double crochet and so form 1 tricot stitch, pick up 1 tricot stitch on each of the following 5 double crochet, making in all 6 tricot on the needle, and leave 24 double crochet at the end to correspond with the 24 left at the beginning, and draw back through the 6 tricot stitches in the ordinary manner. **2nd row**—Drop the tricot stitch off the needle for a moment, draw the wool through the twenty-third double crochet stitch, and the twenty-fourth double crochet stitch, resume the dropped stitch, pick up 5 tricot on 5 tricot stitches of last row, and 2 tricot on two double crochet stitches; making in all 10

eighth, ninth, and tenth double crochet stitches, resume the dropped stitch pick up 9 tricot, 2 together, 6 tricot for the instep, 2 together, pick up 10 tricot on tricot stitches, and 3 tricot on double crochet; 34 tricot on the needle; and draw back. **8th row**—Drop the tricot stitch, pick up a tricot stitch on the fifth, sixth, and seventh double crochet stitches, resume the dropped stitch, pick up 33 tricot on tricot stitches, and 3 tricot on double crochet; 40 tricot on the needle; and draw back. **9th row**—Drop the tricot stitch, pick up a tricot stitch in the first, second, third, and fourth double crochet stitches, resume the dropped stitch, pick up 14 tricot, 2 together, 6 tricot for the instep, 2 together, pick up 15 tricot on tricot stitches, and 4 tricot on double crochet; 46 tricot on the needle; and draw back. **10th row**— Keep the 1 tricot stitch on the needle, increase 1, pick up 17 tricot, 2 together, 6 tricot for the instep, 2 together, pick up 17 tricot, increase 1, pick up 1 tricot; 46 tricot on the needle; and draw back. **11th row**—Pick up 17 tricot,

2 together, 6 tricot for the instep, 2 together, 18 tricot ; 44 tricot on the needle ; and draw back. **12th row**—All plain tricot. **13th row**—Pick up 16 tricot, 2 together, 6 plain, 2 together, 17 plain ; 42 tricot on the needle ; and draw back. **14th row**—Pick up 15 tricot, 2 together, 6 plain, 2 together, 16 plain ; and draw back. **15th row**—Pick up 14 tricot, 2 together, 6 plain, 2 together, 15 plain ; and draw back. **16th row**—Pick up 2 together, 11 plain, 2 together, 6 plain, 2 together, 12 plain, 2 together ; 34 tricot on the needle ; and draw back. Work 5 rows of all plain tricot. **22nd row**—Pick up 2 tricot, increase 1, work plain tricot till within 3 stitches of the end, increase 1, pick up 3 tricot ; and draw back. **23rd row**—Plain tricot. Work 4 rows with increase the same as the twenty-second row. **28th row**—Plain tricot, 44 stitches, and draw back. **29th row**—Plain tricot, and break off the wool. For the **Sole**—Pick up in tricot the 6 stitches of

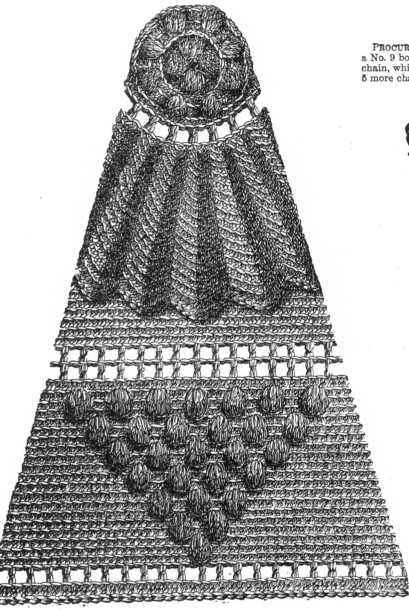

Section of Sexagon Quilt

the foundation chain that you used for the beginning of the toe, and work in plain tricot about 20 rows, or till the sole is about long enough to reach to the back of the boot, decrease one stitch on each side in course of doing the last row, and fasten off ; sew up the back of the leg, then sew the sole neatly in its place, rounding the heel nicely. For the **Frill**—Begin by the seam, with white wool, and do a row of double crochet stitches along the top of the tricot, inserting the hook to take up the perpendicular threads, and join round. **2nd round**—Also with white wool,—Reverse the position of the boot, and hold the row you have just worked towards you, and insert the needle to take the threads that lie between those taken in the last row, that the scollops may turn downwards in the position shown in the engraving,—Do 1 single crochet in the stitch by the needle, miss one stitch, * do 5 treble in the next, miss one, do 1 single crochet in the next, miss one, and repeat from

* to the end of the round, and fasten off. Work three scollops on the front of the leg, beginning just underneath the scollops that run round the top of the boot and going only a little way down, as will be seen in the engraving. **3rd round**—With pale blue wool—Work a line of single crochet along the edge of the stitches of last round, inserting the hook to take the two front threads of the stitches ; break off the wool on the completion of the round. **4th round**—With blue wool—Work upon the round of double crochet stitches, 1 double crochet on the first stitch by the seam, * 3 chain, miss one stitch, 1 double crochet on the next, and repeat from * ; and fasten off at the end of the round. The other boot must be worked in the same manner, but the three scollops on the front of the leg should turn in the opposite direction ; a small blue silk button is then placed on each of these scollops.

CUFF.

WORKED IN TRICOT WITH A CROCHET EDGE.

PROCURE 1 oz. of claret colour single Berlin wool, a No. 8 tricot needle, and a No. 9 bone crochet needle. Commence with the tricot needle by making 31 chain, which is a fair ordinary size to go round the arm, but, if required larger, 5 more chain must be added to allow for one more complete stripe of the tricot

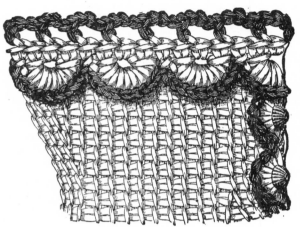

Section of Infant's Boot.

Infant's Boot in Tricot.

pattern. **1st row**—Pick up 1 tricot stitch in each stitch of chain, and you will have 31 stitches on the needle (or the same number with which you began), the tricot must be done moderately loosely, and work back in this manner,—draw through 1 stitch, * do 1 chain, draw through 3 stitches together, do 1 chain, draw through 2 stitches separately, and repeat from * till all the stitches are worked through. **2nd row**—Pick up 1 tricot stitch on the second stitch of previous row, * 1 tricot in the chain stitch, 1 tricot in the little thread at the back of the three stitches that are drawn together, 1 tricot in the next chain stitch, 1 tricot on each of the two plain tricot stitches, and repeat from * to the end, where will be only 1 plain tricot stitch to pick up, and there will be 31 stitches again on the needle, draw back through these as instructed in the first row. Continue working the same as the second row until 11 rows are done. **12th row**—With the crochet needle—work for the edge,—Insert the hook in the second stitch of previous row, draw the wool through and do 3 chain stitches, draw the wool through the last stitch of chain and through the other stitch on the needle, 1 double crochet on the chain stitch of last row, * insert the hook in the little thread at the back of the three stitches that are drawn together and draw the wool through, do 3 chain and draw the wool through the last stitch of chain and through the stitch on the needle, miss the chain stitch, do 1 double crochet on the first of the two plain tricot stitches, 1 picot (as above) on the second of the two plain tricot stitches, 1 double crochet on the chain stitch of last row, and repeat from * to the end of the row, and join *round* by making a single crochet to the beginning of the row. **13th row**—1 double crochet, 3 chain, 1 treble, 1 double crochet, all worked on each double crochet stitch of last row, taking up two front threads, and fasten off at the end of the round. Work a similar edge on the other side of the cuff. Join up the sides of the tricot work. Make the other cuff in the same manner.

Cuff, worked in Tricot with a Crochet Edge.

SLIPPER FOR A CHILD OF EIGHT OR TEN YEARS.

THIS pretty slipper is worked in plain tricot, and is quickly and easily made. The same in a larger size is suitable for lady's wear. Required, single Berlin wool, scarlet, grey, and white, about 1 oz. of each colour, a No. 8 tricot needle, a No. 9 bone crochet needle, a pair of cork soles, a piece of scarlet flannel for lining, and 1½ yards of narrow scarlet ribbon. Begin with the tricot needle and scarlet wool and do 6 chain for the toe. **1st row**—Pick up 1 tricot stitch in the third chain from the needle, 3 in the next (1 in the front, 1 in the back, and 1 in the front again), and 1 in each of the two last, making in all 7 stitches on the needle; draw back in the usual manner, and when 2 stitches remain on the needle take the white wool and draw through the 2 stitches with white, which brings a white stitch on the needle for the beginning of the next row. **2nd row**—With white wool,—Pick up 1 tricot stitch in each of 2 stitches, 3 in the centre stitch (1 in the centre stitch itself and 1 in the horizontal thread on each side it), and 1 in each of the 3 last, making 9 stitches on the needle; draw back, and when 2 stitches remain on the needle take the grey wool and draw through the 2 stitches with grey, and so you get a grey stitch on the needle for the beginning of the next row. **3rd row**—With grey wool,—Pick up 1 tricot stitch in each of 3 stitches, 3 in the centre stitch, and 1 in each of the 4 last, making 11 stitches on the needle; draw back, and when 2 stitches remain on the needle resume the scarlet wool and draw through the 2 stitches with scarlet. You will by this time see how the work is executed, one row with each colour, scarlet, white, and grey, in rotation, and the colour is always changed upon the two last stitches in drawing back. **4th row**—With scarlet,—Pick up 1 tricot stitch in each of 4 stitches, 3 in the centre stitch, 1 in each of 5 stitches, and draw back. **5th row**—With white,—Pick up 1 tricot stitch in each of 5 stitches, 3 in the centre stitch, 1 in each of 6 stitches, and draw back. **6th row**—With grey,—Pick up 1 tricot stitch in each of 6 stitches, 3 in the centre stitch, 1 in each of 7 stitches, and draw back. And continue in this manner, always changing the colour, and always increasing on the centre stitch of every row, till in the **15th row**, which is worked with grey wool, you get 35 stitches on the needle, and sufficient is done for the front of the slipper. **16th row**—Begin the side of the slipper by working with scarlet wool, 14 stitches only, and proceed on 14 stitches till about 20 little rows are done, or until enough is worked to reach to the back of the heel. Work the other 14 side stitches in the same way. Sew the two side pieces together at the back of the heel. A **Trimming** of **Looped Crochet** is worked round the ankle. **1st round**—With grey wool,—Do 1 double crochet stitch and 1 looped stitch alternately; a looped stitch is made by passing the wool three times round the first and second fingers of the left hand, then insert the hook in the tricot and also under the wool that lies over the first finger, draw the wool through and finish as a double crochet stitch. **2nd round**—With scarlet wool,—Work a looped stitch on the double crochet and a double crochet on a looped stitch of last round. **3rd round**—With white wool—Work the same as preceding round. Line the slipper with scarlet flannel, and sew on to the sole. Make the other slipper to correspond. Divide the ribbon, and run a piece through the stitches of double crochet, and tie in a bow in front. Strong useful slippers for a lady or gentleman can be made by working with 3-thread or 4-thread fleecy wool from the above instructions.

Slipper for a Child of Eight or Ten Years.

SHOOTING OR TRAVELLING CAP FOR A LADY.

THIS cap will be found very comfortable to wear in the country or when travelling. In the engraving the tabs are represented as being tied on the top of the cap, out of the way, but they can be let down at pleasure over the ears, and form a complete protection against wind and draughts. A peak in front of the cap rests upon the forehead, and a small plume of looped knitting ornaments the top. Procure a No. 8 bone crochet needle, and 1 oz. of each of two colours in Fleecy wool or double Berlin; grey and dark red are two useful colours and harmonise with almost any dress. Begin with red wool, with 6 chain, and in this pick up 5 stitches, wool over the needle and draw through all the stitches on the needle, do 1 chain to tighten the group, and thus one point neige stitch (or shell stitch) is formed for the centre of the crown of the cap. **1st round**—With red wool,—Do 8 point neige stitches round the centre stitch, and at the end of the round join quite evenly to the beginning, and fasten off. **2nd round**—With grey wool,—Work 16 point neige stitches in the round, and again and always join quite evenly to the beginning, and fasten off securely. **3rd round**—With red wool,—Work 22 point neige stitches in the round. **4th round**—With grey,—Work 28 point neige stitches. **5th round**—With red,—Work 30 point neige stitches. **6th round**—With grey,—Work 30 point neige stitches. **7th round**—With red,—Again work 30 point neige; and now the head of the cap will be sufficiently large. For the **Peak**—**1st row**—With grey wool,—Work 12 point neige stitches over ten point neige of the last round of the cap, and fasten off. **2nd row**—With red wool,—Work 8 point neige stitches on the centre eight of the stitches of last row, and fasten off. For the **Tabs**—Hold the cap the wrong side out, and beginning close by the peak, work with grey wool a row of 4 point neige stitches, and fasten off. **2nd row**—With red wool,—Work a row of 4 stitches over the last small row. **3rd row**—With grey wool,—Again do 4 stitches. **4th row**—With red wool,—Work 3 point neige stitches, which should come over the centre of the four stitches of last row, leaving a little space each side, as the tab is to slant off to a point in the centre. **5th row**—With grey wool,—Work 3 stitches over the three of last row. **6th row**—With red wool,—Work 2 stitches. **7th row**—With grey wool,—Work 1 stitch only. Work the other tab to correspond. Finish off all the margin of the cap, the peak, and the tabs, with a row of double crochet with red wool, on which afterwards a line of single crochet is to be worked with grey to simulate a chain stitch braid. Make a **Plume** of looped knitting with No. 11 knitting needles, casting on 4 stitches, and knitting about 12 rows with alternate colours; sew this on the front of the cap above the peak, as shown in the engraving. From each of the tabs make a short length of chain with parti-coloured wool, which finish off with a small tassel at the end. When the tabs are turned upwards, the right side of the crochet

Shooting or Travelling Cap for a Lady.

is folded on the right side of the cap, as is seen in the illustration, the chain and tassels being tied on the top; but when the tabs are brought over the ears, and tied under the chin, the wrong side of the work appears outside.

WELDON'S PRACTICAL
DRAWN THREAD WORK.

(FIRST SERIES.)

SHOWING NEW STITCHES, DESIGNS FOR BORDERS, CORNERS INSERTIONS, MATS, AND TRAY CLOTHS.

THIRTY-FOUR ILLUSTRATIONS.

The Yearly Subscription to this Magazine, post free to any Part of the World, is 2s. 6d.
Subscriptions are payable in advance, and may commence from any date and for any period.

The Back Numbers are always in print. Nos. 1 to 110 now ready, Price 2d. each, postage ½d. Over 5,000 Engravings.

DRAWN THREAD WORK.

DRAWN THREAD WORK is lately become extremely fashionable for the ornamentation of every description of household linen. It is not by any means a new work, for the very earliest fancy work that ever was invented consisted of drawing certain threads out of linen material and weaving them with a needle round and about the remaining threads to form a pattern, and there is no doubt that the embroidery of fine linen of which we read in Scripture as being used for the vestments of the priests and the hangings of the Temple was worked by drawn threads in various fancy stitches. As time went on, drawn work was introduced into European countries, workers become skilful, fabrics were varied and improved, and much good embroidery was done in Greece, Italy, Russia, Germany, and Spain, under the designation of *Punto tirato* (threads drawn one way of the material), *Punto tagliato* (threads drawn both ways across and across), *Opus tiratum* (fancy open stitches), Dresden point (lace stitches), and other names more especially indicative of the locality in which a particular form of work took a footing. Most of this work was devoted to ecclesiastical purposes. A number of specimens of fine old linen may be seen in the South Kensington Museum, many of which are deftly embroidered with thread drawn from the linen itself, while others are profusely decorated with gold threads and coloured silks, and are so beautifully executed as almost to require a magnifying glass to distinguish the stitches.

Towards the end of the sixteenth century the art of embroidering on linen was taken up in England by the women of the Royal household, and by ladies of high degree, who, being clever in lace-making and delighting in such a dainty accomplishment, introduced lace stitches intermingled with drawn work for the adornment of their apparel and household surroundings; Reticella lace stitches, and

Point lace stitches, such as Point de Bruxelles, Point de Venice, Point D'Esprit, Point Tire, and many others, have thus been gradually incorporated with drawn thread work, and are now used as a filling for cut out spaces, corners, and other purposes, as will appear in the course of the following examples.

Drawn Thread embroidery in its modern form is likely to be very popular, because it is both inexpensive and elegant. The necessary expenditure involves but a certain quantity of linen material, and a few pennyworth of flax thread for working; needles and a sharp pair of scissors are to be found in most ladies' baskets, and the only other requirements are the time necessary for the proper execution of the work, good eyesight, patience, neatness, and exactitude.

Drawn Thread work is principally devoted to such articles of general utility as pocket-handkerchiefs, sheets, pillow-slips, sideboard scarfs, tea and tray cloths, serviettes, dessert d'oyleys, dressing-table covers, towels, night-dress sachets, comb and brush bags, &c., &c.; in fact, anything made of linen, or of any material of which the threads can be readily drawn, can be ornamented with drawn work stitches more or less elaborate according to the skill and patience of the worker. By means of this pretty work, any lady with leisure, combined with the necessary patience and industry, may possess a beautiful array of decorated table linen, and linen for the household, for a merely nominal outlay.

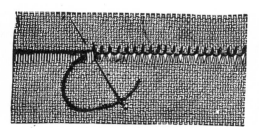

Fig. 1.—Simple Hem-Stitch.

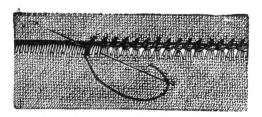

Fig. 2.—Another Way of Working Simple Hem-Stitch.

Many of the most effective specimens of drawn thread work are executed upon fairly coarse linen, and it is not expedient that the very fine work which is so trying to the eyes should be attempted excepting by those who care for it. The new linens which are manufactured purposely for drawn thread work are mostly of rather coarse texture, very evenly woven, and free from dress. The work is very durable, and will wash and clean quite well, time after time, provided the best materials be selected, and care be taken in working to properly secure all edges of the solid linen, and to run in the ends of all the working threads. Most especially must care be taken in the formation of corners, such as the corner illustrated in Fig. 19, and such open spaces in the solid linen as shown in Fig. 22, where the threads which are to be *drawn* have first to be *cut* so as not to interfere with the marginal texture of the linen itself ; for instance, supposing an insertion of the depth of sixteen threads is required to go round a d'oyley, or along the side of a side-board cloth, without extending to the extreme width of the material, you must cut across those sixteen threads perfectly straight with a finely-pointed pair of scissors at the place where you desire the insertion to stop, cut across the same sixteen threads at the opposite end of the insertion, being *very* careful not to cut even one more thread than the required number ; then raise the cut threads one by one with the point of the needle to get a small end to hold, by which to draw the rest of the thread out ; the edges so cut are generally strengthened with buttonhole-stitching. Beginners should practise on a piece of coarse linen, and experiment on patterns in which the threads are drawn all one way of the material, and gradually proceed thence to more elaborate designs. When a piece of work is finished it should be laid between two damp cloths, and ironed with a moderately hot iron.

MATERIALS FOR DRAWN THREAD WORK.

ALMOST any kind of evenly woven linen can be utilised for drawn thread work, but if at all stiff it should be well rubbed between the hands, or if necessary be washed, to render it sufficiently soft to

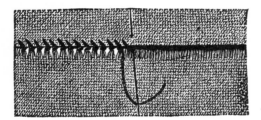

Fig. 3.—A Third Way of Working Simple Hem-Stitch.

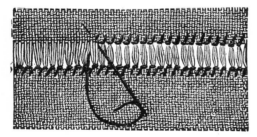

Fig. 4.—Open Hem-Stitch Insertion.

enable the threads to be easily drawn ; a careful ironing between damp cloths after the work is finished will restore its smoothness, take out all creases, and wonderfully improve its appearance.

Various special makes of linen are now manufactured purposely for decorative drawn thread work. Of these "Toile Gros" is very suitable for five o'clock tea cloths, tray cloths, sideboard slips, and many other things. It is woven with strong threads of pure flax, is comparatively easy to work upon, and yet not too coarse for the work to look rich and effective ; it is made in several different widths—viz., 28 inches, 31 inches, and 80 inches, and therefore can be turned to account for almost every purpose of household requirement.

Russian linen is a substantial fabric, with a surface almost as glossy as silk, all the threads both warp and woof are composed of two strands, and in drawing the threads you draw out both strands as one thread, this linen 33 inches wide. Rhodes linen, 14 inches, 22 inches, and 52 inches wide, is of slightly open texture, and therefore is particularly appropriate for light lacy cloths for occasional tables, for buffet-scarfs, piano-scarfs, nightdress sachets, and other articles. Java linen, silesian linen, good single thread flax canvas, tanning cloth, linen gauze, and cambric muslin, are all useful materials for drawn thread work, and selection should be made with due consideration to the purpose to which the work is to be applied.

On no account choose a cheap material with roughness or irregularity in the texture, or the threads will not "draw" properly, and when drawn it will be found that some are thicker than others, and therefore the insertions, although consisting of the same number of drawn threads, will be of uneven width—i.e., those that run warp way of the material will be wider than those that run woof way, or *vice versâ*, which will be fatal to the exactitude of the work, especially if it is desired to form a perfect square.

Drawn thread work is sometimes executed with the threads that are drawn out of the material, or with ravellings therefrom, but lately it is much more usual to employ Harris's flax threads, or Finlayson's threads, both of which can be had in white, cream, and many shades of lovely art colours, and will wash, and clean, and last as long as the material they so successfully beautify. The thread should be selected of size about the same as the threads drawn from the linen on which it is intended to work. Some ladies oppose the introduction of colour into table linen, while others consider that a little colour enhances its appearance. It is entirely a matter of taste, and while it must be admitted that pure white always looks chaste and elegant, the delicate tints in which these flax threads are now manufactured will surely allay all prejudice against their use, the pale blue and pale pink shades are especially commendable. Flourishing thread is much used for drawn work, for which purpose it is very suitable, as it matches well with linen fabric. Crochet cotton, either white or coloured, may be introduced for the coarser parts of the work, for running lines of "crossing" or Punto tirato knots, and for such prominent parts of the patterns as spinning wheels, spiders,

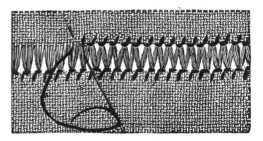

Fig. 5.—Trellis Hem-Stitch.

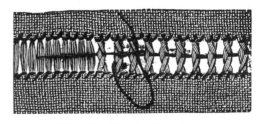

Fig. 6.—Single Crossing.

and stars. Very frequently fast dyed embroidery silks in shades of colours are introduced into a marginal fancy stitching with pleasing effect. Lace thread is used for fine cambric work.

A few crewel needles or short darners must be provided, and also a pair of sharp, finely-pointed embroidery scissors.

STITCHES USED IN DRAWN THREAD WORK.
Fig. 1.—Simple Hem-Stitch.

SIMPLE hem-stitch is the stitch most usually employed for hem-stitching pocket-handkerchiefs, sheets, and other linen articles which need a more ornamental hem than the well-known hem of plain needlework. A hem will, of course, vary in width according to the requirement of the article it is intended to adorn. A pocket-handkerchief hem should be about an inch wide, and to produce this you will require to draw out four threads of the material at a distance of $2\frac{1}{8}$ inches from the margin on all four sides of the material to allow for hem and turning in, and by reason of two of the open lines of drawn threads crossing each other at each end of the fabric, a little square is formed at each corner, as is seen in all bought hem-stitched pocket-handkerchiefs. The turn of the hem must be folded very exactly, to lie perfectly level with the upper edge of the drawn open threads, to which it is sewn in process of hem-stitching. If you are going to hem a sheet a wider hem is generally allowed, sometimes as wide as from three to four inches on best fine linen sheets, but a two-inch hem, or even one inch, will look very well for sheets in ordinary use, and as the hem in this instance will not be carried down the sides, a drawing of five or six threads at a suitable distance from the top and bottom of the sheet will suffice.

The most approved method of working simple hem-stitch is shown in Fig. 1, and a little careful study of the engraving, together with the following explanations, should render it quite easy. In this example the hem is represented as being turned down in position on the upper or right side of the material, and the stitching is executed from right to left along the upper edge of the drawn open threads. Of course it is optional to turn the hem on the wrong side if preferred, but handkerchiefs, sheets, d'oyleys, and such things as are made with fabric both sides alike are generally hemmed in the way here depicted, as the fold looks pretty rather than otherwise. Get your needle threaded with whatever thread you intend working— we will always in these instructions term the working thread "cotton," to avoid confusing it with the threads of the linen material—secure the end of the cotton inside the fold of the hem at the extreme right-hand side of the piece of material, and holding the hem over the first finger of the left hand, bring the needle and cotton out two threads above the fold of the hem, insert the needle

it forms a strengthening ornamental overcast stitch on the margin of the solid linen, it at the same time confines a certain number of open threads into clusters (two, three, four, six, or eight threads in a cluster), according to the requirement of the pattern that is to be worked, as will be explained in succeeding examples.

Fig. 2.—Another Way of Working Simple Hem-Stitch.

THIS hem-stitch very much resembles the hem-stitch of the preceding example, and can be used for the same purposes, but it is worked in a rather different manner, and, on examination of the engraving, it will be seen that the stitches slant obliquely instead of standing perpendicularly upright, besides which the two component parts of each stitch are entwined together. Draw out four threads of linen, and turn down a hem, as instructed in Fig. 1. The hem-stitching is worked from right to left. Secure the end of the cotton inside the fold of the hem at the right-hand side of the piece of material, hold the hem over the first finger of the left hand, and bring up the needle and cotton in the hem two threads above the fold, * hold the cotton under the left-hand thumb, insert the needle in the open insertion two threads to the right from where the cotton is brought out in the hem, and take four open threads on the needle

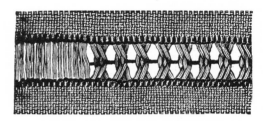

Fig. 7.—Double Crossing.

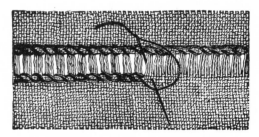

Fig. 8.—Open Buttonhole-Stitch.

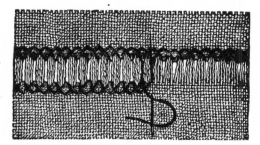

Fig. 9.—Insertion of Cross-Stitch and Spike-Stitch.

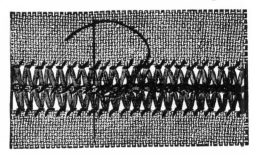

Fig. 10.—Insertion of Hem-Stitch and Cross-Stitch.

between the open threads directly under the place the cotton is brought out, and passing it from right to left take up three open threads on the needle and draw the cotton through, insert the needle in the same place as before, but in a slightly upward direction to pass through the hem in position, as in the engraving, Fig. 1, and bring it out two threads above the fold of the hem straight above the cotton of the stitch just worked and three threads to the left of where the cotton was first brought out, and draw the cotton through, * insert the needle from right to left to take up the next three threads of drawn open linen and draw the cotton through, insert the needle in the same place but turning it in a slightly upward direction through the hem, bring it out straight above the cotton of the stitch just worked, two threads above the fold of the hem, and three threads to the left of where the cotton was before brought out, as represented in the engraving, draw the cotton through, and repeat from * to the end of the line of drawn open threads. You will observe that there are two motions in every stitch; the first motion is taken from right to left in the drawn open threads, and the second motion confines the group of drawn threads in a cluster, secures the hem, and brings the cotton in position for working the next successive stitch. Be careful to make every stitch perfectly true and regular, and draw the cotton close, but not so tight as to pucker the material.

This hem-stitch is very extensively used in drawn thread embroidery to strengthen the upper and lower edge of nearly all open work insertions; it may be made as deep as desired, and while

(as see illustration Fig. 2), and passing the needle above the cotton held by the left-hand thumb, draw the cotton through in a sort of button-stitch loop, insert the needle in the little space you will see at the left of the cluster of threads just drawn together, and bring it out in the hem two threads above the fold and four threads to the left of the last stitch in the hem, and draw the cotton through, and repeat from *. This proceeding clusters four threads together in each stitch, and the stitch in the hem always emerges above the middle of a cluster.

Fig. 3.—A Third Way of Working Simple Hem-Stitch.

As will be seen by reference to the engraving, Fig. 3, this hem-stitch is worked from left to right, and the stitches slant obliquely. It is a very pretty stitch, easy of execution, and may by some workers be preferred to either of the foregoing examples. Prepare the material by drawing out four threads, and turn down a hem as previously instructed. Secure the end of the cotton inside the fold of the hem at the extreme left-hand side of the piece of material; hold the hem over the finger of the left hand, and bring up the needle and cotton in the hem two threads above the fold, * insert the needle from right to left to take up three of the open threads, bringing the needle out exactly under the cotton that proceeds out of the hem, and draw the cotton through; insert the needle in the same space of open threads and bring it up perpendicularly two threads above the fold of the hem, in the position represented in the engraving, which is three threads distant from the last stitch in the hem, and draw the cotton through, and continue from *, taking three threads farther to the right in each consecutive stitch.

Fig. 4.—Open Hem-Stitch Insertion.

THE open hem-stitch insertion represented in Fig. 4 is made by working a line of simple hem-stitch along both the upper and lower edge of an insertion of drawn threads; this method of hem-stitching forms the foundation of numerous elaborate patterns, and serves a twofold purpose, as it not only strengthens each margin of solid linen, but at the same time confines the open threads in even regular clusters. Commence operations by drawing out eight threads. Work from right to left. Secure the end of the cotton with which you intend working on the right-hand side of the linen, near the upper edge of the drawn insertion, either by a knot or by a small invisible stitch on the wrong side of the fabric, bring the needle and cotton out three threads above the open insertion, insert

insertion, which before was at the top, is now at the bottom, and repeat the hem-stitch, taking up the same clusters of threads which you took in the first row, the counting will not now be difficult, as the stitches of the first row will have made a little parting in the open threads between the clusters, to indicate where to place the clusters of the second row.

The art of forming groups and clusters is of very great importance in drawn thread work, and particular attention must always be paid to the working of the *first* row, for upon this, in a measure, the whole beauty of the work depends, and sometimes a very slight inaccuracy will throw out a whole pattern.

Fig. 5.—Trellis Hem-Stitch.

PREPARE the insertion by drawing out eight threads, or more or less, according to the width you desire the insertion to be. Work from right to left. Secure the end of the cotton with which you intend working on the right-hand side of the linen, near the upper edge of the drawn insertion, bring the needle and cotton out three threads above the open insertion, insert the needle between the open threads directly under the place the cotton is brought out, and

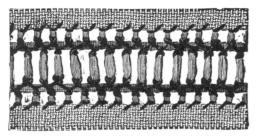

Fig. 11.—Insertion of Double Herringbone.

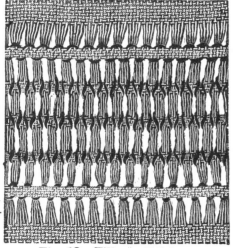

Fig. 12.—Filigree-Stitch.

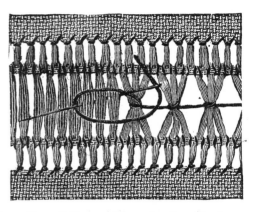

Fig. 13.—Insertion of Drawn Threads, the Clusters confined in Faggots with Punto Tirato Knots.

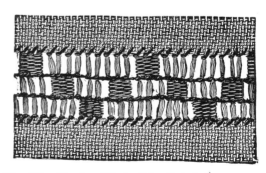

Fig. 14.—Border Worked in Point de Reprise.

the needle between the open threads directly under the place the cotton is brought out, and passing it from right to left, take up three open threads on the needle, and draw the cotton through, insert the needle in the same place, but in a slightly upward direction, and bring it out three threads above the open insertion, straight above the cotton of the stitch just worked, and three threads to the left of where the cotton was first brought out (see position of the needle in Fig. 4), and draw the cotton through. This is practically the same stitch as simple hem-stitch; Fig. 1; but here the stitches are deeper, as they cover three threads of the solid linen instead of only two threads, and thus are better adapted for fancy purposes. Continue working in the same manner to the end of the line of drawn open threads, drawing the cotton close, but not so tight as to pucker the linen, and be very careful to confine the same number of threads in each cluster, or the bars will be irregular, and not perfectly straight. When you reach the end of the line, fasten off the cotton securely by running the end in through some of the worked stitches. Turn the work, so that the edge of the open

passing it from right to left take up four open threads on the needle and draw the cotton through, insert the needle in the same place but in a slightly upward direction, and bring it out three threads above the open insertion straight above the cotton of the stitch just worked and four threads to the left of where the cotton was first brought out, and draw the cotton through. Proceed in the same manner to the end of the row, always grouping four threads in every cluster. When the row is finished turn the work in such a way that the stitched edge of the insertion is now at the bottom and the unworked edge at the top, and work a second row of hem-stitch, sub-dividing the clusters by taking up half the threads of one cluster and half the threads of the next cluster together (see position of the needle in Fig. 5), always taking four threads together, and thereby making the threads slant first one way and then the other, like a trellis.

A variation of this trellis insertion can be made by drawing out a greater number of threads, and grouping six threads, or eight threads (it must always be an even number) in a cluster.

Fig. 6.—Single Crossing.

THIS single crossing is a favourite stitch in drawn thread work as it produces a good effect at the cost of very little labour. Prepare the insertion by drawing out eight, ten, or twelve threads, any even number, and work hem-stitch along the top and bottom edge, grouping the open threads in straight regular clusters of three threads in each cluster, and taking the stitches two threads deep into the margin of the solid linen. When this is satisfactorily accomplished you proceed to "cross" the threads, which is done in this manner—thread your needle with a length of cotton sufficient to run from end to end of the row of drawn open threads (the cotton *can* be joined with a knot if the insertion is too long to take one single thread, but knots in drawn thread work look so bad that it is well to avoid them as much as possible), secure the end of the cotton at the right-hand side of the material with a small invisible stitch at the back of the outer

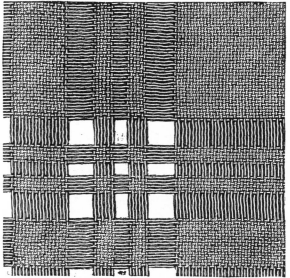

Fig. 15.—Method of Drawing Out Threads both Ways, from Edge to Edge of the Material, to form a Corner.

margin of linen to the right beyond the drawn threads, supposing these threads have been cut to form an outer margin, or if not it must be tied in a knot in the middle of the first cluster of open threads, then having the needle and cotton upon the right side of the work, put the needle from left to right under the second cluster from the cotton, pointing the needle from you, lift it slightly and bring the point of the needle round in such a manner as to take up the first cluster from right to left, and turn the needle to bring the first cluster of threads up clear to the left of the second cluster, this brings the two clusters of threads "crossed" upon the needle, with the needle in the position shown in Fig. 6, draw the cotton through and proceed to cross every two clusters in the same way. The cotton should run easy, exactly midway along the centre of the insertion, and must not be drawn so tightly as to be strained. A very pretty effect can be produced by drawing out threads sufficient to make the insertion an inch or an inch and a half wide, and running a piece of narrow coloured ribbon through the clusters instead of a thread of cotton.

Fig. 7.—Double Crossing.

DOUBLE crossing is more complicated than single crossing, as here four clusters of threads are to be crossed over each other instead of only two. In our example sixteen threads are withdrawn from the linen to make an open insertion exactly half an inch wide, and the hem-stitching is worked very closely and embraces only two threads in a cluster. If you desire to group three or four threads in a cluster, your drawn insertion must necessarily be wider to allow sufficient space for the threads to bend, or "spring," easily over each other in the crossing, or the insertion will not lie as flat as it should. Complete the hem-stitch. Then, having the needle and cotton brought up on the right-hand side of the work, exactly in the centre of the insertion of open threads, proceed for the crossing, thus: Pass the needle from left to right under the third cluster

pointing the needle from you, lift it slightly and pass the point of the needle over the second and first clusters, bringing it round in such a manner as to pick up the first cluster from right to left (not touching the second cluster), bring the first cluster on the point of the needle clear to the left of the third cluster and draw the needle and cotton through, pass the needle from left to right under the fourth cluster, pointing the needle from you, lift it slightly and pass the point of the needle over the second cluster, which you will see peeping out just underneath the cotton, pick this up from right to left on the point of the needle and bring it up clear to the left of the fourth cluster and draw the needle and cotton through, and you will see the double crossing complete, two clusters above the cotton and two clusters below, as shown in the engraving Fig. 7. Another way of performing the operation is as follows: Pass the needle and cotton downwards between the third and fourth clusters, upwards between the second and third, downwards to the right of the first, upwards between the first and second, downwards between the second and third, upwards between the third and fourth, downwards to the left of the fourth, upwards between the second and third, downwards between the first and second, and upwards to the left of the fourth, and the cotton will look like a darning to and fro over the four clusters of threads, draw the cotton up tight, and the clusters will fall into a correct crossing, two clusters above the cotton and two clusters below, as in the engraving. Every group of four clusters is to be manipulated in the same manner. The first method of procedure is recommended as being considerably the quickest and most convenient. The process is rather difficult to describe, but it will not take long to understand if careful attention is given to the instructions, and it is well worth learning, for double

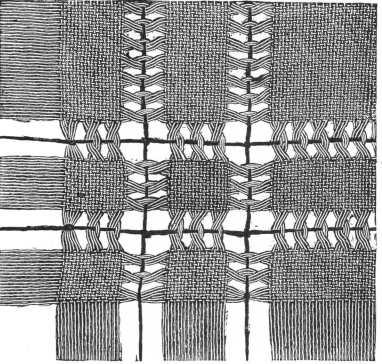

Fig. 16.—The Most Simple Method of Working a Corner.

crossing-stitch is one of the prettiest and most effective stitches in drawn thread work.

Fig. 8.—Open Buttonhole-Stitch.

OPEN buttonhole-stitch is occasionally used to strengthen the edges of drawn thread insertions, and it makes a pretty variation from hem-stitch, for as in hem-stitch the horizontal stitches lie straight along the edge of the open threads and the teeth project as it were into the solid linen, so in open buttonhole-stitch the horizontal stitches lie in a straight line upon the solid linen and the teeth bind a certain number of open threads into clusters. Draw out eight threads. Work from left to right, going first along the lower edge of the insertion. Secure the cotton on the left-hand side of the material close by the lower edge of the insertion, and bring up the needle and cotton in the margin of the solid linen two threads below the edge of the open insertion, * hold the cotton under the left-hand thumb, insert the needle in the open insertion above the place from where the cotton is springing and holding it in a downward direction slanting from left to right, bring the point out two threads below the edge of the open insertion and four threads from the place where the last stitch is already worked, according to the position represented in the engraving, Fig. 8; repeat from * to the end of the row, and fasten off. Turn the work so that the buttonhole-stitched row comes now at the top, and the unworked edge at the bottom, and work again in the same manner, clustering the threads together in regular clusters of always four threads in a cluster, as shown in the illustration.

Fig. 9.—Insertion of Cross-Stitch and Spike-Stitch.

THIS is an effective stitch for ornamenting the edges of an insertion, and it may at any time be used as a substitute for hem-stitch. In our example eight threads are drawn out. The work is executed from left to right along the lower edge of drawn open threads. Secure the cotton on the wrong side of the fabric, and bring up the needle and cotton in the solid linen two threads below the edge of the insertion, insert the needle between the open threads just above the cotton and bring it out with the point towards you two threads below the place it was first brought out, that is, in the solid linen

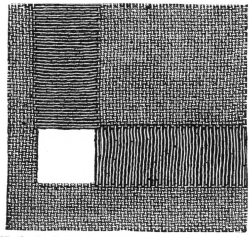

Fig. 17.—Method of Cutting Out Threads to form a Corner and leave a Margin of Solid Linen on the Outside of the Material.

four threads below the edge of the insertion, and draw the cotton through, * insert the needle from right to left to take up four of the drawn threads bringing up the needle in the same space it last was inserted and draw the cotton through, insert the needle, point from you, four threads below the insertion and four threads from the bottom of the first half of the cross-stitch, and bring it up in the open insertion in the same place where the first half of the cross-stitch is worked, as see Fig. 9, and draw the needle and cotton through, insert the needle two threads below the insertion, point towards you, and bring it straight down two threads lower, that is, in the same place where a cross-stitch is already worked, and repeat from *. A tiny straight stitch termed a spike-stitch will be apparent between each cross-stitch. When one side of the work is accomplished, turn the material and work along the opposite side, keeping the threads in straight regular clusters.

Fig. 10.—Insertion of Hem-Stitch and Cross-Stitch.

THIS pretty pattern is rather more elaborate than any of the previous examples, as it is rather wider and consists of two insertions of drawn open threads separated from each other by a narrow strip or bar of solid threads on which cross-stitches are worked, nevertheless it is quite easy to accomplish, and is a useful little insertion for many purposes. To work it, draw out six threads, leave three threads, draw out six threads. Work hem-stitch along the top edge and along the bottom edge of the insertion as shown in the engraving, grouping four threads together in a cluster,

and taking the stitches two threads deep into the margin of the solid linen; the *same* four threads are grouped together in the second row as in the first row of the hem-stitching, and you must count carefully and be sure there is no mistake, or the trellis pattern will not be formed correctly. The cross-stitches which are designed to occupy the whole surface of the three solid threads in the centre of the insertion are worked in the first instance straight along from left to right, and then back from right to left, and in process of working they sub-divide the clusters and thereby produce the trellis pattern. Secure the end of the cotton on the wrong side of the fabric on the left-hand side of the piece of work, and bring up the needle and cotton in between the second and third threads of

Fig. 18.—Tray Cloth, Worked in Six

the first cluster below the three-thread bar, insert the needle in between the second and third threads of the second cluster above the bar and bring it out between the second and third threads of the second cluster below the bar and draw the cotton through, insert the needle in between the second and third threads of the third cluster above the bar and bring it out between the second and third threads of the third cluster below the bar and draw the cotton through, and so on, sub-dividing each cluster in regular order to the end; then work back, inserting the needle in exactly the same position, see how the needle is set in Fig. 10; and you will have a row of crosses on the right side of the linen, and a neat line of small perpendicular stitches on the wrong side.

Fig. 11.—Insertion of Double Herringbone.

THE insertion shown in Figure 11 is suitable for a straight border, or it may be used for the embellishment of d'oyleys and other square articles where the work is not required to be carried to the extreme ends of the material, but may stop short at a certain place to form a corner, where the threads that are to be drawn out are first of all cut away to ensure an inch or more margin of solid linen outside the insertion, after the style of Fig. 19, the corner spaces being afterwards filled up with small wheels or stars, like that represented in Fig. 20, or with other devices according to fancy. To work the insertion of double herringbone, draw out five threads, leave three threads, draw out thirteen, leave three, draw out five.

g, Leaf-Stitch, and Coral-Stitch.

Begin with the herringbone-stitch, working from left to right over the top bar of three linen threads. Attach the end of the cotton securely at the left-hand side in the threads composing the top bar, insert the needle from right to left to take up the six first threads of the wide open insertion and draw the cotton through, insert the needle in the same place again and draw the cotton through, insert the needle from right to left in the top narrow insertion and omitting the three first threads to the left take up the six following threads and draw the cotton through, insert the needle again to take up the same six threads and draw the cotton through ; * insert the needle from right to left to take up the six next threads of the wide insertion and draw the cotton through, insert the needle in the same

position again and draw the cotton through, insert the needle to take up the six next threads of the top narrow insertion and draw the cotton through, insert the needle again in the same position and draw the cotton through, and repeat from * ; this process confines six threads in each cluster, and forms a series of inter-laced herringbone-stitches above the three-thread bar of solid linen, as shown in the illustration, while the only stitches visible on the wrong side of the work are those that confine each cluster of six threads together. When the first row is completed, turn the work, and proceed similarly along the other bar of three solid threads, taking up the same six threads in a cluster along the centre insertion as you took up in the first row that those clusters may stand perpendicularly upright. Complete the insertion by working a row of hem-stitch along the upper and lower edge of the drawn open threads, taking up the same six threads in a stitch as you have already grouped together in the course of herringboning, and making the stitches two threads deep into the margin of the solid linen.

Fig. 12.—Filigree-Stitch.

THIS simple filigree-stitch makes a pretty trimming by itself if arranged in the manner shown in Fig. 12, or it may be incorporated with other stitches in the form in which it is represented in Fig. 13, and again in Fig. 21. When you have done a little piece of the first line you will see that on the *wrong side* it looks just like the second line is represented in the engraving now under notice, and the

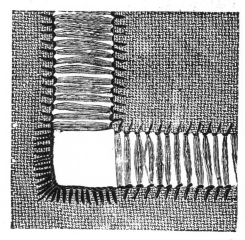

Fig. 19.—Method of Hem-Stitching the Insertion and Overcasting the Corner.

working of the second line looks on the *wrong* side like the first line in the engraving ; thus the pattern is reversible, and looks equally well on one side as on the other, provided the ends of cotton are fastened in neatly. The five rows of filigree work are practically the same stitch, though worked in rather a different manner, according to which side you desire to be uppermost. Draw out seven threads, leave four threads, and repeat the process for the width of the pattern. Work from right to left. For the **first row**—Secure the cotton on the wrong side of the first bar of four solid threads, bring the needle up in the open insertion above the bar of solid threads and draw the cotton through, insert the needle in the open insertion four threads to the left of the cotton and passing it at the back bring it out below the bar of solid threads two threads to the right of where it was inserted, and draw the cotton through, insert the needle four threads to the left of the cotton and passing it at the back bring it out above the bar of solid threads in the same space as the stitch previously worked, and draw the cotton through, insert the needle four threads to the left of the cotton, and passing it at the back, bring it out below the bar of solid threads in the same space as the stitch already worked, and continue doing one stitch above and one stitch below the bar, alternately, to the end of the line. For the **second row**—Wherein the reverse side of the previous row forms the right side of this row—Secure the cotton on the wrong side of the second bar of four solid threads, and bring the needle up in the first little division of the open insertion above the bar of solid threads and draw the cotton through, insert the needle below the bar of solid threads two threads to the right of the cotton, take four threads from right to left on the needle and draw the cotton through, insert the needle above the bar of solid threads in the same place as the previous stitch, take four threads on the needle and draw the cotton through, and continue in this manner inducing the cotton as it crosses the bar, to bend alternately from right to left and from left to right. Work two more rows the same as last row, then do one row similar to the first row, and the insertion, Fig. 12, will be complete. Care should be taken, even in this simple stitch, to avoid drawing one cluster of threads tighter or looser than another cluster, for if this is done the lines will look uneven and the symmetry of the pattern be destroyed, but draw the cotton just sufficiently to confine the threads in groups without distorting the narrow bars of solid linen. A line of open buttonhole-stitch, Fig. 8, worked along the top and bottom edge of the insertion, will be useful to keep the threads of solid linen from getting out of place, and will add to the effectiveness of the border.

Fig. 13.—Insertion of Drawn Threads, the Clusters confined in Faggots with Punto Tirato Knots.

THE Punto tirato knots which are introduced into this insertion are peculiar to drawn thread work, and are used to "knot" or "tie" so many clusters, or so many threads, firmly together in a group.

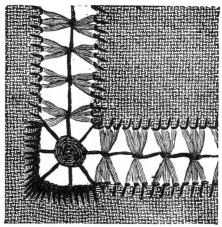

Fig. 20.—Method of Confining the Drawn Threads in Faggot with Punto Tirato Knots and Filling the Corner with a Spider.

The knots are of a similar nature to slip knots, and somewhat resemble the "chain" stitch employed in embroidery. The clusters so knotted together are termed "faggots." The insertion, Fig. 13, is not at all difficult to accomplish, and presents a very handsome appearance when properly worked. Commence by drawing out eight threads, leave three, draw out twenty, leave three, draw out eight. Work a row of simple hem-stitch along the upper and lower margin of the insertion, grouping four threads in every cluster, and taking the stitches two threads deep into the margin of the solid linen. Next, work over the narrow bars of three linen threads, doing the filigree stitch as represented in the centre rows of the previous pattern (Fig. 12), according to the instructions there given; if you consult the engraving, Fig. 13, you will see the same four threads that have been grouped together by the hem-stitching are again grouped together by the filigree-stitch, and therefore the clusters in the narrow insertions stand perfectly straight and regular; the open threads of the wide insertion are grouped into straight clusters also of four threads in a cluster, but these are not perpendicular with the clusters of the narrow insertion, they rather stand intermediately between, as the threads get re-divided by the filigree-stitch. Now for the **Punto tirato**—Get your needle threaded with sufficient cotton to run from end to end of the row of drawn threads, secure the end of the cotton at the right-hand side of the material with a small invisible stitch into the margin of the linen if there is a margin outside the drawn thread insertion; if not, tie the end of cotton in a knot round the centre of the three first clusters of threads to form the first "faggot;" turn the cotton towards the left in front of the three next clusters, retaining it in position by pressure of the left-hand thumb, while with the cotton hanging

downwards, you bring the point of the needle over the cotton held by the thumb, insert it downwards in the upper part of the space between the faggot you have just tied and the faggot that is in process of working, pass it behind the three clusters that are to form this faggot and bring the point up over the cotton that is held by the thumb, it thus presents the appearance of a circular loop, see Fig. 13, draw the needle and cotton through, and draw the loop to the degree of tightness necessary to bind the three clusters in the semblance of a "faggot," at the same time leaving enough cotton to lie evenly across the space between the faggots. Every Punto tirato knot is formed in the same manner. These knots enter largely into the composition of drawn thread patterns; sometimes they are worked with double cotton, sometimes with cotton five or six sizes coarser than that employed in other portions of the embroidery; care and practice are required to keep the cotton in a straight even line, and not too tightly drawn, otherwise the knot itself is sufficiently simple to be very easily acquired.

Fig. 14.—Border Worked in Point de Reprise.

POINT DE REPRISE is one of the stitches appertaining to Guipure d'Art, and which, in common with many other lace stitches, has been introduced into drawn thread work with happy effect. It is a thick stitch, and is worked after the manner of ordinary darning. The same stitch is used in Darned Netting to fill up the meshes and form darned patterns, and it is applied to the same purpose in drawn thread work. All kinds of geometrical designs, vandykes, pyramids, stars, oblongs, &c., &c., may be worked in Point de Reprise; the darning passes in and out through two or more threads or clusters of threads, as may be necessary to produce the pattern that is selected. In our illustration, Fig. 14, the Point de Reprise is carried over three clusters of threads in a vandyked pattern, in which form it makes a useful and pretty border for a tray-cloth or other purpose.

Prepare the border by drawing out sixteen or eighteen threads one way of the material. Work hem-stitching along each edge of the open threads, grouping three threads in a cluster, and taking the stitches two threads deep into the margin of solid linen. Next divide the open insertion into three equal spacings by working a row of

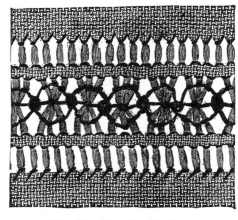

Fig. 21.—Rosette Border.

Punto tirato knots one third distance from the top edge of the insertion, and a second row of Punto tirato knots one-third from the bottom edge, as in the engraving, knotting together the same three threads as are already grouped in the clusters; each cluster must be kept perfectly straight, therefore be careful to draw the knot to just the requisite degree of tightness, but not straining it at all. For the **Point de Reprise**—Begin at the top right-hand corner, securing the end of the cotton in the margin of the fabric; pass the needle over the first cluster, take up the second cluster and draw the cotton through; * point the needle from left to right and pass it under the third cluster, over the second, and under the first, and draw the cotton through; pass the needle over the first cluster and under the second cluster, and draw the cotton through, and repeat from * till the space is full of darned stitches, when pass the needle under the Punto tirato cotton and darn in like manner over the next three clusters in the middle space, and then over three clusters in the lower space; slip the needle up to darn in the middle space again, then darn again in the upper space; and so on, up and down, to the end of the row. Each space must be filled closely and evenly, the cotton should not be drawn tight, for, as shown in the engraving, the clusters of threads must retain their original perpendicular standing.

Point de Reprise is frequently worked over only two clusters of threads, and to do this you simply pass the needle over the first cluster and take up the second, and then pass the needle back over the second cluster and take up the first, and continue the procedure forwards and backwards till the space is full. This method will be illustrated as worked in a wide handsome insertion later on.

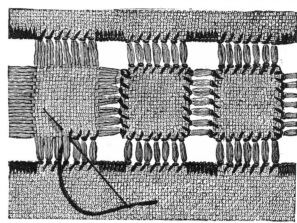

Fig. 22.—Chequered Insertion.

Fig. 15.—Method of Drawing out Threads both ways, from Edge to Edge of the Material, to form a Corner.

TAKE a piece of Toile Gros, Rhodes linen, or whatever other material you intend using, and cut it to the shape of the article you are going to make. The number of threads that are to be drawn will of course depend upon the pattern, but for every pattern it will require that the same number of threads are drawn out each way. Count, say, forty threads from the margin of the material, take the needle and raise the forty-first thread a little way from the margin to loosen it and to get a small end to hold by which to draw the thread completely out, draw out the forty-second thread and six more threads in the same manner, leave the following six threads in their natural state as woven, draw out six threads, leave six threads, draw out eight threads. Do the same along each of the other three sides of the material. Then unravel the outer margin of twenty-three threads to form a fringe round the article, and you will have four drawn corners, as represented in the engraving, together with an open insertion along each side of your material, to embroider with drawn work stitches in any pattern you fancy.

Fig. 16.—The most Simple Method of Working a Corner.

THIS most simple method of working a corner is employed for small occasional table-cloths, antimacassars, and such things as are not subjected to rough usage. It is a light lacy corner, and pretty to look at; but as the edges of the material bordering upon the drawn open insertions are not strengthened by any over-cast stitching, the threads will surely get disarranged after repeated visits to the laundry. If, however, the edges are hem-stitched, the work will wash well and last any length of time. The corner, as illustrated, is intended for the use of those who desire to execute a piece of drawn thread work simply and expeditiously. Having cut a piece of linen material to the size and shape of the article required, count forty threads from the outside margin of the fabric, take the needle and raise the forty-first thread a little distance from the margin to loosen it, and to get a small end to hold by which to draw the thread completely out, draw out the forty-second thread and eight more threads in the same way, leave eighteen threads, draw out ten threads. Do the same along each of the other three sides of the material. Then unravel the outer margin twenty-two threads deep to form fringe. Thus there are eighteen solid threads left between

the fringe and the first open insertion and eighteen solid threads likewise between the two open insertions. Thread a needle with a long length of rather coarse cotton. Tie the end of the cotton in a firm knot round the first six threads of the open insertion, leaving end sufficient to hang to the depth of the fringe, and proceed to "cross" the threads as represented in the engraving, taking three threads over three; the mode of working this single crossing is explained in Fig. 6; carry the crossing on to the end of the row, and finish by tying the cotton in a firm knot round the last six threads, leaving an end to hang to the depth of the fringe. Work the other line of insertion on the same side of the cloth in the same way. Proceed similarly along the other sides of the cloth, but tie a knot as you cross over the cotton of the previous working; this is to keep the two cottons in place as they cross each other in the centre of each open square, and is best managed by keeping the thumb of the left hand upon the cotton till you have drawn the knot exactly into the centre of the square.

Fig. 17.—Method of Cutting out Threads to form a Corner, and leave a Margin of Solid Linen on the Outside of the Material.

ALTHOUGH corners are sometimes formed as instructed in the preceding example, it is very generally required, and is much the best plan, to have a margin or frame of solid linen running round the outside of a cloth, beyond the insertion or border which is worked on all four sides of the cloth. This outer margin or frame may be fringed or hemmed according to taste, either way it adds greatly to the beauty of the article, and also to its durability, as the corners are naturally so much stronger. Fig. 17 shows this method of forming a corner. It is managed in this way: Procure a piece of linen the size desired, say about 24 inches square. We will suppose the

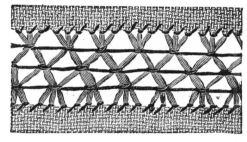

Fig. 23.—Diagonal Threads.

margin on the outside of the cloth is to be two inches deep all round to allow for a hem or fringe, mark this depth at the corners either by running in a thread of coloured cotton or by a line made so L with a black-lead pencil. Begin at one of the corners, count eighteen threads inside from the cotton or line, and cut straight across eighteen threads both ways from the angle, being very careful to count truly, for any mistake will spoil the symmetry of the corner; raise the cut threads one by one with the point of the needle to get a small end to pull by, and draw out all the eighteen threads both ways of the material, cutting them again where they meet the cotton or line at the opposite corners. Repeat the operation, and when complete there will be a square space in each corner, as shown by Fig. 17, and an insertion of drawn open threads will be visible from corner to corner on all four sides of the fabric. If you marked the corners with a piece of cotton, it should now be removed.

Fig. 18.—Tray Cloth, Worked in Single Crossing, Leaf-Stitch, and Coral-Stitch.

A VERY pretty border for a tray cloth, tea-table slip, or sideboard slip, can be worked as shown in Fig. 18. The foundation is an oblong piece of white linen of medium degree of fineness, and the work may be executed with Evans's No. 4 crochet cotton, with rather coarse flourishing thread, or with flax thread, as preferred. Three rows of single crossing are carried round all four sides of the cloth, which also is ornamented with four rows of coral-stitch, besides an embroidery of star-stitches at each corner. The tray cloth represented in the engraving is a small one, measuring 11 inches by 9 inches, but whatever size the cloth is desired to be, the threads must be drawn in the following manner. First, mark out a margin of 1½ inch or 2 inches deep all round the material to allow a frame of solid linen outside the drawn work, part of which will afterwards be unravelled for fringe. Begin at the corner of the material by the mark, cut across sixteen threads from each angle, leave twenty-four threads, cut sixteen, leave twenty-four, cut sixteen. Do the same at end of the other corners, being very careful to cut the same threads. Draw out the cut threads. Work "single crossing" along all the insertions, taking six threads over six; and where the cotton crosses in the open spaces at the corners a Punto tirato knot is tied to retain it in place, see Fig. 18. Work "leaves" on the four squares of solid linen at the corners, thus—pierce a small hole with a stiletto in the centre of each solid square,* bring the needle up in the hole and draw the cotton through steadying the end with your finger or with a knot, put the needle back in the same place and draw the cotton back till a little loop of cotton is produced just long enough to reach to the corner of the square, bring the needle and

Fig. 24.—Point D'Esprit showing the effect of Loops Worked over half the line of Drawn Threads.

cotton from the back upwards through the little loop at the corner, and pass it back at the corner outside the little loop, thus the loop or leaf is held in position, repeat from* for the other three loops, and fasten off neatly at the back of the work. When all the leaf squares are finished proceed to work the coral-stitching as indicated in the illustration; the method of working both coral-stitch and feather-stitch is fully described and illustrated in No. 45 of "Weldon's Practical Needlework Series." Work a row of button-hole-stitch in the margin of solid linen just beyond the outer row of coral-stitch to outline the depth for the fringe and to strengthen the edge thereof; it will be useful to draw a thread or two from the linen as a guide to working the buttonhole-stitch in a perfectly straight line. Withdraw the surplus threads to form fringe, and the article is completed, and only needs a careful ironing to be ready for use.

Fig. 19.—Method of Hem-Stitching the Insertion and Overcasting the Corner.

IN this engraving, Fig. 19, we see the further development of the corner represented in illustration 17. Both edges of the drawn open insertion are strengthened with a row of hem-stitching, grouping three threads in a cluster, and taking the stitches four threads deep into the margin of solid linen. The corner is worked in ordinary buttonhole-stitch overcasting, taking a stitch six threads deep into each alternate thread of the linen.

Fig. 20.—Method of Confining the Drawn Threads in Faggots with Punto Tirato Knots, and Filling the Corner with a Spider.

HERE the corner is represented as finished, the square space is filled with a "Spider," and the clusters of perpendicular threads are confined in "Faggots" with Punto tirato knots. Commence for the knotting by securing the end of the cotton firmly in the fabric by the buttonhole-stitching, exactly opposite the centre of the insertion you are going to work (the way to form faggots by the use of Punto tirato knots has been explained in Fig. 13, and need not be repeated); the line is carried to the buttonhole-stitching on the opposite side.

Repeat along each side of the insertion, and as you cross over the cotton of the previous working tie a knot in the centre of the corner to keep the cotton firm. For the Spider—Commence by darning the end of the cotton through the knot in the centre of the square; take a stitch into the angle of the square and pass the cotton back to the centre, winding it two or three times round the long stitch just formed, take a stitch into the opposite angle of the square and thence back to the centre; do the same at each extremity of the buttonhole-stitching, and you will have a kind of star formed of eight long stitches radiating from the knot that is in the centre of the square; then darn the cotton round and round the knot, over one thread and under one thread, till the spider is as large as you wish, when fasten off neatly on the wrong side.

Fig. 21.—Rosette Border.

FOR this pretty border you will require to draw out eight threads, leave four threads, draw out twenty, leave four, draw out eight. Work simple hem-stitch along the top and bottom of the insertion, grouping four threads together in a cluster, and taking the stitches three threads deep into the margin of the solid linen. Work filigree-stitch on both the bars of four solid threads; description of this stitch will be found in Fig. 12. Now proceed for the centre insertion, which somewhat resembles a series of rosettes. Join on the cotton at the right-hand side of the work, and bind every three clusters together with a Punto tirato knot, the working of which has been already described, see Fig. 13. Next, shape the wheels in this way—Make a Punto tirato knot upon each of the three clusters of the first faggot, about one-third of the distance below the upper bar of filigree-stitch and above the cotton that passes along the middle of the insertion, a Punto tirato knot on the middle cotton in the space between the faggots, a Punto tirato knot upon each of the three clusters of the lower part of the second faggot, a Punto tirato knot on the middle cotton in the space between the faggots, a knot upon each of the three clusters of the upper part of the third faggot, and so on, meandering up and down to the end of the row; the three knots are not made in a perfectly straight line, but rather in a slightly curved direction, resembling the half of a wheel. Another row of knots is to be worked in the same manner, knotting now upon those clusters you before missed, and darning once round the knot that is in the space between the faggots, to form a small spider. The border will now appear complete, as in Fig. 21.

Fig. 25.—Point D'Esprit, showing the effect of the Loops Worked over the entire line of Drawn Threads.

Fig. 22.—Chequered Insertion.

THIS is a bold, effective pattern of chequers or squares; it looks well worked as a border along the sides of a sideboard slip or dressing table cover. Draw out eight threads to form the upper space of open threads, leave twenty-one threads for the chequers, draw out eight threads for the lower space of open threads; then sub-divide the insertion still further to complete the formation of the chequers or squares of solid linen, and to get the line of drawn open threads between each chequer; this is done by cutting away and drawing out certain threads perpendicularly across the insertion, thus—Cut eight threads away along both the top and bottom edge and draw them out; * leave twenty-one threads for a chequer, cut away eight threads along both the top and bottom edge and draw them out, and repeat from * for the length of the insertion; be very careful to cut just exactly the same eight threads at the lower edge of the insertion as you cut at the upper edge, no more nor any less, or the pattern will be spoiled. Having the threads drawn correctly and the needle threaded, commence working at the right-hand side top corner; work eight ordinary buttonhole stitches into the solid linen along the top edge of the small cut away space; work seven hem-stitches sub-dividing the twenty-one drawn open threads into seven clusters of three threads in each cluster, and continue to the end of the row. Then turn the work upside down and proceed along the opposite edge in the same way. When this is done, work completely round each of the square chequers with hem-stitch, taking the drawn threads in clusters of three, which gives seven clusters on each side the square, as is clearly represented in the engraving, Fig. 22.

Fig. 26.—Point Tire.

Fig. 23.—Diagonal Threads.

THIS simple pattern is suitable for a border for serviettes and other articles, and if considered too narrow it may easily be widened by the addition of another drawing of six or eight threads on each side, after the style of Fig. 13 and Fig. 21. To work the border as represented in the engraving, Fig. 23, draw out thirty threads. Work a row of hem-stitch at top and bottom of the open threads, grouping four threads in a cluster, and taking the stitches two threads deep into the margin of solid linen. Begin the diagonal work by securing the cotton at the right-hand side, one fourth below the top line of hem-stitch, and work Punto tirato knots to confine the clusters in groups of three, which gives twelve threads in a group; do not draw the cotton too tight, as there must be sufficient space between the groups for the work to lie nice and flat. When the first row is finished, recommence at the right-hand side by the middle of the insertion, make a Punto tirato knot to confine the first nine threads of the first group, * then a Punto tirato knot to confine the remaining three threads of the first group with the first nine threads of the second group, and continue as from * to the end. Begin again on the right-hand side, and make a Punto tirato knot to confine five threads of the first cluster, then repeat the Punto tirato knots to confine the clusters again in groups of three, combining the remaining four threads from the first knot of the preceding row with the first eight threads from the second knot of the same row. The open threads are now all crossed diagonally, and the border is complete. If you like you can work the three lines of knotting with the *wrong* side of the fabric upwards, and the effect is very good, as then the diagonal threads stand raised above the working cotton instead of the cotton being raised above the diagonal threads.

Fig. 24.—Point D'Esprit: showing the effect of Loops Worked over half the line of Drawn Threads.

POINT D'ESPRIT is a light open stitch peculiar to Guipure d'Art, and it is equally well adapted to drawn thread work, as it suits the character of the work and makes a good " all over " pattern for filling spaces where the threads are drawn both ways from the material, which consequently is transformed into a surface of square open spaces intersected with columns of open threads and small square blocks of solid linen. Very dainty tray cloths, d'oyleys, and

other articles are worked in this stitch, and if very fine linen be employed and the embroidery be done with fine lace thread, the effect is equal to the best lace work. But even if not so fine the pattern is useful for many purposes. In Fig. 24 the stitches of Point D'Esprit are looped round *half* the open threads that separate the square open spaces one from the other, and the loops draw these threads a little aside and a diamond-shaped opening is so formed, as seen in the engraving, Fig. 24. Procure a piece of material, and remove threads both warp and woof way of the fabric, drawing out a certain number, say twelve threads, and leaving intact the same number as you draw out; the drawn out threads must be cut away to make a margin or frame of solid linen all round the outside of the open pattern. You will observe that the fabric now presents the appearance of a variety of squares, an open square space, a solid square, and a square of upright or vertical open threads.

The Point D'Esprit can be worked either in straight lines row by row, or diagonally across and across. Begin by making a knot or a small invisible stitch at the back of the solid linen, bring the needle and cotton up in the centre of one of the square open spaces (preferably a corner space), hold the cotton under the thumb of the left hand, insert the needle downwards in the centre of the bar of twelve open threads turning the point towards you, and bring it out in the open space to form a kind of loose button-stitch loop, and draw the cotton till the threads of the loop lie across each other in the middle of the open space; work a similar button-stitched loop on each of the other three sides of the open space, looping always into six threads which in the present instance is the half of the number of open threads; then pass the needle under the first *thread* of cotton (not the loop-stitch) and draw the cotton through, and so twist the cotton

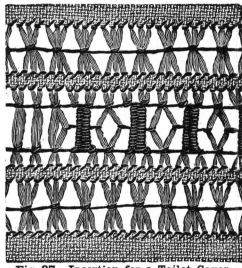

Fig. 27.—Insertion for a Toilet Cover.

round *each* thread which connects the loops of Point D'Esprit; finally join evenly, and return the needle to the wrong side of the fabric, where slip it invisibly along to the next open square space. It will be rather puzzling to a novice to get all four loops of Point D'Esprit shaped exactly alike, and all the same size, but attention and practice will make perfect.

Fig. 25.—Point D'Esprit: showing the effect of Loops Worked over the entire line of Drawn Threads.

THE working of this example is rather simpler than the Point D'Esprit of the preceding example, because here the loops of the stitches are worked over the *entire* line of drawn threads, and therefore, when once the fabric is properly prepared, there is no further counting of threads; also there are no twisted stitches worked round the cotton in the centre of the point. Arrange for the pattern by drawing threads out both ways across the material, six threads to be drawn away, and six threads to be left, alternately, and the drawn away threads must be cut by a marginal line to make a frame of solid linen all round the outside of the pattern. Work stitches of Point D'Esprit to fill each alternate square open space, taking the loops over *all six* of the open threads, as shown in the engraving, Fig. 25; the loops thus made draw the six open threads towards the

Point D'Esprit, and thus each alternate square open space is transformed into a circular space. Many very pretty designs can be arranged by using Point D'Esprit in combination with other fancy stitches.

Fig. 26.—Point Tire.

THIS is a very pretty and exceedingly lacy stitch. As will be apparent from the illustration, more threads are drawn from the fabric than are left in, which makes the open squares larger than the close ones. The open square spaces are traversed diagonally with cotton, and a small knot is tied in the centre of each open space to retain the cotton in position. In the first diagonal line of cotton every small close square is dotted with a small spider or wheel, this is not worked in the next succeeding diagonal line, but occurs again in the next, and in every alternate line. Prepare the material by drawing out ten threads, and leaving four threads, alternately, both

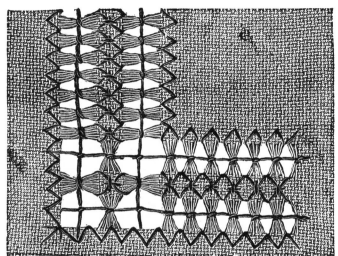

Fig. 28.—Corner and Insertion in Spike-Stitch, Punto Tirato Knots, and Smyrna-Stitch.

ways of the fabric, arranging the drawn threads so as to leave a margin of solid linen as a frame round the outside of the pattern. Then, beginning at a corner, carry a cotton across the open space to the first small close square in a diagonal direction, work a spider or tiny wheel on the square, and go on across the next space to the next small square which work the same, and go on in the same way to the opposite side (or corner) of the foundation. Continue working a line of cotton across every open space in the same direction, but only form spiders in each alternate row. When these lines are worked all over the material in this direction you have to work in the opposite direction, and wherever the second cotton crosses the first a Punto tirato knot is tied in the exact centre of each open square. If you require to make joins in the working cotton all such joins must be effected at the back of one of the small close squares and the ends must be concealed neatly.

Fig. 27.—Insertion for a Toilet Cover.

THE material for working this effective insertion is thus prepared: draw out sixteen threads, leave five threads, draw out twenty-six, leave five, draw out sixteen. Begin by working six rows of hemstitch, that is, doing one row of hem-stitch along each side of each insertion, grouping always three threads in a cluster and taking the stitches two threads deep into the edge of the solid linen. This hem-stitch will cover the whole of the two bars of five solid threads, excepting one single thread in the centre thereof. Next work the top insertion and the bottom insertion with Punto tirato knots, confining three clusters of threads together in faggots (as see

engraving, Fig. 27; instructions for this knotting will be found at Fig. 13). For the centre insertion, which is worked partly in Punto tirato knots and partly in Point de Reprise, proceed in this manner, work first a row of knots a little way below the hem-stitch which borders the insertion, knotting two clusters together all the way along; turn the work and knot along the other side of the insertion to correspond. The pilasters of Point de Reprise, as seen in the engraving, are each darned separately, taking a double cluster of threads for each half of the pilaster, and working from the top, fasten off at the bottom. Pass the needle and cotton over the first double cluster and under the second, then backwards over the second and under the first, and so on, drawing the double clusters together, but not too tightly; when in the middle of the pilaster take up half the cluster of threads (three threads) to the right, pass the cotton once or twice round itself and back to the pilaster again, then take up half the cluster of threads to the left in the same manner: this forms as it were the arms of a cross stretching out on each side the pilaster and draws the half clusters of threads into the shape of an elongated diamond. Fasten off all ends neatly at the back of the work.

Fig. 28.—Corner and Insertion in Spike-Stitch, Punto Tirato Knots, and Smyrna-Stitch.

THIS pretty corner and border shows how several stitches can be combined effectively together to form a pattern. We have spikestitch, Smyrna-stitch (which is a kind of compound cross-stitch), and the ever useful Punto tirato knots. Prepare the material by marking off a certain portion for a margin or frame of solid linen outside the drawn thread work. Then, beginning at the corner, cut across ten threads each way from the angle, leave eight threads, cut across ten threads; the same threads must be cut at each of the other corners, and of course drawn out from one corner to the other, but you had better manage to draw and work nearly the length of two sides first, to ensure getting the pattern in evenly, for all four corners to look just the same as the corner represented in our engraving. Work PUNTO TIRATO KNOTS from margin to margin of the material along the centre of each insertion of drawn open threads, confining six threads together in a cluster, excepting at the corner when going over the eighth thread bar of solid threads where group all the eight threads in one cluster, also knot the cotton where it crosses a previous row of cotton in the middle of an open square. A row of SPIKE-STITCH is prettily arranged as a bordering on each side of the drawn thread insertion; work this from right to left, holding the insertion towards you. Begin on the inside edge by the corner. Secure the end of the cotton by an invisible stitch at the back of the fabric, bring the needle and cotton up in the solid linen three threads each way above the insertion, insert the needle in the open space at the corner and bring it out in an upward direction in the same place where it was brought out to begin with and draw the cotton through,* insert the needle in the small space to the left between the clusters and passing it in an upward direction, bring it out over the centre of the cluster of threads, and five threads above the insertion, and draw the cotton through, insert the needle in the same place as before, and bring it out again in the same place, and repeat from *. Work the same spike-stitch round the outer margin of the insertion. The SMYRNA-STITCH which occupies the bar of eight solid threads in the centre of the insertion may be executed in two different ways; one way is to work two rows of the spike-stitches, just described, in such a manner that the stitches meet together in the form of a cross, and then put a small crossed stitch over the junction of the spike-stitches. Another way, and this, perhaps, is the readiest, is to proceed as in Fig. 10, where ordinary cross-stitch is represented as covering a bar of solid threads, but in the present instance the cross-stitches will be larger, and must afterwards be re-crossed with small stitches, as shown in the accompanying illustration.

WELDON'S PRACTICAL
DRAWN THREAD WORK.

(SECOND SERIES.)

SHOWING NEW STITCHES, DESIGNS FOR BORDERS, HANDKERCHIEFS, CORNERS, INSERTIONS, MATS, AND TRAY CLOTHS.

TWENTY-ONE ILLUSTRATIONS.

Telegraphic Address—
"Consuelo," London.

The Yearly Subscription to this Magazine, post free to any Part of the World, is 2s. 6d.
Subscriptions are payable in advance, and may commence from any date and for any period.

[Telephone—
2745.

The Back Numbers are always in print. Nos. 1 to 106 now ready, Price 2d. each, postage ½d. Over 5,000 Engravings.

DRAWN THREAD WORK.

Fig. 29.—Slanting Hem-Stitch, Double-Rowed.

A HEM-STITCH worked in a slanting direction in two rows, as shown in our illustration, Fig. 29, is a very pretty and suitable embroidery for pocket-handkerchiefs, sheets, and dessert d'oyleys. Three threads are drawn out at such a distance from the margin of the material as you desire for the width of the hem. Turn down the hem as illustrated in Fig 1, No. 52 "Weldon's Practical Needlework Series," and which is devoted to Drawn Thread Work, 1st Series, and proceed with the first row, as follows, before drawing out the threads for the working of the second row. Work from right to left. Secure the end of cotton inside the fold of the hem, and bring up the needle and cotton six threads above the fold of the hem, insert the needle between the open threads three threads to the right of the place the cotton is brought out, and pointing it towards the left take up three open threads on the needle, bringing the needle out in a straight line below the cotton that proceeds out of the fold of the hem, and draw the cotton through, insert the needle in the same place as before but in an upward direction, to pass through the hem and bring it out six threads above the fold of the hem, and three threads to the left of where the cotton was first brought out and draw the cotton through, * insert the needle from right to left to take up the next three threads of drawn open linen and draw the cotton through, insert the needle in the same place in an upward direction and bring it out six threads above the fold of the hem and three threads distant from the preceding stitch and draw the cotton through, and repeat from * When the first row is completed, draw out three threads for the working of the second row, leaving six threads in from the first drawing. Secure the cotton in the line of six solid threads by a small invisible stitch, and bring up the needle

in the first row of drawn open threads in the little space to the left of the first cluster and draw the cotton through, insert the needle in the second row of open threads, three threads to the right of the space where the cotton is brought out, and take up these three threads on the needle, bringing the needle out directly below the cotton that proceeds from the first row of open threads, and draw the cotton through, insert the needle in the second row of open threads in the same place as before and bring it out in the next space in the first row of open threads, and proceed in the same way to the end of the row.

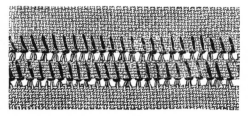

Fig. 29.—Slanting Hem-Stitch, Double-Rowed.

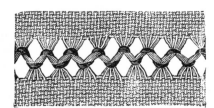

Fig. 30.—Two-Tie Stitch.

Fig. 30.—Two-Tie Stitch.

THIS stitch is very popular for a narrow insertion round pocket-handkerchiefs, d'oyleys, and other articles, and is sometimes used quite by itself, as shown in Fig. 30, and sometimes in combination with other drawn thread insertions. Though apparently simple, great exactness must be observed in working to get the ties in a straight even row Extract eight or more threads to make about the width of $\frac{3}{8}$ of an inch of drawn open insertion. Work from left to right. Bring up the needle to the left of the first drawn thread, then insert the needle from right to left to take up eight of the drawn open threads one-third below the top of the insertion and draw the cotton through, take up the eight threads again in the same place and draw the cotton through; take up the last four threads from right to left one-third above the lower edge of the insertion and draw the cotton through, take up the next four threads to the right with the four threads you last took up, eight threads in all, and draw the cotton through, take up the eight threads again in the same place and draw the cotton through; take up the last four threads from right to left one-third below the top of the insertion and draw the cotton through, take up the next four threads to the right with the four threads you last took up, eight threads in all, and draw the cotton through, take up the eight threads again in the same place and draw the cotton through; and continue thus, working a double tie one-third from the bottom and a double tie one-third from the top of the insertion alternately. Draw the cotton moderately tight, and make all the ties at even distance from the margin of the solid linen, at the same time being careful to keep the cotton as it passes from tie to tie as much to the back of the clustered threads as possible.

Fig. 31.—Binding-Stitch.

BINDING-STITCH is employed as a pretty decorative embroidery over a narrow line or bar of solid linen threads between two rows of drawn open threads, and while it "binds" or holds in place the threads of the bar it is required to ornament, it at the same time groups into clusters the drawn open threads on each side thereof. A simple insertion composed of binding-stitch is represented in Fig. 31,

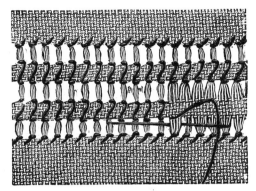

Fig. 31.—Binding-Stitch.

and the stitch may also be advantageously used in combination with other drawn thread stitches. To produce the pattern, Fig. 31, draw out six threads, leave six threads, draw out six, leave six, draw out six. Work a row of hem-stitch at the upper and lower edge of the insertion, as shown in the engraving, grouping four threads in a cluster, and taking the stitches two threads deep into the margin of the solid linen: be especially careful to group the self-same threads into clusters along the lower edge of the insertion as are grouped at the top. The binding-stitch is executed from left to right. Secure the end of the needleful of cotton by making a small stitch on the wrong side of the fabric to the left of the lowest bar of solid linen threads; then bring up the needle and cotton in the lowest row of drawn open threads to the left of the first cluster, insert the needle from right to left to take up the first cluster of threads bringing out the point of the needle in the same space as the cotton was just drawn up and draw the cotton through, hold the cotton under the left-hand thumb, insert the needle from right to left to take up the same four threads in the middle open row and draw the cotton through, insert the needle to the right of the stitch just worked in the middle row and placing it in a downward direction bring it out in the lowest row to the right of the stitch already worked there, * insert the needle from right to left to take up the next four threads of the lowest open row, as shown in the engraving, and draw the cotton through, hold the cotton under the left-hand thumb to keep it from getting twisted, insert the needle from right to left to take up the same four threads in the middle row and draw the cotton through, insert the needle to the right of the stitch just worked in the middle row and bring it out in the lowest row to the right of the stitch that is worked there and draw the cotton through, and repeat from * to the end of the row. Draw the cotton rather tightly each time to confine the stitches closely together in a straight even line but not so tight as to pucker the material. Turn the work, and proceed with the other row of binding-stitch in the same manner.

Fig. 32.—Corner and Border for a Serviette; Spike-Stitch, Hem-Stitch, and Smyrna-Stitch.

THE pattern shown in our engraving is very easy of execution, and yet forms a particularly effective corner and border for a serviette, tray-cloth, or other purpose. The spike-stitch and the hem-stitch are worked simultaneously, and the centre of the insertion is then embellished with Smyrna-stitches. Procure a piece of white linen the size required, and after marking off two inches or three inches to be left as a margin or frame of solid linen outside the work, commence operations by cutting across ten threads each way from the angle of one of the corners, leave eight threads, cut across ten threads; cut the corresponding threads at the next corner to the left, and draw out these threads, and work this side of the serviette before interfering with the threads of the three other sides and before determining the exact situation of the other corners: all four corners have of course to be exactly alike, beginning and ending with an even group of threads, as see illustration, Fig. 32, and if, on completion of the first side, you find you need a few more threads in the last group than the drawing at present permits of, you must make another cut a little farther along, and so provide the additional number required from the portion of material allotted for the outer margin; and similarly on the next side; and when you have two sides worked you will easily see the position for the remaining corner, as the same number of clusters must be got in along the third side as the first, and the fourth as the second. The formation of corners must always be most carefully considered, if they are not correct the beauty of the piece of work is at once spoiled. Now, having the threads drawn out from the first corner along the left-hand side of the serviette, proceed to work the hem-stitch and spike-stitch together, thus—begin at the corner, secure the end of the cotton in the material above the upper insertion of open threads, bring up the needle between the fourth and fifth open threads to the left of the corner space and draw the cotton through, insert the needle in the corner space and bring it up in the solid linen two threads each way above the open insertion, and draw the cotton

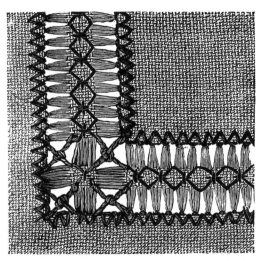

Fig. 32.—Corner and Border for a Serviette; Spike-Stitch, Hem-Stitch, and Smyrna-Stitch.

through, insert the needle again in just the same position, and draw the cotton through, * insert the needle from right to left to take up the four next threads of the open insertion and draw the cotton through, insert the needle in the same place and bring it up in the solid linen over the centre of the cluster of threads and six threads above the insertion and draw the cotton through, insert the needle again in exactly the same position and draw the cotton through, and repeat from * till you reach the corner, where take care to see that an *even* number of clusters are got in along the side of the cloth, and then proceed along the next side in the same manner, and so on till the inner edge is complete all round the cloth. Next, work the lower edge in the same way, and at the corner where the threads are cut do spike-stitch only, as shown in the engraving. The Smyrna-stitches are worked over the bar of eight solid threads in the centre of the insertion and two clusters of drawn threads are embraced in each stitch; begin at a corner, make fast the end of the cotton on the wrong side of the fabric, and bring up the needle and cotton in the small open square to the right of the lower insertion of open threads, insert the needle in the little space between the second and third clusters of the upper insertion and bring it out in a perfectly straight direction in the little space between the second and third clusters of the lower insertion and draw the cotton through, miss two clusters of open threads and insert the needle between the clusters of the upper insertion and bring it out straight below between the clusters of the lower insertion, and continue thus doing half-cross-stitches as far as the corner; then turn, and work back from left to right, inserting the needle in the same places between the clusters, and so forming a row of large cross-stitches; then proceed again from right to left, and work a small cross-stitch over the cross of the previous stitches. A Smyrna-stitch is to be worked on the small solid square in the centre of each corner, and the four open squares are to be filled with " spiders," thus—secure the cotton on the wrong side of the fabric by the corner of the open square and bring the needle and cotton up in the open square,

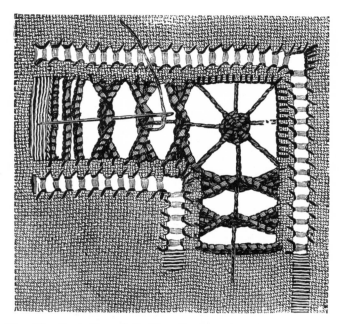

Fig. 33.—Insertion of Bullion-Stitched Bars and a Corner filled with a Spider.

make a stitch in the opposite corner by putting the needle in the margin of solid linen then out in the open space, which makes a long cotton across from corner to corner of the open space, pass the needle and cotton twice under the long stitch so formed, take a similar stitch in the corner to the right and pass the needle and cotton twice under this, then a stitch in the opposite corner and pass the needle and cotton twice under this, then darn once round the crossing of the stitches in the centre of the open square, pass the needle and cotton twice round the cotton with which you began, and so back to the wrong side of the fabric, and fasten off.

Fig. 33.—Insertion of Button-Stitched Bars and a Corner filled with a Spider.

THIS pattern is composed of three rows of open insertions, each worked separately and independently one from the other, with two narrow lines of solid threads intervening and running unbroken round the corner. It is necessary to commence with the most important part of the pattern—i.e., with the wide insertion of button-stitched bars, because here a specified number of threads (twelve) have to be grouped together in each crossed bar, and therefore a sufficiency of threads must be requisitioned to get the groups in evenly from corner to corner, making all four corners alike, as see illustration Fig. 33; and when the wide insertion is correct the two narrow supplementary insertions will fall into their place without much further calculation. Leave space for an outer margin or frame of solid linen (inclusive of ten threads for the narrow insertion to be afterwards worked), and for the wide insertion of button-stitched bars cut across about forty threads, or one inch of material, at the corner, as explained in Fig. 17, No. 52 " Weldon's Practical

Needlework Series," and after drawing out threads to approach nearly but not quite as far as the position for the next corners, strengthen each of the cut spaces with ordinary buttonhole-stitch in the manner represented by Fig. 19, in No. 52 " Weldon's Practical Needlework Series," taking the stitches three threads deep. You will ascertain the actual position for the next corner as you work near enough to it to count the threads requisite to include exactly twelve threads, or three bars, in the last group of crossed button-stitched bars. The **bars** consist each of four open threads clustered together perpendicularly with button-hole stitches, taken as shown in the engraving, Fig. 33, a little distance apart one from the other, working about twelve stitches along each bar, going forwards and backwards, and when you are at the end of a bar insert a stitch sideways into the margin of the solid linen after the manner of a hem-stitch before going on to the next bar. When the corners are all set and the wide insertion worked along the four sides of the cloth, you had better proceed next with the two narrow marginal insertions, and finish off the wide insertion afterwards. Leave six threads of solid linen on each side the wide insertion, and cut across the next four threads at each angle at each of the four corners; draw out the cut threads, and work a simple hem-stitch

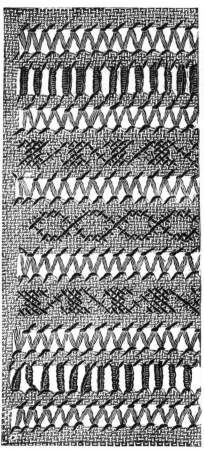

Fig. 34.—Wide Insertion for a Buffet Cloth.

along both edges, clustering four threads in a group, and taking the stitches two threads deep into the solid linen; work a few buttonhole-stitches over the cut threads at each corner. Then, to complete the wide insertion—thread your needle with an extra strong cotton, and secure the end firmly on the right-hand side of the cloth in the buttonhole-stitching opposite the centre of the insertion, and proceed from right to left—three bars are used in each crossing—draw the third bar with the point of the needle over the second and first, bring the first bar quite to the left, and while you hold it a moment with the left-hand thumb, pick up the second bar on the needle between the third and first, with the needle in the position as shown in the engraving, Fig. 33; draw the cotton through, and the " crossing " is complete; repeat the process to the end of the row, carrying the cotton on as far as the outside buttonhole-stitching, and fasten off. Work the other sides in the same manner. For the **Spider**—Commence by tying the end of the cotton across the cotton in the centre of the open square, take a stitch into the angle of the square and pass the cotton back to the centre, turning it two or three times round itself; do the same in each of the other three angles of the square, and you will have a kind of star formed of eight long stitches radiating from the knot that is in the centre of the square; now darn the cotton round and round the knot, passing the needle under each of the four corner stitches and over and under again, which makes a kind of raised rib, and simply passing the cotton over the four other stitches without twisting it at all round them, and when the spider is the size you wish, fasten the cotton off neatly on the wrong side.

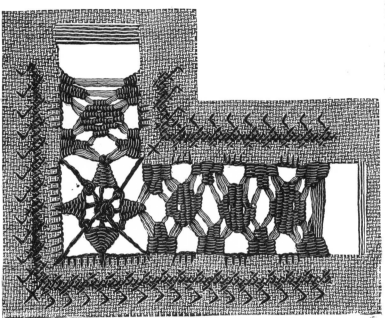

Fig. 35.—Lozenge Pattern Border and Corner.

Fig. 34.—Wide Insertion for a Buffet Cloth.

A BUFFET cloth is usually a straight piece of linen from 2 yards to 2½ yards in length and from 14 inches to 20 inches wide, with deep fringed ends, and only a narrow fringe along the front and back of the cloth. Sometimes the drawn work is executed along each side lengthways of the material, at other times it is arranged across the ends which in this case should hang over at the side sufficiently to show the work. In the illustration, Fig. 34, is given an easy yet very important-looking pattern of drawn-thread insertion combined with cross-stitch, designed expressly for the decoration of a buffet cloth or a sideboard slip; it is exceedingly pretty worked with Harris' blue flax-thread, shade 31, but ordinary flourishing thread can be employed if preferred. Begin at a suitable distance from the margin of the fabric, and draw out eight threads, leave five, draw out eight, leave five, draw out eight, leave eighteen, draw out eight, leave eighteen, draw out eight, leave eighteen, draw out eight, leave five, draw out eight, leave five, draw out eight; this makes eight spaces of drawn out threads for open work, alternated with seven lines of solid linen threads; on the three middle lines of eighteen threads each, a cross-stitch pattern is embroidered, and these may be worked *first* if care be taken to mark out the exact position each line should occupy; the cross-stitches are clearly visible to be copied from the engraving. It is advisable not to extract at once the whole of the threads enumerated above, but to work each open insertion in its turn row by row. For the **First Insertion**—Having drawn out eight threads, work a Trellis hem-stitch, proceeding from right to left, thus—bring the needle and cotton out in the solid linen two threads above the open insertion, * insert the needle between the open threads directly under the place

the cotton is brought out, and passing it from right to left take up four open threads on the needle and draw the cotton through, insert the needle in the same place but in a slightly upward direction, and bring it out two threads above the open insertion straight above the cotton of the stitch just worked and four threads to the left of where the cotton was first brought out and draw the cotton through, and repeat from * to the end of the row; when the row is finished turn the work and do a row of hem-stitch similarly along the side of the drawn open threads but now sub-dividing the clusters by taking up half the threads of one cluster and half the threads of the next cluster together, as see engraving, always taking four threads together, and thereby inducing the threads to slant first one way and then the other, like a trellis. For the **Second Insertion**—This also is worked upon eight drawn open threads, and consists of a series of little upright bars overcast with button-hole-stitch, clustering four threads in each bar, and when at the top and when at the bottom of the bar taking a stitch two threads deep into the margin of the solid linen to simulate the working of a hem-stitch. The third, fourth, fifth, sixth, and eighth insertions are worked in trellis hem-stitch, the same as the first insertion, and the seventh is formed of buttonhole-stitch bars corresponding with those already worked in the second insertion.

Fig. 35.—Lozenge Pattern Border and Corner.

LEAVE space to form an outer margin or frame of solid linen, and commence operations by cutting across thirty threads each way from the angle of the corner, as explained by Fig. 17, in No. 52 "Weldon's Practical Needlework Series;" cut and draw out the same threads somewhere about as far as the position for the next corner, but the actual situation cannot be known until the threads are sub-divided into groups of twelve threads for the lozenge pattern, which must come in at the end of the row the same as at the beginning; count twelve threads from the open space at the first

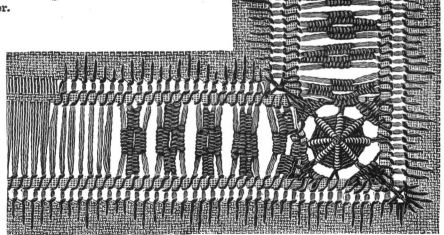

Fig. 36.—Corner and Border Worked in Turrets of Point de Reprise.

corner, and leaving these intact, cut away and draw out six threads perpendicularly across the insertion, leave twelve, cut six, leave twelve, and so on to the end; the twelve threads that are left are the ones used for working the lozenges. Work in **Point de Reprise** upon each group of twelve threads, beginning by the edge of the insertion, take the needle from right to left over four threads, under four, and over four, and then back from left to right under four, over four, and under four, five times; then bring to a point by darning over the four centre threads in two divisions, over two threads and under two, forwards and backwards five times; slip the cotton thence at the back of the work to the edge of the insertion, do four buttonhole-stitches to strengthen the cut space, and continue in the same manner till you come to the end of the row and reach the situation for the next corner. Work similarly along the opposite edge of the insertion. For the **Lozenges** in the **Centre** of the **Insertion**—Darn over two threads from each of the patterns drawing them together in the centre of the space between the patterns and making four darned stitches, then sub-divide to right and left, and darn two of the threads already darned with the two threads next adjoining, sub-divide again and darn the last two threads with the next two threads adjoining, always making four darned stitches, this widens the lozenge to the extent of twelve threads, and you now decrease to a point to correspond, and fasten off neatly at the back of the work; all the lozenges are formed in the same manner. For the **Corner**—The edge must be strengthened with buttonhole-stitch, and the corner is then filled with a diamond shaped star which is commenced by making eight foundation threads across the vacant space, also a foundation thread is run from corner to corner of the star to give three threads to darn upon at each point, in the manner shown in the illlustration, Fig. 35; a small spider is formed in the centre of the star, and a tiny spot is

some little distance and draw them out, so forming the narrow outside insertion; then, leaving four solid threads for the ornamental bar, cut across twenty-eight threads each way for the centre insertion, and when these are drawn out, again leave four solid threads, and cut across four more threads and draw out. The work must be begun at the corner, and the pattern should be got in evenly along the sides of the cloth, making all four corners alike. The inner margin and the outside margin are worked in simple hemstitch, grouping three threads in a cluster, and carrying the stitches over four, seven, nine, and eleven threads respectively on the surface of the linen, to represent a jagged saw-tooth edge. When this is done decorate the bars of four solid threads with binding-stitch, embracing together the same three threads as are grouped in the hem stitching, and fill in the same squares at the corner with a stitch of Point D'Esprit. The turrets of Point de Reprise are next to be worked, beginning at the corner, the mode of working is described by Fig. 27, in No. 52 "Weldon's Practical Needlework Series," darn over the second and third clusters with stitches to and

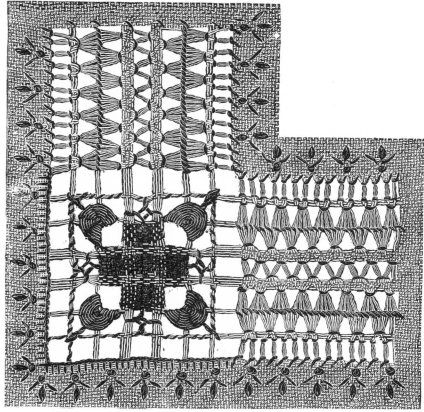

Fig. 37.—Corner and Border for a Five-o'clock Tea-Cloth.

placed where the foundation threads cross each other midway between the points. A border of cross-stitch and Holbein-stitch is worked on each side of the drawn thread insertion, and may easily be copied from the engraving, or any other small pattern may be substituted.

———

Fig. 36.—Corner and Border worked in Turrets of Point de Reprise.

THIS design consists of a wide insertion worked in turrets of Point de Reprise, or darning stitch, flanked on each side with a narrow ornamental bar of four solid threads and a simple narrow open insertion, and the whole, as represented in the engraving, Fig. 36, forms a handsome border for a tea-cloth, toilet-cover, or other purpose. Commence operations at the corner by first cutting across four threads each way of the fabric, cut the same threads again at

fro for one-third the width of the open insertion, darn the first and second clusters for one-third the width, then cross and darn the third and fourth clusters together to correspond, and then finish the turret by darning together the second and third clusters for the remaining one-third space of the insertion, and fasten off neatly. Every group of four clusters is to be treated in the same way. The square open space at the corner is filled with a good sized wheel, for which you make four long foundation stitches across and across, and then proceed to darn, and beginning in the centre of the wheel, pass the needle under two spokes,* then pass it again under the spoke you last went under and also under the next, and repeat from * round and round till the wheel is sufficiently large; the action of passing the cotton in this manner like a cord round every spoke causes the spokes to look high and raised above the surface of the wheel. Do two foundation stitches crossways at each corner of the open space, and fill in by darning from the insertion of binding stitch over the foundation threads and back again till the little corner is well filled.

Fig. 37.—Corner and Border for a Five-o'clock Tea-Cloth.

THIS handsome border consists of seven narrow insertions of drawn threads and, as will be apparent by reference to the engraving, Fig. 37, the work is executed upon the bars of solid linen that intervene between the insertions, and not as in the ordinary way upon the drawn open threads themselves. Almost all the stitches of which the pattern is composed have been already described, and the only difficult part is the corner, which is larger and more elaborate than any we have yet given. The material for

should be pulled out of place. Strengthen the cut edges of the corner with buttonhole-stitching; and work hem-stitch along each edge of the solid linen, grouping four threads in a cluster, and taking the stitches three threads deep into the fabric; an *even* number of clusters must be got in the row from corner to corner. The first, third, fourth, and sixth bars of solid linen are worked in filigree-stitch, see Fig. 12, No. 52 of "Weldon's Practical Needlework Series," grouping the clusters as shown in the engraving, eight threads in a cluster, trellis fashion, excepting along the insertion, where the hem-stitch is already worked, where keep to four threads in a cluster. Work a simple overcast-stitch along the second bar and

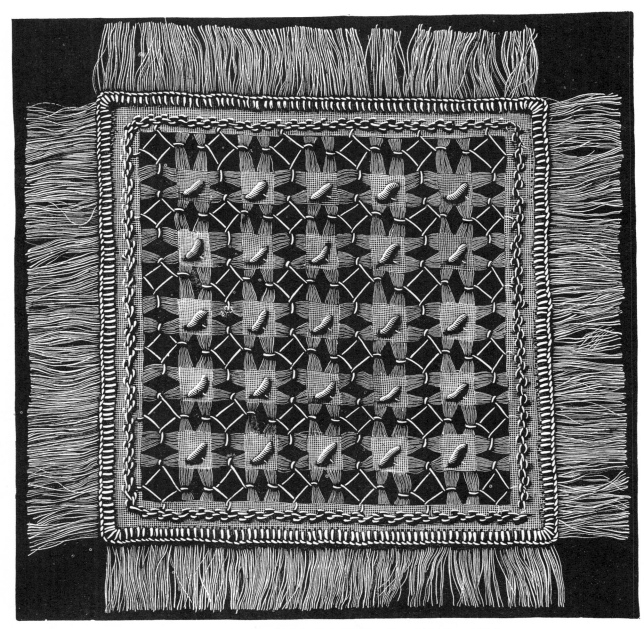

Fig. 38.—D'Oyley Worked in Point D'Esprit and Bullion-Stitch.

the tea-cloth may be Russian linen or Toile Gros, and about two dozen skeins of flax threads, white or coloured, should be procured. Calculate how much space to allow for a margin of solid linen round the outside of the tea-cloth beyond the drawn open threads, and then begin at the angle of the corner, and cut across eight threads, leave two, cut eight, leave two, cut eight, leave four, cut six, leave four, cut eight, leave two, cut eight, leave two, cut eight; cut the same threads again at each of the opposite corners, and draw them out. In practical working it will be safest to draw the threads out row by row as wanted, rather than to extract all at once, in case any

the fifth bar, inserting the needle under the bar between every two open threads. For the **Corner**—Begin by overcasting the outside bars of two solid threads which delineate the boundary of the corner. Then work the "cross" in simple darning-stitch, passing the needle over one thread and under one thread alternately forwards and backwards from right to left and from left to right, as shown in the illustration, and make a stitch of Point D'Esprit across the small open squares adjoining each arm of the cross. Put a foundation thread from angle to angle of each small corner square, and darn a kind of semicircle in the position indicated in the engraving. When the four corners are satisfactorily accomplished, decorate the inner and outer margin of the insertion with an embroidery of French knots, satin-stitch, and crewel-stitch. The tea-cloth may be finished off with a fringe of knotted threads or with a deep border of Torchon lace.

Fig. 38.—D'Oyley Worked in Point D'Esprit and Bullion Stitches.

THE d'oyley, represented in our engraving Fig. 38, is composed

threads, * leave twenty, cut across twenty, and repeat from * till you have made six cut spaces along two sides of the d'oyley counting from the corner, cut across the same identical threads on the other two sides of the d'oyley, and draw them out, and your linen will present the appearance of alternate open squares, solid squares, and squares of upright or vertical threads, ready for embellishing with fancy stitches. Stitches of Point D'Esprit are used upon all the open spaces, working as shown in the illustration four buttonhole loops, each loop embracing ten threads on each side of each open square, and care must be taken to draw the loops to a nice shape, and make them all the same size; for instruction in working Point

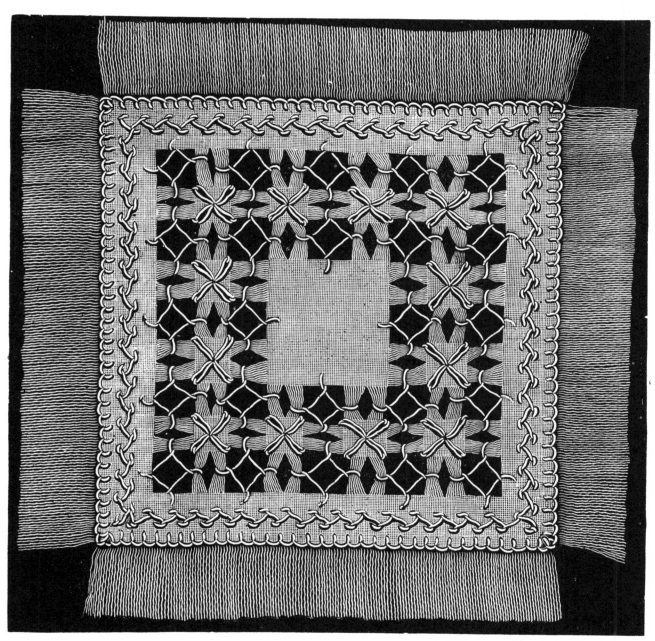

Fig. 39.—D'Oyley Worked in Point D'Esprit and Leaf-Stitch.

of a piece of fine white linen about 7 inches square, effectively worked in drawn thread and fancy stitches with Evans's No. 4 white crochet cotton. First, define a margin 1½ inches deep all round the material to allow for fringe and a frame of solid linen outside the drawn work. An equal number of threads are to be drawn and left; the number will in some degree depend upon the quality of the linen, and the size you have determined for the d'oyley; we will suppose the pattern to consist, as in the original, of a multiple of twenty threads. Begin at the corner, and cut across twenty

D'Esprit turn to Figs. 24 and 25, No. 52 "Weldon's Practical Needlework Series," where all the preliminary details of drawn thread work are fully explained. The bullion-stitches which ornament the surface of the small solid squares can be made simultaneously with the stitches of Point D'Esprit, passing the cotton at the back of the work from one to the other, or they may be worked separately after the Point D'Esprit is finished In either case the procedure is as follows—bring up the needle at one corner of the solid square about four or five threads each way from the margin and draw the cotton through, insert the needle in the opposite corner of the square and bring the point well out in the same place the cotton is, and with the needle standing in this position wind the cotton round the point of the needle ten or twelve times, keeping the twist from falling off by pressure of the left-hand thumb, draw the needle firmly through without disarranging the roll of stitches, pull the cotton gently towards the top of the stitch till the stitch lies in position with the twisted cotton in a close roll upon it, and then insert the needle to the back of the work and pass it along to the place where you intend taking the next stitch. When the centre portion of the d'oyley is accomplished, extract one thread of linen to define the depth to which the fringe may extend, and work a row of simple buttonhole-stitch with a heading straight upon the one drawn thread and the prongs four or five threads deep into the fabric. Do a row of feather-stitch in the space of solid linen between the open-drawn thread work and buttonhole-stitching, and then complete the d'oyley by unravelling the outside threads. Very handsome bed-spreads can be made by alternating squares of open drawn thread work with squares of plain linen decorated with a raised design in Mountmellick embroidery.

cut across the self-same threads on the other two sides of the d'oyley, and draw away the two outside lines of cut threads on all four sides of the d'oyley, and when you have extracted these you will see how far the remaining cut threads must be drawn to permit of the square of solid linen remaining intact in the centre. The open spaces of the insertion are filled with loops of Point D'Esprit worked as explained in the preceding example, Fig. 38. The leaf-stitches which cover the surface of the small solid squares can either be worked simultaneously with the Point D'Esprit, passing the cotton at the back of the work from one to the other, or be put in after the Point D'Esprit is finished; proceed thus—pierce a small hole with a stiletto in the centre of one of the solid squares, * bring the needle and cotton up in the hole, put the needle back in the same place and draw the cotton back till a little loop of cotton is produced just long enough to reach easily to the corner of the square, bring the needle and cotton from the back upwards through this little loop at the corner and pass it back at the corner outside the little loop, thus the loop or "leaf" is held in position—repeat from * for the three other loops, and when the whole of the leaf is finished pass the cotton along the back of the work to the

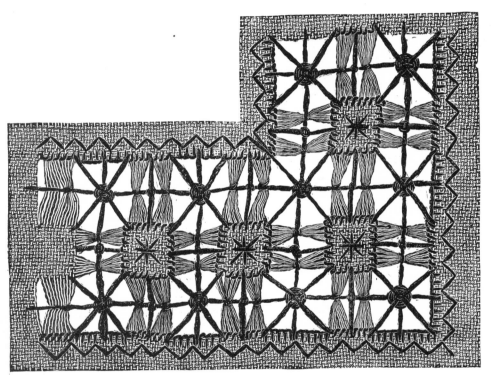

Fig. 40.—Corner and Border in Point Tire and Chequers.

The one style of work sets off the other, and the spread could be lined with pale blue silk or sateen, which would show most effectively through the open spaces of the drawn threads; either of the d'oyleys illustrated in the present issue of our Work Series may with a little arrangement be converted to this purpose with happy effect.

place where you intend working the next stitch. When the insertion is complete, edge the d'oyley with a round of feather-stitching; and beyond that work a round of ordinary buttonhole-stitch to define the margin of solid linen, outside which the threads are to be unravelled for fringe.

Fig. 39.—D'Oyley Worked in Point D'Esprit and Leaf-Stitch.

A VERY pretty d'oyley can be made by working Point D'Esprit and leaf-stitch after the manner of an all-round insertion, leaving a small portion of plain linen in the centre of the square, as shown in Fig. 39. Procure a piece of fine white linen about 7 inches square, and a reel of Evans's white crochet cotton, No. 4. Calculate sufficient space to form an outside margin or frame of solid linen, part of which will be used to unravel for fringe, and commencing at one of the corners, cut across about twenty threads, * leave twenty threads, cut across twenty, and repeat from * till you have made five cut spaces along two sides of the d'oyley, counting from the corner,

Fig 40.—Corner and Border in Point Tire and Chequers.

THE corner and border as illustrated in Fig. 40 is formed by a happy combination of some of the most simple stitches used in drawn thread work, and while in its complete form it is particularly handsome for any purpose for which a drawn thread border is desired, it presents no great difficulty of execution, and may be attempted by any one who has mastered the various stitches of which it is composed; these include hem-stitch, buttonhole-stitch, Punto Tirato knots, spiders, and Point Tire, all of which have been already fully explained and illustrated, see Figs. 1, 13, 20, 22, and 26, in No. 52 of "Weldon's Practical Needlework Series," where will be found every preliminary detail concerning this useful and fashionable work.

Prepare the material by marking off a certain portion for a margin or frame of solid linen outside the drawn thread work. Then, beginning at a corner, cut across sixteen threads each way from the angle, * leave sixteen threads, cut across sixteen threads, and repeat from * till you get to the end of the space that is allotted along the two sides of the material right and left from the corner, cut the self-same threads along the other two sides, and extract the threads of the two outside lines from corner to corner both warp and woof way of the fabric, when you will be able to see how far the remaining threads will need to be drawn out to complete the open pattern along the sides of the material while leaving the centre portion solid and intact. Commence by strengthening the edge of the solid linen along each side of the drawn open threads, doing hem-stitch combined with buttonhole-stitch, the hem-stitch to confine the threads in

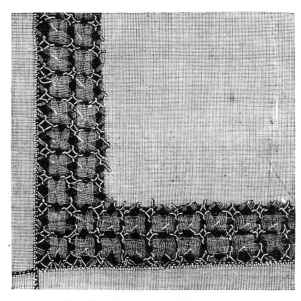

Fig. 41.—Corner of a Handkerchief.

clusters of two threads in a cluster taking the stitches two threads deep into the fabric, and the buttonhole-stitch three threads deep to bind the sides of the cut spaces, as see engraving, Fig. 40. When this is done, work completely round each of the square chequers with hem-stitch in clusters of two threads. The next step is to produce the long straight stitches that cross and re-cross all the open spaces, and to do this you must first proceed along the centre of each of the two outside lines of open spaces straight from corner to corner, making Punto Tirato knots to confine the open threads in faggots of four clusters (eight threads) in a faggot. Work in the same manner, but in short lines, perpendicularly across the insertion, from the buttonhole-stitch on one side to the buttonhole-stitch on the opposite side, and form two faggots of the linen threads that run from chequer to chequer. After this is accomplished, more straight lines have to be run longitudinally between every pair of faggots, in process of which make a knot wherever the cotton crosses a line that has been worked previously, steady the cotton in the hem-stitching that surrounds the chequers, and take one long straight stitch over eight threads in the centre of each square chequer, which straight stitch is the commencement of the leviathan cross-stitch that adorns the surface of each chequer. You must now complete the insertion by running lines vertically across the open spaces from angle to angle, at the same time darning a "spider" in the exact centre of each open space, and finishing the leviathan cross-stitch on each chequer. Ornament the linen on each side of the drawn-thread insertion with a row of wave-stitch as shown in the illustration, or with any other fancy stitching, or cross-stitch border, according to taste.

Fig. 41.—Corner of a Handkerchief.

A POCKET-HANDKERCHIEF may be daintily embroidered, as shown in our engraving, at the expenditure of not too much time and trouble. The work is of course very fine, and requires patience and good

eyesight, but the pleasure of possessing a pretty handkerchief of one's own working will amply repay the labour spent upon it. Procure a square of the best cambric muslin the size you desire the handkerchief to be, and a reel of fine lace thread. Determine the depth for hem, and draw out two or three threads from side to side of the material to denote the distance to which the turning may extend, then fold the hem, and work the hem-stitching according to the instructions, pages 4 and 5, in No. 52 of "Weldon's Practical Needlework Series," where the entire proceeding is fully explained. The whole of the hem-stitching had better be finished before going on to the pattern of Point D'Esprit; for this you will require to extract more threads; begin at one of the corners, cut across six threads from the angle thereof, that is, six threads altogether including the ones already drawn for the hem-stitch, * leave twelve threads, cut across six, and repeat from * to the opposite corner, and do the same along the other sides of the handkerchief. When you have drawn out the threads that are detached by the three first cuttings on each side of each corner you will be able to see how far the open work should extend upon the inside of the handkerchief and will draw more threads accordingly. It will be best, however, not to draw too many threads at one time, but extract by degrees a little distance, work so far, and then extract more. The stitch of Point D'Esprit is the same stitch that is used and explained in the d'oyley, Fig. 39 of the present issue, six threads are grouped together in each loop and the pattern will appear as shown in the engraving, Fig. 41.

Fig. 42.—Corner and Border in Cord-Stitch.

CORD-STITCH consists simply of sewing over and over a certain number of drawn open threads, and it is almost identical with the stitch known in fancy needlework as "overcasting." Many pretty

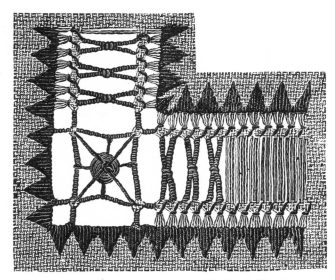

Fig. 42.—Corner and Border in Cord-Stitch.

results can be produced by a judicious use of cord-stitch. The corner and border given in Fig. 42 are suitable for a tray-cloth, table-slip, or toilet-cover. Cut the materials to the size and shape required, and then calculate how much margin to allow round the outside of the cloth beyond the drawn open threads. Begin at a corner, and cut across four threads each way from the angle, leave four threads, cut twenty, leave four, cut four; do the same at the opposite corner, and extract the cut threads. Work a series of indented satin-stitches along each outside margin by the drawn threads, taking one stitch to each thread of the linen, and making the first stitch two threads deep, the next stitch four threads deep, the next six threads deep, the next eight threads, and the next ten threads deep into the solid fabric, and then gradually shorten. Work hem-stitch upon the narrow bar of four solid threads along each *side* of the fabric (not at the corner), grouping four threads together in a cluster, and taking the stitches quite over the bar, as shown in the engraving. At the corner the bars are bound tightly over with cord-stitch in the shape of an Oxford frame, filled in the centre with long foundation stitches, and a wheel in darning-stitch. The **wide insertion** is worked in cord-stitch, thus—secure the end of the cotton firmly in the bar of four solid threads, and sew over and over the first cluster of four threads closely and evenly to nearly the centre of the insertion, where sew over the next cluster together with the first for four or five stitches, then resume on the first cluster sewing it to the bottom of the insertion, slip stitch at the back of the bar to the second cluster and finish this off to correspond with the first: every set of two clusters are "corded" over in this manner, each separately at the top and bottom, and together in the centre, as represented in the engraving.

Fig. 43.—Corner of a Pocket-handkerchief.

THIS pocket-handkerchief is made of fancy cambric, in which certain threads, rather thicker than the ordinary threads of the cambric, are woven at intervals, thereby producing a series of squares; nine of these squares reach along each side of the handkerchief from

surface, such as an antimacassar or bed-spread, with an "all-over" design, introducing various fancy devices in Mountmellick and Crewel-work stitches. A lovely antimacassar or a large ornamental table-cover may be made with Rhodes' linen 22 inches wide to 52 inches wide, with Tammy cloth, or with good fine single thread canvas; while for a bed-spread, if Rhodes' linen is considered too delicate in texture, a wide width of Toile Gros can be called into requisition, and possesses the necessary qualities of firmness and durability. It will be seen that the example Fig. 44 is composed of sixteen squares intersected both warp and woof way of the fabric by lines of drawn open threads; the size of the squares should, of course, vary with the purpose for which the piece of work is intended—that is to say, a considerably larger sized square may be allowed for a bed-spread than would look well for an antimacassar or a table-cover, and the number of clusters into which the open threads are confined, and the boldness of the devices should, of course, vary accordingly. In the example, each square consists of forty-eight threads, and sixteen threads are extracted lengthways and

Fig. 43.—Corner of a Pocket-handkerchief.

corner to corner, and four squares at each corner of the handkerchief are embroidered with drawn thread work, in the manner of the corner shown in the illustration, Fig. 43. A hem, about half an inch deep, is allowed as a margin. Mark the boundary for the hem by drawing out three threads; turn the hem down, and hem-stitch it, as instructed in Fig. 1, No. 52 "Weldon's Practical Needlework Series." The open worked squares are executed in Point D'Esprit, six threads being extracted and twelve threads left, but the number of threads will be likely to vary according to the quality of the cambric, the very finest should be selected, and the threads should be calculated so as to get the pattern as represented in the engraving in each square; the stitch needs no further description as it has already been fully explained in Fig. 24, page 12, of No. 52 of "Weldon's Practical Needlework Series," and by Figs. 38 and 41 in this issue.

Fig. 44.—An Example of Drawn Thread Work in Combination with various Fancy Devices.

OUR present example is intended to show how drawn-thread embroidery can be brought into use for the decoration of a large

widthways intermediately between the squares. A margin of plain solid linen is left outside the piece of work, and part of this is afterwards unravelled to form a nice deep fringe. Work buttonhole-stitches as shown in the engraving to strengthen the cut edges of the drawn open threads. Then *sew* round every margin of the solid linen with simple "over-cast" stitching, grouping eight threads together in clusters, and making six clusters along each side of every square; this may be done in hem-stitch, as Figs. 1, 2, and 3, or after the manner of Figs. 8 and 9, in No. 52 of "Weldon's Practical Needlework Series," if the article is likely to be subjected to much wear; but for a fancy antimacassar or anything of that kind the simple "sewing over" process is most expeditious and quite sufficient. The remainder of the drawn work is executed in Punto Tirato knots, as instructed in Fig. 13, in No. 52 of "Weldon's Practical Needlework Series," confining eight threads together in every knot, and working in straight lines from side to side of the material; a knot is likewise to be formed wherever the cotton crosses itself in the open spaces between the squares, and these are subsequently finished off with wheels and spiders in the manner represented, the method of working which is explained in many of the previous examples where similar wheels and spiders are employed for filling in corners. The squares of solid linen may be more or less ornamented with fancy stitches according to the taste, skill, and patience of the worker. A short description of the devices embroidered upon our model will suffice, as almost any one can design and work small sprays of flowers and leaves, or a little figure, a butterfly, a small basket, a fan, a pair of bellows, a gridiron, or little geometrical designs such as stars, etc., etc., in illimitable variety. The **first square**, beginning at the left-hand top corner, is decorated with a simple spray of leaves, of which the larger group of three is worked in raised satin-stitch, and the smaller leaves in bullion-stitches, the

delineates the eye of the flower, the leaves are both outlined with stem-stitch, and two tiny French knots are placed as filling in the centre of one leaf. The embroidery on the **sixth square** consists of a group of five rings worked in buttonhole-stitch. On the **seventh square** will be found a spray of seaweed very tastefully represented by a mixture of outline-stitch and bullion-stitches. The **eighth square** is occupied with a flower worked in outline-stitch, its centre being filled with a group of French knots. The stem is crewel-stitched, and the two leaves are executed in flat satin-stitch. On the **ninth square** is shown a pretty spray of flowers and leaves, in which satin-stitches, chain-stitches, and a

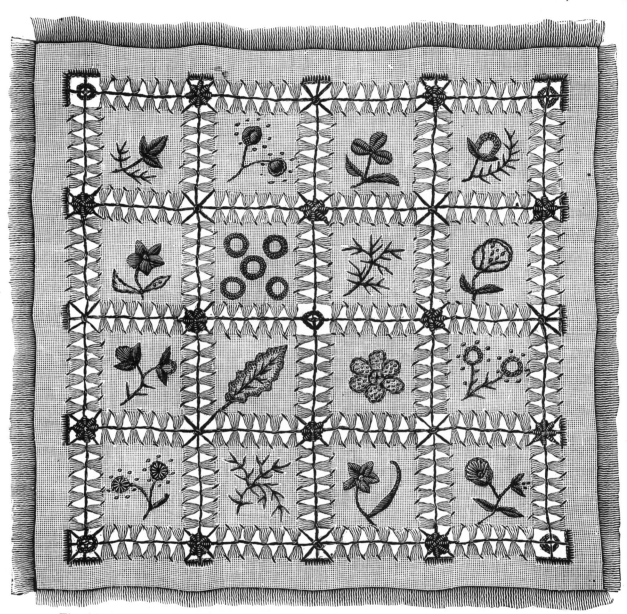

Fig. 44.—An Example of Drawn Thread Work in combination with various Fancy Devices.

stem being executed in crewel-stitch. On the **second square** we see two flower-buds, the one worked in raised satin-stitch and small French knots, the other in satin-stitch surrounded with an outline of crewel-stitch, the circumference of both flowers is delineated with a row of French knots, and the stem is worked in chain-stitch. On the **third square** is a pretty branch executed entirely in satin-stitch with stem of outline-stitch. The **fourth square** is embroidered with a flower worked in satin-stitch and cable-plait-stitch, and a fern-like branch is carried out in bullion-stitches, the stem being crewel-stitch. The **fifth square** shows a pretty primrose-like flower, of which the five petals are worked in raised satin-stitch lengthways round one French knot, which

few spike-stitches are introduced with good effect. The **tenth square** comprises a good-sized leaf with serrated edges, worked in indented buttonhole-stitch and a centre veining of crewel-stitch. On the **eleventh square** is seen a medallion outlined with crewel-stitch and filled in with clusters of tiny French knots. The **twelfth square** has a spray of two flowers worked in conventional style by the use of cable-plait-stitch surmounted with circles of French knots, the leaves are simply formed with long straight spike-stitches, and the stem is depicted with crewel-stitch. The **thirteenth square** contains a very similar spray of flowers, but more closely worked, as the whole centre of each flower consists of a circle of buttonhole-stitches, beyond which the

French knots are arranged, and the spray is completed with one long thin leaf worked in satin-stitch. The seaweed with which the **fourteenth square** is decorated resembles the same subject on the seventh square and is worked in the same kind of stitches. On the **fifteenth square** a little star-like flower is worked in raised satin-stitch, the stitches being taken from the outside to the centre of each of the five petals and making thereby a line or depression down the centre of the petals, while a tiny French knot is placed to simulate the eye, the leaf is long and slender and is executed in over-cast-stitch, the stem is crewel-stitch. The **sixteenth square** shows a bell-shaped flower embroidered in satin-stitch and button-hole-stitch, a small bud worked in satin-stitch and French knots, and two nicely-shaped leaves formed with satin-stitch. The same examples can be repeated should it be desired to extend the piece of work to a greater number of squares, or more can be invented by the worker. The material lends itself equally well to designs worked in cross-stitch if this work be preferred to embroidery.

Fig. 45.—Corner and Border for a Tray-Cloth.

A VERY pretty and lacy pattern for a border for a tray-cloth or other purpose can be made by working according to the accompanying illustration. Arrange the linen material to the size and shape required, determine the position for the first corner, and thence cut across eight threads each way from the angle, leave four threads, cut twelve, leave four, cut twelve, leave four, cut eight. Cut the same threads in relative position towards the next corners, and draw them out. Begin working at the first corner by buttonhole-stitching the two sides where the threads are cut away. Then proceed to work the **pilasters** of **Point de Reprise** in the first insertion of eight open threads; leave the two first threads, darn the four next threads in a pilaster, pass the needle over two threads and under two threads, forwards and backwards, so drawing the four threads together, but not too tightly, when in the middle of the pilaster take up the two threads next to the right, also the two threads next to the left, pass the cotton once round itself and back to the pilaster again, and continue the darning to the bottom of the insertion, make a hem-stitch or two between every pilaster into the margin of the linen on each side, and continue the pattern of pilasters and open diamonds alternately to the end of the row. The same pattern is worked in the other open insertion of eight drawn threads. Next, work a row of hem-stitch along the inner side of the first and third bar of four solid linen threads, grouping three threads in each cluster and taking the stitches two threads deep into the bars. For the **line** of **branching stitches** upon the middle bar of four solid threads, proceed thus—having a knot at the end of the cotton, bring up the needle in the centre of the bar level with the bottom of the first cluster of three drawn threads, insert the needle three threads higher, and bring it out in the open threads to the left level with the top of the first cluster, and draw the cotton through, hold the cotton under the left-hand thumb, insert the needle level with the top of the first cluster in the open threads to the right and bring it out in the centre of the bar at the bottom of the straight stitch you have already worked and over the cotton held by the thumb, and draw through; insert the needle three threads below in the centre of the solid bar and bring it out slanting to the left at the top of the cluster of three open threads and draw the cotton through, hold the cotton under the left-hand thumb, insert the

needle level with the top of the cluster of threads to the right and bring it out in the centre of the bar by the straight stitch last worked and over the cotton held by the thumb, and draw the cotton through, and continue in the same manner; you will find it a particularly easy stitch when you have mastered it, and it has a pretty effect; as you will see by the engraving, Fig. 45, it is worked along the *sides* of the cloth, *not* at the corners. For the **Corners**—First, work a stitch of Point D'Esprit in each of the four small open corner spaces; and then proceed to make long twisted foundation stitches from corner to corner of the block of four larger open squares; a spider is darned round the solid square of four threads in the centre; beyond this another foundation thread is run in the form of a square, and where this crosses one of the other foundation threads and also where it crosses one of the solid bars a circle of darned stitches is grouped making eight spots darned round the centre square. Other and larger spots are darned where the bars of four solid threads cross each other at the angles of the corner. Then, by the help of two foundation stitches placed as in the illustration, a good-sized semi-circular darning is made on each side the corner square, which now is completed. You must be careful to get the pattern in evenly along all four sides of the cloth, so that the other corners may be worked to correspond exactly with this corner. The edges of solid linen by the sides of the drawn-thread work are now to be ornamented with a double row of herringbone-stitching, each stitch taken over six threads of the linen and interspersed with an arrow-head of three spike-stitches at regular intervals, as shown in the illustration.

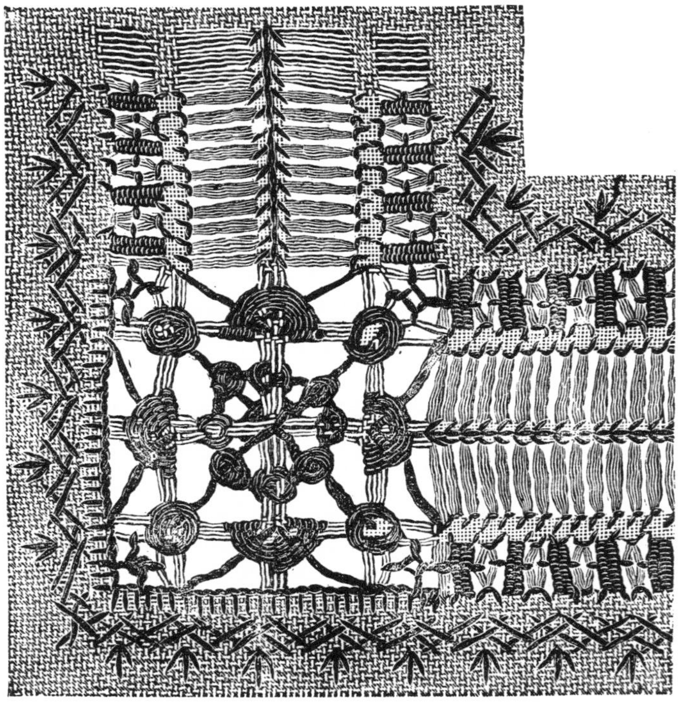

Fig. 45.—Corner and Border for a Tray-Cloth.

WELDON'S PRACTICAL
DRAWN THREAD WORK.

(THIRD SERIES.)

SHOWING ORIGINAL DESIGNS FOR NIGHTDRESS CASE, BRUSH AND COMB BAG, D'OYLEYS, CORNERS, BORDERS, INSERTIONS, &c.

TWENTY-ONE ILLUSTRATIONS.

Telegraphic Address—
"Consuelo," London.

The Yearly Subscription to this Magazine, post free to any Part of the World, is 2s. 6d.
Subscriptions are payable in advance, and may commence from any date and for any period.

[Telephone—
2745.

The Back Numbers are always in print. Nos. 1 to 106 now ready, Price 2d. each, postage ½d. Over 5,000 Engravings.

DRAWN THREAD WORK.

Fig. 46.—Example in Lattice Work and Knotted Piques.

OUR illustration, Fig. 46, shows a pretty design in lattice work, in which a charming and lacy effect is produced by the introduction of knotted piques jutting out on each of the four sides of every little open square. The beauty of this stitch will be at once apparent by reference to Fig. 57, where it is used in the form of an insertion in combination with large diamonds of solid linen. A border for a nightdress satchet, or an all over-piece of work for the centre of a cushion or small tablecloth, may easily be arranged in this style. The piques are simply *knots* tied in the cotton at certain regular intervals of the Point de Reprise. Commence in the manner instructed for working Fig. 52, and proceed obliquely across the linen doing first a perpendicular and then a horizontal bar; the number of Point de Reprise stitches required to fill each bar will of course depend upon the stoutness of the linen and the number of drawn open threads; in example Fig. 46 four threads are drawn and four threads left; six stitches of Point de Reprise are worked over a bar (that is, three stitches over and three stitches under each side of the four thread bar), then a knot is tied in the working cotton close to the bar, and, as shown in the engraving, the needle is passed to the other side of the bar, where a knot is again made, after which the bar is finished with six stitches of Point de Reprise as it began. In some cases it may be sufficient to put only four stitches of Point de Reprise in the bars on each side of the knotted piques, in others as many as eight or ten Point de Reprise stitches may be required; the bars should be just nicely filled with stitches but not crowded, or the effect of the lace or open work of the design will be marred. It forms a pretty border to a solid centre as in Fig. 57.

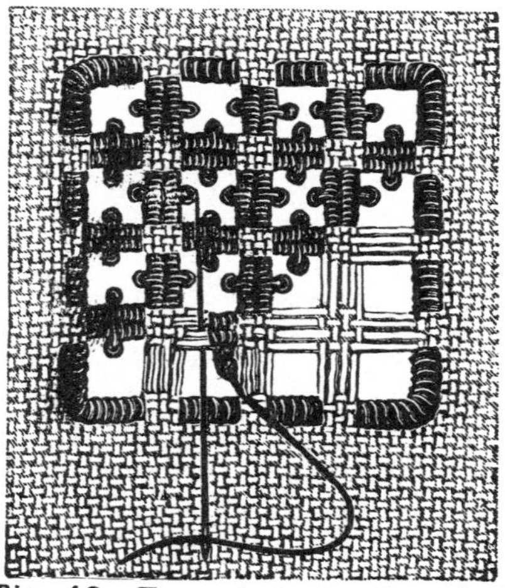

Fig. 46.—Example in Lattice Work and Knotted Piques.

Fig. 47.—Insertion for a Towel.

EMBROIDERED towels are now very generally used in the houses of the wealthy, and as they really are very nice and add considerably to the prettiness of a bedroom, there is no reason why they should not more frequently be seen in the dwellings of the middle-class. Though expensive to buy ready worked, a few handsome towels would cost but little more than ordinary ones if the embroidery could be executed at home, and there are always times when a lady can take up a little fancy work of this description without interfering with more important avocations. Towelling can be purchased with the ends woven specially for decorating with drawn-thread embroidery. The towel from which our sectional engraving is taken is, however, made of plain Russian linen, 20 inches wide, and 60 inches long, and the pattern is executed in the usual manner by drawing out a certain number of threads and working upon those that remain. Harris's red flax-thread, shade 124, size D, is suitable to work with. Reserve six inches of material at each end of the towel below the drawn-thread embroidery, four inches will be afterwards unravelled and knotted into fringe, and the two remaining inches will form a band of solid linen between the fringe and the embroidery. Draw out threads to the extent of half an inch of material, leave three solid threads, draw out half an inch, leave three threads, draw out one inch, leave three threads, draw out half an inch, leave three threads, draw out half an inch, and you will find you have five rows of drawn open threads alternating with four narrow bars of solid linen. Work simple hem stitch along the top and bottom of the insertion, grouping four threads in a cluster and taking the stitches three threads deep into the margin of the solid linen. The first and the fourth bars are now to be worked in the pretty stitch termed "wire" stitch, this is executed from right to left; secure the end of the cotton on the right-hand side of the first bar, and bring up the needle and cotton in the insertion above the bar of three solid threads and four threads from the edge of the towel and draw through, pass the needle over the edge of the towel and bring it up in the place whence it started and draw through, pass the needle again over the edge of the towel and bring it up in the lower insertion two clusters from the beginning and draw through, pass the needle once more over the edge of the towel and bring it up in the upper insertion by the stitch already made and draw through, * insert the needle in the lower insertion by the last made stitch and take up two clusters on the needle and draw through, insert the needle again in the same place and bring it out in the upper insertion by the side of the last stitch and draw through, insert the needle in the lower insertion to the left of the stitch just worked and bring it out in the upper insertion where the cotton is and draw through, insert the needle again in the same place and bring it out in the upper insertion eight threads to the left of the cotton and draw through, insert the needle from right to left to take up eight threads of the upper insertion, bringing the point out where the cotton is and draw through, insert the needle in the lower insertion by the stitch last worked and bring it out in the upper insertion by the cotton and draw through, and repeat from * to the end of the row, where fasten off securely. Work upon the second and third bars of solid linen in herringbone-stitch, taking always four threads on the needle to each stitch and consequently sub-dividing the clusters formed by the wire-stitch. Now the **Middle open insertion** is to be embroidered, tie the cotton on the right-hand side and work a line of Punto Tirato knots along the centre of the insertion, make a knot on the third cluster, a knot on the first cluster, a knot on the fourth cluster, and a knot on the second cluster, all closely together, and drawing the clusters somewhat in the form of the 'double crossing" illustrated Fig. 7, No. 52 of " Weldon's Practical Needlework Series," and repeat the process, leaving enough cotton between the groups to obviate any puckering of the linen. To make the perpendicular stitches between the groups of Punto Tirato knots work thus, — Bring the needle and cotton up in the lower bar of herringbone-stitching close by the little space between the groups, take a stitch perpendicularly in the upper bar of herringbone-stitching and wind the cotton several times round the long perpendicular stitch, passing behind the Punto Tirato cotton, and back to the starting point, where slip the needle along the wrong side of the fabric into the position for working the next stitch. This completes the drawn-thread embroidery. A similar insertion is worked on the other end of the towel. The fringe is formed by unravelling four inches of linen; the threads are separated into groups of eight, the first group and fourth group are knotted together, the third group and sixth group together, and so on, making all the knots in a straight line a short distance below the solid linen; the knotted threads are then sub-divided, and half the threads from one knot are re-knotted with half the threads from the second knot following, when the fringe will appear as shown in the engraving.

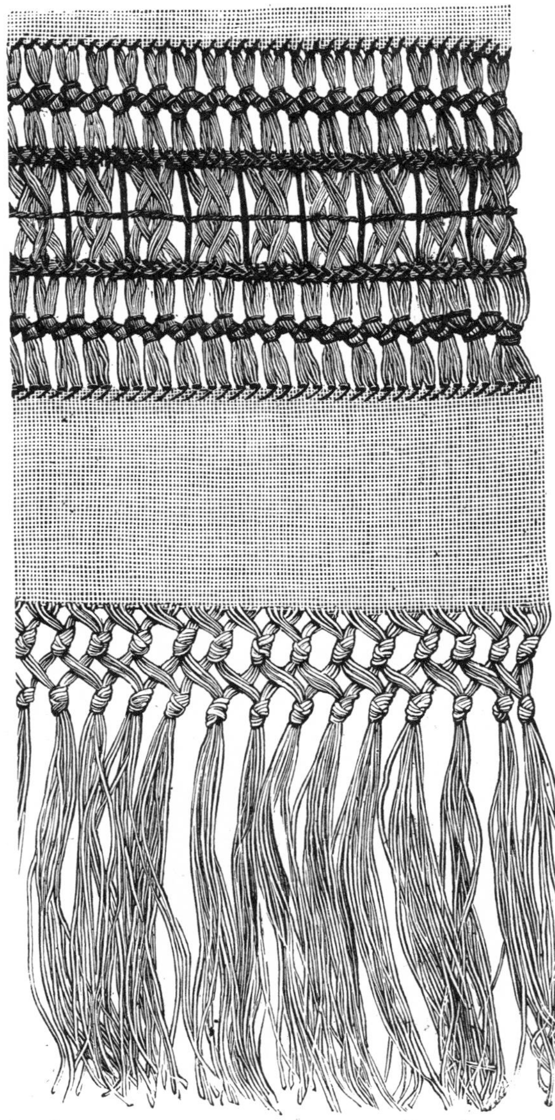

Fig. 47.—Insertion for a Towel.

laundry, as provided the buttonhole-stitching be done strongly round the cut squares there is nothing whatever to fray out. Procure a piece of white linen the size required, and after marking off two or three inches as a margin or frame of solid linen outside the work to be afterwards unravelled for fringe, cut three threads each way from the angle of the corner, draw these three threads out, and proceed to strengthen the corner with buttonhole-stitch and to work hem-stitch all round the cloth on the outer side of the drawn threads, taking four threads in a cluster the first cluster by the corners and three threads in a cluster in all other places, and make the stitches two threads deep. For the **Cut Open Squares**—Count six threads from one side and twenty-nine threads from the other side of the drawn open insertion, and leaving these threads intact, cut away a square of sixteen threads, strengthen the edge of this open square with buttonhole-stitch worked two threads deep rather thickly and closely, and when the buttonhole-stitching is done all round the square make a foundation-stitch to sit angle-ways from the middle of the buttonhole-stitch on one side the open square to the middle of the buttonhole-stitch on the next side, and again from that side to the next, till you get four loops across the square, go round again once or twice to make a firm foundation, and then work buttonhole-stitch over the loops, making a little pique knot in the centre of each loop, in the manner shown in the engraving. The other open square is fashioned to correspond. For the **Square of Solid Embroidery**—This occupies twenty square threads, and leaves four clear threads against the drawn open insertion and three threads against each open square. Bring up the needle and cotton in the centre of the twenty square threads (that is, between the fourteenth and fifteenth threads counting from the angle of the open insertion at the corner), insert the needle in the spot which will be the corner of the square and take two threads on the needle and draw the cotton through, insert the needle again in the place where last inserted and bring it up in the centre and draw the cotton through, you now have one long stitch and one small back-stitch on the surface of the linen, insert the needle by the last back-stitch and take up two threads and draw the cotton through, insert the needle again in the same place and bring it up in the centre and draw the cotton through, and continue in this manner till you get a star-like ray of long stitches extending from the centre of the square over ten threads each way, and surrounded by an edge of ten back-stitches along each side of the square. The **Triangles** are formed by working the half of a solid star-like square, and are specially designed to slant off the corner. This corner is capable of various extensions, as for instance, if the half-squares of solid embroidery were to be finished and the work continued to match the beginning, a good sized perfect square would be produced, which could be used as a square for a corner, while similar squares could be continued in the form of a border; or a number of such squares repeated would make a pretty insertion for the middle of a sideboard slip ; or four squares, with a strip of solid linen between worked in cross-stitch, would make an elegant centre for a cushion or a small tablecloth. It would also work up nicely as corners or a border for a nightdress case or brush and comb bag, or be especially pretty for small d'oyleys, towel corners, &c.

Fig. 48.—Corner for a D'Oyley or Tray Cloth.

OUR engraving, Fig. 48, shows a simple yet very effective corner, executed partly in cut work and partly in solid embroidery; this corner possesses the merit of being easily and quickly worked, and is particularly useful for any article requiring to be much in the

Fig. 49.—Knotted Wheel Insertion.

FOR this pretty insertion you will require to draw out thirty threads, or as many as will make about one inch of open work. Proceed first with simple hem-stitch along the top and bottom of the open threads, grouping two threads in a cluster, and taking the stitches two threads deep into the margin of the solid linen. For the **First row of the Knotted Wheels**—Work Punto Tirato knots along the centre of the insertion, confining five clusters of threads together in faggots, and leaving sufficient cotton to lie evenly across the space left between the faggots. **Second row** —Make a knot upon each of the five clusters of the first faggot a very little way below the top row of hem-stitching, carry the cotton in a straight direction downwards crossing over the cotton that runs along the centre of the insertion, and work a knot upon each of the five clusters of the next faggot a little above the bottom row of the hem-stitching, and continue knotting thus at the top of one group of five clusters and at the bottom of the next group of five clusters to the end of the row. **Third row** —The same as the second row, knotting upon the clusters you before missed. **Fourth row**—This row is worked in the same manner as the first row, making knots on each group alternately on each side of the insertion just inside the knots worked in process of the first row. **Fifth row**—Work knots upon the clusters you omitted working in last row, and as you go across the threads of cotton which lie in the spaces between the faggots pass the needle and cotton in a darning-stitch twice round the cotton that runs along the centre of the insertion, and twice round the bunches of cotton proceeding from the small knots of the wheels, so forming a diamond-shaped spot in the spaces between the faggots, as shown in the engraving, Fig. 49.

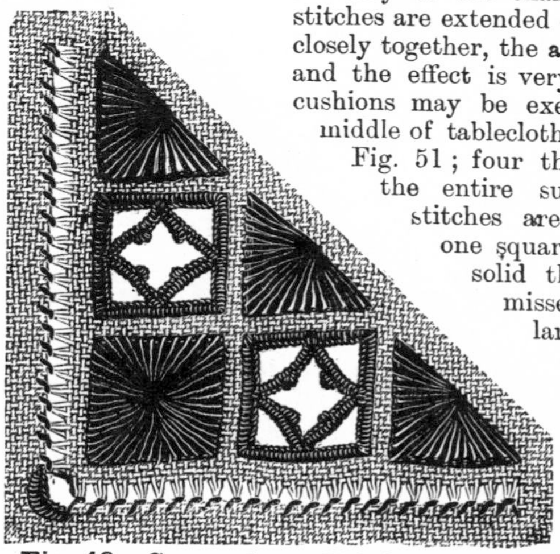

Fig. 50.—Zigzag Insertion.

THIS is a pretty insertion for table linen, and may be widened, if necessary, by the addition of a simple narrow pattern at the top and bottom, or by an edging of ornamental stitches on the margin of the solid linen. Thirty-six threads are drawn out. Work hem-stitch along each edge of the drawn open threads, grouping three threads together in a cluster, and taking the stitches two threads deep into the margin of the linen; the clusters should stand perpendicularly upright. The zigzag pattern is worked in four separate rows, proceeding from right to left. The first row is composed of stitches made alternately one-third distant from the upper edge, and one-third distant from the lower edge of the insertion; secure the cotton on the right-hand side of the material, and pass the needle and cotton three times round the first four clusters of threads one-third below the upper edge of the insertion; tie the cotton in place firmly with a Punto Tirato knot, pass the cotton round the two last of the confined clusters to slip down to bind the cotton three times round four clusters of threads (two already bound and the two next successive) one third from the bottom of the insertion, where tie in place with a knot, pass the cotton round the two last of these confined clusters to slip upwards, and bind and knot four more clusters together, and proceed to the end of the row; these binds or ties may be distinctly seen in the engraving, Fig. 50, right-hand lower illustration on this page, between the stitches of the winding zigzag. For the **second row**—Recommence on the right-hand side, work a knot

on each of the four clusters of threads above the first tie, midway between the tie and the hem-stitching; make a knot on the cluster of eight threads running crossways, make a knot on each of the four clusters below the next tie, make a knot on the cluster of eight threads running crossways, make a knot on each of the four clusters above the next tie, missing two ties from that last worked upon, and continue thus up and down to the end. The **third row** is worked in the same manner, up and down, and where the cotton crosses over the cotton of the last preceding row it is to be turned round it, as seen in the engraving. The **fourth row** makes knots upon those clusters that have been omitted in the course of working the two previous rows, and also twines round the cotton of the last row wherever it crosses the same. This completes the insertion.

Fig. 51.—Example in Fancy Lattice Work.

THE lattice pattern represented in Fig. 51 is worked very similarly to the example Fig 52, but as the Point de Reprise stitches are extended over an open space instead of being drawn closely together, the appearance of the work is considerably altered, and the effect is very elegant and lacy. Very pretty centres for cushions may be executed in lattice work, also stripes for the middle of tablecloths and sideboard slips. To work the example Fig. 51; four threads are drawn and two threads left over the entire surface of the material. Point de Reprise stitches are darned lightly over two squares and missing one square in every third space between the bars of solid threads; the two spaces which thus will be missed between the darnings form as it were one large open block, crossed both perpendicularly and horizontally by two linen threads, foundation threads are added crossing these, as shown in the engraving, and a small spot is then darned in the centre, which adds to the beauty of the design and serves also to bind the threads closely together in the centre of the square.

Fig. 52. — Design in Simple Lattice Work, or Cut Work, otherwise called Point Coupé.

A GREAT number of very beautiful patterns can be formed by a judicious arrangement of small open squares breaking up the surface of the solid linen in a kind of lattice work. Sometimes a whole series of these open squares are employed to cover a good-sized piece of material, in which case the procedure is quite simple, only requiring certain threads to be first cut and afterwards drawn away in each direction, both warp and woof of the fabric, as illustration Fig. 52, which shows four threads withdrawn and four threads left intact. But most frequently the open squares are arranged in such a manner as to force a portion of the solid linen into a prominent pattern while they themselves occupy the position of a ground work, as see Fig. 57, where lattice squares are combined with large diamonds. Patterns of this description are classed under the designation of "Cut" work, or "Point Coupé," and are rather difficult of execution, as very great care must be exercised to cut the right threads in exactly the right place, and moreover to make a clean smooth cut, so that no jagged ends of linen may interfere with the uniformity of the pattern. If the pattern is very elaborate it may be expedient to mark it out with a coloured tacking thread or with a black-lead pencil to prevent any possibility of mistake, for if once any wrong threads are severed the work is ruined. A very sharp fine-pointed pair of scissors must be employed, and it is a good

Fig. 48.—Corner for a D'Oyley or Tray Cloth.

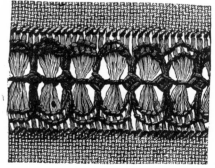

Fig. 49.—Knotted Wheel Insertion.

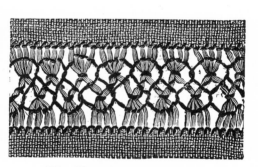

Fig. 50.—Zigzag Insertion.

plan to cut only as much as can conveniently be worked at a sitting, for sometimes the mere folding of the linen if laid by for a few days will disarrange and crease the loose open threads. The method of working simple lattice work, or Point Coupé, needs little description as it will be quite easily understood by reference to the engraving, Fig. 52. After the threads are cut and drawn the outer edge is strengthened and kept in place by an overcast-stitching taken two threads deep into the margin of the linen. The bars are then darned firmly over in the stitch so well-known to all drawn-thread workers as Point de Reprise;—begin at the left-hand top corner and work obliquely, first a perpendicular bar, then a horizontal bar passing the needle and cotton over two threads and under two threads then backwards over the last two threads and under the first two as is represented in one bar in process of working; the cotton should be drawn closely but not too tightly round the linen threads, and it will be well to avoid as far as possible making any joins in the Point de Reprise.

Fig. 53.—Example in Lattice Work and Point Anglais.

In this example the open spaces are rather larger than in the example Fig. 52, and the lattice work is differently executed. Six threads are withdrawn and two threads are left. The two thread bars are sewn over and over in cord-stitch, which is really the same stitch as over-casting, but being worked on a bar between drawn threads it so much resembles a "cord" that the name is particularly appropriate. After securing the cut edge all round the piece of work by means of overcast-stitches, begin the cord-stitch at the left-hand top corner, and proceed in an oblique direction; the first oblique line consists of one perpendicular bar and one horizontal bar, and fasten off; the second oblique line is just twice as long, and when you get in the centre of each horizontal bar you work the cross of Point Anglais upon each of two open squares; this is done by carrying the cotton across and taking a stitch on the opposite side of the square, and then making one cord-stitch round the cotton itself, take a stitch on another side of the square and do a cord-stitch round itself a stitch on the opposite side and a cord-stitch round itself and finally a cord-stitch round the cotton with which you began the Point Anglais, and go back to the centre of the unfinished bar, which now complete in the usual way The third oblique line is worked in simple cord-stitch like the first line, and crosses of Point Anglais are made in the fourth oblique line the same as in the second line, and so on. The pattern is useful for filling in a large space, and may be intermixed with other designs in drawn-thread embroidery, or with solid bands of linen worked in cross-stitch or damask-stitches.

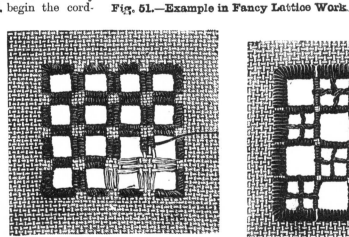

Fig. 52.—Design in Simple Lattice Work or Cut Work, otherwise called Point Coupé.

Fig. 54.—D'Oyley, with a Centre of Fancy Lattice Work.

A MOST elegant d'oyley, made of a piece of linen canvas, and measuring 7 inches square, is elaborately worked in drawn thread and ornamental stitching, as represented in our engraving, Fig. 54. The work may be executed with pale blue, pink, or gold flax-thread, according to taste, or with washing silk, both thread and silk is now

manufactured in fast colours and will wash perfectly. Preserve an outside margin of fifteen threads for the hem, cut across the next two threads at right angles at each corner and draw the threads out; turn down a hem, and proceed to work **hem-stitch** round all four sides of the d'oyley, grouping three threads together in a cluster and taking the stitches two threads deep into the linen, work a few buttonhole-stitches against the cut threads at each corner The **Fancy Lattice Work** in the centre of the d'oyley occupies forty-four threads from right to left and from top to bottom of the design, and the cut work consists in all of twenty-four lattice squares arranged as shown in the illustration, four threads are cut away, and four threads left, and all the little bars are worked in Point de Reprise darning, as see Fig. 52, excepting the eight bars that form the boundary of the four centre squares where, as two extra threads are detached to make each of these squares a trifle larger than the surrounding squares, a cord-stitch, as see Fig. 53, is sewn over the two threads that are left; a line of twisted cotton passes vertically across each of these four centre squares; the surrounding eight squares are filled with stitches of Point D'Esprit; and the remaining twelve squares are left open, and their cut side abutting upon the solid linen is strengthened with buttonhole-stitches taken three threads deep You will observe two dark lines in the engraving defining a **perfect double diamond**, sketch the outline on the linen with a black-lead pencil, and work it rather thickly in crewel-stitch; the space between the two lines is embellished with a series of small stars worked in cross-stitch. The entire surface of the linen between the lattice work centre and the first line of crewel-stitching is occupied with a very pretty piece of

Fig. 51.—Example in Fancy Lattice Work.

open embroidery, two threads drawn away and two threads left, which threads are worked in simple overcast-stitch, one stitch being formed over the surface of every small bar; consult the illustration and observe the way the threads of the linen are cut and drawn to ensure the pattern fitting in nicely from the line of crewel-stitching on one side to the line of crewel-stitching on the opposite side, excepting where intercepted by the lattice design in the centre of the d'oyley. The limit of the

Fig. 53.—Example in Lattice Work and Point Anglais.

Insertion of Ornamental Stitching beyond the diamond is defined by another line of crewel-stitch, which cuts off the corners, and runs parallel with the hem-stitching for a short distance in the centre of each side of the d'oyley; the insertion is embroidered in the first instance by straight lines of cotton marking out a series of small chequers four threads square, and then by three rows of crossed stitches worked diagonally over the small chequers, as shown in the engraving. Work a filling of cross-stitch and Holbein-stitch on the vacant space in the corners. Sew an edging of Torchon lace rather full round the d'oyley, which is now complete.

Fig. 55.—Key Pattern Insertion.

In our engraving, Fig. 55, will be seen an elegant insertion which is a mixture of drawn-thread work and cut work. It may be executed on any description of rather coarse linen, such as Russian linen, or on linen gauze, or single thread-flax canvas. Draw out fifteen threads for the upper open insertion, leave forty-three threads for the present on which afterwards to work the key pattern, and draw out fifteen threads for the lower insertion. Then hem-stitching is done in a new way, and is practically a combination of hemming and back-stitching in one, it has a pretty effect, and is worked from right to left, thus,—Bring the needle and cotton up in the solid linen two threads distant from the open insertion, insert the needle two threads back on the same level and bring it up in the place the cotton springs from, and draw the cotton through, which makes a back-stitch, insert the needle in the drawn open threads even with the top of the back-stitch and bring it up in the solid linen two threads in advance of the cotton and draw through, make another back-stitch, then another hem-stitch, and continue, always embracing two threads at a time to the end of the row. Work the same stitch to correspond on the opposite edge of the insertion, and the threads will be grouped in perpendicular clusters, two threads in each cluster. The clusters are now to be formed into pilasters by a darning of Point de Reprise connecting two clusters together from the top to the bottom of the insertion, and the pilasters are joined together in the centre in sets of three, as shown in the engraving. The crosses may be worked on the completion of each set of three pilasters, or may be added after the row of pilasters is entirely accomplished, according to the pleasure of the worker; the needle and cotton is first of all brought up at the top of the first pilaster, insert it to take up the cotton at the bottom

Fig. 54.—D'Oyley with a Centre of Fancy Lattice Work.

of the third pilaster and draw through, sew the cotton over and over itself to the starting point, and there slip along at the back of the work and bring it out at the top of the third pilaster, insert the needle to take up the cotton at the bottom of the first pilaster, and draw through, and sew the cotton over and over itself to the starting point again, but when in the middle of the "cross," take one stitch to connect this part of the cross to the first part and also to the centre of the group of pilasters. The pilaster insertion on the opposite side of the pattern is then worked to correspond. You next proceed with the **key pattern**, for which forty-three threads are reserved. Leave a bar of six threads of solid linen on each side next against the open drawn-thread insertion (two of which threads are already worked upon by the hem and back-stitching), and

extract four threads horizontally from end to end of the insertion, viz., parallel with the threads already drawn. Now for the first row of the key pattern, beginning on the left-hand side, cut four threads clear away to form a small square space, work overcasting where you cut the threads on the side next the pilaster insertion, and proceed in cord-stitch over two threads at a time, up and down, till fifteen little perpendicular rails are formed, and as you work take an overcast-stitch into the linen at the top and bottom of each rail to keep the bars of solid linen in position, as shown in the engraving, make another small square, work fifteen little perpendicular rails, and repeat the same to the end of the row. The bottom row of the key pattern is worked precisely the same, but the position of the squares is altered, omit working the first thread on the left-hand side, then do twelve perpendicular rails, cut a square, work fifteen rails, and continue, and you will see the squares come five threads to the left of the squares worked in the first row, also the alternate threads are corded together and so the rails fall intermediate between the rails of the first row. Between the two rows of key pattern now worked there remains two rows still to be done, each open row consists of four drawn threads, and each solid bar consists of five threads, and by referring to the engraving you will see that small squares are cut fourteen threads below the squares of the top row, and other squares are cut fourteen threads above the squares of the bottom row, and the intermediate space permits of seven rails being worked in horizontal and eight rails in a perpendicular position, and all the squares are strengthened with overcast-stitching on the two cut sides, and thus the key pattern is perfected.

Fig. 56.—Nightdress Sachet.

THE nightdress sachet represented in our engraving, Fig. 56, is a splendid specimen of drawn-thread embroidery, yet though at first sight it may appear rather elaborate, a fairly competent worker should find no difficulty in executing the design if strict attention be paid to the instructions. The material of which the sachet is composed is a light openly-woven fabric known as Rhodes linen, of which a piece measuring 30 inches by 16 inches will be required; the embroidery is worked with Harris's pale blue flax-thread, shade 31, size E; procure also a piece of blue silk of the same shade for lining, and 3½ yards of pretty Torchon lace about two inches wide for trimming. The sachet is 16 inches wide, and the Rhodes linen is folded in the shape of an envelope, so that the 30-inch length makes the pocket, the back, and the flap of the sachet in one piece. Commence by turning a hem about three-quarters of an inch wide along the end of the linen that is intended for the top of the pocket; when the hem is made the pocket should measure 12 inches deep exactly, run a thread of coloured cotton to denote the place where the linen will be folded to form the bottom of the pocket, and run another thread of cotton to show where the flap is to be turned over. Turn down a quarter-inch hem along the bottom of the flap and also up each side thereof to the place where the sides of the flap meet the top of the pocket, tack this hem in the position in which it should lie, and it will be kept in place ultimately by the hem-stitching of the first row of the drawn-thread work. For the **Insertion**—Begin close by the turned-down hem at the corner of the flap, and cut from the angle across ten threads each way, leave three threads, cut twenty, leave three, cut ten; sever the same threads at the opposite corner, and also at the top of the sachet where the insertion should stop, as there is no occasion to work it down the sides of the back of the sachet, though you can do so if you wish; draw out the cut threads, and you will find you have three rows of open drawn threads separated one from the other by two bars of three solid threads. The threads for the front of the pocket are to be arranged in the same manner, but do not meddle with that until the flap is completed. On the insertion that ornaments the flap of the sachet work a hem-stitching along the inner and outer edge of the drawn open threads, grouping four threads in a cluster, and taking the stitches two threads deep into the margin of the solid linen, and when working by the turned-down hem take the

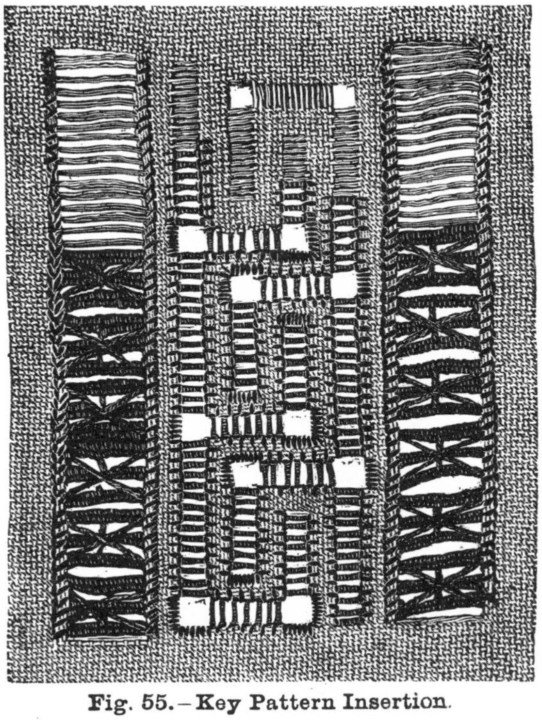

Fig. 55.—Key Pattern Insertion.

stitches right through to sew the hem firmly in its place, do buttonhole-stitching along the two sides of the corner where the threads are cut. Work over the two bars of three solid threads in filigree-stitch, Fig. 12, in No. 52 of "Weldon's Practical Needlework Series," retaining the same four threads in clusters as are already grouped together by the process of the hem-stitching. The two **narrow insertions** are next embroidered with Point de Reprise, making small pilasters of one cluster of drawn threads and leaving the next cluster in its present condition; to work the pilasters you darn in and out over two threads and under two threads till the cluster is full of darned stitches. The next process is to work upon the **wide insertion** of twenty drawn open threads, which threads are already grouped into clusters by the filigree-stitch that is executed over the bars of three solid threads. Secure the cotton to the middle of the first cluster of threads next the corner, and work a row of Punto Tirato knots along the middle of the insertion, confining three clusters of threads together in each knot; when this is done a twining-stitch is worked completely over the wide insertion and over the two solid bars into the clusters that remain in simple perpendicular position between the pilasters; to accomplish this bring up the needle and cotton in the top bar on the right-hand side of the insertion and work from right to left, take

up on the needle the first simple cluster of the top insertion and draw through, * pass the needle in a downward direction over the bar, under the last two threads of the last cluster of the faggot, over the Punto Tirato cotton, under the first two threads of the first cluster of the next faggot, and draw through, pass the needle from right to left under a simple cluster of the lower insertion and draw through, pass the needle in an upward direction over the bar, under the last two threads of the last cluster of the same faggot, over the Punto Tirato cotton, under the first two threads of the first cluster of the next faggot, and draw through, pass the needle from right to left under a simple cluster of the top insertion (the third simple cluster from that last worked under) and draw through, and repeat from * to the end of the row: work two more lines in the same way and you will have a twining-stitch depending from every simple cluster

Fig. 56.—

of the upper and lower insertions; this twining-stitch is very pretty if rightly done. The **Corner** consists of a large centre square, four small squares, and four oblong spaces intersected by the bars of three solid threads; bind the bars over closely and firmly with cord-stitch; then run a foundation thread cornerways across the entire block of squares, and on the foundation darn a small spider in the centre of each small square; put extra foundation threads from side to side of the large centre square and work a star with pyramid points as shown in the engraving; make two parallel foundation threads across each oblong and work them to correspond with the pilasters in the narrow insertions, and between the pilasters put a stitch of Point D'Esprit to connect the pilasters together. Work upon the inside margin of the insertion a line of ornamental stitching, as in the illustration. Work the front of the pocket to correspond with the flap. The words "Bonne Nuit" and the owner's initials or monogram are worked in cross-stitch. Make up the sachet neatly with the blue lining, and trim it all round with Torchon lace set on rather full.

Fig. 57.—Insertion in Lattice Work and Satin-Stitch.

THE insertion represented in our engraving, Fig. 57, affords a very good idea of the manner of combining cut-work with drawn-thread embroidery and satin-stitch; it is a very beautiful pattern, and as far as the actual needlework is concerned is not at all difficult but great care must be taken in cutting the threads so as not to permit any of the open work to trespass upon the space of solid linen required for the formation of the diamonds. The insertion

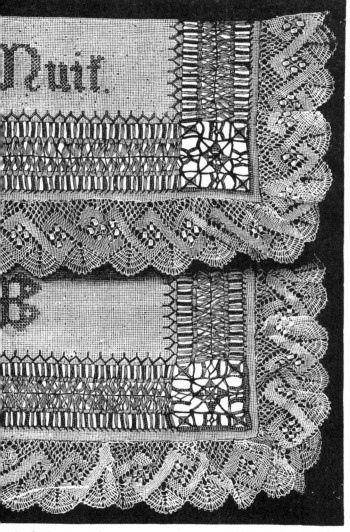

ss Sachet.

occupies sixty-eight threads in depth, and may be carried on to whatever length is desired, and if a corner is needed it can easily be formed without making the slightest alteration in the design. The open work throughout consists of four threads drawn away and four threads left for bars, and the exact termination of the open lattice work and the shaping of the diamonds can be readily understood by consulting the illustration. On each side of the insertion the cut edge is strengthened and kept in place with overcast-stitches taken four threads deep into the margin of the solid linen, and the cut edges of the diamonds are worked in the same way. An example of lattice work and knotted piques in actual working size will be found by turning to Fig. 46, page 1, of the present issue, and as clear instructions are appended the same need not be repeated. The satin-stitch, otherwise called damask-stitch, with which the diamonds are embellished, is worked after the lattice

work is complete, and consists of a series of straight stitches and slanting stitches arranged on the surface of the linen in the form of a star, as shown in the engraving.

Fig. 58.—D'Oyley, with an Open Centre Worked in Lace-Stitches.

EXPERIENCED lace workers will find no difficulty in managing the intricacies of the handsome d'oyley shown in Fig. 58, although it must be confessed it requires skilful and expert handling, together with patience and perseverance, and therefore should not be attempted by a novice. Procure a piece of linen canvas measuring 7 inches square, and several skeins of Harris's flax-thread, size E, either white or coloured as preferred; the model d'oyley is worked with blue, shade 31, and looks exceedingly pretty. In linen canvas about twenty-six threads go to an inch, and if the right kind is obtained the 7 inch square should comprise 184 threads each way, anyhow you must have the stated number of threads in your square

of linen to accommodate the pattern as worked in the original d'oyley. Leave an outside margin of fifteen threads for a hem, cut across the next two threads at right angles at each corner and extract the two threads, turn down a hem, and work hem-stitch round the d'oyley in the usual manner, clustering three threads together, and taking the stitches two threads deep into the hem, strengthen the corners where the threads are cut by a few buttonhole-stitches. Now mark with a thread of cotton the *four* threads in the exact centre of each side the square, these four threads are to be kept intact across from side to side. For the **insertion**—On each side of the four centre threads, and parallel with the hem-stitching, but leaving three solid threads between, cut across eight threads, leave two, cut one thread, draw out the cut threads from side to side of the d'oyley; and now work by the engraving, first of all strengthening the edge where the

Fig. 57.—Insertion in Lattice Work and Satin-Stitch

threads are cut parallel to the hem-stitching by working fourteen cross-stitches in a straight line and over two threads each way so there will be one thread visible between the hem-stitching and the little line of cross-stitches; next work a row of hem-stitches along the one drawn thread taking the head of the stitches into the open space of eight drawn threads, two threads are grouped in a cluster and only fourteen hem-stitches are required to be done, as the insertion of solid linen between the hem and the open lace worked centre is but thirty-four threads wide, and three of these threads are afterwards covered with the buttonhole-stitching by which the open centre is defined. An ornamental binding-stitch is worked to the same depth over the bar of four solid threads in the centre of the insertion. Work Punto Tirato knots along the middle of the eight drawn open threads, tying four threads in a knot, but subdividing the clusters as formed by the binding-stitch so that the threads bend right and left like a trellis. And now, when the bosses are worked in satin-stitch, and the little sprays are worked in cross-stitch, as represented in the engraving, the insertion will be completed, and you will proceed to the centre which is executed entirely in **lace-stitches**. You have a bar of four solid threads running across the centre of the d'oyley, still retain these, and on each side thereof, at the distance of thirty-four threads from the hem-stitching, cut across seventeen threads, leave four threads, cut across eighteen threads, which brings you to the corner, repeat the operation on the other three sides, and remove the cut threads, and you will find you have three bars, each of four solid threads, traversing the open space from side to side. Strengthen the entire edge of the open square with buttonhole-stitching taken three threads deep into the margin of the insertion. The remainder of the design can be better understood by consulting the illustration than by any written description, each bar of four threads is divided, and two threads together are sewn over and over in cord-stitch, and these by the help of Point de Reprise stitches of graduated length are formed into a series of twelve "buds," each bud being tipped with a foundation cotton on which buttonhole-stitches and piques are worked; the centre of the design consists of a lattice of cord-stitch, and foundation-stitches are put in wherever required to supplement the original threads. Finish with Torchon lace sewn on rather full.

Fig. 59.—Brush and Comb Bag.

THE material used for the model is white Russian linen, and if this is procured 33 inches wide,

Fig. 58.—D'Oyley with an Open Centre worked in Lace-Stitches.

straight along above the selvedge of the flap and thence proceeds up each side in the style of a border or insertion; about an inch and a half of solid material is left outside the insertion of drawn threads as a margin on which afterwards to embroider a design in cross-stitch, and a portion of solid linen is left intact in the centre of the flap and affords space for working a monogram or initials. The work on the front of the pocket is similarly arranged. The back of the bag is all plain linen. To **prepare** for **working** the **drawn-thread embroidery**—Fold the linen in half lengthways to discover the precise centre of the bag which mark with a pin or a thread of cotton, and then count towards the side eighty-four threads, which will bring you to the exact position for commencing a corner; now from the angle of the corner cut across six threads each way, that is, six threads in a parallel direction above the selvedge of the flap (and about an inch and a half therefrom) and six threads up the side, leave twelve threads, cut across six threads, and continue this till you have allowed for ten open squares to be formed above the selvedge and eight open squares up the side. Cut the threads on the opposite side to correspond with the first side. Draw away the three lines of cut threads that run parallel nearest to the selvedge, these form the depth of the insertion; draw away three lines of cut threads perpendicularly up each side of the flap, detaching them at the top, as shown in the engraving; you will by this time see how far the side insertions extend towards the centre of the bag and can cut and draw out short parallel threads accordingly. The linen is now **ready for working**, and the insertion presents the appearance of a series of chequers of close and open squares, each close square consisting of twelve solid threads. Strengthen the margin on all sides of the insertion with buttonhole-stitching, taking the stitches four threads deep into the solid linen, in the manner so clearly visible in the illustration. The **stars** are next to be embroidered,—Bring the needle and cotton up in the exact centre of one of the solid linen chequers, insert the needle between the open threads at the corner of the square and bring it up again in the centre and draw through, insert the needle in the

or 36 inches wide, a depth of 10 inches will be sufficient for the bag, as it will be used lengthways, and one selvedge will come at the edge of the flap of the bag and the other selvedge at the top of the opening for the pocket; procure also a piece of pink or blue sateen for lining, 3 yards of binding to sew over the raw edges of the material when making up the bag, 3½ yards of Torchon lace for trimming, a few skeins of white flax-thread or flourishing thread for the drawn work, and some pink or blue flax thread for working the cross-stitch border. You will understand from the illustration how the piece of linen is folded to make the bag, one selvedge is turned up a sufficient distance to afford a good-sized pocket, and the other selvedge is folded down in the position of a flap. The drawn-thread embroidery is executed open threads two threads away from the stitch just made and bring it up again in the centre, and continue taking long stitches at intervals of two threads on each side of the square chequer till twenty-four stitches in all are done, when fasten off neatly; and proceed with similar stars on each of the other chequers. Another piece of drawn-thread insertion is to be executed on the portion of the linen that is intended to be the front of the pocket. When this is done, begin working the cross-stitch pattern upon the

Fig. 60.—Handsome Border, with Corner for a Fancy Tablecloth.

AN evenly woven make of rather coarse white linen may be selected for the tablecloth, or Rhodes linen or flax canvas can be worked upon to produce a pleasing effect; these materials are procurable as wide as 52 inches, but from 36 inches to 45 inches is a fair average size for a cloth for a small fancy table. Calculate the

Fig. 59.—Brush and Comb Bag.

margin of the linen, as shown in the engraving. **To make up the Bag**—Take a piece of sateen for the lining and place it against the wrong side of the linen material, then fold the material into the right shape, and bind the edge all round with binding; lay the head of the lace on the binding and secure the whole in place with a row of feather-stitching.

A nightdress case can be worked to match the comb bag.

depth of solid linen to allow for a margin to be unravelled for fringe, and then begin at the angle of the corner and cut across twenty threads each way in the form of an open square, leave twenty-six threads, and again cut open squares of twenty threads; work buttonhole-stitch closely round the edge of each square, going three threads deep into the solid linen. Make another open square at right angles with these squares, and also make a similar open square in the centre, when, as shown in the engraving, Fig. 60, you will have a block of five open and four solid squares for the corner of the tablecloth ; you will notice the buttonhole-stitching serves two purposes, it strengthens the edge of the five open spaces, and also perfectly outlines the margin of the four solid linen squares, the latter are now to be ornamented with eight long and eight short stitches radiating from the centre in resemblance of a star, in the middle of which a small wheel is darned. Complete the open squares by putting in three foundation threads from corner to corner, and on these work a darning of Point de Reprise in the form of a Greek cross, as is clearly seen in the illustration. For the **Insertion**—Leave intact the four threads that run from the centre of the solid square (these will be in the *middle* of the insertion), and on each side these, and parallel with the buttonhole-stitching, cut across nine threads, leave three threads, cut thirteen, leave three, cut three, and draw the cut threads out to the opposite corner, and you will find six lines of drawn open threads divided by five bars of solid linen. Work hem-stitch on each edge of the insertion, grouping four threads into a cluster, and taking the stitches two threads deep into the margin of the solid linen. Work herringbone along each of the bars of three solid threads, grouping in the narrow insertion the same four threads that are already grouped by the hem-stitching : the clusters of the wide insertion must also stand perpendicularly, and these are afterwards grouped into a single crossing, as Fig. 6, in No. 52 of "Weldon's Practical Needlework Series." The work is now all accomplished excepting the middle bar of four solid threads,—work a row of simple back-stitching straight along the centre of this, taking two threads to each stitch, and at intervals of every four threads, when on a level with the middle of the clusters, make side-stitches branching across each side of the solid bar ; the method of execution is quite clearly delineated in the engraving, and when the scollop-stitches are added the effect is very pretty. The scollop-stitches are worked from left to right, bring the needle and cotton up in the one lowest thread of the bar close by the division of the clusters, * hold the cotton under the left-hand thumb and insert the needle from right to left to take up one cluster of threads, bringing the needle out close below where the cotton springs from and over the cotton that is held by the left-hand thumb, and draw through, and thus make a sort of buttonhole-stitch on the cluster about one-eighth of an inch distant below the bar, now pass the needle upwards under the stitch and draw through to make a perfect "tie," then pass the needle to take up the one lowest thread of the bar close by the next division of the clusters, and repeat from *, keeping the little scollops evenly all along the line ; work similar scollops along the other side of the bar ; and the insertion will be completed.

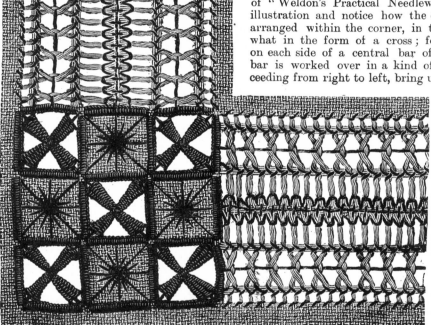

Fig. 60.—**Handsome Border with Corner for a Fancy Tablecloth.**

Fig. 61.—Handsome Corner and Border for a Gipsy Tablecloth.

PROCURE a square of Russian linen or Rhodes linen of the size required for the cloth, also a supply of white or coloured flax-thread for working. Begin by tracing a margin about 4 inches deep all round the piece of material to allow for a fringe and a frame of solid linen outside the border of drawn-thread work. Then proceed

to embroider the several rows of **herringbone-stitching** which, as you will see by the engraving, Fig. 61, run intermediately between the drawn threads. The first row is carried the whole way round the cloth, and you must be very particular to take *two* threads on the needle for each stitch and to leave *two* threads between the stitches, also to embrace three threads in the depth of the herringboning. Leave a space of twenty-four threads, and beginning on the left-hand side close to the outer row of herringboning, work another row, which should stop forty-six threads before you get to the opposite side, where break off the cotton, and resume on the same level at a distance of twenty-two threads, and herringbone twelve stitches to reach to the work already done on the opposite side. Work three other sides of the cloth in the same way. The next row of herringboning corresponds with the row just done from which it is sixteen threads distant. Again resume at a distance of twenty-four threads from the last row, and work from one side to the other side all round the cloth, and thus each corner is completely defined after the manner of the corner shown in the engraving. Now for the **working** of the **corner**—The four open squares which embellish the corners of the large corner square are made by cutting out sixteen threads, the open space is strengthened with buttonhole-stitch and filled with a raised spider, worked as instructed in Fig. 36, No. 53 of "Weldon's Practical Needlework Series." Consult the illustration and notice how the drawn-thread insertion is arranged within the corner, in three separate lines, somewhat in the form of a cross ; four threads are extracted on each side of a central bar of four solid threads, which bar is worked over in a kind of binding-stitch, thus, proceeding from right to left, bring up the needle and cotton in the space between the sixth and seventh threads in the upper insertion · * insert the needle by the first thread and taking six threads on the needle bring up the point in the place where the cotton is and draw through, insert the needle between the third and fourth threads of the lower insertion and take six threads on the needle and draw through, insert the needle again in the same place and bring the point up in the upper insertion six threads to the left of the last stitch and draw through, and repeat from *. The same binding-stitch is worked in the centre insertion on all four sides of the cloth, a little line of six cross-stitches determines the beginning and the end of all the separate rows of the insertions. You now have to work in the spaces where twenty-four threads are left between the rows of herringbone-stitching ; here also the four centre threads are left intact, and eight threads are withdrawn on each side thereof ; both edges of these insertions are embroidered with hem-stitching, grouping two threads in a cluster, and taking the stitches two threads deep into the linen, they therefore come quite close to the herringbone-stitching. The stitch employed to cover the bar in the centre of this insertion is a particularly pretty kind of darning-stitch, and is worked from right to left, in the following manner,— bring up the needle and cotton in the upper insertion in front of the first cluster of threads, pass the needle over the first cluster and take up the second and draw through, pass the needle backwards under the third cluster over the second and under the first and draw through, pass the needle again as you began over the first cluster and under the second and draw through, pass the needle in the little space to the left of the third cluster behind the bar of four solid threads and bring it out to the left of the corresponding cluster in the lower insertion, take another similar perpendicular stitch over the bar, then darn three clusters together on the lower insertion in a similar way, and again cross the bar, and continue thus up and down to the end of the row, when turn the work, and go back, working upon the clusters you before missed; the stitch appears the same on the wrong side of the fabric as on the right side. When the threads of the fabric are unravelled for fringe they should be knotted prettily together, as shown in the towel on page 4 of the present issue.

Fig. 61.—Handsome Corner and Border for a Gipsy Tablecloth.

Fig. 62.—Wide Wheel Pattern Insertion.

THIS handsome wide pattern is composed of three rows of open insertions, the middle row of which is about three times as wide as the upper and lower rows; each insertion is worked quite separately and independently of the other, and a bar of six solid linen threads marks the division between each. Commence first with the **upper insertion**, which occupies eighteen drawn threads, or rather more than half an inch in depth of the material. A peculiar thick stitch is worked along each edge of the insertion in place of the usual hem-stitching—it takes longer to do, but is rather pretty by way of variety. Bring the needle and cotton up at the top left-hand corner, and to bind the open threads into clusters insert the needle to take up the two first threads and with the cotton above the needle draw the needle through, now insert the needle under the stitch just made, with its point towards you, and draw through, which makes a knot clustering two threads together, and continue in the same manner to the end; then do a row of over-sewing upon the row of knot stitches taking up also one thread of the margin of solid linen. For the **Small Wheels**—Work first a row of Punto Tirato knots along the centre of the drawn open threads, binding four clusters of threads together in faggots. Next to form the wheels, make a Punto Tirato knot upon each of the four first clusters above the cotton that passes along the middle of the insertion and about one-third of the distance below the stitching, cross over the middle cotton midway between the faggots, make a Punto Tirato knot upon each of the four next clusters below the middle cotton and about one-third of the distance above the stitching, re-cross the middle cotton, and continue, meandering up and down to the end of the row; the four knots are not made in a perfectly straight line, but are slightly curved, resembling the half of a wheel. Another row is now to be worked in the same way, knotting upon those clusters you before missed, and darning a small ribbed spider on the cotton in the open spaces between the wheels. For the **Middle Insertion**—Extract threads to the depth of one and three-quarter inches, leaving six solid threads below the insertion already worked. Strengthen each edge as in the first insertion but grouping three threads

in a cluster. Then, run a cotton along the exact centre of the insertion, binding eight clusters of threads in a Punto Tirato knot, and be sure to allow a sufficient length of cotton between the knots that the linen may not be puckered at all. Observe in the engraving four parallel lines running above and four below the central line, making altogether nine lines along the drawn open threads. The second line is placed within a little distance of the centre line, and is formed by working two knots, each confining four clusters of threads above the one knot of the first line, then cross the central line, and work two knots below the one knot of the next pattern, re-cross, and proceed up and down; and when this line is finished a similar line is worked, forming knots upon those clusters missed in the preceding line. The fourth line produces three knots above the two knots of the first pattern, interlacing the threads as shown in the illustration, it crosses over the central line, and forms three knots below the two knots of the second pattern, then re-crosses, and continues in the same way to the end; and the fifth line corresponds by knotting upon the clusters missed in the line preceding. The sixth line runs perfectly straight from end to end of the insertion about midway between the central line and the edge, and four knots are worked on each pattern, grouping six threads in each knot. The seventh line is carried along in the same way on the opposite side of the insertion. The eighth line is commenced by making a knot on the crossing of the cotton at the beginning of the row, a knot on the sixth line of cotton, five knots on the first pattern grouping the clusters as in the engraving, a knot on the sixth line of cotton, then cross the central line and do the same on the next pattern on the lower side of the insertion, re-cross the central line, and continue in the same way up and down to the end of the row. The ninth row is worked to correspond. The ribbed wheels are made by darning under and over each of the threads that cross and re-cross in the open spaces between the patterns; begin in the exact centre, pass the needle under two cottons, * pass it again under the last cotton and also under the next following, and repeat from * round and round, till the wheel is sufficiently large,

Fig. 62.—Wide Wheel Pattern Insertion.

when fasten off, and the spokes will appear high and ribbed, as shown in the illustration. And now the middle insertion will be finished. Leave a bar of six linen threads, and work the lower insertion to correspond with the upper.

Fig. 63.—D'Oyley worked in Single Crossing, Star-Stitch, and Coral-Stitch.

THE d'oyley from which our illustration is taken is made of rather fine Irish linen, and measures 6½ inches square, inclusive of fringe. The pattern can easily be worked to whatever size is desired. Prepare the material for working, by first of all marking out a margin 1½ inches deep all round the material, which margin is to form a solid edge of linen outside the drawn work, and also partly to unravel for fringe. Inside the margin the threads are to be arranged thus,—Draw out fourteen threads, leave twenty-four

will not interfere with the drawn open threads, but will only affect the size of the plain linen in the centre of the d'oyley. Work the drawn open insertions in Single Crossing (see Fig. 6 in No 52 of "Weldon's Practical Needlework Series," crossing three threads over four. Work coral-stitch on the bars of solid linen between the drawn threads, as represented in the engraving. Work a star on each of the four solid squares in the corners of the d'oyley, thus,— Pierce a hole with a stiletto in the centre of each of the solid squares, secure the cotton at the back and bring it up in the centre hole, insert the needle at the corner of the square and take up six threads from right to left and draw the cotton through,

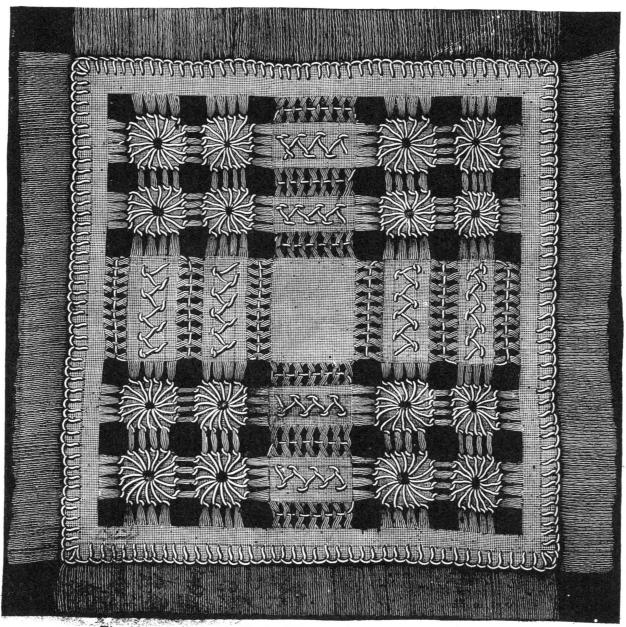

Fig. 63.—D'Oyley worked in Single Crossing, Star-Stitch, and Coral-Stitch

threads, draw out fourteen, leave twenty-four, draw out fourteen, leave forty-nine, draw out fourteen, leave twenty-four, draw out fourteen, leave twenty-four, draw out fourteen. The drawn out threads are of course to be cut away inside the margin or frame of solid linen; the method of doing this has been explained in Fig. 17 and Fig. 22 in No. 52 of "Weldon's Practical Needlework Series." Be careful to count your threads correctly before venturing to cut them, and if on account of difference in the size of the article you intend working the above numeration does not fit in nicely, make the alteration in the *middle of each side* of the material, leaving more or less than the forty-nine, as required : this

insert the needle in the same place as it was inserted before and bring it up in the centre of the square, insert the needle to take up six more threads of open insertion and draw the cotton through, insert the needle again in the same place and bring it up in the centre of the square, and continue, taking up six threads all round the margin of the square, fastening off neatly when complete. When the whole of the insertions are finished, work a line of button-hole-stitching about one inch from the outside of the material, this is to strengthen the edge, and the spare inch is to be unravelled to form fringe. Evans's crochet cotton No. 4 is used for working the model d'oyley, but flax-thread or flourishing thread may be employed if desired

WELDON'S
PRACTICAL NETTING.

(FOURTH SERIES.)

HOW TO NET A NIGHTDRESS CASE, COMB BAG, BILLIARD-BALL POCKET, EAR-CAPS FOR A HORSE, D'OYLEYS, &c.

TWENTY-ONE ILLUSTRATIONS.

The Yearly Subscription to this Magazine, post free to any Part of the World, is 2s. 6d.
Subscriptions are payable in advance, and may commence from any date and for any period.

The Back Numbers are always in print. Nos. 1 to 110 *now ready, Price* 2d. *each, postage* ½d. *Over 5,000 Engravings.*

BAG FOR HOLDING LEMONS.

THIS is a useful bag to have in a kitchen to hold lemons, onions, turnips, &c. The original is made with ordinary red Scotch fingering, but a stronger bag can be netted with pretty variegated twine or with macramé thread. Begin at the bottom of the bag, and using a ¼-inch flat bone mesh, put 18 stitches on a foundation, and tie in a circle, and net round and round. **1st round**—Plain. **2nd round**—Increase in every third loop. Net 2 rounds plain. **5th round**—Increase in every third loop Net 2 rounds plain. And continue thus till the bag attains the circumference you desire it to be, when work all plain netting for about 20 rounds When sufficient is netted to reach the top of the bag, net 1 round taking 2 loops together in 1 stitch, and then 1 plain round. Then take a ½-inch flat mesh, and net 1 round increasing 2 stitches in each loop; and 2 rounds quite plain netting; this will form the frill at the mouth of the bag. Work 2 lengths of crochet chain and run it in double through the last round of the ¼-inch netting to draw up the top of the bag, and to hang it up by. A piece of crinoline steel run through the netting halfway up the bag will expand it into a convenient shape. Finish off the bag with a tassel at the bottom as shown in the engraving

---

BORDER IN DARNED NETTING.

THIS pretty border can be made useful for a variety of purposes. The netting is executed with Coats' crochet cotton No. 12, a flat bone mesh measuring ¼ inch or ⅜ inch wide, and two steel knitting needles, No. 14 and No. 18. Knitting cotton No. 12 is employed for the darning. Begin with crochet cotton and a No. 14 steel needle, and put on sufficient stitches for the length of the border, and net 20 plain rows on which afterwards to darn the pattern as seen in the engraving. **21st row**—With ¼-inch flat mesh,—Net 3 stitches in each loop all along the row. **22nd row**—With No 18 mesh,—

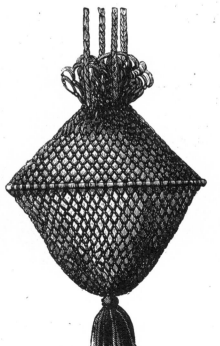

Bag for Holding Lemons.

Net 1 stitch in each loop. **23rd row**—The same. **24th row**—With ¼-inch mesh,—Net 1 stitch in each loop to the end of the row. **25th row**—With No. 14 mesh,—Take 3 loops on the needle and net them together in 1 stitch, and proceed in the same manner all along the row. **26th row**—With the same mesh,—Plain netting. **27th row**—The same; and fasten off. The darned pattern is now to be copied from the engraving and worked along the centre of the twenty plain rows of netting. Many handsome designs in Darned Netting are illustrated in No. 28 of "Weldon's Practical Needlework Series," price 2d. of all booksellers, post free 2½d. from this office.

OPEN PATTERN FOR LONG WINDOW-CURTAINS.

LONG window-curtains, netted in the pattern shown in our illustration, may be very quickly and easily made, as coarse cotton is used and the work is very open, the curtains look very nice when up, and are durable, lasting for many years. Required 1 lb. or more of Strutt's crochet cotton, No. 6, which is almost as thick as a small piping cord, and several skeins of Ardern's crochet cotton, No. 0; also 5 flat bone meshes, measuring respectively 1¼-inch, 1-inch, ½-inch, ¼-inch, and ⅛-inch wide. Commence with any number of stitches with the coarse cotton and the ½-inch mesh, and calculating for the length of the curtain; about from 50 stitches to 60 stitches will make a yard length. **2nd row**—With the same mesh,—Plain netting. **3rd row**—With the 1-inch mesh and Ardern's cotton,—Work 3 stitches in every loop to the end of the row. **4th row**—With the ⅛ mesh and Ardern's cotton, — Plain netting. **5th row** — The same. **6th row** — With 1-inch mesh and Ardern's cotton,—Plain netting. **7th row**—With ½-inch mesh and coarse cotton,—Take up 3 loops together and net them in 1 stitch, and the same all along. **8th row**—With the same mesh and cotton,—Plain netting. Repeat from the third row to the eighth row inclusive until the curtain is the desired width. When it is sufficiently wide, break off the cotton, and along the foundation row of the netting, work **1st row**—With the 1-inch mesh and Ardern's cotton,—3 stitches into each loop. **2nd row**—With ⅛-inch mesh and Ardern's cotton,—Plain netting, 1 stitch in each loop. **3rd row**—The same, and fasten off. **For the Border**—This border is worked along the top and bottom and down the front of the curtain—*i.e.*, on the side where you first left off netting, and not on the side where you last of all netted, which is the back of the curtain. **1st row**—With 1¼-inch mesh and

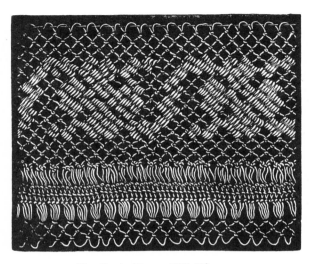

Border in Darned Netting.

Ardern's cotton,—Net 7 stitches altogether in one loop, miss 3 loops, and repeat; the groups of 7 stitches will come into the coarse cotton rows at the top and at the bottom of the curtain. **2nd row**—With ¼-inch mesh and Ardern's cotton,—Net 1 stitch in each of the 6 long loops, and net 1 stitch in the centre loop of the 3 that were missed when working last row, embracing the stitch of last row under the knot. **3rd row**—With the same mesh and cotton,—Plain netting.

EAR-CAPS FOR A HORSE.

THE pair of ear-caps represented in our engraving are most valuable for horses to wear in summer as a preventive to keep flies from their ears, for it is well known that flies will not attempt to pass through the meshes of a net. The model ear-caps are worked with white crochet cotton, Ardern's No. 1, but brown or red cotton can be employed if preferred, and two flat bone meshes, ¼ inch and ⅛ inch wide, are required. Commence by making 6 stitches on a foundation with the ⅛-inch mesh, and tie in a circle, and do 2 rounds of plain netting. **4th round**—Increase by netting 2 stitches in the first loop, net the remainder of the round plain. **5th round**—Increase over the last increase, net the remainder of the round plain. **6th round**—With ¼-inch mesh,—Net 2 stitches into every loop. **7th round**—With ⅛-inch mesh,—Take 2 stitches together on the needle and net them in 1 stitch, and continue in the same way to the end of the round. Net 3 plain rounds, making an increase in each round, over the increase that was previously made. Repeat from the sixth round 8 times, when you will have 50 rounds netted, which is a sufficient length for a cap: fasten off. Make the other ear-cap in the same way. Then proceed for the **Band** which passes across the horse's forehead and connects the two ear-caps together. **1st row**—With ⅛-inch mesh,—Put on 15 stitches. Net 3 plain rows. **5th row**—With ¼-inch mesh,—Net 2 stitches into every loop. **6th row**—With ⅛-inch mesh,—Take 2 stitches together and net them in 1 stitch, and continue the same to the end of the row. Repeat the last two rows 6 times. Then work 4 plain rows as you began. Sew one end of this band to fit against the six centre loops on the *straight* side of the last round of one of the ear-caps, and the other end of the band in the same position on the other ear-cap. Make an ornamental chain of Macramé "double or single knotting,"

if you know it, both stitches being illustrated on page 4, and described on page 5 of No. 7 of "Weldon's Practical Needlework Series," price 2d. of all booksellers, or post free for 2½d. from this office. Otherwise do a simple crochet chain; one piece three inches in length is required for the top of each ear, and two pieces each three inches in length for the bottom of each ear, and these latter chains are knotted together at half their length and then again the plaits are separate; six thick tassels are then to be made, and affixed to the chain as shown in the engraving.

OVAL D'OYLEY EDGED WITH NETTED SHELLS.

THE centre of this d'oyley is composed of an oval of spotted damask linen, measuring 8½ inches long by 5½ inches wide, it is machine stitched with a narrow hem, inside which a round of triple feather-stitching is embroidered with the same sized crochet cotton as that used for the netted edging. The edging is in resemblance of shells; each shell is netted separately, and when all are complete they are sewn to the damask linen centre as represented in the engraving. These d'oyleys are always much admired, and they form a very pleasing adjunct to a dessert-table or to a five-o'clock tea. Procure 2 skeins of Coats' crochet cotton, No. 20, one flat bone mesh ¾ inch wide, and a No. 16 and a No. 17 steel knitting needle. For the **first shell**—Tie a piece of cotton in a circle and pin it to the knee, and with the flat bone mesh net 28 stitches in it; then withdraw the mesh, and *turn* the work, and net in little rows forwards and backwards. **2nd row**—With the No. 17 mesh,—Plain netting, 1 stitch in each long loop of the first row. Work 2 more rows the same. **5th row**—With ¾-inch mesh,—

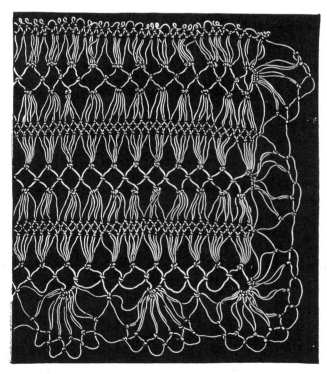

Open Pattern for Long Window-Curtains.

Net 2 stitches into every loop of the preceding row. Net 3 plain rows with No. 17 mesh. **9th row**—With No. 16 mesh,—Net 1 stitch into every alternate loop, and break the cotton off at the end of the row: also break the cotton of the foundation and tie it in a smaller circle, and cut off the tag ends; this finishes one shell. Eight shells are required to go round the d'oyley. When they all are complete, pin them round the damask, arranging them as you wish them to lie, with the end of one shell overlapping about half-an-inch over the adjoining shell, and sew the shells neatly and securely to the margin of the damask.

PLATE D'OYLEY.

THIS is a pretty fancy net d'oyley for a cheese plate or cake dish. Required 2 reels of Evans' crochet cotton, No. 8, a skein of Strutt's No. 12 knitting cotton, and 2 flat bone meshes, measuring $\frac{3}{8}$-inch and $\frac{1}{8}$-inch. Commence with knitting cotton and $\frac{3}{8}$-inch mesh, and for the **1st round** put 30 stitches on a cotton foundation, and tie round. **2nd round**—With crochet cotton and $\frac{1}{8}$-inch mesh,—Net every 3 loops of last round together in 1 stitch, making 10 tufts of stitches for the centre of the d'oyley, and 10 netted stitches in the round. **3rd round**—With knitting cotton and $\frac{3}{8}$-inch mesh,—Work 3 stitches in every loop, 30 stitches in the round.

Ear-Caps for a Horse

4th round—With crochet cotton and $\frac{1}{8}$-inch mesh,—Plain netting. **5th round**—The same. **6th round**—With crochet cotton and $\frac{3}{8}$-inch mesh,—Net 1 stitch in each alternate loop. **7th round**—With knitting cotton and $\frac{3}{8}$-inch mesh,—Net 4 stitches into each loop of last round, and so make 15 bunches of stitches in the round. **8th round**—With crochet cotton and $\frac{1}{8}$-inch mesh, —Plain netting. **9th round**—The same. **10th round**—With crochet cotton and $\frac{3}{8}$-inch mesh,—Net 1 stitch in each alternate loop. **11th round**—With knitting cotton and $\frac{3}{8}$-inch mesh,—Net 4 stitches into every loop of last round, and so make 30 bunches of stitches in the round. **12th round**—With crochet cotton and $\frac{1}{8}$-inch mesh,—Plain netting. **13th round**—The same. **14th round**—With crochet cotton and $\frac{3}{8}$-inch mesh,— Plain netting. **15th round**—With crochet cotton and $\frac{1}{4}$-inch mesh,—Grecian netting. The stitch of Grecian netting is clearly illustrated on page 12, and fully explained on page 8 of No. 21 "Weldon's Practical Needlework Series," and is so well known by most netters that it need not be again explained here. **16th round**—With the same cotton and mesh,—Work in plain netting. **17th round**—With crochet cotton and $\frac{3}{8}$-inch mesh,—Net 1 stitch in each alternate loop. **18th round**—With knitting cotton and $\frac{3}{8}$-inch mesh,—Work 4 stitches into every loop of last round, and so make 60 tufts in the round. **19th round**—With crochet cotton and $\frac{1}{8}$-inch mesh,—Plain netting. **20th round**— The same. **21st round**—With crochet cotton and $\frac{3}{8}$-inch mesh,— Plain netting. **22nd round**—With crochet cotton and $\frac{1}{4}$-inch mesh,—Grecian netting. **23rd round**—Same as the 21st round. **24th round**—Same as the 22nd round. **25th round**—Again with the same cotton and mesh,—Plain netting; and, fasten off at the end of the round. For the **Points**—Still use crochet cotton and the $\frac{1}{8}$-inch mesh,—Tie the end of the cotton to a loop of the netting, work 15 stitches; turn, work 14 stitches; turn, work 13 stitches; turn, work 12 stitches; and so on doing

1 stitch less each time of turning, till you net only 1 stitch at the top of the point, and fasten off. Then, leaving one stitch of last row, tie the cotton on again, and proceed with another point; and continue till 14 points in all are worked round the d'oyley. Darn a little arrow-head pattern with knitting cotton, in every point, as shown in the engraving.

ROUND CHEESE-CLOTH.

REQUIRED, 2 reels of Evans' crochet cotton, No. 16, a few skeins of white flourishing thread, and flat bone meshes measuring $\frac{1}{2}$-inch, $\frac{3}{8}$-inch, and $\frac{1}{4}$-inch, and knitting needles No. 12 and No. 16. Begin in the centre of the cheese cloth with crochet cotton and the $\frac{3}{8}$-inch mesh, and make 36 stitches on a foundation, and join round. **2nd round**—With No. 16 mesh,—Plain netting. **3rd round**— The same. **4th round**—With No. 12 mesh,—Plain netting. **5th round**—The same. **6th round**—With $\frac{1}{4}$-inch mesh,—Net 4 stitches in each alternate loop, making 18 groups of 4 stitches in the round. Net 3 plain rounds with the No. 16 mesh. Net 5 plain rounds with No. 12 mesh. **15th round**—With the $\frac{3}{8}$-inch mesh, —Net 4 stitches in each alternate loop, making 36 groups of four stitches in the round. Net 4 plain rounds with No. 16 mesh. Net 10 plain rounds with No. 12 mesh. **30th round**—With flourishing thread and the $\frac{1}{2}$-inch mesh,—Net 3 stitches in every loop all the way round. **31st round**—With cotton and No. 16 mesh,— Plain netting 1 stitch in each loop. **32nd round**—The same. **33rd round**—With No. 12 mesh,—Net 1 stitch in each of 3 successive loops, miss one loop, and repeat the same. **34th round**— With the same mesh,—Net 1 stitch in each of 2 successive loops, miss the loop over the missed loop of last round, and repeat. **35th round**—With flourishing thread and $\frac{1}{4}$-inch mesh,—Net 1 stitch in one loop, miss the loop over the loop missed in the previous rounds, and repeat; fasten off at the end of this round. Now with the flourishing thread darn the pattern as shown in the engraving; and on completion you will have an elegant cloth to lay under a cheese or in a cake basket.

Oval D'Oyley edged with Netted Shells.

NIGHTCAP.

OUR illustration shows a nicely fitting nightcap for a lady worked in netting and darning. Procure 2 skeins of Coats' crochet cotton, No. 10, and two flat bone meshes measuring respectively $\frac{5}{16}$ inch and $\frac{3}{16}$ inch, or otherwise two steel knitting needles No. 13 and No. 15, also 1 skein of Strutt's No. 10 knitting cotton which is only required for the darning. Begin with crochet cotton, by making 22 stitches on a cotton foundation with the largest mesh, tie the foundation in a circle for the centre of the crown, and net round and round, doing 4 rounds of all plain netting with the smallest mesh. **5th round**—With the largest mesh,—Net 5 stitches in each loop, and there should be 22 bunches of 5 stitches in the round.

6th round—With the smallest mesh,—Plain netting. **7th round**—The same. **8th round**—With the largest mesh,—Plain netting. **9th round**—Take up 4 loops together on the needle and net them in 1 stitch, net 1 stitch in the next loop, and repeat; the four loops that are grouped together are always to come exactly over the five loops below. **10th round**—Still with the smallest mesh,—Net 2 stitches in every loop. Then net 5 plain rounds. **16th round**—With the largest mesh,—Net 6 stitches in one loop, net 1 stitch in each of 3 consecutive loops, and repeat. **17th round**—With the smallest mesh,—Plain netting, 1 stitch in each loop. **18th round**—The same. **19th round**—With the largest mesh,—Plain netting. **20th round**—With the smallest mesh,—Take up the 6 loops together and net them in 1 stitch, net 3 consecutive plain stitches, and repeat. **21st**

For the **Border**—**1st row**—With the smallest mesh,—Net 2 stitches in every loop all along the row. **2nd row**—Net plain and always insert the needle into the upright loop of last row and miss the other loop. **3rd row**—Plain netting into the loops of last row. Net 2 plain rows. **6th row**—With the largest mesh,—Net 3 stitches into every loop *all round* the cap. Work with the smallest mesh 2 rows of plain netting all round the cap. Repeat the last 3 rows of the border to make a frill along the front of the cap, netting 3 stitches into those loops of the first border row that you previously missed, and fasten off. Darn a little pattern with the knitting cotton upon the five plain net rounds and upon the eighteen plain net rows, as shown in the engraving; and run in tapes to keep the cap in shape, and put on strings to tie under the chin.

Plate D'Oyley.

round—Still with the smallest mesh,—Plain netting. **22nd round**—The same. **23rd round**—Which also forms the **1st row** of the **Head**—Still with the smallest mesh,—Net plain along till you come to within 22 loops of the end of the round, leave those unworked to form the back of the cap, and turn the work, and henceforth work in rows, doing 18 plain rows. **19th row**—With the largest mesh,—Net 2 stitches plain, net 4 stitches in the next loop, and repeat. **20th row**—With the smallest mesh,—Plain netting. **21st row**—The same. **22nd row**—With the largest mesh,—Plain netting. **23rd row**—With the smallest mesh,—Net 2 stitches plain, net the 4 loops together in one stitch, and repeat. **24th row**—With the smallest mesh,—Plain netting.

NIGHTDRESS CASE.

THIS nightdress case, with the comb and brush bag to match, is a very useful and pretty accessory for a young lady's toilet; both articles are quite easy to make, and will wash and wear well. Procure 6 skeins of Coats' white crochet cotton, No. 12; 3 flat bone meshes, measuring respectively $\frac{1}{2}$-inch, $\frac{1}{4}$-inch, and $\frac{1}{8}$-inch wide; and half a yard of red Turkey twill for lining, as well as 2 yards of inch wide red ribbon for bag strings. Begin at the bottom of the back of the nightdress case, by putting 100 stitches on a foundation thread with the $\frac{1}{8}$-inch mesh, and net 16 plain rows. **17th row**—With $\frac{1}{2}$-inch mesh,—Plain netting. **18th row**—With $\frac{1}{4}$-inch mesh,—Take up 2 loops together on the needle and net them as 1 stitch, and the same all along, and there will be 50 stitches in this row. **19th row**—With the same mesh,—Plain netting. **20th row**—With $\frac{1}{2}$-inch mesh,—Net 2 stitches in every loop all along the row, which restores the original number of 100 stitches. Net 16 plain rows with the $\frac{1}{8}$-inch mesh. Work the 4 open rows as before. Again net 16 plain rows with the $\frac{1}{8}$-inch mesh. Again work the 4 open rows as before. Net 6 plain rows with the $\frac{1}{8}$-inch mesh. And now begin **shaping the Flap**— **1st row**—Work with the $\frac{1}{8}$-inch mesh in plain netting. **2nd row** —With $\frac{1}{4}$-inch mesh,—Take 2 loops together on the needle and net them in 1 stitch, and repeat the same to the end of the row. **3rd row**—With the same mesh,—Plain netting, and omit 2 loops at the end of the row. **4th row**—With $\frac{1}{2}$-inch mesh,—Net 2 stitches in every loop, and omit 2 loops at the end of the row. Work 4 plain rows with $\frac{1}{8}$-inch, always omitting two loops at

together and net them as 1 stitch, and repeat. **3rd round**— With the same mesh,—Plain netting. **4th round**—With $\frac{1}{2}$-inch mesh,—Net 3 stitches in each loop, and make whatever increase is needed at the corners. **5th round**—With $\frac{1}{8}$-inch mesh,—Plain netting **6th round**—The same. **7th round**—With $\frac{1}{8}$-inch mesh,—Net 1 stitch in each of 5 consecutive loops, miss one loop, and repeat the same; the loop that is missed must be a loop over one of the open spaces between the groups. **8th round**—Net 1 stitch in each of 4 successive loops, miss the loop over the missed loop of last row. **9th round**—Net 1 stitch in each of 3 successive loops, cotton round the mesh, and miss the loop over the missed loop of the preceding row. **10th round**—Net 1 stitch in each of 2 loops, cotton twice round the mesh and miss the loop over the missed loop of last row; and fasten off, this finishes the border. Make up the lining for the nightdress case, and arrange the netting

Round Cheese-Cloth.

the end of each row. Repeat the 4 open rows, omitting 2 or 3 loop at the end of every row. Net 3 plain rows with $\frac{1}{8}$-inch mesh, omitting 2 or 3 loops at the end of each row; and fasten off; this is the end of the flap. For the **Front** of the **Nightdress Case**—Re-commence, and work as for the back, until you get two complete lines of the open netting, and three plain rows of the third line of sixteen plain rows, when fasten off. The front of the nightdress case must be laid level with the back piece, and both be sewn together, the two commencing rows forming the bottom of the case. And now proceed to work the netted **Border** all round the case, taking the needle into both pieces of netting where, along the edge, the work lies double. **1st round**—With $\frac{1}{2}$-inch mesh,—Work 2 stitches into each loop of the netting, and ease at the corners by doing 4 stitches into one or two corner loops. **2nd round**—With $\frac{1}{4}$-inch mesh,—Take up 2 loops

tastefully on it, as shown in the engraving. Put a button and a loop on the flap of the nightdress case to prevent it coming open when not wanted to be open.

SLEEPING CAP.

THIS cap is worked in fancy netting, and is light and comfortable for sleeping. Procure 2 ozs. of Strutt's knitting cotton, No. 10; three flat bone meshes measuring respectively $\frac{1}{2}$-inch, $\frac{3}{8}$-inch, and $\frac{1}{4}$-inch, and two steel knitting needles, No. 12, and No. 14. Begin for the centre of the crown by making 18 stitches on a cotton foundation over the $\frac{3}{8}$-inch mesh, and join in a round. **2nd round** —With No. 14 steel mesh,—Work plain 1 stitch in each loop. **3rd round**—With No. 12 mesh,—Net 1 stitch in each loop, and there should be 18 stitches in the round. **4th round**—With

$\frac{3}{8}$-inch mesh,—Net 8 stitches in one loop, miss one loop, and repeat; and get 9 groups of stitches in the round. Work 4 plain rounds with No. 14 mesh, and 4 plain rounds with No. 12 mesh. **13th round**—With $\frac{1}{4}$-inch mesh,—Leaf netting,—Net 3 stitches in one loop for a leaf, also 3 stitches in the next loop, then net 1 stitch in each of 6 consecutive loops, and repeat the same. **14th round**—With the same mesh,—Plain, and gather the leaf stitches as one loop. **15th round**—Leaf netting,—Work 1 stitch in each of 6 consecutive loops, 3 stitches in one loop for a leaf, and 3 stitches in the next loop, and repeat; these leaf stitches are to come intermediate between the leaves formed in the thirteenth round. **16th round**—Plain, and gather the leaf stitches as one loop. Net 2 plain rounds. **19th round**—With $\frac{3}{8}$-inch mesh,—Net, 5 stitches in one loop, net 1 stitch in each of the two next loops, and repeat. Net 2 plain rounds with No. 14 mesh. **22nd round**—With $\frac{3}{8}$-inch mesh,—Plain netting. **23rd round**—With $\frac{1}{4}$-inch mesh,—Net the 5 increased loops all together in 1 stitch, net 1 stitch in each of the two next loops, and repeat. **24th round**—With the same mesh,—Plain netting. **25th round**—Which also forms the 1st row of the Head—Use the $\frac{3}{8}$-inch mesh,—Net 1 stitch in each of two loops, * net 5 stitches in the loop over the previous bunch of five stitches, net 1 stitch in each of the two intermediate loops, and repeat from *; and at the end of this round leave six bunches of stitches unworked for the back of the cap, and henceforth work in rows backwards and forwards for the head.

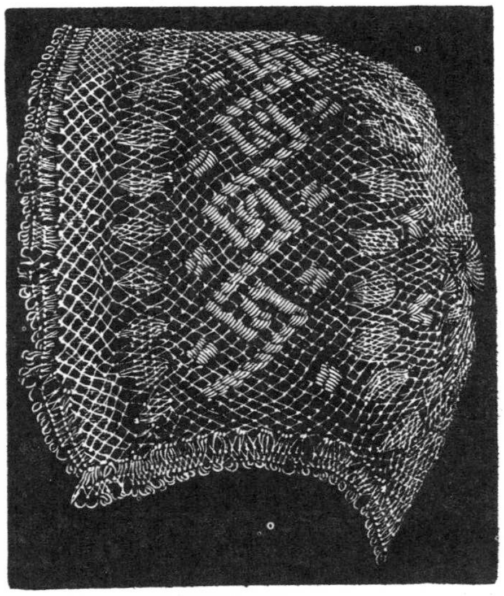

Nightcap.

2nd row—With No. 14 mesh,—Plain netting. **3rd row**—The same. **4th row**—With $\frac{3}{8}$-inch mesh,—Plain netting. **5th row**.—With $\frac{1}{4}$-inch mesh,—Net 1 stitch in each of two consecutive loops, * net the 5 increased loops all together in 1 stitch, net 1 stitch in each of the two next loops, and repeat from*. **6th row**—With the same mesh,—Plain netting. Repeat the last 6 rows. **13th row**—Still with $\frac{1}{4}$-inch mesh—Net 2 stitches into each loop. **14th row**—Net plain, and always insert the needle into the upright loop of last row and miss the other loop. **15th row**—Plain netting into each loop of the preceding row. Now for the **Border: 1st round**—With $\frac{1}{2}$-inch mesh,—Net 2 stitches into each loop all round the cap. **2nd round**—With No. 14 mesh,—Plain netting, increasing a stitch or two on turning the corners. **3rd round**—With No. 12 mesh,—Plain netting. **4th round**—With $\frac{1}{4}$-inch mesh,—Net 1 stitch in each alternate loop all round the cap, and fasten off. Repeat the same 4 rows of border to make a frill along the front of the cap, working the first row into the loops of the thirteenth row that you previously missed, putting 3 stitches into each loop instead of two that the frill may be full. Run a piece of narrow tape into each of the open rows immediately preceding the long stitches of the border, and also run a tape to pass round the back of the cap, securing these all firmly together at the corners with a few stitches. Finish the cap with strings, which can be made of a narrow piece of muslin, or of a strip of plain netting.

BRUSH AND COMB BAG.

Work this comb bag to match the nightdress case. Begin at the bottom of one side of the bag, and with the $\frac{1}{8}$-inch mesh put 60 stitches on a foundation, and net 20 plain rows. Net 4 open rows as instructed in the directions of the nightdress case. Net 18 plain rows with the small mesh. Net 4 more open rows. Net 18 more plain rows, and fasten off. Make the other half of the bag in the same manner. Sew the two pieces together, having the commencing rows at the bottom of the bag, and joining the open rows on the sides quite evenly. Net a border all round the bag in the same way as the border is already worked round the nightdress case. The lining is cut to fit the netting, it has a deep hem at the top with a double running to contain a drawing string, or rather ribbon, to confine the mouth of the bag.

DESIGN IN DARNED NETTING.

For a Splasher, a Short Window Blind, or Antimacassar.

This is an effective design for netting and darning. If for a splasher the work should be mounted on a coloured lining. The

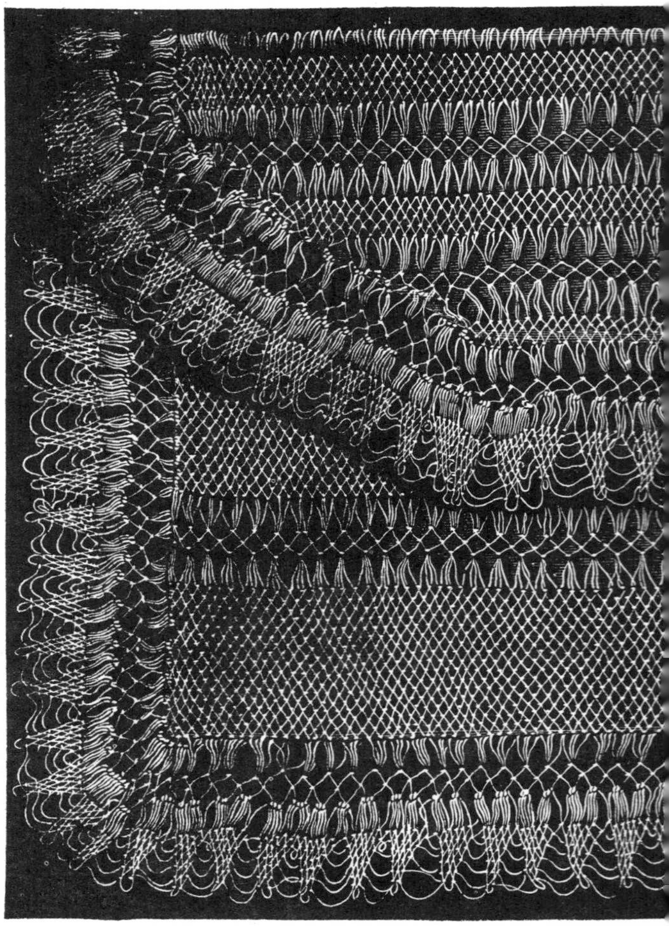

Nig

same pattern is appropriate for an antimacassar to spread over a box ottoman, and may also be used for window blinds. The ground is worked with Coats' crochet cotton, No. 10, and a flat bone mesh, about $\frac{1}{4}$-inch wide. Commence according to the instructions given for "Square," or "Oblong" Netting, in No. 21, Vol. 2, of "Weldon's Practical Needlework Series," and increase a stitch at the end of every row, till you have produced the *width* the article is desired to be; and now by decreasing a stitch on the short side of the netting, and increasing a stitch on the long side, alternately, you *keep it* the same width till the netting is as *long* as required; when you finish it off by squaring the corner. The whole process of doing this is fully explained in the number referred to above, which contains all the preliminary details and instructions in netting. When the foundation is finished, damp it and stretch it, ironing it if necessary, and proceed to darn the pattern with Strutt's No. 12 knitting cotton, being careful to make the stitches all run in the same direction, and lie smoothly and evenly on the meshes of the netting. All four corners are intended to be worked alike, and the sides may be filled in with as many "Scrolls" as the netting will admit, making them meet nicely together in the middle of each side. The centre of the splasher, or antimacassar, is filled with a number of small darned "spots" arranged as a powdering.

OBLONG TRAY CLOTH.

For this pretty cloth you will require 3 or 4 skeins of Coats' crochet cotton, No. 14, and three flat bone meshes measuring respectively ½-inch, ¼-inch, and ⅛-inch wide. Begin for the centre of the cloth by putting 30 stitches on a foundation with the ¼-inch mesh, or as many stitches as will make a cloth of the desired size, any even number, and work in "Honeycomb" netting, which is explained in No. 21 of "Weldon's Practical Needlework Series," and also illustrated with an engraving in full working size. When

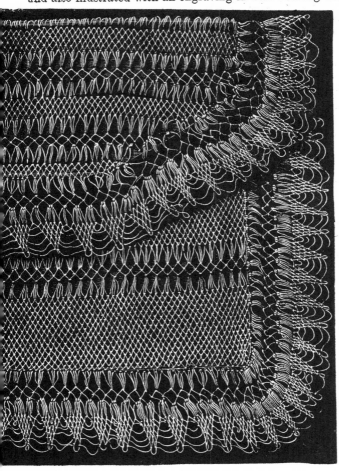

age.

your piece of honeycomb netting is sufficiently large for the centre of the tray-cloth a border is to be netted all round it. For the **Border—1st round**—With ⅛-inch mesh,—Work plain netting all round the centre, putting the stitches in moderately close, yet not to be too full, and make 6 stitches in each of the corners loops to turn easily. Net 3 plain rounds with the same mesh. **5th round** —With ¼-inch mesh,—Plain netting, and increase two or three stitches at each corner. **6th round**—With ⅛-inch mesh,—Plain netting. **7th round**—With the same mesh,—Net 5 plain stitches, net 3 stitches in the next loop, and repeat the same. **8th round**—Net 4 plain stitches, net 3 stitches in the loop in front of the tuft of stitches of last round, net 3 stitches in the next loop, and repeat. **9th round**—Net 3 plain stitches, net 3 stitches in the loop in front of the first tuft of the preceding round; net three

stitches in each of the next two loops, and repeat. **10th round** —Plain netting, and increase at the corners. **11th round**— With ¼-inch mesh,—Net 3 stitches in every loop all round the tray-cloth. **12th round**—With the same mesh,—Take 5 loops together on the needle and net them in 1 stitch, net 1 stitch in the next loop (which is an open loop between the knots), and repeat the same, and so bring the extra loops into the similitude of "leaf" netting. Repeat the last 2 rounds three times. Then net 2 plain rounds with the same mesh. **21st round**—With ½-inch mesh,— Net 8 stitches in one loop, miss one loop, and repeat. **22nd round**—With ⅛-inch mesh,—Net 1 stitch in each of the tall upright loops of the previous round, draw the cotton that passes from group to group *through* the loop that was missed in last round and net a stitch in it, and repeat. **23rd round**—Plain netting with the same mesh. **24th round**—With ¼-inch mesh, —Net 1 stitch in each alternate loop of last round; and this completes the tray-cloth.

DIAMOND PATTERN BORDER.

This pretty diamond pattern border is worked in close fine netting with Evans' crochet cotton, No. 14, a round steel mesh No. 15, and a flat bone mesh ½-inch wide. **1st row**—With No. 15 mesh,—Put stitches on a foundation for the length of the border

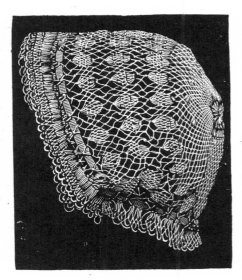

Sleeping Cap.

from end to end, any number divisible by 5. **2nd row**—With the same mesh,—Plain netting. **3rd row**—With ½-inch mesh,— Net 2 stitches in every loop. **4th row**—With No. 15 mesh,— Take up two loops together and net them in one stitch, and work the same all along. **5th row**—With the same mesh,—Plain netting. **6th row**—Begin the diamond,—Net 1 stitch in each of the 2 first loops, * net 3 stitches in the next loop, net 1 stitch in each of 4 successive loops, and repeat from * to the end of the row, where will be only 2 loops to net plain. **7th row**—Net 1 stitch in the first loop, * net 3 stitches in the next loop, 3 stitches in the next loop, and 1 stitch in each of 3 successive loops, and repeat from *, and at the end of the row there will be only 2 loops to net plain; the little tufts in this row must come one on each side of the tuft of the preceding row to widen the diamond. **8th row**—Net 1 stitch in the first loop, * net 3 stitches in each of 3 successive loops to widen the diamond, net 1 stitch in each of the 2 intermediate loops, and repeat from * to the end of the row, when there will be only 1 stitch to net plain. **9th row**—Net 3 stitches in each of 4 successive loops to widen the diamond, net 1 plain stitch, and repeat the same to the end of the row. **10th row**—Net 3 stitches in every loop in succession to the end of the row; this is the centre of the diamond. **11th row**—Net 3 stitches in each of 4 successive loops, net 1 stitch plain and repeat the same to the end of the row. **12th row**—Net 1 stitch in the first loop, * net 3 stitches in each of

3 successive loops, net 1 stitch in each of 2 intermediate loops between the diamonds, and repeat from *, and at the end of the row there will be only 1 stitch to net plain. **13th row**—Net 1 stitch in the first loop, * net 3 stitches in each of 2 loops, net 1 stitch in each of 3 intermediate loops between the diamonds, and repeat from * to the end of the row, where will be 2 plain stitches to net. **14th row**— Net 1 stitch in each of the 2 first loops, * net 3 stitches in the loop on the point of the diamond, net 1 stitch in each of 4 intermediate loops between the diamonds, and repeat from * to the end of the row, where will be only 2 loops to net plain. This completes one line of diamonds. The next row of diamonds are formed in the same manner, but place them intermediately between the diamonds that are already worked, and fill up the space at the beginning and at the end of the row with half diamonds. **24th row**—Still with the small round mesh,—Plain netting. **25th row**—With ½-inch mesh,—Net 4 stitches in every loop. **26th row**—With No. 15 mesh,—Net 2 loops together in 1 stitch all along the row. **27th**

which stitch must be drawn long enough to measure equal length with the preceding stitch ; and net 1 stitch plain, and increase 1 to the end of the round. **3rd round**—Plain netting. **4th round**—The same. **5th round**—Again net and increase as in the second round. **6th round**—With ½-inch mesh,—Plain netting. Net 2 plain rounds with the ¼-inch mesh. **9th round**—With ½-inch mesh,—Plain netting. Net 2 plain rounds with the ¼-inch mesh. **12th round**—With ½-inch mesh,—Plain netting. Net 3 plain rounds with the ¼-inch mesh. **16th round**—With the ½-inch mesh,—Net 18 stitches, and turn the work, and continue on the 18 stitches, leaving the others which are for the front of the pocket. Do 3 rows with ¼-inch mesh on the 18 stitches. **Next row**—Plain netting with ½-inch mesh. Net 2 rows with ¼-inch mesh. **Next row**—With the ½-inch mesh, and with double string,—Net the 18 stitches, and fasten off. The pocket is secured to the billiard table by a strong wire that is passed through the stitches made by the double string netting.

Brush and Comb Bag.

row—With the same mesh,—Plain netting. **28th row**—Still with the same mesh,—Net 1 stitch in each alternate loop.

BILLIARD BALL POCKET.

THESE pockets are placed round billiard tables to hold the balls; they are generally made of white smooth string, or with ecru coloured macramé thread, of medium thickness. Two meshes are required, measuring respectively ½-inch and ¼-inch wide. Commence by putting 8 stitches on a foundation, with the ½-inch mesh, tie in a circle, and net round and round. **1st round**—Plain netting, with the ¼-inch mesh. **2nd round**—With the same mesh,—Net 1 stitch, then increase by netting a stitch into the hole in the second previous row (as shown in the engraving No. 22, page 13, in No. 21, of "Weldon's Practical Needlework Series," which is devoted to the explanation of all the preliminary stitches used in netting),

HOW TO MAKE TWO, THREE, OR MORE STITCHES AND YET HAVE ONLY ONE KNOT.

OUR illustration shows the method in netting of making several stitches in one loop, and yet have only one knot. By this means a pretty fancy stitch can be effected, as represented in the engraving, or the additional stitches may be used simply for the purpose of increasing. To work according to the example, two meshes are employed, the one rather smaller than the other. After putting on the stitches, net the **1st row**—Plain, with the small mesh. **2nd row**—The same. **3rd row**—With the largest mesh,—Put the cotton over the mesh and round the third finger of the left hand 3 times, then cotton under the thumb in the usual way, and pass the needle through all the loops, and under the mesh, and through the stitch of last row to make the knot, and be careful to pull all the stitches level on the mesh before drawing up the knot : the method is the same whether you want three, four, or more stitches made with only one knot. **4th row**—In our example this row is worked by taking all three of the made stitches up together and netting them as 1 stitch; but if you desire to increase, you will of course, net each loop separately. **5th row**—Plain netting. **6th row**—This row is worked similarly to the third row, but here the cotton is only passed round *twice*, which makes *two* stitches with only one knot. **7th row**—Like the fourth row but take two stitches together. **8th row**—Plain netting. Now again work the third, fourth, and fifth rows.

DESSERT D'OYLEY, WITH A BORDER WORKED IN LOOPED NETTING.

REQUIRED, a piece of linen damask cut into a circular shape, and measuring 3½ inches in diameter; this should be hemmed with machine-stitching, and then embroidered round the margin with coral-stitch, from which spike-stitches branch out at intervals on each side. Evans' crochet cotton, No. 14, is employed for the netting, and flat bone meshes ⅜-inch and ¼-inch, and round steel

No. 16 mesh,—Plain netting, 1 stitch in each loop. **14th round**—The same. **15th round**—With No. 14 mesh,—Net 1 stitch in every alternate loop. This completes the d'oyley.

THREE-CORNERED SHAWL, WORKED IN VALENCIENNES NETTING.
(Not illustrated.)

THIS elegant shawl is commenced at the point, and increased gradually in every row till the required size is attained. Procure from 4 ozs. to 6 ozs. of white single Berlin wool, according to the size you desire the shawl to be, and two flat bone meshes, measuring respectively ¼-inch and ½-inch wide. The whole centre of the shawl is worked with the smaller mesh. Commence by putting 2 stitches on a foundation. **2nd row**—Net 1 stitch in the first loop, net 2 stitches in the second loop. **3rd row**—Net 1 stitch in each of the first two loops, net 2 stitches in the last loop. **4th row**—Net 1 stitch in each of the first three loops, and 2 stitches in the last loop. **5th row**—Net 1 stitch in each of the first four loops, and 2 stitches in the last loop. **6th row**—Net 1 stitch in each of the first three loops, net 1 valenciennes stitch—viz., wool over the mesh

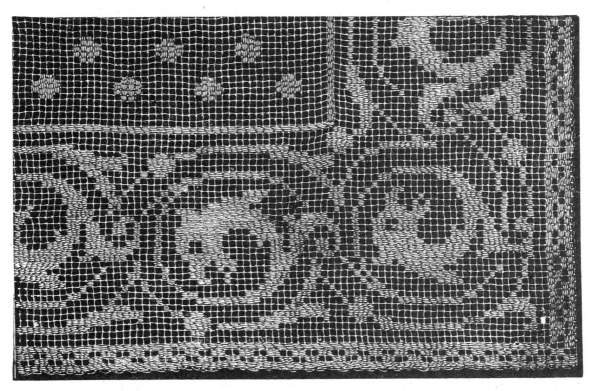

Design in Darned Netting. For a Splasher, Short Curtain, or Antimacassar.

meshes No. 14 and No. 16. **1st round**—Thread a darning needle with a length of crochet cotton, take the No. 16 mesh in the usual manner, and work into the hem of the damask, drawing the needle and cotton through, and manipulating a knot; the stitches must be placed closely together. **2nd round**—With a proper darning needle and No. 16 mesh,—Plain netting. **3rd round**—With No. 14 mesh,—Plain netting. **4th round**—With the ⅜-inch mesh,—Net 2 stitches into every alternate loop. **5th round**—With No. 14 mesh,—Gather 2 loops together in 1 stitch, and repeat the same to the end of the round. **6th round**—With ¼-inch mesh,—Net plain 1 stitch in each loop. **7th round**—With No. 14 mesh,—Looped netting—Pass the cotton twice round the mesh and net 1 stitch in a loop of last round, cotton once round the mesh and net 1 stitch in the same loop, cotton once round the mesh and net another stitch in the same loop, and repeat to the end of the round. **8th round**—Work in the same manner, making the stitches in the long loops of last round. Net 2 more similar rounds. **11th round**—With ¼-inch mesh,—Plain netting, doing 1 stitch in each of the long loops of the previous round. **12th round**—With ⅜-inch mesh,—Net 4 stitches in every loop. **13th round**—With

(not round the fingers), and insert the needle in the work below the knot in the last row but one, and draw the needle and the wool through, do this twice more, and you will have 3 loose loops on the mesh, then pass the wool round the mesh and fingers in the usual way, and net 1 plain stitch in each of the two following loops, and 2 stitches in the last loop. Valenciennes netting is illustrated on page 13, No. 21, of "Weldon's Practical Needlework Series," and a reference to the engraving will be a help to the correct working of this shawl. **7th row**—Net 1 stitch in each of the first three loops, gather the 3 valenciennes loops together with the next loop, and net them in 1 stitch; net 1 stitch in each of the two following loops, and 2 stitches in the last loop. Net two plain rows with increase in the last stitch. **10th row**—Net 1 stitch in each of the first three loops, net a valenciennes stitch in the work below the knot in the last row but one, net 4 plain stitches, a valenciennes stitch, 1 stitch in each of the two following loops, and two stitches in the last loop. **11th row**—Net 1 stitch in each of the first three loops, gather the 3 valenciennes loops together with the next loop and net them in 1 stitch, net 1 stitch in each of the three following loops, gather the next loop and the 3 valenciennes loops together and net them in one stitch, net 1 stitch in each of the two following loops, and two stitches in the last loop. Net 2 plain rows with increase in the last stitch. **14th row**—Net 1 stitch in each of the first three loops, 1 valenciennes stitch, 4 plain stitches, 1 valenciennes stitch (this should come over the valenciennes stitch made in the sixth row), 4 plain stitches, 1 valenciennes stitch, 2 plain stitches, and 2 stitches in the last loop. **15th row**—Net 1 stitch in each of the first three loops, gather the 3 valenciennes loops together with the next loop and net them in 1 stitch, net 1 stitch in each of the three following loops, a gathered stitch, 3 plain stitches, a gathered stitch, net 1 stitch in each of the two following loops, and 2 stitches in the last loop. Net 2 plain rows with increase in the last stitch. The 4 rows constitute the pattern; therefore continue working in the same manner, increasing at the end of every row, which will bring one more valenciennes stitch in each line as you work; and when you get 25 valenciennes stitches in a line the shawl will probably be large enough. For the **Border**—With the ¼-inch mesh,—Work 2 rounds of plain netting round the shawl, increasing five or six stitches on turning the corners. **3rd**

with the ¼-inch mesh, with which put 112 stitches on a foundation, and net 3 plain rows. **5th row**—Take the ⅝-inch mesh, and net with double wool, doing 1 stitch in each loop of the preceding row. Net 2 plain rows with the ¼-inch mesh and single wool. **8th row**—The same as the fifth row. Net 4 plain rows with the ¼-inch mesh and single wool. Repeat from the fifth row till the shawl attains a perfect square. For the **Border**—With the ¼-inch mesh,—Work 2 rounds of plain netting upon the centre of the shawl, increasing sufficiently on turning the corners. **3rd round**—With ⅝-inch mesh,—Net 3 stitches into each loop all round the shawl. **4th round**—With ¼-inch mesh,—Take three loops together on the needle and net them as 1 stitch, and continue the same all round, increasing as needful at the corners. Repeat the last two rounds twice. **9th round**—With ¼-inch mesh,—Plain netting. **10th round**—With 1-inch mesh,—Net 8 stitches in one loop, twist the wool twice round the mesh, miss three loops, and repeat the same to the end of the round. **11th round**—With ¼-inch mesh,—Net 1 stitch in each of the 7 tall upright loops, net 1 stitch in the centre loop of the three loops missed in last round, and confine the long

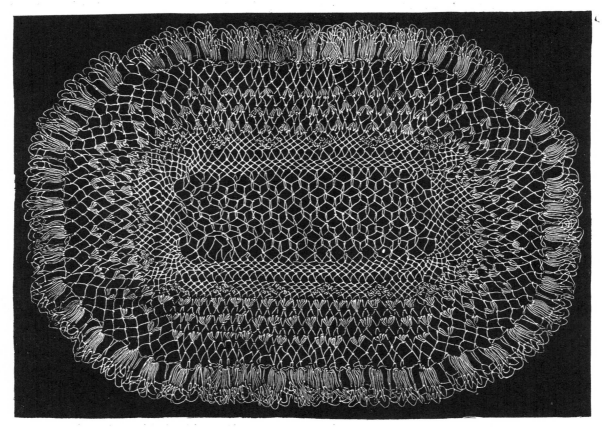

Oblong Tray Cloth.

round—Net 4 plain stitches, net 1 valenciennes stitch, and repeat the same all round the shawl. **4th round**—Plain, and gather the valenciennes loops together with a loop of netting. Work 2 plain rounds. **7th round**—With ½-inch mesh,—Net 3 stitches in each loop. **8th round**—With ¼-inch mesh,—Net 2 loops together in 1 stitch, net 1 stitch in the next loop, and repeat the same. Work 2 plain rounds. **11th round**—With ½-inch mesh,—Net 2 stitches in each loop. **12th round**—With ¼-inch mesh,—Take up 2 loops together and net them in 1 stitch. Work 3 rounds of plain netting. **16th round**—Net 1 stitch in one loop, * pass the wool once round the mesh, miss one loop, net 1 stitch in the next loop, and repeat from * to the end of the round, and fasten off.

NETTED SHAWL, WITH BORDER.
(Not illustrated.)

THIS is a very pretty design in open fancy netting for a shawl. Procure 8 ozs. of grey single Berlin wool and three flat bone meshes measuring respectively ¼-inch, ⅝-inch, and 1-inch wide. Commence

thread of last round as you net the stitch. **12th round**—With the same mesh,—Plain netting. This completes the shawl, which should be damped and stretched and ironed, and is then ready for use.

NETTED VEIL.
(Not illustrated.)

REQUIRED, 4 skeins of fine black purse silk, a No. 15 and No. 13 steel knitting needle, and a ¼-inch and ½-inch flat bone mesh. Begin with No. 15 mesh, with which the whole centre of the veil is netted, and putting 160 stitches on a foundation, work forwards and backwards in all plain netting, till the veil is about 7 inches deep. Then proceed for the **Border—1st row**—With ¼-inch mesh,—Net 2 stitches in each loop down the two sides and along the bottom of the veil, making a few stitches increase on turning the corners. **2nd row**—With No. 13 mesh,—Take up 2 loops together on the needle and net them as 1 stitch. **3rd row**—With the same mesh,—Plain netting. **4th row**—With ¼-inch mesh,—Net 3 stitches in every loop, and increase two or three groups of 3 stitches at the corners. **5th row**—With No. 13 mesh,—Take up 5 loops together on the needle and net them as 1 stitch, net 1 stitch in the next loop, and repeat the same. **6th row**—With the same mesh, —Plain netting. **7th row**—With ¼-inch mesh,—Net two stitches in every loop. **8th row**—With No. 13 mesh,—Take up 2 loops together and net them as 1 stitch. **9th row**—With the same mesh,—Plain netting. **10th row**—With ½-inch mesh, —Net 5

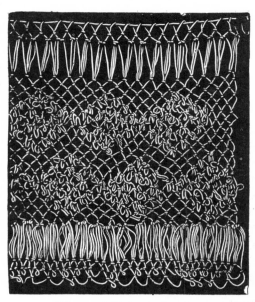

Diamond Pattern Border.

stitches in one loop, miss one loop, and repeat the same down the two sides and along the bottom of the veil, and proceed along the top of the veil, where net 2 stitches in every loop, and join evenly to the beginning of the row ; a few stitches of increase must be arranged to ease at the corners. **11th row**— With No. 13 mesh,—Plain netting, 1 stitch in each loop all round the veil. **12th row**—With the same mesh,—Work plain netting all round the veil.

GIRDLE FOR TENNIS OR POLO.
(Not illustrated.)

PROCURE 5 or 6 skeins of rather coarse crimson purse silk, and a ¼-inch flat bone mesh. Put on 30 stitches, and work in plain netting forwards and backwards, till a length of about 1½ yards is accomplished. Cut some silk into lengths of eight inches, and fringe the ends of the girdle by knotting seven or eight strands into each loop of the netting.

MARKETING BAGS.
(Not illustrated.)

VERY useful bags for marketing are made with brown macramé twine and a ¼-inch flat bone mesh. Put 34 stitches on a foundation cord, and net in rows forwards and backwards, in all plain netting, or in fisherman's netting, till you have done about 22 inches. Fold the netting double, like a book, the fold will form the bottom of the bag. Sew up the sides. Make handles by plaiting a cord, and knot on. Bags for game are netted in the same way with common strong string and a ½-inch wide mesh.

SHORT WINDOW-BLINDS.
(Not illustrated.)

EXCELLENT short window-blinds can be netted with macramé twine of a deep old gold colour. They require to be made as nearly as possible the size of the window sash, putting on sufficient stitches to make the width of the blind, and netting in rows to attain the length. The netting should be stretched on a brass rod at top and bottom.

Billiard Ball Pocket.

BED-REST FOR INVALID.
(Not illustrated.)

PROCURE 1¼ lbs. of Strutt's No. 4 or No. 6 knitting cotton and a ¾-inch flat bone mesh. Commence netting with 20 stitches, and gradually increase 1 stitch at the end of every row till you get 80 or 90 stitches in the row, keep it at this width for about 40 rows, and then decrease 1 stitch at the end of every row, till you again find only 20 stitches, and fasten off. The wide part of the netting is drawn smoothly behind the invalid, and when the narrow ends are secured to the rails at the foot of the bed, either by a tape run through the meshes or by tying the two ends together round the rails, it forms a comfortable and elastic support to the back what sitting up in bed.

ANTIMACASSAR WORKED IN STRIPES OF PLAIN AND HONEYCOMB NETTING.
(Not illustrated.)

THIS antimacassar may be worked with Coats' No. 10 crochet cotton and a flat bone mesh measuring ⅜-inch wide. Put 85 stitches on a foundation, and net 4 plain rows. **1st pattern row**—Net 2 plain stitches, net 2 stitches in each of 10 consecutive loops, net 25 plain stitches, net 2 stitches in each of 10 consecutive loops. Again net 25 plain stitches, and net 2 stitches in each of 10 consecutive loops, and end the row with 3 plain stitches. **2nd row**—Plain netting. **3rd row**—Net 3 plain stitches, * miss one loop, net 1 stitch in the next loop, net 1 stitch in the loop you missed, repeat from * 9 times, net 25 plain stitches, * miss 1 loop, net 1 stitch in the next loop, net 1 stitch in the loop you missed, repeat from * 9 times, again net 25 plain stitches, * miss one loop, net 1 stitch in the next loop, net 1 stitch in the loop you missed, and repeat from * 9 times, and end the row with 2 plain stitches. **4th row**—Plain netting. **5th row**—Work the same as the third row, except that you net 2 plain stitches at the beginning of the row, and 3 plain at the end. **6th row**—Plain netting. Repeat from the third row till the antimacassar is the length required. Then

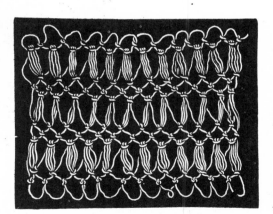

How to make Two, Three, or more Stitches, and yet have only One Knot.

next row—Net 2 plain stitches, net 2 loops together 10 times, net 25 plain stitches, net 2 loops together 10 times, net 25 plain stitches, net 2 loops together 10 times, and end the row by netting 3 plain stitches. Finish with 4 rows of plain netting. Get a skein of No. 10 knitting cotton, and darn a pretty pattern along the centre of the plain netted stripes. The antimacassar may be completed by the addition of a border; either of the borders, illustrated on page 4, No. 33 of "Weldon's Practical Needlework Series," are perfectly suitable, as also are the Alice and Coralline Borders on page 5 of the same issue, which also illustrates the Butterfly Border, an extremely effective design, useful for so many purposes.

LAWN TENNIS BALL BAGS.
(Not illustrated.)

THESE are generally made of string, or of the stout coloured twine which is manufactured purposely for coarse strong netting. A wooden needle is required, and a flat mesh about an inch wide. Put about 30 or 36 stitches on a foundation, and work round and round in all plain netting, or in fisherman's netting, till the bag is half-a-yard deep, when run the string through the loops of the last round of the netting, which is the bottom of the bag, and tie it up close and firm. Finish the top of the bag with a bright red ribbon passed through the foundation stitches, and long enough to hang up the bag by; it can be further ornamented with tufts of red wool tied on to every stitch in every sixth round of the netting.

Another mode of making tennis bags is to commence at the bottom and work thence to the top of the bag. A smaller sized bag can be made by netting 24 stitches in the round, and working to the depth of sixteen inches.

in the engraving No. 2A, on page 6, No. 21, "Weldon's Practical Needlework Series," and increase a stitch in every row, till you bring the work to the width of 1 yard, or from 1½ yards to 2 yards, as required, and keep it the same width (see Oblong Netting, page 7 of the same issue) till the necessary length is attained, when work to a corner, and fasten off.

SLEEPING NET.
(Not illustrated.)

REQUIRED, a skein of Strutt's knitting cotton, No. 10, and flat bone meshes, ¼-inch and ½-inch wide. Commence with the ½-inch mesh, and make 24 stitches on a foundation, and tie in a circle. Work 2 plain rounds with the ¼-inch mesh. **4th round**—With ½-inch mesh,—Net 3 stitches in every loop of last round. Work 4 plain rounds with the ¼-inch mesh. **9th round**—With ½-inch mesh,—Net 2 stitches in every loop of last round. Work round and round in plain netting with the ¼-inch mesh until the net is a con-

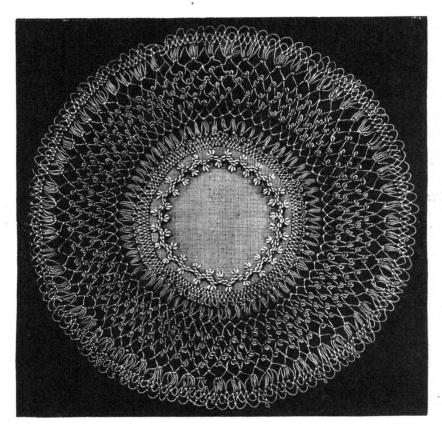

Dessert D'Oyley, with Border of Looped Netting.

MATRIMONY NETTING.
(Not illustrated.)

MATRIMONY netting is very similar to "honeycomb" netting, and is, in fact, almost exactly the same thing. It is worked with any even number of stitches. **1st row**—Plain netting. **2nd row**— Take up the second loop and net a stitch, then net the first loop after passing the needle through the second loop as well as the first to join them firmly together, and so on to the end. **3rd row**—Plain netting. **4th row**—Net 1 plain stitch to begin, then work the matrimony stitches to the end of the row, where will be 1 plain stitch to net. **5th row**—Plain netting. And repeat from the second row for the length required.

NET FOR PROTECTING FRUIT TREES.
(Not illustrated.)

THESE nets are worked with black string especially manufactured for the purpose, and which can be procured from Messrs. Good and Son, King William Street, W., or from the Cotton and Twine Spinning Company, Corporation Street, Manchester; or if made with ordinary string, the netting must afterwards be dipped in gas-tar, to preserve it from rotting in rainy weather. Begin as shown

venient size for the head, when fasten off, and run a piece of narrow white elastic in the last round of the netting.

ANOTHER SLEEPING NET.
(Not illustrated.)

NETTED sleeping nets are highly recommended by medical men as they keep the hair smooth and tidy at night without imparting undue heat to the head. A strong useful net can be made with dark brown purse silk and a mesh ¼-inch wide. Put 20 stitches on a foundation, drawing them up close together, and tie in a circle. **2nd round**—Net 2 stitches in the first loop, 1 stitch in the next loop, and repeat the same, and make 30 stitches in the round. Net 2 plain rounds. **5th round**—Same as the second round, but 45 stitches in the round. Net 4 plain rounds. **10th round**—Again increase the same way as the second round. Now net 6 plain rounds. **17th round**—Again increase a stitch in each alternate loop. And now proceed in all plain netting round and round until the net is the size desired, when if you wish it to be rather orna-mental, you can finish with a round or two of a pretty scollopped border. An elastic run into the last round of the plain netting will keep the net firmly on the head all night.